# Beeton's Practical Encyclopedia of Cookery

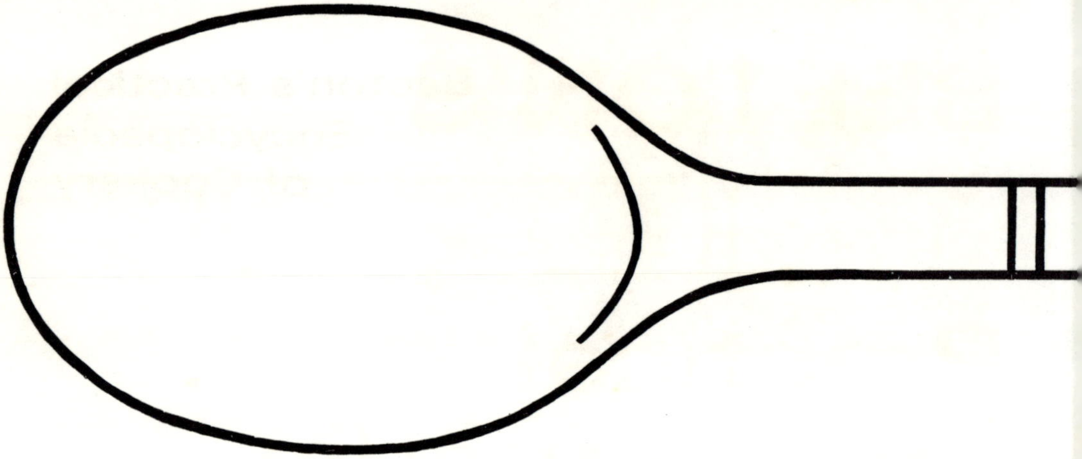

# BEETON'S

# Practical Encyclopedia of Cookery

WARD LOCK LIMITED
*London and Sydney*

## ACKNOWLEDGMENTS

THE PUBLISHER wishes to thank the following for supplying illustrative material: Heinz Home Cookery Service (*front and back pictures on Jacket and Colour Plate 7*); Lincolnshire Canners Ltd (*Colour Plate 1*); Flour Advisory Bureau Ltd (*Colour Plates 3 and 14*); McDougall's Ltd (*Colour Plate 4*); J. W. French and Co. Ltd (*Colour Plate 5*); MacFisheries Ltd (*Colour Plate 8*); Spry Kitchen (*Colour Plate 9*); Nestle Company Ltd (*Colour Plates 12 and 15*); Gas Council (*Colour Plate 16*); Dutch Dairy Bureau (*Plates 4, 28 and 32*); British Farm Produce Council (*Plates 5, 27 and 29*); Bulmer's Cider and F. J. Lyons (*Plate 26*); Danish Food Centre and Danish Lurpak butter (*Plate 31*).

The following also deserve sincere thanks for advising on the text: Mrs. Anna Marais (*on South African dishes*); Mr. R. H. Howorth (*on Russian dishes*); Mr. D. L. Toseland of the Meat and Livestock Commission (*on bacon and ham curing*).





**7063 1413 1**

Made and printed by offset in Great Britain by William Clowes and Sons, Limited,
London and Beccles

# EDITOR'S NOTE

THIS A-Z range of 'the best of Beeton' gives the newcomer to cookery an easy-to-use, comprehensive guide to cookery usage and basic recipes. At the same time, it provides the experienced cook with a valuable series of ready-reference reminders, along with an immense selection of dishes for everyday meals and many attractive ones for dinner parties.

Most of the recipes appear either under the name of the finished dish, e.g. *Lemon Meringue Pie* or under the name of the cooking method used, e.g. *Braised Beef*, *Roast Beef*. All these recipes, ideas and hints are in straight alphabetical order, except in the Appendix which contains general information on the weights and measures used in cookery. References are given to fuller works on specialised topics.

Roast beef or braised? Apple pudding or apricot? All Mrs. Beeton's best known modern recipes appear here in their standard, tested form, so widely used and enjoyed. The method of presenting them in alphabetical sequence enables any cook to vary her cooking method or finished dish easily, to suit the quality or types of products which she has purchased or has in stock.

## AGRO-DOLCE

Bitter-sweet Sauce

| | |
|---|---|
| **1 onion** | **1 tablesp. olive oil** |
| **1 carrot** | **¼ pt. red wine** |
| **1 clove of garlic (optional)** | **⅛ pt. wine vinegar** |
| | **2 oz. sugar** |
| **1 bay leaf** | **2 tablesp. water** |
| **6 peppercorns** | **¼ pt. good meat gravy** |

SWEETENING

**Any one or any mixture of the following to taste: 1 teasp. chopped mint; 1 teasp. finely-shredded candied orange peel; 1 dessertsp. chopped nuts; 1 dessertsp. sultanas; 1 tablesp. grated bitter chocolate**

Chop the onion and carrot, crush the garlic. Cook them with the bay leaf and peppercorns very gently in the oil for 15–20 min. Drain off the oil and add the wine and vinegar. Simmer gently ½ hr. In a separate pan boil the sugar, dissolved in the water until it turns golden brown. Add to this the wine mixture. Add the gravy and any one or any mixture of the sweetening ingredients to taste.

Serve with braised meat.

## ALE PUNCH

| | |
|---|---|
| **1 oz. loaf sugar** | **1 pt. water** |
| **1 lemon** | **2 pt. old ale** |
| **Nutmeg** | **1 gill gin** |
| **Pinch of ground cinnamon** | **1 gill rum** |
| | **1 gill whisky** |
| **3 cloves** | |

Rub the sugar on the rind of the lemon to extract all the zest. Put it into an earthenware bowl or basin together with the strained juice of the lemon, a grate of nutmeg, and the cinnamon. Add the cloves and water, then stir in the old ale, and the spirits. Stir over gentle heat until hot. Strain off the liquid into a punch bowl, place 2–3 thin slices of lemon on top and serve immediately.

## ALLEMANDE SAUCE

*Sauce Allemande*

| | |
|---|---|
| **½ pt. Velouté sauce** | **Salt and pepper** |
| **1 egg yolk** | **Nutmeg** |
| **1 tablesp. cream** | **Lemon juice** |
| **½ oz. butter** | |

Heat the Velouté sauce, preferably in a double boiler. Mix the egg yolk and cream, and stir into the sauce, cook without boiling till the egg yolk thickens. Whisk in the butter, a small pat at a time. Add a pinch of nutmeg, a few drops of lemon juice, season and use the sauce at once.

Serve with any meat, poultry, fish or vegetables.

## ALMOND CHEESECAKES

*Tartelettes aux amandes*

| | |
|---|---|
| **Short crust pastry using 6 oz. flour, etc.** | **2 oz. ground almonds** |
| | **¼ teasp. almond essence** |
| **1–2 dessertsp. jam** | **2 egg whites** |
| **4 oz. castor sugar** | **1 dessertsp. water** |

Roll pastry out thinly, cut into rounds and line patty or bouché tins. Place a little jam in the bottom of each. Mix castor sugar and ground almonds, add essence to egg whites and whisk stiffly. Fold almond mixture into egg white and add water. Half-fill pastry cases with mixture. If desired, place pastry crosses on top of the mixture. Bake in a fairly hot to moderate oven (**375°–350° F., Gas 5–4**).

**16–18 cheesecakes**
**Cooking time—15–20 min.**

## ALMOND CIRCLES

*Cercles d'Amandes*

| | |
|---|---|
| **5½ oz. plain flour** | **½ teasp. almond essence** |
| **Pinch of salt** | |
| **2 oz. butter *or* margarine** | **½ teasp. baking-powder** |
| | **Egg *or* milk to mix** |
| **2½ oz. sugar** | **Glacé icing using 4 oz. icing sugar** |

Sift flour and salt, and rub in the fat. Add sugar, essence and baking-powder and mix to stiff dough with egg or milk. Roll out ¼ in. thick and cut into rings using 2½–1½-in. cutters. Place on a greased baking-sheet and bake in a moderate oven (**350° F., Gas 4**) until lightly browned. When cool spread tops of biscuits with glacé icing and if desired decorate with a sprinkling of "hundreds and thousands".

**40 circles**
**Cooking time—20 min.**

NOTE: Self-raising flour may be used if liked.

### ALMOND FINGERS

*Tranches d'Amandes*

PASTRY

**6 oz. margarine**
**8 oz. plain flour**
**Pinch of salt**
**4 oz. sugar**
**2 oz. cake-crumbs**
**2 oz. ground almonds**
**1 egg yolk**
**Raspberry jam**

TOPPING

**3 egg whites**
**8 oz. castor sugar**
**3 oz. blanched chopped almonds**
**¼–½ teasp. almond essence**

Make the pastry: rub fat into sifted flour and salt; add sugar, crumbs and ground almonds. Mix with egg yolk and enough water to make a stiff consistency. Roll out to ¼ in. thickness and line a shallow baking-tin 13 in. by 9 in. Bake lightly in a moderate oven (**350° F., Gas 4**). When nearly cooked spread with raspberry jam.

Make the topping: whisk egg whites stiffly, fold in sugar, chopped almonds and essence, put into a saucepan and stir lightly till mixture boils. Spread on to pastry, return to oven and bake in a moderate-warm oven at (**350°–335° F., Gas 4–3**), until set and lightly browned. When cold cut into fingers about 3 in. long and 1 in. wide.

**18 fingers**
**Cooking time—about 30–40 min.**

### ALMOND PASTE (ICING) (1)

Almond paste—often called almond icing or marzipan—is used to cover rich cakes before applying royal or glacé icing. It is also used alone to decorate cakes, e.g. Simnel Cake and Battenburg Cake. It is often coloured and flavoured and then moulded into various shapes to be used for cake decoration.

**6 oz. icing sugar and 6 oz. castor sugar *or* 12 oz. icing sugar**
**12 oz. ground almonds**
**Juice of ½ lemon**
**¾ teasp. orange flower water**
**¾ teasp. vanilla essence**
**1–2 egg yolks**

Sieve the icing sugar into a bowl and mix with the ground almonds and castor sugar. Add the lemon juice, essences and enough egg yolk to bind the ingredients into a pliable but dry paste. Knead thoroughly with the hand until smooth.

This quantity of paste is sufficient to cover the top and sides of an 8-in. cake.

NOTE: A whole egg *or* egg whites may be used instead of egg yolks. Egg yolk gives a richer and yellower paste, whilst egg white gives a whiter, more brittle paste. (Economically the yolks can be used for almond paste and the whites used for royal icing.)

### ALMOND PASTE (2) Boiled

**1 lb. loaf sugar**
**¼ pt. water**
**12 oz. ground almonds**
**2 egg whites**

Dissolve the sugar in the water slowly, over a low heat. When the sugar has dissolved, bring to the boil, skim well, and boil to 240° F. Remove from heat and stir briskly until the syrup becomes cloudy. When slightly cooled, add the almonds and then the egg whites. Stir well and then turn on to a marble or enamel slab. Work with a palette knife until the mixture is cool enough to handle. Knead with the hands until smooth.

NOTE: This paste can be coloured and flavoured to taste and is useful for moulding into sweets.

#### To Apply Almond Paste

To cover the top and sides of a rich fruit cake, the cake top should be fairly level and the surface free from loose crumbs.

Brush the top and sides with warm apricot glaze, using a pastry brush. Dredge a little castor sugar on to a clean board and roll out the almond paste to a round which is 4 in. wider than the diameter of the cake. Place the cake in the centre of this with its glazed top downwards and work the paste upwards round the sides of the cake with the hands until it is within ¼ in. of the top edge, i.e. the cake bottom. Using a straight-sided jar or thick tumbler, roll firmly round the sides, pressing slightly with the other hand on the upturned bottom of the cake and turning the

1

Attractive meat and sweet dishes.
This array includes a fruit flan, sea-food chowder, braised pork, country style, an apricot upside-down cake and navarin of lamb.

# BEEF

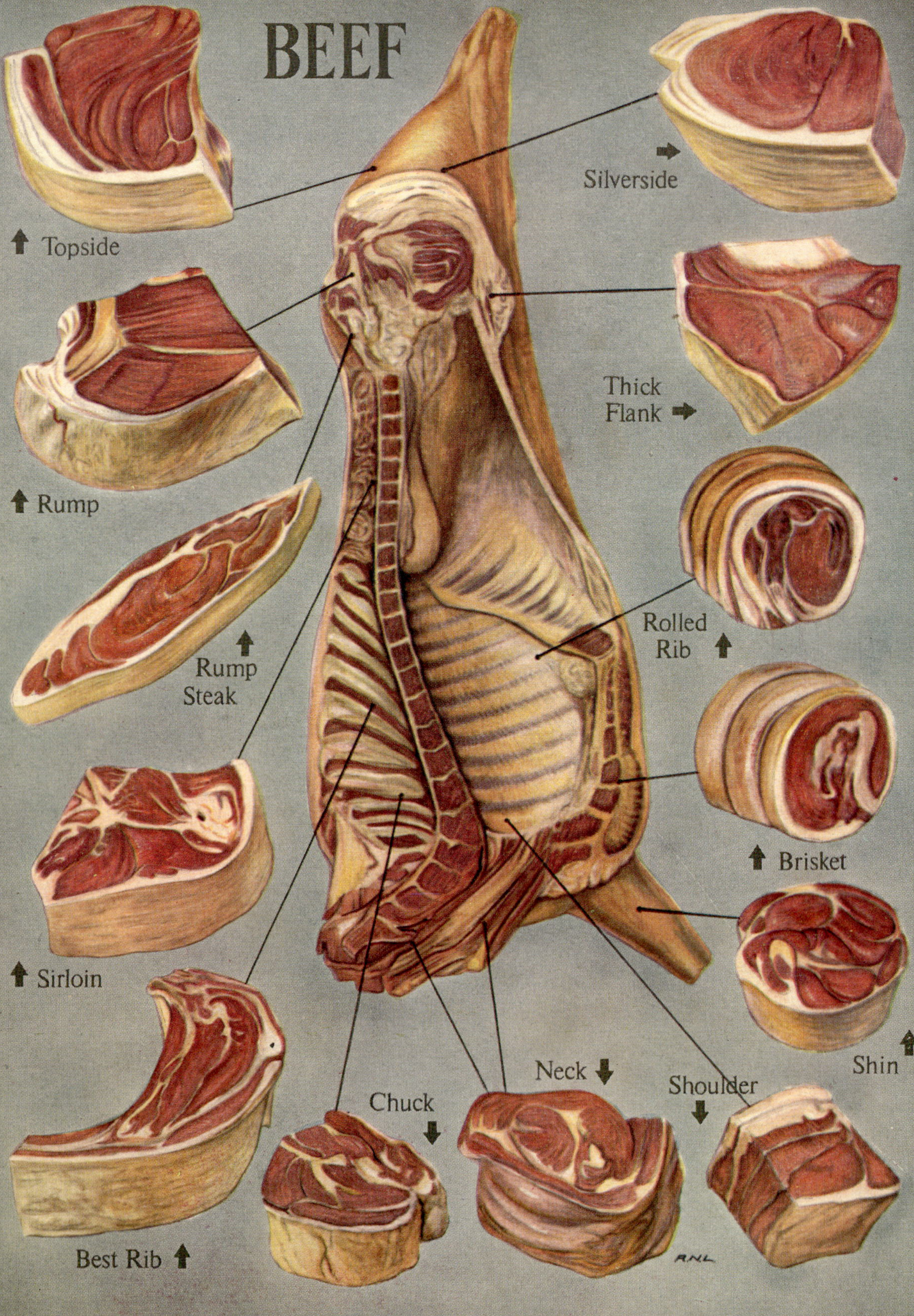
Topside
Silverside
Rump
Thick Flank
Rump Steak
Rolled Rib
Brisket
Sirloin
Shin
Neck
Shoulder
Chuck
Best Rib

**3**
Breads, plain and fancy, can be the housewife's special pride.

←
**2**
Common British cuts of beef.

4

Cakes for tea.
Sultana cake, cream buns, rock buns, madeleines, an orange sandwich cake, eclairs, a chocolate swiss roll and a sponge cake, fruit scones and small cakes. Below, apricot baskets are a more elaborate way of presenting small, rich cakes.

cake round on the sugared board when necessary.

Continue rolling and turning until the sides are straight and smoothly covered and the top edges of the cake are sharp and smooth, when the process is completed and the cake is turned upright.

NOTE: Allow a few days for the almond paste to dry, before putting on the royal icing, or the oil from the almond paste will discolour it. Cover with a clean cloth to protect from dust whilst drying.

## ALMOND PUDDINGS

*Poudings d'Amandes*

**3 oz. butter**
**3 oz. castor sugar**
**3 eggs**
**6 oz. ground almonds**
**3 tablesp. cream *or* top of the milk**

Grease seven or eight dariole moulds.

Cream together the butter and sugar, until soft. Separate the eggs, and work in the egg yolks. Stir in the ground almonds and cream *or* milk. Whisk the egg whites until stiff, and fold them in lightly. Three-quarters fill the moulds with the mixture. Cover with greased paper and steam for ¾–1 hr., until firm.

Turn out and serve with apricot sauce.

**7–8 helpings**

## ALMOND SHORTBREAD BISCUITS

*Biscuits d'Amandes*

**5 oz. butter *or* margarine**
**1 oz. ground almonds**
**8 oz. plain flour**
**1 oz. cornflour**
**3 oz. sugar**

Cream the fat in a bowl, add the almonds. Sift flour and cornflour. Gradually work them into the creamed fat with the sugar, using the hand. Knead on board, roll out ¼ in. thick and cut into rounds or fancy shapes. Allow to firm for 1 hr. then bake in a moderate oven **(350° F., Gas 4).**

**30–36 biscuits**
**Cooking time—20–30 min.**

## ALMOND SHORTCAKE

**4 oz. butter *or* margarine**
**8 oz. wholemeal flour**
**Pinch of salt**
**2 oz. Barbados sugar**
**1 oz. ground almonds**
**½ egg yolk**

Cream fat and sugar; add egg yolk, sifted flour and salt. Add the almonds. Knead all together to a stiff dough. Make into a cake as for Shortbread (Scottish) prick and bake in a warm to cool oven **(335°–310° F., Gas 3–2).**

The dough may be cut into fingers or other fancy shapes and baked as biscuits.

**Cooking time—50–60 min.**

## ALMONDS AS A GARNISH

*See Cake-Making*

*To make almond acorns:* Dip the rounded ends of 8 blanched almonds into raspberry jam so that half is covered with jam; then dip the jammed ends into chocolate nibs.

## ALPINE EGGS

*Œufs à la Suisse*

**4 eggs**
**2 oz. butter**
**6 oz. cheese**
**Finely-chopped parsley**
**Salt and pepper**

Butter a fireproof baking-dish thickly, line it with most of the cheese cut into thin slices and break the eggs over this, keeping the yolks whole. Grate the remainder of the cheese and mix it with the parsley. Season the eggs liberally, sprinkle the grated cheese on top and add the remainder of the butter broken into small pieces. Bake till set.

**4 helpings Cooking time—10 min. (approx.)**

## AMBER JELLY

*Gelée ambrée*

**¾ pt. water**
**1 wineglass sherry (optional)**
**¼ pt. lemon juice (2 lemons)**
**6 oz. loaf sugar**
**1 oz. gelatine**
**3 egg yolks**
**Thin rind of 1 lemon**

Put all ingredients into a pan and allow to soak 5 min. Whisk over gentle heat until near boiling point. Do not boil or the eggs will curdle. Strain through muslin and pour into a prepared mould.

This is a delicious and nutritious sweet for an invalid.

**4–6 helpings Cooking time—½ hr.**

### AMERICAN FISH PIE

**½ lb. cooked turbot, cod *or* other white fish**
**1½ oz. butter**
**½ pt. white sauce**
**1 oz. grated Parmesan cheese**
**Salt and pepper**
**Cayenne pepper**
**¾ lb. mashed potatoes**
**1 egg**
**Nutmeg**

Free the fish from skin and bones, divide it into large flakes and put them into a saucepan with ½ oz. butter, the sauce and some of the cheese. Season with salt and pepper, and a few grains of cayenne, and heat gradually over a low heat. Melt the remaining 1 oz. butter in another pan, add the potatoes and most of the egg, season well with salt and pepper and a little nutmeg. Stir vigorously over the heat until thoroughly hot. Have ready a well-buttered pie-dish, line the bottom and sides thinly with potato purée, using about ½ of it, put in the prepared fish, and cover with the remaining potatoes. Smooth the surface and notch the edges with a knife, giving it the appearance of pastry crust, brush over with egg, sprinkle liberally with grated cheese. Bake in a fairly hot oven (**375° F., Gas 5**) until well browned. Serve hot.

**4–5 helpings**

### AMERICAN FROSTING

**8 oz. granulated sugar**
**4 tablesp. water**
**1 egg white**

Put the sugar and water into a pan, dissolve the sugar slowly in the water and when quite dissolved bring to boiling-point. Boil to 240° F. without stirring. Brush down the sides of the pan with a brush dipped in cold water and remove scum as it rises. Pour on to the stiffly beaten egg white, beating all the time. Continue beating until the icing begins to thicken and coats the back of a spoon thickly. Pour quickly over the cake, spread with a palette knife and work up the icing in swirls.

NOTE: ½ teasp. vanilla essence or lemon juice and a pinch of cream of tartar may be added if liked. The frosting may be used either as a covering or as a filling.

### ANCHOVIES

*Anchois*

Anchovies are small coastal fish of the herring family, abundant in the Mediterranean. Used mainly for making sauce and relishes. Canned fillets are available in this country.

### ANCHOVIES AS AN HORS D'OEUVRE

Lift the rolled or filleted anchovies out of the can—put on to crisp lettuce leaves. If wished coat with chopped parsley, chopped chives and a little cayenne pepper.

Allow about 3 anchovy fillets *or* rolled anchovies per person.

### ANCHOVY BUTTER

*Beurre d'Anchois*

**6 bottled anchovies**
**2 oz. butter**
**Lemon juice**
**Pepper**

Crush the anchovies, rub through a sieve. Mix them smoothly with the butter, add pepper and lemon juice to taste. Sieve and chill.

### ANCHOVY CHEQUER BOARD SALAD

**1 lb. cod fillet *or* other white fish**
**2 tablesp. water**
**2 tablesp. lemon juice**
**1 level tablesp. chopped parsley**
**1 level tablesp. chopped chives**
**Salt and pepper**
**Lettuce leaves**
**1 small can (2 oz.) anchovy fillets**
**Hard-boiled egg *or* olives**

GARNISH

**Radish roses**
**Parsley**

Place the fish in a fireproof dish with the water. Cover and cook in a fairly hot oven (**375° F., Gas 5**) for 20 min.; allow to cool. Remove any skin and bones, flake the fish, then moisten it with the lemon juice and stir in the parsley and chives with seasoning to taste. Arrange neatly on a bed of shredded lettuce, flattening and smoothing the top. Place the anchovy fillets diagonally on top in a squared pattern, filling the spaces with rings of hard-boiled egg or slices of stoned olives. Garnish with radish roses and parsley.

**4 helpings**

## ANCHOVY CROÛTES

*Croûtes d'Anchois*

**1 hard-boiled egg**
**½ teasp. curry paste *or* powder**
**2 oz. butter**
**Toast**
**12 anchovy fillets**
**Paprika pepper**
**Lemon juice**
**Parsley**

Chop the white of the egg finely. Rub the yolk through a fine sieve and combine with the curry paste and butter. Mix to a soft paste. Make the toast thin and crisp, cut it into rounds or triangles and spread on the mixture. Lay on each an anchovy fillet, and season with paprika pepper. Add 2–3 drops of lemon juice, decorate with egg white and parsley. Place them in a hot oven for 3–4 min., then serve.

**12 savouries**
**Cooking time—3–4 min.**

## ANCHOVY EGGS

*Anchois aux Œufs*

**4 hard-boiled eggs**
**1 small can anchovy fillets (well drained)**
**1 teasp. anchovy essence**
**2 tablesp. white sauce or mayonnaise**
**Cayenne pepper**
**Watercress**
**Oil**
**Vinegar**

Cut the eggs across in halves, remove the yolks carefully, and cut off the extreme end of each ½ to enable them to stand firmly. Chop the anchovies and pound with the egg yolks till smooth. Add the anchovy essence, and the white sauce gradually until a moist paste is formed; then season to taste. Fill the egg white cases with the mixture, garnish with watercress seasoned with oil and vinegar.

**About 8 savouries**

## ANCHOVY ROLLS

*Paupiettes d'Anchois*

**1 large thin *or* 2 small thin cucumbers**
**Oil**
**Vinegar**
**Seasoning**
**1 teacup crab *or* lobster meat**
**Mayonnaise**
**Small can anchovy fillets**
**Stuffed olives**
**Parsley**

Peel the cucumbers and cut them into 1-in. thick slices. Cut out the centre portion, place rings on a dish, and pour over a little oil and vinegar; season well. Pound the crab or lobster meat, and mix with mayonnaise. Drain the cucumber shapes and fill the cavity with this mixture. Twist a whole anchovy fillet round each, and place a slice of stuffed olive on top. Garnish with parsley.

**About 10 savouries**

## ANCHOVY SAUCE

*Sauce d'Anchois*

To ½ pt. white sauce made from fish stock *or* water *or* ½ milk and ½ water add 1 *or* 2 teasp. anchovy essence to taste and a few drops of lemon juice and a few drops of carmine to tint the sauce a dull pink.

Serve with fish.

## ANCHOVY TOAST

*Croûtes d'Anchois*

**1 small can of anchovies**
**1 *small* shallot *or* onion**
**1 oz. butter**
**½ teasp. chopped parsley**
**4 eggs**
**Cayenne pepper**
**4 slices buttered toast**

Drain the anchovy fillets, chop them coarsely. Chop the shallot or onion. Heat the butter in a small saucepan, fry the shallot or onion until lightly browned, then add the anchovies, parsley and eggs and season with cayenne pepper. Stir over low heat until the mixture thickens, then pour it on the buttered toast.

**4 helpings *or* 8–10 small savouries**
**Cooking time—3–4 min.**

## ANDALUSIAN SAUCE

*Sauce Andalouse*

**¼ pt. mayonnaise**
**2 tablesp. concentrated tomato purée**
**1 small, sweet, red pepper (pimento)**

Cut the pimento in thin strips and stir into the mayonnaise with the tomato purée.

## ANGEL CAKE

**2 oz. flour**
**4½ oz. castor sugar**
**¼ pt. egg whites**
**Pinch of salt**
**½ teasp. cream of tartar**
**½ teasp. vanilla essence**

Use a 6-in. sandwich cake tin or a funnel tin

which is not greased. Sift the flour and sugar separately three times, then sift the flour with ¼ of the sugar. Put the egg white and salt in a large, clean, dry bowl and whisk until frothy. Sprinkle on the cream of tartar and continue whisking till the white stands up in peaks. Avoid overwhisking so that the white has lost its glossiness. Lightly beat in the sugar and flavouring, then using a tablespoon fold in the sifted flour and sugar carefully and gradually. Pour into tin and gently cut through mixture with a knife to release air bubbles. Bake for 40–45 min. in a very cool oven **(290° F., Gas 1)** increasing the heat to **(335° F., Gas 3)** for the last 10–15 min. Allow the cake to stand in the inverted tin for 30 min. then turn out on to a cooling tray.

NOTE: When top springs back on finger pressure the cake is considered ready.

### "ANGELS ON HORSEBACK"

*Les Anges à Cheval*

**12 oysters**
**12 small thin slices of bacon**
**Paprika *or* cayenne pepper**
**½ teasp. chopped shallot *or* onion**
**½ teasp. chopped parsley**
**Lemon juice**
**12 small rounds of fried bread *or* 4 slices of toast**

Beard the oysters, trim the bacon, cutting each piece just large enough to roll round an oyster, season with paprika or cayenne pepper, sprinkle on a little shallot and parsley. Lay an oyster on each, add a few drops of lemon juice, roll up tightly and secure the bacon in position with a fine skewer. Cook in a frying-pan, under the grill or in a hot oven **(425° F., Gas 7)**, *just long enough* to crisp the bacon (further cooking would harden the oysters), remove the skewers and serve on the croûtes.

**4 helpings *or* 12 small savouries**
**Cooking time—5–10 min.**

### APFELKUCHEN

*German Apple Tart*

PASTRY (Mürbeteig)

**12 oz. flour**
**2 oz. sugar**
**Pinch of salt**
**Pinch of baking-powder**
**6 oz. butter *or* margarine**
**2 eggs**
**A little water, milk *or* white wine**
**A little rolled oats**

FILLING

**2 oz. butter**
**1 dessertsp. flour**
**3 oz. castor sugar**
**Rind of 1 small lemon**
**½ gill cream**
**3 eggs**
**3 oz. blanched almonds**
**4–6 cooking apples**

*To make the pastry:* Sift the flour, sugar, salt and baking-powder on to a baking-board. Cut the butter in rough pieces on to flour. Break eggs into a basin, make a well in the flour and pour the eggs in. Take a long-bladed knife and chop all together until crumbly in appearance. With the hands work into a stiff paste, using a little water, milk or white wine, if necessary. Roll out and line two 9-in. flan or sandwich tins. Spread a thin layer of rolled oats on the pastry to prevent apple juice soaking in later.

*To make the filling:* Melt the butter. Stir into it the flour, sugar, grated lemon rind, cream, beaten egg yolks and mix all well together. Chop the almonds and add half of them to the egg mixture. Peel, core, quarter and slice the apples and arrange them, closely overlapping symmetrically, in circles in the pastry. Beat the egg whites to a stiff snow and with a metal spoon stir them into the egg mixture. Pour the mixture over the tarts. Sprinkle the remainder of the chopped almonds on top. Bake in a fairly hot oven **(375° F., Gas 5)** for about 45 min. Cool slightly and remove on to a wire rack.

**2 tarts, 6–10 helpings** **Time 1½ hr.**

### APPETIZERS

A word being used more and more to replace Hors D'Oeuvre. Appetizers are more varied than Hors D'Oeuvre, which should only consist of small, cold "side" dishes and dainty relishes served before a soup course. Appetizers or "starters" may form the only course before a main meat or fish course. They can consist of hot or cold dishes, such as pieces of a savoury pie, and may be quite substantial.

*See Hors D'Oeuvre, Savouries (Appetizers)*

### APPLE AMBER

*Tarte à la Gelée de Pommes*

**Short crust pastry using 4 oz. flour, etc.**
**2 oz. butter *or* margarine**
**3 oz. brown sugar**

**1½ lb. cooking apples**
**2 tablesp. water**
**Rind of 1 lemon**
**2 eggs**
**2–3 oz. castor sugar for the meringue**

Line the sides of a 1½-pt. pie-dish with the pastry and decorate the edge.

Peel, core and slice the apples; put them in a saucepan and stew with the water and the lemon rind. When soft, pass through a nylon sieve. Return the apple pulp to the pan and re-heat slightly, add the butter, brown sugar and egg yolks. Put the mixture into the lined pie-dish and bake gently in a moderate oven **(350° F., Gas 4)** for about 30 min., until the apple mixture is set. Stiffly whisk the egg whites and fold in 2–3 oz. of castor sugar. Pile on top of the apple mixture, dredge lightly with castor sugar and decorate, if liked, with pieces of angelica and glacé cherry. Bake in a very cool oven **(290° F., Gas 1)** until the meringue is golden brown; about 30–40 min. Serve hot or cold.

NOTE: A good pinch of ground cinnamon and ground cloves can be added to the apples before the butter, sugar and egg yolks, if liked.

**6–7 helpings**

## APPLE AND CELERY STUFFING

**2 oz. chopped salt pork *or* bacon diced *or* pork sausage meat**
**2 onions**
**4 tablesp. chopped celery**
**4 medium cooking apples**
**3 oz. stale bread-crumbs**
**2 tablesp. chopped parsley**
**Sugar to taste**
**Salt and pepper**

Brown the pork, bacon or sausage in its own fat, lift it out of the pan. Chop the onion. In the pork fat cook the onion and celery for 5 min., then remove them. Dice the apples and in the same fat fry them till tender and brown. Mix all the ingredients together.

Use with duck, goose or pork.

## APPLE AND CUCUMBER SALAD

*Salade de pommes et Concombres*

**1 cucumber**
**3 dessert apples**
**Salt and pepper**
**Lemon juice**
**Cream *or* evaporated milk**
**Finely-chopped mint (optional)**

Slice the cucumber thinly; quarter, core and

slice the apples. Season lightly and sprinkle with lemon juice. Stir in a little cream *or* evaporated milk. Pile in a salad bowl. Sprinkle with a little mint, if liked.

**6 helpings**

## APPLE AND POTATO SALAD

*Salade de pommes aux pommes de terre*

**3 dessert apples**
**3 cooked potatoes**
**French dressing (flavoured with mustard)**
**Chopped chives**
**Chopped parsley**

Cut the apples and potatoes into small dice. Mix and dress with French dressing. Pile in a salad bowl and garnish with chives and parsley.

**4–6 helpings**

## APPLE CAKE, DANISH

**20 oz. cooking apples**
**5 oz. sugar**
**3 oz. butter**
**7 oz. breadcrumbs**
**Whipped cream**
**Blackcurrant jelly**

Peel, slice and cook the apples in very little water. Add ½ the sugar. Melt the butter in a frying-pan, add breadcrumbs and rest of the sugar and cook till slightly brown. Well butter a pie-dish. Put a layer of breadcrumb mixture, then applesauce, then breadcrumbs alternately until dish is full—the last layer should be breadcrumbs. Press it firm with a spoon. Cook in a warm oven **(335° F., Gas 3)** for ½ hr. Cool and turn out. Serve lukewarm, covered with ice-cold whipped cream and decorated with spoonfuls of blackcurrant jelly

**6 helpings**

### APPLE CHARLOTTE (1)

*Charlotte de Pommes*

**2 tablesp. browned crumbs (cake *or* bread)**
**6 oz. finely-chopped suet**
**6 oz. white bread-crumbs**
**Grated rind of 1 lemon**
**2 lb. cooking apples**
**4 oz. brown sugar**

Grease a 2 pt. pie-dish with butter and coat with the 2 tablesp. browned crumbs. Mix together the suet, 6 oz. breadcrumbs and lemon rind. Peel, core and slice the apples. Fill the pie-dish with alternate layers of the crumb mixture and apples, sprinkled with sugar, finishing with a layer of crumb mixture. Press down lightly. Cover with greased paper. Bake in a moderate oven (**350° F., Gas 4**) about 1¼–1½ hr., until the apples are soft.

Loosen the edges of the charlotte with a knife and turn out on to a hot dish.

**6–7 helpings**

### APPLE CHARLOTTE (2)

**2 lb. cooking apples**
**4 oz. brown sugar**
**1 lemon**
**8 thinly cut slices of bread and butter**
**Castor sugar**

Grease a 2 pt. pie-dish with butter. Peel, core and slice the apples. Place a layer in the bottom of the pie-dish and sprinkle with sugar, grated lemon rind and lemon juice. Cover with thin slices of bread and butter. Repeat until the dish is full, finishing with a layer of bread and butter. Cover with greased paper. Bake in a moderate oven (**350° F., Gas 4**) for ¾–1 hr.

Turn out of the dish and dredge well with castor sugar before serving.

**5–6 helpings**

### APPLE CRUMBLE

*Pommes au gratin*

**1½ lb. apples**
**4 oz. brown sugar**
**A little grated lemon rind**
**½ gill water (approx.)**
**3 oz. butter *or* margarine**
**6 oz. plain flour**
**3 oz. castor sugar**
**¼ teasp. ground ginger**

Peel, core and slice the apples into a pan. Add ½ gill water, 4 oz. brown sugar and lemon rind. Cook gently with lid on the pan until soft. Place in a greased 2 pt. pie-dish. Rub the fat into the flour until of the consistency of fine breadcrumbs. Add the castor sugar, ground ginger and mix well. Sprinkle the crumble over the apple; press down lightly. Bake in a moderate oven (**350° F., Gas 4**) until golden brown, and the apples are cooked—about 30–40 min., depending on the cooking quality of the apples.

Dredge with castor sugar and serve with custard *or* cream.

NOTE: For apples the same weight of the following may be substituted: **damsons, gooseberries, plums, raspberries** *or* **rhubarb,** and the crumble named accordingly.

**6 helpings**

### APPLE DUMPLINGS—BAKED

*Pommes enrobées*

**Short crust pastry 12 oz. for large apples *or* 8 oz. for small apples**
**2 oz. brown sugar**
**A little grated lemon rind *or* ground cinnamon**
**6 cooking apples**
**12 cloves (optional)**

Make the short crust pastry; divide into six portions, shaping each into a round.

Mix the sugar and grated lemon rind or cinnamon. Peel and core each apple and put it on a round of pastry. Work the pastry round the apple until it is almost covered. Press the cloves, if used, into the centre of the apple; then fill the cavity with the sugar mixture. Seal the pastry edges by moistening slightly with water. Place the dumplings join downwards on a greased baking sheet. Brush them with milk and dredge with castor sugar. Bake for about 30 min. in a fairly hot oven (**400° F., Gas 6**).

**6 helpings**

### APPLE DUMPLINGS—BOILED

*Pommes enrobées*

**6 apples**
**Suet crust pastry using 12 oz. flour, etc.**
**3 oz. moist *or* brown sugar**
**6 cloves**

Core and peel the apples. Divide the pastry into 6 portions and roll each into a round. Put an apple into the centre of the round of pastry and work the pastry round the apple until it nearly meets. Fill the centre of the apple with sugar and a clove. Damp the edges of pastry and join them firmly together. Tie each apple dumpling in the corner of a well-floured pudding cloth. Put the dumplings into boiling water and boil gently, from 40–50 min.

**6 helpings**

## APPLE FRITTERS

*Beignets de Pommes*

| | |
|---|---|
| **1 lb. cooking apples** | **Coating batter** |
| **Castor sugar** | **Lemon juice** |
| **Deep fat** | |

Peel the apples, core them with an apple corer and cut into rings about ¼ in. thick. Put the apple rings on to a plate and sprinkle with lemon juice and sugar. Let them stand for a few minutes. Using a skewer dip them into the batter, then drop them into deep fat which should just be beginning to haze. Cook until golden brown—about 4 min. and then lift out with a skewer.

Dredge well with castor sugar before serving.

**4 helpings**
**Time—20 min.**

## APPLE GINGER JAM

| | |
|---|---|
| **3 lb. apples** | **Juice of 1 lemon** |
| **1 oz. bruised root ginger** | **3 lb. sugar** |
| **1 pt. water** | **4 oz. crystallized ginger** |

Peel, core and cut up the apples, tying the peel, cores and bruised root ginger in muslin. Place the apples, water and bag of peel in the preserving-pan with the lemon juice and cook slowly until tender. Remove the bag of peel after squeezing. Add the sugar, and the crystallized ginger cut into neat pieces. Allow the sugar to dissolve over a low heat and then boil rapidly until setting point is reached. Pot and cover immediately.

**Yield—approx. 5 lb.**

## APPLE JELLY (COLD SWEET)

*Gelée de Pommes*

| | |
|---|---|
| **2 lb. apples** | **2 small lemons** |
| **1 pt. water** | **1½ oz. gelatine** |
| **5–6 oz. sugar** | **4 tablesp. cold water** |
| **2 cloves** | |

Wash apples, cut into quarters and core. Cook with 1 pt. of water, sugar, cloves and grated lemon rind until soft. Soak gelatine in 4 tablesp. cold water for 5 min., then heat until dissolved. Rub apples through a fine sieve, add juice of lemons and taste for further sweetening. Strain gelatine into the purée and stir well. Pour into a wet mould.

**6 helpings**
**Cooking time—15–20 min. Setting time—2–3 hr.**

## APPLE JELLY (PRESERVE)

| | |
|---|---|
| **4 lb. well-flavoured crabapples, *or* cooking apples (windfalls can be used)** | **Flavouring: lemon peel *or* root ginger** |
| | **Sugar** |

Wash the apples and cut up without peeling or coring—just remove any bad portions. Barely cover with water (about 2–3 pt.) and simmer with the chosen flavouring till tender and well mashed (about 1 hr.). Strain through a scalded jelly bag. Bring the strained juice to the boil and test for pectin. Add the sugar (usually 1 lb. sugar to every pint of juice). Stir to dissolve. Boil briskly till setting point is reached.

## APPLE PIE or TART

*Tourte aux Pommes*

| | |
|---|---|
| **Short crust pastry using 6 oz. flour, etc.** | **4 oz. moist sugar** |
| **1½–2 lb. apples** | **6 cloves *or* ½ teasp. grated lemon rind** |

Peel, quarter and core the apples and cut in thick slices. Place half the apples in a 1½-pt. pie-dish, add the sugar and flavouring and pile the remaining fruit on top, piling it high in the centre. Line the edge of the pie-dish with pastry and cover the pie with pastry. Knock up the edges of the pastry with the back of a knife. Bake for 40 min., first in a fairly hot oven (**400° F., Gas 6**), reducing the heat to moderate (**350° F., Gas 4**) when the pastry is set.

Dredge with castor sugar and serve hot or cold.

NOTE: If liked, the pastry may be brushed with egg white and sprinkled with sugar before cooking.

**6 helpings**

APPLE PUDDING—BAKED (1)

*Pouding de Pommes*

**2 lb. cooking apples**
**½ gill water**
**6 oz. castor sugar**
**2 oz. butter *or* margarine**
**1–2 eggs**
**4 oz. breadcrumbs**

Peel, core and cut the apples into slices, stew with ½ gill water until tender. Stir in the sugar, fat, and well-beaten egg. Butter a 2 pt. pie-dish. Coat the bottom and sides thickly with the crumbs. Add the apple pulp and finish with a layer of crumbs. Put a few flakes of butter on the top and bake in a moderate oven **(350° F., Gas 4)** for ¾ hr.

**4–5 helpings**

APPLE PUDDING—BAKED (2)

**5 oz. butter**
**3 oz. demerara sugar**
**1 level teasp. cinnamon**
**1 lb. cooking apples**
**4 oz. sugar**
**1 egg**
**Vanilla essence**
**8 oz. self-raising flour**
**Pinch of salt**
**Milk to mix**

Grease a 2 pt. pie-dish. Melt 1 oz. of the butter, demerara sugar and the cinnamon in a saucepan and add the peeled, cored and sliced apples. Cook for about 5 min. Cream together the remainder of the butter and 4 oz. sugar and beat in the egg. Add a few drops of vanilla essence. Stir in the sifted flour and salt and mix to a dropping consistency with the milk. Put the apple mixture into the bottom of the pie-dish and spread the pudding mixture on top. Bake until firm and set—about 45–50 min., first in a moderate oven **(350° F., Gas 4)** then reduce heat after ½ hr. to warm **(335° F., Gas 3)**.

**4–5 helpings**

APPLE PUDDING—STEAMED

*Pouding de Pommes*

**4 oz. apples (after peeling and coring)**
**4 oz. breadcrumbs**
**4 oz. finely-chopped suet**
**4 oz. moist sugar**
**Pinch of nutmeg**
**Pinch of salt**
**2 eggs**
**¼ pt. milk**

Chop the apples coarsely. Mix together the breadcrumbs, suet, sugar, nutmeg and salt. Add the apples. Beat the eggs. Stir in the eggs and milk, and mix well. Leave to stand for 1 hr. to allow the bread to soak. The mixture should then drop easily from the spoon. If it is too stiff, add a little more milk. Pour into a well-greased basin, cover, and steam for 2 hr.

Serve with custard sauce

NOTE: *See also Fruit Pudding with Suet Crust*

**5–6 helpings**

APPLE SAUCE

*Sauce aux Pommes*

**1 lb. apples**
**2 tablesp. water**
**½ oz. butter *or* margarine**
**Rind and juice of ½ lemon**
**Sugar to taste**

Stew the apples very gently with the water, butter and lemon rind until they are pulpy. Beat them quite smooth or rub them through a hair or nylon sieve. Reheat the sauce with the lemon juice and sweeten to taste.

Serve with roast pork, roast goose or pork sausages. Excellent also as a sweet sauce with ginger pudding.

APPLE SNOW

**2 lb. cooking apples**
**Lemon rind**
**4 oz. sugar**
**1 tablesp. cream (optional)**
**2 eggs**
**½ pt. milk**
**½ oz. castor sugar**
**2 oz. castor sugar**

Peel, core and slice the apples. Stew with the lemon rind in ½ gill water until tender. Put through a fine nylon sieve. Add the 4 oz. sugar and cream, if used. In another bowl separate the eggs. Heat the milk and pour on to the well-beaten yolks; return to the pan and heat gently until the mixture thickens. Add ½ oz. sugar. Put the apple purée into a buttered pie-dish; pour the custard on top. Put into a warm oven **(335° F., Gas 3)** until set —about 40 min. Stiffly-whisk the egg whites; stir in lightly the 2 oz. castor sugar. Pile on top of the mixture. Bake in a very cool oven **(290° F., Gas 1)** until meringue is slightly coloured.

**6 helpings**

APPLE SNOW—COLD

*Pommes à la Neige*

**4 large baking apples (1½ lb.)**
**3 oz. granulated sugar (approx.)**

:hicken. *To make the baskets:* Put an apricot, ·ound side uppermost, on each bun, coat with he jelly, which must be just starting to thicken. ?ipe small stars of whipped cream around the ıpricots. Soak the angelica in warm water, :ut into strips $\frac{1}{4}$ in. wide and long enough to ːrch over the buns to form a "handle". Make wo small holes in each bun with a skewer to :eep the handle in place.

## ıPRICOT FRITTERS

*Beignets d'Abricots*

| | |
|---|---|
| **2 apricot halves (fresh *or* preserved)** | **Castor sugar** |
| **at for frying** | **Ground cinnamon** |

EAST BATTER

| | |
|---|---|
| **$\frac{1}{4}$ oz. yeast** | **6 oz. plain flour** |
| **$\frac{1}{4}$ teasp. castor sugar** | **Pinch of salt** |
| **$\frac{1}{2}$ gill warm milk (approx.)** | **1 oz. melted butter** |

Make the batter by creaming the yeast and ıgar and adding a little milk. Sift together oz. of the flour and the salt into a warm owl. Mix to a batter consistency with the ːast mixture, adding more milk if required. eave to rise until double its size. Meanwhile, rain the apricots from the syrup. When the ough is risen add the rest of the flour and arm milk to make a batter consistency, and ork in the melted butter. Leave to rise again ı a warm place. Coat the apricots thinly ith the batter and place them on a well-uttered paper. Leave in a warm place for ) min. Fry in hot fat until nicely brown.

Drain well and dredge with plenty of castor ıgar and cinnamon, before serving.

**fritters**

## PRICOT GÂTEAU

*Gâteau d'Abricot*

| | |
|---|---|
| **round of genoese pastry *or* rich, light cake 6 in. diameter and 1 in. thick** | **2 tablesp. sieved apricot jam** |
| **ablesp. sherry *or* fruit juice** | **A length of 1 in. wide pale coloured ribbon to tie round the sponge fingers (about 12 in.)** |
| **oz. savoy fingers soft textured** | |

FILLING

| | |
|---|---|
| **1 large can apricots** | **$\frac{3}{4}$ pt. double cream** |
| **$\frac{1}{2}$ pt. lemon jelly tablet** | **Castor sugar to taste** |

DECORATION

**Angelica**

Place the round of cake on a serving plate and sprinkle with the sherry or juice. Trim the sponge fingers so that the sides are quite straight and all are equal in length, with one end trimmed straight across. Melt the $\frac{1}{2}$ pt. jelly tablet in $\frac{1}{4}$ pt. of apricot juice and allow to cool, but not set. Brush inside of trimmed end of each sponge finger to 1 in. in depth with sieved apricot jam; dip one edge only in cool jelly, and press firmly against the side of the round of cake. As each finger is so treated, the jellied edge will be in contact with the dry edge of the adjacent finger, and a firm case may be made without danger of the fingers becoming sodden and crumbling. The rounded, sugary surface of the finger faces outwards. Tie the ribbon round the finished case so that the sponge fingers are held firmly upright, and leave to set.

FILLING: Drain apricots well, and reserve 6 halves for decoration. Cut the remainder into quarters. Whip the cream until the fork leaves a trail; sweeten to taste with castor sugar. Put $\frac{1}{4}$ of the cream into a forcing bag with rose pipe, for decorating (optional). Stir the quartered apricots into the remainder of the cream. Lastly stir in $\frac{1}{8}$ pt. of the liquid jelly, steaming hot. Pour immediately into the sponge-finger case. Arrange the 6 apricot halves (either whole *or* cut as liked) on the top, and pipe cream roses between and around to cover the surface of the cream. Decorate with leaves of angelica.

VARIATIONS: Use fresh *or* canned strawberries, *or* chopped pineapple, *or* fruit-flavoured ice cream, *or* custard cream fillings

## APRICOT GLAZE

| | |
|---|---|
| **2 tablesp. apricot jam** | **1 tablesp. water** |

Sieve apricot jam and water and bring to boiling-point. Use to glaze the top of small cakes, e.g. nougatines, and to stick almond paste to Christmas cakes, etc.

**Rind and juice of 1 lemon**
**½ pt. milk**
**2–3 eggs**
**4 individual sponge cakes**

DECORATION
**Glacé cherries**

Reduce the apples to a purée. The finest flavour is obtained by washing the apples and baking them, dry, in a moderate oven (**350° F., Gas 4**) until quite soft, when the skins and cores may easily be separated from the pulp. Otherwise, peel, core, slice and cook in the minimum amount of water.

Wash the lemon, remove the rind in thin strips, avoiding any white pith, and infuse slowly in the milk. Make a cup custard with this liquid and the egg yolks . Sweeten to taste. Place the sponge cakes, split if liked, in the bottom of a large glass dish and pour the custard over them. Rub the apple-pulp through a fine nylon sieve and sweeten to taste. Add lemon juice to flavour and leave to cool. Whisk the egg whites until quite stiff. Whisk in the apple purée, 1 tablesp. at a time, keeping the foam firm and light. Pile the apple foam on top of the soaked sponge cakes and decorate with glacé cherries.

**6 helpings**

## APPLE SNOWBALLS

*Ballons de Pommes à la Neige*

**To each apple allow:**

**1½ oz. rice**
**½ pt. milk *or* milk and water**
**Pinch of salt**
**1½ oz. sugar**
**1 clove (optional)**

Simmer the rice in the milk with the salt until the rice is tender and all the milk is absorbed. (1 tablesp. of sugar to every pt. of milk may be added if liked.)

Peel and core the apples, keeping them whole. Put a clove (if used) into the centre and stand each apple on a base of cooled rice on a pudding cloth. Fill the centre of the apple with sugar and then cover the apple with rice. Tie the apples in the pudding cloth and drop into boiling water. Boil very gently for about 45 min.

Serve with castor sugar.

**1 apple per helping**

## APPLES AND RICE

*Po*

**3 oz. rice**
**Pinch of salt**
**1½ pt. milk**
**Rind of 1 lemon**
**1 oz. butter**
**3 oz. gran**
**6 cooking**
**2 tablesp.**
***or* butt**

Wash the rice and simmer it (with the salt and strips of lemc tender and most of the milk has b Stir in the butter and granulat remove the lemon rind. Peel apples and place them in a large the cavities with raspberry jam sugar. Carefully fill the spaces apples with rice. Bake in a cool **Gas 2**) for about ¾–1 hr. until tender but not broken.

**6 helpings**

## APPLES AND SAGO

*Pom*

**1 pt. water**
**1 oz. fine sago**
**6 cooking apples**
**3 oz. moist sugar**
**Rind an lemon**
**A few d *or* coc**

Boil the water, sprinkle in the until the sago is clear; about 1

Peel and core the apples, whole. Add the sugar, lemon ju rind in strips and the apples Simmer very gently (with the l until the apples are tender—ab depending on the cooking qualit Lift the apples out on to th remove lemon rind. Add a colouring to the syrup and p round the apples.

**4–5 helpings**

## APRICOT BASKETS

**The basic mixture for rich cakes baked in bun tins**
**1 small can apricots**
**¼ pt. packet lemon jelly**
**A littl swe**
**Piece long**

Whilst the buns are coo apricots from the syrup. Ma to just under ¼ pt. with water, and pour on to the jelly. Sti and leave to cool until it is

### APRICOT JAM
(Fresh Fruit)

**3 lb. fresh apricots**
**½ pt. water**
**3 lb. sugar**

Wash, halve and stone the fruit and put into the preserving-pan with the water. If desired, crack a few of the stones, remove the kernels and blanch them by dipping in boiling water. Add the halved kernels to the pan. Simmer till tender and the contents of the pan are reduced. Add the sugar and stir over a low heat till dissolved. Bring to the boil and boil rapidly until setting point is reached. Skim, pot and cover.

**Yield—5 lb.**

### APRICOT MOULD

*Gâteau d'Abricots*

**1½ pt. milk**
**2½ oz. ground rice**
**1 tablesp. hot water**
**4 tablesp. apricot jam**
**1 oz. castor sugar**
**½ gill double cream**

Heat the milk and when boiling, sprinkle in the ground rice. Cook the rice gently until quite soft—about 7 min., stirring all the time. Stir 1 tablesp. hot water into the apricot jam and sieve. Add to the ground rice and milk. Add sugar to sweeten to taste. Pour quickly into a wet 1½ pt. border-mould. When quite cold and set, turn out and pile sweetened whipped cream into the hollow.

**6 helpings**
**Cooking time—10 min.**
**Setting time—2 hr.**

### APRICOT MOUSSE

**One 10-oz. can apricots**
**1 egg white**
**¼ pt. thick cream**
**2 oz. sugar**

Sieve the apricots; chill for 45 min. Add egg white (unbeaten) to the apricots and beat until light and fluffy. Whip the cream, add sugar gradually, fold into apricots. Freeze until firm.

### APRICOT or PEACH JAM
(Dried Fruit)

This is a popular jam for making in the winter when most other fruits are scarce.

**1 lb. dried apricots *or* peaches**
**Juice of 1 lemon**
**3 lb. sugar**
**2–3 pt. water (2 pt. for peaches, 3 pt. for apricots)**
**2–3 oz. blanched and finely shredded almonds (optional)**

Wash the fruit and put in a basin with the water. Soak for 24–48 hr. Transfer the fruit and water to the preserving-pan and simmer for 30 min., stirring occasionally. Add the sugar, lemon juice and the shredded almonds. Stir over a low heat until the sugar is dissolved. Boil rapidly until setting point is reached. Skim, pot and cover.

**Yield—approx. 5 lb.**

### APRICOT PUDDING—BAKED

*Pouding d'Abricots*

**¾ pt. milk**
**¾ pt. fresh bread-crumbs *or* cake-crumbs**
**Short crust pastry using 5–6 oz. flour, etc.**
**One 12 oz. can *or* 1 bottle of apricots**
**2 oz. castor sugar**
**2 eggs**
**1 glass sherry**
**2–4 oz. castor sugar for the meringue**

Boil the milk, pour it over the bread-crumbs and let them soak for ½ hr. Line the sides of a 2-pt. pie-dish with the pastry.

Strain the apricots, pass them through a fine sieve and add to them 2 oz. sugar, egg yolks, sherry and soaked crumbs. Pour into the pie-dish. Bake in a fairly hot oven (**400° F., Gas 6**) until the pastry is cooked and the filling is set —25–30 min. Whisk the egg whites stiffly, stir in lightly the 2–4 oz. castor sugar and spread this meringue over the top of the pudding. Dredge well with castor sugar and decorate with strips of angelica and cut glacé cherry, if liked. Bake in a very cool oven (**290° F., Gas 1**) until the meringue is crisp and golden, about 30 min.

**6 helpings**

### APRICOT PUDDING—STEAMED

*Pouding d'Abricots*

**6 pieces canned apricots**
**3 oz. butter *or* margarine**
**3 oz. castor sugar**
**2 eggs**
**Rind of ½ lemon**
**3 oz. plain flour**
**¼ teasp. baking-powder**

Grease a 1½ pt. basin. Drain the apricots well and cut them into small pieces.

Cream together the fat and sugar and when

really soft beat in the eggs gradually. Stir in the grated lemon rind, apricots and the sifted flour and baking-powder. Turn the mixture into the basin, cover and steam steadily $1\frac{1}{4}$–$1\frac{1}{2}$ hr.

Serve with apricot sauce.

**4 helpings**

### APRICOT SAUCE

*Sauce à l'Abricot*

| | |
|---|---|
| **½ lb. apricots, fresh *or* canned** | **Lemon juice** |
| **¼ pt. water *or* syrup from can** | **1 teasp. Maraschino (optional)** |
| **1–2 oz. brown sugar** | **1 level teasp. arrowroot** |

Stone the apricots and stew them till soft in the water. When soft rub them through a hair or nylon sieve. Meanwhile crack the stones, scald and skin the kernels. Add sugar, lemon juice, liqueur (if used) and kernels to the sauce. Reheat the sauce, stirring in the arrowroot blended with a little cold water. Bring to the boil and serve the sauce.

*See also Jam Sauce.*

### APRICOT SOUFFLÉ

*Soufflé aux Abricots*

| | |
|---|---|
| **⅜ pt. apricot purée** | **2 oz. castor sugar** |
| **1½ oz. butter** | **Cochineal** |
| **1½ oz. plain flour** | **6 egg whites** |
| **4 egg yolks** | |

Prepare the soufflé tin *or* mould . Make the apricot purée by rubbing either stewed or tinned apricots through a fine sieve and thinning down the purée with some of the syrup.

Melt the butter in the saucepan, add the flour and cook slowly for a few minutes. Stir in gradually the apricot purée; continue cooking until the mixture thickens. Leave to cool. Beat in the egg yolks singly and the sugar. Add a few drops of cochineal to bring up the apricot colouring. Stiffly whisk the egg whites; fold them into the mixture. Pour into the soufflé mould, cover and steam gently, about 50–60 min.

Turn out and serve at once with apricot- or custard- sauce.

**6 helpings**

### APRICOT SYRUP

| | |
|---|---|
| **Sound, ripe apricots** | **Allow 1 lb. loaf sugar to every pt. juice** |
| **Water** | |

Three-quarters fill a large jar with apricots, stoned and cut in halves, add half the kernels. Stand the jar in a pan of boiling water and simmer until the fruit is quite soft and the juice flows freely. Strain off the liquid through a fine sieve or jelly bag, measure it carefully and add sugar in the proportion stated above. Boil up again for 10 min., removing the scum as it rises. Stand aside and when quite cool pour into clean dry bottles. Pour a little olive oil on the top in each bottle, cork securely and seal with bottling wax.

The oil at the top of each bottle must be carefully removed with a piece of clean cotton wool before use. The syrup is usually diluted with plain or aerated water.

**Variations:** Substitute cherries, greengages, peaches, plums or rhubarb for apricots.

### APRICOT TRIFLE

| | |
|---|---|
| **5–6 slices Swiss jam roll** | **1 pt. custard** |
| **1–2 macaroons** | **6 oz. can cream** |
| **2–3 tablesp. sherry** | **1 teasp. gelatine** |
| **1 can apricots** | **2 teasp. boiling water** |
| | **1 oz. blanched almonds** |

Cut the jam roll into small cubes and place with broken macaroons in the bottom of a shallow glass dish; pour the sherry and a little apricot juice over. Cut up some of the apricots and add to the dish; pour over the custard. Allow to set. Whip the cream, adding the gelatine melted in the water. Pile the cream roughly so that it is fairly high in the centre. Decorate with apricots spiked with strips of almonds.

### ARROWROOT PUDDING—STEAMED

*Pouding à l'Arrowroot*

| | |
|---|---|
| **1½ oz. arrowroot** | **½ teasp. vanilla essence *or* grated lemon rind** |
| **1½ pt. milk** | **3 eggs** |
| **2 oz. castor sugar** | |

Mix the arrowroot to a smooth paste with a little of the milk. Boil the remainder of the milk and pour over the arrowroot paste, stirring well. Return to the saucepan, stir, and simmer gently until the mixture thickens. Leave to cool slightly and stir in the flavouring, sugar and well-beaten eggs. Pour into a 2 pt. greased basin, cover with greased paper and steam for 1½ hr.

Turn out and serve with custard or wine sauce.

**6 helpings**

### ARTICHOKE BOTTOMS

*Fonds d'Artichauts*

Where economy need not be considered, one can use only the bottoms or "fonds" of globe artichokes. After cooking, the leaves are carefully pulled out of the artichokes so that the bottoms remain unbroken. These are then served with melted butter, or are stuffed.

### ARTICHOKE SALAD

*Salade d'Artichauts*

**6 cooked globe artichokes (small ones)**
**French dressing *or* Vinaigrette sauce**

When quite cold, serve the artichokes on a suitable dish. Hand the sauce separately.

**6 helpings**

### ASPARAGUS—BOILED

*Asperges au naturel*

**1 bundle of asparagus**
**Salt**
**2 oz. butter**
**Lemon juice**

Trim the hard white ends of the asparagus to suitable lengths for serving. Scrape the stalks with a sharp knife, working downwards from the head. Wash them well in cold water. Tie them into small bundles with the heads in one direction. Re-trim the stalks evenly. Keep them in cold water until ready to cook. Cook very gently, with the heads off the source of heat, in just enough salted boiling water to cover. When tender (in about 15–20 min.), drain and serve on a folded table napkin. Serve with melted butter, seasoned and lightly flavoured with lemon.

NOTE: To ensure that the tender point of the asparagus is not overcooked by the time that the stem is ready, the asparagus should be cooked "standing". This can be achieved in an "asparagus boiler", a narrow very deep pan. A bottling jar half-filled with boiling water, stood in a deep saucepan of boiling water, serves as a very good substitute. The asparagus is placed stems down in the jar and the points cook more slowly in steam only. Allow 30 min. for this method of cooking.

**Allow 6 or 8 medium-sized heads per person**

### ASPARAGUS CREAM SOUP

*Crème d'asperges*

**1 bundle (25 heads) of "sprue" *or* thin asparagus**
**1 pt. white stock**
**1 oz. butter**
**1 oz. flour**
**1 onion**
**Lemon juice**
**Pinch of sugar**
**Salt and pepper**
**⅛ pt. cream**

Cut off the tips of the asparagus and cook them till just tender in a little of the stock—about 10 min.; keep them for garnish. Melt the butter, stir into it the flour, then the stock, and bring to boiling point. Slice the onion and cut the asparagus in short lengths. Add the onion and asparagus sticks to the boiling stock and simmer them very gently till quite tender—30–40 min. Press through a hair or nylon sieve. Add lemon juice and sugar to taste, season. Reheat. Stir in the cream, add the asparagus tips last.

**4 helpings**
**Cooking time—about 50 min.**

### ASPARAGUS—FRENCH STYLE

*Asperges à la Bonne Femme*

**50 heads of asparagus**
**½ pt. milk**
**1 small lettuce—finely shredded and in short lengths**
**1 small onion—parboiled and finely chopped**
**1 bay leaf**
**1 sprig of thyme**
**1 oz. flour**
**1 oz. butter**
**1 egg**
**Salt and pepper**
**1 teasp. lemon juice**
**Croûtes of buttered toast *or* fried bread**

GARNISH

**Chopped parsley**
**Cucumber strips**

Prepare the asparagus (*see Asparagus—Boiled*) and tie into bundles. Bring the milk to boiling-point, put in the asparagus, lettuce, onion, bay leaf, thyme and a little salt. Simmer gently about 20 min. Drain the asparagus well, cut off the points and edible parts of the stalks and keep them hot. Strain the milk and make a white sauce with it and the flour and butter. Cool it slightly, add the beaten egg and cook until it thickens, without boiling. Season and add lemon juice. Pile the asparagus on the croûtes, coat with sauce and garnish with chopped parsley and cucumber strips. Serve as a vegetable entremet *or* as an entrée for a vegetarian dinner.

**Allow 1 croûte for each person and 1 or 2 over**
**Cooking time—30–40 min.**

### ASPARAGUS POINTS

*Pointes d'Asperges*

| | |
|---|---|
| **Asparagus** | **Chopped shallot and chopped parsley (optional)** |
| **Melted butter** | |
| **Salt and pepper** | |

Cut the points and tender green parts of the asparagus into short pieces, place them in slightly salted boiling water, and cook gently 5 to 10 min., according to size and age. Drain well, put the asparagus into a saucepan containing a little melted butter, sprinkle with pepper and toss over heat for a few minutes. Serve as a garnish or a vegetable or as a filling in omelets.

NOTE: It is a mistake to add anything which will impair the delicate flavour of the asparagus but a little chopped shallot and parsley may be fried in the butter before adding the asparagus.

**Allow 12 points per helping**
**Cooking time—15 min.**

### ASPARAGUS ROLLS—HOT

*Petits Pains aux Asperges*

| | |
|---|---|
| **50 heads of asparagus** | **1 egg** |
| **6 small French rolls** | **Salt and pepper** |
| **½ pt. white sauce** | **Lemon juice** |

Cut off the tops of the rolls and scoop out the inside. Heat the shells of crust in the oven till they are very crisp. Cook the asparagus in the usual way, cut off the points and keep them hot and rub the stalks through a fine sieve (stainless metal *or* nylon). Stir the asparagus purée and the beaten egg into the white sauce. Cook until the mixture thickens (without boiling or the egg will curdle). Season well and use a little lemon juice or additional flavour. Fill the crisp rolls, piling the mixture high, garnish the top of each with asparagus points. Put the tops of the rolls on again like lids, and serve very quickly.

NOTE: This dish may be served as a vegetable luncheon dish or as a vegetarian entrée.

**6 helpings**
**Cooking time—about 40 min.**

### ASPARAGUS SALAD, AMERICAN

*Salade d'Asperges Americaine*

| | |
|---|---|
| **2 grapefruits** | **1 tablesp. Worcester sauce** |
| **½ pt. cooked asparagus tips** | **2 tablesp. tomato ketchup** |
| **2 tablesp. lemon juice** | **Salt and pepper** |

Halve the grapefruits and remove the pulp in sections. Mix it with the asparagus tips. Mix the lemon juice, Worcester sauce, tomato ketchup and a little seasoning and pour on to the grapefruit and asparagus. Toss together lightly. Dish and serve very cold.

**4–6 helpings**

### ASPARAGUS SALAD WITH SHRIMPS

*Salade d'Asperges aux Crevettes*

| | |
|---|---|
| **1 small *or* ½ a large bundle of green asparagus *or* can of asparagus** | **½ pt. shrimps (picked)** |
| | **Mayonnaise sauce** |
| | **4 hard-boiled eggs** |

Prepare and cook the asparagus or drain canned asparagus. When cold, cut the tender portions into small pieces and put them into a bowl with the shrimps. Mix lightly with enough mayonnaise sauce to moisten. Serve on a dish in the centre of a border of sliced hard-boiled egg.

**4 helpings**

### ASPARAGUS SANDWICH ROLLS

| | |
|---|---|
| **Thin slices of FRESH brown bread and butter** | **Mayonnaise if wished *or* Hollandaise sauce** |
| **Cooked *or* canned asparagus tips** | **Seasoning** |

Remove the crusts from the bread and butter. Put a well-drained asparagus tip on each piece of bread and butter, adding a little mayonnaise or Hollandaise sauce and seasoning. Roll up firmly. Keep under a damp cloth or cover with aluminium foil until required.

NOTE: If wished the bread and butter can also be spread with demi-sel or soft cream cheese.

### ASPARAGUS SOUFFLÉ

**50 cooked green asparagus heads**
**2 oz. butter**
**1½ oz. flour**
**½ pt. milk**
**2 eggs**
**Salt and pepper**
**2 oz. grated Parmesan cheese**

Heat the butter in a saucepan, stir in the flour, and add the milk. Beat and cook the mixture until it leaves the sides of the pan, then add the egg yolks, and a little salt and pepper. Beat well, add the cheese, fold in the stiffly-whisked egg whites, and lastly the well drained asparagus heads, or the purée from them. Turn into a well-buttered soufflé-dish and bake in a fairly hot oven (**375° F., Gas 5**) for about 20 min.

**3–4 helpings**

### ASPIC CREAM

**1 gill double cream**
**1½ gills aspic jelly**
**1 teasp. lemon juice**
**Pinch of white pepper**
**Pinch of castor sugar**

Put the cream into a basin, stir it with a whisk, and gradually add the aspic, which must be liquid. Add the lemon juice and seasoning and pass through a tammy cloth or fine strainer.

Use for masking entrees, chicken, etc.

### ASPIC JELLY

*Gelée d'Aspic*

**1 qt. jellied veal stock**
**1 oz. gelatine**
**Bouquet garni (parsley, thyme, bay leaf)**
**2 sticks of celery**
**2 egg whites and shells**
**1 glass sherry (optional)**
**¼ pt. vinegar**

Let the stock become quite cold, and remove every particle of fat. Put it into a stewpan with the gelatine, herbs, celery cut into large pieces, the egg whites previously slightly beaten and the shells previously washed and dried. Whisk over heat until nearly boiling, then add the wine and vinegar. Continue the whisking until quite boiling, then reduce the heat and simmer for about 10 min., strain till clear, and use as required.

### ASPIC JELLY (from gelatine)

**2 egg whites and shells**
**1 lemon**
**2 chicken *or* veal bouillon cubes**
**1 qt. water**
**2½ oz. gelatine**
**¼ pt. malt vinegar**
**1 tablesp. tarragon vinegar**
**1 onion**
**1 carrot**
**2–3 sticks of celery**
**Bouquet garni (parsley, thyme, bay leaf)**
**10 peppercorns**
**1 teasp. salt**

Whisk the egg whites slightly, wash the shells; peel the lemon rind as thinly as possible, and strain the juice; crumble the cubes. Put them with the rest of the ingredients into a pan, whisk over heat until boiling, then simmer very gently for about 20 min. Strain through a jelly bag.

NOTE: This jelly is used principally for lining and garnishing moulds. If too stiff it may be diluted with a little water, or sherry, when additional flavour is desired.

### AURORA SAUCE

*Sauce Aurore*

**½ pt. Béchamel sauce**
**Paprika pepper to taste**
**2 tablesp. concentrated tomato purée *or* 1 tablesp. purée of canned pimento (sweet red pepper)**

Add the purée carefully to the hot sauce, reheat without boiling and serve the sauce at once. The sauce should be a deep pink colour.

NOTE: Aurora sauce may also be made with thick Velouté sauce made with fish stock, and with tomato purée added.

Serve Béchamel Aurore with chicken or fish; Velouté Aurore with fish.

### AUSTRALIAN BISCUITS

**3 oz. plain flour**
**2 oz. coconut**
**2 oz. rolled oats**
**1½ oz. sugar**
**1 level teasp. bicarbonate of soda**
**3 oz. lard *or* margarine**
**1 tablesp. golden syrup**
**1 teasp. water**

Sift flour and mix with other dry ingredients.

Melt fat and syrup with water, pour into dry ingredients and mix well. Allow to set. Form into small balls and place well apart on a greased baking-sheet. Bake in a moderate oven (350° F., Gas 4).

**20 biscuits**
**Cooking time—10–15 min.**

## AVOCADO PEARS

These make an unusual ingredient for hors d'œuvre . Halve the pears and remove the stone, then cover the pear halves with oil, vinegar and seasoning. Allow to stand for a while. Alternatively try them filled with prawns .

## AVOCADO PEARS AND PRAWNS

**2 large Avocado pears**
**2 tablesp. olive oil**
**2 tablesp. vinegar**
**Good pinch of salt**
**Good pinch of pepper**
**A little mixed mustard**
**2 teacups (about ½ pt.) shelled prawns**
**Crisp lettuce leaves**
**Lemon**
**Pinch of sugar (optional)**
**¼ crushed clove of garlic (optional)**

Halve the pears. Blend the oil, vinegar and seasonings together. Toss the prawns in this, and then spoon into the pear halves. Put on to crisp lettuce leaves and garnish with wedges of lemon.

A pinch of sugar can be added to the dressing if wished, also a little garlic.

**4 helpings**

## BABAS WITH RUM SYRUP

*Babas au Rhum*

**½ lb. plain flour**
**Pinch of salt**
**½ oz. yeast**
**1 oz. castor sugar**
**1 gill milk**
**4 eggs**
**4 oz. butter**
**2 oz. currants**

RUM SYRUP

**3 oz. granulated sugar**
**1 gill water**
**Rind of ½ lemon**
**1 wineglass rum**
**1 wineglass sherry**

Grease 9 dariole or baba moulds.

Sift the flour and salt into a warm basin. Cream the yeast with a pinch of castor sugar, and add to it the gill of warm milk. Mix this into the flour to form a soft dough. Beat well until the dough leaves the sides of the basin clean. Cover the basin with a damp cloth and leave the dough to rise in a warm (but not hot) place until about twice its size. When the dough has risen sufficiently add 2 eggs, the melted butter and castor sugar, beat well in. Then add the rest of the eggs and the currants and beat again for 5–10 min., until the dough is smooth and glossy. Half-fill the moulds with the mixture. Put them in a warm place until the mixture has risen to the top of the moulds. Bake in a fairly hot oven (425° F., Gas 7) for about 20–25 min. until brown and firm.

Put the granulated sugar and water into a pan with the thinly peeled lemon rind. Boil for 10 min., add the rum and sherry; strain.

Reheat the syrup. Soak the babas in it for a minute; lift them out and serve immediately, with the syrup poured round.

**9 babas**

## BACHELOR'S PUDDING

*Pouding à la Garçon*

**3 oz. dried fruit**
**6 oz. plain flour**
**Pinch of salt**
**1 teasp. baking-powder**
**3 oz. sugar**
**2 oz. breadcrumbs**
**3 oz. finely-chopped suet**
**1 egg**
**Milk to mix (about 1 gill)**

5

Cakes you can use as desserts.
From left to right: feather-iced sandwich cake; strawberry shortcake; small fruit tarts; in the foreground, petits fours.

Wensleydale
Double Gloucester
Cheddar
Blue Stilton
Danish Blue
Camembert
Edam
Cheshire
Parmesan
Leicester
Emmen-thaler
Lancashire
Tôme au Raisin
Caerphilly
Gorgonzola
Sage Derby
Provolone
Roquefort
R.N.Lane

7
Christmas Table.

←
6
This selection of British and foreign cheeses shows you what they look like clearly.

8

Fish dishes.

Attractively cooked, the poached salmon trout above is garnished with cucumber and egg. Below, baked haddock on a bed of rice, garnished with tomatoes and with gay lemon slices.

Grease a pudding basin.

Clean the fruit. Mix together the sifted flour, salt, baking-powder, sugar, breadcrumbs and suet. Stir in the dried fruit. Add the well-beaten egg and some of the milk. Stir, adding more milk as required, until the mixture drops easily from the spoon. Turn the mixture into the basin; cover with greased paper, and steam for 2–2½ hr.

When ready, turn out of the basin and dredge well with sugar.

**4–5 helpings**

### BACON AND HAM

Bacon is obtained from a side of pork from which the head and feet have been removed. The side is salted for a suitable time, and then provides "green" bacon. Much bacon is treated further by smoking. This takes place from 24 to 48 hours in the smoke from a slow-burning hardwood dust such as oak. The chine or back bone is removed before processing, and before slicing the other bones (rib, shoulder and thigh bones).

Strictly speaking, ham is processed pork taken only from the gammon or leg. It is processed, and so preserved, in many different ways; most often by salting and smoking. Hams are made in most countries of Europe, and in the United States. Many European hams are eaten raw, but English hams are usually boiled before use.

### BACON AND POTATO SALAD

| | |
|---|---|
| **6 large new potatoes** | **Mayonnaise sauce** |
| **2 spring onions** | **1 tablesp. finely-chopped parsley** |
| **Salt and pepper** | |
| **2 tablesp. vinegar** | |
| **6 oz. lean bacon** | |

Steam the potatoes and peel after cooking. Dice them while hot and put into a basin with the finely-chopped onions. Season them and baste with the vinegar. Cut the bacon into dice and fry it slowly until browned. Drain from the fat and add to the potatoes; mix lightly with mayonnaise sauce taking care not to break the potato. Dish, sprinkle with parsley.

NOTE: Endive and lettuce may be made into a salad with bacon in the same way but mix with vinegar, salt and pepper only and omit the mayonnaise.

**6 helpings**

### BACON—to fry

Cut the rind off the rashers of bacon. Heat the frying-pan for a few minutes. Place the bacon in the hot pan, reduce the heat and cook for a few minutes. Turn the rashers over and continue cooking until the fat is transparent or crisp, as preferred.

### BACON—to grill

Cut the rind off the bacon rashers. Place the rashers on the grill rack below the hot grill. After a few minutes' grilling, turn and finish cooking.

### BAGELS

Water Doughnuts

| | |
|---|---|
| **½ oz. yeast** | **1 teasp. salt** |
| **1 oz. castor sugar** | **1 egg** |
| **2 oz. margarine** | **1 lb. flour** |
| **1½ teacups water** | **Poppy seeds** |

Cream the yeast with 1 teasp. of the sugar. Put the margarine, water, salt and remaining sugar in a saucepan and place over a gentle heat until margarine is melted; leave till just lukewarm, then mix in the dissolved yeast. Add this mixture with the beaten egg to the flour and knead to a firm dough. Cover with a cloth and leave in a warm place till just beginning to rise. Knead again and roll into small pieces the width of a finger and about 5 in. long. Shape into rings, pinching the ends well together, and leave again on a floured board in a warm place until beginning to rise. Then drop a few at a time in a saucepan ½ full of boiling water and cook gently till they rise to the top. Remove with a fish-slice on to greased baking-sheets and sprinkle with poppy seeds. Bake in a fairly hot oven **(375° F., Gas 5)** till golden brown and crisp—20–30 min.

**20 bagels**

### BAKED APPLES

*Pommes cuites au four*

| | |
|---|---|
| **6 cooking apples** | **½ gill water** |
| **2 oz. demerara sugar** | |

FILLING, choice of:—

1. **2 oz. moist sugar and 2 oz. butter**
2. **Blackcurrant** *or* **raspberry** *or* **strawberry** *or* **apricot jam**
3. **3 oz. stoned dates** *or* **sultanas** *or* **currants** *or* **raisins, 2 oz. moist sugar and 1 teasp. ground cinnamon**

Prepare the filling. Wash and core the apples. Cut round the skin of the apple with the tip of a sharp knife, ⅔ of the way up from the base. Put the apples into a fireproof dish and fill the centres with the chosen filling. Sprinkle with the demerara sugar. Add the water. Bake in a moderate oven **(350° F., Gas 4)** until the apples are soft in the centre —about ¾–1 hr. depending on the cooking quality of the apples.

**6 helpings**

## BAKED AUBERGINE WITH CHEESE

*Aubergine au Parmesan*

| | |
|---|---|
| **4 aubergines** | **½ pt. Béchamel sauce** |
| **1 heaped tablesp. grated Parmesan cheese** | **Salt and pepper** |
| | **1 tablesp. breadcrumbs** |
| | **½ oz. butter** |

Parboil the aubergines for 10 min., then slice rather thickly, remove the seeds, if any, and arrange slices neatly in a fireproof dish. Mix the cheese into the Béchamel sauce, season to taste, and coat the aubergines with it. Cover lightly with the breadcrumbs, sprinkle the surface with the melted butter. Bake in a fairly hot oven, **(375° F., Gas 5)** for ½ hr.

**6 helpings**

## BAKED BEETROOT

**Small young beetroots**

Wash the beetroots carefully. If the skin has been damaged in any way, cover the damaged part with a little flour and water paste. Put them into a baking-dish and bake in a moderate oven **(350° F., Gas 4)**, until tender, about 1 hr. This method is excellent for young beetroots, all the flavour and sweetness of the beetroot being retained.

NOTE: The beetroots may be wrapped in greased papers or covered with aluminium foil before baking.

## BAKED CALF'S HEART

*Cœur de Veau rôti*

| | |
|---|---|
| **A calf's heart** | **Flour for dredging** |
| **4 oz. veal forcemeat** | **½ pt. brown gravy** |
| **2 oz. fat** | |

GARNISH

| | |
|---|---|
| **Rashers of bacon** | **Forcemeat balls** |
| **Parsley** | |

Wash the heart thoroughly under running cold water or in several changes of cold water. Cut off flaps and lobes and remove any pieces of gristle. Cut away the membrane which divides the 2 cavities and see that the inside is quite free from blood. Soak in cold water for ½–1 hr. Wash again and dry well. Fill the inside with the forcemeat and sew up the ends with fine string. Heat the fat in a roasting-tin and put the heart in it. Baste well and cover with greased paper. Bake for about 1½ hr. in a fairly hot oven **(375° F., Gas 5)**. Turn and baste often, and ½ hr. before serving remove the paper, dredge well with flour, re-baste and put back in the oven. When ready, place on a hot dish and use the fat and flour in the tin to enrich or form the base for the brown gravy. Garnish with rashers of bacon which have been fried or grilled, and sprigs of parsley. If liked, some of the stuffing can be made into balls and cooked for the last ½ hr. with the heart and served as garnish.

**4 helpings**

## BAKED CARP

*Carpe farcie*

| | |
|---|---|
| **1 carp** | **Butter for basting** |
| **Egg and breadcrumbs** | |

FORCEMEAT

| | |
|---|---|
| **8 sauce oysters** | **1 shallot** |
| **3 anchovies, boned** | **Salt** |
| **2 tablesp. breadcrumbs** | **Cayenne pepper** |
| **1 teasp. finely-chopped parsley** | **1 egg yolk** |

SAUCE

| | |
|---|---|
| **1 oz. butter** | **1 tablesp. lemon juice** |
| **1 tablesp. flour** | **½ tablesp. Worcester sauce** |
| **¾ pt. good stock** | |
| **1 teasp. mixed mustard** | |

Clean and scale the fish. Remove the beards of the oysters and simmer for 15 min. in a little fish stock or water. Cut the oysters into small pieces, but do not cook them; also cut the anchovies into small pieces. Mix together the breadcrumbs, oysters, anchovies, parsley, finely-chopped shallot and seasoning; add the egg yolk, the liquor of the oysters and the stock in which the oysterbeards were simmered. Put the forcemeat inside the fish and sew up the opening; brush over with egg and coat with breadcrumbs. Place in a baking-dish and cook gently for about 1 hr., basting frequently with hot butter. To make the sauce: melt the butter in a saucepan, stir in the flour, add the stock and stir until the sauce boils. Simmer for 2–3 min. then add the mustard, lemon juice, Worcester sauce and the liquor (strained) in which the fish was cooked. Garnish the fish with cut lemon and parsley, and serve the sauce in a sauceboat.

NOTE: The fish may be stuffed with veal forcemeat instead of oyster forcemeat if liked.

**4–5 helpings**
**Cooking time—1¼–1½ hr.**

## BAKED CONGER EEL

*Congre cuit au Four*

**2 lb. conger eel**
**Suet forcemeat** *see* **Baked Stuffed Plaice**
**Butter** *or* **fat**
**Flour**

Wash and dry the fish thoroughly, skin and stuff with forcemeat and bind it with tape. Melt the butter or fat in a baking-dish or tin, put in the fish and baste well. Bake gently for 1 hr., basting occasionally with fat and dredging the surface with flour.

Serve with the gravy poured round, or if preferred with tomato, brown caper, or a suitable fish sauce.

**4–5 helpings**

## BAKED CORN ON THE COB

*Maïs rôti*

**6 ears** *or* **cobs of corn, freshly picked**
**2 oz. butter**
**Seasoning**

*Method 1.* Remove outer and inner husks and the silk. Melt the butter in a roasting dish. Roll the cobs in it, so that they are lightly coated with butter. Season. Roast in a fairly hot oven **(375° F., Gas 5)** turning them frequently.

**6 helpings**
**Cooking time—35 min. (approx.)**

*Method 2.* Prepare as above but place the cobs in the roasting dish (without butter) and just cover them with milk. Bake for about 45 min. Drain; season with salt and pepper. Toss in melted butter and place under a hot grill for a few minutes before serving.

**6 helpings**
**Cooking time—1 hr. (approx.)**

## BAKED CUSTARD

*Crème cuite au four*

**1½ pt. milk**
**Flavouring**
**3 eggs**
**1½ oz. castor sugar**

Beat the eggs with the sugar. Add the warmed milk and flavouring. Strain into a greased pie-dish. Stand the pie-dish in a tray of warm water and bake slowly in a warm–moderate oven **(335°–350° F., Gas 3–4)** until the custard is set in the centre, about 50 min.

**6 helpings**

## BAKED CUSTARDS

*See Custard and Custard Mixtures.*

## BAKED EGG IN SPINACH

**2 oz. creamed spinach**
**Seasoning**
**1 egg**
**½ tablesp. cream** *or* **milk**
**¼ oz. butter**

GARNISH
**Triangles of crisp toast**

Put the spinach into an individual dish. Season. Break egg carefully, pour on to spinach. Pour cream on top, add butter and season. Bake for 10 min. near the top of a fairly hot oven **(375° F., Gas 5)**.

Serve at once—with a spoon.

**1 helping**
**Cooking time—10 min.**

## BAKED EGGS

*Œufs en Cocotte*

Heat one cocotte (a special little dish manufactured for this purpose) for each person.

Add a little butter or cream, break an egg into each, season to taste, and place the cocottes in a pan of boiling water to come half way up their sides. Cover the pan and place in a moderate oven **(350° F., Gas 4)**. Cooking time when the eggs are in thin china dishes will be 6–7 min.; allow 8–9 min. with thicker dishes.

*Œufs sur le Plat*

These are usually cooked in small dishes, one for each person, but the dish can be larger provided that the egg whites do not spread out too much when broken in, otherwise they will cook before the yolks. Heat the dish, add butter, eggs and seasonings as for Œufs en Cocotte. Place the dish in a moderate oven **(350° F., Gas 4)** and cook until the white is set but soft, and the yolk shows through a film of white. This will take about 5 min.; time will vary according to the thickness of the eggs and dish.

## BAKED GRAYLING

*Ombre rôti*

**2 medium-sized grayling**
**Butter for basting**
**Salt and pepper**
**1/3 pt. melted butter sauce**

Empty, wash and scale the fish. Dry well, place in a baking-dish in which a little butter has been previously melted and baste well. Season with salt and pepper, cover with a greased paper and bake gently for 25–35 min., basting occasionally. Make the melted butter sauce very thick and a few minutes before serving strain and add the liquor from the fish. Place the fish on a hot dish, strain the sauce over and serve.

**4 helpings**

## BAKED HADDOCK AND ORANGE

*Aiglefin au Four aux Oranges*

**1 orange**
**1½ lb. fillet of haddock**
**Salt**
**Juice of 1 lemon**
**2 level teasp. cornflour**
**½ level teasp. sugar**

Grate the rind from the orange, remove pith and cut pulp across into slices. Cut the fish into convenient portions for serving and arrange in a greased dish. Sprinkle with a little salt, add the lemon juice and arrange the slices of orange over the top. Cover with greased paper and cook in a fairly hot oven **(400° F., Gas 6)** for 15–20 min. Strain off the liquor and make up to ¼ pt. with water. Blend the cornflour with this, add the grated orange rind and sugar and bring to the boil, stirring constantly. Boil gently for 3 min., correct the seasoning and serve with the fish.

**4 helpings**

## BAKED HADDOCK WITH CUCUMBER SAUCE

**One 14-oz. carton fillets of haddock**
**½ pt. milk**
**1 oz. margarine**
**1 oz. flour**
**¼ cucumber**
**Salt and pepper**

Partially thaw and separate the fillets and divide into suitable portions for serving. Place in a baking-tin, cover with the milk and bake for 20 min. in a fairly hot oven **(375° F., Gas 5)**. When cooked, remove the fillets on to a serving dish and keep hot. Make a sauce, using the margarine, flour and the milk in which the fish was cooked. Just before serving add the diced cucumber and season to taste. Pour over the fish and serve at once.

**3–4 helpings**

## BAKED HADDOCK WITH RICE AND OLIVE STUFFING

*Aiglefin au Four farci au Riz et aux Olives*

**One 2–3 lb. fresh haddock—cleaned**

STUFFING

**2 oz. butter**
**1 onion**
**2 sticks celery**
**4 oz. cooked rice**
**¼ level teasp. sage**
**¼ level teasp. thyme**
**1½ oz. stuffed olives, chopped**
**Salt and pepper to taste**

GARNISH

**Cooked rice**
**Tomatoes**
**Lemon**
**Creamed potatoes**
**Parsley**

Scale the haddock and trim the fins and tail. Leave the head on, but remove the eyes. To make the stuffing, melt the butter in a pan, add the finely-chopped onion and celery and sauté for about 3 min. Add the rice and the remaining ingredients and cook gently for a further 3 min. Stuff the fish with this mixture then place the fish, with the tail curled inwards, in a well-greased baking-tin. Cover with greased paper and bake in a fairly hot oven (**375° F., Gas 5**) for 30–40 min. Serve on a bed of rice garnished with quarters of tomatoes, lemon wedges, creamed potatoes and parsley.

**4–6 helpings**

### BAKED HAKE STEAKS

*Darnes de Merluche cuites au Four*

**4 medium-sized hake steaks**
**Flour**
**Salt and pepper**
**1 teasp. finely-chopped parsley**
**1 teasp. finely-chopped onion**
**1 oz. butter**

Wipe the steaks and place them side by side in a greased baking-dish. Dredge well with flour, season with salt and pepper, sprinkle over the parsley and onion and add the butter in small pieces. Bake gently for ½ hr., basting occasionally, then place the fish on a hot dish, strain the liquor over it and serve.

**4 helpings**

### BAKED HALIBUT

*Flétan rôti*

**2 lb. halibut, cut in one thick slice**
**Salt and pepper**
**Flour**
**1 oz. butter *or* dripping**

Wipe the fish well, sprinkle liberally with salt and pepper and dredge with flour. Place in a baking-dish or pie-dish, add the butter in small pieces and bake gently for about 1 hr. Serve on a hot dish with the liquid from the fish strained and poured round.

**4–5 helpings** **Cooking time—30–40 min.**

### BAKED HAM

*Jambon rôti*

**A ham**
**Flour**
**Brown sugar**
**Cloves**

Soak the ham in water for at least 12 hr. Wipe well and trim off any rusty bits. Coat with a flour and water paste crust which must be sufficiently thick all over to keep in the gravy. Place the ham in a fairly hot oven (**400° F., Gas 6**) for about 15 min., then reduce heat to cool (**310° F., Gas 2**) and cook for the remainder of the time allowing 30 min. per lb. Remove the crust and skin, score squares in the fat and place a clove in each square, sprinkle brown sugar over the fat. Garnish the knuckle with a paper frill. Pieces of ham will need less time to cook.

### BAKED HAM LOAF

**8 oz. ham**
**4 oz. browned breadcrumbs**
**2 oz. sultanas**
**1 large cooking apple**
**4 oz. corned beef**
**1 tablesp. finely-chopped parsley**
**1 teasp. grated lemon rind**
**Pinch of allspice**
**Pinch of grated nutmeg**
**Salt and pepper**
**2 eggs**
**Milk**

Well grease a bread-tin and coat with browned breadcrumbs. Wash the sultanas well; peel, core and grate the apple. Mince the ham and corned beef and mix with the parsley, lemon rind, breadcrumbs, apple, sultanas, allspice, nutmeg and seasoning. Bind with the beaten eggs and a little milk if needed. Carefully put into the prepared bread-tin and bake in a cool oven (**310° F., Gas 2**) for about 40 min. Serve hot with gravy, or cold with salad.

**6 helpings**

### BAKED HAM SLICE

*Jambon rôti*

**1½–2 lb. slice uncooked ham *or* gammon 1–1½ in. thick**
**½ teasp. dry mustard**
**¼ teasp. cinnamon**
**2 tablesp. brown sugar**
**Milk**

Mix the mustard, cinnamon and brown sugar and spread on both sides of the ham. Place in a casserole and add sufficient milk to barely cover the ham. Cook in a cool oven (**310° F., Gas 2**) for ¾ hr.

**6 helpings**

### BAKED HARE

*Lièvre aux Truffes*

**1 young hare**
**6 oz. pickled pork**
**6 oz. veal**
**1 shallot**
**A little good stock**
**Salt and pepper**
**1 glass sherry (optional)**
**½ lb. truffles *or* mushrooms**
**Fat for basting**
**1 pt. Espagnole sauce**

Prepare hare as directed in notes on trussing hares. Chop and pound pork, veal and shallot, until smooth; moisten with a little good stock, season to taste, add sherry if used. Dice truffles or mushrooms, reserve 1 tablesp. and add remainder to stuffing. Press stuffing lightly into body of hare, sew up the opening, truss into shape and cover back with 2 or 3 folds of greased paper. Baste well with hot fat, bake in a fairly hot oven (**375°–400° F., Gas 5–6**) 1–1¼ hr., basting frequently. About 20 min. before serving, remove paper and allow back to brown. Heat remainder of truffle in the Espagnole sauce. If mushrooms are used, allow these to cook in the sauce, and serve sauce separately.

**5–6 helpings**

### BAKED HERRING ROES

*Laitance de Harengs au gratin*

**1½ oz. butter *or* margarine**
**4 small mushrooms**
**1 small shallot *or* onion**
**½ teasp. chopped parsley**
**Lemon juice**
**Few drops anchovy essence**
**Seasoning**
**½ gill thick white sauce**
**8 fresh soft roes**
**2 tablesp. breadcrumbs**

Brush the inside of 8 small ramekin dishes or individual scallop shells with a little butter. Chop the mushrooms coarsely; chop the shallot or onion finely. Heat 1 oz. butter in a saucepan, put in the mushrooms, shallot and parsley and cook gently. When tender, remove from the pan, leaving any surplus butter in the pan, and put the mixture into the dishes or shells. Add a little lemon juice, anchovy essence and seasoning to the white sauce and pour a little over the mushroom mixture. Re-heat the butter in the pan and cook the roes until tender. Put on top of the mixture in the cases and top with breadcrumbs and tiny knobs of butter. Bake in a hot oven for 7 min. or under a hot grill for about 3–7 min. until the crumbs are brown.

**8 savouries**

### BAKED JAM ROLL

**12 oz. plain flour**
**1 teasp. baking-powder**
**Pinch of salt**
**6 oz. finely-chopped suet**
**Jam**

Mix the flour, baking-powder, salt and suet with sufficient water to make a soft, but firm, dough. Roll the dough into a rectangle about ¼ in. thick. Spread with jam almost to the edges, damp the edges and roll up lightly. Seal the edges. Put on to a well-greased baking sheet. Cook in a fairly hot oven (**400° F., Gas 6**) until cooked through; about 1 hr.

**6 helpings**

### BAKED JERUSALEM ARTICHOKES

*Topinambours rôties*

**2 lb. Jerusalem artichokes**
**Lemon juice *or* white vinegar**
**Salt and pepper**
**Dripping**

Prepare and parboil the artichokes 5 min. Drain them and shake the pan over heat to dry them. Put into hot dripping in a roasting tin or in the tin containing the roast joint. Roll the artichokes in the fat and cook in a fairly hot oven (**375° F., Gas 5**) till brown and tender (about 1 hr.) turning them during cooking. They will not be a good colour but are of excellent flavour.

**4–6 helpings**

**Cooking time—to parboil, 5 min.; to bake about 1 hr.**

### BAKED LOBSTER

*Homard au Gratin*

**1 boiled lobster**
**1½ oz. butter**
**½ teasp. finely-chopped shallot**
**2–3 tablesp. white sauce**
**1 dessertsp. finely-chopped parsley**
**Juice of ½ lemon**
**Pinch of nutmeg**
**Salt and pepper**
**1 egg**
**Browned breadcrumbs**

Remove the lobster meat from the shells (*see* above) and mince or chop it coarsely. Clean the two halves of the large shell. Melt the butter in a saucepan, fry the shallot for 2–3 min. without browning, then add the lobster meat, white sauce, parsley, lemon juice, nutmeg and salt and pepper to taste. Stir and heat until thoroughly hot. Beat the egg slightly, add it to the mixture and cook until it begins to bind. Put the mixture into the shells, cover lightly with brown breadcrumbs, put 3–4 very small pieces of butter on top and bake for 10–15 min. in a moderate oven (**350° F., Gas 4**).

**4–5 helpings** **Cooking time—½ hr.**

## BAKED MACKEREL

*Maquereau au Four*

**2 large-sized mackerel**
**Veal forcemeat**
**1 oz. butter *or* sweet dripping**
**Flour**
**Salt and pepper**

Clean the fish and take out the roes. Stuff with the forcemeat and sew up the opening. Put them with the roes into a fireproof dish. Add the butter or dripping, dredge with flour, sprinkle well with salt and pepper and bake for 30–40 min., basting occasionally.

Serve with parsley sauce, or melted butter to which a little lemon juice has been added, and finely-chopped parsley.

**3–4 helpings**

## BAKED MUSHROOMS

*Champignons au beurre*

**18–24 flap mushrooms**
**Salt and pepper**
**Powdered mace**
**Butter *or* margarine**

Wash the mushrooms under running water, peel the caps and trim the ragged ends of the stalks. Put into a baking-dish, gills of the mushrooms uppermost, sprinkle with salt and pepper and a very little mace and put a tiny piece of butter on each. Cover and cook 25–30 min. in a fairly hot oven (**375° F., Gas 5**).

If possible, cook in a fireproof glass dish with a lid and serve in the same dish, thus retaining all the flavour of the mushrooms.

**6 helpings**

## BAKED ONIONS

*Oignons rôtis*

**6 large onions**
**Salt and pepper**
**A little margarine *or* butter**
**A little milk**

*Method 1.* Peel the onions and cook in boiling, salted water 20 min. Drain and place in a fireproof dish. Sprinkle with salt and pepper. Put a small pat of margarine *or* butter on the top of each and pour enough milk in the dish to come ⅓ of the way up the onions. Cover with a greased paper. Bake in a moderate oven (**350° F., Gas 4**) until tender,

basting frequently with the milk. Serve with any milk and onion liquor in the dish.

**6 helpings**
**Cooking time—to bake the onions about 1½ hr.**

*Method 2.* Boil the onions till tender, in their skins. Drain and dry in a cloth and wrap each onion in well-greased paper or in silicone paper. Bake in a moderate oven (**350° F., Gas 4**) for an hour. Unwrap and serve in their skins with butter or margarine.

**6 helpings**
**Cooking time—to boil 1½ hr.; to bake 1 hr.**

*Method 3.* Trim off the roots of the onions, wipe, but do not skin. Put a little margarine, butter *or* dripping in a fireproof dish, or roasting-tin. Place the onions in it and bake until tender in a fairly hot oven (**375° F., Gas 5**). Take out the onions and peel them. Put them back in the dish, season with salt and pepper, and baste well, using a little extra fat if necessary. Reheat for 10 min.

**6 helpings** **Cooking time—to bake 1½–2 hr.**

## BAKED PARSNIPS

*Panais rôtis*

**2 lb parsnips**
**Salt**
**Dripping**

Prepare the parsnips, cut off the thin end and leave whole, cut the thick end lengthwise, then across, i.e. into quarters. Boil the parsnips in just enough salt water to cover, for 10 min. Strain off the water and dry the parsnips over a low heat. Put into hot dripping in a roasting-tin, or in the tin containing the roast joint. Roll the parsnips in the fat and cook till brown and tender—¾–1 hr., turning them during cooking. The high sugar content of the parsnips gives them an excellent flavour and a very pleasant brown colour when baked.

### BAKED PIKE

*Brochet farci*

**1 medium-sized pike (about 4 lb.)**
**4 oz. veal forcemeat**
**1 egg**
**Brown breadcrumbs**
**Butter *or* fat for basting**

Wash, clean and scale the fish and remove the fins and gills. Fill the inside with forcemeat, sew up the opening, brush over with beaten egg and coat with breadcrumbs. Sometimes the fish is trussed in a round shape, the tail being fastened in the mouth with a skewer. Before putting the fish in the oven it should be well basted with hot fat or butter, and as this fish is naturally dry it must be frequently basted and kept covered with greased paper while cooking. Bake gently for 40–45 min.

**8–10 helpings**

### BAKED POTATOES—IN THEIR JACKETS

*Pommes de terre en robe de chambre*

**6 large potatoes**
**Butter *or* margarine *or* bacon fat**

Scrub the potatoes, rinse and dry them. Brush with melted butter, or margarine or bacon fat or rub with a greasy butter paper. Prick with a fork. Bake on the shelves of a fairly hot oven (**375° F., Gas 5**) until soft—about 1½ hr., turning them whilst they are cooking. Cut a cross in the top of each, insert a pat of butter or margarine. Serve in a hot vegetable dish.

**6 helpings** **Cooking time—about 1½ hr.**

### BAKED SALMON

*Saumon à l'Italienne*

**2 lb. salmon (middle) (approx.)**
**Salt and pepper**
**Grated nutmeg**
**2 small shallots**
**1 teasp. chopped parsley**
**A little butter**
**1 small glass claret *or* cider (optional)**
**Génoise *or* tomato sauce**

Cut the fish into 2–3 even-sized slices and place in a well-buttered fireproof dish. Season with salt, pepper and a little grated nutmeg. Chop the shallots and sprinkle over with the parsley. Dot a little butter on top of the fish. Moisten with the wine or cider (if used), and bake for about 15 min. in a fairly hot oven (**375° F., Gas 5**), basting the fish frequently. When done, dish up and pour some Génoise or tomato sauce over the slices of salmon. Use the essence left in the dish in which the fish was baked to flavour the sauce.

**6–8 helpings**

### BAKED SCALLOPS

*Escalopes cuites au Four*

**4 large scallops**
**Cider (optional)**
**2½ oz. bacon fat *or* margarine**
**2 oz. breadcrumbs (approx.)**
**1 teasp. finely-grated onion**
**A little lemon juice**
**Salt and pepper**
**Grating of nutmeg**
**Sprigs of watercress *or* parsley**

Prepare the scallops Separate the roes (orange tongue) and place in a casserole with just enough cider or water to prevent sticking and a shaving of fat on top; cover. Melt the rest of the fat, add sufficient breadcrumbs to give a moist texture then add onion, lemon juice and seasoning. Cut the scallops in half horizontally; season. Cover the bottom of each shell with a thin coating of the breadcrumb mixture and place the fish on top. Coat with the remaining breadcrumb mixture. Bake shells and roes in a fairly hot oven (**375° F., Gas 5**) for 25–30 min. Serve each fish garnished with a roe and a sprig of watercress or parsley.

**4 helpings**

### BAKED SEA BREAM

*Brème de Mer rôtie*

**1 bream about 2 lb. weight**
**Salt and pepper**
**Cayenne pepper**
**2 oz. butter *or* cooking fat (approx.)**

Thoroughly wash the bream, but do not remove the scales, dry thoroughly with a clean cloth. Season inside and out with salt and pepper and place in a well-greased baking-dish. Place the butter in small pieces on the fish and bake in a fairly hot oven (**375° F., Gas 5**) for a little more than 30 min.

**4 helpings**

### BAKED SOLE WITH SHRIMPS

*Sole aux Crevettes*

**1 medium-sized sole**
**¼ pt. picked shrimps**
**1 teasp. anchovy essence**
**1 egg**

**1 dessertsp. white breadcrumbs**
**Cayenne pepper**
**Salt**
**A little white sauce *or* milk**
**Brown breadcrumbs**
**A little butter**

Remove the skin from the sole, make an incision down the centre as for filleting, and raise as far as possible the flesh on each side. Chop the shrimps coarsely, add the breadcrumbs, cayenne, salt (if necessary), anchovy essence, half the egg and sufficient white sauce or milk to moisten. Press the mixture lightly inside the fish, and instead of drawing the two sides together, fill the gap between them with forcemeat and flatten the surface of it to the level of the fish. Brush over with the remainder of the egg, coat lightly with pale-brown breadcrumbs. Place in a fireproof dish, dot with a few small pieces of butter and bake for about 20–25 min. in a fairly hot oven **(375° F., Gas 5).**

**2–3 helpings**

### BAKED STUFFED FRESH HERRINGS

*Harengs frais farcis et cuits au Four*

**6 herrings**
**2 tablesp. breadcrumbs**
**1 tablesp. finely-chopped suet**
**1 teasp. chopped parsley**
**¼ teasp. grated lemon rind**
**Salt and pepper**
**Milk**

Wash and split the herrings and remove the backbone. Mix together the breadcrumbs, suet, parsley and lemon rind, season to taste and add enough milk to moisten. Season each herring with salt and pepper, spread on a thin layer of the forcemeat and roll up tightly, beginning with the neck. Pack closely in a greased pie-dish, cover with greased paper and bake 30–40 min. in a moderate oven **(350° F., Gas 4).** Serve hot.

**5 helpings**

### BAKED STUFFED PLAICE

*Plie farcie*

**1 medium-sized plaice**
**2 tablesp. white breadcrumbs**
**1 tablesp. finely-chopped suet**
**1 dessertsp. finely-chopped parsley**
**¼ teasp. mixed herbs**
**A pinch of nutmeg**
**Salt and pepper**
**1 egg**
**Milk**
**Pale brown breadcrumbs**
**A little butter *or* fat**

Mix the white breadcrumbs, suet, parsley, herbs and nutmeg together, season well with salt and pepper, add ½ the egg and enough milk to moisten thoroughly. Make an incision down the centre of the fish as for filleting, raise the flesh each side as far as possible and fill with forcemeat. Instead of drawing the sides of the fish close together, fill up the gap with forcemeat and flatten the surface to the level of the fish with a knife. Brush over with the remaining egg, coat lightly with pale brown breadcrumbs, put into a fireproof dish and dot a few small pieces of butter on top. Bake for 20–30 min. in a moderate oven **(350° F., Gas 4).**

NOTE: The forcemeat may be varied by using shrimps or oysters.

**3–4 helpings**

### BAKED AND STUFFED POTATOES

*Pommes de terre farcies*

**6 large potatoes**

STUFFING, choice of:

(1) **3 oz. grated cheese; 1 oz. butter *or* margarine; a little milk; seasoning; nutmeg**
(2) **3 oz. chopped, fried bacon; a little milk; seasoning**
(3) **3 oz. mashed, cooked smoked haddock; chopped parsley; lemon juice; a little milk; nutmeg**
(4) **2 boned kippers, cooked and mashed; a little milk**
(5) **2 oz. grated cheese; 1 oz. butter; chopped parsley; a little milk; seasoning; 2 egg yolks stirred into the filling; 2 egg whites folded in at the end**

Scrub, rinse and dry the potatoes and grease as in preceding recipe. With a small sharp knife, cut through the skin of the potatoes to give the appearance of a lid. Bake as for Potatoes in Jackets. Lift off lids carefully, scoop out cooked potato from skins, including lids, taking care not to split the skins. Mash the potato in a basin and add the ingredients of any one of the stuffings listed above. Mix well and season thoroughly. Fill the potato skins with the mixture, piling it high. Fork the tops and brush with a little egg, or sprinkle with a little grated cheese (if an ingredient of the stuffing). Put back in the oven and bake till thoroughly hot and golden brown. Serve in a hot dish garnished with parsley and with the skin "lids" replaced, if liked.

NOTE: A stuffing consisting of cooked minced meat in a sauce or gravy, *or* of cooked mixed vegetables *or* flaked fish in a sauce may replace the floury meal of the potato entirely. The latter should then be mashed and served separately *or* mashed and piped round the opening of the potato after it has been stuffed and before returning it to the oven.

**6 helpings**
**Cooking time—about 2 hr.**

## BAKED STUFFED TROUT

*Truite rôtie au Four*

**2 large trout**
**Veal forcemeat**
**3 oz. butter**
**1 oz. flour**
**1 dessertsp. capers**
**1 teasp. lemon juice**
**½ teasp. anchovy essence**
**Salt and pepper**

Clean, scale, empty and dry the fish. Make the forcemeat stiff. Stuff the trout with forcemeat, and sew up or skewer the openings. Place in a baking-tin or dish with 2 oz. of butter and bake in a moderate oven **(350° F., Gas 4)** for about ½ hr., basting frequently. Fry the flour and the rest of the butter together. When the fish is ready, remove it to a hot dish and strain the liquor in the baking-dish on to the flour and butter. Stir until boiling and smooth, then add the capers, lemon juice, anchovy essence and season to taste. Simmer for 2–3 min., then pour over the fish and serve.

**5–6 helpings**

## BAKED TOMATOES

*Tomates rôties*

**6 large tomatoes**
**A little butter *or* margarine**
**Salt and pepper**
**Castor sugar**
**Finely-chopped tarragon (optional)**

Wash the tomatoes and cut them in halves. Put them in a greased, deep fireproof dish. Season and sprinkle each with a pinch of sugar and a pinch of chopped tarragon, if used. Put a tiny piece of butter on each or cover with a well greased paper. Bake in a moderate oven **(350° F., Gas 4)** until soft—about 20 min.

**6 helpings**

## BAKEWELL TART

**Short crust pastry using 4 oz. flour, etc.**
**1 egg**
**2 oz. ground almonds**
**2 oz. cake-crumbs**
**Raspberry jam**
**2 oz. butter**
**2 oz. sugar**
**Almond essence**
**Icing sugar**

Line a 7-in. flan ring or a pie-plate with the pastry. Place a good layer of raspberry jam on the bottom. Cream together the butter and sugar till thick and white. Beat in the egg and add the ground almonds and cake-crumbs and a few drops of almond essence. Spread the mixture on top of the jam and bake in a fairly hot oven **(400° F., Gas 6)** for about ½ hr.

Sprinkle icing sugar on top and serve hot or cold.

**5–6 helpings**

## BAKING

When a housewife describes her domestic activity as "doing a baking" she usually means that she is replenishing her stocks of bread, scones, buns, cakes and, sometimes, dishes made with pastry.

Baking is an interesting branch of cookery, giving satisfaction to the producer as well as the consumer. In the craft of baking, there are fortunate people who seem able, without any apparent effort, to produce baked goods of a high standard. They possess a "light hand".

However, less lucky people can acquire the same skill if they approach the craft with a good background knowledge of the general requirements for success, together with the determination to "try again" if necessary.

For various forms of baking, *see Bread and Bread-Making*, *Cake-Making*, *Gingerbreads*, *Scones*, *Yeast*, *Use of*, *etc.*

## BAKING AS A COOKING METHOD

*See Cooking Methods,*

## BAKING FISH

*See Fish*

## BAKING POWDER, TO MAKE

Mix well together 2 oz. ground rice, 2 oz. bicarbonate of soda and 4½ oz. cream of tartar *or* 2 oz. tartaric acid, and pass them through a fine sieve. Keep in an air-tight tin.

BAKING-POWDER BREAD

| | |
|---|---|
| **1 lb. plain flour** | **Milk to mix to light spongy dough—average ½ pt.** |
| **1 teasp. salt** | |
| **2 oz. lard *or* margarine** | |
| **2 round *or* 4 level tablesp. baking-powder** | |

Sift the flour and salt and rub in the fat until quite fine. Add the baking-powder and mix very lightly with the milk. Shape into small loaves or bake in two greased 6-in. cake-tins. Put into a hot oven **450°–425° F., Gas 8–7**).

**Cooking time (Small loaves)—10–15 min.**
**(Large loaves)—25–30 min.**

BALMORAL TARTLETS

*Tartelettes à la Balmoral*

| | |
|---|---|
| **Short crust pastry using 4 oz. flour, etc.** | **½ oz. chopped glacé cherries** |
| **2 oz. butter** | **½ oz. shredded candied peel** |
| **2 oz. sugar** | **1 teasp. cornflour** |
| **1 egg** | **Icing sugar** |
| **1 oz. cake-crumbs** | |

Line 12 patty tins with pastry. Cream the butter and sugar until thick and white and beat in the egg yolk. Add the cake-crumbs, cherries, peel and cornflour and mix well. Whisk the egg white till stiff and fold lightly into the mixture. Fill the patty tins with the mixture, and bake in a fairly hot oven (**400°–375° F., Gas 6–5**) for about 20 min.

Dredge with icing sugar and serve cold.

**12 tartlets**

BANANA BREAD

| | |
|---|---|
| **3 oz. margarine** | **3 eggs** |
| **6 oz. sugar** | **3 bananas** |
| **12 oz. flour** | **1 teasp. bicarbonate of soda** |
| **Pinch of salt** | |

Cream margarine and sugar. Add flour, salt and eggs alternately. Peel and mash bananas and add to mixture with soda. Bake in a fairly hot oven (**375° F., Gas 5**).

**Cooking time—30–40 min. (approx.)**

BANANA CHUTNEY—BERMUDA

| | |
|---|---|
| **1 lb. Bermuda onions** | **Pinch of salt** |
| **¾ lb. chopped dates** | **½ lb. raisins** |
| **6 bananas** | **2 cups fruit syrup (apricot or peach)** |
| **1½ cups vinegar** | |
| **¼ lb. crystallized ginger** | |

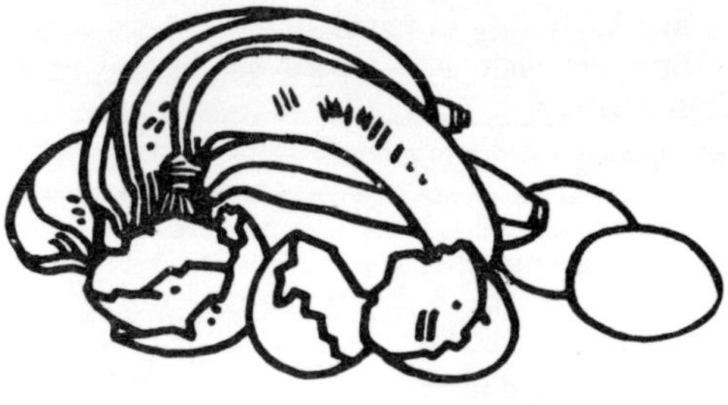

Chop the onions and dates. Peel and mash the bananas. Put onions, dates and bananas into a saucepan and add vinegar; simmer 20 min. Add chopped ginger, salt, raisins and fruit syrup. Cook till thick.

**Cooking time—30–40 min.**

BANANA CORNFLAKE PUDDING

| | |
|---|---|
| **2 oz. butter** | **6 bananas** |
| **2 oz. cornflakes** | **Juice of 1 lemon** |

Grease a fireproof dish with some of the butter and sprinkle with half the cornflakes. Peel the bananas, slit them in half lengthwise, then across. Dip them in lemon juice and put into the dish, cover with the rest of the cornflakes; dot with butter and bake in a moderate oven (**350° F., Gas 4**) for 20 min.

**6 helpings**

BANANA CUSTARD

*Crème aux Bananes*

| | |
|---|---|
| **1 pt. cup custard** | **1 lb. bananas** |

Make the custard and when cooked add the sliced bananas. Leave to stand for 3–4 min. Pour into a dish or into individual glasses and serve.

**Time—25 min.**

BANANA FRITTERS

*Beignets de Bananes*

| | |
|---|---|
| **4 firm bananas** | **Frying-fat** |
| **Coating batter** | **Castor sugar** |

Prepare the batter. Cut each banana lengthwise and across the middle, making four portions. Coat with batter. Fry in hot fat, which is just beginning to haze.

Sprinkle well with castor sugar and serve immediately.

**6 helpings**

### BANANA ICE CREAM

*Glace à la Crème de Bananes*

| | |
|---|---|
| **3 bananas** | **½ pt. cream *or* ¼ pt. cream and ¼ pt. ice cream custard (1) *or* (2)** |
| **2 tablesp. lemon juice** | **3–4 oz. castor sugar** |

Peel and slice the bananas, cover with lemon juice. Pass fruit through a nylon sieve. Add the half whipped cream, cold custard if used, and sugar. Chill and freeze.

**6 helpings**

### BANANA JELLY WITH CREAM

*Gelée de Bananes à la Crème*

| | |
|---|---|
| **1 pt. lemon *or* orange jelly** | **6 bananas** |
| **½ oz. peeled pistachio nuts** | **¼ pt. double cream** |

Make the jelly and allow to cool. Chop green pistachio nuts finely and stir into 2 tablesp. jelly. Set the nut jelly in the bottom of a mould. Beat the bananas to a purée and half-whip the cream. Stir the banana purée into the remaining jelly ; add cream and fold together lightly. Fill up the mould and turn out when set.

**6 helpings**
**Cooking time—5 min.**
**Setting time—2 hr.**

### BANANA MOULD

*Gâteau de Bananes*

| | |
|---|---|
| **2 oz. cornflour** | **2 egg yolks** |
| **2 pt. milk** | **½ teasp. vanilla essence** |
| **2 oz. castor sugar** | **2 bananas** |

Blend the cornflour with a little milk and heat the remainder of the milk. Proceed as for cornflour mould, cooking well. Stir in the sugar, cool, and add the beaten yolks. Re-cook until the mixture thickens, stir well. Stir in the vanilla essence, add the thinly-sliced bananas and pour into a wetted mould.

**6 helpings**
**Cooking time—10–12 min.**
**Setting time—2 hr.**

### BANANA PUDDING

*Pouding de Bananes*

| | |
|---|---|
| **1½ oz. butter *or* margarine** | **6 oz. plain flour** |
| **6 oz. castor sugar** | **¾ gill of top of the milk *or* cream** |
| **3 eggs** | **3 bananas** |

Cream the fat and sugar together until soft. Beat in the egg yolks. Stir in the sifted flour and milk (or cream) alternately. Add the thinly sliced bananas. Whisk the egg whites to a stiff froth, and add them lightly to the rest of the ingredients. Pour the mixture into a well-buttered dish. Bake in a warm oven (335° F., Gas 3) for ¾–1 hr. until the pudding is firm and golden brown.

**6–7 helpings**

### BANANA SALAD

*Salade de Bananes*

| | |
|---|---|
| **6 bananas** | **Chopped parsley** |
| **Lemon juice** | **Watercress** |
| **Mayonnaise sauce *or* salad dressing** | **French dressing** |

Cut the bananas into rounds ⅛ in. thick and put them into a salad bowl containing about 1 tablesp. lemon juice. Mix lightly, and pile in the dish. Coat with salad dressing or mayonnaise, sprinkle with parsley. Arrange watercress around the dish and sprinkle it with French dressing.

NOTE: Coarsely chopped walnuts may be added to this salad.

**6 helpings**

### BANANA SNOW PUDDING

| | |
|---|---|
| **1 oz. gelatine** | **¼ cup fresh lemon and lime juice** |
| **¼ cup cold water** | **3 egg whites** |
| **1 cup boiling water** | **3 bananas** |
| **1 cup sugar** | |

Soften gelatine in the cold water for 5 min., then dissolve in boiling water. Add sugar and juices. Chill until slightly thickened then whip till frothy. Fold in egg whites. Arrange sliced bananas in a large mould. Turn in gelatine mixture and chill until firm.

### BANANA SPLIT

| | |
|---|---|
| **6 bananas** | **¼ pt. whipped sweetened cream** |
| **1 pt. vanilla ice cream *or* 1 family brick** | **2 oz. chopped walnuts** |
| **½ pt. melba sauce** | **8 maraschino cherries** |

Peel bananas, split in half lengthways and place in small oval dishes. Place two small scoops or slices of ice cream between the halves of bananas. Coat the ice cream with melba sauce; sprinkle with chopped nuts. Decorate with piped cream and cherries.

### BANANAS BAKED WITH RUM AND COCONUT

| | |
|---|---|
| **8 ripe bananas** | **3 oz. brown sugar** |
| **1 oz. margarine** | **1 tablesp. lemon juice** |
| **Pinch of salt** | **½ cup water** |
| **6 oz. coconut** | **½ glass of rum** |

Peel the bananas, cut in half lengthways. Spread out on a flat fireproof dish and dot with pieces of margarine. Scatter salt, coconut and sugar over. Sprinkle with lemon juice. Bake in a warm oven (**335° F., Gas 3**) for 10–15 min. Add water and rum and continue baking for 5 min.

**6 helpings**

### BANANAS (SAVOURY)

Peel and cut the bananas in halves or quarters, season with salt and Paprika pepper (mixed). Melt some butter in a sauté-pan and cook the bananas for 10–15 min. Drain, sprinkle with finely-chopped parsley, dish up and serve hot.

### BANBURY CAKES

*Petits gâteaux à la Banbury*

**Rough puff pastry using 8 oz. flour, etc.**
***or* puff *or* flaky pastry may be used**

FILLING

| | |
|---|---|
| **Small 1 oz. butter *or* margarine** | **4 oz. currants** |
| **½ oz. plain flour** | **½ oz. chopped candied peel** |
| **¼ nutmeg (grated) *or* ¼ teasp. ground cinnamon** | **2 oz. brown sugar** |
| | **2 tablesp. rum** |

GLAZE

| | |
|---|---|
| **Egg white** | **Castor sugar** |

*To make the filling:* melt the fat, stir in the flour and spice and cook for a minute or two. Remove from the heat, add the fruit, sugar and rum.

Roll the pastry out ¼ in. thick and cut into 3-in. rounds. Place a spoonful of filling in the centre of each, damp the edges and gather them together to form a ball; turn over so that the smooth side is uppermost. Roll each out and shape into an oval shape 4 in. by 2½ in.; make 3 cuts in the centre. Put the cakes on a greased tin and bake in a hot oven (**425° F., Gas 7**).

Brush with the egg white and dust immediately with castor sugar. Return to the oven for a few minutes, to frost the glaze.

**14 cakes**
**Cooking time—20 min.**

### BARBECUE OF RABBIT

*Lapin grillé*

| | |
|---|---|
| **1 very young rabbit** | **2 tablesp. good gravy** |
| **Salt and pepper** | **1 tablesp. lemon juice** |
| **Olive oil *or* butter** | **1 teasp. French mustard** |

GARNISH

| | |
|---|---|
| **Slices of lemon** | **Fried parsley** |

Cut off the head of the rabbit. Allow the rabbit to lie in salted water for 1 hr.; dry it thoroughly. Score the back and legs closely, season, brush with olive oil *or* melted butter. Heat the gravy, add to it lemon juice and mustard, correct the seasoning. Grill the rabbit 20–25 min., basting and turning it frequently. Divide into neat joints and place on a hot dish. Pour the sauce over; garnish.

**3–4 helpings**

### BARBEL

*Barbeau*

| | |
|---|---|
| **1–2 barbel, according to size** | **2 tablesp. vinegar** |
| | **Juice of 1 lemon** |
| **1 tablesp. salt** | **Bouquet garni** |
| **2 small onions, sliced** | **Grated nutmeg to taste** |
| **2 anchovies** | **Pinch of mace** |

Soak the fish in slightly salted water for 2–3 hr. Put into a fish-kettle or saucepan with warm water and the salt, and poach gently until done. Take 1 pt. of the water in which the fish was cooked and add to it the other ingredients. Simmer gently for about 15 min., then strain, and return to the saucepan. Put in the fish and let it heat gradually in the flavoured liquor.

**4 helpings**

### BARLEY CREAM SOUP

| | |
|---|---|
| **1½ oz. cream of barley *or* patent barley** | **½ teasp. yeast *or* meat extract (if needed)** |
| **½ pt. milk** | **Salt and pepper** |
| **1 qt. well flavoured stock** | **Grated nutmeg** |
| **1 oz. butter *or* margarine** | **2 egg yolks** |
| | **½ gill cream** |

As for Barley Soup but add the egg yolks and cream mixed with ½ gill of the milk, at the end of cooking; reheat without boiling.

NOTE: Cream of Rice, Minute Tapioca, Oat Flour, Fine Sago and Farola may all be used for this recipe instead of Patent Barley.

### BARLEY PUDDING

*Orge au lait*

| | |
|---|---|
| **4 oz. pearl barley** | **2 eggs** |
| **2 pt. milk** | **2 oz. sugar** |
| **Pinch of salt** | **Grated rind of 1 lemon** |
| **2 oz. butter *or* margarine** | |

Wash and blanch the barley by putting it into a saucepan with enough cold water to cover well. Bring quickly to the boil, strain, and rinse in cold water. Leave the barley to soak overnight in just enough cold water to cover. Put it into a saucepan with the milk, salt and butter and simmer slowly until the barley is tender, about 1 hr. Leave to cool slightly. Separate the eggs. Stir into the barley the sugar, egg yolks and grated lemon rind. Stir in lightly the stiffly-whisked egg whites. Pour into a buttered pie-dish and bake in a moderate oven (**350° F., Gas 4**) for 20–30 min., until nicely browned.

**6 helpings**

### BARLEY SOUP

*Potage au crème d'orge*

| | |
|---|---|
| **1½ oz. cream of barley *or* patent barley** | **1 oz. butter *or* margarine** |
| **½ pt. milk** | **½ teasp. yeast *or* meat extract (if needed)** |
| **1 qt. well flavoured stock** | **Salt and pepper** |
| | **Grated nutmeg** |

Blend the barley with the milk. Boil the stock with the fat and the yeast or meat extract, stir it into the barley and milk, return all to the pan and simmer until the barley thickens and becomes clear. Stir all the time as the barley easily forms lumps. Season very carefully, adding the merest trace of nutmeg.

Serve with croûtons of fried bread, handed separately.

**6 helpings**
**Cooking time—20–30 min.**

### BARLEY WATER

| | |
|---|---|
| **2 oz. pearl barley** | **Thinly-peeled rind of ½ a small lemon** |
| **2–3 lumps of sugar** | **1 pt. boiling water** |

Cover the barley with cold water. Boil for 2 min. to blanch, then strain. Place the barley, sugar, and lemon rind in a jug. Pour in the 1 pt. boiling water. Cover closely. When cold, strain and use.

NOTE: This forms a nutritious, agreeable drink, and it is also largely used to dilute milk, making it easier to digest.

**1 generous helping**
**Cooking time—5 min.**

### BARONESS PUDDING

*Pouding à la Baronne*

| | |
|---|---|
| **4 oz. finely-chopped suet** | **1 rounded teasp. baking-powder** |
| **6 oz. stoned raisins** | **Pinch of salt** |
| **8 oz. plain flour** | **1 gill milk (approx.)** |
| **2 oz. castor sugar** | |

Grease a 1½ pt. pudding basin. Prepare the suet and raisins.

Mix together the sifted flour, baking-powder and salt with the raisins, suet and sugar. Add enough milk to mix to a soft dropping consistency. Put the mixture into the basin; cover with a greased paper. Steam 1½–2 hr.

Serve with custard, brandy- *or* lemon-sauce *or* well-dredged with sugar.

**6 helpings**
**Cooking time—1½–2 hr.**

## BASQUE CABBAGE AND BEAN SOUP

| | |
|---|---|
| **¼ lb. haricot beans** | **1 clove of garlic** |
| **2 onions** | **1 qt. water** |
| **½ lb. white cabbage** | **Salt and pepper** |
| **1 oz. pork *or* bacon fat** | **A few drops of vinegar** |

Soak the beans overnight in the water. Slice the onion, shred the cabbage. In a deep pan fry the onions very slowly till brown, in the fat, add the cabbage and shake the pan over gentle heat for a few minutes. Add the crushed garlic, the beans and water. Simmer the soup for 3-4 hr. until the beans are quite soft. Season and add a few drops of vinegar.

**4-6 helpings**
**Cooking time—3-4 hr.**

## BÂTARDE SAUCE (Quickly made)

| | |
|---|---|
| **¾ oz. butter** | **A little milk *or* cream** |
| **¾ oz. flour** | **2 oz. butter** |
| **½ pt. boiling water** | **Lemon juice** |
| **2 egg yolks** | **Salt** |

Melt the butter, add the flour, pour in all the boiling water and whisk briskly. Mix the egg yolks and milk or cream, stir these into the sauce, below boiling point, and thicken without boiling. Whisk in the butter, flavour and season the sauce.

Serve at once.

## BATH BUNS

| | |
|---|---|
| **1 lb. plain flour** | **Good ½ oz. yeast** |
| **½ teasp. salt** | **3 oz. sugar** |
| **3 oz. fat—margarine and lard** | **2 eggs** |
| | **1½-2 gills warm milk** |

GLAZE

| | |
|---|---|
| **1 tablesp. water** | **1 dessertsp. sugar** |

Mix salt with warmed flour and rub in fat. Mix in most of the sugar. Mix to a light dough with yeast creamed with remainder of sugar, egg and milk. Put to rise till double its size, then knead lightly. Divide into 24 pieces and shape each 3½-4 in. long and 1 in. wide. Place fairly close together (so that they join up in baking) on greased baking-sheets and prove 15 min. Bake in a hot oven (**425° F., Gas 7**) 10–15 min.

To make the glaze—boil together the water and sugar until *slightly syrupy*. Brush the buns immediately they come from the oven so that the syrup dries on.

Dredge thickly with castor sugar. Break buns apart before serving.

NOTE: 2 oz. sultanas and 1 oz. chopped peel may be worked into the dough after it has risen.

**24 buns**
**Cooking time—10–15 min.**

## BATTENBURG CAKE

*Gâteau Battenbourg*

**2 Victoria sandwich cakes made in oblong tins, one white and the other coloured pink *or* Patriotic cake**
**1 tablesp. apricot glaze**
**Almond paste , using 3 oz. ground almonds etc.**

DECORATION

| | |
|---|---|
| **Glacé cherries** | **Angelica** |

Cut the cake into strips 8–9-in. long and 1½ in. square at ends—2 pink and 2 white pieces will be needed. Join these together with apricot glaze to make a square end having pink and white pieces alternately. Roll almond paste into an oblong, wide enough and long enough to wrap round the cake leaving the ends open. Trim edges of almond paste. Spread top of cake with apricot glaze and invert on to almond paste. Spread the remaining three sides with glaze, roll up firmly and join almond paste neatly. To decorate, pinch the two top edges between thumb and forefinger. Mark the top of the cake lattice fashion with a knife and decorate with cherries and angelica.

## BATTER PUDDING

| | |
|---|---|
| **½ lb. plain flour** | **1 pt. milk** |
| **¼ teasp. salt** | **1 tablesp. cooking fat *or* lard** |
| **2 eggs** | |

Sift the flour and salt into a basin. Make a well in the centre of the flour and break the eggs into this. Add about a gill of the milk. Stir gradually working the flour down from the sides and adding more milk, as required, to make a stiff batter consistency. Beat well for about 5 min. Add the rest of the milk. Cover and leave to stand for 30 min. Put the fat into a Yorkshire pudding tin and heat in the oven until hot. The fat should just be beginning to smoke. Quickly pour in the batter and leave to cook in a hot oven (**425° F., Gas 7**) at the top of the oven until nicely browned. Reduce the heat to **375° F., Gas 5**, and finish cooking through for 10–15 min.

Serve with jam sauce.

**6 helpings**
**Time (Large pudding)—35–40 min.**
**(Individual puddings)—20–25 min.**

## BATTER PUDDING WITH APPLES

**½ lb. plain flour**
**¼ teasp. salt**
**2 eggs**
**1 pt. milk**
**1 lb. apples**
**2 oz. granulated sugar**
**¼ teasp. ground cinnamon *or* grated lemon rind**
**½ oz. butter**

Prepare the batter as for Batter Pudding. Cover and leave to stand for 30 min.

Core, peel and slice the apples thinly. Sprinkle them with the sugar and cinnamon *or* lemon rind. Spread them over a well-greased Yorkshire pudding tin. Pour the batter over, flake the butter on top, and bake in a hot oven (**425° F., Gas 7**) until brown, 20–25 min. Reduce the heat to **375° F., Gas 5**, and finish cooking. Dredge with sugar before serving.

**6 helpings** **Cooking time—30–40 min.**

## BATTERS FOR COATING

(1)

**2 oz. plain flour**
**Pinch of salt**
**1 dessertsp. salad oil *or* oiled butter**
**½ gill warm water**
**1 egg white**

Sift together the flour and salt. Mix to a smooth consistency with the oil and water. Beat well and leave to stand for at least 30 min. Just before using, stiffly whisk the egg white and then stir it lightly into the batter.

(2)

**4 oz. plain flour**
**Pinch of salt**
**1 tablesp. salad oil *or* melted butter**
**1 gill warm water (approx.)**
**1 teasp. baking powder**

Sift together the flour and salt. Mix to a smooth consistency with the oil and water until the mixture is thick enough to beat. Beat well; then add water until the mixture is of a consistency to coat the back of a wooden spoon. Leave to stand for at least 30 min. Just before using, stir in the baking powder.

(3)

**4 oz. plain flour**
**Pinch of salt**
**1 egg**
**1 gill milk**

Sift together the flour and salt. Make a well in the centre of the flour and add the egg and some of the milk. Mix gradually to a stiff consistency, using more milk as required. Beat well. Add the rest of the milk. Leave to stand for about 30 min. before using.

## BEAN CROQUETTES

**Boiled haricot beans (left-overs can be used)**
**Breadcrumbs**
**Onion**
**Salt and pepper**
**Egg**
**Oil to fry**

Mash or sieve the beans, add sufficient breadcrumbs to make them stiff enough to mould, a little fried chopped onion and pepper and salt. Shape them into balls or flat cakes, egg and crumb them and fry in hot deep oil. Serve with sauce or brown gravy poured round, and garnish with fried parsley.

The croquettes are best eaten hot.

NOTE: Split peas or lentils can be substituted for the beans if preferred. Parsley and herbs, or grated lemon rind can be added if liked.

## BEAN SPROUTS

**1 lb. bean sprouts**
**1 tablesp. oil**
**1 tablesp. soya sauce**
**1 tablesp. water**

Break off roots from bean sprouts and wash under running water. Heat oil in a saucepan and add sprouts. Fry for about 1 min. Add soya sauce mixed with water. Cover pan and simmer.

**Cooking time—6 min.**

## BEANS—FRENCH METHOD OF COOKING

*Haricots Verts à la Maître d'Hôtel*

**1½ lb. French beans**
**2 oz. butter *or* margarine**
**Juice of ½ lemon**
**1 tablesp. chopped parsley**
**Salt and pepper**

Cook as in preceding recipe, drain well and shake in the pan until most of the water has

9

Four foreign dishes.
First, pizza, a famous Italian dish. Second, one of the most popular salads—Russian salad. The third picture shows a French fricassée of chicken, and the fourth (at the side) shows goulash from Austria and Hungary.

10
Hot and cold sweets.
In the foreground, a cold mould and a hot chocolate pudding. Beyond, ice cream with chocolate sauce and a hot chocolate soufflé.

→

11
Common British cuts of lamb or mutton.

# LAMB

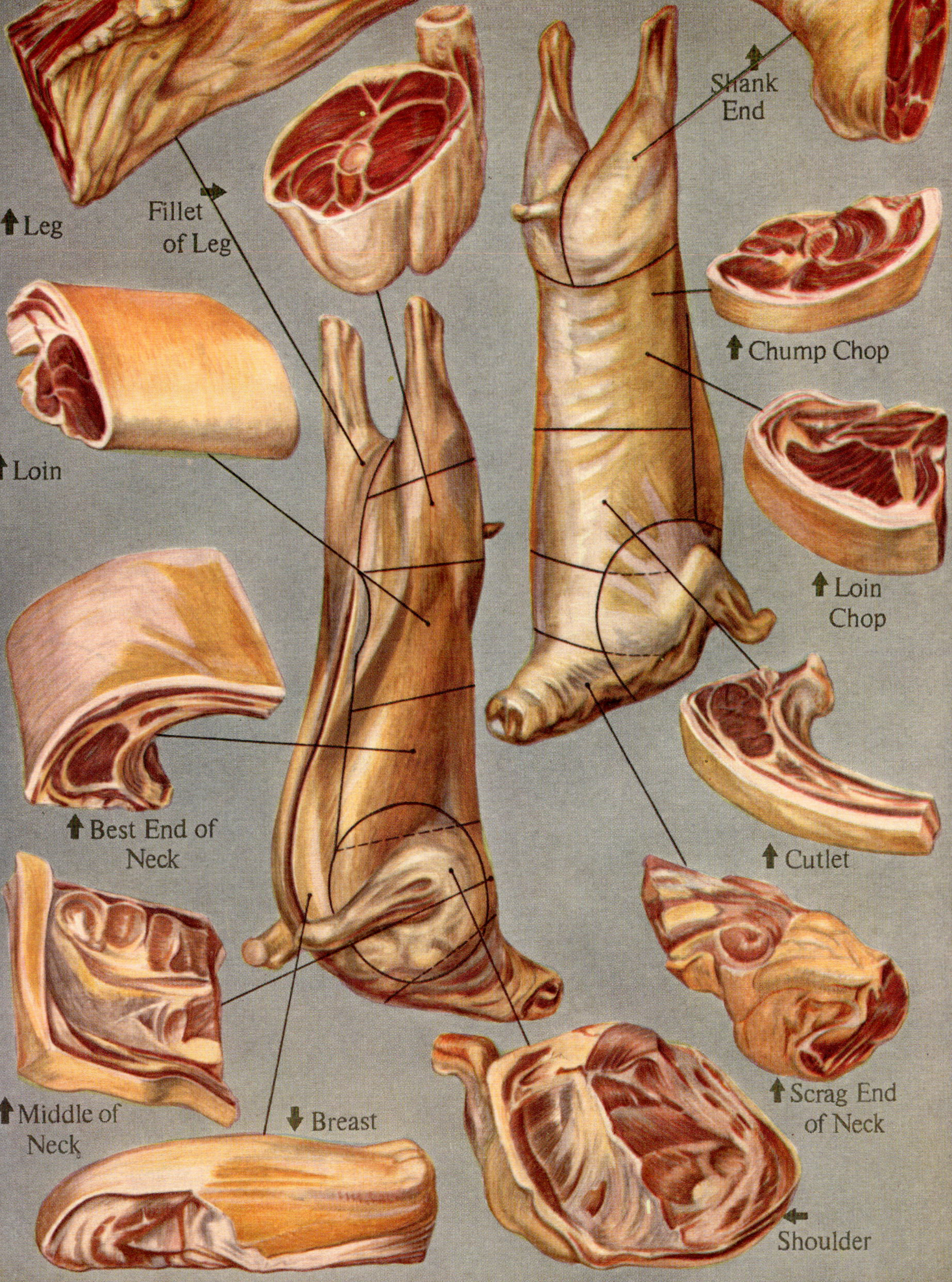

Leg
Fillet of Leg
Shank End
Chump Chop
Loin
Loin Chop
Best End of Neck
Cutlet
Middle of Neck
Breast
Scrag End of Neck
Shoulder

12

Meringue foam features in both these sweets: lemon meringue pie above, and apple snow below.

⟶

13

Common British cuts of pork.

# PORK

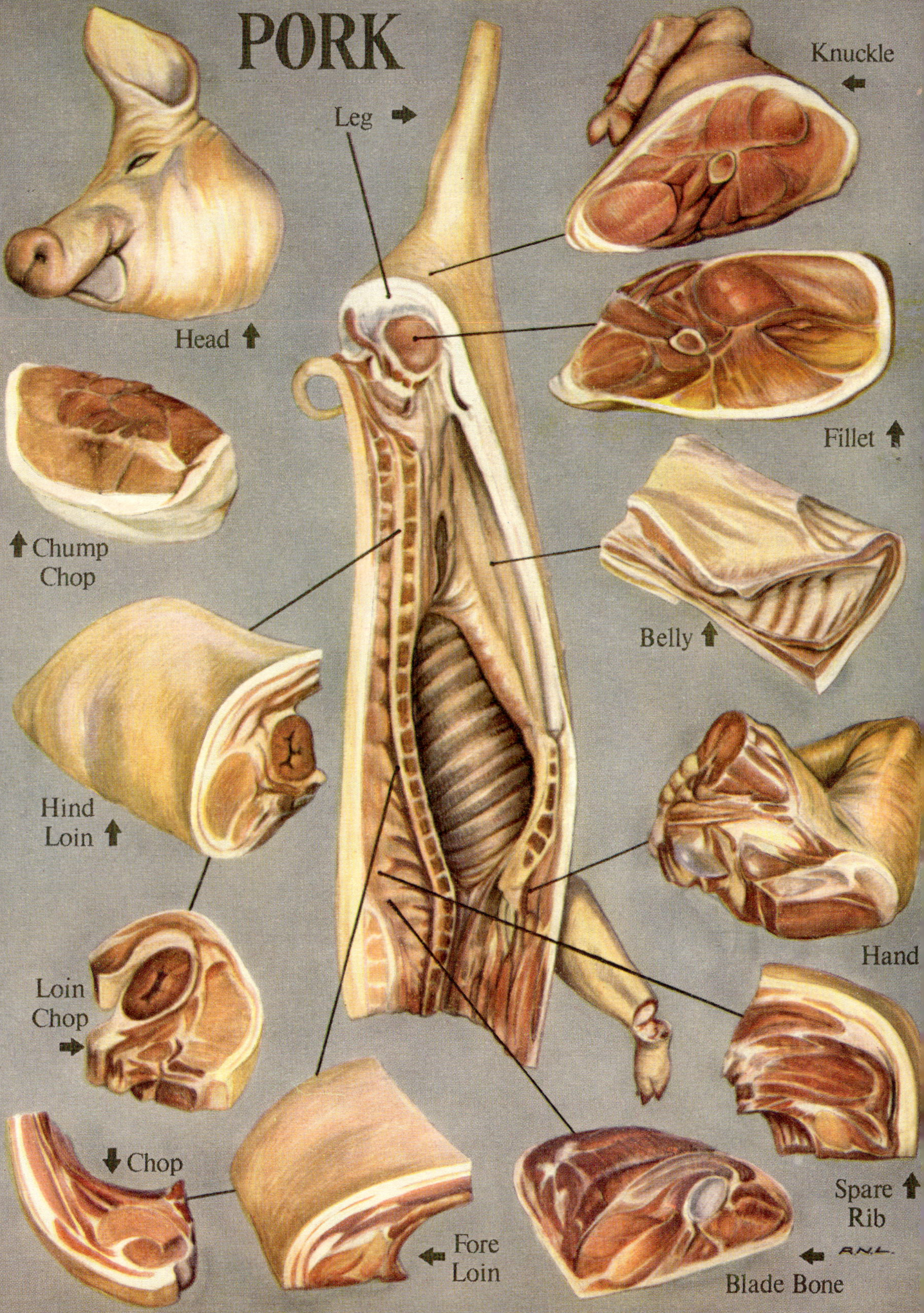
Leg
Knuckle
Head
Fillet
Chump Chop
Belly
Hind Loin
Hand
Loin Chop
Spare Rib
Chop
Fore Loin
Blade Bone
A.N.L.

14
Sandwiches.
Tempting sandwiches and two savoury sandwich loaves make a gay spread.

15

Sweet Dishes for summer days. Below, a cold chocolate soufflé, decorated with piped cream. At left, apricot trifle, quickly made and delicious.

**16**

Soups and vegetables.
Above, colourful soups—tomato, green pea and broad bean purée, with a bowl of peas and grated cheese. Below a dish of mixed vegetables.

evaporated. Add butter, parsley, lemon juice and seasoning and shake over heat for a few minutes. Serve immediately.

**4–6 helpings**
**Cooking time—15–20 min.**

### BEARNAISE SAUCE

| | |
|---|---|
| **1/4 pt. Béchamel sauce** | **1/8 pt. white wine *or* wine vinegar** |
| **2 shallots** | **2–3 egg yolks** |
| **Sprig of tarragon** | **4 oz. butter** |
| **Sprig of chervil** | **2 teasp. lemon juice** |
| **6 peppercorns** | **Salt and pepper** |

Chop shallots and herbs. Put wine in a very small pan with the shallots, herbs and peppercorns and simmer gently till reduced by ½, then strain. Mix egg yolks and sauce and heat them in a double boiler or in a basin over a pan of hot water. Add the wine and whisk in the butter, a pat at a time, until all is absorbed. The water must not be allowed to boil or the sauce will curdle. Season sauce and add lemon juice, add a little chopped tarragon and chervil and use sauce at once. Serve with grilled meat.

### BÉCHAMEL SAUCE

*French White sauce*

| | |
|---|---|
| **1 pt. milk** | **Salt** |
| **1 small onion** | **6 peppercorns** |
| **1 small carrot** | **A small bunch of herbs** |
| **2 in. celery stick** | **2 oz. butter** |
| **1 bay leaf** | **2 oz. flour** |
| **1 clove** | **1/8 pt. cream (optional)** |
| **1 blade of mace** | |

Warm the milk with the vegetables, herbs, salt and spices, and bring it slowly to simmering point. Put a lid on the pan and stand it in a warm place on the cooker to infuse for ½ hr. Strain the milk, melt the butter, add the flour, cook this roux for a few minutes without browning it. Stir the flavoured milk gradually into the roux. Bring the sauce to boiling point, stirring vigorously. For an extra smooth result, wring the sauce through damp muslin. If cream is used, add it to the sauce just at boiling point and do not reboil it.

Serve with chicken, veal, fish or white vegetables.

NOTE: Béchamel sauce may be made with ½ white stock and ½ milk, the result will have a good flavour but will not be so creamy in texture.

**Cooking time—40 min.**

### BEEF

Beef is obtained from adult bovine animals, often called "cows" by town-dwellers. In fact, a cow is a mother animal. Having borne young and fed them, her muscles have been much exercised. The more milk she has yielded, either to feed her calves or for milk production, the less fat has been available for her own body. Beef from a cow is therefore, usually lean and tough. It is also, as a rule, a darker colour than beef from animals bred for eating.

It is not true, as many believe, that cow beef can be recognized because the fat is yellowish in colour. The colour of the fat is dictated by the breed of the animal and its pasture. Cows fed on grass during the summer have darker fat at the end of that period than in spring because there has been more carotene in their feed.

Cows which have not yet borne calves are called heifers. Their beef is indistinguishable from bullock or ox beef to most laymen, and like the flesh of all female animals, has the merit for the buyer of having a lighter bone structure than beef from male animals.

The father of cattle is the bull. Bull beef is rarely sold in retail shops as it is strongly flavoured and dark. Young bull meat is, however, popular with some sections of the Jewish community. It is usually well fatted, but needs careful and special cooking because of its strong flavour.

The prime supplier of good quality beef is the ox or bullock. These terms both apply to a male animal castrated at an early age. The operation produces a quiet animal whose main interest is feeding. As a result, its muscles get little exercise and every opportunity to lay down fat.

Beef flesh should, ideally, be bright red when freshly cut. But after a short exposure to the air, this lustrous colour disappears, and the beef takes on a colour hard to describe.

The term "creamy red" may give some idea of it.

A beef carcase (that is, the body after the removal of head, feet, skin and intenral organs) is split down the backbone into two halves called sides. Each side is then divided into two halves, being cut through between the tenth and eleventh rib bones. (These cuts and cutting processes are called "London" style. Where it is necessary, reference will be made in recipes to the terms used in other areas.)

The piece of a beef carcase that contains the forelimb and the first ten rib bones is called the forequarter. The other half of the side is called the hind quarter.

### The Hind Quarter

The cuts into which a hindquarter is divided can be understood best by reference to the accompanying diagram.

(1) The **undercut** or **fillet** is the most suitable meat for frying. Having a very delicate flavour it is unsuitable for any other treatment. There are, however, only 5–7 pounds of fillet in a carcase of 600–700 lb.

(2) The **sirloin** may be considered to be the next most suitable frying cut, and is preferred to fillet by many people. In England, the most usual practice is to roast the sirloin.

(3) **Rump steak** is the most common frying cut, and the prime end of the rump is to be found in the small slices which are removed from the hip-bone.

(4) The **topside**, the muscle of the inside leg, (5) and the **top rump**, the muscle of the front part of the thigh, are suitable for slow frying being taken from the highest quality of fat animal. In nearly all cases, however, they are, together with the rump, better cooked in the oven with a small quantity of water.

The muscle of the outside of the thigh and the buttock is sold as **silverside** (6). Today this joint is oven roasted, but it is really suitable only for casseroling if tenderness is desired.

For those who like beef fat, (7) the **hindquarter flank** (the belly of the animal) yields a cheap and delicious joint for boiling or a casserole.

(8) The **leg of beef** is only suitable for boiling. It may be cut in two ways. In strips it shows clearly the structure of working muscle being sheathed with white or transparent connective tissue which is gathered together at the ends into thick pieces of white gristle. If cut in slices it exhibits "lines" where the various sheaths of connective tissue have been cut across. There is little to choose between the leg and the foreleg or shin except that the leg is larger and will yield bigger pieces of meat for stewing where this is required.

### Steak

Several terms are now in growing use for various types of beef steaks. They are not new terms and some have already been mentioned.

**Fillet:** This term is used in two ways. Correctly it refers to the meat found beneath the blade part of the loin bones. It is also used for the continuation of this same muscle which is part of a whole unboned rump steak or steakpiece. This part is properly called the undercut. Fillet or undercut may be served in several ways and under several names.

**Châteaubriand:** A very thick piece of fillet sufficient for two people and cut at the time of serving into two portions.

**Tournedos:** Thick slices of fillet for one person. Usually $\frac{3}{4}$ in. thick and a nice round shape, they are perhaps the most usual way in which the steak is cooked. They are sometimes tied to preserve their shape.

**Noisettes:** Neatly trimmed, round or oval shapes of fillet between half and three-quarters of an inch in thickness.

**Mignons:** Very fine fillet steaks which should be cooked quickly. These are often referred to as minute steaks.

**Porterhouse:** A steak from the wing end (wing rib) of the sirloin or forerib. In fact a slice from the part of the loin which contains no undercut or fillet.

**T-bone steak:** A steak cut through the sirloin so that it contains on one side at least, the "T"-shaped loin bone. It has two "eyes", that of the loin meat and that of the fillet.

**Entrecote:** This is a sirloin steak without the undercut and without the bone. In other words the eye meat of the loin cut into steaks.

All these steaks may be served in many different ways. For example an ordinary Châteaubriand is dipped in olive oil, salted, peppered and grilled. Garnished with hearts of artichoke, stuffed braised lettuce and Maître d'Hôtel butter it becomes *Châteaubriand Marquise*. If you sauté a sirloin steak with mushrooms and shallots in butter and then make a sauce of the vegetables with dry white wine and thick gravy it is an *Entrecôte Forestière*. With red wine instead of white and marrowbone cooked in the sauce it becomes *Entrecôte Bordelaise*. A mignon or minute steak cooked quickly in butter with a little Worcester sauce and chopped parsley is a *Bœuf Minute Diane*. The methods of cooking tornedos are legion. For example *Tournedos Andalouse* is served with grilled tomatoes on buttered toast garnished with aubergines, small onions and Madeira sauce. Cooked in butter and served with a sauce of tomatoes, mushrooms and shallots poured over the top it becomes *Tournedos Chasseur*.

### The Fore Quarter

As in the case of the hindquarter, the diagram explains the position of the various cuts. Commencing with:

(9) the **flank** and (10) **brisket**, which are the muscular extension of the belly of the animal towards the chest, we find two joints suitable for salting and boiling, and for casseroling. When tender they may be finished for a short while in a very hot oven to simulate the flavour and appearance of roast beef. Whether purchased with the bone or boneless they are extremely economical joints. Properly cooked they yield a slice of meat little fatter than that obtained from the sirloin of the same animal, and have the advantage of providing at the same time an extremely fine and nutritious beef dripping.

The remarks made above about leg of beef apply equally well to (11) the **shin** or **foreleg.**

(12) The **sticking** or **neck** of the animal and (13) the **clod** or front chest muscles provide meat suitable for casseroling rather than boiling. These cuts contain less connective tissue than the shin or leg and may be distinguished from the chuck steak and blade bone by the fact that in the same animal they contain less evidence of marbling fat.

(14) The **chuck** and **blade bone** lie on the dividing line between casserole steak and roasting meat. Though sold for stewing, they need a shorter cooking time than any other cut of oven stewing meat with the possible exception of the top rump and topside.

The **foreribs** (15) are merely an extension of the sirloin and the **backribs** (16) an extension of the forerib. Since they are nearer to the harder working part of the animal than the sirloin (the forequarter is more exercised in feeding by the constant lifting and dropping of the head), they require rather more care in roasting, that is to say a lower heat, a longer time, and the addition of a little water to the pan.

The last cuts of the forequarter, the **top ribs** (17) and **flat ribs** (18) come halfway between the two types of cut and may be very slowly roasted. It is interesting here to note that the top ribs possess the peculiar quality of swelling up when placed in a hot oven. This is the reason for the colloquial term "oven busters" which is applied to this cut. In some parts of the country they are often referred to as "rising ribs".

## BEEF A LA MODE

*Bœuf à la mode*

| | |
|---|---|
| **2 lb. rump of beef** | **1 oz. butter *or* fat** |
| **1 glass claret** | **10 button onions** |
| **Juice of ½ lemon** | **1 oz. flour** |
| **1 small onion** | **1½ pt. stock** |
| **2 cloves** | **2 bacon rashers** |
| **Salt and pepper** | **2 carrots** |
| **Bouquet garni** | |

Trim and bone the meat. Place it in a bowl with a marinade made from the claret, lemon juice, finely-chopped onion, cloves, salt, pepper and bouquet garni. Leave for 2 hr., basting frequently. Melt the fat in a stewpan, drain the beef well and fry until brown. Fry the button onions at the same time. Remove both from the pan, add the flour and fry until nut brown. Then add the stock and the marinade in which the meat was soaked and stir until boiling. Replace the meat and the onions and season to taste. Cover the meat with the bacon rashers. Add the carrots, thinly sliced, and cook gently for 2½ hr., stirring occasionally. When tender, place on a hot dish, strain the liquid in the saucepan and pour over the meat.

**8 helpings**

### BEEF AS MOCK HARE

**1¼ lb. stewing steak**
**4 oz. fairly fat bacon**
**Seasoned flour**
**1 onion stuck with 3 cloves**
**¾ pt. stock**
**Bouquet garni**
**1 tablesp. redcurrant jelly**
**½ gill port (optional)**
**1 dessertsp. chopped pickle**
**Salt and pepper**

GARNISH

**Fried *or* baked forcemeat balls**
**Parsley**

Wipe and trim the meat and cut into 1-in. squares. Dice the bacon, fry in a saucepan, then remove from pan. Toss the meat in seasoned flour and fry until nicely browned. Add the onion stuck with cloves, stock and bouquet garni and cook slowly until tender, 1½–2 hr. Remove the onion and bouquet garni, add the redcurrant jelly, port (if used), chopped pickle, and seasoning if required.

Serve on a hot dish. Garnish with forcemeat balls and chopped parsley.

**6 helpings**

### BEEF BROTH

*Croûte-au-pot*

**1 carrot**
**1 turnip (small)**
**1 onion**
**1 clove of garlic (optional)**
**1 oz. butter *or* margarine**
**1 qt. brown stock *or* bone stock**
**Salt and pepper**
**½ small cabbage**
**A sprig of parsley**
**A few chives**
**Grated nutmeg**
**6 thin slices of French roll**

Scrub and peel the carrot and turnip, peel the onion and crush the garlic (if used). Slice the vegetables in thin rounds. Melt the fat and in it cook the vegetables gently for 10 min with a lid on the pan. Add the stock (boiling) and ½ teasp. salt. Simmer the whole for 30 min.

Meanwhile wash the cabbage, shred it finely and chop the parsley and chives. Add the cabbage to the broth and simmer for 20 min. longer; then add seasoning, a little grated nutmeg, and the chopped parsley and chives. Toast or bake the slices of roll till golden and put one in each soup plate or cup; pour the hot soup over them. If liked, grated cheese may be handed with this soup.

**4–6 helpings** **Cooking time—50 min.**

### BEEF CREOLE

**2 lb. beef**
**1 teasp. salt**
**1 teasp. pepper**
**3 rashers fat bacon**
**2 lb. onions**
**2 lb. fresh tomatoes**
**1 pepper**

Season the meat. Place on the rashers of bacon in an earthenware casserole. Cover with sliced onions, tomatoes and pepper. Simmer slowly.

**6 helpings** **Cooking time 3½–4 hr.**

### BEEF HASH

*Hachis de Bœuf*

**1 lb. cold roast beef**
**2–3 oz. streaky bacon**
**2 onions**
**1 oz. butter *or* fat**
**¾ pt. mixed Spanish and tomato sauce**

GARNISH

**Croûtes of fried *or* toasted bread**
**Parsley**

Trim and cut the meat into thin slices. Dice the bacon, slice the onions; melt the fat and fry them until light brown. Add the sliced meat and pour the mixed sauces over. Heat thoroughly without boiling for about ½ hr. If liked this dish can be prepared and served in a casserole and heated in the oven.

Serve neatly garnished with croûtes and parsley.

**6 helpings**

### BEEF SAUSAGES

*Saucisses de Bœuf*

**2 lb. lean beef**
**1 lb. beef suet**
**¼ teasp. powdered allspice**
**Salt and pepper**
**Sausage skins**
**Fat for frying**

Mince the beef and grate the suet finely or

use shredded suet. Add the allspice, salt and pepper to taste and mix well. Press the mixture lightly into the prepared skins and prick well with a fork. Fry in hot fat until well browned and cooked. If preferred the mixture may be shaped into small cakes and floured before being fried.

### BEEF STROGONOFF

| | |
|---|---|
| **2 lb. fillet of beef** | **¼ lb. mushrooms** |
| **Flour** | **2 oz. butter** |
| **Salt and pepper** | **A little brown stock** |
| **1 large onion** | **½ pt. sour cream** |

Cut the beef into small very thin pieces and shake in a wire sieve with a mixture of flour, salt and pepper. Chop the onion. Heat the butter in a saucepan and fry the onion until golden brown. Add the beef and chopped mushrooms, fry a little and then moisten with the stock. Stir, and continue cooking for about 15–20 min. Pour over the sour cream, re-heat and serve.

**6 helpings**
**Time—40 min.**

### BEEF TEA

| | |
|---|---|
| **1 lb. gravy beef (flank *or* skirt of beef)** | **1 pt. water** |
| | **½ teasp. salt** |

Cut all fat from the meat. Put the meat into a jar, basin or top of a double saucepan, add the water and salt. Stand in or over a pan of water and allow to simmer for 2–3 hr. Put through fine strainer or muslin. Allow to cool; remove any fat on top of beef tea. Re-heat *without boiling*—serve with biscuits or toast.

NOTE: This must be stored in a cool place. If this is not possible, then make freshly each time.

**2–3 helpings**
**Cooking time—2–3 hr.**

### BEEF TEA CUSTARD

| | |
|---|---|
| **1 egg** | **¼ pt. beef tea** |
| **1 egg yolk** | **Salt** |

Beat the egg and egg yolk thoroughly together. Pour on to it the beef tea and season to taste. Have ready a well-buttered cup, and pour in the mixture. Cover with a buttered paper and stand the cup in a saucepan containing a little boiling water. Steam very gently for about 20 min. Turn out carefully. Serve either hot or cold, or cut into dice, and serve in broth or soup.

**1 generous helping**
**Cooking time—20 min.**

### BEEFSTEAK PIE

*Pâté chaud de Bœuf à l'Anglaise*

| | |
|---|---|
| **1½ lb. lean beefsteak** | **Flaky, rough puff *or* short pastry, using 8 oz. flour, etc.** |
| **Seasoned flour** | |
| **2 onions** | |
| **Stock *or* water** | **Egg *or* milk** |

Wipe the meat, remove the skin and superfluous fat and cut meat into small cubes. Dip the cubes in the seasoned flour and place in a pie-dish, piling them higher in the centre. Peel and finely-chop the onions; sprinkle them between the pieces of meat. Sprinkle any remaining seasoned flour between the meat. Add enough stock or water to ½ fill the dish. Roll out the pastry ¼–½ in. thick to the shape of the pie-dish, but allow an extra 2 in. all round. Cut a strip about ¾ in. wide from around the edge of the pastry to cover the rim of the pie-dish. Dampen the rim, place the strip of pastry around with the cut side out and allow it to overlap the rim a little. Damp the join and the rest of the pastry and cover with the pastry lid. Press the edges lightly together. Trim, make a small round hole in the centre of the pie, and decorate with pastry leaves. Brush with beaten egg or milk. Place in a hot oven (**450° F., Gas 8**) until pastry is set and then reduce heat, if necessary place the pie on a lower shelf and cover with greased paper to prevent pastry becoming too brown. Heat the stock. Make a hole in the pie and pour in the hot stock before serving.

**6 helpings**
**Cooking time—about 2 hr.**

### BEEFSTEAK AND KIDNEY PIE

*Pâté chaud de Bœuf et Rognons à l'Anglaise*

As for Beefsteak Pie, but add 2 sheep's or 6 oz. ox kidneys. Soak the kidneys, remove the skins and cores and cut into slices. Then proceed as directed in the preceding recipe, adding the sliced kidneys with the steak and onions.

**BEEFSTEAK AND KIDNEY PUDDING**

*Pouding de Bœuf et de Rognon*

As for Beefsteak pudding but add 2 sheep's or 6 oz. ox kidneys. Soak the kidneys, remove the skins and cores and cut into thin slices 3 in. by 2 in. Dip in seasoned flour, place a slice of kidney on each slice of meat, roll up tightly and place the rolls on end in the basin. Proceed as directed for Beefsteak Pudding.

**BEEFSTEAK AND POTATO PIE**

*Pâté de Bœuf et de Pommes de Terre*

As for Beefsteak Pie, adding potatoes to taste. Cut the meat in slices and dip in the seasoned flour. Cut the potatoes into slices. Place a layer of sliced potato on the bottom of the pie-dish, season, and cover with a layer of meat. Add a little onion, finely chopped. Repeat with layers of potato, meat, onion and seasoning until the dish is full. Add stock or water to ⅓ the depth of the dish. Then cover with pastry and cook as directed for Beefsteak Pie.

**BEEFSTEAK PUDDING**

*Pouding de Bœuf à l'Anglaise*

**1½ lb. good stewing steak**
**Seasoned flour**
**Suet pastry using 8 oz. flour, etc.**
**3 tablesp. stock *or* water (approx.)**

Wipe the meat; remove any superfluous skin and fat. Cut the meat into narrow strips or cubes and dip in the seasoned flour. Cut off ⅓ of the pastry for the lid. Roll the remainder out into a round about ¼ in. thick and line a greased pudding basin with it. Press well in to remove any creases. Half-fill the basin with the prepared meat and add the stock or water. Then add the remainder of the meat. Roll out the pastry reserved for the lid. Damp the edges, place the lid on top and press the edges well together. Cover with greased greaseproof paper if pudding is to be steamed, or with a pudding cloth if it is to be boiled. Place in boiling water and steam for about 3½ hr.—keep the water boiling, if necessary add more *boiling* water; *or* boil for 3 hr. Serve in the pudding basin, or turn out on to a hot dish.

**6 helpings**

**BEETROOT CASSOLETTES**

*Cassolettes de Betterave*

**1 large cooked beetroot**
**Vinegar**
**Oil**
**Seasoning**

FILLING

**Small can anchovy fillets (well drained)**
**3–4 gherkins**
**1 hard-boiled egg**
**Salt and pepper**
**1 teasp. chopped parsley**
**1 teasp. chopped chives if available**
**Pinch of mixed herbs**

Cut 8 or so small cassolette shapes from the cooked beetroot, and cover them in vinegar, oil and seasoning. Prepare the filling by cutting the ingredients into thin strips, retaining the egg yolk for garnish. Season with a pinch of salt and pepper, oil and vinegar, and mix with the parsley and other herbs. Drain the cassolettes and fill them with the anchovy mixture. Dish up, garnish with egg yolk.

**8–9 savouries**

**BEETROOT SALAD**

*Salade de Betterave*

**2 cooked beetroots**
**French dressing**
**Grated horseradish**

Slice or dice the beetroot and arrange neatly. Baste with French dressing, after sprinkling with freshly grated horseradish.

NOTE: If preferred, dry mustard may be added to the French dressing and the horseradish omitted.

**6 helpings**

**BEIGNETS DE CHOUXFLEURS**

Cauliflower Fritters

**2 large cauliflowers**
**1 tablesp. salt to 2 qt. water**
**Olive oil**
**A few sprigs of parsley**
**Salt and pepper**
**Coating batter**
**Frying-fat**

Trim and wash the cauliflowers and ½ boil them in salt and water. Drain the cauliflowers thoroughly, divide into sprigs, place in a dish, sprinkle with olive oil, chopped parsley and seasoning. Allow to stand for 10–15 min. Then dip them in the batter, and fry in lightly-smoking deep fat, taking care that they do not stick to each other.

Serve in pyramidal shape garnished with sprigs of parsley.

**8 helpings**

### BERCY SAUCE

*Sauce Bercy*

**½ pt. Velouté sauce made with *fish stock* for fish dishes *or* with *veal stock* for meat dishes**
**2 shallots**
**⅛ pt. white wine**
**1 oz. butter**
**1 dessertsp. chopped parsley**

Chop the shallots and cook them gently in the wine until reduced by half. Add to this the sauce and reheat it. Whisk in the butter just at boiling point and add the parsley.

### BEVERAGES FOR INVALIDS

*See Invalid Cookery, and recipes for the type or flavour of beverage required.*

### BICARBONATE OF SODA AS A RAISING AGENT

*See Bread and Bread-Making*

### BIERSUPPE

Beer Soup

**2 slices stale bread with crusts removed**
**1 qt. Lager beer**
**Salt**
**1 oz. sugar**
**Ground cinnamon *or* lemon peel *or* a few caraway seeds**
**2 egg yolks**

Break the bread into small pieces and put into a saucepan. Add the beer and bring to the boil, whisking all the time. Add salt to taste, the sugar and lemon rind or caraway seeds if used. Simmer gently for 15 min. Beat the egg yolks in a large bowl. Pour the soup, which must be below boiling point, gradually over the eggs in the bowl, whisking all the time. Stir in ground cinnamon if used, remove lemon peel, if used.

**6 helpings** **Cooking time—25 min.**

### BIGARADE SAUCE

*Sauce Bigarade*

**½ pt. Espagnole sauce**
**½ Seville orange**
**½ lemon**
**⅛ pt. red wine (optional)**
**Salt**
**Cayenne pepper**
**Pinch of sugar**

Remove the outer orange rind, avoiding the pith, and cut the rind in neat, thin strips. Cover it with a little cold water; stew till just tender; then strain. Squeeze the orange and lemon juice into the sauce, add the orange rind, reheat, add the wine, if used, season and add sugar to taste.

Serve with roast duck, goose, wild duck, pork or ham.

### BIRDS AS FOOD

There is no bird, nor any bird's egg, that is known to be poisonous though they often become unwholesome because of the food that the birds eat. This can at any time change the quality of the flesh, even in birds of the same breed.

Wild ducks and other aquatic birds are often rank and fishy-flavoured. Pigeons fatten and waste in the course of a few hours. The pronounced flavour of grouse is said to be due to the heather shoots on which they feed.

For methods of dealing with birds, *see Poultry, Game Birds and Carving.*

### BIRTHDAY CAKE

*Gâteau de Fête*

**4 oz. butter *or* margarine**
**4 oz. moist brown sugar**
**1½ oz. golden syrup**
**2 eggs**
**6 oz. plain flour**
**⅛ teasp. salt**
**1 level teasp. baking-powder**
**1 level teasp. mixed spice**
**11 oz. mixed fruit—sultanas, currants, glacé cherries**
**2 oz. candied peel *or* marmalade**
**½ gill milk (approx.)**

Line a 6–7-in. cake-tin with greaseproof paper. Cream fat, sugar and syrup thoroughly. Whisk eggs and add alternately with the sifted flour, salt and baking-powder, beating well with each addition. Add remaining ingredients and fruit, which has been mixed with a little of the flour. Mix to a fairly soft consistency with milk and place in the cake-tin. Bake for ½ hr. in a moderate oven **(350° F., Gas 4)** and a further 2–2½ hr. in a cool oven **(310°–290° F., Gas 2–1)**.

NOTE: This cake can be coated with almond paste and decorated with royal icing

**Cooking time—about 3 hr.**

### BISCUITS

In the United States, scones are often called biscuits; and what the British call biscuits are known as cookies, if "raised" like buns, or wafers, if flat.

A basic recipe for British-style biscuits is the one for *Shrewsbury Biscuits*. For other biscuit recipes, see the recipe for the type or flavour required, e.g. *Almond Biscuits*.

### BISHOP'S NIGHTCAP

| | |
|---|---|
| **1 orange** | **½ teasp. powdered cloves** |
| **12 cloves** | **1 lemon** |
| **½ teasp. mace** | **½ pt. water** |
| **½ teasp. ground ginger** | **¼ lb. sugar** |
| **½ teasp. ground cinnamon** | **1 bottle of port** |
| **½ teasp. allspice** | |

Stick the cloves into the orange, put into a fireproof bowl, cover closely and roast until a rich brown colour. Put the mace, ginger, cinnamon, allspice, powdered cloves and the thinly-peeled rind of the lemon into an enamel saucepan containing the water and bring to the boil. Simmer gently for ½ hr.

Strain off the liquid through a fine sieve and stir in the strained juice of the lemon and the sugar. Now add the roasted orange and port and heat up again but do not allow to boil. Serve hot.

### BISQUE AUX HUÎTRES

Oyster soup

| | |
|---|---|
| **1 doz. oysters, fresh *or* canned** | **½ glass white wine** |
| **1 qt. fish stock** | **Salt and pepper** |
| **¼ pt. cream** | **Lemon juice** |
| **1 oz. butter** | **Grated nutmeg** |
| **1 oz. flour** | **1 egg yolk** |

Add the beards, buttons and liquor of the oysters (fresh or canned) to the simmering fish stock. Cut the oysters into halves and cover them with the cream. Melt the butter in a deep pan, stir in the flour, then the fish stock and oyster liquor and the wine. Simmer the liquid for ½ hr. Season carefully, adding a little lemon juice and nutmeg to taste. Strain the soup through a fine sieve. Mix the egg yolk with the cream. Boil the soup, remove it from the heat and stir in the egg yolk, cream and halved oysters. Cook the egg without boiling.

**6 helpings**
**Cooking time—40 min. for fish stock**
**40 min. for bisque**

### BISQUE DE CREVETTES

Shrimp soup

| | |
|---|---|
| **1½ pt. fish stock in which the shells of the shrimps have been cooked** | **Grated nutmeg** |
| **3 tablesp. fresh bread-crumbs** | **1 glass white wine *or* cider** |
| **2 oz. butter** | **1 egg yolk** |
| **1 pt. cooked shrimps** | **¼ pt. cream *or* milk, *or* ½ cream and ½ milk** |
| **1 teasp. lemon juice** | **Salt and pepper** |

Heat ½ pt. of the fish stock and in it soak the breadcrumbs. Melt ½ oz. butter in a deep pan and in it toss the shrimps over gentle heat for 5 min. Add lemon juice, nutmeg, bread-crumbs and ½ pt. stock, heat gently for 5 min., beat in the rest of the butter. Pound this paste and rub it through a wire sieve. Gradually add the wine and the rest of the fish stock and bring to boiling point. Mix the egg yolk with the milk or cream. Season the soup carefully, remove it from the heat, stir in the egg and cream mixture and cook this without allowing the soup to boil.

**4–6 helpings**
**Cooking time—40 min. for fish stock**
**15–20 min. for the bisque**

### BISQUE D'HOMARD

Lobster soup

| | |
|---|---|
| **The shell, trimmings and a little of the flesh of a medium-sized lobster** | **¼ pt. white wine** |
| **1 onion** | **1¾ pt. fish stock** |
| **1 carrot** | **Salt and pepper** |
| **1 clove of garlic** | **1 tablesp. cooked lobster coral** |
| **1 bay leaf** | **2 oz. butter** |
| **1 blade of mace** | **1 oz. flour** |
| **Lemon juice** | **¼ pt. cream** |
| **1 teasp. anchovy essence** | **A few drops carmine if needed** |

Crush the shell; flake the rough pieces of flesh as finely as possible, keeping neat pieces of the better parts for garnish. Slice the vegetables finely, put them into a pan with the spices, flavouring, shell, flaked lobster and the wine. Heat all quickly and cook briskly for a few minutes. The alcohol in the wine should extract much of the flavour from the lobster and vegetables. Add the stock, and salt, bring to boiling point; simmer 1 hr. Strain through a wire sieve, and rub through the sieve any of the scraps of lobster that are still firm. Pound the lobster coral with 1 oz. butter and rub through a nylon sieve. Melt the other 1 oz. butter, stir into it the flour, then the strained stock, bring to boiling point. Whisk in, just at boiling point, the lobster butter, then stir in the cream, off the heat. Season carefully, colour if necessary to obtain a deep orange-pink, reheat without boiling, adding any neat pieces of lobster.

NOTE: Live lobster may be used

**4–6 helpings Cooking time—40 min. for fish stock**
**1 hr. 20 min. for bisque**

### BISQUES

Bisques are fish soups of a thick, creamy consistency usually made from molluscs or crustaceans, the flesh of which is pounded and sieved to form a purée.

### "BLACK" BUTTER

*Beurre Noir*

**Butter** **Vinegar**

Heat the required amount of butter till brown but not burnt, strain, add a dash of vinegar. Use hot.

### BLACKBERRY AND APPLE JAM

**¾ lb. sour apples (weighed when peeled and cored)**
**½ pt. water**
**2 lb. blackberries**
**3 lb. sugar**

Slice the apples and stew them till soft in ¼ pt. of the water. Pick over the blackberries, add the other ¼ pt. of water and stew slowly in another pan till tender. Mix the 2 cooked fruits together. Add the sugar, heat gently until dissolved, then boil rapidly until setting point is reached. Skim, pour into warm, dry jars and cover.

**Yield—5 lb.**

### BLACKBERRY AND APPLE JELLY

**4 lb. blackberries**
**4 lb. cooking apples**
**2 pt. water**
**Sugar**

Rinse the fruit. Cut up the apples without peeling or coring. Simmer the blackberries and apples separately with the water for about 1 hr., until the fruits are tender. Mash well and allow to drip through a jelly bag. Measure the juice. Bring to the boil, then stir in the sugar (usually 1 lb. to each 1 pt. of juice). Boil briskly till set.

### BLACKBERRY or BLACKCURRANT SYRUP

*To each lb. of fruit allow:*
**1 lb. loaf *or* preserving sugar and 1 tablesp. water**

*To each pt. syrup allow:*
**1 small glass brandy**

Place the fruit, sugar and water in a large jar with a close-fitting cover, stand the jar in a saucepan of boiling water, and cook gently for 2 hr. Strain the juice, measure it, put it into a preserving pan or stewpan (preferably an enamelled one), and boil gently for 20 min., skimming carefully meanwhile. To each pt. of syrup add a small glass of brandy, let it become quite cold, then bottle for use.

### BLACKCOCK FILLETS À LA FINANCIÈRE

*Filets de Petit Coq de Bruyère à la Financière*

**2 blackcocks**
**1 medium-sized onion**
**1 small carrot**
**½ turnip**
**¼ pt. stock**
**3 rashers of bacon**
**½ pt. brown sauce**
**12 button mushrooms**
**1 glass sherry *or* Madeira (optional)**
**Salt and pepper**

Joint birds and cut into fillets. Slice vegetables and lay these in a sauté-pan with the bacon; put the fillets on top. Add the stock, cover with a buttered paper and close-fitting lid, simmer gently 30 min. Make brown sauce, add mushrooms (if fresh, fry first in butter), and wine (if used); season to taste; keep sauce hot.

When fillets are cooked, arrange on a hot dish, strain the sauce over and use mushrooms and bacon for garnishing.

**5–6 helpings**

### BLACKCURRANT ICE CREAM

*Glace à la Crème de Cassis*

**½ lb. ripe blackcurrants**
**3 oz. castor sugar**
**¼ pt. water**
**Rind and juice of 1 lemon**
**Few drops of carmine**
**½ pt. ice cream custard**
**¼ pt. cream**

Place blackcurrants, sugar and water, peel and strained juice of lemon and a few drops of carmine in a pan and allow to just boil. Pass through a nylon sieve. Add the custard and partly freeze. Add the whipped and sweetened cream and finish freezing.

**6 helpings** **Time—2½ hr.**

### BLACKCURRANT JAM

**2 lb. blackcurrants**
**1½ pt. water**
**3 lb. sugar**

Remove currants from the stalks. If the fruit is dirty, wash it thoroughly and drain. Put into the preserving pan with the water, and stew slowly till the skins are soft. *This will take at least ½ hr., probably more.* As the pulp thickens, stir frequently to prevent burning. Add the sugar, stir over a low heat until dissolved, then boil rapidly till setting point is reached. (Test for set at intervals after about 10 min. rapid boiling). Skim, pour into dry, warm jars and cover.

NOTE: This is a good jam for beginners—it sets very easily. But beware of adding the sugar too soon, otherwise hard, "boot-button" currants will result. Try adding 1 tablesp. blackcurrant jam when cooking curry; it helps to darken the curry and gives a good flavour.

### BLACKCURRANT JELLY (PRESERVE)

**4 lb. ripe blackcurrants**
**2½ pt. water**
**Sugar**

Remove the leaves and only the larger stems and wash the blackcurrants. Place in the preserving-pan, add 1½ pt. water, and simmer gently till thoroughly tender. Mash well, then strain the pulp through a scalded jelly bag, leaving it to drip undisturbed for at least 15 min. Return the pulp left in the jelly bag to the pan, add another pint of water and simmer for ½ hr. Tip this pulp back into the bag and allow to drip for 1 hr. Mix the first and second extracts together. Measure the juice into the cleaned pan, bring to the boil. Then add 1 lb. sugar to each pint of juice and stir till dissolved. Boil briskly, without stirring, until setting point is reached. Remove the scum, then immediately pour the jelly into warm jars.

### BLACKCURRANT VINEGAR

**4 qt. sound, ripe blackcurrants**
**2 pt. picked and washed young currant leaves**
**Loaf sugar**
**White wine vinegar**
**Brandy**

Put the fruit and currant leaves into a preserving-pan and crush and stir them over gentle heat until the juice flows freely. Strain the juice off through a fine sieve, measure and add 12 oz. sugar for every pt. of juice. Bring to the boil and cook for 20 min., removing the scum as it rises. Stand aside until cold, then measure and add 3 gills white wine vinegar for every pt. of syrup. Finally add 1 gill of brandy for every qt. of liquid. Bottle, cork, seal and store in a cool, dry cupboard.

### BLACKCURRANT WHIP

*Gelée de Cassis fouettée*

**¼ pt. blackcurrant purée and ½ pt. water *or* ¾ pt. blackcurrant juice**
**½ oz. gelatine**
**Sugar to taste**

Heat the gelatine slowly in the juice *or* purée and water until dissolved. Add sugar if necessary. Cool, then whisk briskly until a thick foam is produced. When the whisk leaves a trail in the foam, pile quickly into a glass dish.

**6 helpings**
**Time—½ hr.**

## BLANQUETTE OF LAMB

*Blanquette d'Agneau*

| | |
|---|---|
| **2 lb. fleshy lamb-loin, neck *or* breast** | **Stock *or* water** |
| **Salt and pepper** | **1½ oz. butter** |
| **1 large onion** | **1 oz. flour** |
| **Bouquet garni** | **1 egg yolk** |
| **6 peppercorns** | **2 tablesp. cream *or* milk** |
| **Pinch of grated nutmeg** | |

GARNISH

| | |
|---|---|
| **Croûtes of fried bread *or* fleurons of pastry** | **Button mushrooms** |

Cut the meat into pieces about 2 in. square and put into a stewpan with salt, sliced onion, herbs, peppercorns and nutmeg. Just cover with cold stock or water and simmer until tender—about 2 hr. When the meat is cooked, melt the butter in a saucepan and stir in the flour. Cook for a few minutes without browning. Strain ½ pt. liquor from the meat and add to the blended flour and butter. Stir until boiling then simmer for 3 min. Beat together the egg yolk and cream and add to the sauce. Stir and cook gently for a few minutes, do not allow to boil or it may curdle. Correct the seasoning. Arrange the meat on a hot dish, piling it high in the centre and strain the sauce over.

Garnish with neatly shaped croûtes of fried bread or fleurons of pastry and grilled mushrooms. Serve hot.

**5–6 helpings**

## BLANQUETTE OF TURKEY

*Blanquette de Dinde*

| | |
|---|---|
| **¾–1 lb. cold turkey** | **1 oz. flour** |
| **1 small onion** | **¾ pt. stock *or* water** |
| **1 blade of mace** | **Pinch of nutmeg** |
| **Salt and pepper** | **2 tablesp. cream *or* milk** |
| **1½ oz. butter** | **1 egg yolk** |

Cut turkey into neat pieces. Place some turkey bones, the sliced onion, mace and seasoning in a pan, cover with stock or water, simmer at least 1 hr. Melt butter in a saucepan, stir in flour, cook 3 min. without browning, stir in hot strained stock. Simmer 10 min., season to taste, add nutmeg and pieces of turkey, allow to heat thoroughly—about 20 min. Mix cream *or* milk with egg yolk, stir in a little of the hot liquid, return all to pan, heat gently without boiling for about 5 min.

Serve hot.

**4 helpings**

## BLINIS

*Russian Pancakes*

| | |
|---|---|
| **½ lb. flour** | **Pinch of salt** |
| **¼ lb. rye flour** | **½ teasp. sugar** |
| **1½ pt. milk** | **2 eggs** |
| **1 oz. yeast** | **Butter for frying** |
| **2 oz. butter** | |

Sift the flour and rye flour into a bowl. Warm a little of the milk, slightly, and stir in the yeast. Make a well in the centre of the flour and pour into it the yeast and milk moving into it a little flour from the sides. Cover and stand in a warm place for about 1 hr. Warm the rest of the milk slightly, melt the butter and add both to the yeast in the centre of the flour. Add the salt, sugar and both egg yolks and mix thoroughly together into a smooth batter. 20 min. before using, beat the egg whites to a stiff snow, fold into the batter. Fry—as pancakes—in a little butter, in a very small pan.

Serve very hot with ice-cold caviare or sour cream and melted butter—handed separately.

**6 helpings**
**Time—2 hr.**

## BLOATER TOAST

*Croûtes à la Yarmouth*

| | |
|---|---|
| **2 bloaters with soft roes** | **Cayenne pepper** |
| **1½ oz. butter** | **8 squares of buttered toast *or* 2 large pieces of toast** |
| **1 egg** | |
| **Salt** | |

Remove the roes, grill the bloaters, free them from skin and bone, then chop or rub them through a fine sieve. Heat 1 oz. of butter in a small saucepan, add the fish, and when hot put in the egg, season to taste, and stir over a low heat until the mixture thickens. Meanwhile divide the roes into 8 pieces, and fry them in the remainder of the butter. Spread the fish mixture on the toast, place the roe on the top, and serve as hot as possible.

**2 helpings *or* 8 small savouries**
**Cooking time—5 min.**

## BLOATERS—GRILLED

Split the bloaters open and remove the backbone, then either fold each bloater back into shape, or leave them opened out flat and place 2 together with their insides facing. Rub over with a little oil or fat and grill as for kippers.

## BLUEBERRY GRUNT

| | |
|---|---|
| **2 cups blueberries** | **½ teasp. salt** |
| **½ cup sugar** | **2 tablesp. sugar** |
| **2 tablesp. lemon juice** | **¼ cup shortening** |
| **2 cups plain flour** | **¾ cup milk (approx.)** |
| **4 teasp. baking-powder** | |

Put the blueberries, ½ cup of sugar, lemon juice and 1 cup of water into a pan and bring to boil, stirring continuously. Boil for 3 min. Sift together the flour, baking-powder and salt, add the 2 tablesp. sugar. Cut in the fat and mix with milk to make a soft dough. Drop the dough over the boiling fruit, cover and simmer for 10 min. without raising the lid.

## BOILED BACON

*Petit lard bouilli*

Soak the bacon for at least 1 hr. in warm water—if very dry or highly salted longer is needed, and the water should be changed. Scrape the underside and the rind as clean as possible. Put into a pan with cold water, just to cover. Bring slowly to the boil and remove any scum. Simmer gently until tender, allowing about 25 min. per lb. and 25 min. over, e.g. 2 lb. will take 75 min. or 1 hr. 15 min. if a thick piece, and rather less if a thinner piece. Take joint out and remove the skin—this comes off easily when the bacon is done. If to be eaten cold, allow to cool in the water in which it was cooked. To finish—drain well then sprinkle the fat thickly with a mixture of browned breadcrumbs and brown sugar.

Note: Bacon can be cooked very successfully in a pressure cooker. Remove the trivet, cover joint with water, bring to boil then throw the water away. Cover again with water and pressure cook at 15 lb. pressure, allowing 12 min. per lb.

## BOILED BEEF—Unsalted

*Bœuf bouilli*

| | |
|---|---|
| **2½–3 lb. brisket, aitchbone *or* round of beef** | **A bunch of herbs** |
| **Salt** | **Carrots** |
| **3 cloves** | **Turnips** |
| **10 peppercorns** | **Onions** |
| | **Suet dumplings (optional)** |

Wipe the meat with a damp cloth and tie into a neat shape with string. Put into a pan and cover with boiling salted water. Bring to the boil again and boil for 5 min. to seal the surface. Reduce to simmering point, add the cloves, peppercorns and herbs and simmer for the remainder of the time, allowing 20 min. per lb. and 20 min. over. Skim when necessary. Add the sliced vegetables allowing enough time for them to be cooked when the meat is ready. Place the meat on a hot dish. Remove string and re-skewer meat if necessary. Arrange vegetables neatly round and serve some of the liquid separately in a sauce boat.

If suet dumplings are to be served, put them into the liquor ½ hr. before serving.

Note: In boiling meat a certain proportion of the nutritive qualities escape into the water, the liquor therefore should be utilised for soup, when it is not too salty for the purpose. With this end in view the liquor should be reduced to the smallest possible quantity by using a pan just large enough to contain the joint, with barely sufficient water to cover.

## BOILED BEETROOT

**Beetroots**

Wash the beetroots very carefully, but do not break the skins, or they will lose colour and flavour during cooking. Put them into sufficient boiling water to cover them and boil them gently until tender, 1½–2½ hr. according to size and age. Unless to be served as a hot vegetable, leave them to cool in the cooking water before rubbing off the peel. If to be served hot, serve them with melted butter.

Beetroots are cooked most successfully and quickly in a pressure cooker, taking 15–40 min. according to size and age, with the cooker set at 15 lb. pressure.

**Cooking time (in a pressure cooker)**—*small*

beetroots 15 min., *medium* beetroots 20 min., *large* beetroots 35–40 min.

## BOILED BREAST OF MUTTON

*Poitrine de Mouton*

| | |
|---|---|
| **A breast of mutton** | **½ teasp. mixed herbs** |
| **2 tablesp. breadcrumbs** | **Salt and pepper** |
| **1 tablesp. finely-chopped suet** | **A little milk** |
| **1 dessertsp. chopped parsley** | **Stock *or* water with vegetables, 10 peppercorns, and salt** |

Remove all the bones and surplus fat; flatten the meat and season well. Make the stuffing by mixing the breadcrumbs, suet, parsley, herbs, salt and pepper together. Moisten with milk. Spread the mixture on the meat, roll up lightly and bind securely with string. Put into the boiling stock or water and vegetables, and simmer for 2–3 hr., according to size.

Pour caper sauce over the meat, if liked.

NOTE: Leg and neck of mutton can be cooked in the same way.

**6–8 helpings**

## BOILED BRUSSELS SPROUTS

*Choux de Bruxelles au naturel*

| | |
|---|---|
| **1½ lb. Brussels sprouts** | **1 oz. butter *or* margarine (optional)** |
| **Salt** | |

Choose small, close, sprouts. Remove shabby outer leaves by cutting the end, then make a cross cut on the bottom of each stalk. Soak in cold water, containing 1 teasp. of salt per quart, for 10 min. only. Wash thoroughly under running water if possible. Choose a suitably sized pan and put in enough water to ¼ fill it only, with ½ teasp. salt to 1 pt. of water. When boiling, put in half the sprouts, the largest ones if variable in size, put on lid and bring quickly to boil again. Add rest of sprouts and cook until all are just tender, with the lid on the pan all the time. Drain in a colander and serve immediately in a hot vegetable dish or toss in melted butter before serving. Sprouts should be served quickly as they soon cool.

NOTE: By this method the sprouts retain their maximum colour, flavour and nutritive value.

On no account should soda be used in the cooking of green vegetables.

**6 helpings**
**Cooking time—15 min.**

## BOILED CABBAGE

*Choux au naturel*

| | |
|---|---|
| **1 large, fresh cabbage (about 2 lb.)** | **Salt** |

Cut across the end and remove only the very thick, coarse piece of stalk and shrivelled or discoloured outer leaves. Pull off the green leaves and put to soak, with the heart cut into 4 pieces, in cold water with 1 teasp. of salt per quart of water. Soak for 10 min. only. Wash thoroughly under running water if possible. Choose a suitably-sized pan and put in enough water to ¼ fill it only, with ½ teasp. of salt to 1 pt. of water. Cut out the stalk from the green leaves and heart of the cabbage, shred it and put on to cook with the lid on the pan. Shred the green outer leaves and add these to the pan. Replace lid and bring to boil again quickly, while shredding the cabbage heart. Add the heart to the pan a handful at a time so that the water barely goes off the boil. Cook with lid on pan until the cabbage is just tender. Drain well in a colander but do not press out liquid. Serve in a hot dish and send to table immediately.

NOTE: *See Boiled Brussels Sprouts*

**6 helpings**
**Cooking time—10–15 min.**

## BOILED CARDOONS

*Cardons au naturel*

| | |
|---|---|
| **2 lb. cardoons** | **Salt** |
| **¾ pt. white sauce** | **1 tablesp. lemon juice** |

Discard the outer stems, which are very tough. Cut the inner stalks into 3-in. lengths, remove the prickles, cover with boiling salted water and lemon juice and cook very gently for 15 min. Drain and rub off the skins with a cloth. Put into fresh, boiling salted water and continue to cook very gently for another 1–1¼ hr. Drain well and coat with white sauce. Serve immediately.

**6 helpings**
**Cooking time—1¼–1½ hr.**

**BOILED CAULIFLOWER WITH WHITE SAUCE**

*Choufleur à la Sauce blanche*

**1 large cauliflower**
**½ pt. white sauce made with ½ milk and ½ cauliflower water**
**Salt**

Trim off the stem and all the leaves, except the very young ones. Soak in cold water, head down, with 1 teasp. salt per qt. of water, for not more than 10 min. Wash well. Choose a suitably sized pan and put in enough water to ¼ fill it, with ½ teasp. salt to 1 pt. water. Put in cauliflower, stalk down, and cook with lid on pan until stalk and flower are tender. Lift out carefully and drain. Keep hot.

Coat the cauliflower with the sauce and serve immediately.

NOTE: To reduce cooking time, the cauliflower may be quartered before cooking or broken into large sprigs.

**6 helpings**
**Cooking time—20–25 min.**

**BOILED CHICKEN—TURKISH STYLE**

*Poulet bouilli à la Turque*

**1 chicken *or* fowl**
**1 oz. butter**
**1 finely-chopped shallot**
**½ pt. tomato sauce**
**1 teasp. cornflour**
**Salt and pepper**

GARNISH

**½ lb. boiled rice**

Truss and boil the chicken, cut into neat joints, remove skin. Melt the butter, fry shallot lightly, add tomato sauce, heat it, then add the pieces of chicken, simmer gently for 35 min. Correct the seasoning. Blend the cornflour, with a little cold water or stock, add it to the sauce and boil for 3 min.

Arrange a border of boiled rice in a hot dish, put in the chicken, strain the sauce over.

**6 helpings**
**Cooking time—2–2½ hr.**

**BOILED CORN ON THE COB**

*Maïs bouilli*

**6 ears *or* cobs of corn freshly picked**
**Seasoning**
**Butter**

Remove the outer husks of the corn. Open the tender, pale green inner husks and take away all the silk surrounding the corn. Replace the inner husk and tie securely; place the ears in a saucepan with sufficient boiling water to cover them. Simmer gently 15–20 min. Drain and remove strings and husks. Serve with melted, seasoned butter. The flavour is always best if the corn is torn from the cob with the teeth, each guest being supplied with melted butter in which to dip the corn. Eating it this way is most pleasant but very messy.

**6 helpings**
**Cooking time—about 20 min.**

**BOILED CUSTARDS**

*See Custard and Custard Mixtures.*

**BOILED EGGS**

Boiling eggs is a simple job, but not everyone does it perfectly. There are three ways of doing it; a good cook finds the method that suits her best, and sticks to it.

*Method 1.* Bring sufficient water to cover the eggs to the boil. Gently place the eggs in the water, set the egg-timer, or make a note of the time, and cook from 3–4½ min., according to taste. Take out the eggs, tap each lightly, once, with the back of a spoon, and serve.

*Method 2.* Put the eggs into a pan containing cold water and bring to the boil. When boiling point is reached, start timing. Cooking will take a little less time than with Method 1.

*Method 3.* This method is, in effect, "coddling", and it produces an egg with a softer white than if actually boiled. Have a pan of boiling water ready, put in the eggs, cover the pan and turn off the heat. Let the pan stand for 6–8 min., according to the degree of softness required.

*Hard-Boiled Eggs*

For a really hard-boiled egg, cook by either Method 1 or 2, boiling for about 12 min. Then take out the eggs and put them under cold running water to cool them as quickly as possible. This prevents discolouration around the yolk.

### BOILED FOWL

*Poulet bouilli*

**1 fowl**
**1 onion**
**1 carrot**
**½ lemon**
**Salt**
**Bouquet garni**
**1½ oz. butter**
**1½ oz. flour**
**¾ pt. stock**

GARNISH

**Truffle *or* mushroom**
**Sprigs of parsley *or* sieved yolk of hard-boiled egg**

Truss the fowl, inserting some pieces of vegetable in the body.. Rub breast of bird with lemon, wrap in buttered paper and put in pan with sufficient stock or water to cover. Add remainder of vegetables (sliced), salt and bouquet garni and cook gently until fowl is tender (about 2 hr.). Meanwhile melt butter in a saucepan, add flour and cook without browning; gradually stir in the stock and boil for 10 min., stirring all the time; season. Use some of the liquor from stewpan if no stock is available. Remove trussing string from fowl.

Place on a hot dish, coat with sauce; garnish.

**5–6 helpings**

### BOILED FRENCH or RUNNER BEANS

*Haricots Verts au Naturel*

**1½ lb. French *or* runner beans**
**1 oz. butter *or* margarine**
**Salt**

Wash, top and tail and string the beans. Do not cut up French beans *or* young runner beans as they lose their flavour in cooking. For older scarlet runners, slice thinly, or, for better flavour, cut into diamonds, i.e. slice them in a slanting direction. Have ready just enough boiling salted water to cover them and cook them with the lid on the pan. When tender (15–20 min.), drain and reheat in butter or margarine. Serve immediately.

**4–6 helpings**

### BOILED GLOBE ARTICHOKES

*Artichauts au naturel*

**6 globe artichokes**
**Salt**
**1 tablesp. lemon juice**
**½ pt. Hollandaise sauce**
***or* ½ pt. mushroom sauce**
***or* 2 oz. melted butter**

Soak the artichokes in cold, salt water for at least 1 hr. to ensure the removal of all dust and insects. Wash them well. Cut off the tails and trim the bottoms with a sharp knife. Cut off the outer leaves and trim the tops of the remaining ones with scissors. Put into a pan with just sufficient boiling water to cover them, adding salt and the lemon juice. Cook until tender, 15–45 min., according to size and freshness (when cooked the leaves pull out easily). Test frequently after 15 min. as they are apt to break and become discoloured if over-cooked. Remove from water and drain them well by turning them upside down.

Serve with Hollandaise sauce *or* melted butter *or* mushroom sauce.

**6 helpings**
**Cooking time—15–45 min.**

### BOILED HALIBUT

*Flétan bouilli*

**3–4 lb. halibut**
**Salt**
**1 lemon**
**Parsley**
**½ pt. anchovy *or* shrimp sauce**

Add salt to hot water in the proportion of 1 oz. to 1 qt., and put in the fish. Bring slowly to boiling-point and simmer very gently for 30–40 min., or until the fish comes away easily from the bone. Drain well, arrange on a hot dish garnished with slices of lemon and parsley, and serve the sauce separately.

**8–12 helpings (*or* 3 helpings per lb.)**
**Cooking time—30–40 min.**

### BOILED HAM (1)

*Jambon bouilli*

**Ham**
**Glaze *or* raspings**
**Brown sugar**

If the ham has been hung for a long time and is very dry and salt, soak for 24 hr., changing the water as necessary. For most hams about 12 hr. soaking is sufficient. Clean and trim off the rusty parts. Put into a saucepan with sufficient cold water to cover and simmer gently until tender, allowing 30 min. per lb. When cooked, remove the ham and strip off the skin. Sprinkle the ham with a mixture of equal quantities of raspings and brown sugar. If to be eaten cold, after removing skin, put the ham back into the water until cold to keep it juicy. Before serving, sprinkle on the raspings and sugar, or glaze, if preferred.

NOTE: To ensure that the ham is sweet insert a sharp knife close to the bone—when withdrawn there should be no unpleasant smell.

### BOILED HAM (2)

**One 2 lb. ham**
**Vinegar**
**1 onion**
**1 head of celery**
**1 turnip**
**A bunch of savoury herbs**
**Raspings**

Prepare the ham as in the preceding recipe and let it soak for a few hours in vinegar and water, mixed together in the proportion of 1 teasp. of vinegar to 1 pt of water. Then put the ham into cold water and bring to the boil. When boiling add the sliced vegetables, and herbs. Simmer gently until tender, allowing 30 min. per lb.

Then remove the skin, cover the ham with raspings and put a paper frill round the knuckle.

### BOILED HARICOT BEANS

*Haricots de Soisson au beurre*

**½ lb. haricot beans**
**1 oz. butter *or* margarine**
**Salt and pepper**
**Chopped parsley**

Soak the beans overnight in boiling water. Drain them and well cover with cold, salted water. Bring slowly to boiling point and simmer very slowly until tender, 2–2½ hr. Drain off the water and shake them gently over the low heat to dry them. Toss them in butter and season with pepper and salt. Serve hot, sprinkled with freshly chopped parsley.

**6 helpings**

### BOILED JERUSALEM ARTICHOKES

*Topinambours au naturel*

**1½–2 lb. Jerusalem artichokes**
**White vinegar *or* lemon juice**
**Salt**
**¾ pt. white sauce**

Scrub, scrape and rinse the artichokes, using 1 teasp. of white vinegar or lemon juice in each water to keep the vegetable white. Put into sufficient boiling, salted water to cover the vegetable, adding 1 teasp. white vinegar or lemon juice to each quart of water. Simmer gently till just tender, about 20 min. Drain well and serve in a hot vegetable dish with the white sauce poured over.

**5–6 helpings**
**Cooking time—about 20 min.**

### BOILED LEEKS

*Poireaux au naturel*

**12 leeks**
**Salt**
**¾ pt. white sauce**

Trim off the roots and outer leaves and as much of the tops as necessary. Split from the top to within 1 in. of the bottom. Wash very thoroughly under running water, separating each leaf with the fingers to ensure that no grit is left between the leaves. Drain and tie in bundles. Boil in as little water as possible (barely enough to cover), with 1 teasp. salt to 1 pt. water. Cook until tender—30–40 min. Drain well and coat with white sauce made with ½ milk and ½ leek water.

**6 helpings**

### BOILED LENTILS

*Lentilles bouillies*

**¾ lb. lentils**
**Bouquet garni**
**1 ham bone (if available) *or* bacon rinds**
**1 onion**
**1 clove**
**Salt and pepper**
**½ oz. butter *or* margarine**

Put the lentils into cold water with the herbs, ham bone, onion stuck with the clove, and a little salt. Bring to boiling point and cook until the lentils are soft—about 1 hr. Strain the lentils, toss in a little melted butter *or* margarine; season and serve. If preferred, sieve the lentils before tossing in butter.

**6 helpings**

### BOILED MACKEREL WITH PARSLEY SAUCE

*Maquereau bouilli au Persil*

**2 large mackerel**
**Salt**
**Parsley sauce**

Remove the roes, wash the fish, put them into the pan with just sufficient hot water to cover and add salt to taste. Bring the water gently to near boiling-point, then reduce heat and cook very gently for about 10 min. If cooked too quickly, or too long, the skin is liable to crack and spoil the appearance of the fish. The fish is sufficiently cooked when the skin becomes loose from the flesh. Drain well, place the mackerel on a hot dish, pour a little parsley sauce over and serve the remainder of the sauce separately.

**4 helpings** **Cooking time—10–15 min.**

## BOILED ONIONS

*Oignons bouillis*

**6 large onions**
**Salt and pepper**
**¾ pt. white sauce**
**Lemon juice**

Cut off the root and top of the onion, the brown skin and inner layer of skin. Put into cold water, bring to the boil and strain if a mild flavour is required. Put into boiling water (just enough to cover) with 1 teasp. salt to 1 pt. of water. Boil gently 1½–2 hr. according to size. Make a white sauce with ½ milk and ½ onion water. Season and flavour with a little lemon juice. Coat the onions and serve very hot.

**6 helpings** **Cooking time—1½–2 hr.**

## BOILED PERCH

*Perche bouillie*

**4 perch**
**Salt**

The scales of perch are rather difficult to remove; the fish can either be boiled and the scales removed afterwards, or a better method is to plunge the fish into boiling water for 2–3 min. then scale.

Before cooking, the fish must be washed in warm water, cleaned, and the gills and fins removed. Have ready boiling water to cover the fish, add salt to taste, put in the fish, reduce heat and simmer gently for 10–20 min., according to size. Serve with Hollandaise or melted butter sauce.

NOTE: Tench may be cooked the same way, and served with the same sauces.

**4–5 helpings**

## BOILED OX TONGUE

*Langue de Bœuf bouilli*

**1 ox tongue**
**1 onion**
**1 carrot**
**1 turnip**
**A bunch of mixed herbs**

Wash the tongue thoroughly and soak for about 2 hr. If the tongue is dry and rather hard soak for 12 hr. If pickled, soak for about 3–4 hr. Put the tongue into a large pan of cold water, bring slowly to the boil, skim and add the onion, carrot, turnip and bunch of herbs. Cook gently, allowing 30 min. per lb. and 30 min over. When ready, lift out tongue, remove the skin very carefully.

The tongue can then be garnished with tufts of cauliflower or Brussels sprouts and served hot with boiled poultry or ham.

*To serve cold* (1). After skin has been removed, shape tongue on a board by sticking a fork through the root and another through the top to straighten it. Leave until cold, trim and then glaze. Put a paper frill around the root and garnish with parsley. Decorate with a savoury butter if liked.

*To serve cold* (2). When skin has been removed put the tongue in a bowl or flat tin, curling it round tightly, cover with stock, put a saucer on top and press with a weight on top. Leave until cold, then turn out.

## BOILED PHEASANT

*Faisan bouilli*

**1 pheasant**
**Stock *or* water**
**1 onion**
**1 carrot**
**½ small turnip**
**Bouquet garni**
**1pt. Oyster sauce**

FORCEMEAT

**12 small oysters**
**2 tablesp. breadcrumbs**
**1 tablesp. chopped suet**
**½ tablesp. chopped parsley**
**Nutmeg**
**Salt, cayenne pepper**
**1 egg**

Open and beard oysters. Add them with their liquor to breadcrumbs, finely chopped suet and parsley, season with nutmeg, salt and pepper and bind with egg. Prepare, stuff, and truss the bird as for roast chicken. Wrap it in well-greased paper and immerse it in boiling stock *or* water. When the stock reboils add the sliced vegetables and bouquet garni to the pan; simmer gently about 1 hr.

Remove trussing strings and serve on a hot dish with a little oyster sauce poured round, serve the remainder of the sauce in a sauce-boat.

If preferred, chestnut stuffing may be substituted for oyster stuffing, or the bird may be cooked with some pieces of vegetable in the body instead of stuffing, and served with celery *or* oyster sauce.

Should the bird be required cold, it will be better left to cool in the pan of liquid.

**4–5 helpings**

### BOILED PICKLED PORK

| | |
|---|---|
| **A joint of pickled *or* salt pork** | **1 onion** |
| **Broad beans** | **½ turnip** |
| **10 peppercorns** | **Salt** |
| **1 carrot** | **Parsley sauce** |

Soak the beans over night. Soak the meat in cold water. Cover the pork with cold water and simmer gently, allowing 25–30 min. per lb. and 25–30 min. over. When the liquid is boiling, add the peppercorns, and the carrot, onion and turnip cut in thick slices. About ½ hr. before the pork is cooked, cook the beans in boiling salted water, simmer gently until tender but whole. Drain the beans well and coat with parsley sauce. Pease pudding or peas may be served in place of the beans if liked. Serve the pork in a hot dish, garnished with the vegetables.

The liquor in which the pork is cooked can be made into good pea soup.

### BOILED POTATOES

*Pommes de terre au naturel*

| | |
|---|---|
| **2 lb. even-sized potatoes** | **Salt** |
| | **Chopped parsley** |

Scrub the potatoes. Peel thinly. Rinse and put into a saucepan with sufficient *boiling* water just to cover them and 1 teasp. salt to each quart of water. Boil gently 25–40 min. according to age and size. Test with a fine skewer and if tender, drain off the water and put the saucepan back on a very low heat, with the lid tilted to allow steam to escape. Serve hot, sprinkled with chopped parsley.

NOTE: The potatoes have a better flavour if boiled in their skins. In this case peel off a thin strip of skin, round the middle of each potato. This facilitates skinning after cooking.

**6 helpings**
**Cooking time—25–40 min.**

### BOILED POTATOES—IRISH WAY

*Pommes de terre à l'Irlandaise*

| | |
|---|---|
| **2 lb. potatoes** | **Salt and pepper** |

Boil the potatoes in the usual way but without peeling them. When cooked, add sufficient cold water to the pan to reduce the temperature of the cooking water several degrees below boiling-point. Leave 2–3 min. Pour off the water. Cover the potatoes with a folded cloth, and stand the pan near the heat until the steam has evaporated. Peel them quickly and serve in an uncovered dish, so that the steam can escape, otherwise the potatoes may be watery.

**6 helpings** **Cooking time—about 40 min.**

### BOILED PUDDINGS

*See Puddings.*

### BOILED RABBIT

*Lapin bouilli*

| | |
|---|---|
| **1 rabbit** | **6 peppercorns** |
| **1 onion** | **1 teasp. salt** |
| **1 carrot** | **Onion sauce** |
| **½ turnip** | **Bacon** |
| **Bouquet garni** | |

Truss the rabbit (see notes on trussing, rabbits put it into boiling water. When the water re-boils, add the vegetables cut in pieces, the bouquet garni, peppercorns and salt. Cook gently for 45–60 min.—until the rabbit is tender. Remove the skewers.

Serve the rabbit, coated with onion sauce. Any extra sauce serve separately. Fried or boiled bacon may be served separately *or* the bacon may be rolled, grilled, and used as garnish. The liquor in which the rabbit is cooked may be made into broth or soup.

**4 helpings**

## BOILED SALMON

*Saumon bouilli*

**Salmon**
**Salt**
**Boiling water**

Scale and clean the fish, and put into a saucepan or fish-kettle with sufficient *boiling* water to just cover, adding salt to taste. The boiling water is necessary to preserve the colour of the fish. Simmer gently until the fish can be easily separated from the bone. Drain well. Dish, garnished with cut lemon and parsley. Serve with lobster, shrimp or other suitable sauce, and a dish of thinly-sliced cucumber.

**Allow 4–6 oz. per helping**
**Cooking time—allow 10 min. per lb.**

## BOILED SALMON—in Court Bouillon

**Salmon**

COURT BOUILLON
**To each quart of water allow:**

**1 dessertsp. salt**
**1 small turnip**
**1 small onion**
**½ leek**
**1 strip of celery**
**6 peppercorns**
**Bouquet garni**

Put into the pan just enough water to cover the fish, and when boiling add the prepared vegetables and cook gently for 30 min. In the meantime, wash, clean, and scale the fish and tie it loosely in a piece of muslin. Remove any scum there may be on the court bouillon, then put in the fish and boil gently until sufficiently cooked (the time required depends more on the thickness of the fish than the weight; allow 10 min. for each lb. when cooking a thick piece, and 7 min. for the tail end). Drain well, dish, garnished with parsley.

Serve with sliced cucumber, and Hollandaise, caper, shrimp or anchovy sauce.

**Allow 4–6 oz. per helping**

## BOILED SALSIFY

*Salsifis bouillis*

**2 lb. salsify**
**White vinegar** *or* **lemon juice**
**Salt**
**¾ pt. white** *or* **Béchamel Sauce**

Wash and scrape the roots, using vinegar or lemon juice in the water (see Boiled

Jerusalem Artichokes). Scrape gently so that only the outside peel is removed. Cut into 4-in. lengths, cook and serve as for Jerusalem Artichokes

**6 helpings**
**Cooking time—30–40 min.**

## BOILED SHEEP'S TONGUES

*Langues de Mouton bouillies*

**4–5 sheep's tongues**
**Stock**
**Salt and pepper**
**1 oz. butter**
**½ oz. flour**
**½ pt. stock**
**A few capers (optional)**
**1 tablesp. sherry (optional)**

Soak the tongues well in salt water for 1 hr., then blanch and dry them. Put into a pan, cover with stock, season, and simmer for about 2 hr. until tender. When cooked, remove skin, trim the roots and divide each tongue lengthwise into 3. Make a sauce with the butter, flour and the ½ pt. stock. A few roughly chopped capers may be added if liked. When thickened and boiling, add the tongues and reheat with the sherry and seasonings to taste.

Serve very hot within a circle of spaghetti, spinach or potatoes.

**6 helpings**

## BOILED SKATE

*Raie au Naturel*

**One 5–8 oz. piece of skate wing**
**Salt**

Wash the skate, put into a saucepan containing sufficient salted warm water to just cover, and simmer gently for about 15 min. or until the fish separates easily from the bone. Drain well, dish and serve with shrimp, lobster or caper sauce.

**1 helping**

## BOILED SPINACH

*Purée d'Épinards*

**3 lb. spinach** **Salt and pepper**
(*a*) **1 oz. butter** *or* **margarine and a little cream** *or*
(*b*) **a roux: 1 oz. butter** *or* **margarine and 1 oz. flour** *or*
(*c*) **a panada: 2 rounded teasp. cornflour and 1 gill spinach liquor**

GARNISH

**Fleurons of pastry,** *or* **sieved egg yolk,** *or* **crescents of fried bread**

Proceed as for Vegetable Purée, and drain well. Chop finely with a stainless knife or rub through a hair, nylon or stainless metal sieve. Reheat with either (*a*) the butter and a little cream if liked, *or* (*b*) with the roux, *or* (*c*) with the panada. Season well. Serve hot. Garnish if liked, with fleurons of pastry, sieved egg yolk *or* crescents of fried bread.

NOTE: If the spinach is to be sieved, the central rib need not be stripped from the spinach. A little grated nutmeg may be added for additional flavour.

**5–6 helpings**
**Cooking time—25 min.**

## BOILED TURKEY

*Dinde bouillie*

**1 turkey**
**1 lb. sausage meat**
**Stock** *or* **water**
**2 onions**
**2 carrots**
**1 small turnip**
**Bouquet garni**
**Salt**
**1 pt. celery sauce**

GARNISH

**Veal forcemeat**
**Boiled celery**
**Egg and breadcrumbs**

Stuff the turkey with seasoned sausage meat, truss for boiling Place the bird in a large pan, cover with boiling stock *or* water; add large pieces of onion, carrot, turnip, the bouquet garni and a little salt. Cover, boil gently until tender—about 2½ hr. for 9 lb. bird (this may vary considerably—test the thigh of the bird with a thin skewer). Make forcemeat into small balls, egg and crumb, fry in deep fat, also cook celery and make sauce. Remove trussing strings from bird. Garnish with forcemeat balls; and serve celery and sauce separately.

Boiled ham *or* tongue is usually served with this dish.

## BOILING

*See Cooking Methods,*

## BOILING FISH

*See Fish*

## BOILING WATER CAKE

**1 gill water**
**½ teasp. mixed spice**
**4 oz. raisins**
**4 oz. lard**
**4 oz. brown sugar**
**½ lb. plain flour**
**¼ teasp. salt**
**1 level teasp. baking-powder**
**2 level teasp. bicarbonate of soda**
**1 tablesp. hot water**

Grease a 7-in. cake-tin and line the bottom with greaseproof paper. Boil water, spice, raisins and lard together for 3 min. then cool. Add sugar and sift in flour, baking-powder and salt. Dissolve soda in 1 tablesp. hot water, mix well into other ingredients. Pour into cake-tin and bake in the middle of a fairly hot oven (**400° F., Gas 6**), reduce heat to moderate (**350° F., Gas 4**) after 15 min.

**Cooking time—1–1½ hr.**

## BOMBES OF CHICKEN

*Petites Bombes de Volaille*

**Clarified butter**
**Chopped parsley**
**½ lb. raw chicken**
**1 oz. flour**
**½ oz. butter**
**½ gill water**
**1 egg**
**Salt and pepper**
**2 tablesp. cream** *or* **milk**
**½ pt. Béchamel sauce**

Have ready the bombe (small) moulds, thickly coated with clarified butter warmed, and sprinkle the entire surface with finely-chopped parsley.

Mince or chop chicken finely. Melt butter in a small saucepan, stir in flour, add water, boil well. Turn panada or culinary paste on to a plate to cool. Pound chicken in a bowl until smooth, add panada gradually, then add egg. Season the mixture, rub it through a fine wire sieve. Add slightly-whipped cream *or* milk. Pipe mixture into moulds. Place these in a saucepan, containing boiling water to about half their depth, cover with buttered paper, put on lid, simmer gently 20–25 min.

Arrange in 2 rows on a hot dish, pour hot sauce round and serve.

**10–12 bombes**

## BONE STOCK OR HOUSEHOLD STOCK FOR SOUPS AND SAUCES

### (Also called Second Stock)

**Cooked *or* raw bones of any kind of meat or poultry**
**Cooked or raw skin, gristle and trimmings of lean meat**
**Clean peelings of carrots, turnip, mushrooms**
**Salt**
**1 outside stick of celery**
**1 onion**
**1 bay leaf**
**Peppercorns**

Break or chop the bones to 3-in. pieces and put them with the skin and trimmings into a strong pan. Cover with cold water and add ½ teasp. salt to each quart of water. Bring slowly to simmering point. Add the vegetables, including a piece of outer brown skin of onion, if a brown stock is required. Simmer for at least 3 hr., without a lid on top heat, or covered in a slow oven. Bones may be cooked until they are porous and so soft that they crumble when crushed, but they should be strained and cooled at the end of each day, the vegetables removed at once, and fresh water added next day. If the stock is not required at once it must be cooled quickly, kept cold—preferably in a refrigerator; and used within 24 hr. even in cool weather or within 3 days if kept in a refrigerator.

In warm weather it must be made as required and used at once. These precautions are necessary because stock provides an excellent medium for the growth of bacteria which can cause food-poisoning. Before use, skim the fat from the top of the stock. This fat may be clarified with other meat fat, or used as needed in meat cookery.

**Quantity—1½ pt. from each 1 lb. bones, etc.**

## BONED AND STUFFED LEG OF MUTTON

*Gigot de Mouton farci*

**A small leg of mutton, boned**
**2 oz. ham *or* bacon**
**2 shallots**
**4 tablesp. breadcrumbs**
**2 tablesp. finely-chopped suet**
**1 teasp. chopped parsley**
**½ teasp. powdered mixed herbs**
**½ teasp. grated lemon rind**
**1 saltsp. grated nutmeg**
**Salt and pepper**
**1 egg**
**A little milk**
**Brown sauce *or* gravy**

Finely chop the ham or bacon and shallots, and mix well together with the breadcrumbs, suet, parsley, mixed herbs, grated lemon rind and nutmeg. Season to taste. Moisten with beaten egg and a little milk to bind the mixture lightly together. Press the mixture into the cavity left by removing the bone and secure in a neat shape with string. Roast in a moderate oven (**350° F., Gas 4**); allow 25 min. per lb. and 25 min. over. Serve with brown sauce.

## BONNE FEMME SOUP

*Potage Bonne Femme*

**½ lettuce, a few leaves of sorrel, chervil, watercress *or* tarragon *or* a mixture of these, 1½ in. length cucumber; to make ¼ pt. in all**
**½ oz. butter**
**1 qt. white stock**
**½ oz. flour**
**¼ pt. milk**
**Salt and pepper**
**Lemon juice**
**2 egg yolks**
**⅛ pt. cream**

Shred the lettuce and other leaves finely. Cut the cucumber into match-like strips. Melt the butter in a deep pan and fry the vegetables very gently for 3 min. Add the stock, boiling, to the vegetables and simmer for 10 min. Blend the flour with ½ the milk, stir this into the soup and cook till the flour thickens. Season very carefully, add lemon juice to taste and cook slightly. Mix the remaining milk with the egg yolks and cream, add these to the cooked soup and cook till the egg yolks thicken, but do not allow to boil.

Serve at once.

**6 helpings**
**Cooking time—20 min.**

## BORDELAISE SAUCE

*Sauce Bordelaise*

**½ pt. Espagnole sauce**
**1 carrot**
**2 onions *or* shallots**
**1 clove of garlic**
**¼ pt. good stock**
**6 peppercorns**
**1 bay leaf**
**Sprig of thyme**
**Parsley stalks**
**Sprig of tarragon**
**¼ pt. red *or* white wine**
**Lemon juice**
**Cayenne pepper**
**1 teasp. chopped chervil**
**1 teasp. chopped parsley**

Chop the vegetables, crush the garlic. Put stock, vegetables, spices and herbs into a small saucepan, bring slowly to simmering point and simmer until the liquid is reduced to a sticky consistency. Add the wine and again reduce the liquid slightly. Add the Espagnole sauce, boil then strain the sauce. Add lemon juice to taste, season and just before serving add the chopped chervil and parsley.

Serve with beef, pork, ham or duck.

### BORTSCH, POLISH or RUSSIAN BEETROOT SOUP

| | |
|---|---|
| **4 raw beetroots** | **Shredded white leek, cabbage, beetroot, celery to make ½ pt. in all** |
| **1 qt. brown stock** | **Salt and pepper** |
| **1 onion stuck with 1 clove** | **Grated nutmeg** |
| **Bunch of herbs** | **¼ pt. sour cream *or* 1 bottle yoghourt** |
| **A few caraway seeds** | |
| **1 oz. goose fat *or* bacon fat** | |

Slice 3 of the beetroots and simmer them in the stock with the onion, clove, herbs and caraway seeds for about 1 hr. or until the colour has run into the soup and the flavour is no longer raw. Melt the fat and in it cook the shreds of vegetable and the finely-grated 4th beetroot very gently for 10–15 min. Strain the stock and press the juice out of the beetroots into it. Add the shreds of vegetable and finish cooking them in the soup. Season, add a trace of nutmeg to the soup. Beat the sour cream or yoghourt into the hot soup but do not allow it to boil; *or* put a spoonful of yoghourt or sour cream into each soup plate before pouring in the soup.

**6 helpings**
**Cooking time—1½ hr.**

### BORTSCHOK

*"Little Bortsch"*

| | |
|---|---|
| **1 qt. strong beef *or* chicken stock** | **3 large beetroots** |
| **1 carrot** | **3 oz. butter** |
| **1 onion** | **1 tablesp. vinegar** |
| **1 stick of celery** | **Salt and pepper** |

Put the stock to boil. Peel and cut up the carrot, onion, celery and 2 of the beetroots into very thin strips. Fry them in the butter, remove and add to the stock. Add vinegar and simmer all slowly for 1 hr. Peel and grate finely the remaining beetroot (raw) and add to the soup, bringing to boil for a few minutes. Pour through a sieve, season with salt and pepper. Serve either hot or iced, with cream or sour cream in a sauceboat. If hot, beetroot quenelles should also be served in the soup.

**6 helpings**

### BOSTON PORK CASSEROLE

| | |
|---|---|
| **1¼ lb. lean pork** | **1 tablesp. sugar** |
| **4 oz. haricot beans** | **1 tablesp. golden syrup** |
| **1 grated carrot** | **½ teasp. dry mustard** |
| **Salt and pepper** | **½–1 pt. white stock** |
| **2 diced celery sticks** | **6 potatoes** |

Soak the beans over night. Place them in a casserole with the neatly diced pork and all the other ingredients except the potatoes. The stock should just cover the mixture. Cover with a lid and cook in a cool oven (**310° F., Gas 2**) for 4 hr. Add more stock if needed. About 1 hr. before it is ready, place 6 even-sized potatoes on the top. Return to the oven and cook until tender. Serve hot.

**6 helpings**

### BOTTLING FRUIT, MEAT, VEGETABLES, ETC.

Like canning, this is a specialized form of cookery. The reader interested in it should refer to *Mrs Beeton's Cookery and Household Management* where it is treated in some detail.

### BOUCHÉES

*See Pastry-Making*

### BOUDINETTES OF VEAL

*Boudinettes de Veau*

| | |
|---|---|
| **3 lb. spinach** | **1 egg yolk** |
| **6 oz. lean cold cooked veal** | **Salt and pepper** |
| **2 oz. lean ham *or* tongue** | **Pig's caul** |
| **1 oz. grated cheese** | **½ pt. good gravy** |
| **2 tablesp. cream** | **Flour for dredging** |
| | **Meat glaze** |

Cook the spinach and rub through a fine sieve. Mince the veal and ham or tongue very finely and put into a small pan with 1 tablesp. of the spinach purée, the cheese, cream and egg yolk. Mix thoroughly with a wooden spoon, season to taste and cook very slowly for 3–4 min., stirring the whole time. Then turn the mixture on to a plate and leave to cool. Cut the caul into pieces 3½ in. square, shape the mixture into 1½-in. squares and wrap them in the pieces of caul. Bake for 7–8 min. in a fairly hot oven **(375° F., Gas 5).** Put the rest of the spinach into a pan, add 2 tablesp. gravy, dredge with a little flour, season with salt and pepper and re-heat. Arrange in an oblong on a hot dish. Brush the boudinettes with meat glaze and arrange them on the spinach, pour the hot gravy round.

**6 helpings**

### BOUILLABAISSE

NOTE: This, the most famous of all fish soups is made chiefly in the South of France, different districts having particular recipes. It is a kind of thick stew of fish which should include a very wide mixture of different kinds of fish. The original French recipes use many fish not available in Great Britain. The following recipe is adapted to use the available fish. In order to get a wide enough variety a large quantity must be made.

*A mixture of* 8 *to* 10 *different kinds of fish, e.g.:*

| | |
|---|---|
| **Whiting** | **John Dory** |
| **Red mullet** | **Monk fish** |
| **Crawfish *or* lobster** | **Crab** |
| **Conger eel *or* eel** | **Bass** |
| **Gurnet** | **Sole** |

*To every* 2 *lb. fish allow:*

| | |
|---|---|
| **1 large onion** | **A sprig of fennel *or* tarragon** |
| **1 leek** | **1/8 teasp. saffron** |
| **1 clove of garlic** | **Salt and pepper** |
| **2 tomatoes** | **1/4 pt. olive oil** |
| **1 bay leaf** | **1/4 pt. white wine** |
| **A sprig of parsley** | |
| **A sprig of savory** | |

*To each portion of bouillabaisse allow:*

**1 thick slice of French roll**

Clean the fish, cut them into thick slices and sort them into 2 groups, the firm-fleshed kind and the soft kind. Chop the onion; slice the leek; crush the garlic; scald, skin and slice the tomatoes. In a deep pan make a bed of the sliced vegetables and the herbs, season this layer. Arrange on top the pieces of firm-fleshed fish; season them and pour over them the oil. Add to the pan the wine and enough cold water or fish stock barely to cover the top layer of fish. Heat as quickly as possible to boiling point and boil briskly for 8 min. Now add the soft pieces of fish, forming a fresh layer. Boil for a further 5 min. Meanwhile toast the slices of bread and arrange them in the bottom of the soup tureen or individual bowls. Pour the liquid over the bread and serve it as a fish bouillon. Serve the mixture of fish separately.

NOTE: The vegetables and herbs are for flavour only, and need not be served, the olive oil should be distributed over the pieces of fish if cooking has been brisk enough.

The mixture suggested would probably weigh 4 lb.

**Sufficient for 8–10 helpings**
**Cooking time—15–20 min.**

### BOUQUET-GARNI or BUNCH OF FRESH HERBS or FAGGOT OF HERBS

| | |
|---|---|
| **1 sprig of thyme** | **1 small bay leaf** |
| **1 sprig of marjoram** | **A few stalks of parsley** |
| **1 small sage leaf (optional)** | **A few chives (optional)** |
| **1 strip of lemon rind (optional)** | **Sprig of chervil (optional)** |

Tie all the herbs into a bunch with thick cotton or fine string, leaving a long piece free, which may be used to tie the bunch to the handle of the pan. Alternatively the herbs may be tied in a small square of muslin and fastened with string or cotton, as before.

### BRAINS AND EGG ON TOAST

*Cervelles sur Croûtes*

| | |
|---|---|
| **3 sheep's brains** | **1 oz. butter** |
| **Salt and pepper** | **1 teasp. chopped parsley** |
| **1 hard-boiled egg** | |
| **Buttered toast** | |

Soak the brains in salt water for ½ hr. and remove the blood and membranes with salt. Wash thoroughly and tie in muslin. Cook for 15 min. in the muslin in boiling water to which a little salt has been added. Shell and chop roughly the hard-boiled egg. Prepare and butter the toast and keep it hot. Drain the brains and chop roughly. Melt the butter in a pan and in it heat the brains and egg thoroughly. Then add the parsley and serve hot at once on the toast.

**6 helpings**

### BRAINS ON TOAST

**2–3 oz. calf's *or* lamb's brains**
**$\frac{1}{2}$ oz. butter**
**$\frac{1}{2}$ oz. flour**
**$\frac{3}{4}$ gill milk**
**Seasoning**
**Slice of toast**

GARNISH

**Slice of lemon**
**Parsley**

Put brains in a saucepan. Cover with cold water, bring to boil and simmer for 5–10 min. until tender. Remove from liquid, chop finely. Heat butter in a saucepan, stir in flour. Cook for several minutes, then gradually add milk. Bring to boil, cook until smooth, add brains and seasoning. Pile on to hot toast, garnish with parsley and lemon.

NOTE: Instead of toast the brains can be served on mashed potatoes.

**1 helping**
**Cooking time—15 min.**

### BRAISED BEEF

*Bœuf braisé*

**3 lb. brisket of beef**
**1 large carrot**
**1 large turnip**
**18 button onions**
**2 leeks**
**A few sticks of celery**
**$\frac{1}{4}$ lb. fat bacon rashers**
**1 oz. dripping**
**Bouquet garni**
**6–12 peppercorns**
**Salt**
**Stock**

Wipe and trim the meat and tie into a good shape. Dice a little of the carrot and turnip and put aside with the onions for garnish. Thickly slice the remainder of the carrot, turnip, leeks and celery and fry slightly in a stewpan with the bacon trimmings in the hot dripping. Place the meat on top and cover with slices of bacon. Add the bouquet garni and peppercorns tied in muslin, salt to taste and enough stock to nearly cover the vegetables. Cover with a well-fitting lid and cook as slowly as possible for about 3 hr., basting occasionally and adding more stock if necessary. When nearly ready, cook the diced vegetables and onions separately in well-flavoured stock. Make a brown gravy adding any strained stock left in the stewpan. Place the meat on a hot dish, remove string and garnish with the diced vegetables and onions. Serve the gravy separately.

### BRAISED BEEF IN ASPIC

*Filet de Bœuf Braisé en Gelée*

**$1\frac{1}{2}$ lb. fillet of beef previously braised**
**1 jar of meat paste**
**French mustard**
**$1\frac{1}{4}$ pt. aspic jelly**
**Cooked peas**
**Cooked carrots**

It is better to braise the beef the previous day if possible and allow it to become quite cold. Trim into an oblong shape and cut lengthwise into slices. Spread each slice alternately with meat paste and mustard, put the slices together again and press between 2 boards. Set a layer of aspic jelly at the bottom of a cake- or bread-tin and decorate with cooked peas and rings of cooked carrots. Pour on another layer of cold, liquid aspic jelly and allow it to set. Place the prepared beef on top, fill up the mould with aspic jelly and allow to set. Unmould on to an oval dish and decorate with chopped aspic. Serve with salad and mayonnaise.

**6 helpings**

### BRAISED CALVES' SWEETBREADS

*Ris de Veau braise*

**2 calves' heart sweetbreads**
**1 oz. fat**
**1 small onion**
**1 small carrot**
**$\frac{1}{2}$ small turnip**
**Bouquet garni**
**6 peppercorns**
**Salt and pepper**
**$\frac{3}{4}$ pt. stock**
**Croûte of fried bread**

Prepare the sweetbreads as follows: wash and soak in cold water for 1–2 hr. until free from blood. Put into a pan, cover with cold water, bring to boil and simmer for 3–5 min. then plunge into cold water. Discard fat and skin and any gristle. Press between 2 plates to retain shape.

Melt the fat in a stewpan or meat-tin, add the sliced vegetables and fry for about 10 min., then add the bouquet garni, peppercorns, salt and pepper and almost cover with stock. Place the sweetbreads on top of the vegetables and cover with greased greaseproof paper. Bring to the boil, baste the sweetbreads well and cook in a moderate oven **(350° F., Gas 4)** for about 1 hr. with the lid on. Add more stock as necessary and baste occasionally. Meanwhile cut a croûte of bread 2 in. thick and fry until golden brown. Drain well.

Place the croûte on a hot dish with the sweetbreads on top.

**6 helpings**

## BRAISED CELERY

*Céléri braisé*

| | |
|---|---|
| **4 heads of celery** | **Glaze (if available)** |
| **Stock** | |

MIREPOIX

| | |
|---|---|
| **½ oz. dripping** | **Bouquet garni (thyme, marjoram, sage, parsley)** |
| **½ oz. bacon** | **1 blade of mace** |
| **2 large carrots** | **6 white peppercorns** |
| **1 small turnip** | **1 bay leaf** |
| **2 onions** | **Salt** |

Trim the celery but leave the heads whole. Wash them well and tie each securely. Prepare the mirepoix. Fry the bacon in the dripping in a large saucepan, then fry all the vegetables cut in pieces ¾ in. thick, until lightly browned. Add herbs, spices and ½ teasp. of salt and enough stock to come ¾ of the way up the vegetables. Bring to boiling-point. Lay the celery on top. Baste well with the stock in the pan and cover closely with greased paper or metal foil. Put on lid and cook until the celery is soft (about 1½ hr.). Baste several times during cooking. Dish the celery and keep hot. Strain the liquor, put it back in the pan and add 1 teasp. of glaze if available. Reduce by boiling quickly until of glazing consistency. Pour over the celery.

NOTE: Use the coarse outer stems of the celery for soups. A few pieces may be cut up and fried for the mirepoix. The cooked mirepoix can be served sprinkled with parsley as a separate vegetable dish or if sieved and thinned down with stock it makes an excellent soup.

**4–8 helpings, according to the size of the celery heads**

## BRAISED CHICORY

*Barbe-de-Capucin braisé*

| | |
|---|---|
| **6 large heads of chicory** | **Glaze, if available** |
| **Stock** | **Mirepoix** (*see Braised Celery,*) |

Prepare and blanch chicory.

Braise and serve as for Braised Celery.

**4–6 helpings**
**Cooking time—1–1¼ hr.**

## BRAISED DUCK—WITH CHESTNUTS

*Canard braisé à la française*

| | |
|---|---|
| **1 duck** | **¾ pt. Espagnole sauce** |
| **1 pt. stock** | **1 glass port wine (optional)** |
| **Larding bacon (optional)** | **1 dessertsp. redcurrant jelly** |
| **2 oz. butter** | |

MIREPOIX

| | |
|---|---|
| **2 onions** | **Bouquet garni** |
| **1 small turnip** | **6 black peppercorns** |
| **2 carrots** | **2 cloves** |
| **1 stick celery** | |

STUFFING

| | |
|---|---|
| **1 lb. chestnuts** | **Salt and pepper** |
| **1 Spanish onion** | **1 egg** |

Boil chestnuts, remove skins and chop or mince nuts finely for stuffing. Cook Spanish onion in water until tender, chop finely, add to chestnuts, season well and bind with egg. Stuff duck with chestnut mixture, truss, lard with bacon, if liked. Slice vegetables for mirepoix (foundation), place in a large saucepan with butter, lay duck on vegetables, cover pan, fry gently for 20 min.; then add bouquet garni, spices, and enough stock to come three-quarters of the depth of mirepoix. Cover with a buttered paper, put on lid, simmer gently until duck is tender—abour 2 hr. Add more stock if necessary to prevent burning. Heat Espagnole sauce, add wine (if used) and jelly, re-heat and season to taste. Remove paper and trussing string from duck, and place it in a hot oven (**425°–450° F., Gas 7–8**) to crisp the bacon.

Serve on a hot dish, with a water-cress garnish, if liked; serve sauce separately.

**4–5 helpings**
**Cooking time—about 3 hr. in all**

## BRAISED ENDIVE

*Chicorée braisé*

| | |
|---|---|
| **6 heads of endive** | **Mirepoix** (*see Braised Celery,*) |
| **Stock** | |

**Glaze, if available**

Cut off the stumps of the endive and discard any outer leaves that are discoloured or tough. Wash in several waters, then parboil in salted water 10 min. to remove bitter flavour. Drain well; pressing out water with the fingers. Braise and serve as for Braised Celery.

**6 helpings**
**Cooking time—approx. $1\frac{1}{2}$ hr. altogether**

## BRAISED LEG OF MUTTON

*Gigot de Mouton braisé*

| | |
|---|---|
| **A small leg of mutton** | **Bouquet garni** |
| **2 onions** | **10 peppercorns** |
| **1 turnip** | **2 shallots** |
| **2 carrots** | **$1\frac{1}{2}$ oz. butter** |
| **1 oz. dripping** | **$1\frac{1}{2}$ oz. flour** |
| **Stock** | **Salt and pepper** |

Thickly slice the onions, turnip and carrots. Melt the dripping in a saucepan and sweat the sliced vegetables in it with the lid on, over a gentle heat for 5–10 min. Almost cover with stock or water, add the bouquet garni and peppercorns. Place the prepared meat on top, put a piece of greased greaseproof paper on top of the pan and cover with a good-fitting lid. Cook gently for $3–3\frac{1}{2}$ hr., basting occasionally with the stock and adding more stock if necessary. About $\frac{1}{2}$ hr. before serving, chop the shallots very finely, melt the butter and fry the shallots lightly. Then add the flour and cook until a good brown colour. Keep the meat hot, strain the stock and make up to 1 pt. Add the stock to the browned flour and butter and stir until boiling. Season to taste and pour a little over the meat. Serve the remainder in a sauce-boat.

Cooked tomatoes, mushrooms, diced turnips and carrots, peas, timbales of spinach or green pea purée are all suitable garnishes for this dish.

If preferred, the leg may be boned and the cavity filled with a forcemeat made as follows: equal quantities of ham and trimmings from the leg finely chopped, finely-chopped onion and a little garlic if liked. Allow an extra $\frac{1}{2}$ hr. for cooking.

**8–12 helpings**

## BRAISED LEEKS

*Poireaux braisés*

| | |
|---|---|
| **12 leeks** | **Mirepoix** (*see Braised Celery,*) |
| **Stock** | |
| **Glaze, if available** | |

Prepare leeks.

Braise and serve as for Braised Celery.

**4–6 helpings**
**Cooking time—$1\frac{1}{2}$ hr.**

## BRAISED LETTUCES

*Laitue braisé*

| | |
|---|---|
| **6 heads of lettuce** | **Mirepoix** (*see Braised Celery,*) |
| **Stock** | |
| **Glaze, if available** | |

Braise as for Braised Endive

## BRAISED MUTTON CUTLETS

*Côtelettes de Mouton braisées*

| | |
|---|---|
| **6 cutlets from the best end of neck** | **2 sticks of celery** |
| **Larding bacon** | **Bouquet garni** |
| **1 onion** | **$1\frac{1}{2}$ oz. dripping** |
| **1 carrot** | **$\frac{1}{2}$ pt. stock** |
| **$\frac{1}{2}$ turnip** | **Salt and pepper** |
| | **Meat glaze** |

Trim and flatten the cutlets. Insert about 5 strips of larding bacon into the lean part of each cutlet. Thickly slice the vegetables and lightly fry them with the bouquet garni in the dripping. Then add stock to $\frac{3}{4}$ cover them; season to taste. Lay the cutlets on top, cover with greased paper and a good fitting lid. Cook gently for about 50 min. adding more stock as necessary. When cooked, brush one side of the cutlets with meat glaze and put into a hot oven to crisp the bacon.

Serve on a bed of mashed potato garnished with diced vegetables. Tomato or caper sauce are suitable for serving with this dish.

**6 helpings**

## BRAISED NECK OF VEAL

*Carré de Veau braisée*

| | |
|---|---|
| **$2\frac{1}{2}$ lb. best end of neck of veal** | **1 blade of mace** |
| **$1\frac{1}{2}$ oz. fat** | **12 peppercorns** |
| **2 oz. bacon** | **Salt and pepper** |
| **2 onions** | **Stock** |
| **2 carrots** | **$\frac{3}{4}$ oz. flour** |
| **1 small turnip** | **Meat glaze** |
| **Bouquet garni** | **1 tablesp. capers** |
| **2 cloves** | **1 teasp. lemon juice** |

Detach the short pieces of rib bones which have been sawn across and fold the flap under. Melt $\frac{3}{4}$ oz. of the fat in a stewpan and fry the bacon and vegetables slightly. Add the bouquet garni, cloves, mace, peppercorns, and seasoning, nearly cover with stock and bring slowly to the boil. Place the meat on the bed of vegetables, cover with greased paper and a well-fitting lid and cook gently for about 2 hr., adding more stock as necessary and basting occasionally. Then place in a moderate oven **(350° F., Gas 4)** for $\frac{1}{2}$ hr., removing the lid for the last 15 min. Meanwhile melt the remaining $\frac{3}{4}$ oz. fat in a small pan, add the flour and fry gently until nut brown. When the meat is tender, remove to a hot dish, brush over with glaze and keep hot. Strain the liquid, add to the brown roux and stir until smooth. Add more stock if necessary and simmer for 5 min. Add the capers and lemon juice, season to taste and serve separately. Garnish the meat with the vegetables and serve very hot.

**6 helpings**

### BRAISED ONIONS

*Oignons braisés*

| | |
|---|---|
| **6 large onions** | **Mirepoix** (*see Braised Celery*) |
| **Stock** | |
| **Glaze, if available** | |

Prepare and blanch the onions. Braise and serve as for Braised Celery.

NOTE: If small onions, shallots, or button onions are to be braised, tie them loosely in a muslin bag before placing on the mirepoix, so that they are easy to remove after cooking.

**6 helpings**
**Cooking time—1¾–2 hr.**

### BRAISED PIGEONS—FRENCH

*Compote de Pigeons*

| | |
|---|---|
| **3 pigeons** | **Bouquet garni** |
| **¼ lb. raw ham *or* bacon** | **1 carrot** |
| **12 shallots *or* 1 onion** | **½ turnip** |
| **1½ oz. butter** | **1 oz. flour** |
| **1 pt. good stock** | **Salt and pepper** |

Truss pigeons for roasting, dice ham or bacon and peel shallots (slice a large onion). Melt butter, fry pigeons, bacon and onions until well-browned. Add stock, bring to boiling point; add the bouquet garni, diced carrot and turnip. Cover and allow to simmer steadily until pigeons are tender—1–1½ hr. Blend flour with a little cold water *or* stock, add to pan. Bring to boiling-point, stirring continuously, re-cover and allow to simmer for 10 min. Season to taste, skim off any excess fat. Remove pigeons, cut away trussing strings and split birds in half. Serve on a hot dish, pour sauce over, garnish with bacon and vegetables at each end.

**6 helpings**

### BRAISED PORK, COUNTRY STYLE

| | |
|---|---|
| **4 pork chops** | **Salt and pepper** |
| **4 tablesp. cider** | **2–3 large dark mushrooms** |
| **Bouquet garni** | **1 breakfastcup *or* A1 can garden peas** |
| **3 onions** | **1 breakfastcup *or* A1 can beetroots** |
| **2 cooking apples** | **6–8 oz. noodles** |
| **Good pinch of ground cinnamon** | |

Trim off rind and excessive fat and quickly fry chops in them until golden brown. Place in a casserole, add cider and bouquet garni, cover and cook gently on the cooker or in a cool oven **(310°–335° F., Gas 2–3)**. Meanwhile, pour off excess fat from frying-pan; peel, chop, then fry the onions and apples for a few minutes. Add the cinnamon and water to cover them, put on a lid and simmer until soft. Sieve, season to taste and turn on to the chops. Cover and cook for 1¾–2 hr. in all, adding the thickly-sliced mushrooms ½ hr. before the end. Heat the peas and beetroots separately. Trickle the noodles in salted boiling water and boil until, on testing a piece, the centre is still slightly firm. Drain the noodles, peas and beetroots. Dish the noodles with the chops on top and garnish with the mushrooms, peas and beetroots.

### BRAISED PORK PIECES—CHINESE

| | |
|---|---|
| **1 lb. pork** | **1 piece of ginger** |
| **1 oz. lard** | **1 teasp. sugar** |
| **1 cup soya sauce** | |

Cut pork into cubes. Melt lard in a saucepan and fry pork, turning constantly. Cover with soya sauce and cook for a few minutes, stirring continuously. Add 1½ cups of water and heat to boiling-point. Add ginger. Cover and simmer over a low heat. Add sugar when almost cooked.

**6 small helpings** **Cooking time—1½ hr.**

### BRAISED SHEEP'S TONGUES

*Langues de Mouton braisées*

**4 sheep's tongues**
**1 oz. butter *or* margarine**
**1 onion**
**1 turnip**
**1 carrot**
**2 sticks of celery**
**Bouquet garni**
**6 peppercorns**
**½ pt. stock**
**2 bacon rashers**
**Meat glaze**

Prepare the tongues.
Melt the fat in a stewpan and add the roughly sliced vegetables. Put on a tightly fitting lid and toss for 10 min. over a very low heat. Lay the tongues on top, add the bouquet garni, peppercorns and enough stock almost to cover the vegetables. Place the bacon on top of the tongues. Cover with greased greaseproof paper, and the lid, and cook gently for about 2 hr. or until the tongues are tender. When ready skin the tongues, cut in halves lengthwise and brush with warm glaze. Place on a greased paper in a baking-tin and put in a warm oven for a few minutes to reheat.

Serve on a bed of mashed potatoes or spinach purée. Serve with brown sauce.

**6 helpings**

### BRAISED SWEETBREADS

**2 oz. lamb's sweetbreads**
**½ oz. butter**
**½ oz. flour**
**¼ pt. good brown stock**
**Seasoning**
**1 bay leaf**
**Pinch of herbs**
**1 dessertsp. sherry**

Put the washed sweetbreads into a pan of water. Bring to boil and simmer for 10–15 min. Drain off liquid, skin and chop sweetbreads. Heat butter in pan; stir in flour and cook for several minutes. Add stock. Bring to boil and cook until thickened. Add the sweetbreads, seasoning, bay leaf and herbs. Simmer for 10 min. Remove bay leaf, add sherry. Serve with creamed potatoes.

**1 portion**
**Cooking time—25 min.**

### BRAISING

*See Cooking Methods,*

### BRANDY BUTTER (Hard sauce)

**3 oz. butter**
**6 oz. icing sugar *or* 4½ oz. icing sugar and 1 oz. ground almonds**
**1 teasp.–1 tablesp. brandy**
**1 whipped egg white (optional)**

Cream the butter till soft. Sift the icing sugar and cream it with the butter till white and light in texture. Mix in the almonds if used. Work the brandy carefully into the mixture. Fold the stiffly-whipped egg white into the sauce.

Serve with Christmas or other steamed puddings.

NOTE: This sauce may be stored for several weeks in an airtight jar. It makes an excellent filling for sweet sandwiches.

### BRANDY PUDDING

*Pouding au Cognac*

**1 oz. glacé cherries**
**1 stale French roll**
**2 oz. macaroons *or* ratafias**
**4 oz. castor sugar**
**1 wineglass brandy**
**4 eggs**
**½ pt. cream**
**½ pt. milk**
**½ teasp. grated lemon rind**
**Grated nutmeg**

Grease and decorate a mould or basin with the halved cherries. Line the mould with thin slices of roll. About ½ fill the mould with alternate layers of macaroons and thinly sliced roll; adding a few cherries, 1 oz. sugar and the brandy. Mix the eggs, cream and milk together; add the rest of the sugar, the lemon rind and a little nutmeg and pour the whole into the mould. Let it stand for 1 hr. Then cover and steam gently for 1½ hr. Serve with lemon sauce.

**6–7 helpings**

### BRANDY SAUCE (1)

*Sauce au Cognac*

**1 level teasp. arrowroot *or* cornflour**
**¼ pt. milk**
**1 egg yolk**
**⅛ pt. good brandy**
**1 teasp. sugar, Barbados if possible**

Blend the arrowroot with a little cold milk. Heat the rest of the milk and when boiling stir it into the blended arrowroot. Return mixture to pan and bring to boiling point. Mix together the egg yolk, brandy and sugar. Cool the arrowroot sauce a little, then stir into it the egg mixture. Cook without boiling until the egg yolk thickens.

### BRANDY SAUCE (2)—RICH

**¼ pt. thin cream**
**2 egg yolks**
**1 dessertsp. light Barbados sugar**
**⅛ pt. good brandy**

Mix all the ingredients in a basin. Set the basin over a saucepan of boiling water and whisk steadily until the mixture thickens.

### BRANDY SNAPS

**2½ oz. sugar**
**1 oz. butter *or* margarine**
**1 oz. golden syrup**
**1 oz. plain flour**
**1 level teasp. ground ginger**

Cream sugar, fat and syrup, and stir in the sifted flour and ginger. Make into 12–16 small balls and place well apart on greased baking-sheets. Bake in a cool oven **(310° F., Gas 2)** until rich brown colour. Allow to cool slightly, remove from sheet with a knife and, while soft enough, roll round the handle of a wooden spoon, remove when set. The snaps may be filled with sweetened and flavoured cream.

**12–16 Brandy snaps**
**Cooking time—10–15 min.**

### BRAWN

**A pig's head weighing about 6 lb.**
**2 tablesp. salt**
**¼ teasp. powdered cloves**
**⅛ teasp. powdered mace**
**1½ lb. lean beef**
**1 teasp. pepper**
**1 onion**

Clean the head well and soak in water for 2 hr. Place in a saucepan with the rest of the ingredients and almost cover with cold water. Boil for about 3 hr. or until quite tender. Take out the head and remove all the flesh. Put the bones back into the liquid and boil quickly until well reduced so that it will form a jelly when cold. Roughly chop the meat with a sharp knife, work quickly to prevent the fat settling in and put into a wet mould, basin or cake-tin. Pour some of the hot liquid over the meat through a strainer. Leave until quite cold and turn out when set.

The liquor in which the meat was cooked will make excellent soup, and the fat, if skimmed off and clarified well will answer the purposes of lard.

### BREAD AND BREAD-MAKING

Bread has been described as the staff of life, and the housewife is certainly very dependent on it. It is served in some form at most meals. One must stress however that its consumption together with that of other starchy foods is often greater than our bodies require. Eating too much bread is therefore one of the causes of overweight.

Bread is obtained by baking a mixture of flour, water and salt which is made porous and light by yeast or some other means of aeration. Bread which is not aerated is called "unleavened" bread. It is used by the Jews at many special religious feasts, and by many other peoples.

Flour used for bread-making in Britain is most often obtained from wheat. A white flour is obtained when all the outer husk is removed before grinding. *Wholemeal* flour comes from the entire grain ground down. Its keeping quality is less good because the flour contains more fat, but it is widely thought more nutritious. For bread-making a "strong" flour is considered desirable. i.e. a flour with a high protein (gluten) content. Other flours are used in breadmaking but usually with some wheat flour since wheat contains more gluten than any other flour.

Oat flour, barley flour, maize (corn starch), potato and banana flour can all be used for bread-making.

#### Yeast

Most bread dough is "raised" by using yeast. The yeast most used in the home is compressed yeast. When in good condition, it has a beery smell and is a fresh putty colour.

In order to produce carbonic acid gas for "raising" starches, yeast requires warmth, moisture and food. Its action can be retarded by cold, by contact with salt and a high concentration of sugar, and it can be killed entirely by great heat, e.g. too hot water for mixing. One ounce of yeast should raise 1½ lb. of flour in 1 hr.

Compressed yeast can be stored in a refrigerator for a week or two.

Another form of yeast is described as "dry, granular" yeast. This yeast keeps without refrigeration. It can be bought in tins, and instructions for use are stated on the tin or package. The required amount of yeast is mixed with warm water, not *hot* water, and it is allowed to stand without stirring for five minutes. It is stirred however before being added to the flour.

It is important to remember that whatever further liquid is being added to mix the required dough, all the prepared yeast must be put in first.

For more information about yeast, *see Yeast, Use of*

**Other Raising Agents Used in Baking**

**Sour Milk is a raising agent,** especially for steamed breads. It is not widely used otherwise.

**Baking-powder** is a leavening or raising agent produced by the mixing of an acid reacting material, e.g. tartaric acid and sodium bicarbonate—this is generally blended with some starchy material. The ideal baking-powder gives the most gas ($CO_2$) for the least volume and weight of powder. It gives the gas slowly when cold and increasingly in the cooking dough—this means that some doughs may be left standing before baking. The baking-powder should leave a tasteless and harmless residue in the bread, etc., and it should not deteriorate in the tin with keeping. Baking-powder is used in the proportion of one to three teaspoonfuls to each pound of flour, depending on the richness of the mixture—usually the plainer the mixture (fewer eggs, less fat) the more baking-powder is required.

**Egg powders** are just coloured baking powders and must not be confused with dried egg.

**Eggs (fresh)** act as raising agents because when beaten they possess the property of holding air which expands on heating.

**Bicarbonate of Soda and Cream of Tartar** (without starchy material as in baking-powders) are used in the making of scones, etc. The proportion used in scones is one teaspoonful bicarbonate of soda and two and a quarter teaspoonfuls cream of tartar to one pound of flour, or equal quantities if sour milk (acid) is used. It is most important to combine the soda with the correct amount of cream of tartar, or the excess soda will affect the colour and taste of the food. The cream of tartar and the bicarbonate of soda only act upon one another in the presence of moisture. So they must be kept dry if they are to retain their strength.

Bicarbonate of soda is used sometimes without the cream of tartar, e.g. in the making of gingerbread or treacle pudding where the resulting dish is required to be brown.

**Self-Raising Flour** may be used for some things; in this case the raising agent has been added to the flour and usually no more is required. Self-raising flour is more expensive than plain flour but it has an appeal for some amateurs because they feel more confident when they use it.

## BREAD AND BUTTER FRITTERS

*Beignets de Pain beurré*

**Coating batter**
**6 thin slices of bread and butter**
**Jam**
**Fat for frying**
**Castor sugar**
**Ground cinnamon**

Make the batter. Spread the slices of bread and butter well with jam. Make into sandwiches and cut into four. Dip into the batter and fry in fat which is at least 1 in. deep and which is just showing signs of smoking or hazing. Turn and fry to a golden brown. Drain well.

Dredge with plenty of castor sugar and cinnamon.

Serve immediately.

**4–5 helpings**
**Cooking time—5 min.**

## BREAD AND BUTTER PUDDING

*Pouding au Pain beurré*

**6 thin slices of bread and butter**
**3 eggs**
**1½ oz. sugar**

| | |
|---|---|
| **2 oz. sultanas *or* currants *or* stoned raisins *or* chopped candied peel** | **1½ pt. milk** |

Grease a 2 pt. pie-dish. Cut the bread into squares or triangles and put them neatly in the dish. Remove the crust, if preferred. Sprinkle the fruit over. Beat the eggs with the sugar, add the milk and pour over the bread; it should only half-fill the dish. Leave to soak at least 30 min. Bake in a moderate oven (**350° F., Gas 4**) until the custard is set; about 1 hr.

**5–6 helpings**

### BREAD PUDDING—BAKED

| | |
|---|---|
| **8 oz. stale bread** | **1 oz. chopped peel** |
| **4 oz. currants *or* raisins *or* sultanas** | **½ teasp. mixed spice** |
| **2 oz. brown sugar** | **1 egg** |
| **2 oz. finely-chopped suet** | **A little milk** |

Break the bread into small pieces and soak in cold water for at least ½ hr.; then strain and squeeze as dry as possible. Put into a basin and beat out the lumps with a fork. Add the dried fruit, sugar, suet, peel and mixed spice and mix well. Add the egg and enough milk to enable the mixture to drop easily from the spoon. Put into a greased tin. Bake in a warm oven (**335° F., Gas 3**) for about 1 hr.

When done, turn out on to a hot dish. Dredge with sugar and serve with custard or vanilla sauce.

**5–6 helpings**

### BREAD PUDDING—BOILED OR STEAMED

| | |
|---|---|
| **6 oz. raisins *or* currants** | **Good pinch of ground nutmeg** |
| **3 oz. finely-chopped suet** | **3 oz. castor sugar** |
| **1 lb. stale bread** | **1 egg** |
| **2 oz. chopped candied peel** | **¼ pt. milk (approx.)** |

Any scraps of stale bread can be used for this. Grease a basin, clean the fruit and prepare the suet. Break the bread into small pieces, cover with cold water and leave to soak

for at least ½ hr. Strain and squeeze the bread dry; beat out all the lumps with a fork. Add the suet, fruit, nutmeg and sugar. Mix to a stiff consistency with the egg and milk. Put into the basin; cover. Steam *or* boil for 2 hr.

**5–6 helpings**

### BREAD AND ROLLS MADE WITH YEAST

All breads and rolls other than Quick Breads are aerated by yeast. Full details will be found under Bread and Bread-Making, Yeast, Use of, and the recipes for the various types and flavours of bread raised with yeast, e.g. White Bread, Hot Cross Buns.

### BREAD AND ROLLS MADE WITHOUT YEAST

*See Bread and Bread-Making, Quick Breads, and the recipe for the type or flavour of bread desired, e.g. Baking Powder Bread.*

### BREAD SAUCE

*Sauce au Pain*

| | |
|---|---|
| **1 large onion** | **2 oz. dry white bread-crumbs** |
| **2 cloves** | **½ oz. butter** |
| **1 blade of mace** | **Salt and pepper** |
| **1 bay leaf** | **2 tablesp. cream (optional)** |
| **4 peppercorns** | |
| **1 allspice berry** | |
| **½ pt. milk** | |

Put the onion and spices into the milk, bring them very slowly to boiling point. Cover the pan and infuse over a gentle heat for ½–1 hr. Strain the liquid. To it add the crumbs and butter, and season to taste. Keep the mixture just below simmering point for 20 min. Stir in the cream if used, serve the sauce at once.

Serve with roast chicken or turkey.

## BREAD SOUP, WELSH «BRYWAS» or LANCASHIRE «BREWIS»

**1 qt. stock *or* broth *or* liquor from any boiled meat**
**½ lb. crusts of bread**
**Salt and pepper**

Boil ½ pt. of the stock and add to it the bread crusts, cover the pan and keep the mixture hot for ½ hr. or until the bread is soft enough to mash. Mash the bread with a potato masher or sieve it. Stir into the bread purée the rest of the stock, simmer for 20 min. Season well and sieve. Success depends on the flavour of the stock.

**6 helpings**
**Cooking time—50 min.**

## BREADCRUMBS, TO MAKE

*Fresh white breadcrumbs:* Remove the crusts from some bread that is at least 1 day old and either rub the bread through a fine wire sieve, or grate it; or rub between the palms of the hand until fine crumbs are obtained; the crusts are not used. Note: Fresh crumbs will not keep.

*Dried white breadcrumbs* are fresh white breadcrumbs which have been dried slowly. They may be dried in a very cool oven, or left in a warm place until thoroughly dry. They will keep for several weeks if kept in an air-tight tin or jar.

Any crumbs left over from egging and crumbing should be dried in the oven, passed through a sieve, and kept in an air-tight tin or jar for future use.

*Browned breadcrumbs or raspings:* Put the crusts or any pieces of stale bread in a moderate oven (**350° F., Gas 4**) and bake them until golden and crisp. Then crush them with a rolling-pin or put them through the mincer. Store in an air-tight tin or jar. Use for coating croquettes, fish cakes, rissoles, or for covering au gratin dishes.

*Fried Breadcrumbs:* Put some fresh, fine white breadcrumbs in a frying-pan or baking-tin, with a little butter; season with salt and pepper, and either fry or bake until well browned. Drain well on kitchen paper and serve hot with roast game.

## BREAKFAST

The day's first meal is substantial in many British households. It may consist of a hot or cold cereal dish, followed by a cooked dish of eggs, sometimes with bacon, fish or meat. This is followed by toast or bread with butter, and with marmalade or honey. Tea or coffee is drunk with this repast.

## BREAST OF LAMB—MILANAISE

*Poitrine d'Agneau à la Milanaise*

**A breast of lamb**
**Salt and pepper**

MIREPOIX

**2 onions**
**2 carrots**
**½ turnip**
**½ oz. dripping**
**1 oz. fat bacon**
**Bouquet garni**
**Stock**

MACARONI À LA MILANAISE

**6 oz. macaroni**
**4 oz. mushrooms**
**2 oz. butter *or* fat**
**2 oz. cooked ham**
**2 oz. cooked tongue**
**1 glass white wine *or* stock**
**2 tablesp. tomato purée *or* sauce**
**1 dessertsp. flour**
**3 oz. grated cheese**

Braise the breast of lamb as follows: bone the meat and season well with salt and pepper. Roll tightly and secure with string. Prepare the mirepoix by cutting the onions, carrots and turnip into thick pieces. Melt the dripping in a stewpan and gently fry the vegetables with the fat bacon with the lid on the pan for 10 min. Add the bouquet garni and sufficient stock to almost cover the vegetables. Bring to the boil. Place the meat on top of the mirepoix, cover with greaseproof paper and put on the lid. Cook slowly for about 2 hr. until meat is tender. Baste frequently.

While the meat is cooking prepare the macaroni à la Milanaise as follows: break the macaroni into 2-in. lengths. Cook in boiling, salted water or stock for 20 min. or until tender, then drain well. Wash and peel the mushrooms and cut into fine shreds. Put the mushrooms in a saucepan with ½ the butter and cook for a few minutes. Meanwhile cut the ham and tongue into strips and add to the mushrooms with the wine or stock and simmer for a few minutes. Now add the macaroni and tomato purée or sauce, and season carefully. Cook again until nearly dry. When ready, add the remainder of the butter mixed with the flour, this will bind the mixture together. Stir with a fork until cooked. Remove from heat and stir in the cheese. (The mixture must not boil after the cheese has been added.)

Arrange the macaroni in the centre of a hot dish and place the meat on top.

**5-6 helpings**
**Cooking time—about 2½ hr.**

### BREDIE—TOMATO

*South African stew*

| | |
|---|---|
| **2 onions** | **12 ripe tomatoes** |
| **1½ oz. butter *or* fat** | **A small piece of red chilli** |
| **2 lb. thick rib of mutton** | **A little sugar** |
| **Tomato stew** | **Salt and pepper** |

Chop the onions finely. Melt the fat in a broad shallow saucepan. Add onions, and brown lightly. Cut meat in small pieces, and add to onions. Stir well until all pieces are thoroughly seared. Remove skins from tomatoes by pouring boiling water over them, the skins can then be easily removed, chop up the flesh into small pieces and add to meat. Add the skin of the red chilli finely chopped, cover and simmer on the side of the stove for about 2 hr. Just before serving, add sugar, salt and pepper.

NOTE: No water is required if tomatoes are used, as they are sufficiently watery. A little boiling water is added to the meat if a bredie of any of the other vegetables, e.g. cabbage, cauliflower, potatoes, French beans, is desired. The meat is simmered in the same way, but the other vegetables are not added until ½ hr. before serving. They should be cut up into small pieces, added to the meat and allowed to cook gently, with frequent stirrings. More boiling water may be added, a little at a time, if the bredie becomes too dry, but it should never be allowed to become watery.

### BRIDGE ROLLS OR SANDWICH BUNS

**1 lb. flour, etc., as for Milk Bread, using 1–2 eggs in mixing the dough**

Make the dough as for Milk Bread and divide raised dough into required number of pieces; roll each piece into long finger-shaped buns about 3–3½ in. long. Place on warmed greased baking-sheets and pat down a little to make a good shape. Put the rolls touching one another so that they bake with soft edges. Prove for 10 min., brush with egg and milk and bake in a hot oven (**425° F., Gas 7**).

**45–50 rolls**
**Cooking time—8–10 min.**

### BRILL

*Barbue*

| | |
|---|---|
| **1 small brill** | **Salt** |
| **Lemon juice** | **Vinegar** |

Clean the brill, cut off the fins, and rub a little lemon juice over it to preserve its whiteness. Barely cover the fish with warm water, add salt and vinegar to taste and simmer gently until done (allow about 10 min. per lb.). Garnish with cut lemon and parsley, and serve with either lobster, shrimp, Hollandaise or melted butter sauce.

NOTE: This fish is also nice baked or grilled.

**Allow 4–6 oz. per helping**

### BRIOCHE ROLLS

| | |
|---|---|
| **1 lb. plain flour** | **4 eggs** |
| **½ teasp. salt** | **1 oz. castor sugar** |
| **½ oz. yeast** | **6 oz. margarine** |
| **2–3 tablesp. tepid water** | |

Sift the warmed flour and salt into a basin, make a well in the middle and pour in the creamed yeast and tepid water. Allow to sponge in a warm place for about 30 min. Add the eggs, sugar and slightly warmed margarine and mix all together with additional tepid water to make a soft pliable dough. Allow dough to rise 1–2 hr., until it has doubled its size. Take ⅔ and divide it into 20–24 large balls. Divide the remaining ⅓ into 20–24 small balls. Grease patty tins, place a large ball on each tin and flatten slightly, make a small depression, damp it and fix a small ball on top. Put the little finger through the centre. Leave the rolls in a warm place to prove for 20 min. Brush with egg and sprinkle with salt, or if wanted sweet, with sugar. Bake in a hot oven (**425° F., Gas 7**).

**20–24 rolls**
**Cooking time—15–20 min.**

## BRISKET OF BEEF

*Poitrine de Bœuf à la Flamande*

| | |
|---|---|
| **3 lb. brisket of beef** | **Allspice** |
| **Bacon rashers** | **Peppercorns** |
| **2 onions** | **Stock *or* water** |
| **Bouquet garni** | **¾ pt. brown sauce** |
| **2 cloves** | **2 carrots** |
| **1 blade of mace** | |

Wipe and trim the meat. Cover the bottom of a stewpan with rashers of bacon, place the meat on them and lay more bacon on top. Add the onions, bouquet garni, cloves, mace, allspice, peppercorns and trimmings from the vegetables. Nearly cover with stock or water. Cover closely and cook very gently for 2½–3 hr., adding more boiling liquid if necessary. In the meantime make the brown sauce, using stock from the stewpan if liked. Peel and dice the carrots and cook them separately. Place the meat on a hot dish, remove any string and re-skewer if necessary. Glaze and garnish with the diced carrots. Serve with the sauce.

## BRITTANY SAUCE

*Sauce Brétonne*

| | |
|---|---|
| **½ pt. Espagnole sauce** | **½ oz. butter** |
| **2 onions** | **2 tablesp. sieved, cooked haricot beans** |

Chop the onions and cook gently in butter until quite soft, without browning them. Add this mixture with the beans to the Espagnole sauce and reheat.

Serve with meat.

NOTE: This sauce may also be made with a foundation of Normandy sauce to serve with fish.

## BROAD BEAN PURÉE

*Purée de Fèves*

| | |
|---|---|
| **1 pt. shelled broad beans *or* if very young, 1 pt. beans in the pod** | **1 sprig of savory** |
| **1 oz. lean bacon scraps and rinds** | **¼ pt. milk** |
| **½ oz. butter** | **Cornflour to thicken** |
| **1 onion** | **Salt and pepper** |
| **1 pt. stock** | **Sugar** |
| | **Lemon juice** |
| | **1 teasp. chopped parsley** |

Unless the beans are young, boil them for 10 min. in salted water and remove the skins. In a deep pan fry the bacon, butter and onion together for 10 min., add the stock and savory and when boiling add the beans. Simmer until the beans are soft, about 20 min. unless very old. Rub through a sieve, stir the milk into the purée and measure the soup. For each 1 pt. of soup blend ½ oz. cornflour with a little cold milk, stock or water, and stir into the soup. Cook until the soup is thickened. Season, add sugar and lemon juice to taste. Sprinkle the parsley over.

Decorate with piped double cream or a few cooked beans, if liked.

**4 helpings** **Cooking time—45–50 min.**

## BROAD BEAN SALAD

*Salade de fères*

| | |
|---|---|
| **1 pt. very small, young broad beans, cooked** | **Rounds of young carrots (cooked)** |
| **French dressing *or* Vinaigrette sauce** | **Finely-chopped savory *or* chives** |

Dress the cold broad beans with French dressing or vinaigrette sauce. Garnish with rounds of cooked young carrots and sprinkle with a little chopped savory or chopped chives.

**4–6 helpings**

## BROAD BEANS WITH CREAM SAUCE

*Fèves à la Poulette*

| | |
|---|---|
| **2 lb. broad beans** | **1 lump of sugar** |
| **½ pt. veal *or* chicken stock** | **1 egg yolk** |
| **A bunch of herbs (thyme, sage, savory, marjoram, parsley stalks)** | **¼ pt. single cream *or* evaporated milk** |
| | **Salt and pepper** |

Shell the beans and cook them in the stock with the lump of sugar and the bunch of herbs. When the beans are tender, lift out the herbs. Beat the egg yolk with the cream and stir it carefully into the saucepan. Reheat, stirring all the time until almost simmering. Season and serve at once. If preferred, the herbs may be finely chopped and left in the sauce.

If the beans are really large strain them from the liquid when they are tender and skin them before returning them to the thickened sauce.

**4–6 helpings**
**Cooking time—20–40 min.**

## BROAD BEANS WITH PARSLEY SAUCE

*Fèves à la Maître d'Hôtel*

| | |
|---|---|
| **2–3 lb. broad beans** | **2–3 savory leaves (if available)** |
| **Salt** | **Parsley sauce** |

Wash the beans and shell them. If not to be cooked immediately, cover down with some of the washed pods as this prevents the skins of the beans from drying out and becoming slightly toughened. Cook gently in just enough boiling salted water to cover, with the savory leaves in the water. When tender, 15–35 min. according to size and age, drain well. Make a good parsley sauce with ½ milk and ½ bean water and well flavoured with lemon juice. Reheat the beans in the sauce and serve immediately.

NOTE: When really young, broad beans should have heads, tails and strings removed as for runner beans, and be cooked whole in the pods. The pods are eaten after tossing them in melted butter. The pod is quite tender, with an excellent flavour, and a very economical dish can be produced by this method.

When really mature, it is often necessary to skin the beans after cooking and before tossing them in the parsley sauce.

**4–6 helpings (according to yield)**

## BROAD BEANS WITH SPANISH SAUCE

*Fèves à l'Espagnole*

| | |
|---|---|
| **2 lb. broad beans** | **6 *or* 8 button mushrooms** |
| **¾ pt. good brown stock** | **1 oz. butter *or* margarine** |
| **1 small onion (finely-chopped)** | **1 oz. flour** |
| **2 *or* 3 sprigs of thyme** | **1 teasp. parsley (finely-chopped)** |
| **1 bay leaf** | **Lemon juice** |
| **Salt and pepper** | |

Shell the beans and cook them in the boiling stock with the onion, thyme, bay leaf and a little salt. Meanwhile, fry the mushrooms in the butter, without browning. Add them to the pan containing the cooked beans, leaving the butter behind. Add the flour to the butter and cook until it is golden brown. Stir into it the beans, mushrooms and stock, having lifted out the sprig of thyme and the bay leaf. Stir over heat until just boiling. Add parsley and lemon juice and season carefully. Serve very hot.

If liked, garnish the dish with bacon rolls and crescents of fried bread. Vegetarians could substitute vegetable stock for the meat stock and garnish with small dice of nut meat fried in oil.

**4–6 helpings** **Cooking time—35–40 min.**

## BROILING

*See Cooking Methods,*

## BROTHS

*See Soups.*

## BROTSUPPE

Bread Soup

| | |
|---|---|
| **1 qt. meat *or* vegetable stock** | **Salt and pepper** |
| **¼ lb. stale brown *or* white bread** | **Nutmeg** |
| | **2 eggs** |

Put the stock to boil. Break the bread into small pieces, including crusts, and put into a saucepan. Pour the boiling stock over the bread. Add salt, pepper, a little nutmeg and simmer all gently for 15 min. Beat eggs well in a large bowl. Gradually pour the soup, which must be below boiling-point, over the eggs, stirring vigorously all the time.

**6 helpings** **Cooking time—25 min.**

## BROWN CAPER SAUCE

*Sauce aux Câpres Brunes*

| | |
|---|---|
| **½ pt. Espagnole sauce *or* Brown sauce** | **1 teasp. caper vinegar** |
| **1 onion *or* shallot** | **1 teasp. anchovy essence** |
| **1 tablesp. halved capers** | **Cayenne pepper** |
| | **Lemon juice to taste** |

Chop the onion or shallot and simmer it in the sauce for 10 min. then strain. Add the other ingredients, reheat the sauce.

Serve with steak, kidneys or fish.

## BROWN SAUCE

*Sauce Brune*

| | |
|---|---|
| **1 small carrot** | **1 oz. flour** |

1 onion
1 oz. dripping
1 pt. household stock
Salt and pepper

Thinly slice the carrot and onion. Melt the dripping and in it slowly fry the onion and carrot until they are golden brown. Stir in the flour and fry it even more slowly till it is also golden brown. Stir in the stock, bring to simmering point, season then simmer for ½ hr. Strain the sauce before use. As the frying of the flour is a long process extra colour may be given to the sauce by adding a piece of brown onion skin, or a little gravy browning or a little meat or vegetable extract which will also add to the flavour.

**Cooking time—40 min.–1 hr.**

### BROWN STEW

*Ragoût brun*

**1½ lb. neck of beef**
**Vinegar**
**2 carrots**
**1 turnip**
**2 onions**
**1½ oz. dripping**
**1½ oz. flour**
**1½ pt. stock *or* water**
**Salt and pepper**

Wipe the meat and trim off any skin and superfluous fat. Cut the meat into pieces suitable for serving and place in a dish with the vinegar. Leave for about 1 hr., turning 2 or 3 times; then drain well and dry. Cut the carrots and turnip into dice or Julienne strips for garnishing and keep the trimmings. Slice the onions. Heat the fat in a saucepan and fry the meat quickly until lightly browned then remove from the pan. Fry the sliced onion until lightly browned; add the flour and cook slowly, mixing well, until a good brown colour. Add the water or stock and bring to the boil stirring all the time. Replace the meat, add the vegetable trimmings and seasoning, cover with a lid and simmer gently for about 2½ hr. or until the meat is tender. Before serving, cook the diced carrots and turnip separately. Arrange the meat in the centre of a hot dish and pour the gravy over. Garnish with the drained, diced vegetables.

**6 helpings**

### BROWN STOCK FOR SOUPS AND SAUCES
(Also called First Stock)

**2 lb. veal and beef bones, mixed**
**1½ teasp. salt**
**1 carrot**
**1 lb. shin beef (lean only)**
**3 qt. cold water**
**1 stick of celery**
**1 onion**
**½ teasp. peppercorns**

Scrape the bones, remove fat and marrow and wash the bones in hot water. Wipe the meat with a damp cloth and cut it into small pieces, removing any fat. Put all into a pan and add the cold water and salt. Soak for ½ hr. Bring very slowly to simmering point and simmer 1 hr. Add the vegetables whole, including a piece of outer, brown skin of onion, and simmer for a further 3 hr. Strain the stock through a metal sieve and cool it. The remaining meat may be used in any dish requiring cooked meat. The bones should be used for household stock.

**Quantity—5 pt.** **Cooking time—at least 4 hr.**

### BROWNING

**¼ lb. sugar**
**¼ pt. water (approx.)**

Dissolve the sugar very slowly in 1 tablesp. water, then boil it quickly till it is a dark brown. Add a little water and warm this gently till the caramel dissolves, then add enough water to make a thin syrup. Bring this to boiling point, cool and bottle it. Use for colouring brown soups, sauces or gravies.

A better method of producing a brown colour and a good flavour is to fry the vegetables and meat, and often the flour, until all are of a pleasant nut-brown colour.

### BRUSSELS SPROUTS AU JUS

*Choux de Bruxelles au Jus*

**1½ lb. Brussels sprouts**
**1 pt. stock**

Prepare and cook sprouts.

Using stock instead of water and half the quantity of salt. Drain and dish the sprouts. Reduce the stock to a thin glaze by quick boiling and pour it over the sprouts.

**6 helpings**
**Cooking time—15–20 min.**

### BRUSSELS SPROUTS SALAD—COOKED

*Salade de Choux de Bruxelles*

**2 lb. small, compact Brussels sprouts, cooked**

**French dressing** *or* **salad dressing**
**Beetroot**

Toss the sprouts lightly in the dressing and pile them in a salad bowl. Garnish with a border of diced or neatly sliced beetroot.

**6 helpings**

## BRUSSELS SPROUTS SALAD—UNCOOKED

*Salade de Choux de Bruxelles*

| | |
|---|---|
| **1 lb. very young Brussels sprouts** | **Salt** |
| | **French dressing** |

Prepare the brussels sprouts in the usual way, taking care to discard any coarse leaves. Shred very finely. Sprinkle with a little salt and dress with French dressing.

**6 helpings**

## BRUSSELS SPROUTS WITH CHESTNUTS

*Choux de Bruxelles aux Marrons*

| | |
|---|---|
| **1½ lb. Brussels sprouts** | **3 oz. ham** |
| **1 dozen cooked chestnuts** | **4 tablesp. cream** |
| | **Salt and pepper** |

Boil the sprouts and drain them.
Cook the chestnuts separately and chop them. Put the sprouts, chestnuts, finely chopped ham and cream into a warm casserole. Put on the lid and reheat gently in a moderate oven **(350° F., Gas 4).**

**6 helpings**
**Cooking time—in the oven, 15 min.**

## BUCK RAREBIT

**As for Welsh Rarebit, but top each slice of cooked Welsh Rarebit with a poached egg and serve at once.**

## BULLOCK'S HEART— STUFFED AND BAKED

*Cœur de Bœuf—farci et cuit au Four*

| | |
|---|---|
| **1 bullock's heart** | **1 oz. flour** |
| **Veal forcemeat** *or* **sage and onion stuffing** | **1 pt. stock** *or* **vegetable water** |
| **2–3 oz. dripping** | **Redcurrant jelly** *or* **apple sauce** |

Wash the heart thoroughly under running water or in several changes of cold water. Cut off the flaps and lobes and remove all pieces of gristle. Cut away the membrane which separates the cavities inside the heart and see that it is quite free from blood. Soak for at least ½ hr. Drain and dry the heart thoroughly and stuff with the forcemeat or stuffing. Sew up the ends with fine string and place in a baking-tin with smoking hot dripping. Baste well and cook in a warm to moderate oven **(335°–350° F., Gas 3–4)** for 3 hr. Baste frequently and turn occasionally. When tender remove the string, place the heart on a hot dish and keep hot. Pour away most of the fat retaining about 1 tablesp. of the sediment. Add 1 oz. flour and stir and cook until brown. Add 1 pt. of stock or vegetable water, gradually at first, blend well and stir until boiling. Boil for 4 min. Pour a little round the heart and serve the rest separately. Serve redcurrant jelly with the heart if it is stuffed with veal forcemeat and apple sauce if sage and onion stuffing is used.

**6 helpings**

## BUBBLE AND SQUEAK

| | |
|---|---|
| **Thin slices of cold roast** *or* **boiled meat** | **Cold greens of any kind** |
| **Dripping** | **Salt and pepper** |
| **1 shredded onion** | **Vinegar (optional)** |
| **Cold mashed potatoes** | |

Heat some fat in a frying-pan and put in the meat and fry quickly on both sides until lightly browned. Remove and keep hot. Fry the onion until browned, add the potatoes and greens which have been mixed together and well seasoned. Stir until thoroughly hot, add a little vinegar if liked, and turn on to a hot dish. Place the meat on top and serve.

NOTE: The name Bubble and Squeak is now often given to a dish of re-heated vegetables without meat.

**Cooking time—about 20 min.**

## BUN LOAF

| | |
|---|---|
| **½ lb. plain flour** | **1 oz. peel** |
| **½ teasp. salt** | **½ oz. yeast** |
| **1 oz. margarine** *or* **lard** | **½ teasp. sugar** |
| **¼ teasp. mixed spice** | **1¼ gills warm milk** *or* **enough to make a very soft mixture** |
| **1 oz. sugar** | |
| **1–2 oz. currants** *or* **sultanas** | **1 egg** |

Mix salt with warmed flour, and rub in the fat. Add the spice, 1 oz. sugar, currants and peel. Cream the yeast with the ½ teasp. sugar, add the dry ingredients and mix with the milk and egg to a very soft consistency. Pour into a well-greased 6-in. cake-tin and allow to rise almost to the top of the tin. Place in the top middle of a hot oven (**425° F., Gas 7**) for 10 min., then reduce heat to fairly hot (**375° F., Gas 5**) and bake an extra 20 min. until golden brown and cooked through. Brush the top with sugar and water glaze (1 dessertsp. sugar to 1 tablesp. water boiled to slight syrup), and dust with castor sugar. Avoid over-raising.

**Cooking time—30 min.**

## BUNS OR COOKIES

*See also Plain Cakes and Buns.*

### Basic Recipe

(Self-raising flour can be used for any of the following, in which case omit the raising agent.)

| | |
|---|---|
| **1 lb. plain flour** | **3 teasp. baking-powder** |
| **¼ teasp. salt** | **2 eggs** |
| **2–6 oz. margarine *or* lard *or* dripping** | **1–1½ gills milk *or* enough to make a stiff consistency** |
| **4–6 oz. sugar** | |

Sift flour and salt into bowl, cut in fat with round-bladed knife, then rub with finger tips till quite fine. Add sugar and baking-powder. Mix with egg and milk to a stiff consistency. (The fork with which the buns are mixed should stand up in the mixture.) Divide into pieces and form into rocky heaps on a greased baking-sheet. Bake in a hot oven (**450°–425° F., Gas 8–7**).

**24–32 buns**
**Cooking time—10–15 min.**

### Variations of Basic Recipe

**Chocolate Buns**

Add 1–1½ oz. cocoa to the flour and 1 teasp. vanilla essence with the milk.

**Coconut Buns**

Mix in 4 oz. desiccated coconut with the sugar.

**Ginger Buns**

Add 2 small teasp. ground ginger to the flour and add 4 oz. chopped or grated crystallized ginger with the sugar.

**Lemon Buns**

Add 1 teasp. lemon essence with the milk. Turn mixture on to floured board and make into a roll. Divide into 24 pieces, form into balls, brush with egg *or* milk and sprinkle with coarse sugar.

**London Buns**

Add 2 oz. chopped peel and 2 teasp. grated lemon rind when adding the sugar and form mixture into balls as for lemon buns. Glaze and sprinkle with coarse sugar. Place 2 pieces of lemon *or* orange peel on top of each bun.

**Nut Buns**

Add 4 oz. chopped nuts when adding the sugar.

**Raspberry Buns**

Form basic mixture into 24 balls, make a hole in each bun and place a little raspberry jam in the hole. Close the opening, brush with milk *or* egg and sprinkle with coarse sugar.

**Rock Buns**

Add 4–6 oz. currants and 2 oz. chopped peel when adding the sugar.

**Seed Buns**

Add 2 dessertsp. caraway seeds with the sugar.

## BUTTER

Butter is made from cream and consists largely of fat globules massed in clusters. 80% of the content of butter is usually fat, the remaining 20% being composed of protein and milk sugar together with minerals and Vitamins A and D.

Butter may be made with either "sweet" (i.e. fresh) cream or "sour" (ripened) cream.

The main butter-producing and exporting countries are Australia, Denmark, France, the

Netherlands and New Zealand. Large quantities are also made in Great Britain, Canada, Eire, Finland, Sweden and the United States. The different types of grass and breeds of cattle cause the colour, texture and flavour of the butter to vary from country to country.

### To Choose Butter

The butter you buy depends largely on your personal taste, on its price and on what the butter will be used for. Butter imported from New Zealand or Australia is usually made from "sweet" cream, while most Dutch and Danish butter is made from "ripened" cream. The former butters have a firm, cold texture and are usually brighter in colour than the Dutch and Danish ones which are soft and fine-textured. Both kinds may be sold "fresh" or unsalted, or may have salt added.

A firm butter is better for making all but very rich pastries. but soft butter is easier to cream for cakes. Ripened butters are best for confectionery—toffee, fudge, etc.—because of their marked flavour.

Unsalted butter is best for butter icings and butter cream, for cold desserts and also for frying.

### Storing Butter

Butter is best stored in its wrapper, and, like milk, should be kept in a cool dark place, away from strong odours and flavours. If you have no refrigerator, an earthenware dish or butter cooler will usually keep butter in good condition.

## BUTTER BEAN PURÉE

**6 oz. butter beans**
**1 qt. water *or* bone stock**
**A few scraps of bacon *or* a bacon bone *or* a few bacon rinds**
**1 onion**
**2 sticks of celery**
**½ small turnip**
**1 medium-sized potato**
**½ oz. bacon fat**
**A bunch of herbs**
**1 blade of mace**
**½ pt. milk**
**Salt and pepper**

Wash the beans, boil the stock or water. Soak the beans in the stock or water all night. Chop the bacon and slice the vegetables. Melt the fat in a deep pan and fry very gently the

bacon, onion, celery, turnip and potato for 10 min. Add the water or stock, beans, herbs and mace; bring all to boiling point and simmer for 2 hr. or until the beans are quite soft. Remove the herbs, sieve the vegetables and stir the milk into the purée. No starch thickening, other than the potato, should be needed. Reheat and season carefully.

**6 helpings**
**Cooking time—2½ hr.**

## BUTTER, TO CLARIFY

**Put the butter into a saucepan, heat it slowly, removing the scum as it rises, and when quite clear, pour it carefully into clean and dry jars, leaving the sediment behind.**

**Clarified butter, or as it is sometimes called, oiled or melted butter, is often served instead of sauce with fish, meat and vegetables; it is also used to moisten the surface of many things grilled or cooked "au gratin"; for oiling moulds and baking-tins; and for sealing potted meats.**

**To de-salt butter: Put into a bowl and pour over boiling water. Leave until cold. The butter will then have risen to the top of the water and can be lifted off. The water will have washed out the salt.**

## BUTTER CRUST

For boiled puddings

**1 lb. plain flour**
**Pinch of salt**
**6 oz. butter**
**Cold water to mix**

Sift the flour and salt and, using a knife, mix to a smooth paste with cold water, adding the water gradually. Roll out thinly. Place the butter over it in small pieces and dredge lightly with flour. Fold the pastry over, roll out again.

Use as required.

## BUTTER ICING (BUTTER CREAM)

**2 oz. butter *or* margarine**
**3 oz. icing sugar**
**Flavouring**
**Colouring**

Cream the butter or margarine. Add the sugar gradually and cream together. Beat until smooth, creamy and pale. Add flavouring and colouring to taste.

NOTE: In cold weather the butter may be warmed slightly to facilitate creaming but do not allow it to oil.

### FLAVOURINGS

**Almond:** Beat in ¼ teasp. almond essence.

**Chocolate:** Dissolve 1 oz. chocolate in 1 tablesp. water and beat in, *or* beat in 1 dessertsp. cocoa and a few drops of vanilla essence.

**Coffee:** Beat in 1 dessertsp. coffee essence.

**Jam:** Add 1 tablesp. strong flavoured jam, e.g. plum, raspberry.

**Lemon:** Beat in 1 dessertsp. strained lemon juice.

**Orange:** Beat in 1 teasp. strained orange juice.

**Vanilla:** Beat in ½ teasp. vanilla essence.

**Walnut:** Add 2 oz. chopped walnuts and 1–2 teasp. coffee essence.

## BUTTERED EGGS—INDIAN STYLE

*Œufs brouillés à l'Indienne*

**3 hard-boiled eggs**
**½ oz. butter**
**½ teasp. curry powder**
**Cayenne pepper**
**2 raw eggs**
**Salt and pepper**
**Browned breadcrumbs**

Cut the hard-boiled eggs, crosswise, in rather thick slices. Place them in a well buttered gratin dish or baking-dish, in which they may be served, and sprinkle the curry powder and a few grains of cayenne over them. Slightly beat the raw eggs, season with salt and pepper, and pour them into the dish. Cover the surface lightly with browned breadcrumbs, add a few pieces of butter, then bake in a moderate oven **(350° F., Gas 4)** for about 10 min. Serve as hot as possible.

**4–5 helpings**

## BUTTERFLY CAKES

**The basic mixture for rich cakes (small) cooked in greased bouchée tins**
**1 gill sweetened and flavoured cream**
**A little jam**

Cut a thin slice from the top of each cake, cut each slice in 2 to make wings; dredge with icing sugar. Spread cut top of cake with a little red jam, pipe a large rosette of beaten cream on this and place wings in position.

**10–12 cakes**

## BUTTERS, SAVOURY

*See Savouries, Savoury Butters (General Method) and the recipe for the flavour required, e.g. Anchovy Butter.*

## BUTTERSCOTCH MOULD

*Gâteau de Caramel au Beurre*

**1 oz. cornflour**
**1 pt. milk**
**5 oz. soft brown sugar**
**1 oz. butter**
**2 egg whites**
**1 teasp. vanilla essence**

Blend cornflour and make as for cornflour mould ( cold ). Melt the sugar in a thick pan, stir in the butter and pour into the cornflour mixture. Beat well. Stiffly whisk egg whites and beat 2 tablesp. into the cornflour mixture to soften it a little. Fold in the remaining foam very lightly. Flavour with vanilla and pile into a glass dish *or* mould, and chill.

**6 helpings**
**Cooking time—20 min.**

## BUTTERSCOTCH SAUCE

**4 oz. moist, dark brown sugar**
**¼ pt. water**
**1 oz. butter**
**1 strip of lemon rind**
**1 teasp. arrowroot**
**A few drops of vanilla essence**
**A few drops of lemon juice**

Dissolve the sugar in the ¼ pt. water, add the butter and lemon rind and boil for 5 min. Remove lemon rind. Blend the arrowroot with 2 teasp. water; thicken the sauce with the blended arrowroot. Add vanilla and lemon juice to taste.

**Beefsteak Pudding.**

Cut the beefsteak into strips or cubes and toss in seasoned flour.

Cut off $\frac{1}{3}$ of the pastry for the lid, roll out the remainder into a round of about $\frac{1}{4}$ inch thickness.

3 Line the greased pudding basin with pastry, pressing out creases.

4 Fill with meat, adding the stock. Damp the edge of the pastry, roll out the lid and place on the top.

5 Press the edges together, cover with greased greaseproof paper.

6 Place in boiling water and steam.

1

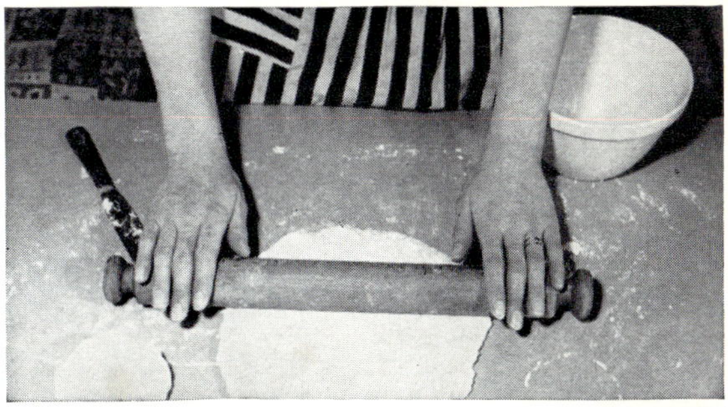

2

3

4

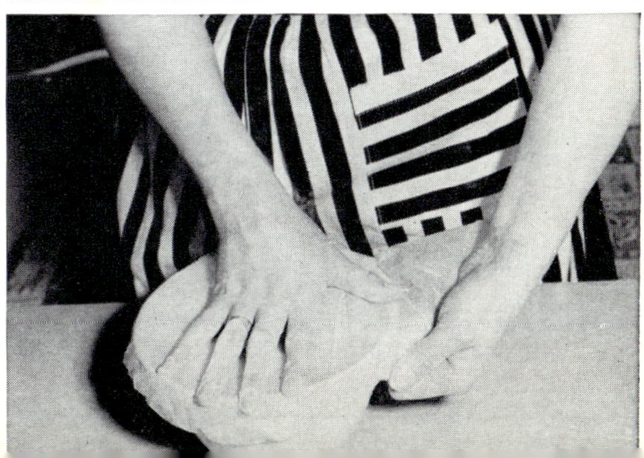

5

6

Cake tins, moulds, etc.

1 patty tins; 2 éclair tins; 3 raised pie mould; 4 caramel mould; 5 dariole or castle pudding mould; 6 and 8 vol-au-vent cutters; 7 madeleine or shell mould; 9 border or ring mould; 10 set of fluted pastry cutters; 11 gugelhupf or fluted timbale mould; 12 soufflé dish; 13 cutlet bat; 14 set of cake decoration markers; 15 cake decoration markers; 16 jelly mould.

## CABBAGE SALAD

*Salade de chou*

**1 lb. of the heart of a white cabbage**
**Salt**
**French dressing**

Prepare the cabbage in the usual way. Shred very finely. Sprinkle with a little salt and dress with French dressing.

**6 helpings**

## CABBAGE SOUP

*Potage aux Choux*

**1 lb. young cabbage with a good heart**
**1 onion**
**2 oz. fat bacon rashers**
**1 clove of garlic (if liked)**
**1 large tomato**
**1½ pt. stock *or* vegetable boilings *or* water in which mild pickled pork *or* bacon has been cooked**
**A few caraway or dill seeds (optional)**
**1 oz. minute tapioca**
**Salt and pepper**
**A very little grated horseradish**
**½ pt. milk *or* 1 bottle yoghourt**

Wash, dry and shred the cabbage; chop the onion and the bacon; crush the garlic, skin and chop the tomato. In a deep pan fry the bacon slowly until the fat runs freely, add the shredded vegetables and shake them over gentle heat for 5 min. Add the stock, boiling, caraway seeds if used, and simmer until the cabbage is very soft. Sprinkle and stir in the tapioca and cook it till clear and soft. Season and flavour to taste. Stir in the milk *or* yoghourt and reheat without boiling.

Serve with grated cheese handed separately.

**6 helpings**
**Cooking time—about 40 min.**

## CABINET PUDDING

*Pouding de Cabinet*

**6 individual sponge cakes *or* 12 savoy biscuits**
**1 pt. milk**
**4 eggs**
**8 ratafias**
**1 oz. castor sugar**
**A few drops of vanilla essence**

DECORATION

**Angelica**
**Glacé cherries**

Grease a 1 pt. soufflé (straight-sided) mould and put a round of greased paper in the bottom, to fit exactly. Decorate the bottom of the mould with a bold design of cherries and angelica. Line the sides with slices of cut sponge cakes. Crumble the trimmings of cake and ratafias and put them into the mould.

Add the sugar to the milk and warm slightly. Add the well-beaten eggs and vanilla essence. Pour the mixture into the mould and leave to stand for about 1 hr., if time allows. Cover with greased paper and steam gently 1–1¼ hr. Remove paper, turn out, and peel off top paper,

Serve with jam sauce.

**6 helpings**
**Cooking time—1–1¼ hr.**

## CAKE-MAKING

One can classify cakes by the way the cake mixture is made.

(*a*) Plain cakes and buns where the fat is rubbed in, and the proportion of fat to flour is small, e.g. rock buns.
(*b*) Plain cakes where the fat is melted, e.g. gingerbread.
(*c*) Rich cakes, where the fat and sugar are creamed together because the proportion of fat to flour is larger, e.g. queen cakes, sandwich cakes, Dundee cake. Note that the proportion of sugar, fruit and eggs to a pound of flour is also larger.
(*d*) Sponge cakes, where there is a large proportion of egg, with or without fat, e.g. Swiss roll.
(*e*) Miscellaneous cakes, which belong to none of the categories above, e.g. jap cakes, brandy snaps.

### Preparation of Tins

(*a*) For small cakes, grease tins with clarified fat.
(*b*) For sponge cakes (but not Swiss roll) grease the tin with clarified fat and dust the greased tin with equal quantities of

castor sugar and flour mixed. This gives a crisp outside to the cake.

(*c*) Line large cake tins as described below. Even for plain cakes, line the bottom with paper. Treat sandwich tins in the same way. The richer the cake and the longer it must bake, the thicker the lining should be. The lining protects the cake while baking, and prevents it being over-cooked on the outside before the centre is cooked.

Tins can be lined with foil or with silicone-treated paper. In the latter case, they need not be greased.

A square tin takes about the same amount of mixture as a round tin whose diameter is 1 in. longer than one side of the square tin. This means that a 7 in. diameter round tin holds about the same amount as a 6 in. square tin.

Any difference in the depth of tins must be taken into account when calculating baking times. On the whole, smaller, deeper cakes require longer baking than shallow wide ones of the same weight and volume.

*To line a tin—round or square*

1. Cut a single or double piece of lining material to fit the bottom of the tin. Take care that it is no bigger than the bottom, or it will spoil the shape of the cake.
2. Measure the circumference of the tin and cut a strip, single or double, long enough to line the sides of the tin, allowing for an overwrap. Make the strip 2 in. deeper than the height of the tin.
3. Fold up 1 in. along the bottom of the strip and cut this 1 in. fold with diagonal cuts so that it will "give" and shape well into the roundness of the tin. Paper for a square tin need not be snipped in this way. It should, however, be mitred at the corners—two pieces are easier to fit than one.
4. Place the strip round the sides of the tin with the cut edge on the bottom of the tin. Fit in the bottom piece. Grease the lined tin with clarified fat if necessary.

*To line a Swiss roll tin*

Cut a piece of greaseproof paper large enough to fit the base and sides of the tin neatly. If the paper is made higher than the sides of the tin it may prevent the heat from browning the top of the roll. Bisect each corner by cutting down 1½ in. Fit the paper into the tin and grease it carefully.

### Ingredients Used in Cake-Making

**Flour:** In cake-making a less glutinous (viscid protein) flour can be used than that which is required for bread-making. For large solid rich cakes where a close texture is desired, it is always advisable to use plain flour plus baking-powder or bicarbonate of soda, as required. The richer the cake and the more eggs used, the less baking-powder will be needed, in some cases, none at all.

**Self-raising flour:** This may be utilized for some of the smaller cakes, and cakes of the sandwich and spongy types where the texture of the finished article is more "open" than for large fruit cakes. As the raising agent content varies in different brands of flour, it is sometimes necessary to add extra baking-powder, an average quantity being one rounded teaspoonful to each pound of flour.

*For cake-making, flour should always be sifted.*

**Rice-flour:** Is used, e.g. in the making of shortbread, macaroons, etc.

**Cornflour:** Sometimes called cornstarch, is another type of flour sometimes used with plain flour. Its addition tends to produce a cake which is rather short and dry, crumbles easily and "melts" in the mouth.

**Fats:** *Butter* gives the best flavour, particularly in the case of large rich cakes and shortbreads. If it is too expensive, *margarine* proves a good substitute; it is easily creamed. *Lard* is flavourless and should only be used alone where highly flavoured ingredients are introduced, e.g. spices and black treacle. Lard is 100% fat and this must be taken into account when considering proportions. A point to note is that it does not hold air well when creamed, and for this reason also, it is unsuitable for the making of many cakes. Lard is good for making pastry.

There are on the market fats described as "all purpose" fats. These fats have air finely dispersed through them, which helps to give a quick start when creaming. When using these "all purpose" fats the "fork mix" method is recommended by the manufacturers as being speedy and economical of utensils—it means that a fork is used to distribute the fat and mix to required consistency. Because both margarine and butter contain water, it is claimed that these "all purpose" shortenings are more economical, e.g. where 4 oz. margarine or butter is given in a recipe, 3–3½ oz. of the shortening will be sufficient. Butter or margarine has been suggested for most of the recipes in this book, but the cook can use any fats she likes as long as the correct proportions are kept. The quantity of fat in the recipe, when replaced by "all purpose" fat should be reduced by about one fifth.

**Sugar:** *Castor sugar* is best for most cakes; *granulated sugar* is apt to give a speckled appearance. *Moist brown sugar* is satisfactory for gingerbread and cakes where a good dark brown colour is required. *Loaf sugar* crushed down to suitable small-sized pieces is effective when sprinkled on the top of yeast mixtures such as "S" buns, bath buns, etc.

*Icing sugar*, being very fine, is used mostly for icings—glacé, royal, almond paste, etc.; it can be introduced successfully into short-crust pastry and some mixtures.

**Eggs:** All eggs should be fresh. New-laid eggs are best for sponge cakes and meringues. Eggs may be whisked with a fork, small whisk or wheel whisk. It is usually enough to whisk till the liquid flows freely and is frothy. In making large cakes the eggs may be added whole one at a time, each being beaten in very thoroughly to the creamed fat and sugar. The housewife who possesses an electric mixer will find the work much simplified and expenditure of time and energy greatly reduced.

**Fruits:** The methodical housewife washes fruit as soon as possible and after drying it *slowly* in a warm place (otherwise it becomes hard), stores it in suitable jars until required for use. It is best to buy *dried fruit* when the grocer gets in his fresh stock. Dry-cleaning of fruit with flour is not a good idea. No adverse results should arise from washing the fruit immediately before use, so long as it is very thoroughly dried on a clean cloth. If it is put into the cake wet, it will tend to sink to the bottom of the cake. Stones must always be removed from *raisins*; drop the stones into a basin of hot water to prevent the sticky stones from adhering to the fingers.

The sugar is removed from *peel* before shredding and chopping. Citron peel is best for putting on top of a madeira cake.

*Glacé cherries* are very heavy and for most cakes it is advisable to cut them into pieces.

*Angelica* (a candied stem) is used more as decoration but it can be chopped as peel and used in a cake.

**Caraway Seeds:** These should be used with care; they make a delicious cake but are not universally popular.

**Nuts:** *Almonds* must be blanched to remove the skins. Put the nuts into cold water and bring almost to boiling point; pour away the water and run plenty of cold water over them. Pinch off the skins and rub the nuts dry in a soft cloth. They are usually either chopped or shredded but if for the top of a Dundee cake, etc., they are generally split into halves and distributed over the top of the cake with the rounded side up.

*To brown almonds:* Blanch, skin, shred and place on an oven tray, put in a moderate oven. Turn frequently till a good golden colour. Allow to cool and store in a jar.

*To make almonds shine:* Brush them over with egg white and dry off in the oven.

*Coconut*—desiccated or shredded. Desiccated coconut may be included in cake mixtures or used to coat a cake already brushed with jam or spread with butter or glacé icing. Shredded, it may be used for decoration.

*Pistachio nuts:* Skin by immersing in hot water for a minute or two, then cut or chop. Thin cross-sections, three together, can be used as shamrock in decoration, or the finely chopped nuts can be sprinkled for green decoration.

*Walnuts* are not blanched; they may be chopped up to go into the mixture or left whole for decorating an iced cake. Walnuts can also be used to coat the sides of an iced sandwich cake, sieved apricot jam being used to make the nuts stick to the sides.

**Manufactured decorations:** These include silver or coloured balls (dragées), crystallized violets, mimosa, rose petals, chocolate shreds and flakes, "hundreds and thousands", marzipan fruits and flowers, glacé fruits, etc. Several kinds of confectionery can be used.

### Aids to Success in Cake-Making

1. Always have necessary utensils and ingredients collected before beginning to make a cake.
2. Line tins carefully.
3. Prepare the oven so that it is at the correct temperature when required.
4. Measure accurately.
5. Follow instructions implicitly.
6. Cream fat and sugar very thoroughly with a wooden spoon or with the hand, until light and fluffy and white in colour. Warm the fat slightly to facilitate creaming. Do not melt it since melted fat does not hold air.
7. Make sure that you obtain the proper consistency.
8. Place cake in correct position in oven.
9. Do not let anxiety override your judgment and open oven door unnecessarily.
10. Remember that temperature is maintained in an electric oven for much longer than in a gas one—this is important in baking a cake.
11. Test carefully for readiness. See below.
12. Allow cake to cool on a rack where there is circulation of air—if laid on a solid board it will become damp and sodden underneath.

### Points to Remember

1. Have correct proportions. Fat and sugar are liquefying ingredients, therefore the richer the cake, the less liquid, such as milk, is required. It is better to add water instead of milk in the sandwich cake type of mixture.
2. For cakes of a sponge type, e.g. sandwich cake, as much as possible of the egg should be added to the creamed fat without the addition of flour, unless the mixture appears to be curdling. For fruit cakes, where a close texture is required, add egg and flour alternately.
3. For rich cakes add the fruit at the end, mixed with some of the flour to help to keep the fruit suspended in the cake.
4. Generally speaking, the plainer the cake, the hotter the oven; the richer the cake, the cooler the oven. Bake small cakes in the top or the hottest part of the oven, larger cakes in the middle, and very large cakes in the lower part of the oven. Cakes must not be placed over the flame at the sides of a gas oven or too near the element in an electric oven. Never bake a cake on a browning sheet.
5. Avoid opening the oven door before a cake has begun to set. Do not slam the door—this is especially important with sponge mixtures and gingerbreads.

### Tests for Readiness

The time given for baking cakes is always approximate, since ovens vary.

1. Open the oven door carefully and just enough to test the cake quickly. The cake should be well risen and evenly browned.
2. Touch the surface lightly and, if it seems firm to the touch, the cake is done. If the impression of the finger remains the cake is not ready.
3. Insert a warm skewer into the cake; if it comes out dry the cake is ready.
4. If the cake is already shrinking from the sides of the tin it is probably over-baked.

### Reasons for Some Common Failures

1. *A coarse textured cake* results from the use of too much raising agent.
2. *A damp and heavy cake* may be due to:
   (*a*) incorrect proportion of ingredients
   (*b*) too much orange or lemon juice added to the mixture
   (*c*) the oven has been too cool
   (*d*) the cake has been cooled too rapidly, making it damp

(*e*) the cake may have been packed into a tin before it has cooled sufficiently, so causing dampness.

3. *Fruit sunk to the bottom of a cake*, may be due to:
   (*a*) incorrect proportions of ingredients—too much liquefying material, e.g. sugar
   (*b*) too much baking-powder
   (*c*) oven too slow
   (*d*) the use of wet fruit.

More information on cake-making will be found under the various types of cakes, e.g. *Gingerbreads, Sandwich Cakes.*

### CAKES AND BUNS, PLAIN

*See Plain Cakes and Buns.*

### CALF'S BRAINS AU GRATIN

*Cervelles de Veau au Gratin*

**1 set of calf's brains**
**½ pt. white sauce**
**6 button mushrooms**
**1 tablesp. cream**
**½ teasp. lemon rind**
**2 oz. finely-grated cheese**
**White breadcrumbs**
**Parsley**

Prepare the brains as directed for Calves' Brain Cakes and cut into small pieces. Put the sauce in a small saucepan, add the brains and chopped mushrooms and heat without boiling. Remove from the heat and add the cream, seasoning if necessary and the lemon rind. Have ready 6 greased scallop shells and sprinkle them with breadcrumbs. Put some of the mixture in each shell and sprinkle with more crumbs. Cover with grated cheese and brown quickly under the grill. Serve at once garnished with parsley.

**6 helpings**

### CALF'S FOOT BROTH

**1 calf's foot**
**3 pt. water**
**Rind of 1 lemon**
**Salt and pepper**
**Egg yolks** (*see below*)
**Milk**

Wash the foot. Simmer in the water for 3 hr; then strain into a basin. When cold, remove the fat. Re-heat the broth with 2–3 strips of lemon rind, which must be removed as soon as the broth is sufficiently flavoured. Add salt and pepper to taste. To each ½ pt. of broth allow 1 egg yolk and ½ gill of milk. Stir over low heat until thickened. Do not allow to boil or the egg will curdle. Store in a very cool place.

**6 generous helpings** **Cooking time—3 hr.**

### CALF'S FOOT JELLY

**1 calf's foot**
**2 pt. water**
**Salt and pepper**
**1 large lemon**
**1 egg white and shell**
**Pinch of powdered cinnamon**
**2 cloves**
**½ wineglass sherry (optional)**

Wash and blanch the calf's foot; cut into pieces. Put in a pan with the 2 pt. water and seasoning. Simmer for 3–4 hr., removing scum if necessary. Strain and measure stock. If more than 1 pt., boil until reduced to this quantity. Allow to cool, remove fat. Return to pan with rind and juice of the lemon, egg white and shell, cinnamon, cloves and sherry (if used). Simmer for 10 min. Strain or put through a jelly bag. Store in a cool place.

**3–4 helpings**
**Cooking time—4 hr. (approx.)**

### CALF'S LIVER—HUNGARIAN STYLE

*Foie de Veau à la Hongroise*

**1½ lb. calf's liver**
**Flour**
**Salt and paprika pepper**
**2 oz. butter**
**2 tablesp. finely-grated onion**
**1½ gills fresh *or* sour cream**

Wash the liver well in tepid salt water, remove any skin and tubes and dry well. Cut into ½-in. slices and dip into flour which has been well seasoned with salt and paprika pepper. Fry in hot butter quickly on both sides, then more slowly until tender. Fry the onion for about 5 min. Remove the liver and arrange the slices down the centre of a hot dish—keep hot. Pour away the surplus fat from the pan, add the cream to the onion in the pan, heat slightly, season to taste and pour over the liver. Sprinkle with paprika.

**6 helpings**

### CALVES' KIDNEY WITH SCRAMBLED EGGS

*Rognons aux Œufs brouillées*

**3 calves' kidneys (small)**
**2 shallots *or* 1 small onion**
**½ gill sherry (optional)**
**5–6 eggs**
**1 gill milk**

| | |
|---|---|
| **3½–4 oz. butter** | **Salt and pepper** |
| **½ pt. Espagnole sauce** | **Parsley** |

Prepare the kidneys.

Trim and cut into very thin slices and season well. Chop the shallots or onion very finely, melt 1 oz. butter in a pan and fry them lightly. Then add the slices of kidney, frying these quickly on both sides and shaking the pan well. Pour off any surplus fat. Pour the Espagnole sauce over the kidneys, add the sherry if used and cook slowly for 15 min. Beat up the eggs and add the milk and seasoning. Arrange the kidney in a circle on a hot dish and keep hot. Keep the sauce hot. Heat the remaining butter and scramble the eggs gently until the mixture starts to thicken. Pile the scrambled egg in the centre of the circle of kidneys and pour the hot sauce round. Sprinkle with parsley and serve at once.

**6 helpings**

## CANADIAN PUDDING

*Pouding Canadien*

| | |
|---|---|
| **1 oz. stoned raisins** | **Rind of 1 small lemon** |
| **6 oz. corn meal** | **2 oz. sugar** |
| **2 pt. milk** | **3 eggs** |

Grease, then decorate a basin with the raisins. Mix the meal with a little of the cold milk; infuse the lemon rind in the remainder of the milk for 15 min. Remove the lemon rind; pour the boiling milk over the blended corn meal, stirring well. Return to the pan, add the sugar, and simmer gently for 10 min. When cool, add the well-beaten eggs. Pour the mixture carefully into the decorated mould. Cover. Steam slowly for 1½–2 hr. until firm to the touch.

**6–7 helpings**

## CANDIED AND CRYSTALLIZED FRUITS

Shop-bought candied fruits are expensive luxuries. One can save pounds by making them at home from fresh fruit, bought when it is in season and cheap. In most years, for example, there are cheap, well-flavoured pineapples and small peaches.

Scarcely any skill is needed to produce professional-looking results. But one needs a diligent nature: it is necessary to spend a few minutes looking after the fruit practically every day for many days. Impatient attempts to speed-up the process would shrivel and toughen the fruit. The water in the fruit must diffuse out slowly; it must be replaced gradually by a syrup which is steadily increased in strength. In this way, the fruit is slowly impregnated with sugar but remains plump and tender.

The method is described in detail in *Mrs Beeton's Cookery and Household Management*.

## CANNED AND BOTTLED VEGETABLES

*See Vegetables.*

## CANNING AND BOTTLING

These forms of preserving fish, fruit, meat and vegetables are a specialized form of cookery. Mistakes can be dangerous, leading to food poisoning. The reader interested in canning or bottling should therefore study a specialized book on the subject or refer to *Mrs Beeton's Cookery and Household Management* where it is treated in some detail.

## CAPER SAUCE

*Sauce aux Câpres*

To ½ pt. white sauce made with broth from boiled mutton *or* ½ broth and ½ milk, add 1 tablesp. capers and 1 teasp. vinegar in which the capers were pickled.

Serve with boiled mutton or fish.

## CARAMEL CUSTARD

*Crème au Caramel*

| | |
|---|---|
| **4 eggs** | **A few drops of vanilla essence** |
| **1 oz. castor sugar** | |
| **¾ pt. milk** | |

CARAMEL

| | |
|---|---|
| **3 oz. loaf sugar** | **½ gill cold water** |

Have ready a warm charlotte *or* plain mould and a thickly-folded band of newspaper to encircle it so that the mould can be firmly held in one hand. Prepare the caramel by heating the loaf sugar and water together, stir until it boils, then remove the spoon and allow to boil without stirring until it is golden brown. Pour the caramel into the warm mould and twist round until the sides and base are well coated with caramel.

Work together the eggs and sugar without beating them and pour on to them the warmed milk. Add the vanilla essence. Strain the custard into the mould and cover with greased paper. Steam very slowly for about $\frac{3}{4}$ hr. until the custard is firm in the middle; *or* the caramel custard may be baked by leaving it uncovered, standing it in a tray of warm water, and baking in a warm oven (**335° F., Gas 3**) until the custard is set in the centre: about 40 min. Turn out carefully, so that the caramel runs off and serves as a sauce.

NOTE: Small caramel custards can be made in dariole moulds; cook for about 20 min.

**6 helpings**

### CARAMEL MOULD

*Gâteau de Caramel*

| | |
|---|---|
| **1 lemon** | **3 oz. ground rice** |
| **1½ pt. milk** | **1 oz. castor sugar** |

CARAMEL

| | |
|---|---|
| **2 oz. loaf *or* granulated sugar** | **1 tablesp. cold water** |

Heat a tin charlotte or soufflé mould and have ready a thickly folded band of newspaper so that the hot tin may be encircled with it and held firmly in one hand. Melt loaf sugar in the water in a thick, very small pan, and when dissolved, boil quickly until it becomes dark golden brown. Do not stir. Pour at once into the hot tin mould, and rotate quickly to coat the sides and base of the mould. Finally, place mould on a firm flat board so that excess caramel may flow to the base and set level. Keep in a warm place, as draughts may cause the caramel coating to crack.

Cut thin strips of lemon rind and infuse in the milk, slowly. Remove the rind when the milk boils, sprinkle in the rice, stirring all the time and cook until grain is soft and smooth, about 8–10 min. Sweeten to taste. Pour into the coated mould and leave in a cool place to set. Turn out and serve with cream.

**6 helpings**

### CARAMEL PUDDING

| | |
|---|---|
| **3 oz. loaf *or* granulated sugar** | **2 oz. bread (weighed with crusts removed)** |
| **3 tablesp. water** | **3 eggs *or* 4 egg yolks** |
| **1 pt. milk** | **1 dessertsp. sugar** |

DECORATION

**Little cream if permitted**

Put the sugar and water into a strong pan; stir until sugar has dissolved. Boil steadily, without stirring until brown caramel. Cool slightly. Add cold milk. Heat together *slowly* until milk has absorbed caramel. Do not boil. Cut bread into small dice; pour over it the caramel liquid. Leave to stand for 30 min. Add well-beaten eggs and sugar. Pour into a greased basin or mould. Cover with greased paper. Steam gently—*never* allow water to boil—for approximately 2 hr. until the pudding is firm. Turn out and serve hot or cold decorated with cream.

**5–6 helpings**

### CARAMEL RICE PUDDING

*Pouding Caramel au Riz*

| | |
|---|---|
| **4½ oz. rice** | **2 eggs** |
| **1½ pt. milk** | **1½ oz. castor sugar** |
| **Pinch of salt** | |

CARAMEL

| | |
|---|---|
| **3 oz. loaf sugar** | **½ gill water** |

Heat a charlotte mould and have ready a thickly folded band of newspaper so that the hot mould may be encircled with it and held firmly in one hand. Prepare the caramel by heating the loaf sugar and water together; stir until it boils; then remove the spoon and allow to boil without stirring until golden brown. Pour the caramel into the warm charlotte mould and twist round, until the sides and base are well coated with the caramel. Wash the rice and simmer in the milk, with the salt, until the rice is soft and all the milk has been absorbed. Cool slightly and add the beaten eggs and sugar. Turn into the caramel-lined mould, cover with greased paper and steam for 1 hr. until firm.

Serve either hot or cold.

**6 helpings**

### CARAMEL SAUCE

*Sauce au Caramel*

| | |
|---|---|
| **2 oz. sugar *or* golden syrup** | **½ pt. custard sauce** |
| **⅛ pt. water** | **Lemon juice *or* vanilla essence** |

Put the sugar and 2 tablesp. water in a small

pan; dissolve the sugar over gentle heat, then boil the syrup so made until it is a deep golden brown. Add to the caramel the rest of the water and leave it in a warm place to dissolve. If golden syrup is used heat it without water until of a golden-brown colour, then dissolve it in the water. Add the dissolved caramel to the custard sauce and flavour to taste.

### CARDINAL SAUCE

**¼ pt. Béchamel sauce**
**¼ pt. well-reduced fish stock**
**Cayenne pepper**
**Salt**
**⅛ pt. cream**
**1 dessertsp. lemon juice**
**1–2 oz. lobster butter**

Heat sauce and stock together and season to taste. Just below boiling point stir in cream and lemon juice and whisk in the lobster butter, a small pat at a time. Do not allow sauce to boil. This sauce should be bright scarlet. Serve with lobster or other fish.

NOTE: Cardinal sauce may be made with Velouté sauce made from fish stock, instead of the Béchamel sauce and stock.

### CARPET-BAG STEAK

**4 lb. piece of topside, pocketed for stuffing**

STUFFING

**1½ oz. butter**
**12–18 oysters**
**¼ lb. fresh mushrooms**
**6 oz. white breadcrumbs**
**1 tablesp. chopped parsley**
**Grated rind of ½ lemon**
**Salt and paprika**
**1 egg**

Heat the butter and into it toss the oysters and roughly chopped mushrooms; cook for 5 min. Transfer to a basin and mix in the breadcrumbs, parsley, lemon rind and seasoning. Stir in the beaten egg. Press the mixture into pocket in steak and sew or skewer edges together. Roast in a warm oven (**335° F., Gas 3**) to prevent shrinkage for 2 hr. Serve with roast potatoes and pumpkin.

**6 helpings**

### CARRACK SAUCE

**1 clove of garlic**
**4 anchovies**
**1 tablesp. chopped pickled walnuts**
**½ pt. vinegar**
**1 dessertsp. mushroom ketchup**
**1 dessertsp. any good commercial savoury sauce**
**1 dessertsp. good chutney, chopped**

Crush and pound the garlic; crush and sieve the anchovies. Mix all the ingredients well together; bottle the sauce. Shake it frequently. Store 1 month before use.

Serve with cold meat.

### CARROT SALAD

*Salade de Carottes*

**3 large carrots**
**1 lettuce**
**French dressing**
**Finely-chopped parsley**

Grate the carrots finely and serve on a bed of lettuce leaves. Sprinkle with the French dressing. Garnish with chopped parsley.

NOTE: Grated, raw carrot can be used with success in many salads. It should be grated very finely to be digestible and sprinkled with lemon juice or French dressing as soon as grated to retain its bright colour.

**6 helpings**

### CARROTS—COOKED FOR FOOD VALUE

**1½ lb. carrots**
**1 oz. butter *or* margarine**
**½ teasp. salt**
**½–1 gill boiling water**
**Chopped parsley**

Cut off the green tops, scrub and scrape the carrots. Slice them thinly if old carrots (or leave whole if really young). Fat steam the carrots for 10 min., i.e. shake them in the melted fat, well below frying temperature, with the lid on the pan until the fat is absorbed. Add the liquid (less for young carrots) and the salt, and simmer gently until the carrots are tender—15–30 min. according to age of carrots. Serve hot, with the small amount of liquid remaining, and garnished with parsley.

NOTE: This method should be employed for cooking most root vegetables, e.g. parsnips, turnips, swedes, onions, etc., and should replace "boiling". Both flavour and food value are conserved.

**6 helpings**

## CARROTS—GERMAN STYLE

*Carottes à l'Allemande*

**1½ lb. carrots**
**2 oz. butter *or* margarine**
**1 dessertsp. finely-chopped onion**
**1 pt. stock**
**1 oz. flour**
**Nutmeg**
**1 tablesp. chopped parsley**
**Salt and pepper**

Prepare and cook the carrots as in preceding recipe, using 1 oz. butter, but add the onion and use the stock for cooking. Pour the carrots into a colander, retaining the liquid and making it up to ¾ pt. Melt the other ounce of butter, stir in the flour and cook until browned. Add the ¾ pt. stock and stir till boiling. Add the carrots to the boiling stock, stir in the grated nutmeg and parsley, season. and serve.

**6 helpings** **Cooking time—¾–1 hr.**

## CARROTS WITH CREAM

*Carottes à la crême*

**1½ lb. young carrots**
**1 oz. butter *or* margarine**
**½ teasp. salt**
**½–1 gill boiling water**
**Salt and pepper**
**Chopped parsley**
**1 tablesp. cream**

Proceed as for Carrots—Cooked for Food Value. Stir in the cream just before serving.

**6 helpings** **Cooking time—20–35 min.**

## CARROTS WITH PARSLEY SAUCE

*Carottes à la Maître d'hôtel*

**1½ lb. carrots**
**1 oz. butter *or* margarine**
**½ teasp. salt**
**½–1 gill boiling water**
**¾ pt. parsley sauce**

Cook the carrots as for Carrots—Cooked for Food Value. Drain off the liquid, make up to ½ pt. with milk, and make the parsley sauce. Coat the carrots and serve immediately.

**5–6 helpings** **Cooking time—about 45 min.**

## CARVING

Carving is neither an art nor a science but an acquired skill. Many people are deterred from carving by lack of confidence. They consult literature on the subject, and are put off by directions which make it seem necessary to possess the knowledge and skill of a surgeon.

Carving is, in fact, quite simple. All you need is a sharp knife, and—of course—a suitable piece of meat (or fish).

A sharp knife is essential. A blunt one forces you to exert heavy pressure. This dents the meat and makes it much harder to cut evenly and thinly. It also means that, if the knife slips, you are almost certain to cut yourself. A sharp knife can be used lightly, and is much easier to keep under control.

A keen carver gets himself a really good quality knife and an oilstone.

When "stoning" or steeling a knife to sharpen it, remember that the cutting edge should taper very finely. Therefore, the blade should not make an angle of more than 15° with the stone or steel while sharpening the knife. (Roughly speaking, if the blade edge rests on the stone, and its back edge rests on the thumb, which in its turn is touching the stone, the knife will lie at the correct angle to the stone.)

The not-so-keen carver can purchase many different good knives which will keep their edge well provided they are only used for carving meat.

A knife is essentially a very finely toothed saw and it should be used in the same way, that is, drawn back and forth through the meat it is cutting. Never try to push even a sharp knife through meat without this sawing action. If the knife is sharp, the backward and forward motions can be long and light. In this way less jagged slices are removed. Try to keep the knife at the same angle all the way through the joint and try to take a slice of equal thickness. This is not always possible, as with the first cuts from a roast joint of beef.

Try always to cut across or away from yourself. Protect the left hand by using a fork, preferably a proper carving fork with a stout thumb piece.

Carving at table is nowadays fairly uncommon. But the appearance of a finely browned joint which is carved before the guests does add greatly to the sense of occasion, and with very little practice can be successfully attempted by anyone . . . with a sharp knife.

**Carving Beef**

When carving rolled joints of beef, leave the string and skewers in position on the joint until you have carved down to them and then if there are many, only remove those which impede the progress of further carving. Joints on the bone are carved from the outside fat towards the bone. When this is reached the knife is turned upwards and the slices gently detached. With sirloin and ribs try to carve the outside rib muscles first as these are better eaten hot. Save the central least cooked meat to be eaten cold for it will have a better flavour. As with most butchers' meat carve across the grain or run of the muscle. Generally this means cutting parallel to the rib bone. With boneless joints the obvious way to carve is usually the correct way.

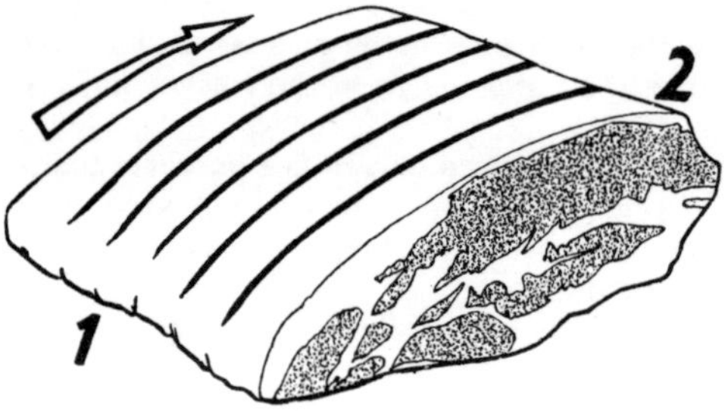


*Fig. I.—Brisket of Beef*

**Aitchbone of Beef:** Set the joint on the wide flat base. Take small slices towards the bone parallel to the base until a thick slice is being cut across the whole joint. At the end of each slice turn the knife blade upwards to separate the meat from the bone.

**Beef Tongue:** *Unpressed*, cut nearly through across the tongue at the thick part, and then serve a fairly thick slice. The carving may be continued in this way towards the point until the best portions of the upper side are served. The fat which lies about the root of the tongue can be served by turning it over. If *pressed*, carve thinly across the top, parallel to the round base.

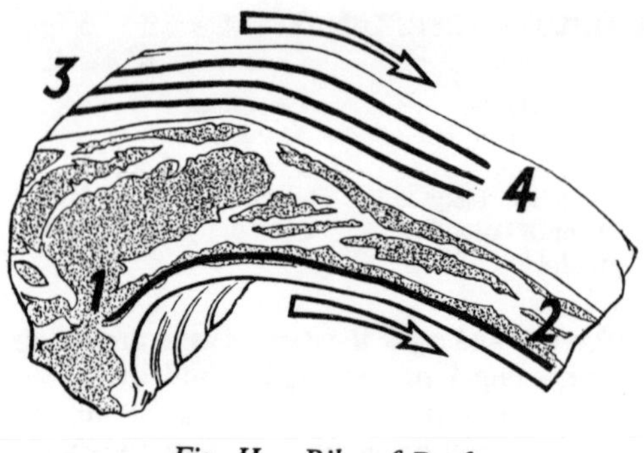


*Fig. II.—Ribs of Beef*

**Brisket of Beef** (*see* Fig. I): The joint should be cut evenly and firmly across the bones (1)–(2), in slices the whole width of the joint.

**Ribs of Beef** (*see* Fig. II): Cut slices off the sides, starting at the thick end (3) and through to the other (4). The joint will be more easily cut if before commencing to carve, the knife is slipped between the meat and the bone from (1) to (2).

**Round of Beef** (*see* Fig. III): A round of beef, or ribs rolled, are not so easily carved as some joints. A thin-bladed and very sharp knife should be used. Off the outside of the joint, at its top, cut a thick slice first, leaving the surface smooth; then thin and even slices should be carved to leave a level-topped joint.

*Fig. III.—Round of Beef*

**Sirloin of Beef** (*see* Fig. IV): Sirloin is seldom carved "on the bone" today. If it is,

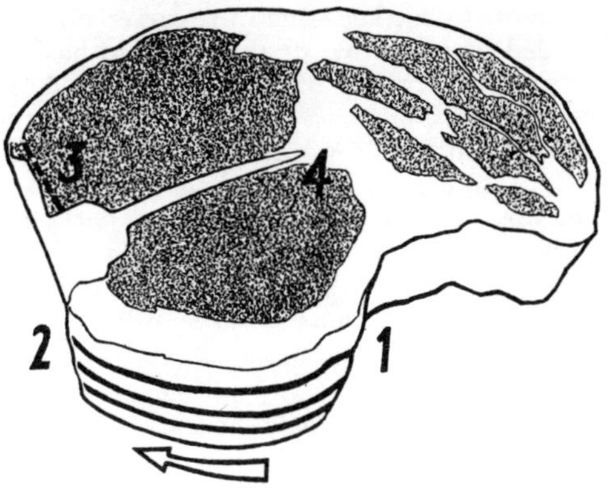


*Fig. IV.—Sirloin of Beef*

the carver should first slice the fillet or undercut into a suitable number of pieces. (1–2). It is best eaten hot (being rather flavourless cold). When the fillet has been used, turn the joint over, loosen the meat from the backbone (3) and carve down towards the blade of the bone (4).

### Carving Veal

**Breast of Veal:** The breast of veal consists of two parts—the rib-bones and the gristly brisket. These two parts should first be separated by sharply passing the knife through the centre of the joint; when they are entirely divided, the rib-bones should each be detached separately and served. The brisket can be helped by cutting pieces from the centre part of the joint. If it is boned and stuffed, carve it by cutting downwards across the end of the rolled joint.

**Fillet of Veal:** The carving of this joint is similar to that of a round or roll of beef. The stuffing is inserted between the flap and the meat and a small portion of this should be served on each plate.

**Knuckle of Veal:** This is carved in the same way as a leg of lamb.

**Loin of Veal:** As is the case with a loin of mutton, the careful jointing of a loin of veal is more than half the battle in carving it. The butcher should be asked to do this. When properly jointed there is little difficulty in separating each chop. Each should carry a piece of the kidney and kidney fat.

### Carving Mutton and Lamb

Legs are cut perpendicularly to the bones inside the leg. Once one has been attempted the remainder will be easy. In the case of loins ask the butcher to "chine" them or saw across the blade parts of the bone or ask him to chop it through the joints for serving in cutlets. Should it be forgotten, use an old knife and knock the blade through between the joints where they are separated by white discs of gristle. Mutton, and to a lesser extent lamb, should always be served as quickly as possible and on very hot plates. The speed is necessary because the flavour of mutton is soon lost. The heat is required because mutton and lamb fat have a higher melting point than other animal fats and on a cold plate soldify, leaving a semi-solid fat that coats the palate producing a "furry" or diminished sense of taste.

**Fore-Quarter of Lamb:** In carving a fore-quarter of lamb, separate the shoulder from the breast by raising the shoulder, into which the fork should be firmly fixed. It will come away easily by cutting round the outline of the shoulder and slipping the knife beneath it. The shoulder should be served cold. The remainder of the joint is then ready to be served as cutlets carved from the ribs.

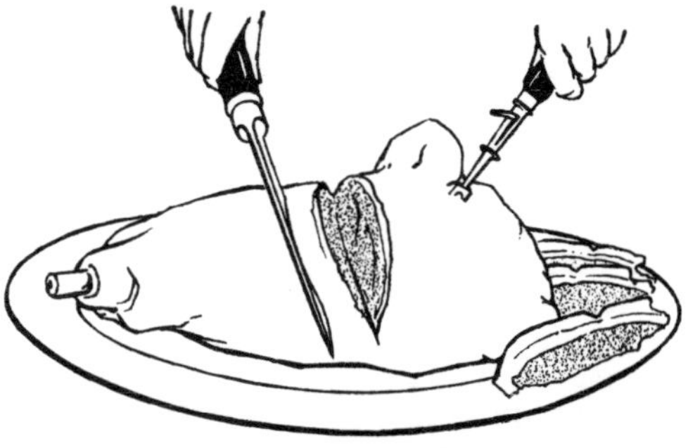

*Fig. V.—Leg of Lamb*

**Leg of Lamb** (*see* Fig. V): This joint is almost invariably carved by cutting a "V"-shaped piece down to the bone in the middle of the leg. Slices are then taken alternately from either side. Those from the thin or knuckle end will be the best cooked. The fat will be found near the bottom corner of the thick end.

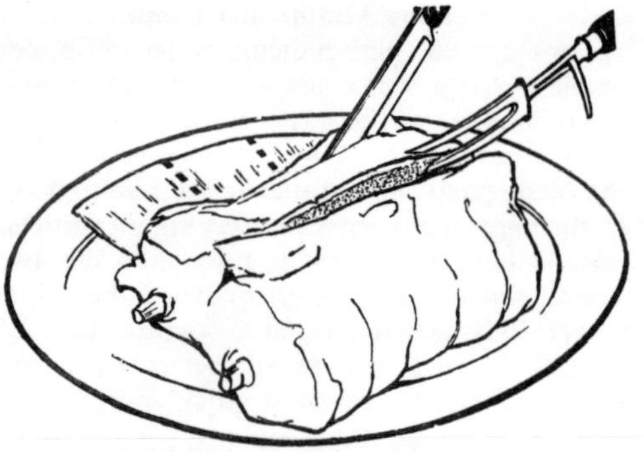

*Fig. VI.— Saddle of Mutton*

**Loin of Mutton:** Loin, and other similar joints, should be well jointed. Examine the loin before cooking it, and carefully joint any part that has been neglected. The knife should be inserted in the white gristle of the joint, and tapped between the bones with a steel or small hammer.

**Saddle of Mutton** (*see* Fig. VI): This consists of two loins connected by the spinal bone. The method adopted in carving this joint, contrary to the general rule of cutting meat across the grain, is carved across the ribs, in slices running parallel with the backbone and the fibres or grain of the meat. Each long slice should be cut across into two or three pieces, according to its length; and with each portion is usually served a small piece of fat cut from the bottom of the ribs where the joint rests on the dish, and some good gravy. Redcurrant jelly or mint sauce is served separately.

**Shoulder of Mutton:** The joint should be raised from the dish and slices cut parallel to the face of the meat (*see* Fig. VII). Lay the joint down and carve the meat lying on either side of the bladebone from the knuckle end. (Fig. VIII).

**Carving Pork**

The remarks made about jointing loins of lamb are true of loins of pork. When carving a joint with crackling, remove a section of crackling first. Only remove as much as will expose that part of the joint to be carved hot.

**Ham:** In cutting a ham the carver must be guided by economy, or the desire to have at once, fine slices out of the prime part. To be economical commence at the knuckle end, and cut off thin slices towards the thick part of the ham, slanting the knife from the thick part to the knuckle. To reach the choicer parts, the knife, which must be very sharp and thin, should be carried quite down to the bone, at the centre of the ham.

**Leg of Pork:** This joint, which is such a favourite one with many people, is easy to carve. The knife should be carried sharply down to the bone, clean through the crackling, in exactly the same way as that described for leg of mutton. Carving is easier if a section of the crackling is removed.

**Loin of Pork:** As with a loin of mutton, it is essential that a loin of pork should be properly jointed before cooking, and the crackling must be scored. Divide into neat, even chops.

**Sucking Pig:** A sucking pig seems, at first sight, an elaborate dish, or rather animal, to carve; like small poultry it is mainly jointed rather than sliced. It is usually prepared by

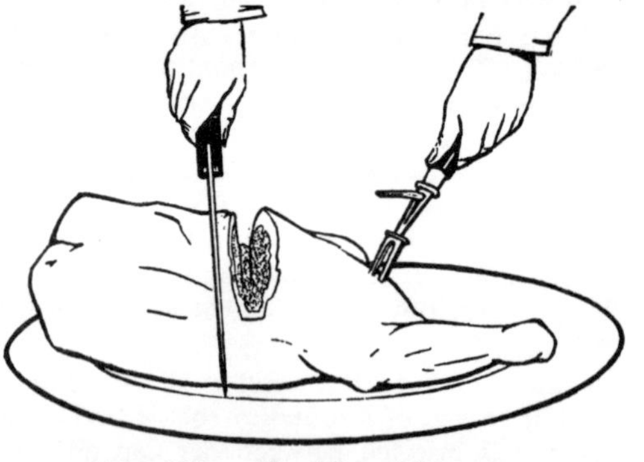

*Fig. VII.—Shoulder of Mutton*

splitting in half, and the head is separated from the body. Separate the shoulder from the carcase, in the same way that the shoulder of a forequarter of lamb is raised. Then take off the hind leg; the ribs are then open to the knife and may be served as two or three helpings.

**Carving Poultry**

Larger birds are usually jointed at the wings

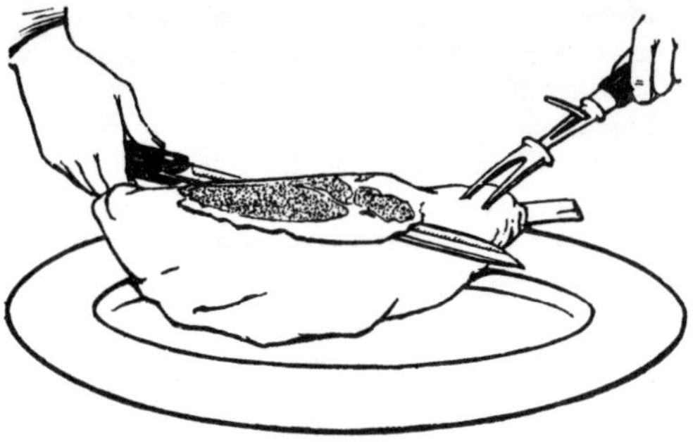

*Fig. VIII.—Shoulder of Lamb*

and legs which are served as portions or carved into slices. This is made easier if before the bird is placed on the table a small pointed knife is worked between each joint. The joints occur at the natural bends of the limb and are quite easy to discover. When all else fails at a first attempt they are quite easily broken open, but the carving is rather more dignified if this is done out of sight in, say, the kitchen.

**Roast Duck:** A young duck or duckling is carved in the same way as a chicken. First remove the wings, then the breast should be cut off the bone in one slice, or several slices if very plump. The legs are next removed and divided at the joints. The foot, and the bone to which it is attached, is today rarely left on the dressed bird.

**Boiled** *or* **Roast Fowl** (*see* Fig. IX): Though the legs of a boiled fowl may be hidden beneath the skin, the method of carving is not affected, and the following directions may be applied to birds either roasted or boiled. The fork should be inserted firmly in the breast of the bird (1)–(2) and with a sharp knife a downward cut made between the thigh and the body, after which an outward turn of the blade of the knife usually detaches the leg sufficiently to allow the joint connecting it to the body to be easily severed. Some carvers "open" the joints with a small knife before the bird is sent to table. With the fork still inserted in the breast, the next step should be to remove the wings (3)–(4). In doing this a good carver will contrive, by cutting widely, but not too deeply, over the adjacent part of the breast, to give to the wing the desired shape without depriving the breast of much of its flesh. When carving a large fowl the breast may be sliced (5)–(6), otherwise it should be separated from the back by cutting through the rib-bones near the neck. The breast should be cut across in half, thus providing two portions, to which may be added, when a larger helping is desired, a slice off the thigh. Cut lengthwise into rather thin slices, the legs may be served as several portions or part portions. To conclude the carving, the back should be turned over with the cut side to the dish, and if the knife is pressed firmly across the centre of it, and the neck raised at the same time with the fork, the back is easily dislocated about the middle. To remove the sockets of the thigh-joints (the side-bones to which are attached choice morsels of dark-coloured flesh) unless the joints have previously been opened, the tail part of the back must be stood on end, and held firmly with the fork, while the bones are cut off on either side. A fowl when boned and stuffed is usually cut across in slices.

*Fig. IX—Roast Fowl*

**Roast Goose:** If the bird is large carve only the breast and save the legs and wings for cold or rechauffé dishes.

**Pigeon:** The knife is carried entirely through the centre of the bird, cutting it into two precisely equal and similar parts. If it is necessary to serve three, a small wing should be cut off with the leg on each side. There will be sufficient meat on the breast for a third portion.

**Roast Turkey:** A small turkey may be carved in the same way as a large fowl. No bird is more easily carved than a large turkey, for the breast alone may, when properly carved, supply several helpings. If more meat is required than the breast provides, the upper part of the wing should be served. When it is necessary for the legs to be carved, they should be severed from the body and then cut into slices. The forcemeat in the crop of the bird should be carved across in thin slices; and when the body is stuffed serving is easiest with a spoon.

### Carving Game

**Blackcock:** The brains of this bird were once considered a delicacy. The head is sometimes still trussed on one side of the bird. The breast and the thigh are the best parts, the latter may be cut lengthwise into thin slices, or served whole.

**Grouse:** Grouse may be carved in the way first described in carving partridge. The backbone of the grouse, as of many game birds, is considered to possess the finest flavour.

**Roast Hare** (*see* Fig. X): Place the hare on the dish with the head at the left hand. Cut along the spinal bone from about the centre of the back to the end (1)–(2). Then cut through the side and middle, and remove this portion. Cut off the hind leg (3)–(4) and afterwards the foreleg or wing. It is usual not to serve any bone and the flesh should be sliced from the legs and placed alone on the plate. Plenty of gravy should accompany each helping; otherwise this dish, which is naturally dry, will lose half its flavour.

**Partridges:** There are several ways of carving this bird. The usual method is to carry the knife sharply along the top of the breastbone and cut it through, dividing the bird into two equal parts. When smaller portions are desired the legs and wings may be easily severed from the body in the way described for boiled fowl, while the breast, if removed intact, will provide a third helping. Another easy and expeditious way of carving birds of this description is to cut them through the bones lengthwise and across, thus forming four portions. A piece of toast should accompany each portion of bird.

**Pheasant:** The choice parts of a pheasant are the breast and wings. The various joints of the birds are cut in exactly the same way as those of a roast fowl.

**Plover:** Plover may be carved like woodcock, being trussed and served in the same way as woodcock.

**Ptarmigan,** *see* Partridge.

**Rabbits:** In carving a boiled rabbit, the knife should be drawn on each side of the backbone, the whole length of the rabbit, thus separating the rabbit into three parts. Now divide the back into two equal parts, then cut off the leg and next the shoulder.

A roast rabbit is rather differently trussed from one that is meant to be boiled; but the carving is nearly similar. The back should be divided into as many pieces as it will yield, and the legs and shoulders can then be separated.

**Snipe:** One of these small but delicious birds may be served whole or cut through the centre into two portions.

**Teal** and **Widgeon,** *see* Wild Duck.

**Haunch of Venison:** The thick end of the joint should be turned towards the carver and slices taken parallel to the dish on which the joint rests. Venison, like mutton, should be cut and served quickly.

**Wild Duck:** The breast alone is considered by epicures worth eating, and slices are cut; if necessary, the leg and wing can be taken off as for a fowl.

**Woodcock:** *see* Partridge.

### Carving Fish

**Brill** and **John Dory,** *see* Turbot.

**Cod:** Cut in fairly thick slices through to the centre bone and detach just above it. The parts about the backbone and shoulders are the firmest.

**Crab,** *See Fish*

**Eel and all flat fish:** The thickest parts of the eel are considered the best.

**Lobster** *See Fish*

**Mackerel:** First cut along the backbone of the fish. Then insert the fish-knife at this part and cut through, separating the upper half of the fish, which may be divided; when the fish is of moderate size serve for two helpings only. Next remove the backbone, tail and head, and divide the lower half.

**Plaice:** First run the knife down the centre of the fish. Then cut downwards to the bone and remove "fillets" from each side. Next take away the backbone and head of the fish, and divide the lower half in the same way.

**Salmon:** First run the knife down the centre of the back and along the whole length of the fish. Then cut downwards from the backbone to the middle of the fish, cut through the centre and remove the piece from the back. Next cut the lower part of the fish in the same way. A slice of the thick part should always be accompanied by a smaller piece of the thin from the belly, where the fat of the fish lies.

**Sole:** The usual way of serving this fish is to cut quite through, bone and all, distributing it in fillets or smallish pieces. The middle part is generally thought better than either head or tail. The head should be cut off and not laid on a plate.

**Turbot:** First slice down the thickest part of the fish, quite through to the bone, and then cut slices out towards the sides of the fish. When the carver has removed all the meat from the upper sides of the fish, the backbone should be raised, and the under side served in portions.

**Whiting, Haddock, etc.:** Whiting, pike, haddock and similar fish, when sufficiently large, may be carved in slices from each side of the backbone in the same way as salmon; each fish serving for four or more slices. When small, they may be cut through, bone and all, and served in nice pieces. A small whiting is served whole; a middle-sized fish in two pieces.

### CASSEROLE OF MUTTON

*Casserole de Mouton*

| | |
|---|---|
| **1½ lb. middle neck of mutton** | **Salt and pepper** |
| **1 onion** | **Suet pastry using 4 oz. flour, etc.** |
| **Good gravy *or* stock** | |

Cut the meat into neat chops and remove the bones and surplus fat. Place the meat in a casserole so that it is about half full. Thinly slice the onion and place on top and barely cover with gravy or stock. Season carefully. Cover and cook gently in a moderate oven (**350° F., Gas 4**), for about 1½ hr. Roll the suet pastry to the shape of the casserole—but slightly smaller. Lay the pastry on top of the meat, replace the lid and cook gently for 1 hr.

*Fig. X.—Roast Hare*

longer. Before serving, divide the pastry crust into suitable portions.

NOTE: If a casserole is not available this may be cooked in a saucepan on top of the cooker.

**6 helpings**

### CASSEROLE OF VEAL

*Veau en Casserole*

| | |
|---|---|
| **1½ lb. lean stewing veal** | **2 doz. button mushrooms** |
| **1 pt. thick Velouté sauce** | **Salt and pepper** |
| | **2 teasp. lemon juice** |

GARNISH

| | |
|---|---|
| **Bacon rolls** | **Crimped slices of lemon** |

Wipe and trim the meat, discarding any skin or fat. Cut into neat pieces and put into a casserole. Bring the sauce to boiling point and pour over the veal, adding the mushrooms and seasoning. Stand the casserole in a pan of water and simmer very gently in a warm to moderate oven (**335°–350° F., Gas 3–4**) for about 1½ hr. When tender, stir in the lemon juice, place the grilled bacon rolls on top, and garnish with lemon. Serve in the casserole.

**6 helpings**

### CATALAN SOUP

| | |
|---|---|
| **2 oz. bacon** | **1 glass white wine** |
| **2 Spanish onions** | **Thyme** |
| **1 sweet pepper** | **Parsley** |
| **1 stick of celery** | **Salt and pepper** |

## *Cauliflower Cream Soup*

| | |
|---|---|
| **2 large potatoes** | **Nutmeg** |
| **2 large tomatoes** | **2 egg yolks** |
| **1 qt. stock** | **⅛ pt. milk** |

Chop the bacon, slice the onions very thinly. Melt the fat of the bacon in a deep pan and fry the onions and bacon together till golden brown. Slice the pepper and celery very thin, cut the potatoes and skinned tomatoes into thick slices, add them to the pan, shake over gentle heat for 5 min. Add the stock, wine and herbs and boil the soup, then simmer gently for ½–¾ hr. until all the vegetables are soft. Season, add a trace of grated nutmeg, and cook the soup slightly. Mix the egg yolks and milk and stir them into the soup. Cook the egg yolks without boiling.

**4–6 helpings**
**Cooking time—1½ hr.**

### CAULIFLOWER CREAM SOUP

*Purée de Choufleur* or *Crème de Choufleur*

| | |
|---|---|
| **1 medium-sized cauliflower about ¾–1 lb. after trimming** | **1 blade of mace** |
| **1 onion** | **1 bay leaf** |
| **1 oz. butter *or* margarine** | **¼ pt. milk** |
| **1 pt. white stock** | **Cornflour to thicken** |
| **Lemon juice** | **Salt and pepper** |
| | **1 egg yolk** |
| | **⅛ pt. cream** |

Remove the green leaf from the cauliflower but keep all the stalk. Continue as for Vegetable Purée carefully. The cauliflower should be cooked for the shortest time possible or its flavour will be spoilt.

### CAULIFLOWER SALAD—COOKED

*Salade de Choufleur*

| | |
|---|---|
| **1 large cauliflower** | **Vinaigrette sauce** |

Steam the cauliflower then divide carefully into small sprigs. Arrange the sprigs neatly in a salad bowl and pour the sauce over while the cauliflower is still warm. Serve when quite cold.

**6 helpings**

### CAULIFLOWER SALAD—UNCOOKED

*Salade de Choufleur*

| | |
|---|---|
| **1 medium-sized cauliflower** | **Mayonnaise sauce *or* salad dressing** |
| **1 small bunch of radishes** | **Lettuce leaves** |

Grate the raw cauliflower and the radishes, leaving a few radishes for decoration. Mix with mayonnaise or salad dressing and pile on a bed of crisp, young lettuce leaves. Garnish with finely-cut, overlapping rounds of radishes.

NOTE: Tomato mayonnaise is excellent with this salad.

**6 helpings**

### CAULIFLOWER WITH CHEESE

*Choufleur au gratin*

**1 large cauliflower**
**¾ pt. cheese sauce**
**Salt**
**1 heaped tablesp. grated cheese (dry Cheddar)** *or* **1 dessertsp. grated Cheddar cheese and 1 dessertsp. grated Parmesan cheese**

Cook the cauliflower as in preceding recipe, drain well and dish up in a fireproof dish. Coat with thick cheese sauce. Sprinkle with grated cheese and immediately brown under a hot grill or in the top of a hot oven (**425° F., Gas 7**). Serve immediately.

**4 helpings**
**Cooking time—25–30 min.**

### CELERIAC WITH WHITE SAUCE

*Céléri-rave à la Sauce blanche*

| | |
|---|---|
| **3 roots of celeriac** | **Salt** |
| **¾ pt. good white sauce** | **Lemon juice** |

Scrub the root well, then peel thickly. (If the roots are spongy discard them as useless.) Cut into ½-in. slices and stew them slowly in boiling, salted vegetable stock or water till tender—about 45 min. Drain. Make a good white sauce with ½ pt. milk and cooking liquid. Season and add a little lemon juice. Coat the celeriac and serve immediately.

NOTE: The vegetable stock can be water in which onions, Jerusalem artichokes, etc., have been cooked.

**6 helpings**
**Cooking time—45 min. approx.**

### CELERY CURLS

Cut 2–3 pieces of celery about 2 in. long. Cut lengthwise in very fine shreds or shred by

Crab, to dress.

1 Wipe the crab with a damp cloth and remove the claws and legs by twisting inwards and towards you. 2 Place the thumbs under the tail flap and push upwards until the body breaks away from the shell. 3 and 4 Remove the mouth and stomach bag with the thumbs as shown. 5 Ease round the inside of the shell to loosen the meat, and turn it into a basin.

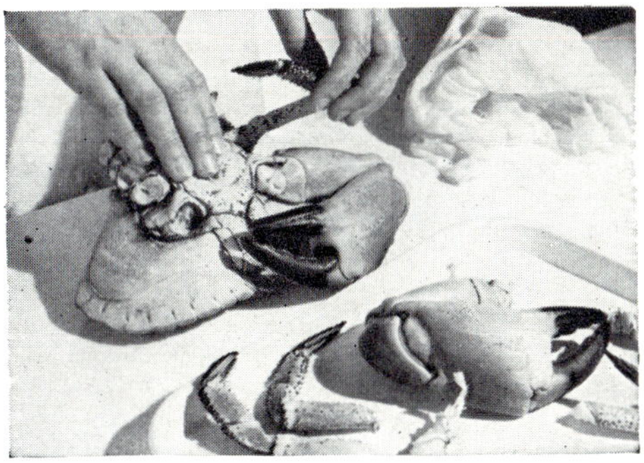
1

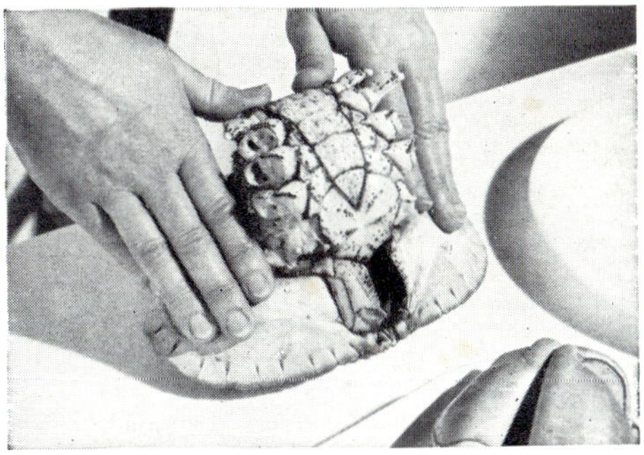
2

3

4

5

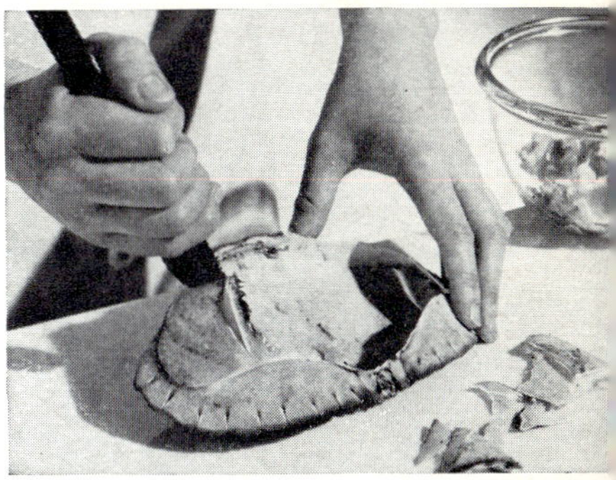
6

7

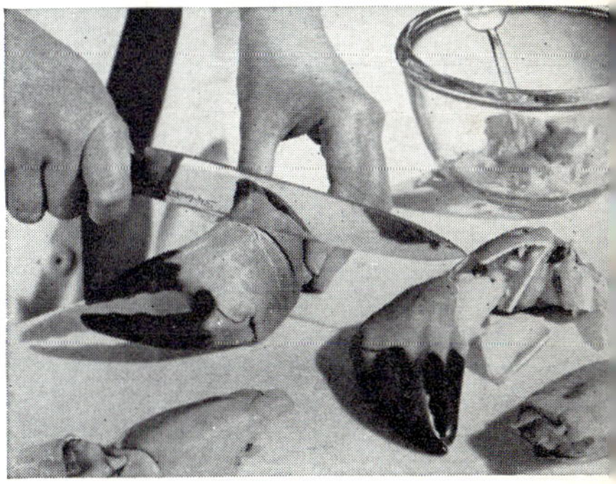
8

6 Trim shell by tapping "false" lines round shell cavity with a knife handle and press with the thumbs till edges of shell will break away. 7 Remove "dead men's fingers". Remove meat. Scoop white meat from leg sockets, keeping free of bone. 8 Twist off joint from both claws and empty meat into a basin. With the back of a heavy knife tap sharply round the centre of the broadest part of the claws till the shell cracks apart.

Cheese is the basis of many excellent savouries.

drawing the pieces lengthwise over a coarse grater. Put the shreds into very cold water (iced if possible) and leave for ½ hr. Drain the curls well.

### CELERY SALAD (1)

*Salade de Céleri*

| | |
|---|---|
| **2–3 celery hearts** | **Crisp lettuce leaves** |
| **Mayonnaise sauce *or* tomato mayonnaise** | **Chervil** |
| | **Tarragon** |

Shred the tender sticks of celery and mix with the mayonnaise. Pile on the crisp lettuce leaves. Sprinkle with chopped chervil and tarragon and decorate with curls of celery.

**6 helpings**

### CELERY SALAD (2)

*Salade de Céleri*

| | |
|---|---|
| **1 head of celery** | **Good pinch of salt** |
| **Mayonnaise** | **Good pinch of pepper** |
| **Chopped parsley** | **1 hard-boiled egg** |

Wash the celery and cut into tiny pieces. Toss in mayonnaise, adding chopped parsley and seasoning. Arrange in a dish or on plates and garnish with finely-chopped hard-boiled egg and more parsley.

**About 6 helpings**

### CELERY SAUCE

*Sauce Céleri*

| | |
|---|---|
| **6 outside sticks of celery, leaves and all** | **Seasoning** |
| **½ pt. water** | **1–2 tablesp. cream (optional)** |
| **Butter** | **1–2 drops lemon juice** |
| **Flour** | |

Cut the celery in very short lengths, simmer the pieces in the water till quite soft. Rub the celery through a sieve. Make a white sauce ( carefully ) with the celery purée for liquid. Cream is an excellent addition, stirred in at boiling point, off the heat.

Serve with mutton or rabbit.

### CELERY SOUP or CELERY CREAM SOUP

*Crème de Céleri*

| | |
|---|---|
| **1 lb. outer sticks of celery** | **Lemon juice** |
| **1 onion** | **¼ pt. milk** |
| **¾ oz. butter *or* margarine** | **Cornflour to thicken** |
| **1 pt. white stock** | **Salt and pepper** |
| | **⅛ pt. cream (optional)** |

Proceed as for Vegetable Purée. Cook the celery without boiling or it will become stringy and difficult to sieve. If cut in ½-in. lengths it is easy to sieve.

**4 helpings**
**Cooking time—1 hr.**

### CELERY WITH CHEESE

*Céléri au gratin*

| | |
|---|---|
| **2 large heads of celery** | **1 heaped tablesp. dry, grated Cheddar cheese *or* 1 dessertsp. dry, grated Cheddar cheese and 1 dessertsp. grated Parmesan cheese** |
| **¾ pt. cheese sauce** | |
| **Salt** | |

Cook the celery as for Celery with White Sauce. Coat with thick cheese sauce. Sprinkle with grated cheese and brown under a hot grill or in the top of a hot oven (**425° F., Gas 7**). Serve immediately.

**6 helpings**
**Cooking time—1 hr.**

### CELERY VINEGAR

| | |
|---|---|
| **½ lb. celery *or* ½ oz. celery seed** | **1 pt. vinegar, wine *or* white** |
| | **½ teasp. salt** |

Chop the celery if used. Boil the vinegar with the salt. Pour the hot vinegar on to the chopped celery or seed, cover and leave till cold. Bottle and leave the vinegar for 3 weeks, then strain and re-bottle. Cork securely.

Use in salad dressings.

### CELERY WITH WHITE SAUCE

*Céléri à la Sauce blanche*

| | |
|---|---|
| **2 large heads of celery** | **Salt** |
| **½ pt. good white sauce** | **Lemon juice** |

Trim off the green tops of the celery, reserving a few pale green ones. Remove the very tough outer stalks. Separate the other stalks and wash or, if necessary, scrub in cold water. Rinse and reserve the tender hearts for eating raw. Scrape the stalks to be cooked, cut into suitable lengths for cooking and tie in bundles. Stew in barely sufficient boiling water, slightly salted, to cover the celery. If possible, cook in vegetable water from cooked artichokes, onions etc. When tender (in about 1 hr.), drain. Make a good white sauce with ½ milk and ½ cooking liquid. Season and add a little lemon juice. Coat the celery with the sauce, garnish with some of the pale green leaves and serve immediately.

NOTE: The celery may be cooked in milk, with the addition of 1 finely chopped onion. When cooked, the celery may be served as above, with the addition of 2 tablesp. of cream to the sauce just as the pan is removed from the heat.

**4–6 helpings**
**Cooking time—1 hr.**

## CEREAL MOULDS AS COLD SWEETS

These cold sweets or desserts consist of whole or ground cereals, milk, sugar, flavouring and sometimes a little gelatine to make sure the mould sets firmly. These dishes are easily digested and are well suited to young children and invalids. Care must be taken during the cooking of the starch to avoid too much evaporation of liquid otherwise the consistency may be too stiff. A small nut of butter added during the cooking improves both flavour and texture.

Whole grain, such as rice (Carolina or Carolina-type), large sago, large tapioca and barley, should be simmered gently in the milk until every grain is soft and the milk is almost absorbed. To accomplish this without burning, and without too much evaporation, use (*a*) a double saucepan, *or* (*b*) a thick-bottomed pan, standing over low heat or in a cool oven.

Keep covered and stir occasionally to ensure even cooking of the grain. Cooking time 1½–2 hr.

Small grain, such as semolina, ground rice, small sago and tapioca should be sprinkled dry into near-boiling milk and cooked gently until the grain is soft and clear. Continuous stirring is necessary to ensure smoothness, and excessive evaporation must be avoided by keeping the heat low. Cooking time 10–15 min.

Powdered grain, such as cornflour, arrowroot, custard powder and flour should be blended with sufficient cold milk to make a thin cream. Heat the rest of the milk almost to boiling-point and pour on to the blended grain, stirring continuously. Pour back into the pan and boil gently, still stirring, until all the starch grains are quite cooked. Cooking time 4–5 min.

The consistency of cereal mixtures ready for moulding should be such that if a spoonful is dropped back on to the surface of the hot mixture, it will merge into it only when gently shaken. This should be achieved either by further evaporation if the consistency is too slack or by adding a little milk if too stiff. A cereal mould of too stiff a texture is very unpalatable, but if too thin it may be poured into a bowl and served semi-set.

Choose china or glass moulds for preference, as the cold wetted surface causes instant gelatinization of the surface starch and imparts a clean, glossy surface to the mould when turned out. Pour in quickly, and from a slight height so that, by its own weight, the mixture can drive all the air out of the mould and force itself into the hollows of the shape. This will ensure a well-formed mould free from holes. If cereal mixtures are to be set in border moulds, which are metal, a little margarine *or* butter *or*, best of all, pure olive oil, should be used to grease the inside. A sharp tap on the side of this type of mould should be all that is necessary to dislodge the mixture.

A china or glass mould may be turned out quite cleanly if the cereal mixture is first gently loosened from the lip of the mould with the tips of the fingers, then inverted on to the hand and dislodged by a sharp jerk of the wrist. If the surface of the dish is moistened the mould can be moved to an exact position.

## CEREALS, PASTA

Success in cooking cereal dishes depends largely upon giving the cereal, which is normally rather tasteless, a pleasant texture and a full appetizing flavour. The dishes are useful for providing filling meals cheaply.

## CEYLON LOBSTER CURRY

**1 large lobster**
**1 large cucumber**
**1 small coconut**
**3 oz. chopped onions *or* shallots**
**1 clove garlic very finely-chopped**
**2 oz. butter**
**1 dessertsp. thinly-sliced green ginger**
**¼ pt. fish stock**
**1 dessertsp. rice flour**
**1 teasp. ground turmeric**
**½ teasp. each sugar, ground cloves and ground cinnamon**
**1 teasp. salt**
**1 teasp. lemon juice**

Peel the cucumber, cut it lengthwise into quarters, across into pieces 2 in. long, and carefully remove the seeds. Have ready a saucepan of salted boiling water, put in the cucumber, cook gently until ¾ done, then drain well. Break the coconut in half, saving the milk from inside, and scrape or chop the white part of the nut finely. Pour ⅓ pt. boiling water over the coconut, let it stand for 20 min., then strain off the liquid, and put it aside. Cover the grated nut again with ⅓ pt. boiling water, let it remain for at least ½ hr., then strain through fine muslin 2 or 3 times squeezing the nut well each time. In a saucepan fry the onions and garlic lightly in hot butter, add the ginger, stock, rice flour, turmeric, cinnamon, cloves, sugar and salt, stir and cook very slowly for 15 min. then put in the pieces of lobster and cucumber, cover closely, and let the saucepan stand away from heat for ½ hr. so that the contents may become thoroughly impregnated with the flavour of the curry-sauce. Then re-heat, add the first infusion of the coconut, and the lemon juice, bring to boiling-point.

**3-4 helpings**

## CHAMPAGNE CUP

**1 bottle of champagne**
**2 bottles of soda water**
**A few strips of lemon rind**
**½ teasp. Maraschino**
**1 liqueur glass brandy**
**1 teasp. castor sugar (optional)**

Chill the champagne and soda water for 1 hr. When ready to serve, put the strips of lemon rind into a large glass jug, add the Maraschino and brandy, pour in the champagne and soda water; serve at once. If sugar is added it should be stirred in gradually.

## CHARLOTTE RUSSE

As for Gooseberry Charlotte, but fill the prepared mould with Italian cream using a flavouring of vanilla *or* sherry.

## CHARLOTTES

Charlottes are moulds lined with bread or sponge fingers, savoy fingers or wafers. They are usually filled with a sweet cream mixture, although savoury charlottes are known.

Choose a mould with straight sides for making a charlotte.

## CHÂTEAUBRIAND STEAK

*Château-Briand grillé*

**A double fillet steak not less than 1½ in. thick**
**Olive oil *or* melted butter**
**Salt and pepper**

Wipe the steak, remove any sinew or skin. Cover the meat with a cloth and beat carefully. Brush over with oil or melted butter and season. Place under a red-hot grill and cook both sides quickly. Reduce heat slightly and cook, turning frequently. The steak should be well browned but slightly underdone.

Serve immediately on a hot dish with Maître d'hôtel butter and potato straws or with gravy, demi-glace, tomato or Béchamel sauce.

## CHEESE

Cheese is the natural way of preserving milk's nourishment.

Many cheeses are made like junket or "curds and whey" by adding a little rennet to fresh milk. The most valuable part of the milk becomes solid—the "curd"—and the watery part, or "whey", separates from it.

This curd contains a higher proportion of fat than when milk is allowed to go sour and make curds naturally. In souring, much of the milk's fat remains in the whey, and the resulting cheese has a lower calorific value.

Like butter and cream, most cheese is now made in creameries but the principles of making it remain the same as those used in farmhouses. Production in creameries makes it possible to ensure the same rigid controls with regard to standards and hygiene that exist in other branches of the dairy industry.

### Nutritional Value of Cheese

All classes of cheese contain a high proportion of protein. An ordinary fat cheese consists of one-third protein, one-third fat and one-third water with large amounts of calcium and riboflavin (one of the B vitamins) and worth-while quantities of vitamins A and D. Cheese, therefore, has an extremely high nutritional value.

This nutritional value varies with the proportion of milk and cream used in the manufacture of the different cheeses. The higher the proportion of cream, the greater the fat content, while cheeses made from skimmed milk have little fat but a large amount of protein.

### Digestibility of Cheese

It is now generally agreed that, provided certain rules are followed in preparing and cooking cheese, it can be easily digested by most people.

Before cooking, cheese should be finely divided by grating or chopping. It should be very well chewed if eaten raw. The eating of some form of starch aids the digestion and, as starch is usually accompanied by some vegetable protein, it is strongly recommended by nutritionists. If animal and vegetable protein are eaten together, more value is obtained from both than if they are taken separately.

### Soft and Hard Cheeses

Generally speaking, cheeses made from skimmed milk are hard. There is one notable exception to this—Cottage Cheese, made from soured skimmed milk. Soft cheeses contain more water than hard cheeses, partly because the latter are subjected to higher temperatures and pressures during their manufacture.

It is almost impossible to classify cheeses beyond this stage because so many factors can affect the finished product. The type of soil in the district; the fat content of the milk; the acidity of the curd at various stages of cheese-making; the amount of pressure and the length of time for which it is applied; all these factors and others contribute to the individuality of each cheese. Therefore, although the principles are the same, no two types of cheese are made in exactly the same way.

### To Choose Cheese

One's own taste and smell are the best indications of a cheese's quality and palatability. People's preferences vary so much that there is much to be said for the old adage, "Taste and try before you buy".

This is not possible when buying modern processed cheese in packets. However, these are so bland and similar in flavour that they are unlikely to offend most people.

### Storage Hints

Cheese keeps well if it is stored in a polythene bag to prevent it drying out. It should be kept in a cool place (50°–60°) or in a refrigerator. If refrigerated, cheese must be allowed to come to room temperature before use. It should have at least 1–2 hr. to reach this.

### Serving Cheese

Cheese is often served as a separate course and, where possible, a variety of types should be offered. They should be attractively arranged on a cheese-board or large plate and accompanied by bread rolls or a choice of biscuits. Vegetables such as watercress, radishes, small onions or celery go well with cheese and make an attractive addition. Many people like a little butter with cheese. Stilton Cheese deserves special mention because it is so often incorrectly served. It should be cut horizontally—not scooped from the centre. Port may be served *with* it but should not be poured *into* it.

### Kinds of Cheese

There are well over 400 different kinds of cheese but those in the following list are among the best known.

*English cheeses*

**Caerphilly Cheese** is the small white cheese which originated in a small Glamorgan village but is now made in the West of England. It has a mild, creamy taste and a smooth springy texture. Welsh miners like it because it is moist and salty.

**Cheddar Cheese** is the best known of all English cheeses but is now made all over the world. A good Cheddar is solid and firm, pale yellow in colour with a succulent "nutty" taste.

**Cheshire Cheese** has a keen, tangy flavour and an open texture. There are red, white and blue varieties, "Old Blue" being the richest and rarest. It has been produced in England since the twelfth century.

**Cream Cheese** is always very mild in flavour. It must be eaten fresh as it will not keep for very long and is therefore normally made up in small quantities.

**Derby Cheese** is another mild, creamy cheese with a smooth texture. If allowed to mature for 4–6 months, it develops a fuller flavour. **Sage Derby** is given extra flavour with layers of finely-chopped sage leaves.

**Double Gloucester Cheese** is a pungent, smooth-textured cheese somewhat similar to Cheddar, but fuller in flavour. It is straw-coloured or light red.

**Lancashire Cheese** is especially famous for its toasting qualities. It has a crumbly and fairly soft texture which makes it easy to spread, while its flavour is clean and mild.

**Leicester Cheese** is a fine dessert cheese with a mild flavour which becomes more piquant with maturity. It is rich red in colour and has a soft, crumbly texture.

**Stilton Cheese** is famous the world over. The rich, mellow, strong-flavoured Blue Stilton is creamy white in colour with plenty of blue veins and a wrinkled brown coat. The texture should be open and flaky and the body soft and slightly moist. A creamy, young White Stilton has a mild flavour and is popular in the North Country.

**Wensleydale Cheese** has a unique lingering, sweet flavour. Its texture is velvety and, when mature, is creamy enough to spread. The White Wensleydale is most common but small quantities of Blue Wensleydale are also made.

*Scottish cheese*

**Dunlop Cheese** is the principal Scottish cheese. Its flavour is not unlike that of Cheddar but it has a closer texture and is more moist.

*Danish cheeses*

**Danish Blue Cheese** is a semi-hard cheese made from whole milk. It is ripened by blue-green mould which gives it a mottled appearance. The texture is creamy and the flavour mellow. Its official name is Danableu.

**Samsoe Cheese** is another Danish cheese made from whole milk. It is mild and creamy with a nutty flavour. Like some Swiss cheese, it has a number of holes, or eyes.

*French cheeses*

**Brie Cheese** has become popular in England. It is not unlike Camembert.

**Camembert Cheese** is a rich cream cheese from Brittany. It is small and flat, pale yellow in colour and has a rough rind.

**Roquefort Cheese** is very rich French cheese. Strictly speaking it should be made from ewe's milk but similar types are made in other countries from other kinds of milk. The flavour is sharp and peppery while the appearance is of white curd with mottled blue veins. It has to be kept a considerable time before ripening.

**Tôme au Raisin Cheese** is a rich cream cheese which also comes from France. The outside is coated with grape pips which impart a unique flavour to the cheese.

*Italian cheeses*

**Bel Paese** is the name given to the best known of a group of Italian table cheeses. They are uncooked, soft, sweet and mild. The ripening period is short—about 6 weeks. Bel Paese is made from whole milk and the finished product is wrapped in tinfoil.

**Gorgonzola Cheese** is the principal blue-veined cheese from Italy. It now has counterparts in many other countries. The interior has blue-green veins mottling the creamy cheese and its coat resembles a form of clay. The ripening period is at least 3 months and sometimes extends to a year.

**Mozzarella Cheese** is a soft, plastic-curd cheese that was originally made from buffalo's milk. Made mainly in Southern Italy, it is now produced from cow's milk as well. Used mainly in cooking, this cheese has little or no ripening period and is shaped into rather irregular spheres.

**Parmesan Cheese** is the name given to a group of very hard cheeses which originated in Italy but are now made in some other countries. Made entirely from skimmed cow's milk, their high flavour is largely due to the pasturage but also to the long maturing period —from 6 months to 4 years. This cheese becomes very hard and then grates easily. It is often sold in powdered form, and keeps almost indefinitely.

**Provolone Cheese** is made in many parts of Italy. It is light in colour, mellow and smooth, cuts without crumbling and has a delightful flavour. This cheese is made in many shapes and sizes—each having a special name. It becomes strongly flavoured with age.

*Dutch Cheeses*

**Edam Cheese** originated in the Netherlands. It may be semi-soft or hard, and is a sweet-curd cheese made from cows' milk in which the fat content has been slightly reduced. It has a mild, clean flavour and a firm but rather crumbly texture.

**Gouda Cheese** is similar to Edam but contains more fat. Its shape is almost spherical. Like Edam, it has a bright red coating when exported.

*Swiss Cheeses*

**Ennenthaler Cheese** is a famous Swiss cheese similar to Gruyere in that it has an elastic body in which holes develop. However, its nut-like sweetish flavour is milder.

**Gruyère Cheese** takes its name from a Swiss village, although much Gruyère cheese is now made in France. Made from whole milk, it has a sharp flavour. The body is elastic in texture, and as the cheese ripens, holes or "eyes" develop in it.

**Processed Cheeses** are usually sold in tinfoil or plastic wrapping, in separate portions or slices. The cheese has been specially treated to prevent it ripening or deteriorating during storage.

For Cheese dishes, *see the recipe for the flavour or style of dish required, e.g. Cheese Onion Spread, Cheese Soufflé.*

## CHEESE AIGRETTES

*Aigrettes au Parmesan*

**2 oz. butter**
**½ pt. water**
**4 oz. flour (plain *or* self-raising)**
**3 oz. grated cheese (preferably Parmesan)**
**2 eggs**
**Pinch of salt**
**Pinch of pepper**
**Deep fat for frying**

GARNISH

**Grated cheese**
**Cayenne pepper**

Put the butter and water into a small saucepan; when boiling add the sifted flour, and stir vigorously over heat until the panada leaves the sides of the pan quite clean. Remove from heat and mix in the cheese, egg yolks, beating each one in separately, add seasoning to taste, and lastly stir in the stiffly whisked egg whites. Turn the mixture on to a plate, and when cold drop small rough pieces of it into hot fat, do not allow to fry too quickly or the outside will become too brown before the inside is sufficiently cooked. On the other hand, if the fat is too cold it soaks into the paste and the aigrettes are greasy. As the success of this dish depends chiefly on the frying, the greatest possible care should be taken. Drain well, then arrange the aigrettes in pyramid form on a savoury d'oyley and sprinkle with Parmesan cheese and cayenne pepper.

**About 24 savouries**
**Cooking time—about 4 min. for each batch**

## CHEESE AND SARDINE FINGERS

**1 small can sardines in oil**
**½ teacup breadcrumbs**
**Seasoning**
**½ teasp. mixed mustard**
**2 oz. grated Cheddar cheese**
**A little margarine *or* butter if necessary**
**4 slices buttered toast**
**1 tomato**

**1 teasp. Worcester sauce**

Mash the sardines very well, and season. Mix the oil from the can of sardines with the breadcrumbs, seasoning, mustard, Worcester sauce and cheese. If there is not sufficient oil to give a soft mixture then add a little margarine or butter and cream well. Spread the mashed sardines on the slices of toast, and cover with the crumb mixture. Put under a hot grill for a few minutes until crisp and golden brown. Garnish with a small piece of tomato.

**4 helpings *or* 8 small savouries**
**Cooking time—4 min.**

### CHEESE AND ONION PIE

| | |
|---|---|
| **Short crust pastry using 8 oz. flour, etc.** | **½ oz. flour** |
| **3 small onions** | **Salt and pepper** |
| | **4 oz. cheese** |
| | **2 tablesp. milk** |

Parboil the onions whilst making the pastry. Line an 8-in. fireproof plate with half the pastry. Mix the salt and pepper with the flour. Slice the onions and dip in the seasoned flour, spread them over the bottom of the lined plate. Grate the cheese and sprinkle it over the onion, add the milk. Wet the edge of the pastry, put on the cover and press the edges firmly together. Knock up the edges, decorate as desired and brush over with milk. Bake in a hot oven (**425° F., Gas 7**) for about 40 min.

NOTE: This can be made as an open tart if liked, use 4 oz. flour, etc., for the pastry.

**6–8 helpings**

### CHEESE BREAD — Plait

As for Milk Bread, adding 3–4 oz. finely grated cheese with the dry ingredients. Bake as for Bread Plait.

### CHEESE D'ARTOIS

*D'Artois au Parmesan*

| | |
|---|---|
| **1 egg** | **Puff pastry using 4 oz. flour, etc.** |
| **4 oz. grated cheese** | **Egg yolk** |
| **1 oz. butter** | **Parsley** |
| **Salt and pepper** | |

Beat the yolk and white of the whole egg slightly, add 3 oz. of cheese, butter (melted), and season rather highly with salt and pepper. Roll the pastry out thinly, cut it in 2, spread the mixture over one ½, and cover with the other ½. Place carefully on a greased baking-sheet, score it in 1 in. deep strips, brush over with egg yolk, sprinkle with remainder of grated cheese, and bake for about 10 min. in a hot oven (**425° F., Gas 7**). When ready cut through the scores, pile on a hot dish, and serve. Garnish with parsley.

**12–15 savouries**

### CHEESE FINGERS WITH CAYENNE

| | |
|---|---|
| **4 oz. finely-grated cheese** | **½ saltsp. salt** |
| **4 oz. butter** | **½ saltsp. cayenne pepper** |
| **4 oz. flour** | |

Rub the butter into the flour and add grated cheese, salt and cayenne pepper. Mix well together and add sufficient water to make a stiff paste. Roll out to about ¼ in. thick and cut into fingers 3½ in. long by ¾ in. wide. Transfer to a greased baking-sheet and bake in a warm oven (**335° F., Gas 3**) until crisp and lightly browned. Serve either hot or cold.

**10 helpings** **Cooking time—30–45 min.**

### CHERRY PUDDING

*Pouding aux Cerises*

| | |
|---|---|
| **1 lb. cooking cherries** | **2 oz. castor sugar** |
| **½ gill water** | **Pinch of salt** |
| **3 oz. moist sugar** | **3 eggs** |
| **3 oz. plain flour** | **Grated rind of ½ lemon** |
| **2–3 tablesp. milk (approx.)** | **Pinch of ground cinnamon** |
| **1 gill cream *or* milk** | |

Stone the cherries and stew them very gently (to keep them whole) in a small saucepan with the water and moist sugar. Allow to cool. Blend the flour with the 2–3 tablesp. of milk, so that it is smooth and "runny". Boil the cream *or* milk and add to it the blended flour, beating well to keep the mixture smooth. Bring to the boil again and add the castor sugar and salt. Cool the mixture. Separate the eggs. Beat the egg yolks into the mixture. Add the lemon rind and cinnamon, and lastly the stiffly-whisked egg whites. Put into a well-greased mould or pie-dish a layer of cherries and a layer of mixture alternately until the mould is full. Cover with greased paper.

Bake in a fairly hot oven (**400° F., Gas 6**) for about 40 min.

Serve with a sweet sauce or fruit syrup.

**5–6 helpings**

## CHEESE MERINGUES

*Meringues au Parmesan*

| | |
|---|---|
| **2 egg whites** | **2 oz. grated Parmesan cheese** |
| **Pinch of cayenne pepper** | **Deep fat for frying** |
| **Pinch of salt** | **A little Parmesan cheese for garnish** |

Whisk the egg whites to a very stiff froth. Add a good seasoning of cayenne and a little salt to the cheese, then stir it lightly into the whisked egg whites. Have ready a deep pan of hot fat, drop in the mixture in small teaspoonfuls, and fry until nicely browned. Drain well, and serve sprinkled with Parmesan cheese and more cayenne pepper.

**About 14 savouries** **Cooking time—5 min.**

## CHEESE OMELET

*Omelette gratinée au Parmesan*

| | |
|---|---|
| **3 eggs** | **1 tablesp. cream *or* milk** |
| **1 tablesp. grated Parmesan cheese** | **Salt and pepper** |
| | **1 oz. butter** |

Whisk the eggs well, then add the cheese, cream and a little salt and pepper. Have the butter ready heated in an omelet pan, pour in the egg mixture, and stir over heat until the eggs begin to set. Then fold one half over the other, making it crescent shaped, or fold the sides towards the middle in the form of a cushion. Allow the omelet to brown slightly, then turn on to a hot dish, serve immediately.

**2 helpings** **Cooking time—4–5 min.**

## CHEESE ONION SPREAD

*See Savouries (Appetizers).*

## CHEESE PASTRY

For savoury pies and canapés

| | |
|---|---|
| **4 oz. flour** | **3 oz. butter** |
| **Pinch of dry mustard** | **3 oz. Parmesan cheese** |
| **Pinch of salt** | **1 egg yolk** |
| **Cayenne pepper** | **2 teasp. cold water** |

Sift flour, mustard and seasonings. Cream butter till very soft and white. Add flour, grated cheese and enough egg yolk and water to mix to a stiff dough. Bake in a fairly hot oven (**400° F., Gas 6**).

## CHEESE POTATOES

| | |
|---|---|
| **½ lb. potatoes** | **A little salt** |
| **2 oz. finely-grated cheese** | **1 tablesp. milk** |

Cook the potatoes and mash well. Beat in the cheese, seasoning and enough milk to make a creamy mixture. Serve with a green vegetable or a tomato.

## CHEESE PUDDING

*Pouding au Fromage*

| | |
|---|---|
| **2 eggs** | **Pinch of pepper** |
| **4 oz. grated cheese** | **½ pt. milk** |
| **1 teasp. mixed mustard** | **1 oz. breadcrumbs** |
| **Pinch of salt** | |

Beat the eggs slightly, add to them the cheese, mustard, salt and pepper. Boil the milk, pour over the eggs then add the breadcrumbs. Pour into a pie-dish or soufflé dish and bake for 25–30 min. in the centre of a fairly hot oven (**375° F., Gas 5**). Serve at once. If baked in 4 or 5 individual dishes allow approximately 15 min.

**4–5 helpings**

## CHEESE RAMAKINS

*Ramequins de Fromage*

| | |
|---|---|
| **1 tablesp. breadcrumbs** | **1 oz. butter** |
| **Milk** | **1 egg** |
| **1 oz. grated Parmesan cheese** | **Salt and pepper** |
| **1 oz. grated Cheshire cheese** | **Mace** |

Barely cover the breadcrumbs with boiling milk and leave to stand for 10 min. Stir well. Add cheeses, butter, egg yolk and seasoning to taste. Beat until the mixture is quite smooth. Whisk the egg white to a stiff froth and fold it into the mixture. Pour into well-greased ramakin dishes and bake in a hot oven (**425° F., Gas 7**) until set.

**4–6 helpings**
**Cooking time—15 min.**

## CHEESE SAUCE

To ½ pt. white sauce medium made with vegetable boilings *or* milk *or* ½ milk and ½ vegetable liquid, add 2 heaped tablesp. grated cheese, seasoning, mixed English *or* French mustard and a grain or two of cayenne pepper.

Add the cheese to the cooked, seasoned sauce at boiling point. Do not reboil the sauce, use at once.

### CHEESE SOUFFLÉ

*Soufflé au Fromage*

| | |
|---|---|
| **A little butter for greasing** | **3 oz. grated cheese** |
| **1 oz. butter** | **Pinch of salt** |
| **1 oz. flour** | **Pinch of cayenne pepper** |
| **¼ pt. milk** | **1–2 egg whites** |
| **2 eggs** | |

Coat a soufflé dish well with butter and tie round it a well-buttered, thickly folded piece of paper to support the soufflé when it rises above the level of the dish. Melt the 1 oz. butter in a pan, stir in the flour, add the milk, and boil well. Remove from heat, and mix in the 2 egg yolks, beat well, then stir in the cheese and add seasoning to taste. Whisk all the egg whites to a stiff froth, add them lightly to the rest of the ingredients, pour the mixture into the soufflé dish, and bake in a moderate oven (**350° F., Gas 4**) for 30–35 min. Serve in the dish in which it is baked. Serve immediately.

**5–6 helpings** **Cooking time—35 min.**

### CHEESE STRAWS

**Cheese pastry using 3 oz. flour, etc.**

Roll out pastry thinly, cut into strips about 4 in. long and about ⅛ in. wide, and from the trimmings cut out some rings of about 1¼ in. diameter. Bake in a fairly hot oven (**400° F., Gas 6**) until crisp. Cool on the baking-sheet. Fill each ring with straws and arrange neatly on a dish.

**18 straws** **Cooking time—10 min.**

### CHELSEA BUNS

| | |
|---|---|
| **½ lb. plain flour** | **½ oz. currants *or* sultanas** |
| **¼ teasp. salt** | **½ oz. chopped candied peel** |
| **1 oz. lard *or* margarine** | **1 oz. sugar** |
| **½ oz. yeast** | |
| **1 gill warm milk** | |

Mix flour and salt; rub in fat, cream yeast and add to flour, with warm milk. Beat well and put to rise to double its size. Knead risen dough lightly and roll out in a square of about 10 in. Sprinkle with the fruit and sugar and roll up like a Swiss roll. Cut roll into 7 pieces and put cut side uppermost. Place buns in a greased 8 in. sandwich cake tin so that they will join together when cooked and allow to prove till up to the top of the tin. Brush with milk or egg, bake in a hot oven (**425° F., Gas 7**)

### CHERRY CAKE

*Gâteau aux Cerises*

| | |
|---|---|
| **9 oz. butter *or* margarine** | **1 level teasp. baking-powder** |
| **9 oz. sugar** | **4 oz. glacé cherries** |
| **3 eggs** | **½ teasp. vanilla essence** |
| **¾ lb. plain flour** | **Milk to mix** |
| **¼ teasp. salt** | |

Line a 7-in. cake-tin with greaseproof paper. Cream the fat and sugar until light and creamy and gradually beat in the eggs, one at a time. Add a little flour if curdling takes place. Sift together flour, salt and baking-powder. Chop cherries into pieces (leaving a few whole for decorating the top) and mix with a little of the flour. Stir into the creamed fat the flour, cherries, essence and enough milk to make a dropping consistency. Put into the cake-tin and place a few cherries lightly on the top. Bake in a moderate oven (**350°–335° F., Gas 4–3**). Avoid making mixture too soft.

**Cooking time—1½–1¾ hr.**

### CHERRY CAKE, RICH

*See Rich Cakes, Large, Various.*

### CHERRY CAKES, SMALL

*See Rich Cakes, Small, Various.*

### CHERRY SALAD

*Salade de Cerises*

| | |
|---|---|
| **1 lb. Morello cherries** | **1 dessertsp. brandy *or* Kirsch** |
| **1 tablesp. olive oil** | **Finely-chopped tarragon** |
| **1 teasp. lemon juice** | **Finely-chopped chervil** |
| **3 or 4 drops of tarragon vinegar** | **1 teasp. castor sugar** |

Stone the cherries. Crack some of the stones and mix the kernels with the cherries. Mix the oil, lemon juice, vinegar, brandy or kirsch, a very small quantity of tarragon and chervil and the sugar. Pour over the cherries.

Serve with roast game or duck.

**4–6 helpings**

## CHERRY SAUCE

*Sauce aux Cerises*

**½ lb. freshly-stewed *or* bottled cherries, morellos for preference**
**¼ pt. juice in which cherries were cooked *or* bottled**
**Sugar to taste**
**2 tablesp. redcurrant jelly**
**Pepper**
**1–2 teasp. vinegar**
**2 tablesp. red wine**
**½ teasp. arrowroot (optional)**

Stone the cherries. Heat all the ingredients together and simmer the sauce till the juice is slightly syrupy, or blend the arrowroot with 1 teasp. cold water and add it to thicken the liquid.

Serve with braised game or rabbit.

## CHERRY TARTLETS

*Tartelettes de Cerises*

**Rich short crust pastry using 6 oz. flour, etc.**
**1 can bright red cherries**
**¼ pt. fruit syrup**
**1½ oz. loaf sugar**
**Lemon juice to flavour**
**1 teasp. arrowroot**
**Carmine**
**Sweetened, whipped cream**

Line 15 patty tins or boat-shaped moulds with the pastry. Bake them "blind" (*see Pastry*)in a fairly hot oven (**400° F., Gas 6**) until set. Remove the weighted paper and return the tartlet cases to the oven for 2–3 min. to dry the pastry. Drain the juice from the cherries and remove the stones. Place a layer of cherries in the tartlet cases. Dissolve the sugar in the fruit syrup and boil for 5 min. Blend the arrowroot with the lemon juice, add to the syrup stirring all the time and boil for 2 min. till the syrup is clear. Add a few drops of carmine to colour. Pour a little syrup over the cherries and allow to set. Decorate with piped, sweetened whipped cream.

NOTE: The syrup must be stirred and boiled gently.

**15 tartlets**

## CHESTNUT PURÉE

*Purée de Marrons*

**2 lb. chestnuts**
**Veal *or* chicken stock**
**½ oz. butter**
**1 tablesp. cream**
**Seasoning**

Peel and skin chestnuts as in standard recipes. Put them into the boiling stock with a little salt and stew gently until tender (use barely enough stock to cover). Strain. Put the chestnuts through a wire sieve. Put them back into the pan, add the butter and enough of the cooking liquor to give a thick purée. Add the cream and season carefully. Serve in a hot vegetable dish. Put tiny pieces of butter on the surface to prevent a crust forming, if the purée must be kept waiting.

**4–6 helpings**
**Cooking time—1¼ hr. (approx.)**

## CHESTNUT PURÉE SOUP

*Purée de Marrons*

**1 lb. chestnuts after peeling (about 1½ lb. in shells)**
**1 onion**
**1 oz. butter**
**1 qt. stock**
**Lemon juice**
**Salt and pepper**
**A little yeast *or* meat extract**
**A pinch of sugar**
**A pinch of cinnamon**
**Grated nutmeg**
**¼ pt. cream (optional)**

Make an incision in the rounded sides of the chestnuts then drop them into fast boiling water and boil for 15 min. Drain them and while still warm remove shells and skins. Add the spices so sparingly that they cannot be recognized but merely enhance the chestnut flavour. No added thickening is required except the cream which is optional.

## CHESTNUT SAUCE

*Sauce aux Marrons*

**½ lb. chestnuts**
**¾ pt. stock**
**1 oz. butter**
**A trace of ground cinnamon**
**A small strip of lemon rind**
**Salt and pepper**
**⅛ pt. cream (optional)**

Score the rounded side of the shells of the chestnuts and bake or boil them for 15–20 min. Remove shells and skins. Simmer the chestnuts until soft in the stock, about ½ hr. Rub them through a fine wire sieve. Reheat the sauce with the butter and flavourings, season to taste. Add the cream just below boiling point. Serve at once.

Serve with roast chicken or turkey.

## CHESTNUT STUFFING

**2 lb. chestnuts**
**¼–½ pt. stock**
**2 oz. butter**
**Salt and pepper**
**A trace of powdered cinnamon**
**½ teasp. sugar**

Slit the chestnuts and bake or boil them for 20 min. Remove shells and skins. Stew the chestnuts till tender in sufficient stock barely to cover them. Rub them through a fine wire sieve. Add the butter, seasoning, flavouring, sugar and sufficient stock to make a soft dough.

Use for roast turkey, also good with chicken.

## CHESTNUTS, TO COOK—AU JUS

*Marrons au jus*

**2 lb. chestnuts**
**2 cloves**
**1 small onion**
**1 outside stick of celery**
**1 bay leaf**
**1 blade of mace**
**1 pt. good brown stock**
**Cayenne pepper**
**Salt**
**1 dessertsp. glaze (if available)**
**Fleurons of pastry**

Take a sharp knife and make an incision in each chestnut, in the shell only. Put into a saucepan and cover with cold water. Bring to the boil and cook for 2 min. Drain and peel and skin them while very hot. Stick the cloves into the onion and put chestnuts, onion, celery, bay leaf and mace into the boiling stock. Season. Simmer about 1 hr. until the chestnuts are tender. Strain and keep the chestnuts hot. Return stock to pan, add the glaze if available and reduce to a glazing consistency. Pile the chestnuts in a hot vegetable dish, pour the glaze over and decorate with fleurons of pastry.

**6 helpings**
**Cooking time—1¼ hr.**

## CHICKEN À LA MARENGO

*Poulet sauté à la Marengo*

**1 chicken**
**¼ pt. olive oil**
**1 pt. Espagnole sauce**
**Salt and pepper**
**2 ripe tomatoes**
**½ glass sherry (optional)**
**1 doz. button mushrooms**
**6 stoned olives**
**1 truffle**

GARNISH

**Fleurons of pastry *or* croûtes of fried bread**
**Olives**
**Truffle**
**Mushrooms**

Joint and dry chicken Remove skin and excess fat. Fry joints in oil until golden brown, drain well, pour away oil. Heat Espagnole sauce with tomato pulp, add chicken, sherry (if used), whole olives and mushrooms, truffle in large pieces, and season. Simmer gently until chicken is tender—about ¾ hr.

Pile in centre of hot dish, strain sauce over and garnish. Place fleurons *or* croûtes round the dish.

**6 helpings**

## CHICKEN À LA MINUTE

*Poussin à la Minute*

**3 baby chickens (poussins)**
**2 oz. butter**
**1 oz. flour**
**Salt and pepper**
**½ pt. milk (approx.)**
**4 button onions**
**2 egg yolks**
**¼ pt. cream**

Cut the prepared chickens into quarters. Melt the butter in a saucepan, fry chicken in butter until golden brown. Sprinkle with flour, salt and pepper and stir until flour is golden brown. Just cover with boiling milk, add the blanched onions, cover tightly and cook gently until tender—about ½ hr. Remove onions, remove chicken and keep hot. Stir egg yolks and cream together; add to pan; heat gently until thick. Return chicken and continue to heat without boiling for a few more minutes. Correct seasoning and serve.

**6 helpings**
**Cooking time—about ¾ hr.**

## CHICKEN BROTH

*Bouillon de Volaille*

**1 small old fowl**
**3–4 pt. water to cover**
**Salt and pepper**
**1 onion**
**1 blade of mace**
**A bunch fresh herbs (thyme, marjoram, parsley stalks)**
**Lemon rind**
**1 bay leaf**
**1 tablesp. rice (optional)**
**1 tablesp. finely-chopped parsley**

Wash and joint the fowl, break the carcase bones, scald and skin the feet and wash the giblets. Put the pieces of fowl and the giblets into a pan and cover them with cold water. Add ½ teasp. salt to each quart of water and bring the whole very slowly to simmering point. Add the onion, peeled whole, the mace, herbs, lemon rind and bay leaf, and simmer very gently for 3–4 hr. Strain the broth through a colander, return it to the pan and sprinkle into it the washed rice, if used. Simmer for a further 20 min.

Meanwhile, the meat may be removed from the chicken bones and cut into small cubes, to be returned to the broth before serving, or the chicken may be finished and served as a separate dish. Just before serving the broth, season to taste and add the chopped parsley.

**8 helpings** **Cooking time—3–4 hr.**

## CHICKEN CREAM SOUP

*Potage à la crème de volaille*

| | |
|---|---|
| **1 oz. cream of rice** | **Salt and pepper** |
| **¼ pt. milk** | **1 teasp. lemon juice** |
| **1 qt. chicken stock** | **Grated nutmeg** |
| **A few pieces of cooked chicken** | **2 egg yolks** |
| | **2 tablesp. cream** |

Blend the "cream of rice" with ½ the milk and a little stock. Boil the stock and into it stir the blended rice and milk. Simmer the mixture for 20 min. or until the mixture has thickened. Cut the chicken into ¼-in. dice and heat these in the soup. Season and add lemon juice and a trace of nutmeg. Mix the egg yolks with the rest of the milk and the cream. Strain this mixture into the soup and thicken without boiling.

**4–6 helpings**
**Cooking time—30 min.**

## CHICKEN CREAMS (Cold)

*Crèmes de Volaille à la Gelée*

| | |
|---|---|
| **½ lb. cooked chicken** | **Salt and pepper** |
| **2 tablesp. white sauce** | **½ oz. gelatine** |
| **1 tablesp. sherry (optional)** | **½ pt. aspic jelly** |
| | **½ gill cream** |

FOR COATING MOULDS:

| | |
|---|---|
| **Aspic jelly** | **Selection of: peas, truffle, red pepper, tomato, hard-boiled egg, cucumber** |
| **Cream** | |

Prepare 1 large mould (approx. 5 in. diameter, 3–4 in. deep) *or* 8 individual moulds:

(1) Coat moulds thinly with aspic jelly, decorate with the chosen garnish, and set with a little more aspic.

(2) If liked, the moulds may now be lined with aspic cream, i.e. equal quantities cream and aspic jelly mixed together—about ¼ pt. of each.

Chop and pound chicken until smooth; add sauce and sherry (if used) gradually. Season, and sieve if required very smooth. Dissolve gelatine in aspic jelly, cool, add to chicken. Fold in stiffly-beaten cream, pour mixture into mould. When set, dip mould a few times in warm water, wipe, and unmould the cream.

Serve with a dressed salad, *or* in a border mould of salad. (*See Dutch or Flemish Salad.*)

**6 helpings**
**Setting time—2–3 hr.**

## CHICKEN CROQUETTES

*Croquettes de Volaille*

| | |
|---|---|
| **8 oz. cold chicken *or* fowl (boned)** | **2 oz. cooked ham *or* tongue** |
| **1 truffle (optional)** | **1 oz. butter** |
| **1 tablesp. cream *or* milk** | **1 oz. flour** |
| **1 teasp. lemon juice** | **¼ pt. stock** |
| **Salt and pepper** | **Egg and fresh breadcrumbs** |
| **6 button mushrooms** | |

Chop the chicken and ham *or* tongue finely. Melt the butter in a saucepan, stir in flour, stir in stock slowly, boil 3–5 min. Add all other ingredients, chopping the mushrooms and truffle, turn on to a plate to cool. Form into cork-shapes, coat with egg and fresh breadcrumbs, fry until golden brown in hot deep fat. Drain and serve on a dish-paper.

**6 helpings** **Cooking time—15 min.**

## CHICKEN EN CASSEROLE

*Poulet en Casserole*

| | |
|---|---|
| **1 chicken** | **1 shallot** |
| **1 oz. flour** | **2 oz. chopped mushrooms** |
| **Salt and pepper** | **1 pt. stock** |
| **2 oz. butter *or* dripping** | |
| **4–6 oz. streaky bacon** | |

Joint the chicken, dip joints in flour and seasoning. Melt the fat in a casserole; fry the bacon, cut in strips; add chicken, mushrooms and chopped shallot. Fry until golden brown, turning when necessary. Add hot stock, sufficient just to cover the chicken, simmer until tender—about 1½ hr. Correct the seasoning.

Serve in the casserole.

**6 helpings**

## CHICKEN FORCEMEAT

*Farce de Volaille*

**½ lb. raw boneless chicken**
**1 oz. butter**
**1 oz. flour**
**½ gill stock**
**1 egg**
**Salt and pepper**
**Nutmeg**

Melt the butter, stir in the flour, add stock (chicken stock if possible), boil 3–5 min., allow panada to cool. Chop and pound chicken, add egg and panada gradually, season well. Sieve if required very smooth.

NOTE: Before moulding or shaping the force, test the consistency (it should not crack when handled and should retain an impression of the spoon). If necessary, soften with cream *or* milk.

Use for quenelles, cutlets, boudins, bombes, timbales.

## CHICKEN JELLY

*Gelée de Volaille*

**1 chicken *or* fowl**
**Salt and pepper**

Joint the chicken, place the pieces in a casserole with 1 pt. cold water and a little seasoning. Cover. Cook in a warm oven **(335° F., Gas 3)** for 2 hr. Cut flesh from bones in thin slices, arrange the meat in a wetted mould or pie-dish leaving as much space as possible at the sides and between the layers for stock. Place the bones, trimmings and stock in a pan, boil rapidly for ½ hr. Strain this stock, season it, and pour over the chicken. Leave to set.

Turn out, and serve with suitable accompaniments.

**6 helpings**

## CHICKEN LEGS AS CUTLETS

*Cuisses de Volaille en Côtelettes*

**2 chicken legs**
**Salt and pepper**
**8 peppercorns**
**½ pt. stock**
**2 onions sliced**
**2 carrots sliced**
**1 small turnip sliced**
**Bouquet garni**
**2 rashers of bacon**
**½ pt. Espagnole sauce**
**Glaze (optional)**

Remove thigh-bones from chicken, but leave drumsticks, season the meat. Fold the skin under, and shape as much like a cutlet as possible. Wrap each leg in muslin, and fasten securely. Place vegetables, bouquet garni and peppercorns in a saucepan, add sufficient stock to barely cover the vegetables. Lay the chicken on the vegetables, covering each piece with bacon. Lay a piece of greased paper on top, and put on a tightly-fitting lid. Simmer gently until tender, about 1¼–1½ hr. Remove muslin, dish the chicken and pour the sauce over.

For an alternative method of serving: remove the pan-lid about 15 min. before the chicken is cooked, place the pan in a hot oven **(400°–425° F., Gas 6–7)** to brown the meat. Glaze the legs and pour the sauce round.

**2 large helpings**

## CHICKEN LIVER PATTIES

*Pâtés de Foie de Volaille*

**4 chicken livers**
**1 oz. butter**
**Rough-puff pastry using 4 oz. flour, etc.**
**Salt and pepper**
**¼ pt. brown sauce**
**Egg *or* milk**

Remove gall, wash and trim livers, then cut into small pieces. Toss the pieces in butter over a low heat for 5 min. Line patty tins with ½ the pastry, put in the liver, season well, and add a little brown sauce to each. Cover with pastry, brush with egg *or* milk, bake in a fairly hot oven **(375° F., Gas 5)** for 20–30 min. Serve hot or cold.

**4–6 helpings**

## CHICKEN MAYONNAISE

*Mayonnaise de Volaille*

**1 cold boiled chicken *or* fowl**
**½ pt. aspic jelly**
**¾ pt. mayonnaise sauce**
**Truffle *or* pickled walnut**
**Chervil**

Joint cooked chicken, remove skin and excess fat, and as much bone as possible. Trim joints to a neat shape. Melt aspic jelly; when almost cool, blend ¼ pt. carefully into mayonnaise. A smooth glossy sauce will be obtained by passing it through a tammy cloth, (i.e. a piece of well-washed flannel). This is most easily done by twisting the ends of the cloth containing the sauce in opposite directions. Place the pieces of chicken on a wire cooling-tray, and mask them with the sauce when it is of a good coating consistency. Use a small ladle or tablespoon. Decorate when almost set with cut shapes of truffle (pickled walnut is cheaper, but must previously be drained on clean blotting-paper) and chervil, *or* other colourful garnish. Mask with a thin layer of the remaining aspic jelly.

Arrange on a bed of dressed salad, *or* on a dish flooded with coloured aspic. Decorate the edge of the dish with endive, cucumber and blocks of aspic jelly, if liked.

**6 helpings**

## CHICKEN MOUSSE

**3 egg yolks**
**1 tablesp. gelatine**
**1 teacup chicken broth**
**Salt and pepper**
**1 teacup cooked chicken, minced finely**
**1 teacup double cream lightly whipped**
**¼ teacup mayonnaise**

Soak the gelatine for 5 min. in ½ cup broth. Beat the egg yolks and stir lightly in the remaining broth, add salt and pepper, cook in top of a double boiler, stirring constantly until thickened to custard consistency. Stir in the dissolved gelatine. Pour this over the chicken until the mousse begins to set. (This operation is speeded up if the chicken is put in a basin stood in cold water or cracked ice.) Then fold in the cream and mayonnaise. Turn into a mould which has been moistened with cold water. Chill until set.

To serve, turn out and garnish with watercress and lettuce.

**4 helpings**
**Cooking time—45 min. (approx.)**

## CHICKEN PIE

*Pâté de Volaille à l'Anglaise*

**1 large *or* 2 small chickens**
**Veal forcemeat**
**Rough puff pastry using 8 oz. flour, etc.**
**Salt and pepper**
**½ lb. ham *or* bacon**
**2 hard-boiled eggs**
**¾ pt. chicken stock**
**Egg for glazing**

Joint chicken, boil bones, gizzards, and trimmings for stock. Parboil the chicken liver, chop finely and mix with veal forcemeat. Cut ham into strips and eggs into sections. Make pastry. Arrange chicken and other ingredients in layers in a 1 pt. pie-dish, seasoning each layer carefully, then three-quarters fill the dish with stock. Cover pie-dish with pastry, decorate and glaze with beaten egg yolk. Bake 1½—2 hr. until meat is cooked. Until the pastry is set, have the oven hot (**425° F., Gas 7**), then lower the heat (**350°–375° F., Gas 4–5**) until cooking is complete. Before serving, add remainder of hot stock to pie.

**6–8 helpings**
**Cooking time—about 2½ hr.**

## CHICKEN PILAFF

*Pilau de Volaille*

**1 chicken *or* fowl**
**3 pt. stock *or* 3 pt. water and 2 lb. scrag-end neck of mutton**
**2 large Spanish onions**
**1 carrot**
**1 blade mace**
**6 black peppercorns**
**4 oz. butter**
**6 oz. Patna rice**
**Salt and pepper**
**1 tablesp. curry paste**
**2 small onions (shallots)**

Joint and trim the chicken, put the backbone, giblets, bones and trimmings and stock (*or* water and the mutton cut into small pieces) into a saucepan; add outside layers of Spanish onions, carrot, mace and peppercorns. Simmer gently 2–3 hr., strain. Dice remainder of Spanish onions, fry in a saucepan until lightly browned in 2 oz. of the butter, add the washed and drained rice, 1½ pt. stock and seasoning. Cook gently until rice has absorbed stock. Fry chicken slowly in remaining butter until lightly brown, put into rice with curry paste and mix well, retaining the butter. Cook gently until chicken and rice are tender, adding more stock if necessary. Cut small onions into rings, fry until golden brown in the butter in which the chicken was fried.

Pile the pilaff on a hot dish, pile rings of fried onion on top. Serve very hot.

**6 helpings**
**Cooking time—about 1½ hr., excluding stock**

## CHICKEN PILLAU—INDIAN

**1 boned chicken**
**6–8 oz. rice**
**3 oz. ghee *or* butter**
**Stock**
**2 onions**
**2 hard-boiled eggs**
**Salt and pepper**
**Cayenne pepper**
**White sauce**

Wash, drain and dry the rice, fry it in 1½ oz. hot ghee or butter until lightly browned. Cover with stock, and cook till soft, adding more stock when necessary; but when ready the rice should be rather dry. Dice the onions and hard-boiled eggs. Fry the onions in the remainder of the ghee, add the rice, eggs and seasoning to taste, and stuff the chicken with the mixture. Braise the chicken gently, and serve coated with a good white sauce.

**5 helpings** **Cooking time—2¾ hr.**

## CHICKEN PURÉE (SOUP)

*Potage à la Princesse*

*For the stock:*

**1 boiling fowl *or* carcase, giblets, skin and legs of a fowl**
**¼ lb. lean bacon**
**2 onions**
**1 carrot**
**3 qt. water**
**Salt and pepper**
**A bunch of herbs: parsley, thyme, marjoram**
**1 bay leaf**
**1 blade of mace**
**6 peppercorns**
**Lemon juice**
**A strip of lemon rind**

*For each quart of chicken stock:*

**1 oz. butter *or* margarine**
**1 oz. flour**
**Lemon juice**
**Nutmeg**
**½ gill cream *or* milk**

Prepare the fowl, chop the bacon, peel and slice the vegetables; put into a large pan with the water, salt, herbs, spice, lemon juice and rind. Cook until the flesh of the chicken is absolutely white; the addition of lemon juice makes the flesh tender more quickly. Cool the stock and skim off all fat. Mince 4 oz. of the cooked chicken and moisten it with a little stock. Rub it through a coarse wire sieve. Melt the fat, stir into it the flour then the stock a little at a time; boil well. Stir the hot soup gradually into the chicken purée. Season lightly with lemon juice, salt, pepper and a trace of nutmeg. Add the cream or milk and reheat without boiling.

**4–6 helpings**
**Cooking time—stock 3–4 hr.; soup 10 min.**

## CHICKEN RISSOLES

*Rissoles de Volaille*

**4 oz. cooked chicken**
**2 oz. cooked ham *or* tongue**
**4 small mushrooms**
**1 truffle (optional)**
**½ oz. butter**
**½ oz. flour**
**¼ pt. white stock**
**1 tablesp. cream *or* milk**
**Salt and pepper**
**Rough-puff pastry using 4 oz. flour, etc.**
**Egg and breadcrumbs**
**Frying-fat**

Chop chicken and ham finely, dice mushrooms and truffle. Melt the butter in a saucepan, stir in flour, add stock gradually, stir and boil until cooked. Add chicken mixture to sauce, re-heat, season, then add mushrooms and truffle, stir in cream or milk and allow to cool. Roll pastry very thinly, cut into rounds about 2 in. in diameter. Place 1 teasp. of mixture on to half the rounds, dampen the edges, put other pastry rounds on top, and seal well. (Alternatively, cut 4 in. rounds, put mixture on each and fold in half.) Coat rissoles with egg and breadcrumbs, fry in hot deep fat until golden brown, then drain well.

**4–6 helpings**
**Cooking time—about 25 min. to cook sauce and to fry**

## CHICKEN SALAD

*Salade de Volaille*

**¾ lb. cold cooked chicken**
**3 tablesp. chopped celery**
**1 hard-boiled egg**
**1 tablesp. salad oil**
**1 tablesp. vinegar**
**Seasoning**
**6 tablesp. mayonnaise sauce**

GARNISH—selection of:

**Gherkins**
**Capers**
**Anchovy fillets**
**Stoned olives**
**Lettuce**

Cut chicken into neat pieces; mix with celery, the chopped egg white, salad oil, vinegar and seasoning. Allow to stand 1 hr. Stir in the mayonnaise. Pile mixture on a bed of lettuce, garnish with a selection of the ingredients suggested, and sprinkle the sieved egg-yolk over.

Chill before serving.

**4 helpings**

## CHICKEN SAUTÉ CHASSEUR

**3½–4 lb. tender chicken**
**1 tablesp. olive oil**
**2 oz. butter**
**1 oz. shallots**
**6 oz. button mushrooms**
**½ glass white wine**
**3 tomatoes**
**½ pt. thin Espagnole sauce**
**Salt and pepper**
**1 sprig of tarragon**
**1 sprig of chervil**
**1 sprig of parsley**

Joint and trim the chicken. Heat the olive oil with ½ the butter in a shallow saucepan. Place in the joints of chicken and nicely colour brown all over. Lower heat and cook gently until tender, allowing approximately 12–15 min. for white joints (i.e. wings and breast) and 20 min. for the dark joints (legs—i.e. drumsticks and fat part of leg). Remove joints from saucepan, neatly arrange on serving dish and keep hot. Put the chopped shallots in the saucepan and cook gently without colouring. Then add the thinly-sliced mushrooms and cook until light brown. Moisten with the white wine, simmer 1 min. then add the diced flesh of the peeled tomatoes and the Espagnole sauce. Season. Simmer for 8–10 min. Stir in the chopped tarragon leaves, chervil and parsley. Work into the sauce the remainder of the butter; do not re-boil. Pour the sauce over the chicken; sprinkle with a little of the herbs and serve.

## CHICKEN SOUP

**1 boiling fowl (3–4 lb.)**
**2½ pt. water**
**1 small onion**
**Pinch of salt**
**2 slices of ginger**

Pour water (cold) into a heavy pot and put in fowl. Bring to boiling-point. Add chopped onion, salt and ginger. Reduce heat and simmer for about 3 hr.

## CHICKEN SOUP NOODLES

**2 oz. minced, raw ham**
**6 oz. minced, raw chicken**
**3 spring onions**
**2 pt. chicken stock**
**½ lb. cooked noodles**
**2 slices of ginger**

Simmer ham, chicken, ginger and chopped onions for 10 min. in the stock. Add noodles 2 min. before soup is cooked.

## CHICKEN OR GAME STOCK FOR SOUPS AND SAUCES

**Carcase of chicken *or* game bird**
**Cleaned feet of bird**
**Giblets**
**Salt**
**Cold water to cover**
**1 onion**
**White peppercorns**

Make as for Brown Stock.

## CHICKEN VOL-AU-VENT

*Vol-au-Vent de Volaille*

**6 oz. cooked chicken**
**Puff-pastry using 8 oz. flour, etc.**
**2 oz. cooked ham *or* tongue**
**2 truffles (optional)**
**2–4 oz. mushrooms**
**Salt, pepper, nutmeg**
**½ pt. Béchamel sauce**
**Egg *or* milk to glaze**

Prepare pastry, roll out to ¾ in. thickness; cut into a round or oval shape and place on a wet baking sheet. Cut an inner ring through half the depth of the pastry and brush top of pastry (not sides) with beaten egg. Bake in a hot oven (**425°–450° F., Gas 7–8**) until well risen, firm and brown—about 25 min. Dice chicken and ham, slice mushrooms and truffles; add all these to the Béchamel sauce, season well and heat thoroughly. Lift centre from vol-au-vent case and reserve for lid, clear any soft paste which may be inside, fill with the mixture, and replace lid. See method of making a vol-au-vent case.

A separate piece of pastry the size of the lid may be baked with the large case, and used as a lid for the filled case; this has a better appearance.

**6 helpings**

## CHICORY AND WHITE SAUCE

*Barbe-de-Capucin à la Sauce blanche*

**6 large heads of chicory**
**¾ pt. good white sauce**
**Salt**
**Lemon juice**

Cut off the end of the chicory and the outer leaves. Split each head to within ½ in. of the end and wash well between the leaves. Blanch, by bringing to the boil in just enough water to cover and boiling 5 min. Drain, then tie the heads together in bundles of 2 and cook in boiling salted water until just tender. Finish and serve as for Celery with White Sauce

**6 helpings**
**Cooking time—30–40 min.**

## CHICORY SALAD

*Salade de Barbe-de-Capucin*

| | |
|---|---|
| **6 heads of chicory** | **French dressing** *or* **Vinaigrette Sauce** |

Prepare, wash and drain the chicory well, having split each head in ½ lengthwise. Toss in the French dressing.

NOTE: Chicory cut in shreds may be added to many salads, its crisp texture making it a very pleasant addition. It is most useful as a substitute for celery when the latter is of poor quality or out of season.

**6 helpings**

## CHICORY SOUP

| | |
|---|---|
| **2 large heads of chicory (Witloof) also called Belgian Endive** | **1 blade of mace** |
| **1 oz. butter** | **Salt and pepper** |
| **1 onion** | **Lemon juice** |
| **1 pt. white stock** | **¼ pt. milk** *or* **cream;** *or* **½ milk and ½ cream** |
| **½ oz. flour** | **1 egg yolk** |
| **A bunch of herbs** | |

Cut the chicory in ¼-in. slices and cook it with the onion gently in the butter for 10 min. Continue as for asparagus soup, reserving a few shreds of cooked chicory for garnish. Lemon juice added with the stock improves the flavour. The chicory must not be allowed to boil or it will become tough and stringy.

**4 helpings**

## CHIFFONADE DRESSING

| | |
|---|---|
| **2 hard-boiled eggs** | **1 teasp. very finely-chopped shallot** |
| **2 tablesp. very finely-chopped parsley** | **French dressing** |
| **2 tablesp. very finely-chopped red pepper** | |

Chop the eggs very finely. Add the parsley, red pepper and chopped shallot and enough French dressing to give the desired consistency. Use very cold.

## CHILDREN'S FARE

*See Children's Food.*

## CHILDREN'S FOOD

Strong bones and teeth, good eating habits and a healthy appetite are things most mothers desire for their children. The time to start creating them is when a child takes his first "solid" food.

### Feeding Young Children

Between the ages of 9 months and 7 years, a child's body forms bones, teeth, muscles, blood etc. very rapidly. At the same time, he has only a limited capacity for food, and a small appetite compared with a young adult. His food must therefore give him as much nourishment as possible in a small bulk.

During this period, too, he is learning by imitation, and copies the feeding habits of those around him. As he grows older, he often comes to share the family meal, so the housewife has the problem of adapting some recipes to suit him and his needs. She must either prepare special dishes for him, or use ones suitable for him which the whole family can share.

The following notes will help her to overcome the problems this may present.

1. Make sure that the family diet contains plenty of foods for building strong muscles, blood, bones and teeth, e.g. meat (including liver), fish, eggs, milk and Vitamins A and D.
2. See that every main meal includes fresh fruit or juice, and vegetables.
3. Allow the child to satisfy his appetite with fats, cereals, bread (including whole-grain), and sugar only after foods from 1 and 2 have been eaten.
4. Give a young child small portions, so that he is not discouraged by facing amounts of food he cannot manage. Remove any food uneaten after a reasonable time without comment.
5. Allow some meals to be taken with the family if possible so that the child copies good feeding habits and enjoys the community feeling of the meal.
6. When serving a new food, i.e. one that is new to the child, particularly if it has a new

texture, serve a *very small* amount for the first and second times before increasing it. Sometimes as little as ½ teasp. is sufficient for a first taste. If this is rejected, do not comment, but repeat on successive days especially in the case of "important" foods such as liver, brown bread, fruit, etc., or those which are served frequently to the family and are suitable.

**Adapting the Family Meal to the Child**

1. Where the meal contains "bulky" foods, e.g. clear soups, stalky or stringy fruit and vegetables, or starchy bulk in pies, cheese dishes, puddings, potato dishes, etc., these should be adapted, not necessarily omitted.

(*a*) *Soup:* Add grated cheese or sieved meat or fish to a small quantity of clear soup. Add finely shredded fresh or fresh-cooked green vegetables just before serving.

(*b*) *Starchy foods:* Remove pastry, potato crust, excess fat from meat. Where, for instance, grilled sausage, fish cakes or rissoles are being served for the main meal reserve a little of the cooked meat or fish and serve it plain for the child or grill a small lamb's kidney, piece of lean bacon or fish roe after the main meal is cooked. If a starchy oven-cooked dish is being served for the family, e.g. toad-in-the-hole, a cheese custard for the child could be cooked at the bottom of the oven at the same time.

2. Young children should not be given highly seasoned foods, e.g. curry, bottled sauces and spiced meat dishes. Curry is often served with boiled rice, and finely grated cheese may be added to the cooked rice or to mashed potato, and gently warmed before serving for the child's meal.

**Feeding the Older Child**

As the child's capacity for food increases and the appetite grows with a more active life, the mother's task is a little easier. The child can eat the family meals without extra preparation. Providing that a good appetite is maintained and satisfied, the diet will tend to be more easily balanced. It must be remembered, however, that the teenage child needs more protein foods for building his fast-growing body than the adult, and more energy-producing foods for his abundant energy. This means that the child's main meal at this age should be bigger than that needed by the adults of the family and should contain a larger share of meat, fish or other proteins. Having satisfied these needs it is unlikely that feeding at this age will go far wrong provided that the child is offered a *varied* freshly prepared diet.

**Party Dishes for Children**

Party dishes for young children must be simple. Small children do not eat a lot, nor like elaborate food. Serve simple, small cakes and biscuits which they can handle themselves, Jellies and ice cream are always popular. Remember to make a cake—especially a birthday cake—look like a cake, even if it is decorated in the shape of a toy.

**Party Dishes for Teenagers**

Teenagers like simple food too. They tend to like savouries as much as sweets, and sausage rolls, crisps and so on are usually popular. If the food is simple to prepare and serve, many teenagers will enjoy helping to get it ready and served.

## CHOCOLATE BUNS

*See Buns or Cookies*

## CHOCOLATE CAKES, SMALL

*See Rich Cakes, Small, Various.*

## CHOCOLATE CREAM

*Crème au Chocolat*

**4 oz. plain chocolate**
**½ pt. milk**
**3 egg yolks *or* 1 whole egg and 1 yolk**
**2–3 oz. castor sugar**
**½ oz. gelatine**
**4 tablesp. water**
**1 teasp. vanilla *or* coffee essence**
**½ pt. double cream**

Grate the chocolate and dissolve in the milk. Beat eggs and sugar until liquid and make a thick pouring custard with the flavoured milk, straining back into the pan to cook and thicken. Do not allow to boil or the eggs may curdle. Allow to cool. Soak gelatine in the water for 5 min., then heat to dissolve. Stir the vanilla *or* coffee essence gently into the cooled custard, and add the dissolved gelatine, stirring again as it cools. Whip the cream and fold lightly into the custard mixture just before setting. Pour into a prepared mould or into glass dishes.

**6 helpings**
**Setting time—1–2 hr.**

## CHOCOLATE, TO DRINK

*See Cocoa.*

## CHOCOLATE FILLING

| | |
|---|---|
| **3 oz. butter** | **½ oz. plain chocolate** |
| **5 oz. icing sugar** | **2 teasp. milk** |

Cream the butter and gradually work in the sugar. Heat the chocolate in the milk until dissolved. Cool slightly then stir into the creamed butter and sugar. Mix well.

## CHOCOLATE ICE CREAM

*Glace au Chocolat*

| | |
|---|---|
| **4 oz. plain chocolate** | **1 gill cream** |
| **½ gill water** | **1–2 teasp. vanilla essence** |
| **½ pt. custard** | |

Break chocolate roughly, place in pan, add water. Dissolve over low heat. Add melted chocolate to the custard. Cool. Add the half-whipped cream and vanilla to taste. Chill and freeze.

**6–8 helpings**

## CHOCOLATE ICING

| | |
|---|---|
| **3 oz. chocolate (preferably couverture *or* plain chocolate)** | **8 oz. icing sugar** |
| | **½ gill water** |

Break the chocolate into small pieces, put into a small bowl over a bowl of warm water and allow to dissolve. Add the sieved icing sugar and water, stir until well mixed and smooth. Use as required.

*See Butter Icing.*

## CHOCOLATE MOUSSE

| | |
|---|---|
| **4 eggs** | **4 oz. plain *or* vanilla chocolate (sweetened)** |

Melt the chocolate with 1 tablesp. water (*or* black coffee) in a pan over a very low heat. Stir until smooth. Meanwhile separate the eggs and beat the yolks. Stir the melted chocolate into the yolks. Whip the whites very stiff and fold them into the chocolate. Make sure they are perfectly blended. Turn into a serving dish, or 4 individual dishes and leave to cool. Unless in a hurry, it is best not to put chocolate mousse in a refrigerator.

**4 helpings**
**Cooking time—15 min. (approx.)**

## CHOCOLATE PUDDING—BAKED

| | |
|---|---|
| **6 oz. plain flour** | **4 oz castor sugar** |
| **Pinch of salt** | **1 oz. cocoa** |
| **1 rounded teasp. baking-powder** | **1 egg** |
| | **Milk to mix** |
| **3 oz. butter *or* margarine** | **A few drops of vanilla essence** |

Sift together the flour, salt and baking-powder. Rub in the fat. Add the sugar and cocoa; mix well. Add the beaten egg and milk and mix to a dropping consistency. Add the vanilla essence. Put into a greased tin or pie-dish. Bake in a fairly hot oven (**375° F., Gas 5**) for 30–40 min.

Dredge well with castor sugar and serve with chocolate *or* custard sauce.

**6 helpings**

## CHOCOLATE PUDDING—STEAMED (1)

*Pouding au Chocolat*

| | |
|---|---|
| **8 oz. plain flour** | **1 oz. cocoa** |
| **1 teasp. baking-powder** | **2 eggs** |
| **Pinch of salt** | **Milk to mix** |
| **4 oz. butter *or* margarine** | **A few drops of vanilla essence** |
| **4 oz. castor sugar** | |

Grease a 2 pt. basin.

Sift together the flour, salt and baking-powder. Rub in the fat. Add the sugar and cocoa. Mix to a soft dropping consistency with the beaten eggs and milk. Add vanilla essence to taste. Put the mixture in the basin; cover. Steam for 2 hr. Serve with chocolate sauce.

**6 helpings**

## CHOCOLATE PUDDING—STEAMED (2)

| | |
|---|---|
| **3 oz. plain chocolate** | **A few drops of vanilla essence** |
| **2 tablesp. milk** | |

**6 oz. butter**
**6 oz. castor sugar**
**3 eggs**
**6 oz. plain flour**
**¾ teasp. baking-powder**

Grease a mould or basin.

Grate the chocolate and heat with the milk in a small saucepan until dissolved. Cream the butter, sugar and melted chocolate together. Add a few drops of vanilla essence. Beat in the eggs. Sift in the flour and baking-powder and mix to a soft dropping consistency. Pour the mixture into the mould *or* basin. Steam for 2 hr. Serve with custard, chocolate, *or* sherry sauce .

**6 helpings**

### CHOCOLATE RICE MOULD

*Gâteau de Riz au Chocolat*

**6 oz. rice**
**2 oz. cocoa** *or*
**3 oz. chocolate**
**1 qt. milk**
**4 oz. castor sugar**
**Vanilla** *or* **coffee essence** *or* **1 teasp. brandy** *or* **rum**
**1 oz. fresh butter**

Make as the basic recipe for Whole Rice Mould, blending the cocoa with a little of the warm milk. If chocolate is used, chop roughly and add to the mixture ½ hr. before moulding. Flavour with essences *or* spirits just before moulding.

**6 helpings**
**Cooking time—2–3 hr.** **Setting time—2 hr.**

### CHOCOLATE SANDWICH CAKE —EGGLESS

**1 oz. butter** *or* **margarine**
**2 oz. sugar**
**2 tablesp. golden syrup**
**1 level teasp. bicarbonate of soda**
**1–1½ gills milk**
**6 oz. self-raising flour**
**1 oz. cocoa**
**Pinch of salt**
**Chocolate butter icing**

Cream together the fat, sugar, and syrup, and dissolve the soda in the milk. Sift together flour, salt and cocoa. Add flour and milk alternately to the creamed fat mixture—the consistency should be that of a thick batter. Place the mixture in a prepared 8-in. sandwich cake-tin and bake in a fairly hot oven (**375°–350° F., Gas 5–4**). When cool spread the top of the cake with butter icing, smooth with a knife and decorate by marking with circles or lines.

**Cooking time—40 min.**

### CHOCOLATE SAUCE (1)—PLAIN

*Sauce au Chocolat*

**3 oz. bitter chocolate** *or* **cooking chocolate** *or* **1 heaped tablesp. cocoa**
**½ pt. water**
**¼ oz. cornflour** *or* **custard powder**
**Sugar if required**
**Vanilla essence**
**1 teasp. rum (optional)**
**A few drops of coffee essence (optional)**

Break the chocolate in rough pieces and warm them gently with a very little water. When melted, beat the chocolate mixture till smooth, adding the rest of the water gradually. Thicken the sauce with the cornflour or custard powder blended with a little cold water. Flavour and sweeten to taste.

If cocoa is used, mix it with the dry cornflour before blending with water.

### CHOCOLATE SAUCE (2)—RICH

**¼ lb. chocolate**
**½ pt. milk**
**2–3 egg yolks**
**Vanilla essence**
**1 teasp. rum**
**Sugar, if required**
**1 egg white (optional)**

Dissolve the chocolate in the milk. Make a custard with the egg yolks and the chocolate-flavoured milk—*see Custard Sauce*. Flavour and sweeten to taste. If liked one egg white may be whipped to a stiff froth and folded into the finished sauce.

### CHOCOLATE SAUCE FOR ICE CREAM

*Sauce de Chocolat*

**1 rounded dessertsp. cornflour**
**2 rounded dessertsp. cocoa**
**3 rounded dessertsp. sugar**
**½ pt. water**
**3 drops vanilla essence**
**½ oz. butter**

Blend together the cornflour, cocoa and sugar with a little of the water. Boil remaining water and pour on to blended mixture. Return to pan and boil for 2 min., stirring all the time. Add vanilla and butter.

Serve hot or cold.

## CHOCOLATE SOUFFLÉ—HOT

*Soufflé au Chocolat*

**2 oz. finely-grated plain chocolate**
**3/8 pt. milk**
**1½ oz. butter**
**1½ oz. plain flour**
**4 egg yolks**
**3 oz. castor sugar**
**½ teasp. vanilla essence**
**5 egg whites**

Prepare the soufflé tin *or* mould. Dissolve the chocolate in the milk. Melt the butter, add the flour and let it cook for a few minutes without colouring. Add the milk and beat well until smooth. Reheat until the mixture thickens and comes away from the sides of the pan. Allow to cool slightly. Beat in the egg yolks well, one at a time, add the sugar and vanilla essence. Stiffly whisk the egg whites and fold them lightly into the mixture. Turn into the mould; cover, and steam very gently for about 1 hr.

**6 helpings**

## CHOCOLATE SUNDAE

**½ pt. chocolate ice cream *or* 1 small brick**
**½ pt. chocolate sauce**
**½ pt. vanilla ice cream *or* 1 small brick**
**2 oz. chopped walnuts**
**¼ pt. sweetened whipped cream**
**8 maraschino cherries**

Place a scoop of chocolate ice cream in 6–8 sundae glasses; coat with chocolate sauce. Place a scoop of vanilla ice cream on top; coat with chocolate sauce. Sprinkle with chopped nuts. Pipe with cream. Decorate with cherries.

## CHOCOLATE SWISS ROLL

*Bûche au Chocolat*

As for Swiss roll, with the addition of 2–3 teasp. cocoa sifted with the flour.

When the roll is cooked, turn on to sugared paper, place a piece of greaseproof paper on top and roll up. When the roll has cooled, unroll it gently and spread with vanilla butter icing. Roll up again. Dust with castor sugar.

## CHOPPED HERRING

**2 salt herrings**
**1 large apple**
**1 small onion**
**3 tablesp. breadcrumbs**
**1 tablesp. salad oil**
**½ teasp. castor sugar**
**Pepper**
**Lettuce leaves**
**2 tablesp. vinegar**
**1 hard-boiled egg**

Soak the herrings in cold water overnight; then wash thoroughly; remove bones and chop to a pulp. Peel and grate apple and onion and add to the herrings, together with the breadcrumbs, vinegar, salad oil, sugar and a dash of pepper, and mix thoroughly. Serve on lettuce leaves sprinkled with chopped hard-boiled egg, either as hors d'œuvres or as an accompaniment to cold fried fish.

**5–6 helpings**

## CHOPPED LIVER

**½ lb. chicken *or* calves' liver**
**2 tablesp. chicken fat**
**1 small onion**
**1 hard-boiled egg**
**Salt and pepper**
**Lettuce leaves**

Fry the liver gently in the chicken fat till tender, then remove from the pan. Skin and chop the onion and fry this until soft, but not brown. Put the liver and hard-boiled egg through the finest cutter of the mincing machine, then add the onion with the fat in which it was cooked, season with salt and pepper and mix to a paste. Serve on lettuce leaves garnished with hard-boiled egg, as an hors d'œuvre or as a spread for canapés or sandwiches.

**4–5 helpings** **Time—about 20 min.**

## CHOUX PASTRY

*Pâte à choux*

For Cream buns, Cream puffs and Éclairs

**4 oz. plain flour**
**½ pt. water**
**1/8 teasp. salt**
**2 oz. butter *or* margarine**
**½ teasp. vanilla essence**
**1 egg yolk**
**2 eggs**

Sift and warm the flour. Place water, salt and fat in a pan, and bring to boiling-point. Remove from heat, add flour all at once and beat well (using a wooden spoon) over the heat again, until it becomes a smooth soft paste and leaves the sides of the pan clean. Remove from the heat, add vanilla and egg yolk immediately and beat well. Add the other two eggs one at a time, beating thoroughly between each addition. (It is important to get the first of the egg in while the mixture is hot enough to cook it slightly, otherwise it becomes too soft.) Use as required.

Bake in a fairly hot oven (**400°–425° F., Gas 6–7**).

## CHRISTMAS BREAD

*Pains de Noël*

| | |
|---|---|
| **1 lb. plain flour** | **¾ oz. yeast** |
| **¼ teasp. salt** | **3 eggs** |
| **4 oz. margarine** | **1½–2 gills warm milk** |
| **½ teasp. cinnamon** | **4 oz. sultanas** |
| **¼ teasp. mixed spice** | **4 oz. raisins** |
| **3 oz. sugar** | **2 oz. currants** |

Sift together the warmed flour and salt; rub in the margarine. Add other dry ingredients (not fruit) to flour and mix to a light dough with the yeast creamed with a little of the sugar, eggs and milk. Beat well. Put to rise to double its size then work in the fruit. Put into greased tins (two 6 in. *or* one 8 in. *or* 10 in.) and allow to prove till well up in the tin. Bake in a fairly hot oven (**400°–380° F., Gas 6–5**) for ¾–1¼ hr. depending on size of loaf. When loaf is almost ready, brush over with sugar and water glaze. Return to oven for 5 min.

**1 large or 2 small loaves**
**Cooking time—50–80 min.**

## CHRISTMAS CAKE

*Gâteau de Noël*

| | |
|---|---|
| **8 oz. butter *or* margarine** | **5–6 eggs** |
| **8 oz. castor sugar** | **1 lb. currants** |
| **½ teasp. gravy browning** | **8 oz. raisins** |
| **8 oz. plain flour** | **4 oz. glacé cherries** |
| **⅛ teasp. salt** | **2 oz. chopped peel** |
| **1 level teasp. mixed spice** | **4 oz. blanched, chopped almonds** |
| **½ level teasp. baking-powder** | **Milk, if necessary** |
| | **4–5 tablesp. brandy (optional)** |

Line an 8-in cake-tin with greaseproof paper.

Cream fat and sugar until white; add gravy browning. Sift together flour, salt, mixed spice and baking-powder. Add egg and flour alternately to the creamed fat, beating well between each addition. Stir in the prepared fruit, almonds and if necessary, add a little milk to make a heavy dropping consistency. Place the mixture in the cake-tin and tie a piece of paper round the outside of the tin. Smooth the mixture and make a depression in the centre. Bake in a warm oven (**335° F., Gas 3**) for ½ hr. then reduce heat to **290° F., Gas 1** for a further 3–3½ hr. Allow to firm before removing from tin and when cold remove paper. Prick bottom of cake well and sprinkle brandy over. Leave for a few days before icing .

**Cooking time—4 hr.**

## CHRISTMAS CAKE, NELL'S

| | |
|---|---|
| **8 oz. butter *or* margarine** | **2 teasp. rum *or* lemon juice** |
| **8 oz. soft brown sugar** | **1 teasp. almond essence** |
| **1 level teasp. black treacle** | **1 level teasp. baking-powder** |
| **4 eggs** | **8 oz. currants** |
| **10 oz. plain flour** | **8 oz. sultanas** |
| **¼ teasp. salt** | **1 oz. chopped mixed peel** |
| **1 level teasp. soluble coffee powder *or* essence** | **1 oz. chopped glacé cherries** |
| **1 level teasp. mixed spice** | **8 oz. chopped valencia raisins** |
| **½ level teasp. ground ginger** | **1 oz. blanched chopped almonds** |
| **1 teasp. vanilla essence** | |

Line a 7–8-in. cake-tin with greaseproof paper smoothly Cream the fat and sugar well and add the treacle. Beat the eggs and add a small amount to the fat, beat well. Sift the flour, salt, coffee powder and spices. Stir into the creamed fat a tablespoonful of the spiced flour, add some more egg, beat well and add a second tablespoonful of the spiced flour. Add the rest of the egg gradually, beating well between each addition. Add vanilla, rum or lemon juice, almond essence and coffee essence if used. Stir in the rest of the flour and baking-powder and lastly add the dried fruits and almonds. Put the mixture into the prepared cake-tin and bake in the middle of a warm oven (**335° F., Gas 3**) for 1 hr.; reduce to very cool (**290° F., Gas 1**), for last 2 hr.

When cool remove paper and store in a tin for 2–3 weeks. Cover with almond paste and royal icing.

NOTE: One pouring coating of royal icing will be sufficient, using 1¼ lb. icing sugar.

**Cooking time—3 hr.**

## CHRISTMAS PUDDING (1)

*Pouding de Noël*

**6 oz. finely-chopped suet**
**6 oz. raisins, stoned and halved**
**6 oz. sultanas**
**6 oz. currants**
**1½ oz. whole almonds**
**3 oz. plain flour**
**Pinch of salt**
**¼ teasp. grated nutmeg**
**3 oz. breadcrumbs**
**6 oz. moist brown sugar**
**3 oz. chopped candied peel**
**Grated rind of 1 lemon**
**2 eggs**
**1 small wineglass brandy, sherry, stout *or* fruit juice (optional)**
**A little milk**

Grease two 1½ pt. basins; finely chop or shred the suet, clean the fruit, blanch, skin and chop the almonds.

Sift the flour, salt and nutmeg into a mixing bowl. Add the breadcrumbs, suet, sugar, dried fruit, peel, grated lemon rind and almonds. Beat the eggs well, and stir them and the flavouring (if used) into the mixture. Add milk and mix to a soft dropping consistency. Put the mixture into the basins; cover; steam for 5–6 hr.

## CHRISTMAS PUDDING (2)—FRUITARIAN

## PLUM PUDDING (Without suet)

**½ lb. figs**
**8 oz. peeled sweet almonds**
**4 oz. shelled Brazil nuts**
**4 oz. pine kernels**
**4 oz. currants**
**8 oz. raisins, stoned and halved**
**4 oz. sultanas**
**2 small cooking apples**
**1 teasp. mixed spice**
**4 oz. moist brown sugar**
**½ lb. breadcrumbs**
**4 oz. chopped candied peel**
**Pinch of salt**
**Rind and juice of 1 large lemon**
**4 oz. butter *or* margarine**
**4 oz. honey**
**3 eggs**

Grease two 1½ pt. basins. Wash, chop (or mince) the figs; chop the nuts; prepare the dried fruit; core, peel and chop the apples.

Mix together the fruit, nuts, spice, sugar, breadcrumbs, candied peel, salt and grated lemon rind. Warm the butter and honey together. Beat the eggs and add them to the butter and honey. Stir into the dry ingredients. Add the lemon juice and stir well to thoroughly mix the ingredients. Put the mixture into the basins; cover. Boil for 3 hr.

**12 helpings**

## CHRISTMAS PUDDING (3)—RICH

**10 oz. sultanas**
**10 oz. currants**
**½ lb. raisins**
**2 oz. sweet almonds (skinned and chopped)**
**1 level teasp. ground ginger**
**½ lb. plain flour**
**Pinch of salt**
**1 lb. soft brown sugar**
**½ lb. mixed finely-chopped candied peel**
**1 level teasp. mixed spice**
**1 level teasp. grated nutmeg**
**½ lb. breadcrumbs**
**10 oz. finely-chopped *or* shredded suet**
**6 eggs**
**½ gill stout**
**Juice of 1 orange**
**1 wineglass brandy**
**½ pt. milk (approx.)**

Grease three 1 pt. pudding basins. Prepare the dried fruit; stone and chop the raisins; chop the nuts.

Sift the flour, salt, spice, ginger and nutmeg into a mixing bowl. Add the sugar, breadcrumbs, suet, fruit, nuts and candied peel. Beat the eggs well and add to them the stout, orange juice and brandy, and stir this into the dry ingredients adding enough milk to make the mixture of a soft dropping consistency. Cover and boil steadily for 6–7 hr. Take the puddings out of the water and cover them with a clean dry cloth and, when cold, store in a cool place until required.

When required, boil the puddings for 1½ hr. before serving.

**3 puddings (each to give 6 medium helpings)**

## CHRISTMAS PUDDING (4)—INEXPENSIVE

**1 apple**
**1 lb. mixed dried fruit (sultanas, currants, raisins)**
**4 oz. plain flour**
**1 oz. self-raising flour**
**6 oz. mixed chopped candied peel**
**Juice and rind of 1 lemon**
**2 eggs**
**Milk to mix**

**Pinch of salt**
**4 oz. breadcrumbs**
**4 oz. moist brown sugar**
**½ lb. shredded suet** ***or*** **finely-chopped suet**
**A little caramel** ***or*** **gravy browning**
**A few drops of almond essence**

Grease two small basins or one large basin; peel, core and chop the apple; prepare the dried fruit.

Sift together the plain flour, self-raising flour and salt into a mixing bowl. Add the breadcrumbs, dried fruit, sugar, suet, candied peel and grated lemon rind. Beat the eggs and milk together and stir them into the dry ingredients with the lemon juice, adding more milk to make the mixture of a soft dropping consistency. Add a little caramel *or* gravy browning to slightly darken the mixture (about a level teasp.), and the almond essence. Mix well in. Turn into the basin, cover and boil for 4 hr.

**12 helpings**

## CHRISTMAS PUDDING SAUCE

**2 eggs**
**⅛ pt. rum** ***or*** **brandy**
**1½ oz. castor sugar**
**⅛ pt. water**

Whisk all the ingredients in a basin placed over a pan of boiling water. Whisk vigorously all the time until the sauce is thick and frothy. Serve at once.

## CHURROS

**½ pt. water**
**4 oz. butter**
**2 oz. sugar**
**Pinch of salt**
**4 oz. flour**
**Vanilla** ***or*** **other flavouring**
**2 eggs**
**Oil for frying**

Put the water in a thick saucepan over heat. Cut butter into pieces and add to water. Add sugar and salt to water. Sift the flour thoroughly. When water boils, remove from heat and stir in the flour and flavouring. Replace over heat and stir vigorously allowing the mixture to cook until it leaves the sides of the pan and does not stick to the spoon. Remove from heat and allow to cool a little. Meanwhile beat the eggs and beat them in a little at a time to the cooled mixture. Put the oil in a deep pan to heat. Put the mixture into a forcing bag with pipe rather less than ½ in. in diameter and when the oil is very hot press out long strips and let them drop into the oil. They will form various twisted shapes. Cook until golden brown, then remove and drain well. Dredge thoroughly with castor sugar.

## CIDER CUP

**1 bottle of cider**
**1 bottle of soda water**
**1 liqueur glass brandy**
**A few thin strips of cucumber rind**
**A few thin strips of lemon rind**
**1 dessertsp. lemon juice**
**1 dessertsp. castor sugar** ***or*** **to taste**

Chill the cider and soda water for ½ hr. Put the brandy, cucumber and lemon rind, lemon juice and sugar into a large jug, add the chilled cider and soda water. Serve at once.

## CLARIFYING FATS

*See Cooking Methods,*

## CLARET DRESSING

**¼ pt. claret**
**1 teasp. lemon juice**
**1 clove of garlic**
**1 teasp. finely-chopped shallot**
**Salt and pepper**

Mix all the ingredients together and leave to stand overnight. Strain and pour over a salad previously tossed in a little salad oil.

## CLEANING FISH

*See Fish*

## CLEAR SHRED ORANGE MARMALADE

**3 lb. Seville oranges**
**2 lemons**
**1 sweet orange**
**6 pt. water**
**Sugar**

Wash the fruit, dry and cut in half. Squeeze out the juice and strain, keeping back pulp and pips. Scrape all the white pith from the skins, using a spoon, and put pips, pulp and white pith into a bowl with 2 pt. water. Shred the peel finely with a sharp knife and put this into another bowl with 4 pt. water and the juice. Leave all to stand 24 hr. Strain the pips, etc., through a muslin bag and tie loosely. Put the bag and strained liquor, the peel and juice into the preserving-pan and bring to simmering point. Simmer for 1½ hr. until the peel is tender. Remove from the heat and squeeze out the muslin bag gently. For a very clear jelly, allow to drip only. Measure 1 lb. sugar to each pint juice and allow the sugar to dissolve completely over a low heat. Bring to the boil and boil rapidly until a set is obtained (20–25 min.). Remove from the heat and cool until a skin forms on the surface. Pour into hot jars and cover immediately.

**Yield—approx. 10 lb.**

## CLEARED JELLIES AS COLD SWEETS

Cleared jelly is filtered through a foam of coagulated egg whites and crushed egg-shells. The pan, whisk and metal jelly-mould to be used must first be scalded. The egg whites are lightly whisked until liquid, then added with the washed and crushed egg-shells to the cooled jelly. The mixture is heated steadily and whisked constantly until a good head of foam is produced and the contents of the pan are hot but not quite boiling. The albumen in the egg-whites and egg-shells coagulates at 160° F., and as the hardened particles rise to the surface they carry with them all the insoluble substances with which they come in contact, forming a thick "crust" of foam. The correct temperature is reached when the foam begins to set, and care must be taken not to break up, by whisking too long, a completely coagulated foam. The whisk is removed, and heating continued to allow the foam "crust" to rise to the top of the pan. The heat is then lowered and the contents of the pan left to settle in a warm place, covered with a lid, for 5–10 minutes. The jelly is then poured through a scalded jelly cloth while the cloth is still hot, into a scalded bowl below. The bowl of strained jelly is replaced with another scalded bowl, and the jelly re-strained very carefully by pouring through the foam "crust" which covers the bottom of the cloth and acts as a filter. If the jelly is not clear and brilliant when a little is taken up in a highly-polished spoon, the filtering must be repeated immediately.

The filtering is most easily carried out using a jelly bag and stand made for the purpose, but if these are not available the 4 corners of a clean cloth can be tied to the legs of an upturned stool, and a bowl placed below the cloth.

It must be remembered that repeated filtering will cool the jelly considerably and, if done too often, will result in a very poor yield of clear jelly as it will tend to solidify in the cloth. The jelly stand should be placed in a warm position during filtering and draughts should be excluded from the filter by covering the stand with a blanket. A metal container filled with hot water "planted" in the filter will assist in keeping the jelly liquid, but if the filter is at all disturbed by doing this, the resulting jelly will be cloudy, caused by the filter being broken up.

Careful filtering produces a jelly of clear brilliance, a necessary quality for lining moulds and setting decorations and fruit.

### Moulds for Cleared Jellies

All moulds must be scrupulously clean, and should be scalded, as the merest trace of grease may cause cloudiness.

### Lining a Mould

To line a mould thinly and evenly with jelly, it is essential that it should be rotated quickly; therefore it is better to choose a round mould and to prepare a bed of crushed ice, into which the mould is set on its side in such a position that it can be "spun" by the thumbs. Care must be taken to prevent ice from entering the mould during spinning.

The jelly should be cold but liquid, and enough should be used to coat the side from the base to the lip—two to three tablespoonfuls. Surplus jelly should be drained from the mould while still liquid, otherwise a ridge will form in the lining. Two thin coats are preferable to one thick one, and, as speed is essential in acquiring a thin coat, spinning should be practised with an empty mould.

### Decorating a Mould

Decorations may be placed in the base or on the lined sides of a mould, and must be covered by another thin coating of jelly before the "filling" is put in, otherwise, when the mould is turned out, they will appear to have sunk into the filling.

When the sides of the mould are set, use a teaspoon to place jelly in the base. On no account should jelly be poured into the mould, as bubbles of air can very easily be entrapped and appear as holes when the jelly is turned out. Any bubbles which do form should be gently lifted out with a teaspoon.

Decorations should be chosen for their colour contrast, or if they are decorating a cream, they can indicate the flavour of the cream filling. In either case, they must be very neatly cut. Pistachio nuts, blanched, skinned and cut into thin slices, give a clear bright green trefoil shape ideal for leaves. Angelica, on the other hand, is almost invisible because it is translucent. If this is used, it must be cut rather thickly to be effective. Candied and glacé fruits, too, are not always colourful enough. But the black skin of prunes and the red and yellow of plums and apricots are very effective if cut into tiny petals, rounds and diamonds. Each piece of decoration is dipped into cold liquid jelly before being set in place. Two hat-pins will be found most suitable for this meticulous work.

**Filling the Mould**

Moulds should always be filled to the brim, and if when moulding a cream there is insufficient cream to do this, the space should be filled with jelly. The reason for this is that when the mould is jerked to release its filling a "drop" of a mere half-inch may be enough to break the delicate texture.

**To Unmould Jellies**

*See Unmoulding Jellies and Creams.*

**To Chop Jelly**

Chopped jelly used as a decoration must be very clear and be chopped cleanly with a wet knife on wet greaseproof paper so that the light is refracted from the cut surfaces as from the facets of a jewel. The more coarsely the jelly is chopped, the better is the effect, for whilst large pieces refract the light, finely-chopped jelly has a slightly opaque appearance.

## COATING BATTERS

*See Batters for Coating.*

## COCIDO

**1 lb. smoked pork *or* home-cured bacon**
**1 cabbage heart**
**1 green pepper**
**1 lb. butter beans *or* haricot *or* any other dried beans, soaked**
**6 carrots**
**6 small onions**
**2 small turnips**
**6 tomatoes**
**¼ lb. rice *or* dried peas *or* lentils**
**Salt**
**2 qt. water**

Cut the pork into cubes and put into a thick pan. Add the beans. Chop the carrots, onions and turnips and add to the pan. Shred in strips the cabbage and green pepper and add. Slice the tomatoes and add. Sprinkle in the rice, peas or lentils, and add salt to taste. Cover with the water and simmer gently for about 3 hr., making sure that the lid of the pan is tight.

NOTE: If fresh peas or beans are used they should be added about half way through the cooking. There are many variations served in Spain, and chicken, cooked sausage, game and any seasonable vegetables may be used but some sort of pork and beans are typical.

**6 helpings**

## COCK-A-LEEKIE or COCKIE-LEEKIE

**1 small boiling fowl**
**¼ lb. prunes**
**Salt and pepper**
**1 lb. leeks**

Soak the prunes 12 hr. in ½ pt. water. Clean the fowl and truss it, wash the giblets, scald and skin the feet. Put the fowl, giblets and sufficient cold water to cover them in a pan, bring very slowly to simmering point, add 2 teasp. salt. Wash and trim the leeks thoroughly and cut them into thin rings. Add the leeks to the broth after 1 hr. cooking and simmer for 2–3 hr. more. Half an hour before serving add the soaked prunes; simmer till they are just tender but not broken. Lift out the fowl and the giblets and feet. Cut some of the flesh of the fowl into small cubes and return these to the broth. (The rest of the bird may be served with a suitable sauce as a separate course). Season the broth carefully and serve it with the prunes.

**Cooking time—3 hr.**

## COCOA AND CHOCOLATE

Cocoa is prepared from the seeds of *Theobroma cacao*, a tree grown in South America, Africa, West Indies and Asia. Chocolate was introduced into Europe by the

Spaniards, and it reached England during the latter half of the seventeenth century. Columbus brought it to Europe in 1520. Cocoa possesses to some extent the stimulating properties of tea and coffee, but it differs from them in that it also contains a considerable amount of fat and albuminous matter. It is, as its name implies, food as well as drink.

**To make cocoa**

Allow 1½ teasp. cocoa to ¼ pt. milk and ¼ pt water. Mix the cocoa smoothly with a little cold water, boil the remainder of the water and the milk, and pour these on the blended cocoa, stirring well.

**To make Drinking Chocolate**

Various proprietary brands of powdered chocolate are now on the market, which when mixed with hot milk or milk and water provide a nourishing drink. Alternatively, grated block chocolate may be substituted for powdered chocolate. Sweeten and use in the same proportions as proprietary brands of powdered chocolate.

### COCONUT BUNS

*See Buns or Cookies*

### COCONUT CAKES, SMALL

*See Rich Cakes, Small, Various.*

### COCONUT CONES

**2 egg whites**
**5 oz. castor sugar**
**5–6 oz. desiccated coconut**
**1 teasp. ground rice *or* semolina**

Beat the egg whites stiffly, stir in the other ingredients. Make into small cone shapes or, if desired, pack the mixture into wet egg-cups and turn out on to a greased baking-sheet. Bake in a cool oven **(310° F., Gas 2)** until fawn colour.

NOTE: If desired, cones may be coloured pink by adding carmine to egg whites while whisking.

**12–14 cones**

### COCONUT CREAM PIE

**6 oz. semi-sweet biscuits**
**2 level teasp. castor sugar**
**2 oz. butter *or* margarine**
**1 level tablesp. golden syrup**

FILLING

**¾ pt. milk**
**3 oz. cornflour**
**Pinch of salt**
**2 oz. sugar**
**1 egg yolk**
**1 oz. butter**
**Few drops of vanilla essence**
**1½ cups shredded coconut**

Crisp biscuits in the oven if necessary. Crumble finely. To make pie shell: cream together fat, sugar and syrup. Gradually work in the biscuit crumbs. Press the mixture firmly on the bottom and round the sides of a 7-in. shallow pie-dish.

To make the filling: put the milk on to boil. Sift cornflour and salt, add sugar and mix with a little cold milk. Stir into the hot milk and cook slowly until thick, stirring constantly. Put into a basin placed over boiling water or in the top of a double boiler, cover and cook for a further 5 min. Add the lightly beaten egg yolk slowly and cook for 1 min. Add the butter, stir in vanilla to taste, and coconut. Allow to cool then turn into the pie shell. Place in refrigerator and leave until set.

### COCONUT CUSTARD PIE

**Plain pastry using 6 oz. flour, etc.**
**4 eggs**
**6 oz. sugar**
**Salt**
**1 cup shredded coconut**
**3 cups milk**

Line a 9-in. deep pie-plate with pastry, making a high raised rim. Beat the eggs well. Mix together eggs, sugar and salt. Gradually stir in milk. Add shredded coconut. Pour into pastry-lined pie-plate and bake in hot oven **(425° F., Gas 7)** for 10 min., then reduce heat to moderate **(350° F., Gas 4)** for 25–30 min.

### COCONUT PUDDING

*Pouding de Noix de Coco*

**6 oz. flour**
**Pinch of salt**
**1 rounded teasp. baking-powder**
**2 oz. butter *or* margarine**
**2 oz. sugar**
**2 oz. desiccated coconut**
**1 egg**
**Milk to mix**

Grease a 1½ pt. pudding basin. Sift together the flour, salt and baking-powder. Rub in the fat and add the sugar and coconut. Mix to a soft dropping consistency with the beaten egg and milk. Put the pudding mixture into the basin and cover with a piece of greased paper. Steam for 1½–2 hr.

**4–6 helpings**

## COD À LA MAÎTRE D'HÔTEL

*Cabillaud à la Maître d'Hôtel*

**2 lb. cod (cold remains can be used)**
**4 oz. butter**
**1 teasp. finely-chopped onion**
**1 teasp. finely-chopped parsley**
**Juice of ½ lemon**
**Pepper and salt**

Poach the cod, and afterwards remove skin and bone and separate the flesh into large flakes. Melt the butter in a saucepan, add the onion, and fry for 2–3 min. without browning. Add the parsley, lemon juice, a good pinch of pepper, salt and the fish. Heat until quite hot, shaking gently all the time, then serve.

**5–6 helpings**
**Cooking time—30–40 min.**

## COD À LA PROVENÇALE

**2 lb. middle cut cod (approx.)**
**Salt and pepper**
**½ pt. Velouté *or* other rich white sauce**
**1 gill white stock**
**2 small shallots**
**A small bunch of parsley**
**Bouquet garni**
**1 egg yolk**
**2 oz. butter**
**1 teasp. anchovy paste**
**1 teasp. chopped parsley**
**2 teasp. capers**

Wash and wipe the fish well and place in a saucepan. Season with pepper and salt, and add the sauce, stock, finely-chopped shallots, bunch of parsley and the bouquet garni. Simmer slowly until the fish is done, basting occasionally. Remove the fish to a hot dish, and keep it warm. Reduce the sauce until the desired consistency is obtained. Remove the herbs, add the egg yolk, work in the butter, and pass through a strainer. Return to a smaller saucepan, add the anchovy paste, chopped parsley and capers, stir over heat for a few minutes but do not allow to boil, then pour over the fish.

**5–6 helpings**
**Cooking time—35–40 min.**

## COD STEAKS

*Tranches de Cabillaud*

**Four 4–6 oz. cod steaks**
**Fat for frying**
**Flour**
**Salt and pepper**
**Parsley**

Make a rather thin batter of flour and water, season well with salt and pepper. Melt sufficient clarified fat or dripping in a frying-pan to form a layer about ½ in. deep. Wipe the fish, dip each piece separately in the batter, place these at once in the hot fat, and fry until light-brown, turning once during the process. Drain well, and serve garnished with crisply-fried parsley. If preferred, the fish may be coated with egg and breadcrumbs and fried in deep fat.

Serve with anchovy or tomato sauce.

**4 helpings**

## CODDLED EGG

**1 new-laid egg**

Place the egg in boiling water, put on the lid, and let the saucepan stand for 7–8 min. where the water will keep hot without simmering.

An egg cooked in this manner is more easily digested than when boiled in the ordinary way.

**1 helping**

## CODFISH BALLS

**1 lb. codfish**
**3 lb. potatoes**
**2 eggs**
**1 tablesp. margarine**
**Pinch of pepper**
**Juice of Bermuda onion**
**Breadcrumbs**
**Deep fat for frying**

Soak fish for 3–8 hr. Shred, then simmer for 10 min. Boil potatoes and when cooked mash with a fork. Add fish, 1 beaten egg and margarine, pepper and the onion juice. Mix well. Roll into balls and dip in egg and breadcrumbs. Fry in deep fat.

**6 helpings**
**Time—½ hr. (approx.)**

## COD'S ROE

*Laitance de Cabillaud*

**1 lb. cod's roe**
**Salt**
**Vinegar**
**Melted butter sauce *or* other white sauce**
**A little milk *or* cream**
**Brown breadcrumbs**

Wash and wipe the cod's roe and poach for 10 min. in water with a little salt and vinegar. Dice the roe and put into melted butter sauce or other white sauce diluted with a little cream or milk. Butter 3–4 scallop shells, put in the roe, cover with brown breadcrumbs and brown in the oven, or serve on hot buttered toast.

**3–4 helpings**

### COFFEE CREAM

*Crème au Café*

| | |
|---|---|
| **3 egg yolks *or* 1 whole egg and 1 yolk** | **4 tablesp. water** |
| **2–3 oz. castor sugar** | **2–3 teasp. coffee essence** |
| **½ pt. milk** | **½ pt. double cream** |
| **½ oz. gelatine** | |

Beat the eggs and sugar until liquid. Heat the milk almost to boiling point and pour over the egg mixture. Strain the egg and milk back into the pan, and cook gently until thick, stirring all the time. Allow to cool. Soak the gelatine in the water for 5 min., then heat to dissolve. Stir the coffee essence into the cooled custard, and add the dissolved gelatine, stirring again as it cools. Whip the cream and fold lightly into the custard mixture just before setting. Pour into a prepared mould or into glass dishes.

**6 helpings**
**Setting time—1–2 hr.**

### COFFEE

According to legend coffee was discovered about 1200 years ago by a young goat-herd in Arabia, who noticed that his goats became more lively after eating the berries and leaves of a certain tree. In 1570, coffee became firmly established as the most popular beverage in Arabia and Turkey, from whence it soon spread to Europe. It was brought to London by Daniel Edwards, a merchant, whose servant, Pasqua Rosee, a Greek, was trained in the art of roasting and preparing it. This servant, under the patronage of Edwards, established the first coffee-house in London.

#### To Make Coffee

To make perfect coffee the beans should be roasted and ground just before they are to be used. When this is impracticable, it is better to buy the beans and grind only as many as are required for immediate use. The beans should be stored in an airtight container. If a coffee mill is not available, buy only a small quantity of ground coffee at a time (to avoid loss of flavour) and store it in an airtight container.

Allow 2 heaped dessertsp. coffee (or 2 of the coffee measuring spoons sponsored by the Coffee Publicity Association) and ½ pt. freshly boiled water for each person. Some people also add a pinch of salt.

*Method 1*: Warm an ordinary china jug, put in the ground coffee, pour on to it the boiling water, and stir vigorously. Allow the jug to stand for 1 min., then skim off any floating coffee grains, stand for a further 4 min., closely covered, where the contents will remain just below boiling-point. The coffee can then be poured slowly or strained into another warmed china jug and used at once.

*Method 2*: Put the coffee with the water into an enamel saucepan and bring almost to the boil. Reduce the heat and simmer very gently for 3 min. Dash in 1 teasp. cold water to help the grounds to settle. Strain into a warmed coffee pot or jug.

*Method 3*: Use a percolator and fine- or medium-ground coffee. Into the percolator put as much fresh cold water as is required and bring to the boil. Put the coffee into the basket and insert it in the percolator, cover, and return to heat. Allow to percolate *gently* for 6–8 min.

*Method 4*: The vacuum method. The equipment for this method consists of 2 containers plus a source of heat. Put the required amount of cold water into the lower container and place on the heat. Put the filter in the upper container and the required amount of fine- or medium-ground coffee, in the upper container. Allow the water in the lower container to boil, then reduce heat (if electric switch off) then insert upper bowl with a slight twist to ensure a tight fit. Some vacuum models can be assembled completely before placing on the heat. When the water has risen into the upper container (some water will always remain in the lower container) stir well. In 1–3 min. (fine-ground coffee will require the shorter time) turn off heat; remove electric models from unit. When all the coffee has been drawn into the lower container, remove upper container and serve.

*Method 5: Café filtre.* Heat a coffee pot or individual cups, place the finely-ground coffee in the strainer over the coffee pot and slowly pour over freshly-boiled water and allow to drip through. When the water has dripped through remove strainer—if the coffee is not strong enough filter again.

Equipment for making coffee should always be kept scrupulously clean.

Coffee may be served black (*Café Noir*) or with milk (*Café au Lait*) or with cream (*Café Crème*). When serving *Café au Lait* it is usual to pour the 2 liquids into the cup at the same time. *The milk should be hot but not boiled.*

Liqueurs such as Kirsch, Cognac or liqueur brandy, as well as one or two of the following: Bénédictine, Chartreuse, Kümmel, Curaçao, Cherry Brandy or other sweet liqueur are often served with coffee at formal dinners.

There are several patent coffee powders on the market with which one can make a quick cup of coffee. Full instructions for their use are printed on the tin. Coffee is also sold in liquid form.

*To make iced coffee:* Make the coffee in the usual way, put into a closely-covered non-metal container, then chill for not *more* than 3 hr. in a refrigerator. Chill the milk separately. Just before serving add milk to coffee, sweeten to taste, mix in a shaker or beat with a whisk.

*To make burnt coffee:* Allow 3 good teasp. coffee to each ½ pt. water, and prepare according to any of the preceding methods. Sweeten it rather more than ordinarily, and strain into small cups. Pour a little brandy into each over a spoon, set fire to it, and when the spirit is partly consumed the flame should be blown out, and the coffee drunk immediately.

## COFFEE ICE CREAM (1)

*Glace Crème au Café*

**½ pt. cream**
**½ pt. custard**
**2 tablesp. liquid coffee**
**2 oz. castor sugar**

Half whip the cream. Add the custard, coffee and sugar. Mix well. Chill and freeze.

**6 helpings**

## COFFEE ICE CREAM (2)

**3 teasp. instant coffee**
**½ gill hot water**
**½ pt. cream**
**3 oz. castor sugar**

Dissolve the coffee in the hot water. Cool. Half whip the cream and add castor sugar. Fold in the dissolved coffee. Chill and freeze.

**6 helpings**
**Time—2½ hr.**

## COFFEE LAYER CAKE

**4 oz. butter**
***or* margarine**
**4 oz. castor sugar**
**2 eggs**
**8 oz. plain flour**
**1 teasp. baking-powder**
**2 teasp. soluble coffee powder**
**3 tablesp. milk**

MOCHA ICING

**2 teasp. soluble coffee powder**
**2 oz. chocolate**
**4 tablesp. water**
**3 oz. butter *or* margarine**
**1 lb. icing sugar**

DECORATION

**Almonds**

Cream the fat and sugar until very light and add the eggs one at a time with a dessertsp. of flour—beat well. Sift the flour, baking-powder and coffee powder and fold lightly into the mixture with the milk. Pour into 2 greased sandwich tins and spread evenly. Bake in a fairly hot oven (**375° F., Gas 5**) for 35-40 min. until firm. Cool.

*To make the mocha icing:* dissolve coffee powder and grated chocolate in the almost boiling water. Cream the margarine and 2 tablesp. of the sugar. Beat well. Add the rest of the sugar and liquid alternately, beating until it is smooth and easy to spread.

Cut the two cakes across in half, and sandwich the halves together with some of the icing, spreading the rest of the icing on the top and sides and frost or "rough up" with a fork. Decorate with blanched almonds.

## COFFEE SAUCE

*Sauce au Café*

**¼ pt. very strong coffee**
**1 egg yolk**
**Sugar to taste**

| | |
|---|---|
| **¼ pt. milk** | **Vanilla essence (optional)** |
| **1 heaped teasp. cornflour *or* custard powder** | **1 teasp. rum (optional)** |

Thicken the coffee and milk with the cornflour or custard powder (*see Cornflour Sauce*). Cool the sauce, add the egg yolk and cook it without boiling. Sweeten and flavour to taste.

### COFFEE WHIP

*Gelée de Café fouettée*

| | |
|---|---|
| **1 pt. milk** | **¾ oz. gelatine soaked and dissolved in 4 tablesp. water** |
| **1 tablesp. coffee essence** | **1–2 egg whites (optional)** |
| **Sugar to taste** | |

DECORATION

**Chopped nuts**

Heat together the milk, coffee essence and sugar. Heat the gelatine in the water until dissolved then cool slightly. Add to the cooled coffee-flavoured milk. Whisk strongly. If egg whites are used, whisk them until liquid and slightly frothy, and stir into the cool jelly just before whisking. When thick, pile into a dish and scatter chopped nuts over the top.

**6 helpings**
**Cooking time—10 min.**
**Setting time—½ hr.**

### COLD BUTTERMILK SOUP (SWEET)—SCANDINAVIAN

| | |
|---|---|
| **3 pt. buttermilk** | **Grated rind of ½ lemon** |
| **2 egg yolks** | **Whipped cream** |
| **3 tablesp. sugar** | |
| **A little lemon juice** | |

Put the egg yolks in the soup tureen, add the sugar and stir well for at least 5 min. till white and frothy. Add the lemon juice and rind. Pour in the buttermilk, whipping briskly. Put on ice. Just before serving add the whipped cream.

**6 helpings**

### COLD COOKERY

Today, cold cookery usually involves using a refrigerator.

Many refrigerator recipes require no cooking at all. Others call for preliminary cooking before freezing or chilling the prepared dish.

For instructions on making ice cream in a refrigerator, *see Ices.* For other cold dishes, see the recipe in the text for the type or flavour of dish required.

### COLD SWEETS

*See Sweet Dishes.*

### COLE SLAW

| | |
|---|---|
| **1 small white cabbage** | **1 tablesp. flour** |
| **¼ pt. vinegar** | **Pinch of salt** |
| **½ oz. butter** | **1 egg** |
| **1 teasp. celery seed** | |

Shred the cabbage finely, discarding stalk and outer leaves. Warm the vinegar and butter, put in the cabbage, sprinkle in the celery seed, flour and salt, and cook gently for a few minutes. Add lightly beaten egg, stir and cook for 3–4 min. Cool, chill in refrigerator.

**3–4 helpings**

### COLLEGE PUDDING

*Pouding de Collège*

| | |
|---|---|
| **4 oz. flour** | **3 oz. finely-chopped suet** |
| **½ teasp. baking-powder** | **3 oz. castor sugar** |
| **Pinch of salt** | **2 oz. currants** |
| **½ teasp. mixed spice** | **2 oz. sultanas** |
| **4 oz. breadcrumbs** | **1–2 eggs** |
| | **1 gill milk (approx.)** |

Grease 6–7 dariole moulds. Sift together the flour, baking-powder, salt and spice. Add the breadcrumbs, suet, sugar, currants and sultanas, and mix well together. Well beat the eggs. Add to the dry ingredients and mix to a soft dropping consistency, adding milk as required. Half-fill the moulds with the mixture. Bake in fairly hot oven (**375° F., Gas 5**) for about 25 min.; *or* cover with greased paper and steam for 35–40 min.

Serve with wine-, orange-, brandy- or custard-sauce.

### COLLOPS OF VEAL

*Paupiettes de Veau*

| | |
|---|---|
| **1½ lb. fillet of veal** | **Butter *or* fat for frying** |
| **6 bacon rashers** | **¾ oz. flour** |
| **Salt and pepper** | **½ pt. stock *or* water** |
| **4 oz. veal forcemeat** | **1 tablesp. lemon juice** |
| **Egg and breadcrumbs** | **Pinch of ground mace** |

GARNISH

**Slices of lemon** **Fried forcemeat balls**
**Parsley**

Cut the meat into very thin strips about 3 in. by 2 in. After removing the rind place the bacon rashers on a board and stretch with a palette knife. Cover each piece of meat with a piece of bacon, season well, spread lightly with forcemeat and roll up. Coat with egg and breadcrumbs and fry gently in hot fat. If forcemeat balls are to be used for the garnish, fry them at the same time. Drain well and keep hot. Pour away surplus fat, leaving about ¾ oz. in the pan and any sediment. Add the flour and cook until light brown. Add boiling stock or water, lemon juice, a pinch of mace and seasoning to taste and simmer gently for 5 min., then strain. Arrange the collops on a hot dish.

Garnish with sliced lemon, sprigs of parsley and fried forcemeat balls. Serve the sauce separately.

**6 helpings**

## CONFECTIONERS' CUSTARD

**½ pt. milk**
**¾ oz. cornflour**
**2 yolks *or* 1 whole egg**
**1 oz. sugar**
**½ teasp. vanilla essence**

Blend the cornflour with the milk, stir in the egg yolks and sugar, and cook over a gentle heat until thick. Beat in the vanilla. Allow to cool.

## CONGER EEL PIE

*Pâté de Congre*

**1 small conger eel**
**Salt and pepper**
**1 teasp. finely-chopped onion**
**1 teasp. powdered mixed herbs**
**1 teasp. finely-chopped parsley**
**1 tablesp. vinegar**
**Rough puff *or* puff pastry, using 4 oz. flour, etc.**

Wash and dry the fish thoroughly, remove all skin and bones and cut into neat pieces. Place in layers in a pie-dish, sprinkling each layer with salt, pepper, onion, herbs and parsley. Add water to ¾ fill the dish and mix with it the vinegar. Cover the pie-dish with pastry and bake in a very hot oven (**450° F., Gas 8**) until pastry is set then reduce heat to moderate (**350° F., Gas 4**).

Serve either hot or cold.

**6–8 helpings** **Cooking time—about ¾–1 hr.**

## CONSOMMÉ AUX BETTERAVES

Clear Beetroot Soup

**1 qt. first white stock**
**1 small raw beetroot**
**1 small onion, scalded**
**1 stick of celery**
**1 egg white**
**4 peppercorns**
**Salt**
**½ glass sherry**
**A few drops of carmine**

GARNISH

**1 steamed egg white**

Prepare the vegetables as usual, peeling the beetroot and cutting it into thick slices. Put all ingredients except sherry and carmine into a pan and clear as for consommé with egg Steam the egg white for garnish in a small greased basin till just firm, cut it into tiny dice or fancy shapes, rinse these in hot water. Tint the soup clear pink, add the sherry and the garnish and serve. Hand separately sour cream or yoghourt.

**4–6 helpings**
**Cooking time as for consommé**

## CONSOMMÉ À LA CELESTINE

Clear Soup with Cheese Pancakes

**1 qt. consommé**

CHEESE PANCAKE BATTER

**½ oz. flour**
**½ teasp. melted butter**
**½ teasp. grated Parmesan cheese**
**1 teasp. chopped parsley**
**½ beaten egg**
**⅛ pt. milk**
**Salt and pepper**

Make a pancake batter with the ingredients. Fry very thin pancakes in the usual way and rinse them in hot water. Cut them in short strips ¼ in. wide, and serve them in the hot consommé.

**6 helpings**

## CONSOMMÉ À LA DUBARRY

Clear Soup Dubarry style

**1 qt. consommé made from first chicken stock**

GARNISH

| | |
|---|---|
| **4 chopped Jordan almonds** | **Salt and pepper** |
| **Royal custard** *See Soups.* | **1 tablesp. tiny sprigs cauliflower** |
| | **½ oz. Patna rice** |

Add the blanched and finely-chopped almonds to the royal custard; season carefully. Steam the custard, cut it into ⅛-in. dice. Boil the cauliflower sprigs in salted water till just done. Wash, blanch and boil rice; drain it. Add all garnishes to the boiling consommé and serve.

**6 helpings**

## CONSOMMÉ À L'INDIENNE or CONSOMMÉ À LA MULLIGATAWNY

Clear Mulligatawny soup

| | |
|---|---|
| **1 qt. first brown stock** | **1 small apple** |
| **2 level tablesp. curry powder** | **1 egg white** |
| **1 small onion** | **Juice of ½ lemon** |
| | **Salt** |

GARNISH

**2 oz. cubes of cooked chicken**

Mix the curry powder with a little of the stock. Add the peeled, chopped onion and apple with the curry paste and egg white to the stock. Clear the stock without whisking surface. Flavour the consommé to taste with lemon juice and salt. It is as well to make certain that the curry flavour is strong enough during the clearing process as no curry powder can be added later. Heat the dice of chicken for a few minutes in the consommé before serving.

**6 helpings**

## CONSOMMÉ FRAPPÉ

Iced clear soup

Iced consommé may be made from either beef or chicken stock, in either case veal bones added to the stock will give a better jellied result. To serve it iced, the stock is cleared in the usual way and must be most carefully seasoned, it is then allowed to cool, sherry is added and finally it should be put in a refrigerator or packed into a colander with ice for 1–2 hr. before serving. It should be a soft jelly.

*Consomme a la Madrilene*

SUITABLE GARNISHES:

**Chopped parsley, chives and tarragon** *or* **chervil to taste**
*or* **tiny dice of raw cucumber**
*or* **chopped hard-boiled egg white**
*or* **small squares of the fleshy part of scalded tomato**

To serve consommé frappé the jelly should be lightly whipped so that it is not quite solid, and served with its garnish in soup cups.

See also consommé aux Betteraves, Consommé Carmen (without the rice) and Consommé Madrilène which are very refreshing iced.

## CONSOMMÉ À LA JULIENNE

**1 qt. consommé**

GARNISH

| | |
|---|---|
| **1 tablesp. shreds of carrot** | **1 tablesp. shreds of green leek** |
| **1 tablesp. shreds of turnip** | |

Cut the shreds $\frac{1}{16}$ in. thick and 1–1¼ in. long. Boil them separately for a few minutes till just tender, drain them and put them into the soup tureen, pour on to them the hot consommé.

**6 helpings**

## CONSOMMÉ À LA MADRILÈNE

| | |
|---|---|
| **1 qt. first brown stock** | **1 bay leaf** |
| **1 lb. tomatoes** | **¼–½ lb. lean beef** |
| **1 green pepper** | **1 egg white** |
| **1 clove of garlic** | **1 carrot** |
| **Parsley stalks** | **1 onion** |
| **Thyme** | **1 stick of celery** |

Cut up the tomatoes and green pepper. Tie the herbs together in a small piece of muslin. Shred and soak the beef in ¼ pt. water. Whip the egg white slightly. Put all ingredients into a pan and simmer very gently for 1 hr. Strain as usual. To garnish cut tiny dice from the firm flesh of skinned tomato, 2 tablesp. to the quart.

Serve the consommé hot or iced; if iced it should be almost liquid and may therefore need whisking a little.

**6 helpings**

## CONSOMMÉ DE QUEUE DE BOEUF

Clear Oxtail soup

**1 ox tail**
**1 lb. shin of beef**
**3 qt. water**
**1 carrot**
**1 onion**
**1 stick of celery**
**1 blade of mace**
**6 peppercorns**
**3 teasp. salt**
**1 egg white**
**Sherry (optional)**

GARNISH

**Small rounds from the thin end of the tail**
**1 tablesp. tiny dice of carrot**

Joint the tail, remove solid fat, cover the tail with cold water, bring to the boil, drain and rinse it. Make the stock with the water and vegetables in the usual way, season. Take the required amount of stock and a few pieces of the thin end of the tail for the soup; keep the rest of the tail and stock for other dishes. Clear the measured stock with the egg white, and strain Add sherry to taste. Cook the diced carrot separately and add with the pieces of tail to the boiling consommé.

## CONSOMMÉ ROSÉ

Pink clear soup

**4 raw beetroots**
**Sugar**
**1 qt. water *or* stock**
**3 carrots**
**1 stick of celery**
**1½ lb. tomatoes *or* 1 large can of tomatoes**
**1 onion**
**1 bay leaf**
**1 clove garlic**
**1 clove**
**1 egg white**
**Salt and pepper**

Scrub and peel the beetroots, slice and sugar them and cook in the water or stock till soft, then lift them out to be used in salad. Cool the stock, add the other vegetables and spices. Beat the egg white and add to the stock. Bring slowly to simmering point and simmer very gently for 1 hr. Strain through a linen cloth. Season and reheat.

This soup may be served hot or cold. If cold, ¼ oz. gelatine should be dissolved in a little stock and added to the whole before cooling.

**6 helpings**

## CONSOMMÉ AUX TOMATES

Clear tomato soup

**1 qt. consommé with 2 large tomatoes added during clearing**

GARNISH

**Tiny dice of vegetable, if liked**

The brown stock is cleared in the usual way with the addition of the tomatoes cut in small pieces. The long method of clearing the stock should be used for greater flavour. Add the vegetables to the boiling consommé.

**6 helpings**

## CONSOMMÉ VERT

Clear Green soup

**1 qt. white *or* chicken stock**
**2 tomatoes**
**A bunch of green herbs: marjoram, thyme, basil**
**1 egg white**

GARNISH

**1 tablesp. shreds of lettuce**
**1 tablesp. shreds of spinach *or* sorrel**
**1 tablesp. small green peas**
**1 dessertsp. shreds of cucumber rind**
**6 leaves of mint**
**6 leaves of chives**
**Lemon juice**
**½ glass dry white wine (optional)**
**A few leaves of chervil**

Skin and dice the flesh of the tomatoes. Add with the herbs to the boiling stock. Clear as for consommé with the egg white .

Cook the well shredded vegetables and the green peas separately in a little boiling stock till just tender. Chop the mint and the chives. Have the consommé boiling and to it add the cooked shredded leaves and peas with the stock in which they were cooked. Reheat for 1 min. only. Immediately before serving add a little lemon juice, the wine and the mint and chives. Float on the top of each portion of consommé one leaf of chervil.

**6–8 helpings**
**Time—to cook garnish, about 20 min.**

**COOKIES**

*See Buns or Cookies*

**COOKING METHODS**

There are two basic methods of cooking food:

(*a*) in water

(*b*) in fat.

Either may be a constituent of the food itself, or may be added as a cooking medium.

The water methods include boiling, poaching, stewing and steaming.

Cooking in fat aims at producing a crisp, dry-surfaced food, and is therefore usually described as cooking by "dry" methods.

### Cooking in Water

**Boiling**

This means "bubbling" or ebullition, and actual boiling is only used on rare occasions, such as for the deliberate evaporation of sugar syrups, meat stock when making a fumet or glaze, chutneys and sauces. Also when cooking rice and Italian pasta to be served whole and well drained, when plenty of water should be used for evaporation and absorption. Green vegetables should also be cooked as quickly as possible, but in only sufficient depth of water to provide steam, and with a lid firmly in place.

All foods should be put into water at 212° F., with perhaps the possible exception of old potatoes, which tend to cook too quickly on the outside. The use of hot water shortens cooking time, saves fuel and helps to impart stronger colour and flavour to food.

The rate of boiling must be adjusted to the structure of the food.

**Stewing**

This term is used when food is cooked slowly in a small quantity of water or other liquid, either in the oven or on top of the cooker. "Casserole" cookery involves the use of a sauce as the liquid, as it is not practical to thicken the contents of a casserole after cooking unless it is truly fireproof. Stewing is a very economical method of cooking as all the flavours are retained and the lengthy process renders the toughest food digestible. Thick pans or casseroles with tight lids are essential to prevent evaporation, and seasoning must be done at the beginning. Food to be stewed should be cut into pieces to expose more surface to the moderate heat of the liquor. Birds and rabbits should be jointed, meat cut *across* the fibres, fruit quartered or, if small, left whole. The consistency of the liquor when the dish is ready should be just thick enough to coat the solid ingredients and so keep them moist in the serving dish. They should be visible and not completely submerged in an excessive amount of liquid. Thickening is achieved by the use of blended flour, etc., or by the inclusion of potatoes which fall during cooking.

Approximate proportion of ingredients: 1 lb. meat to $\frac{3}{4}$ pt. water.

*A stew should never be boiled.*

**Steaming**

Here food is cooked in steam from boiling water or from the food itself, in which case it is enclosed in a container surrounded by steam or boiling water. For example, small pieces of food (fish) wrapped in buttered paper may be steamed between two plates over a pan of boiling water, as for invalids. Foods cooked in steam must be covered to protect them from condensing steam, which would make them sodden, and they will require longer cooking than if boiled; usually half as long again. Water providing the steam must be kept boiling and replenished with *boiling* water when necessary, especially for puddings, otherwise they will be heavy.

**Poaching**

The process of poaching is similar to that of boiling, except that the liquid must not bubble and the food is only just submerged, the temperature being just below boiling point.

### Cooking in Fat

**Roasting**

Roasting and grilling are similar methods applied to large and small pieces of food respectively when a quick, fierce heat is used. These methods are suitable only for top quality flesh foods, as these are composed of thin muscle-fibres and even-graining of fine fat, which is quickly released by heat.

The ideal weight of a joint for high temperature roasting is approximately 4 lb. The oven must be hot when the food is put in. Joints which require to be cooked through, such as joints of pork, veal and mutton, will need a reduced temperature after the first ½ hour. Tender joints of beef and lamb should be cooked quickly so that the interior is served pink.

The oven should be pre-heated to 450° F., Gas 8, and the joint should be placed on a trivet in a tin in the middle of the oven. The trivet is necessary to raise the joint from the fat and thus prevent spitting fat splashing the inside of the oven.

Joints lacking in fat such as veal, and poultry, may be kept moist by basting.

**Slow roasting or pot roasting**

This method is used for joints of poor quality meat, when the temperature should not exceed 360° F., Gas 4. The meat is cooked on a trivet in a roasting tin in the oven or on a trivet in a saucepan with a little fat and a *very* small quantity of liquid—either stock or water. It should be covered with a lid or aluminium foil to retain the steam. If the meat is cooked in a pan it may be browned first in hot fat to give it a good colour and flavour. If cooked in the oven, uncover the joint for the last ½ hour. As these joints are cooked at a lower temperature there is less evaporation and therefore more moisture is retained in the tissues of the meat and this helps to soften the coarser muscle-fibres. The inclusion of vegetables (onions) flavours the steam, and the use of strips of green bacon placed over the top of the joint will moisten the flesh, and help to brown the surface.

**Braising**

The method is the same as for slow roasting but the cover is removed half an hour before serving and the heat of the oven increased to allow the top to brown. Alternatively the meat may be fried to brown the surface before being placed in the cooking container. The meat is cooked on a bed of roughly sliced vegetables in a little stock. The layer of vegetables, chosen for flavour, should be sufficiently thick to support the joint above the level of the stock so that the meat is steamed. Bacon rinds, bones, mushroom trimmings and a bouquet garni are used for flavouring the dish, especially immature meat such as veal. After dishing, a suitable accompanying sauce can be produced from the strained vegetable liquor, diluted with water, thickened with blended flour or cornflour and made piquant with tomato purée, wine, cider, etc.

**Grilling or broiling**

This involves the use of a well-heated radiant; charcoal imparts the finest flavour and is used extensively for portable grills and rotisseries in America where barbecue cooking is so popular. For indoors, the electrically operated infra-red grill and rotisserie is considered to be the best equipment yet designed to produce meat of the finest flavour by searing and crisping the outside while retaining all the juices inside. As the food being grilled is spitted, it is essential that it is carefully arranged on the spit so that turning is smooth. If not, the food will not cook evenly and the machine will be strained. Gas and electrically heated fixed grills must be preheated to an even, glowing heat before food is placed under them. Grill-cuts should not be less than 1 inch thick and should be seasoned and brushed with fat before being cooked. Both sides of the food are exposed to the heat to coagulate the surface protein and sear the flesh.

This forms a seal on the outside which retains the juices. Further cooking may entail placing the food further away from the heat to allow it to penetrate more slowly. Food must not be pierced after the seal has formed so two spoons should be used to turn the meat if tongs are not available. Delicate-skinned food, such as fish, may be grilled successfully if wrapped in thickly-greased foil or parchment and placed in the bottom of the grill-pan. This prevents charring of the skin and retains all the juices.

**Frying**

Frying resembles grilling in that only small pieces of food are cooked and the process is quick. In fact, the "pan-broiling" of America is comparable to dry-frying, when the hot pan is used to draw fat from the food. Fats chosen for frying must be capable of being heated to a temperature of 400° F. approximately, without burning or disintegrating. Commercially prepared frying fats, clarified dripping and some vegetable oils are all suitable. ALL fats must be heated slowly so that the heat spreads throughout the depth of fat evenly, or the fat at the bottom of the pan burns before the frying temperature of the whole fat has been reached.

ALL food must be dried before being placed in hot fat, either by shaking in a towel, as for chipped potatoes, or by dusting with seasoned flour, oatmeal, etc., as for oily fish, or by coating with a medium which will dry on contact with hot fat, such as egg and breadcrumbs, batter or pastry. Wet foods, like fish fillets, must be dried with flour before being coated, or the coating may be dislodged by the steam forming underneath it. The choice of a coating depends on the nature of the food and the method of frying. All foods fried in deep fat should be coated unless they are starchy, such as potatoes and doughnuts, to prevent any flavour of them escaping into the fat, so making it unfit for further use.

A pan of deep fat is considerably hotter than shallow fat and food is consequently cooked at a higher temperature. Immediate sealing should prevent adulteration of the fat so that it may be used for many differently-flavoured foods at a time: e.g. fish, apple fritters, cutlets. A frying basket aids the removal of food from deep fat. It should fit loosely in the pan, and must be heated with the fat so that food does not stick to it when put in, and so that it does not cool the fat by being lowered into the pan cold. Never overload the basket; only sufficient food to cover the bottom should be fried at once to avoid cooling the fat too much.

Draining after frying is essential, first over the pan, then on absorbent paper, before dishing on a dish-paper.

The temperature of fat can be tested simply, by frying a cube of day-old bread. If it becomes golden brown in 1 minute, the fat is approximately 360° F., in ½ minute the fat is approximately 380° F. N.B. A fat thermometer must be heated gradually in the fat and cooled slowly after use.

Generally speaking, raw foods are fried at the lower temperature to ensure thorough cooking, and re-heated foods at the higher one as they are merely heated and only the coating is actually cooked. Potato crisps are cooked at the higher temperature, but thicker potato slices, such as are used for soufflé potatoes, need the lower temperature for cooking, followed by immersion in fat at the higher temperature for "puffing" them out.

All fat must be kept clean, otherwise food will taste of impurities, as a little fat is always absorbed. Strain the fat through a fine mesh after each use, and clarify occasionally.

Foods fried in shallow fat must be thin enough for complete cooking merely by being turned over during frying. Turn with spoons to avoid piercing the seal and drain well when lifting from the pan.

**Sautéing**

Sautéing is a French term applied to the practice of shaking food in fat while it is frying. It may be used as a preliminary method of developing the flavour of vegetables for sauces and soups, or as a method of cooking complete in itself, as in the cooking of kidneys. A well-flavoured fat must be used, as it is absorbed: butter, chicken fat rendered down, etc. A lid is used to keep in the steam to assist with the cooking of raw food, but cooked food such as sliced potatoes is usually turned in the melted fat with a fork.

**Baking**

Baking in an oven subjects food to the heat radiated from the walls and top, to convection currents of hot air, and to heat conducted along shelves, baking-sheets and tins, steel skewers, etc., which is a very dry heat. There are occasions when a water bath is included for the purpose of providing insulation against this, as in baked custard.

## COOLGARDIE STEW—AUSTRALIAN

**1½ lb. topside steak**
**2 hard-boiled eggs**
**1 onion**
**1 heaped tablesp. flour**
**Salt**
**Cayenne pepper *or* curry powder**
**1 egg**
**½ lb. bacon rashers**
**Flour**
**1 lb. tomatoes**
**Juice of 1 lemon**
**1 pt. stock *or* water**

Cut the steak into thin 5-in. lengths. Chop the hard-boiled eggs and onion and mix them with the 1 tablesp. flour, seasonings and beaten egg. Remove rind from bacon and cut bacon into 3 in. lengths. Roll a teaspoonful of egg mixture in each strip of bacon, and then in one of the pieces of steak. Secure with a toothpick. Toss in flour and seer in hot fat. Transfer from pan to casserole, add the tomatoes, skinned and sliced, lemon juice and stock or water. Place in a moderate oven (**350° F., Gas 4**) and allow to cook for 2 hr. Remove toothpicks. Serve with macedoine of vegetables and creamed potatoes.

**4 helpings**

## CORN FRITTERS

**One 5-oz. carton sweet corn**
**2 oz. self-raising flour**
**Pinch of salt**
**1 egg**
**4 tablesp. milk**
**Fat for frying**

Cook the corn according to the directions on the carton, drain and cool. Make a batter with flour, salt, well-beaten egg and milk and stir in the cooled corn. Fry tablespoonfuls of the mixture in a little hot fat until crisp and golden brown on both sides, drain, serve hot.

Serve plain as an accompaniment to fried or grilled chicken, or sausages and bacon; serve with lemon juice and sugar, or with jam or syrup for a sweet.

**12 fritters**

## CORNFLOUR CAKE, RICH

*See Rich Cakes, Large, Various.*

## CORNFLOUR CUSTARD

**½ oz. lightweight cornflour *or* custard powder**
**½ pt. milk**
**1 dessertsp. sugar**
**Flavouring**
**1 egg yolk**

Blend the cornflour with a little of the cold milk. Boil the rest of the milk with thinly cut lemon rind if used for flavouring. Remove rind and stir the boiling liquid into the blended cornflour. Rinse the pan and return the sauce to it. Just bring it to boiling point for custard powder; boil for 3 min. for cornflour. Sweeten and flavour the sauce unless lemon rind has been used. Cool the sauce, add the egg yolk and sugar and cook gently until the egg thickens without boiling. At once pour out of the pan into a basin or the sauceboat. Flavour and add extra sweetening if required.

## CORNFLOUR MOULD

*Gâteau à la crème de maïs*

**3 oz. cornflour**
**2 pt. milk**
**2 oz. castor sugar**
**Flavouring (*see below*)**

Blend cornflour with a little cold milk to a thin cream. Boil remainder of milk and pour on to the blended cornflour, stirring continuously. Return mixture to the pan and heat until boiling. Cook gently for 4 min., stirring all the time. Add sugar to taste, and flavouring essences, if used. Pour quickly into a wetted mould. Turn out when set.

**6 helpings**
**Cooking time—15 min.**
**Setting time—2 hr.**

FLAVOURINGS

**Lemon *or* orange**: Infuse thinly-cut strips of lemon *or* orange rind with the milk. Remove rind before pouring milk on to cornflour.

**Chocolate**: Blend 1½ oz. cocoa with the cornflour. Extra sugar may be desired, and also a flavouring of vanilla, rum *or* coffee essence.

**Coffee**: Add 1 tablesp. coffee essence with the sugar, and taste before adding more, as essences vary in strength.

**Custard**: Add beaten egg yolk to cooled mixture and re-heat until cooked ; *or* replace 1 oz. cornflour with 1 oz. custard powder.

## CORNFLOUR SAUCE

**½ pt. milk**
**½ oz. cornflour**
**1 dessertsp. sugar**
**Lemon rind *or* any flavour to blend with the flavour of pudding which it accompanies**

Blend the cornflour with a little of the cold milk. Boil the rest of the milk with the thinly cut lemon rind if used. Remove rind and stir the boiling liquid into the blended cornflour. Rinse the pan and return the sauce to it. Bring to boiling point and boil for 3 min. Sweeten and flavour the sauce, unless lemon rind has been used for flavouring.

### CORNISH PASTIES

**¼ lb. raw meat**
**¼ lb. potatoes**
**½ teasp. finely-chopped onion**
**Mixed herbs to taste**
**Salt and pepper**
**2 tablesp. gravy *or* water**
**Short crust pastry, using 8 oz. flour, etc.**

Mince the meat finely. Dice the potatoes. Add the onion, herbs, salt, pepper and gravy to the meat and potatoes, and mix well together. Divide the pastry into 8 equal portions and roll them out ¼ in. thick, keeping the portions as round as possible. Pile the mixture in the centre of each piece of pastry, wet the edges and join them together on the top to form an upstanding frill, prick them with a fork. Bake in a hot oven (**425° F., Gas 7**) for 10 min., then reduce heat to moderate (**350° F., Gas 4**) and cook for about 50 min. longer.

**5–6 helpings**

### COTTAGE SOUP

**½ oz. butter**
**1 teacup grated mixed vegetables**
**¾ pt. water**
**1 level dessertsp. flour**
**¼ pt. milk**
**⅛ level teasp. yeast extract**
**2 level teasp. salt**
**2 level tablesp. grated cheese**
**1 level teasp. chopped parsley**

Melt the butter and add the grated vegetables. Cover with a lid and toss over gentle heat for 1 min. Add the water and cook 10 min. with the lid on. Blend the flour with the milk and add to the soup with the yeast extract and salt and cook 5 min. Add the cheese and parsley and serve.

(This soup is suitable for children and invalids.)

### COUPE JACQUES

**½ pt. vanilla ice cream**
**1 peach**

**½ pt. strawberry ice cream**
**2 oz. peeled grapes**
**1 banana**
**2 oz. raspberries**
**¼ pt. sweetened whipped cream**

Place one portion of vanilla ice cream and one portion of strawberry ice cream in a deep dish. Chop and mix the fruit and place over the ice cream. Garnish with piped whipped cream.

**6–8 helpings**

### CRAB SALAD

*Salade de Crabes*

**1 large cooked crab *or* 2 small cooked crabs**
**2 celery hearts *or* the heart of 1 endive**
**2 tablesp. olive oil**
**2 tablesp. tarragon vinegar**
**1 tablesp. chilli *or* caper vinegar**
**1 dessertsp. chopped parsley**
**Salt and pepper**
**Crisp lettuce leaves**
**2 hard-boiled eggs**
**1 tablesp. capers**
**12 stoned olives**
**Anchovy butter**

Cut the meat of the crabs into convenient-sized pieces. Shred the celery or endive, add to the crab meat and mix lightly with the oil, vinegar, parsley and seasoning. Serve on a bed of lettuce leaves; garnish with slices of hard-boiled egg, capers and olives stuffed with anchovy butter.

**6 helpings**

### CRAB SAUCE

*Sauce de Crabe*

**½ pt. white sauce made from fish stock in which crabshell, claws and legs have been simmered**
**Meat from a small cooked crab**
**Cayenne pepper**
**Salt**
**A few drops of lemon juice**

Stir the soft crab meat and the chopped white meat into the hot sauce, season, add lemon juice and simmer for 5 min.

### CRABS

Crabs are on sale all the year round, but are at their best from May to October. It is usual to buy crabs which have been boiled by the fishmonger. Choose crabs which are heavy for their size and which are not "watering" or sound "watery" when shaken. Avoid crabs which are attracting flies, especially around the mouth, as this is a sign of deterioration; choose a crab which looks and smells fresh. A crab should look clean and wholesome—if the shell is dark the meat will invariably be dark. The hen crab may be distinguished from the cock crab by its broader tail flap. Normally the flesh of the cock crab is more reliable for quality than the hen, the cock crab usually yields more meat for its size and is therefore a more economical buy. Avoid crabs that are less than 4½ inches across the shell. An average crab about 6 inches across should weigh 2½–3 lb., this will be found sufficient for 4 people. It is illegal to sell "berried" or "rush" crab.

Crabs are normally served in salads or in hot made-up dishes.

#### TO PREPARE A CRAB

After wiping well with a damp cloth, place the crab on its back with tail facing, and remove claws and legs by twisting them in the opposite way to which they lie. Place the thumbs under flap at tail and push upwards, pull flap away upwards so that the stomach contents are not drawn over the meat, and lift off. (The fishmonger will always do this on request.) Reverse the crab so that the head is facing, then press on the mouth with the thumbs, pushing down and forward, so that the mouth and stomach will then come away in one piece. Remove the meat from the shell by easing round the inside edge of the shell to loosen the tissues with the handle of a plastic teaspoon, and the meat will then come away easily. Keep the dark and the white meat separate. With the handle of a knife, tap sharply over the false line around the shell cavity, press down and it will come away neatly. Scrub and dry the shell, then rub over with a little oil. Remove the "dead-men's fingers" (the lungs) and discard, then scoop out the meat from the claw sockets. Scoop out as much as possible but keep it free of bone. Twist off first joint of large claws and scoop out meat. Tap sharply round the broad shell with back of knife until halves fall apart. Cut the cartilage between the pincers, open pincers and meat will come away in one piece.

### CRANBERRY SAUCE

**½ lb. cranberries**
**¼–½ pt. water**
**Sugar to taste**

Stew the cranberries till soft, using ¼ pt. water and adding more if needed. Rub the fruit through a hair or nylon sieve. Sweeten to taste. For economy, half cranberries and half sour cooking apples make an excellent sauce.

Serve with roast turkey, chicken or game.

### CRANBERRY-RAISIN PIE

**Plain pastry using 8 oz. flour, etc.**
**8 oz. cranberries**
**8 oz. seedless raisins**
**6 oz. sugar**
**½ oz. flour**
**Dash of salt**
**1 oz. butter**

Line a deep 9-in. pie-plate with pastry, reserving about ⅓ of pastry for crust or decoration. Cut cranberries in halves. Mix together fruits and dry ingredients and turn into pastry-lined plate. Dot with butter and adjust top crust, or arrange lattice of pastry strips over top. Bake in a very hot oven (**450° F., Gas 8**) for 10 min., then reduce heat to moderate (**350° F., Gas 4**) for 30–40 min.

### CRAYFISH *Écrevisses*

Crayfish, which must not be confused with crawfish, are similar to lobsters, only much smaller. The flesh is most delicate in flavour. They are extremely useful for hors d'œuvres as well as for serving in salads. There are several kinds, the best being those which are quite red under the claws. Shell and serve on crisp lettuce, garnished with lemon or tossed in mayonnaise.

#### TO BOIL CRAYFISH

Wash thoroughly, remove the intestinal cord, then throw the fish into fast boiling salted water. Keep boiling for about 10 min.

## CREAM

Cream is made from the concentrated fat in milk, and the standards of butterfat content are laid down as follows:

**Single Cream** (sometimes known as pouring or coffee cream): not less than 18%; **Double Cream** (sometimes known as thick or whipping cream): not less than 48%; and **Canned Cream**: 23% (usually sterilized). **Clotted Cream** has been heat-treated so that the liquid in it is reduced and the butterfat content is a minimum of 48%—though it is often nearer 60%.

Provided the condition of the cream is good, and heat-treatment has been given, chilled cream can be stored for up to five days in perfect safety. It is illegal to add preservatives and fresh cream means, literally, fresh cream.

Single cream will not whip unless helped by the addition of a stiffly whisked egg white. Really fresh cream will not whip as well as that which is 24 hours old. It is best to use it straight from a refrigerator for whipping although it should not be too cold when served.

Cream as a food has a high energy value and its easy digestibility makes it useful in a sickroom diet.

*See also Devonshire Cream.*

## CREAM BISCUITS

**2 oz. margarine**
**2 oz. sugar**
**½ teasp. vanilla essence**
**2½ oz. plain flour**
**1½ oz. custard powder *or* cornflour**
**½ egg (approx.)**
**Vanilla butter icing using 3 oz. icing sugar, etc.**

Cream the margarine, sugar and flavouring. Sift flour and custard powder, and add to the creamed margarine. Mix with enough egg to make a stiff but pliable dough. Roll out thinly on a floured board and cut into fingers 1 in. by 3 in. Bake in a moderate oven (**350° F., Gas 4**) until crisp but still cream in colour. When cold, sandwich pairs together with vanilla butter icing.

NOTE: The use of a ridged roller gives an attractive and more unusual surface to the biscuits.

**12–16 doubles**
**Cooking time—20 min.**

## CREAM BUNS

*Petits Choux à la Crème*

**Choux pastry using 4 oz. flour, etc.**
**Icing sugar**

FILLING

**½ pt. sweetened double cream flavoured with vanilla essence *or* confectioner's custard *or* mock cream may be used**

Put the pastry into a forcing bag and pipe balls on to a greased baking-sheet using a 1-in. vegetable pipe, or shape the mixture with a spoon into piles and bake in a fairly hot oven (**425°–400° F., Gas 7–6**) for 30 min. (do not open the door), then move to a cooler part of the oven for about 10 min. until dried inside. Split the buns and remove any damp mixture. When cold fill with whipped cream and dust with icing sugar.

**12 buns**
**Cooking time—40 min.**

## CREAM CHEESE

Although not regarded as a true cheese, cream cheese is often made at home. It is usually ready to eat after 2 days, but it should be made only in small quantities as it will not keep as long as other types of cheese.

*Double Cream Cheese.* The fat content of the cream should be high—between 50% and 60%—and, after cooling to 50° F., add 1½ oz. salt for every 4 pt. double cream. The cream may then be left to sour naturally or starter may be added to hasten this process. Leave to stand in a cool place for 12 hr. Place a strong linen cloth over a large basin and pour the cream into the cloth. Gather the four corners and tie a piece of string round them (using a slip knot) to form a "bag". Hang the bag over the basin in a cool place (*not* a refrigerator) with a good draught. Every 4 or 5 hr., open the bag and scrape the sides. When drainage is complete, the cheese may be shaped into small portions (usually about 1–2 oz.), wrapped and stored in a refrigerator.

*Single Cream Cheese.* The fat content of the cream should be between 20% and 40%. Heat the cream to 80° F. and add ¼ teasp. cheese-making rennet (to which 1 teasp. cold water has been added) to every 4 pt. single cream.

Leave for about 3 hr. until a curd has formed. Transfer the mixture to a strong linen cloth placed over a basin and hang it up to drain, keeping it at a temperature of about 60° F. Leave for 24 hr. and then scrape the sides of the cloth. Transfer the bag and basin to a cool place (*not* a refrigerator) and leave to hang until drainage is complete. Make up in small portions, wrap and store in a refrigerator.

### CREAM CHEESE FLAN

**Short crust pastry using 6 oz. flour, etc.**
**¼ oz. gelatine**
**2 tablesp. water**
**⅛ pt. milk**
**1 egg yolk**
**2 teasp. sugar**
**4 oz. cream cheese**
**¼ teasp. grated lemon rind**
**1 tablesp. lemon juice**
**¼ pt. cream**

Line an 8-in. flan ring with the pastry and bake "blind". Soak the gelatine in the water for 2–3 min. Heat the milk and dissolve the gelatine in it. Beat together the egg yolk and sugar and add the hot milk. Combine with the cheese, stir in lemon rind and juice. Cool. Whip the cream and fold into cheese mixture. Pour into baked flan case; chill for 2 hr.

### CREAM DRESSING USING SOUR CREAM

**Sour, thick cream**
**Salt and pepper**
**Mixed mustard *or* French mustard**
**Castor sugar**

Stir the cream until smooth. Flavour with salt, pepper, mustard and castor sugar. Add a little milk or top of the milk if too thick.

### CREAM AND EGG SALAD DRESSING

**2 raw egg yolks**
**Salt and pepper**
**1 level saltsp. mixed mustard**
**2 tablesp. salad oil**
**2 tablesp. double cream**
**1 tablesp. wine *or* malt vinegar**
**1 teasp. tarragon vinegar**
**½ teasp. finely-chopped onion *or* spring onion *or* chives**

Add salt, pepper and mustard to the raw egg yolks and stir with a wooden spoon in a small basin until the yolks are thick. Add the oil drop by drop, beating the mixture vigorously; stir in the cream, then beat in the vinegar slowly. Stir in the onion.

### CREAM GRAVY

**2 tablesp. butter**
**2 oz. flour**
**1 cup light (single) cream**
**2 tablesp. meat drippings**
**½ teasp. salt**
**Pepper to taste**

Melt butter in a saucepan and stir in flour. Gradually add light cream. Stir until mixture thickens. Add meat drippings and seasonings. Cook for 3 min. longer. Place over hot water and cover tightly to prevent crust from forming.

### CREAM HORNS

*Cornets de Crème*

**Puff *or* flaky pastry using 4 oz. flour, etc.**
**Raspberry jam**
**1 gill sweetened and flavoured cream**
**Chopped pistachio nuts**

Roll pastry out ⅛ in. thick and cut into strips ½ in. wide and 12–14 in. long. Moisten strip with water and wind round the cornet mould from the point upwards keeping moist surface on the outside. Finish final overlap on under side of tin and trim neatly. Allow to stand for 1 hr. Place horns on baking-sheet, brush over with egg and milk and place in a hot oven (**425° F., Gas 7**) until nicely browned and cooked through. Remove tins and return horns to oven to dry for a few minutes. When cool, place a little jam in each horn, pipe a rosette of cream on top and sprinkle with nuts.

**7–8 horns**
**Cooking time—15–20 min.**

### CREAM OF PEANUT SOUP

**6 oz. peanut butter**
**1 onion**
**2 sticks of celery**
**1 qt. milk**

Heat the peanut butter in a pan. Chop the onion and celery and add to the pan. Cook for 5 min. Add milk and heat.

**6 helpings** **Cooking time—15 min.**

### CREAM SALAD DRESSING

**½ level teasp. mixed mustard *or* French mustard**
**1 level saltsp. salt**
**1 saltsp. castor sugar**
**4 tablesp. double cream**
**1 tablesp. vinegar (wine *or* malt with a little tarragon)**

Mix the mustard, salt and sugar smoothly together. Stir in the cream. Add the vinegar drop by drop, beating mixture all the time.

### CREAM SAUCE

| | |
|---|---|
| **½ pt. Béchamel sauce** | **Lemon juice to taste** |
| **Cayenne pepper** | **⅛ pt. cream** |
| **Salt** | |

Heat the sauce; add cayenne, salt and lemon juice. Stir cream into seasoned sauce, just below boiling point. On no account allow sauce to boil or it will curdle. Serve at once, with chicken, veal, fish or delicately-flavoured vegetables.

### CREAM SCONES

| | |
|---|---|
| **8 oz. plain flour** | **2 level teasp. cream of tartar** |
| **¼ teasp. salt** | **½ gill milk** |
| **3 oz. butter *or* margarine** | **½ gill cream** |
| **1 level teasp. bicarbonate of soda** | |

Sift flour and salt and rub in the fat, add the raising agents. Mix to a light dough with milk and cream. Roll out ½–¾ in. thick, cut in rounds with cutter 2–2½ in. in diameter, place on greased baking-sheet and brush with milk or egg wash. Bake in a very hot oven **(450° F., Gas 8)**.

**12 scones** **Cooking time—10–15 min.**

### CREAM OF SPINACH SOUP

| | |
|---|---|
| **One 11-oz. carton chopped spinach** | **¾ oz. flour** |
| **¾ oz. margarine** | **1 pt. milk** |
| **1 level teasp. grated onion** | **Salt and pepper** |

Cook the spinach according to the directions on the carton, then pass the spinach and liquor through a sieve. Melt the margarine and add the onion, fry gently without browning until soft, add the flour and cook for 2 min. Add the milk and bring to the boil, stirring all the time. Boil gently for 5 min. Add the spinach purée, adjusting to the correct consistency with a little more milk if necessary; add seasoning to taste and reheat.

NOTE: ¼ level teasp. grated nutmeg may be added to the soup as an alternative flavouring to the onion.

**4–5 helpings**

### CREAM OF TARTAR AS A RAISING AGENT

*See Bread and Bread-Making*

### CREAMED BUTTER (for sandwiches)

| | |
|---|---|
| **8 oz. butter** | **Salt and pepper** |
| **1 gill double cream** | **Cayenne pepper** |
| **Mustard** | |

Beat the butter to a cream. Whip the cream stiffly and add it lightly to the butter. Season to taste with mustard, salt and pepper or cayenne.

### CREAMED HAM ON TOAST

| | |
|---|---|
| **6 oz. cooked ham** | **¼ teasp. dry mustard** |
| **½ pt. white sauce** | **Salt and pepper** |
| **3 hard-boiled eggs** | **6 slices buttered toast** |

Dice the ham. Add to the white sauce, the chopped ham, sliced eggs, mustard and seasoning to taste. Serve hot on toast with stuffed olives.

**6 helpings**

### CREAMED LOBSTER

*Homard à la Newbury*

| | |
|---|---|
| **1 small cooked lobster** | **Pinch of pepper** |
| **1 oz. butter** | **Pinch of grated nutmeg** |
| **2 egg yolks** | **8–10 small rounds of fried bread *or* toast; *or* 2–3 slices of toast** |
| **½ gill cream *or* creamy white sauce** | |
| **Good pinch of salt** | **Parsley** |

Remove the flesh of the lobster from the body and claws, and cut this into flakes. Cook in the butter for about 5 min. only—no longer as this toughens the lobster meat. Add the beaten egg yolks and cream or white sauce, the seasonings and nutmeg, and heat gently until the mixture thickens. Put on to the rounds of bread and garnish with parsley.

NOTE: Canned lobster could be used for this dish.

### CREAMED RICE

*Riz à la Crème*

To 1 pint of cold rice mould, add whipped cream *or* cream and custard, to produce a soft, creamy consistency. Pour into serving dishes and flavour and decorate in any of the following ways:

1. **Chocolate**: Grate chocolate coarsely over the top.
2. **Coffee**: Stir in coffee essence to taste.
3. **Orange**: Stir in finely-grated orange rind just before serving.

4. **Fruit**: (fresh, canned, preserved *or* stewed e.g. peaches, pineapple, dessert apples, dates.)
   (*a*) Drain the fruit from the juice, chop or shred, and stir into the rice.
   (*b*) Arrange fruit attractively on top of the rice, either in slices, quarters, halves *or* even a purée. The dish may be finished by piling up on top a meringue border and drying it to a golden brown in a cool oven **(310° F., Gas 2)** *or* finished as for Peach Condé (see below).

**4 helpings**

## CREAMS AS COLD SWEETS

Creams in the form of cold sweets or desserts can be of two types—full creams and half-creams.

### Full Creams

These consist wholly of cream flavoured with essence or liqueurs, set with gelatine.

### Half Creams

**Half-Creams (also known as Bavarois or Bavarian Creams)** consist of custard and cream, flavoured with fruit purée, juice, an essence or similar substance.

Fresh cream cannot be equalled in texture and flavour by any synthetic substance, but substitutes can be used if care is taken. Some well-known substitutes are:

(*a*) **Evaporated, sweetened or condensed milk.** Boil the can of milk unopened for 20 min., then cool it quickly. The milk will then keep for several weeks in a refrigerator, provided the can is not opened. This means that several cans can be boiled at one time, and can be kept until needed.

(*b*) **Synthetic Cream.** This should be whipped as it is. Any sugar needed to sweeten it should be stirred or folded in after it is whipped.

Adding milk, custard, cream or ice cream to any jellied liquid increases its density. Less gelatine is therefore needed to set one pint of it. A quarter of an ounce may even be enough to set a pint of a really thick mixture of cream and rich custard. The gelatine, dissolved in a little hot water, must be added when almost cooled. If it is too hot, it makes the cream lose some of its lightness. If it is too cold, it sets in small hard lumps before it can be evenly distributed in the main mixture. (If this happens, whip the cream over a bowl of hot water.)

Egg also has a thickening capacity, since it coagulates when heated and is then able to hold liquid. One egg will "set" a quarter of a pint of liquid. So, if eggs are added to jellies or creams to make them more nourishing, the amount of gelatine should be reduced accordingly.

The smoothness of cream mixtures depends largely on the speed and lightness with which their ingredients are blended. To achieve a smooth texture, they must be combined when they are of a similar consistency. Do not try to mix a stiff preparation with a semi-liquid one. Custard should be cooled until its consistency is like that of the jelly or fruit purée being used. Cream should be whipped to a similar stage. (If the cream is over-whipped, it may turn to butter, especially in hot weather.) Fresh, whipped cream should be folded in to a mixture very lightly. Air is incorporated in it while it is whipped, and this will be lost if it is stirred briskly or for long.

If ice cream is used, it may be necessary to warm the mixture while blending it in, as its low temperature may cause the mixture to set before additional milk, cream or custard can be added.

**Moulds** for full and half-creams should be made of metal, and if they are to be decorated, should be lined with jelly. For instructions on lining a mould with jelly, and for decorating and filling it, *see Cleared Jellies*. For instructions on turning it out, *see Unmoulding Jellies and Creams*.

## CRÈME AUX FRUITS

### Basic Recipe

| | |
|---|---|
| **½ pt. fruit purée** | **½ oz. gelatine** |
| | **4 tablesp. water *or* thin fruit juice** |
| **½ pt. thick, rich custard** | |
| **Castor sugar to sweeten** | **Colouring (optional)** |
| **Lemon juice (optional)** | **½ pt. double cream** |

Purée the fruit through a very fine sieve—nylon mesh if possible, as fresh fruit is acid.

Blend with the cool custard, sweeten, and flavour with lemon juice if required. Soak the gelatine in the water *or* juice for a few minutes and heat to dissolve. Pour, while steaming hot, into the custard and fruit mixture, and stir to keep well blended until the mixture begins to feel heavy and drags on the spoon. Colour if necessary. Stir in, lightly, the whipped cream and pour into a prepared mould.

NOTE: **apricots, blackcurrants, damsons, gooseberries, greengages, peaches, raspberries** *or* **strawberries** may be used for the purée, and the cream named accordingly.

**6 helpings**
**Setting time—1–2 hr.**

## CRÈME DE RIZ

| | |
|---|---|
| **1 pt. milk** | **2 tablesp. cold water** |
| **2 oz. ground rice** | **2 oz. castor sugar** |
| **½ oz. powdered gelatine** | **Flavouring** |
| | **¼–½ pt. double cream** |

Heat the milk and when boiling, sprinkle in the rice. Cook gently, stirring continuously, until quite soft and smooth—15–20 min. Avoid too much evaporation. Soak gelatine in the 2 tablesp. cold water, for 5–10 min., then warm until dissolved. Sweeten and flavour the rice, stir in the gelatine and allow to cool, stirring lightly from time to time. When quite cool, but not set, fold in the whipped cream. Pour into a cold wet mould and leave to set.

NOTE: This recipe may be used for whole rice, or for semolina.

**4 helpings**
**Cooking time—½ hr.**
**Setting time—2 hr.**

## CREOLE CHICKEN GUMBO

| | |
|---|---|
| **3 oz. margarine** | **Pinch of salt** |
| **1 green pepper** | **Pinch of pepper** |
| **1 lb. okra** | **2 tablesp. chopped parsley** |
| **1 small onion** | **1 cup diced cooked chicken** |
| **1 qt. chicken stock** | |
| **1 lb. tomatoes** | |

Heat the margarine in a saucepan. Chop the green pepper, okra and onion, and fry in hot margarine. Add chicken stock and tomatoes.

Simmer for 15 min. Season to taste. Add parsley and chicken.

**Cooking time—25–30 min.**

## CRÊPES SUZETTE

| | |
|---|---|
| **½ pt. batter** | **Brandy** *or* **rum** |
| **Icing sugar** | |

FILLING

| | |
|---|---|
| **2 oz. butter** | **2 teasp. orange juice** |
| **3 oz. castor sugar** | **1 teasp. lemon juice** |
| **Rind of ½ orange, grated** | **1 tablesp. Kirsch** *or* **Curacao** |

Make the batter and leave it to stand. Cream together the butter and sugar for the filling until very soft, then work in the orange juice, orange rind, lemon juice and liqueur. Make a very thin pancake, spread with some of the filling, roll up and dredge with icing sugar. Put into a warm place while the rest of the pancakes are being made. Just before serving pour over the rum or brandy and light up. Serve immediately.

## CROISSANTS

| | |
|---|---|
| **1 lb. plain flour** | **½ pt. warm milk and water** |
| **½ teasp. salt** | **3 oz. margarine** |
| **½ oz. yeast** | |
| **1 teasp. sugar** | |

Make as for Milk Bread ( basic ), omitting margarine. When the dough has risen to double its size, roll out on a floured board three times its width and spread with ⅓ of the margarine, in small pieces. Dredge lightly with flour, fold up ⅓ and down ⅓ (as for flaky pastry) and seal the edges. Repeat with the other ⅔ of margarine. Put the dough in a warm place again to rise for 30 min. Roll the dough out like pastry ⅛ in. thick, and cut into 12 pieces 5 in. square. Turn the squares over so that the smooth side comes outside and damp the surface very lightly with warm water. Beginning at one corner, roll up the square, pressing the opposite corner over to make it stick to the roll. Bend the two ends towards each other to form a crescent. Place on greased trays and allow to prove 15 min. Bake in a fairly hot oven (**425° F., Gas 7**). Brush with egg yolk and milk when almost ready, then dry them off.

**12 croissants**
**Cooking time—15–20 min.**

### CROÛTES AND CROÛTONS

*To make croûtes:* Croûtes, used as bases for entrees, are usually cut to the size of the dish in which they are to be served. Cut them from stale bread, discard the crusts, and fry or toast.

*To make croûtons:* Small croûtons for garnish or savouries should be cut from slices of stale bread about ½ in. thick, in round, oval, square, triangle or heart shapes. Fry in clarified fat (preferably butter) until lightly brown, drain well and keep hot and crisp until required. They can be toasted if liked.

### CROÛTES OF HERRING ROES

*Croûtes de Laitance de Harengs*

| | |
|---|---|
| **Toast** | **1 lemon** |
| **Butter** | **Cayenne pepper** |
| **Anchovy paste** | **Lemon** |
| **8 fresh herring roes** | **Parsley** |

Cut the toast into rounds or triangles and butter then spread liberally with anchovy paste. Melt about 1 oz. butter in a pan and fry the roes until lightly browned. Drain well, then put on to the prepared toast, sprinkle with lemon juice and cayenne pepper. Garnish with slices of lemon and parsley.

NOTE: Frozen or canned roes can be used instead of fresh roes. Frozen roes should be defrosted then fried, but since canned roes are already cooked they need to be just browned in the butter.

**2 helpings *or* 8 small savouries**
**Cooking time—5 min.**

### CRUNCHIES

| | |
|---|---|
| **4 oz. butter *or* margarine** | **1 tablesp. golden syrup** |
| **2½ oz. sugar** | **5 oz. rolled oats** |

Melt fat, sugar and syrup in a saucepan and stir in the oats. Spread on a greased baking-sheet with a raised edge, 7 in. by 13 in. to within ½ in. of the edge. Place in a moderate oven (**350° F., Gas 4**) and bake until a good brown colour and firm. Cut into fingers before completely cold.

**16 crunchies**
**Cooking time—20–30 min.**

### CRYSTALLIZED FRUIT

*See Candied and Crystallized Fruit.*

### CUCUMBER

*Concombre*

| | |
|---|---|
| **1 large cucumber** | **Vinegar *or* white wine vinegar** |
| **Salt** | **Chopped parsley** |
| **Salad oil** | |

Peel the cucumber thinly if wished and cut into thin slices. Place the slices on a dish, and sprinkle with salt, cover, and let them remain for 1–2 hr. Drain well, dish up on small glass dishes, season with a little salad oil and vinegar. Sprinkle parsley over and serve.

**10–12 helpings**

### CUCUMBER, AS A VEGETABLE WITH SAUCE

*Concombre à la Poulette*

| | |
|---|---|
| **2 large cucumbers** | **¾ pt. white sauce** |
| **1 oz. butter *or* margarine** | **1 egg** |
| **1 teasp. finely-chopped shallot** | **1 teasp. finely-chopped parsley** |
| | **Salt and pepper** |

Peel the cucumber and steam it until tender (about 20 min.). Drain well and cut into 1-in. slices. Melt the butter in a saucepan, put in the shallot and cook it without browning. Add the sliced cucumber, toss over heat for a few minutes, then stir in the white sauce. Just before boiling-point is reached, add the well-beaten egg and parsley, stir and cook gently until the egg thickens. Season and serve hot.

**6 helpings**
**Cooking time—30 min. approx.**

### CUCUMBER CREAM SOUP

*Crème de Concombre*

| | |
|---|---|
| **1 lb. cucumber** | **Salt and pepper** |

| | |
|---|---|
| **1 oz. butter** | **Lemon juice** |
| **6 spring onions** | **Green colouring** |
| **1 oz. flour** | **A sprig of mint** |
| **1 pt. white stock** | **A sprig of parsley** |
| | **1/8 pt. cream** |

Peel the cucumber, reserve a 2-in. length for garnish, slice the rest. Melt the butter in a deep pan and cook the onions gently, without browning for 10 min. Stir in the flour, then the stock and bring to boiling point. Add the sliced cucumber and cook till tender. Sieve through a nylon sieve. Season and add lemon juice to taste. Cut the 2-in. piece of cucumber into ¼-in. dice and boil these in a little stock or water till just tender and add them to the finished soup. Five minutes before serving the soup add the mint and parsley. Tint the soup pale green. Stir the cream into the hot soup immediately before serving.

**4 helpings** **Cooking time—20–30 min.**

### CUCUMBER SALAD

*Salade de Concombre*

| | |
|---|---|
| **1 large cucumber** | **Chopped parsley** |
| **Salt** | **Chopped tarragon** |
| **French dressing** | |

Slice cucumber . Put on a china plate and sprinkle with salt. Tilt the plate slightly so that the water may drain off easily and leave for ½ hr. Rinse quickly in a colander and drain. Dish and pour over the French dressing. Sprinkle with parsley and tarragon.

**6 helpings**

### CUCUMBER SALAD À L'ESPAGNOLE

| | |
|---|---|
| **1 large *or* 2 small cucumbers** | **Olive oil** |
| **1 large red pepper (capsicum)** | **Vinegar** |
| **Salt and pepper** | **Chopped chervil** |
| | **Chopped parsley *or* chives** |

Peel the cucumber thinly, cut in halves lengthwise and remove the seedy portion. Cut the cucumber into very fine slices or small cube shapes. Cut the red pepper into fine strips and mix with the cubes of cucumber. Season with salt and pepper, and add enough olive oil and vinegar to season, also the finely-chopped chervil. Mix carefully, sprinkle with parsley or chives and dish up.

**8–10 helpings**

### CUCUMBER SAUCE

*Sauce au Concombre*

| | |
|---|---|
| **½ oz. butter** | **Lemon juice** |
| **½ a cucumber** | **Sugar** |
| **1 tablesp. stock** | **Nutmeg** |
| **¼ pt. Béchamel sauce** | **Green colouring** |
| **Salt and pepper** | **2 tablesp. cream** |

Melt the butter in a saucepan, slice the cucumber and slowly cook the slices in the butter for 10 min. Add the stock and continue cooking until the cucumber is soft. Rub the cucumber through a hair or nylon sieve. Return the purée to the saucepan and simmer with any of the butter and liquid remaining, until reduced a little. Stir the hot Béchamel sauce and the cucumber purée together; season and flavour to taste; colour the sauce. Lastly stir in the cream at boiling point, do not reboil. Use the sauce at once.

Serve with salmon and other fish, veal or poultry.

### CULINARY HERBS AND THEIR USES

*See Appendix*

### CUP CUSTARD

To make ¾ pt.

| | |
|---|---|
| **½ pt. milk** | **1 oz. castor sugar** |
| **Flavouring: lemon rind *or* vanilla essence** | **2 tablesp. double cream (optional)** |
| **1 egg and 1 yolk *or* 3 egg yolks** | |

Warm the milk, infusing the lemon rind if used. Mix eggs and sugar to a liquid. Pour the warmed milk over the eggs and strain the custard into a pan previously rinsed with cold water. Cook the custard gently until the eggs have coagulated and thickened the milk. To ensure that this occurs evenly and forms a smooth creamy texture, stirring should be brisk and thorough. If the custard is cooked in a saucepan, a wooden spoon will be found most suitable for this as the thick edge of the spoon works smoothly over the base of the pan, keeping it clear. If the custard is cooked in a double saucepan over hot water, a whisk is better as thickening takes place from the sides as well as from the base. Do not let the custard boil. When the custard coats the spoon, pour into a cool bowl, and add the vanilla if used. Add the cream (if used) and stir in lightly. Stir frequently during cooling so that a skin does not form on the surface.

NOTE: A thinner pouring custard can be made by using 1 pt. milk and 2 eggs.

**Time—15 min.**

## CURRANT PUDDING

*Pouding aux Groseilles*

**12 oz. plain flour**
**2 rounded teasp. baking-powder**
**Pinch of salt**
**6 oz. currants**
**6 oz. finely-chopped suet**
**1½ gill water (approx.)**
**Lemon**
**Castor sugar**

Sift together the flour, salt and baking-powder. Add the suet and currants and mix with the water to make a soft pliable dough. Form into a roll and put into a floured pudding cloth. Roll up loosely and tie at each end to form a sausage-shape. Put the pudding into boiling water and let it boil gently for 2–2½ hr. Turn out and serve with cut lemon and plenty of castor sugar.

**6 helpings**

## CURRIED BEEF

*Kari de Bœuf*

**1½ lb. lean beef**
**2½ oz. butter *or* fat**
**1 large onion**
**1 sour apple**
**2 teasp. curry powder**
**1¼ oz. flour**
**1½ pt. strained stock *or* coconut infusion**
**1–2 teasp. curry paste**
**2 teasp. chutney**
**Salt and pepper**
**4–6 oz. patna rice**
**Juice of ½ lemon**
**2 teasp. jam *or* jelly**

GARNISH

**Paprika**
**Gherkins**

Cut the meat into 1-in. cubes. Melt the fat in a stewpan; fry the meat lightly on both sides, then remove and keep hot. Peel and chop the onion; peel, core and slice the apple. Fry them in the fat until golden brown. Add the curry powder and flour and fry gently for 5 min. Add the strained stock or coconut infusion, curry paste, chutney and seasoning; stir until boiling. Replace the meat, cover closely, and simmer gently for 1½–2 hr. Meanwhile, boil the rice in boiling salted water for about 15–20 min. Drain on a sieve, separate the grains by pouring boiling water over; dry thoroughly. Arrange in a border on a hot dish. Add lemon juice, jelly and extra seasoning if required, to the curry. Pour the curry into the middle of the rice border. Garnish. If preferred the rice may be served separately.

**6 helpings**

## CURRIED COD

*Cabillaud au Kari*

**2 lb. cod**
**2 oz. butter**
**1 medium-sized onion**
**1 tablesp. flour**
**1 dessertsp. curry powder**
**1 pt. white stock (fish *or* bone)**
**1 tablesp. lemon juice**
**Salt and pepper**
**Cayenne pepper**

Wash and dry the cod, and cut into pieces about 1½ in. square. Melt the butter in a saucepan, fry the cod slightly, then take out and put aside. Add the sliced onion, flour and curry powder to the butter in the saucepan and fry 15 min., stirring constantly to prevent the onion becoming too brown, then pour in the stock. Stir until boiling then simmer gently for 20 min. Strain and return to the saucepan, add lemon juice and seasoning to taste, bring nearly to boiling-point, then put in the fish. Cover closely, and heat gently until the fish becomes thoroughly impregnated with the flavour of the sauce. An occasional stir must be given to prevent the fish sticking to the bottom of the saucepan.

NOTE: Remains of cold fish may be used for this dish in which case the preliminary frying may be omitted.

**5–6 helpings**

## CURRIED CRAB

*Kari de Crabe*

**1 good-sized crab**
**Mustard**
**1 shallot *or* onion**
**½ apple**
**1 oz. butter *or* other good cooking fat**
**½ pt. curry sauce**
**4 oz. well-boiled rice**

Remove the meat from the crab, including the claws, flake it up and sprinkle a little dry mustard over it. Peel and finely chop the shallot or onion; peel, core and chop the apple. Melt the butter in a saucepan and lightly fry the shallot and apple. Fry for a few minutes

Duck, roasted or braised, is typically English.

Fish preparation—cleaning and filleting plaice.

1 Cut off the fins of the plaice with a pair of kitchen scissors.

2 Cut open the belly, and remove and discard entrails. Remove the head with a semi-circular cut.

3 Slit the flesh from head to tail down the line of the backbone.

4 Insert the knife in the slit and separate the flesh from the bone, keeping the knife pressed against the bone. Remove second fillet.

5 Turn the fish over and remove the other two fillets as described above.

1

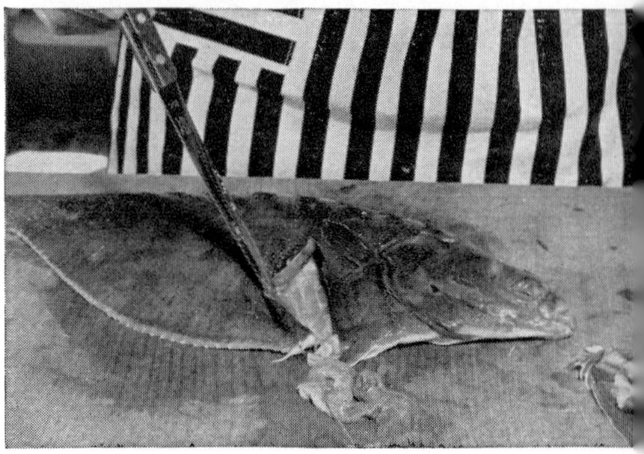

2

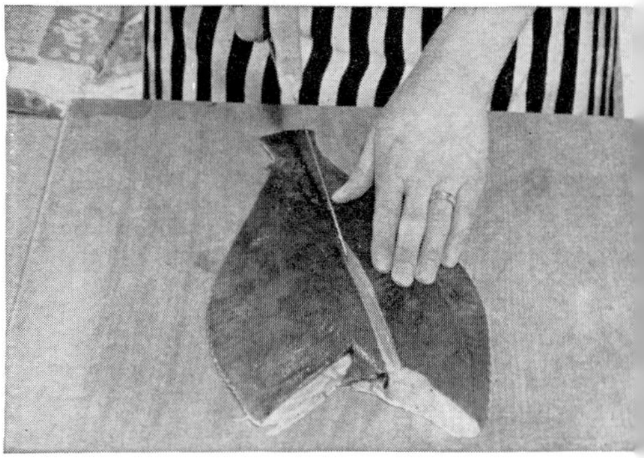

3

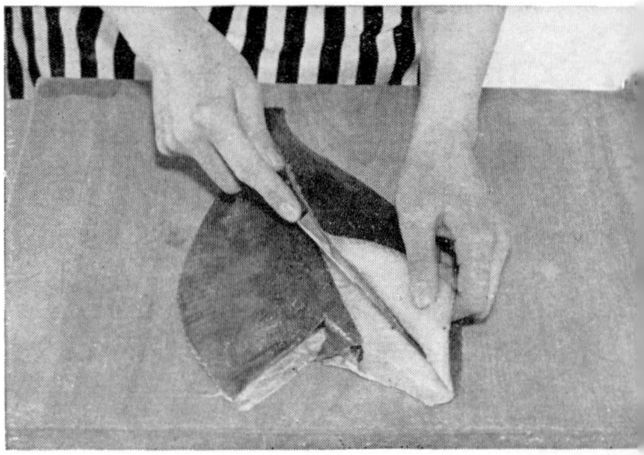

4

5

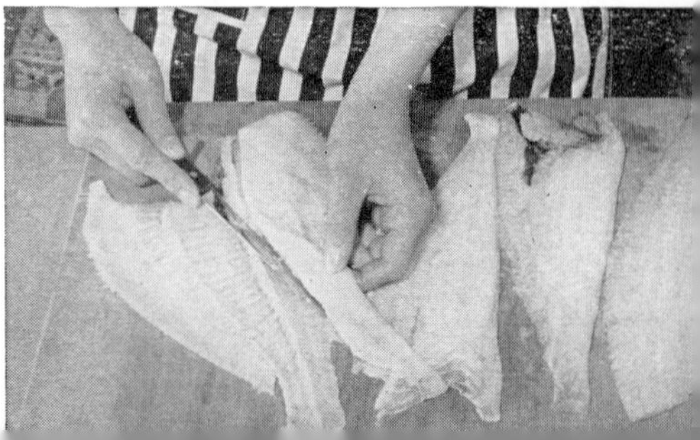

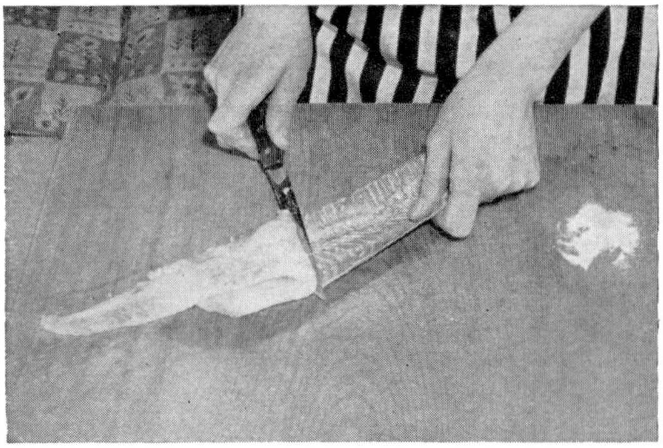

6

6 To skin the fillets, dip the fingers of the left hand in salt, take a firm hold of the tail, and with the knife peel the flesh away from the skin, keeping the edge of the knife pressed hard against the skin.

only, then add the curry sauce and lastly the crab meat. Re-heat and serve on a hot dish in the centre of a border of rice.

**3-4 helpings**

## CURRIED CHICKEN

*Kari de Volaille*

| | |
|---|---|
| **1 chicken** | **1 dessertsp. chutney** |
| **2 oz. butter** | **1 tablesp. lemon juice** |
| **1 chopped onion** | **Salt and pepper** |
| **1 dessertsp. flour** | **1 oz. sultanas** |
| **1 tablesp. curry powder** | **1 oz. blanched almonds** |
| **1 dessertsp. curry paste** | **1 dessertsp. desiccated coconut** |
| **¾ pt. white stock** | **2 tablesp. cream *or* milk (optional)** |
| **1 chopped apple** | |

GARNISH

| | |
|---|---|
| **Fans of lemon** | **Red pepper** |
| **Gherkin fans** | |

Divide chicken into neat joints, remove skin, fry joints lightly in hot butter, remove from saucepan and drain. Fry onion lightly, add flour, curry powder and paste, and fry very well, stirring occasionally. Stir in stock, bring to boil. Put in all other ingredients except the cream, put in chicken joints. Have the coconut tied in muslin, and remove after 15 min. Simmer gently about 1½ hr., adding a little more stock if necessary. Dish the chicken, add the cream to the sauce and pour the sauce over the chicken, straining if liked. Garnish.

ACCOMPANIMENTS: Dry boiled Patna rice sprinkled with paprika pepper, mangoe chutney, Bombay Duck, Poppadums, fresh grated coconut, gherkins, pickled pimentoes. These are served separately, not in the dish with the curry. Bombay Duck and Poppadums are grilled before serving.

**6 helpings** **Cooking time—1¾ hr.**

## CURRIED EGGS

*Œufs au Kari*

| | |
|---|---|
| **4 hard-boiled eggs** | **1 teasp. curry powder** |
| **4 oz. cooked rice** | **⅓ pt. stock *or* milk** |
| **1 small onion** | **Salt** |
| **1 oz. butter** | **Lemon juice** |
| **1 teasp. flour** | |

Prepare the rice (drain well), shell the eggs and cut them into quarters. Chop the onion finely and fry lightly in the butter, sprinkle in the flour and curry powder, and cook slowly for 5–6 min. Add the stock or milk, season with salt and lemon juice and simmer gently for ½ hr. Then add the eggs and let them remain until thoroughly heated and serve. The rice may be arranged as a border, or served separately.

**4 helpings**
**Cooking time—45 min. (approx.)**

## CURRIED FISH

| | |
|---|---|
| **2 lb. fish** | **¼ oz. fenugreek** |
| **½ lb. onions** | **1 clove of garlic** |
| **½ oz. each of green chillies, dried chillies, green ginger, turmeric, cumin seeds, coriander seeds** | **1 dessertsp. salt** |
| | **2 oz. ghee *or* butter** |
| | **½ pt. fish stock *or* milk** |
| | **Juice of 2 tamarinds** |

Slice the onions. Put ½ the onions into a bowl, add the dried chillies, ginger, turmeric, cumin, coriander, fenugreek, finely-chopped garlic, and salt, and pound until smooth. Fry the remaining onions in hot ghee until lightly browned, add the fish previously washed, well-dried and cut into small slices, fry lightly, then add the stock or milk, the pounded ingredients, the juice of the tamarinds, and the green chillies, and cover closely. Cook slowly for 20 min. then serve with plainly-boiled rice.

**5 helpings**

## CURRIED FOWL

*Poulet à l'Indienne*

| | |
|---|---|
| **Remains of 2 cold roast fowls** | **¾ pt. stock** |
| | **1 sliced apple** |
| **1 sliced onion** | **1 teasp. chutney *or* redcurrant jelly** |
| **2 oz. butter** | |
| **1 tablesp. flour** | **1 dessertsp. lemon juice** |
| **1 tablesp. curry powder** | **Salt and pepper** |

Cut fowl into neat pieces (use bones and trimmings for stock). Fry sliced onion lightly in butter in a saucepan, stir in flour and curry powder, cook 3 min. Stir in stock, bring to boil. Add sliced apple, chutney, lemon juice and seasoning; simmer gently for ½ hr. Put in fowl, keep hot but not simmering for ½ hr. Dish fowl, pour sauce over (strain if liked).

Garnish and serve accompaniments as for Curried Chicken.

## CURRIED FRIED FISH—SOUTH AFRICAN

*Ingelegde Vis*

**1 good firm fish**
**4–5 onions**
**2–3 oz. curry powder**
**2 oz. castor sugar**
**2 oz. salt**
**½ oz. ground ginger**
**2–3 red chillies**
**24 coriander seeds**
**2 qt. vinegar**

Cut the fish into small steaks; fry (preferably in oil), drain and cool. Peel the onions, cut them into rings and fry a delicate brown. Put into a saucepan with all the other ingredients except the fish, bring to the boil and boil for a few minutes. Lay the fried fish in layers in a jar, pouring over each layer some of the curry mixture. Take care to have it well corked or sealed. This will keep for months and is excellent for lunch or supper.

## CURRIED MUTTON

**2 lb. lean mutton**
**¼ oz. green ginger**
**2 oz. ghee *or* butter**
**Salt**
**½ lb. onions**
**1 clove of garlic**
**⅛ teasp. ground cloves**
**⅛ teasp. ground cardamoms**
**½ teasp. black pepper**
**⅓ pt. cream**
**½ lb. ground almonds**
**½ teasp. saffron**
**Juice of 5 limes**

Cut the meat into small thin slices. Pound the green ginger with a little ghee, season it well with salt, and rub it into the meat. Let it stand for ½ hr. Meanwhile heat the rest of the ghee in a large saucepan and fry the sliced onions until lightly browned. Put the meat into the saucepan, add the garlic very finely-chopped, ground cloves, cardamom seeds and pepper, and fry until the meat is cooked, taking care the onions do not burn. Add the cream, ground almonds, saffron, lime juice, and salt to taste, cover closely, and cook as slowly as possible for 20 min. Serve with plainly-boiled rice.

**5–6 helpings**

## CURRIED PRAWNS

*Crevettes à l'Indienne*

**2 doz. prawns**
**1½ oz. butter**
**1 small onion**
**1–1½ level dessertsp. curry powder (depending on strength)**
**1 level dessertsp. flour**
**½ pt. stock**
**1 sour apple**
**1 tablesp. grated coconut**
**Salt**
**1 teasp. lemon juice**

Shell the prawns and put them aside. Melt the butter in a saucepan, fry the chopped onion without browning, then add the curry powder and flour and fry slowly for at least 20 min. Add the stock, coarsely chopped apple, coconut and a little salt. Simmer gently for ½ hr., then strain and return to the saucepan. Season to taste, add the lemon juice, put in the prawns and when thoroughly hot serve with well-boiled rice.

**4 helpings**
**Cooking time—about 1 hr.**

## CURRIED RABBIT

*Lapin au Kari*

**1 rabbit**
**2 oz. butter**
**1 chopped onion**
**1 dessertsp. flour**
**1 tablesp. curry powder**
**1 dessertsp. curry paste**
**¾ pt. white stock**
**1 chopped apple**
**1 dessertsp. chutney**
**1 tablesp. lemon juice**
**Salt and pepper**
**1 oz. sultanas**
**1 oz. blanched almonds**
**1 dessertsp. desiccated coconut**
**2 tablesp. cream *or* milk (optional)**

GARNISH

**Fans of lemon**
**Red pepper**
**Gherkin fans**

Wash, dry and joint the rabbit. Heat the butter in a saucepan, dry joints lightly, remove and drain. Fry onion lightly, add flour, curry powder and paste, and fry very well, stirring occasionally. Stir in stock, bring to boil. Put in all other ingredients except the cream, put in rabbit joints. Have the coconut tied in muslin, and remove after 15 min. Simmer gently about 1½ hr., adding a little more stock if necessary. Add cream or milk (if used).

Dish the rabbit, pour the sauce over, straining if liked. Garnish. For accompaniments see Curried Chicken .

**3–4 helpings**

## CURRIED SCRAMBLED EGGS

**4 eggs**
**1 small onion**
**½ oz. butter**
**1 teasp. curry powder**
**Salt**
**¼ pt. milk**
**Buttered toast**
**Lemon juice**

Chop the onion finely. Melt the butter in a stewpan, add the onion and fry for 2–3 min.;

sprinkle in the curry powder, let this cook for a few minutes, stirring meanwhile. Beat the eggs slightly, season with salt, add the milk, pour the mixture into the stewpan and stir until the eggs begin to set. Have ready squares of well-buttered toast, pile the egg mixture lightly on them, sprinkle with lemon juice and serve at once.

**4 helpings**
**Cooking time—15 min. (approx.)**

### CURRIED SHRIMPS

*Crevettes au Kari*

**½ pt. shrimps—** ***unshelled***
**¼ pt. water**
**1 oz. butter *or* margarine**
**1 shallot *or* tiny onion**
**1 teasp. curry powder**
**1 teasp. flour**
**1 tablesp. cream *or* top of milk**
**1 teasp. lemon juice**
**Parsley**
**Toast**

Shell the shrimps and put the shells into a saucepan with the water and simmer for about 10 min. to get the flavour from the shells. Meanwhile melt the butter in another saucepan, add the finely-chopped shallot or onion and fry gently until tender. Work in the curry powder and flour and cook for several minutes, then add the strained shrimp stock. Bring to the boil and cook until slightly thickened, then put in the shrimps and heat for a few minutes. Remove from the heat and when no longer boiling whisk in the cream and lemon juice. Pour into 4 small dishes, garnish with chopped parsley and serve with crisp toast.

This makes an excellent hot hors d'œuvre.

**4 helpings**
**Cooking time—15–20 min.**

### CURRIED VEAL

**1½ lb. lean veal**
**2½ oz. butter *or* margarine**
**2 onions**
**2 apples**
**1 clove of garlic (optional)**
**1 oz. flour**
**1–2 heaped teasp. curry powder**
**1½ pt. light stock *or* coconut infusion**
**2 heaped teasp. curry paste**
**2 heaped teasp. chutney**
**Salt**
**6 oz. rice**
**2 heaped teasp. redcurrant jelly**
**Lemon juice**
**Cayenne pepper**

GARNISH

**Chilli skins *or* paprika pepper**
**Sliced gherkin**
**Crimped slices of lemon**
**Parsley**

Trim, wipe and cut the meat into 1-in. cubes. Heat the fat and fry the meat lightly until sealed and lightly browned. Then remove. Fry the finely-chopped onions and apples and the minced garlic for about 7 min. without browning too much. Add the flour and curry powder to the apple and cook for at least 5 min. to get rid of the raw flavour. Add the stock or coconut infusion, curry paste, chutney and salt and whilst stirring bring slowly to the boil. Return the meat to the pan and simmer very slowly for about 2 hr., stirring occasionally. Cook the rice and arrange as a border on a hot dish and keep hot. Add to the curry the redcurrant jelly, lemon juice, cayenne pepper to taste and place in the centre of the dish. Garnish with chilli skins or paprika pepper, gherkin, lemon and parsley.

NOTE: Curry can be served with any of the following accompaniments: pappadums; slices of hard-boiled egg; cubes of cucumber in coconut milk; green olives; Bombay duck; shredded coconut; cubes of salted almonds; sliced banana; variety of chutneys; fresh melon; chillies; silver onions; guava jelly; preserved ginger; diced pineapple.

**6 helpings**

*To make coconut infusion*

Add 1½ pt. boiling water to 2 heaped tablesp. coconut. Infuse for 15–20 min., strain and use as stock.

### CURRY BUTTER

**4 oz. butter**
**1 heaped teasp. curry powder**
**½ teasp. lemon juice**
**Salt to taste**

Cream the butter then stir in the curry powder and lemon juice. Beat well and add salt to taste.

### CURRY, RICE FOR

Put ½ lb. Patna rice in a saucepan with sufficient cold water to cover. Bring to the boil, then strain, and hold the strainer under running cold water until the rice is thoroughly washed. Have ready 3–4 pt. boiling salted water, put in the rice, and cook for 12–15 min., then turn into a colander. Rinse with hot water, cover with a clean dry cloth, and leave in a warm place until dry (½–¾ hr.) stirring occasionally with a fork.

The above is the better method of boiling rice for curry, but if time is short the following method cuts out the first boiling. Drop the dry rice into sufficient fast boiling salted water to keep it moving in the pan, boil for 7–10 min. Drain and dry as above.

## CURRY SAUCE

*Sauce Indienne*

**1 medium-sized onion**
**1 oz. butter *or* margarine**
**1 small cooking apple**
**½ oz. curry powder**
**½ oz. rice flour *or* flour**
**½ pt. white stock, coconut infusion (see below) *or* water**
**½ teasp. black treacle**
**1–2 teasp. lemon juice**
**1 dessertsp. chutney**
**Salt**

Chop the onion, put it into a saucepan and fry it very gently in the butter for 10 min. Chop the apple and cook it in the butter with the onion for a further 10 min. Stir in the curry powder and heat it for a few minutes. Add the flour and then stir in the liquid. When boiling, add all the other ingredients and simmer the sauce for at least ½ hr., or better 1½ hr.

*To make the coconut infusion:* Soak 1 oz. dessicated *or* fresh grated coconut in ½ pt. water for a few minutes, bring slowly to boiling point and infuse it for 10 min. Wring the coconut in a piece of muslin to extract all the liquid.

## CUSTARD AND CUSTARD MIXTURES

Basically, these are made from a mixture of eggs and milk, cooked just enough to "set" the mixture. Custards can be cooked by "boiling", baking or steaming but they must be cooked very slowly since over-cooking makes the mixture curdle. A custard which is to be turned out from a mould needs at least the equivalent of four eggs to each pint of liquid to "set" it. If it has less, it may break when turned out.

Custards may be savoury or sweet.

### Pouring Custards

Pouring custards are made by heating the mixture to a point just below boiling point, and by stirring keeping it below boiling point, until the beaten eggs cook evenly throughout the mixture. Using a double saucepan lessens the risk of curdling.

### Baked Custards

Grease a pie dish well. Place it in a tray of warm water, and bake the custard slowly in the oven at about **335° F., Gas 3,** until it is set. Take it out of the water at once to prevent further cooking.

### Steamed Custards

Grease the basin for the custard thoroughly, and cover the custard with greased paper to prevent condensing steam dripping into it. Only a very gentle flow of steam should be maintained.

## CUSTARD CREAM

**1 pt. milk**
**2 eggs**
**1 dessertsp. sugar**
**A few drops of almond *or* vanilla essence**
**½ gill cream**
**¼ oz. agar-agar**

Make a custard in the usual way, adding the cream afterwards. Dissolve the agar-agar according to the directions, and strain whilst hot (not boiling) into the hot custard. Stir well and pour immediately into a mould previously rinsed out with cold water. Leave until set.

**4–5 helpings**

## CUSTARD, ECONOMICAL (SWEET)

*Crème Anglaise*

(*To make* 1 *pt.*)

**1 teasp. cornflour**
**1 pt. milk**
**1 oz. sugar**
**1 egg**
**Flavouring: lemon rind *or* vanilla essence**

Blend cornflour with 1 tablesp. of the milk and heat the remainder, infusing the lemon rind if used. Remove the rind, pour the hot milk over the blended cornflour, stirring to keep smooth. Replace in saucepan and cook thoroughly by boiling gently for 2 min. stirring continuously. Add the sugar and allow to cool slightly. Beat the egg, mix with a little of the hot mixture, then add to the contents of the saucepan and cook for a few minutes until thickened. Stir in the vanilla if used. Serve hot *or* cold.

**4 helpings** **Time—20 min.**

### CUSTARD FOR ICE CREAM

*See Ice Cream Custard.*

### CUSTARD PIE

*Tourte à la Crème*

**3 level tablesp. cornflour**
**1½ pt. milk**
**3 eggs**
**1½ oz. castor sugar**
**A little grated nutmeg**
**Short crust pastry using 6 oz. flour, etc.**

Blend the cornflour with a little of the cold milk and put the rest of the milk to boil. Pour the boiling milk on to the blended cornflour, stirring well. Return to pan, re-boil 2–3 min.; remove from heat. Work together the eggs and sugar, and when the cornflour mixture is cooler add this to the worked eggs.

Line a 9-in. flan ring or a shallow heat-proof glass dish with short crust pastry and prick the base finely. Pour in the custard mixture, dust with a little grated nutmeg, if liked, and bake in a fairly hot oven (**375° F., Gas 5**) until the pastry is browned, then reduce the heat to **335° F., Gas 3,** until the custard is set —45 min.

### CUSTARD SOUFFLÉ

*Soufflé à la Crème*

**Butter**
**3 oz. plain flour**
**¾ pt. milk**
**4 eggs**
**2 oz. castor sugar**

Well butter a pie-dish. Melt 3 oz. butter in a saucepan, add the flour and stir over the heat until well cooked but not coloured. Add the milk; beat well until smooth. Reheat stirring continuously until the mixture thickens and comes away from the sides of the pan. Let it cool slightly. Beat in the egg yolks singly and add the sugar. Stiffly whisk the egg whites and fold them lightly into the mixture. Turn into the pie-dish and bake in a fairly hot oven (**375° F., Gas 5**) for 25–30 min.

Serve with a wine- or fruit-sauce.

**6 helpings**

### CUSTARD TARTLETS

*Tartelettes à la Crème cuite*

**Short crust pastry using 6 oz. flour, etc., and add 1 teasp. castor sugar**
**2 small eggs**
**1 tablesp. sugar**
**1¾–2 gills milk**
**Grated nutmeg**

Line 13–14 patty tins or small tart tins with the pastry. Lightly whisk the eggs, add sugar and warmed milk. Strain custard into prepared tins and grate a little nutmeg on top. Bake in a fairly hot to moderate oven (**375°–350° F., Gas 5–4**). Allow to cool before turning out of tins.

**13–14 tartlets**
**Cooking time—20–30 min.**

### CUTLETS OF SALMON À LA MORNAY

*Filets de Saumon à la Mornay*

**2 slices of salmon ¾–1 in. thick**
**1 onion**
**2½ oz. butter**
**½ pt. fish stock**
**Bouquet garni**
**Salt and pepper**
**1 oz. flour**
**¼ pt. cream**
**1 tablesp. grated Parmesan cheese**
**1 dessertsp. lemon juice**

Chop the onion coarsely. Melt half the butter in a shallow saucepan, fry the onion and the salmon quickly on both sides, then add the stock (boiling), the bouquet garni and salt and pepper. Cover closely, and simmer gently for 20 min. Meanwhile, melt the remainder of the butter in another saucepan, add the flour and cook for 4 min. When the fish is done, transfer it to a hot dish and keep warm. Strain the stock on to the flour and butter and stir until boiling. Simmer for 5 min., then add the cream, cheese, lemon juice and seasoning to taste. Pour the mixture over the fish and serve.

**5–6 helpings**

## *Dairy Produce*

### DAIRY PRODUCE

*See Butter, Cream, Devonshire Cream, Margarine, Milk, etc.*

### DAMSON JAM

| | |
|---|---|
| **$2\frac{1}{2}$ lb. damsons** | **3 lb. sugar** |
| **$\frac{3}{4}$–1 pt. water** | |

Remove the stalks, wash the damsons and put into the pan with the water. Stew slowly until the damsons are well broken down. Add the sugar, stir over a low heat till dissolved, bring to the boil, then boil rapidly. Remove stones as they rise to the surface (a stone-basket clipped to the side of the pan is useful for holding the stones, and allows any liquid to drip back into the pan). Continue boiling rapidly until setting point is reached. (Test for set after about 10 min. boiling.) Skim, pour into dry, warm jars and cover.

**Yield—5 lb.**

### DAMSON TART

*Tourte aux Prunes de Damas*

| | |
|---|---|
| **Short crust pastry using 6 oz. flour, etc.** | **$1\frac{1}{2}$ lb. damsons** |
| | **4 oz. demerara sugar** |

Half-fill a $1\frac{1}{2}$-pt. pie-dish with damsons, sprinkle on the sugar, pile the remaining damsons on top, piling them high in the centre. Line the edge of the dish with pastry and cover it with pastry, brush lightly over with cold water, dredge with castor sugar, and bake in a fairly hot oven (**400° F., Gas 6**).

**5–6 helpings**
**Cooking time—about 1 hr.**

### DANISH HERRING (for Smørrebrød) D.

| | |
|---|---|
| **Herrings** | **Sugar** |
| **Onions** | **Vinegar** |
| **Peppercorns** | **2–3 bay leaves** |
| **Salt** | |

Wash and clean some good herrings. Slit them down the back and remove the back-bone. Cut them in neat pieces and place a layer in a fireproof dish. Cover this layer with rings of raw onions, whole peppercorns, salt and a good sprinkling of sugar. Repeat with more fish, onions and flavouring until the dish is $\frac{3}{4}$ full. Cover with vinegar and water ($\frac{3}{4}$ vinegar to $\frac{1}{4}$ water) and add the bay leaves; then cover with a lid and cook in a cool oven (**310° F., Gas 2**) for 1 hr. Leave the herring to cool in the vinegar. Serve 2–3 slices on a piece of buttered bread. Decorate with the slices of onions.

### DANISH SALAD

*Salade Danoise*

| | |
|---|---|
| **4 tomatoes** | **$\frac{1}{4}$ pt. pickled button onions** |
| **1 lb. cooked French beans** | **Mayonnaise sauce** |
| **$\frac{1}{2}$ pt. cooked green peas** | **Sprigs of dill** |

Skin and slice the tomatoes; cut the beans into thick slices. Mix the beans, peas and onions with mayonnaise sauce. Pile on a dish and garnish with sliced tomato and sprigs of dill.

**4–6 helpings**

### DATE PUDDING

| | |
|---|---|
| **8 oz. plain flour** | **3 oz. castor sugar** |
| **Pinch of salt** | **6 oz. chopped stoned dates** |
| **1 rounded teasp. baking-powder** | **1 egg** |
| **3–4 oz. butter *or* margarine** | **Milk** |

Grease a basin. Sift together the flour, salt and baking-powder. Rub the fat into the flour. Add the sugar and dates and mix well together. Mix to a soft dropping consistency with the egg and milk. Put into the basin. Cover with a greased paper and steam for $1\frac{1}{2}$ hr. until firm in the centre.

**6 helpings**

### DATE ROLY POLY

*Roulade aux Dattes*

| | |
|---|---|
| **6 oz. dates** | **$\frac{1}{4}$ teasp. salt** |

| | |
|---|---|
| **12 oz. plain flour** | **4–6 oz. finely-chopped suet** |
| **2 rounded teasp. baking-powder** | **Water to mix** |

Chop the dates. Sift together the flour, baking-powder and salt. Add the suet and dates. Add sufficient water to mix to a soft, but firm, dough. Form into a roll and place at the end of a well-floured pudding cloth. Roll up loosely and tie firmly at either end, into a sausage-shape. Drop into boiling water and simmer 2–2½ hr.

Serve with custard.

NOTE: For dates the same weight of the following may be substituted—**currants, sultanas,** stoned **raisins** or **figs,** and the pudding named accordingly.

## DATE AND WALNUT CAKE

*Gâteau aux Dattes et aux Noix*

| | |
|---|---|
| **¾ lb. plain flour** | **2 level teasp. cream of tartar** |
| **¼ teasp. salt** | **4 oz. chopped dates** |
| **4½ oz. butter** *or* **margarine** | **1½ oz. chopped walnuts** |
| **5 oz. sugar** | **2 eggs** |
| **A little grated nutmeg** | **1½–2 gills milk (approx.)** |
| **1½ level teasp. bicarbonate of soda** | |

Sift flour and salt and rub in the fat. Add the other dry ingredients and mix with the eggs and milk to a dropping consistency. Put into a greased 8-in. tin and bake in a fairly hot oven **(375° F., Gas 5).** Reduce heat to moderate **(350° F., Gas 4** after 15 min.

**Cooking time—1¼–1½ hr.**

## DEMI-GLACE SAUCE

Half glaze

| | |
|---|---|
| **½ pt. Espagnole sauce** | **¼ pt. juices from roast meat** *or* **¼ pt. stock and 1 teasp. good beef extract** *or* **meat glaze** |

Boil the sauce and meat juices together until well reduced. Skim off any fat before serving the sauce.

Serve with meat, poultry, game etc.

## DESSERT

Dessert is the last course to be served at formal dinners. It is composed principally of fruits in season, nuts (with or without raisins) and (sometimes) ices, petits fours or dessert biscuits, dainty sweets and bonbons. Sometimes, salted almonds are served too.

Before being arranged on its dish, dessert fruit should be well washed and dried with a clean cloth. It can be polished slightly with the cloth.

Grapes, peaches, nectarines, plums, cherries, apples, pears, oranges, dates and figs can all be served as dessert. The fruit looks most attractive presented on a dish lined with green leaves, and it can even form part of the table setting in this case. If dessert is to be handed round, it is served after the table has been cleared. Dessert plates, knives and forks are placed before each person before serving the fruit.

On the Continent, fruit is often served as, or instead of, a sweet course.

In the United States, the pudding or sweet course is usually referred to as the dessert, and this custom is coming more and more into favour in Britain.

## DEVILLED BUTTER

*Beurre à la Diable*

| | |
|---|---|
| **2 oz. butter** | **¼ teasp. curry powder** |
| **¼ teasp. cayenne** | **¼ teasp. ground ginger** |
| **⅛ teasp. pepper** | |

Pound all the ingredients together, then rub through a fine sieve.

## DEVILLED CHICKENS' LIVERS

*Foie de Volaille à la Diable*

| | |
|---|---|
| **4 chickens' livers** | **Pinch of salt** |
| **1 shallot** *or* **small onion** | **8 small rashers of bacon** |
| **½ teasp. chopped parsley** | **4 croûtes of fried bread** |
| **Pinch of cayenne pepper** | |

Wash and dry the livers, cut them in halves. Finely chop the shallot or onion and mix with the parsley, cayenne pepper and salt. Sprinkle this mixture over the livers. Wrap the rashers of bacon round the livers, and fasten them in position with skewers. Bake in a moderate oven **(350° F., Gas 4)** for 7–8 min., or cook under the grill. Remove the skewers, put 2 bacon rolls on each croûte of bread, and serve as hot as possible.

**4 helpings**

### DEVILLED CHICKENS (POUSSINS)

*Poussins à la Diable*

**1 poussin per portion**
**1 dessertsp. olive oil**
**Salt and pepper**
**Pinch of ground ginger**
**Pinch of mustard**
**1 teasp. chopped parsley**
**1 teasp. chopped shallot**

Split and skewer the baby chicken, sprinkle with the olive oil. Season with salt, pepper, ginger and mustard and sprinkle the parsley and shallot over. Allow to stand for about 1 hr., turning occasionally. Grill until tender.

Serve very hot.

### DEVILLED CRAB

*Crabe à la Diable*

**1 medium-sized crab**
**1 teacup of bread-crumbs**
**1 teasp. mixed mustard**
**1 teasp. Worcester sauce**
**1 tablesp. oiled butter**
**Cayenne pepper**
**Salt to taste**
**Cream *or* milk**
**2 tablesp. breadcrumbs**
**Extra butter**

Remove the crab meat from the shell and claws, clean the shell and put it aside. Chop the meat of the crab, add the breadcrumbs, mustard, sauce, butter and a very liberal seasoning of cayenne and salt. Mix well, if necessary moisten with a little milk or cream, then turn the whole into the prepared shell. Cover lightly with breadcrumbs, add a few small pieces of butter, and brown in a fairly hot oven **(375° F., Gas 5).**

**3 helpings**
**Cooking time—15 min.**

### DEVILLED OYSTERS

*Huîtres à la Diable*

**1 dozen oysters**
**Salt**
**Cayenne pepper**
**1 oz. butter**

Open the oysters carefully so as to preserve as much of the liquor as possible, or ask your fishmonger to open them for you and leave them in their shells. Sprinkle lightly with salt, and more liberally with cayenne, and put a small piece of butter on top of each one. Place the oysters on a baking sheet and put in a hot oven until thoroughly heated.

Serve with sliced lemon and thin brown bread and butter.

**3–4 helpings** **Cooking time—4 min.**

### DEVILLED SHEEP'S KIDNEYS

*Rognons à la Diable*

**6 sheep's kidneys**
**1½ oz. butter *or* fat**
**1 tablesp. chopped onion**
**Salt**
**Cayenne pepper**
**3 teasp. chutney**
**2 teasp. lemon juice**
**½ teasp. mixed mustard**
**¼ pt. stock**
**2 egg yolks**
**Breadcrumbs**
**Buttered toast *or* potato border**

Skin and well wash the kidneys. Split open and remove the cores. Cut the kidneys into neat pieces. Melt the fat in a small pan, put in the onion and cook without browning. Then add the kidney, salt, cayenne, chutney, lemon juice, mustard and stock. Cover and stew for a short time over moderate heat until the kidney is cooked. Cool slightly and stir in the egg yolks. Sprinkle in enough bread-crumbs to make a soft consistency and correct the seasoning. Serve on buttered toast or in a mashed potato border.

**6 helpings**
**Cooking time—about 20 min.**

### DEVILLED SMOKED SALMON

**½ lb. smoked salmon (approx.)**
**3–4 slices toasted bread**
**1 oz. fresh butter**
**Salt and pepper**
**Curry butter**

Trim the slices of toast, cut each into 3 even-sized pieces and butter one side of each. Sprinkle with salt and pepper, cover with thin slices of smoked salmon, then spread with curry butter. Place in a hot oven for a few minutes. Dish up neatly, garnish with sprigs of parsley and serve hot.

**5–6 helpings**

### DEVILLED TOMATOES

*Tomates à la Diable*

**6 tomatoes**
**2 oz. butter *or* margarine**
**Cayenne pepper**
**½ teasp. mixed mustard**

| | |
|---|---|
| **Yolks of 2 hard-boiled eggs** | **A little sugar** |
| **Salt** | **2 tablesp. vinegar** |
| | **2 eggs** |

Peel and slice the tomatoes and cook them slowly in a saucepan with ½ oz. of the butter. Mix the rest of the butter with the hard-boiled egg yolks, stir in the salt, pepper, mustard, about 1 saltsp. of sugar and the vinegar. Lastly add the beaten eggs. Put the mixture into another small pan and stir over a gentle heat until it thickens. Re-season. Place the tomatoes in a hot dish and pour the sauce over them.

**5–6 helpings**
**Cooking time—about 30 min.**

## DEVILLED TURKEY

*Dinde à la Diable*

| | |
|---|---|
| **¾ lb. cold roast turkey** | **½ pt. piquant sauce** |

DEVILLED BUTTER

| | |
|---|---|
| **1 oz. butter** | **½ saltsp. curry paste** |
| **½ saltsp. cayenne** | **Pinch of ground ginger** |
| **½ saltsp. black pepper** | |

Mix together all the ingredients for the devilled butter. Divide the turkey into portions convenient for serving, remove all skin, score the flesh deeply, spread lightly with the devilled butter and leave 1 hr. (Leave longer if a highly-seasoned dish is desired.) Grill meat about 8 min. Serve sauce separately.

**3–4 helpings**

## DEVILLED TURKEY LEGS

*Cuisses de Dinde à la Diable*

| | |
|---|---|
| **2 turkey legs** | **Mixed mustard** *or* **French mustard** |
| **Salt and pepper** | **Butter** |
| **Cayenne pepper** | |

Remove skin from turkey, criss-cross with deep cuts. Sprinkle well with seasoning and a little cayenne, if required very hot. Spread with mixed mustard (*or* French mustard) pressing well into the cuts and leave for several hours. Grill 8–12 min. until crisp and brown, spread with small pieces of butter mixed with cayenne, and serve immediately.

**4 helpings**

## DEVILS ON HORSEBACK

| | |
|---|---|
| **1–2 chicken livers** *or* **equivalent of calf's liver** | **8 well-drained canned prunes** |
| **Butter** | **8 short thin rindless rashers streaky bacon** |
| **Salt and pepper** | **4 small bread squares** |
| **Cayenne pepper** | **Olives stuffed with pimento** |

Gently cook the liver in a little butter, then cut it into 8 pieces. Season well and dust with a few grains of cayenne pepper. Stone the prunes and stuff with the liver. Stretch the bacon to double its size with the flat of a knife. Encircle each prune in a piece of bacon and secure with a cocktail stick. Grill all over or bake in a very hot oven. Fry the bread in shallow bacon fat and drain well. Remove sticks and place the "devils" on the bread. Garnish with a pimento-stuffed olive.

**4 helpings**

## DEVONSHIRE CREAM

Before starting to make Devonshire Cream at home, fresh milk should be allowed to stand for some hours. In very cold weather, this period should be 12 hours but about half that time is sufficient if the weather is warm.

The milk should be heated, in a milk pan, until it is quite hot but not boiling. Boiling coagulates the protein and a skin will form on the surface. The more slowly the milk is heated, the better will be the result. The time required depends upon the size and shape of the pan and the amount of heat applied but slight movement on the surface of the milk indicates that it is sufficiently scalded.

When scalding is completed, the pan should at once be transferred to a cold place and left there until the following day. The cream can then be skimmed off the surface.

## DEVONSHIRE RUM

| | |
|---|---|
| **Cold Christmas pudding** | **½ oz. castor sugar** |
| **1 oz. cornflour** | **1 egg** |
| **1 pt. milk** | **Wineglass of rum** |

Grease a pie-dish and fill it with strips of pudding crossed lattice fashion. Mix the cornflour smoothly with a little of the milk. Put the rest of the milk on to boil. When boiling remove from the heat and add the blended cornflour, slowly, but stirring thoroughly to prevent lumps forming. Return to heat and cook for 3 min. Add the sugar, beaten egg and the rum. Pour the sauce over the pudding. Bake gently in a moderate oven (**350° F., Gas 4**) until the mixture is set.

If preferred, the pudding may be steamed for 2 hr. in a basin.

**6 helpings**
**Cooking time (baked)—½ hr.**
**(steamed)—2 hr.**

## DHÂLL

| | |
|---|---|
| **½ pt. lentils** | **3 onions** |
| **¾ pt. stock** | **1 tablesp. curry powder** |
| **2 oz. ghee** | **Boiled rice** |

Wash and dry the lentils, cover them with stock, simmer gently until tender, adding more stock gradually, but when finished they should be quite dry. Heat the ghee in a saucepan, slice the onions and fry until lightly browned. Sprinkle in the curry powder, stir for a few minutes, then add the lentils. Cook gently for about 20 min. Serve with boiled rice.

**Cooking time—1–1¼ hr.**

## DIABETIC FOODS

The diabetic sufferer must of course always be guided by his diet sheet and by his doctor's instructions. If the housewife is in any doubt about using a particular recipe for him, the Diabetic Association will advise her.

Most egg dishes are suitable for a diabetic diet. Milk, cheese, fish and meat are also valuable foods.

The carbohydrate value of most leafy green vegetables is minute, so the patient can enjoy salads, cooked green vegetables and many vegetable soups.

The following notes may be useful in planning a diet sheet:

1 pint of milk contains 30 grams carbohydrate, 24 grams protein, 24 grams fats, so the moment one drinks or adds ¼ pint milk to a soup then 7½ grams carbohydrate, 6 grams protein and 6 grams fat are added.

¼ oz. flour (¾ level tablespoonful) used in thickening a soup or stew gives 5 grams carbohydrate and 1 gram protein but no fat.

⅙th oz. sugar (1 good teaspoonful) gives 5 grams carbohydrate but no added protein or fat.

## DOUGH BUNS — Dinner

**1 lb. plain flour, etc., as for Milk Bread**

Make the dough as for Milk Bread then divide risen dough into required number of pieces. Shape each into a round, making sure that the underside is smooth. Place on a greased baking-sheet and flatten slightly—keep good shape. Prove for 10–15 min. then brush over with beaten egg and milk. Bake in a hot oven (**425° F., Gas 7**).

**20–24 buns**
**Cooking time—10–15 min.**

## DOUGHNUTS

| | |
|---|---|
| **½ lb. plain flour** | **½ oz. yeast** |
| **¼ teasp. salt** | **½–¾ gill warm milk** |
| **2 oz. margarine *or* ¾ oz. lard and 1 oz. margarine)** | **1 egg** |
| | **Cinnamon sugar for coating** |
| **1 oz. castor sugar** | **Fat for deep frying** |

Rub the fat into the warmed flour and salt; add sugar, having taken out ½ teasp. to cream the yeast. Add the warm milk and egg to the creamed yeast and pour into the flour. Mix well (do not make too soft as the dough is to be cut out), and put to rise to double its size. Knead lightly and roll out ½ in. thick. Cut into rings, using 2½–2¾ in. cutter for outside and 1½–1¾ in. for inner ring, and prove on warm tray for 5 min. Drop into very faintly smoking fat and cook 5 min.; drain well and toss in castor sugar *or* sugar mixed with ground cinnamon to taste.

NOTE: Proving may be unnecessary, the first doughnuts may be ready to fry by the time the last are cut out.

**14–16 doughnuts**

*Alternative Method:* Divide dough into 12. Roll each piece into a ball and place a glacé cherry or a little jam in the middle. Prove 10 min. and proceed as above.

## DOUGHNUTS WITHOUT YEAST

**8 oz. plain flour**
**$1/8$ teasp. salt**
**$1\frac{1}{2}$ oz. butter *or* margarine**
**$1\frac{1}{2}$ oz. sugar**
**A little grated lemon rind**
**$1\frac{1}{2}$ teasp. baking-powder**
**1 egg**
**$3/4$ gill milk *or* enough to make a light dough**

Mix flour and salt, rub in fat. Add other dry ingredients and mix to a light dough with egg and milk. Roll out on a floured board $\frac{1}{2}$ in. thick, cut out and fry as for yeast doughnuts.

NOTE: 2 small level teasp. cream of tartar may be used and 1 small level teasp. bicarbonate of soda instead of baking-powder.

**12–16 doughnuts**

## DRESSED CRAB

*Crabe froid*

**One $2\frac{1}{2}$–3 lb. crab**
**Salt and pepper**
**Fresh breadcrumbs (optional)**
**A little lemon juice (optional)**
**French dressing**

GARNISH

**1 hard-boiled egg**
**Parsley**

Pick the crab meat from the shells (see crabs ). Mix the dark crab meat with salt and pepper, fresh breadcrumbs and a little lemon juice if liked. The breadcrumbs are optional but they lessen the richness and give a firmer texture. Press the mixture lightly against the sides of the previously cleaned shell. Flake up the white meat, mix with French dressing and pile in the centre of the shell. Garnish with sieved egg yolk, chopped egg white, chopped parsley, sieved coral if any, and decorate with small claws. Make a necklace with the small claws, place on a dish and rest the crab on this. Surround with salad.

**4 helpings**

## DRESSED LOBSTER

*Homard froid*

Prepare the boiled lobster ready for use . Leave the meat in the shell and arrange the two halves on a bed of salad. Garnish with the claws. Serve with oil and vinegar handed separately. Piped lobster butter may be used to garnish the shell, if wished.

## DRESSING POULTRY

*See Poultry.*

## DRIED PEAS

**Dried peas**
**2 qt. boiling water to each 1 lb. peas**
**$\frac{1}{2}$ level teasp. bicarbonate of soda *or* a piece of washing soda the size of a cherry**

Pour the boiling water on to the required weight of peas, add the soda, and leave to soak overnight.

Rinse the peas thoroughly after soaking, cook in plenty of boiling, salted water until the peas are soft—1–$1\frac{1}{2}$ hr. approximately.

To improve the flavour, add a sprig of mint, bunch of herbs (a small sprig of marjoram, sage, thyme and a few parsley stalks) or an onion stuck with 2 or 3 cloves.

## DRIED VEGETABLES

*See Vegetables.*

## DROPPED SCONES

**6 oz. plain flour**
**$1/8$ teasp. salt**
**$1\frac{1}{2}$ oz. sugar**
**2 eggs**
**1 gill milk (approx.)**
**1 level teasp. bicarbonate of soda**
**2 level teasp. cream of tartar**

Mix flour, salt and sugar together, add eggs and enough milk to make a thick batter. Beat well. Stir in the dry bicarbonate of soda and cream of tartar. Drop in spoonfuls on a hot greased girdle—allow 1 dessertsp. for a small scone and 1 tablesp. for a large one. Drop from the point of the spoon to keep the scone a good shape. When there are bubbles appearing and the scone is brown on the underside, turn with a broad knife, straighten the edges and brown on the second side. Cook for 2 min. and cool in a tea-towel.

**12–20 scones**

## DRYING AND SALTING

These methods of preserving food are a specialized form of cookery. They are described fully in *Mrs Beeton's Cookery and Household Management.*

## DUCHESS POTATOES

*Pommes de terre Duchesse*

**1 lb. old potatoes**
**1 oz. butter *or* margarine**
**Cream *or* top of milk**
**2 yolks *or* 1 whole egg**
**Salt and pepper**
**Grated nutmeg**

Prepare and cook the potatoes as for Boiled Potatoes. Put through a sieve. Mash with the fat, beaten egg and sufficient cream to give a smooth mixture, which stands up in soft peaks when drawn up with the wooden spoon. Season well and add grated nutmeg. Pipe through a star vegetable pipe, on to a greased baking-sheet. Sprinkle with a little beaten egg and bake in a hot oven (**400° F., Gas 6**), until crisp and brown. Serve in a hot uncovered dish.

Note: If a "pipe" is not available, keep the mixture a little stiffer and shape on a floured board into small cork shapes, diamonds, rounds or triangles. Decorate the tops with criss-crosses made with the back of a knife.

If more convenient, the mixture may be shaped or piped on to the tin and left in a cool place for baking at a later time.

**6 helpings** **Cooking time—to bake, 15 min.**

## DUCHESS PUDDING

*Pouding à la Duchesse*

**½ oz. pistachio nuts**
**3 oz. macaroons**
**3 oz. butter *or* margarine**
**3 oz. castor sugar**
**3 eggs**
**4 tablesp. orange marmalade**
**1 level dessertsp. ground rice**

Grease a mould (or 1½ pt. pudding basin) with butter. Blanch, peel and chop the pistachios roughly; sprinkle half of them round the sides and bottom of the mould. Crush the macaroons.

Cream together the fat and sugar. Separate the eggs. Work in the egg yolks and marmalade. Stir in the macaroons. Stiffly whisk the egg whites and fold them in lightly. Sprinkle in the ground rice and the rest of the pistachios at the same time. Put the mixture into the mould; cover. Steam slowly for 1¼–1½ hr.

Serve with marmalade sauce.

**5–6 helpings**

## DUCK EN CASSEROLE

*Canard en casserole*

**1 duck**
**¾ oz. flour**
**Salt and pepper**
**4 oz. mushrooms**
**4 shallots**
**¾ pt. stock (approx.)**
**½ pt. green peas**
**1 teasp. chopped mint**

Cut duck into joints, remove all skin, dip the joints in seasoned flour. Place duck, chopped mushrooms and chopped shallots in a casserole. Just cover with stock, put on a tightly-fitting lid and cook in a fairly hot oven (**375°–400° F., Gas 5–6**) about ¾ hr. Add shelled peas and mint and continue cooking until duck is tender—about another ½ hr. Correct seasoning.

Serve from the casserole.

**4–5 helpings**

## DUCK WITH PEAS—FRENCH

*Caneton au Petits Pois*

**3½–4 lb. duck**
**12 spring *or* button onions**
**2 oz. butter**
**8 oz. lardoons (streaky bacon)**
**¾ pt. veal *or* chicken stock**
**1 qt. fresh peas**
**Bouquet garni**
**Salt and pepper**
**Sugar**
**1 small globe lettuce (optional)**

Parboil the spring or button onions and the lardoons. Drain off. In a saucepan large enough to hold the duck, heat the butter, add the onions and lardoons, and quickly toss to a nice light brown colour. Remove from saucepan. Place the duck in the saucepan and also colour well all over; then remove. In the saucepan put ⅓ of the stock and boil down to ½ its quantity, then add the remainder of the stock, with the duck, onions, lardoons, peas and bouquet garni. Lightly season with salt and pepper and a pinch of sugar. Bring to the boil, then place in a fairly hot oven (**375° F., Gas 5**) to cook, with the lid on. Baste from time to time. Approximate time of cooking, 45 min. Remove duck and place on a dish; surround with peas and the remainder of the garnish. Lightly reduce the cooking liquor by boiling, then pour it over the duck. A shredded or whole lettuce can be added to the duck and peas when cooking. In the latter case it is cut into quarters when serving and placed on the peas.

**5–6 helpings**

## DUCK AND RED CABBAGE

*Canard au Chou rouge*

**Trimmings of 2 cold roast ducks**
**½ red cabbage**
**2 oz. butter**
**Good gravy *or* stock**
**Salt and pepper**
**1 tablesp. vinegar**

Wash and drain cabbage, shred it finely and cook gently for 1 hr. with the butter, in a tightly-covered pan, adding gravy *or* stock if necessary to prevent burning; season well. Divide duck into neat joints and heat the pieces in a little gravy. Add vinegar to the cabbage—turn on to hot dish.

Arrange the duck on top, and serve with good gravy.

## DUCK—ROUENNAISE STYLE

*Canard à la Rouennaise*

**1 large "Rouen" duck**
**2 oz. butter**
**1 tablesp. chopped shallot**
**1 dessertsp. flour**
**½ pt. stock**
**1 glass claret (optional)**
**Bouquet garni**
**Lemon juice**

STUFFING

**Heart and liver of the duck**
**2 tablesp. breadcrumbs**
**1 teasp. chopped parsley**
**1 small onion**
**1 oz. butter**
**Salt and pepper**

Prepare stuffing: remove gall bladder from liver, wash liver and heart, chop finely. Parboil onion, chop finely and add to liver and heart with breadcrumbs, parsley, melted butter and seasoning. Stuff duck with this mixture, truss, and fry with chopped shallot in the butter, until brown. Remove duck, stir in flour and brown it, stir in stock, bring to boiling-point, add claret (if used). Replace duck in pan, add bouquet garni and lemon juice, cover with a tightly-fitting lid. Cook in a moderate oven (**350° F., Gas 4**) until duck is tender—1–1½ hr. Remove trussing strings, joint the duck but keep it in shape.

Serve on a hot dish with sauce strained over.

**4–5 helpings**
**Cooking time—1½ hr.**

## DUCK SALAD

*Salade de Canard*

**½ a cold duck**
**1 small heart of celery**
**Salt and pepper**
**3 tablesp. French dressing**
**2 slices unpeeled orange**
**1 cabbage lettuce**
**½ bunch watercress**
**Mayonnaise sauce**
**1 teasp. chopped parsley**
**1 teasp. chopped olives (optional)**

Cut the duck into 1-in. dice, and the celery into fine strips. Mix in a basin with seasoning and 2 tablesp. French dressing and leave to stand. Cut the orange slices into quarters or eighths. Line the salad bowl with lettuce leaves and sprigs of cress. Decorate with the orange sections and baste with 1 tablesp. French dressing. Place the duck mixture in the centre and cover with a thin layer of mayonnaise. Sprinkle with parsley and olives.

**6 helpings**

## DUNDEE CAKE

**7 oz. butter *or* margarine**
**7 oz. castor sugar**
**¾ lb. plain flour**
**¼ teasp. salt**
**12–16 oz. mixed fruit—currants, raisins sultanas**
**3–4 eggs**
**1 level teasp. baking-powder**
**Milk *or* water as required**
**Blanched almonds**

Line a 7–8-in. cake-tin with greaseproof paper (oiled). Cream the fat and sugar till light. Sift together flour and salt and mix the fruit with a small amount of the flour. Add the eggs and flour alternately to the creamed fat, beating well between each addition. Mix baking-powder with the last lot of flour, stir in the fruit and if necessary add a little milk *or* water to make a heavy dropping consistency. Put into the cake-tin, make a slight depression in the centre and spread some split blanched almonds over the surface. Bake in a moderate oven (**350° F., Gas 4**), reduce heat after ¾ hr. to warm to cool (**335°–310° F., Gas 3–2**).

**Cooking time—2½ hr.**

ECCLES CAKES

**Flaky *or* rough puff pastry, using 6 oz. flour, etc. *or* trimmings may be used**
**½ oz. butter *or* margarine**
**¼ oz. sugar**
**2 oz. currants**
**¾ oz. chopped peel**
**¼ teasp. mixed spice**
**A little grated nutmeg**

Roll out pastry ¼ in. thick, cut into 4-in. rounds. Cream fat and sugar, add currants, peel and spice and place a good teasp. of the mixture in the centre of each round of pastry. Gather the edges together, pinch firmly, and form into a flat cake; reverse the cake and roll gently till the fruit begins to show through. Make two cuts on top of each, brush with water and dust with castor sugar. Bake in a hot oven (**425° F., Gas 7**).

**12–14 cakes**
**Cooking time—20 min.**

ÉCLAIRS

**Choux pastry**
**½ pt. double cream *or* confectioner's custard *or* mock cream**
**Sugar to sweeten**
**Vanilla essence**
**Chocolate *or* coffee glacé icing**

Grease a baking-sheet. Place the pastry in a forcing bag with a large plain pipe (¾ in. to 1 in.), and pipe mixture out on to the greased sheet in 4-in. lengths, cutting off each length with a knife dipped in hot water. Bake in a hot oven (**425°–400° F., Gas 7–6**) until risen and crisp (do not open the door during this time). Reduce heat and move to a cooler part of the oven, until éclairs are light and dry inside, about 30 min. altogether. Place on a cooling tray and slit open. When cold fill the cavities with stiffly-whipped, sweetened cream flavoured with vanilla. Spread tops with chocolate or coffee glacé icing thinly. Put the icing on in a straight line, using a teaspoon—hold the éclair in a slanting position when doing so.

**9–10 éclairs** **Cooking time—30 min.**

EGG AND BRANDY (or WINE)

**1 egg**
**Castor sugar to taste**
**1 tablesp. hot *or* cold water**
**1 tablesp. brandy *or* a small glass port *or* sherry**

Beat the egg well in a cup, add a little sugar, and the water, brandy, port or sherry, and mix well. Strain into a tumbler and serve.

**1 helping**

EGG BUTTER FOR SAVOURIES

*See Savouries (Appetizers).*

EGG CROQUETTES

*Croquettes aux Œufs*

**4 hard-boiled eggs**
**6 mushrooms**
**1 oz. butter**
**½ oz. flour**
**½ gill milk**
**Salt and pepper**
**Pinch of nutmeg**
**A little flour and milk for coating**
**Breadcrumbs**
**Fried parsley**

Chop the eggs finely. Chop the mushrooms roughly and fry them lightly in the butter, stir in the flour, add the milk and boil well. Now put in the eggs, add seasoning and nutmeg, mix well over heat, then spread on a plate to cool. When ready to use, shape into balls, coat carefully with a batter (milk and flour mixed to the consistency of cream), cover with breadcrumbs and fry in hot fat until golden brown. Drain well and serve garnished with fried parsley.

**4 helpings**

EGG CUSTARD SAUCE

**1 egg *or* 2 egg yolks**
**½ pt. milk**
**1 level tablesp. castor sugar**
**Lemon rind *or* vanilla essence to flavour**

Beat egg thoroughly. Pour hot milk slowly over egg. Return to saucepan, straining if necessary. Add lemon rind if used, and sugar. Simmer over a very low heat until the custard thickens sufficiently to coat back of wooden spoon. Remove lemon rind; stir in a few drops of vanilla essence if used. *Never* allow to boil. A double saucepan can be used if liked. Serve hot or cold.

**2 helpings** **Cooking time—about 15 min.**

## EGG DISHES

Egg dishes are very varied. Eggs also form an important ingredient in many dishes such as savoury flans, which are named after some other main ingredient which flavours the dish, e.g. Cheese Onion Pie. For ways of cooking eggs, *see Baked Eggs, Boiled Eggs, Custards, etc.* For other dishes, *see the recipe for the type of flavour of dish required, e.g. Meringues, Cream and Egg Salad Dressing, Coffee Ice Cream.*

## EGG FLIP

**1 tablesp. brandy *or* sherry**
**¼ pt. milk**
**A little castor sugar (optional)**
**1 egg white**

Mix the brandy or wine and the milk together in a tumbler. If liked, add a little castor sugar. Beat the egg white to a stiff froth, stir it lightly into the flavoured milk and serve.

**1 helping**

## EGG KROMESKIS

*Cromesquis d'Œufs*

**3 hard-boiled eggs**
**⅛ pt. white sauce**
**1 tablesp. chopped tongue *or* ham**
**½ teasp. finely-chopped truffles**
**Salt and pepper**
**5 thin pancakes**
**Frying fat**
**Coating batter**

Chop the eggs coarsely, add the sauce, tongue, truffles and seasoning. Stir over heat for a few minutes. Let the mixture cool, then divide it into pieces the size and shape of a cork, and enfold in squares of pancake. Dip separately into batter, fry in hot fat until nicely browned, drain well and serve.

**3–4 helpings**
**Cooking time—40 min. (approx.)**

## EGG NOG

**1 tablesp. sherry *or* brandy**
**1 tablesp. cream**
**Castor sugar to taste**
**1 egg white**

Put the wine or brandy in a tumbler, add the cream and a little sugar and mix well. Whisk the egg white to a stiff froth, stir it lightly into the contents of the tumbler, and serve.

**1 helping**

## EGG POWDER

*See Bread and Bread-Making*

## EGG SALAD (1)

*Salade aux Œufs*

**5 hard-boiled eggs**
**Oil**
**Vinegar**
**Salt and pepper**
**Lettuce**
**Parsley**

Shred finely or cut into small julienne strips the whites of the hard-boiled eggs. Rub the yolks through a coarse sieve, and mix with oil, vinegar, salt and pepper, then add the shredded egg white and blend carefully. Place on lettuce leaves, sprinkle over a little chopped parsley and serve.

**5–6 helpings**

## EGG SALAD (2)

**4 hard-boiled eggs**
**½ gill thick mayonnaise**
**½ teasp. anchovy essence**
**Tiny pieces of tomato**
**Tiny pieces of gherkin**
**Lettuce**

Cut the eggs into halves or quarters. Mix together the mayonnaise and the anchovy essence, turn the eggs upside down and coat the white outside with the mayonnaise mixture. Arrange tiny pieces of tomato or gherkin on top. Lift on to crisp lettuce leaves.

**4–5 helpings**

## EGG SAUCE

*Sauce aux œufs durs*

**½ pt. white sauce made with milk**
**1 hard-boiled egg**
**1 teasp. chopped chives, if liked**

Chop the hard-boiled egg, stir it, with the chives, into the hot, well-seasoned sauce. Reheat the whole.

### EGG SOUP

*Potage à la Royale*

**1 oz. macaroni**
**¾ oz. butter**
**¾ oz. flour**
**1½ pt. stock**
**Trace of nutmeg**
**1 bay leaf**
**A little yeast *or* meat extract**
**Salt and cayenne pepper**
**2 egg yolks**
**⅛ pt. milk**
**⅛ pt. cream**

Boil the macaroni until very soft, cut it into ¼-in. lengths. Melt the butter, stir in the flour, then the stock and bring to the boil. Add the spices, yeast or meat extract and the macaroni and season the soup. Mix the egg yolks, milk and cream and add to the soup well below boiling point. Cook the egg yolks without allowing the soup to boil.

Serve with grated cheese.

**6 helpings**
**Cooking time—15 min.**

### EGG STUFFING FOR SAVOURIES

*See Savouries (Appetizers).*

### EGG WASH, TO MAKE

Lightly beat together ½ teasp. salt and 1 egg with a fork. Use for glazing.

### EGG WHITE, TO WHISK

All utensils must be perfectly clean and free from grease, and once the process has been started it must be carried through without a break. Separate the egg whites from the yolks so that the whites are perfectly clean and free from egg yolk. Put the whites into a basin with a pinch of salt, then whisk until they stand up in firm peaks.

### EGGING AND CRUMBING

*Egging and crumbing:* Food is often given a protective coating of egg and breadcrumbs before frying.

An egg, slightly beaten, is often used, but better results may be obtained by adding 1 teasp. salad oil, 1 dessertsp. milk and a little salt and pepper. Mix these together in a deep plate. Lightly flour the food to dry it, dip each piece individually in the egg coating and then toss lightly in plenty of crumbs held in a piece of kitchen paper, pressing them on firmly with the hand or knife blade. Shake off the loose crumbs. Use fine crumbs as they will adhere more firmly than coarse ones.

White breadcrumbs should be used for coating uncooked food and browned breadcrumbs (raspings) for coating food which is already cooked and only requires heating.

### EGGS IN BAKED POTATOES

**6 eggs**
**3 large potatoes**
**⅓ pt. (approx.) Béchamel *or* White sauce**
**1 oz. grated cheese**
**Breadcrumbs**
**½ oz. butter**

Scrub the potatoes, bake them, cut in halves and scoop out the greater part of the inside. Poach the eggs and trim them neatly. Put a little sauce in each halved potato, and add an egg. Mix the remainder of the sauce with half the cheese and spread it lightly over the eggs. Sprinkle first with breadcrumbs, then with cheese, add little bits of butter. Brown the surface in a hot oven and serve.

**6 helpings** **Cooking time—1½ hr. (approx.)**

### EGGS, TO COOK

*See Baked Eggs, Boiled Eggs, etc.*

### EGGS À LA DREUX

*Œufs à la Dreux*

**4 eggs**
**¼ lb. lean cooked ham**
**1 dessertsp. finely-chopped parsley**
**½ oz. butter**
**Cayenne pepper**
**Salt**
**4 small rounds buttered toast**

Chop the ham finely, add the parsley and mix. Coat 4 deep patty tins thickly with butter, and cover them completely with a thin layer of ham mixture. Break an egg into each tin, taking care to keep the yolk whole. Sprinkle with a little cayenne pepper and salt, and add a small piece of butter. Place the patty tins in a deep baking-tin, surround them to half their depth with boiling water, and cook in a moderate oven (**350° F., Gas 4**) until the whites are set. Cut the rounds of toast to the size of the patty tins, dish the eggs on them.

**4 helpings** **Cooking time—10 min. (approx.)**

Flan Cases ("Blind" Baking).

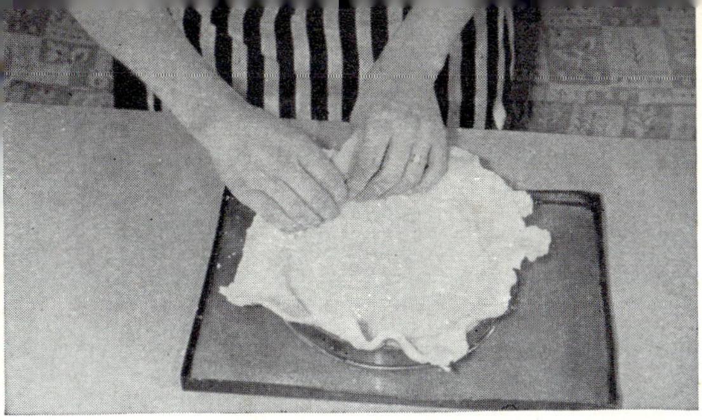

1 Roll out the pastry and line a greased flan ring with it. Press to fit bottom and sides so that no air bubbles form underneath.

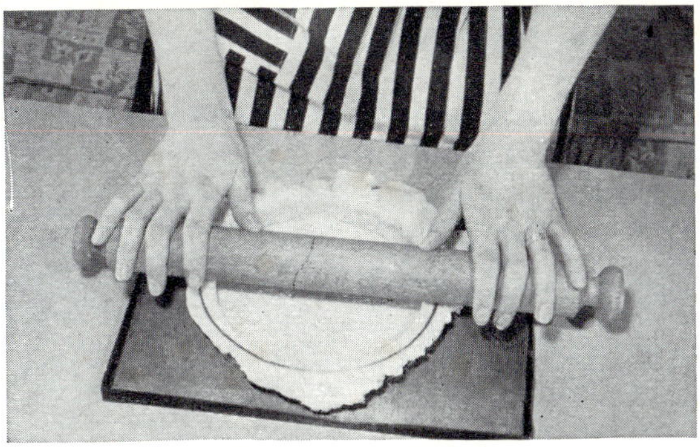

2 Trim off surplus pastry by rolling across with the rolling-pin or cut it off with a sharp knife.

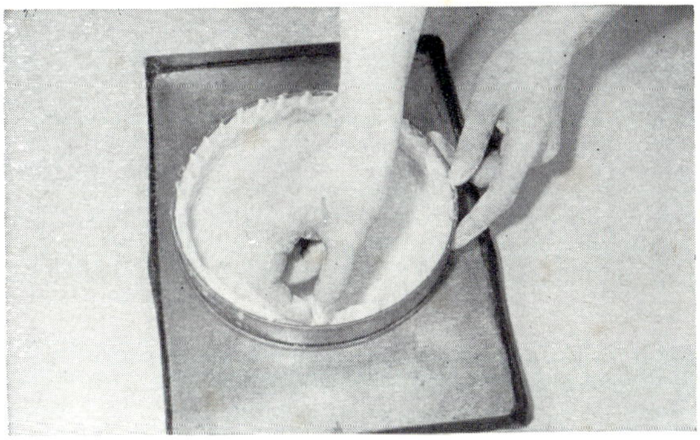

3 Decorate the top edge by pinching and twisting the pastry between the first finger and the thumb.

4 Cover bottom of flan with a piece of greaseproof paper and weight it to keep shape during baking.

5 Remove paper, rice, beans, etc., and flan ring when pastry is cooked.

Fruit Pie.

1 Fill the dish with fruit. Roll out the pastry a little larger than the pie-dish; cut off a strip from the edge to fit the dish rim.

2 Moisten edge of the pie-dish. Place strip on rim with cut edge inwards and dampen the strip.

3 Lift pastry lid with the rolling-pin to prevent stretching it and place on dish. Press strip and cover well together, trim off surplus pastry with sharp knife.

4 Knock up edge of pastry with the back of a knife held horizontally.

5 Scallop edge with the back of a knife, pressing lightly with thumb.

6 Raise the pie edge to make a few gaps to allow the steam to escape.

1

2

3

4

6

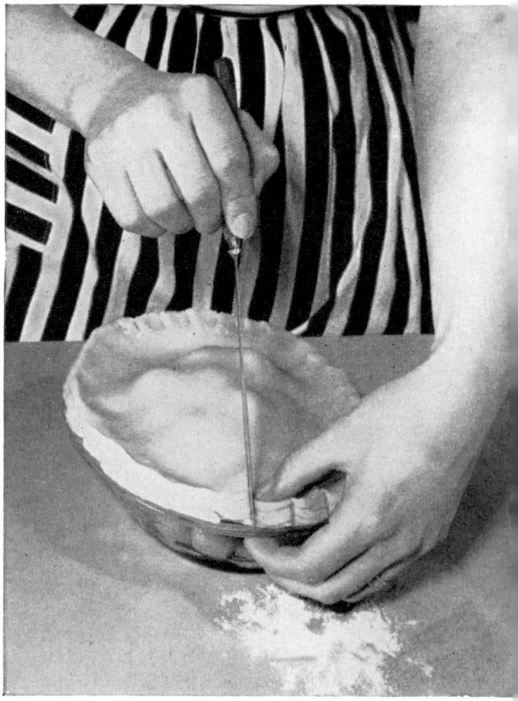

5

## EGGS À LA MAÎTRE D'HÔTEL

**3 eggs**
**2 oz. butter**
**1 dessertsp. flour**
**¼ pt. milk**
**Salt and pepper**
**1 teasp. chopped parsley**
**1 teasp. lemon juice**

Melt 1 oz. butter in a saucepan, stir in the flour, add the milk and boil for 2 min. Have ready the eggs boiled hard, remove the shells, cut each egg in 4 or 8 pieces, and arrange them neatly on a dish. Season the sauce to taste, whisk in the remainder of the butter, add it gradually in small pieces, stir in the parsley and the lemon juice, then pour the sauce over the eggs.

Serve as quickly as possible.

**2–3 helpings**
**Cooking time—20 min. (approx.)**

## EGGS MORNAY

*Œufs à la Mornay*

**4–5 hard-boiled eggs**
**1 oz. butter**
**Nutmeg**
**Salt and pepper**
**1½ oz. grated cheese**
**¼ pt. white sauce**

Cut the eggs into thick slices, place them on a well-buttered fireproof dish, sprinkle them lightly with nutmeg and more liberally with salt and pepper. Add 1 oz. cheese to the sauce and pour it over the eggs. Sprinkle thickly with cheese, and add a few tiny pieces of butter. Brown the surface in a hot oven or under the grill and serve.

**4–5 helpings**
**Cooking time—5 min. (approx.)**

## EGGS—POLONAISE STYLE

*Œufs à la Polonaise*

**4–5 eggs**
**1 teacup small dice of bread**
**Butter**
**1 tablesp. cream (optional)**
**1 teasp. finely-chopped parsley**
**1 teasp. finely-chopped chives**
**Salt and pepper**

Fry the bread in butter and drain well. Beat the eggs, add the cream (if used), parsley, chives, bread, salt and pepper, and pour the preparation into a pan containing 2 tablesp. butter. Stir over heat until the mixture is thick enough to spread, then drop it in spoonfuls into hot butter, fry, drain well and serve.

**5–6 helpings**
**Cooking time—15 min. (approx.)**

## EGGS STUFFED WITH PRAWNS

*Œufs farcis aux Crevettes*

**4 hard-boiled eggs**
**12 large *or* 18 small prawns**
**1½ oz. butter**
**1 tablesp. mayonnaise**
**Pinch of salt**
**Pinch of pepper**
**Pinch of cayenne pepper**
**1 tablesp. grated Parmesan cheese**

Cut the shelled eggs across in halves, cut off their extreme ends so that they stand firmly and remove the yolks. Put the prawns into a basin, add the egg yolks, pound until smooth; add the butter and mayonnaise, season to taste, then fill the egg cases. Sprinkle the surface with Parmesan cheese, place a prawn head in the centre of each.

**8 savouries**

## EEL SOUP

*Soupe aux Anguilles*

**1 lb. eel**
**1 onion**
**1 oz. butter**
**1 qt. water**
**A bunch of herbs**
**1 blade of mace**
**1 strip of lemon rind**
**1 teasp. lemon juice**
**1 oz. flour**
**Salt and pepper**
**¼ pt. cream *or* milk**

Clean and cut the eels into small pieces. Slice the onion. Melt the butter in a saucepan and gently fry the onion and eel for 10 min. without browning them. Add the water, bring to simmering point; add herbs, mace, lemon rind and juice, and seasoning. Simmer very gently till the eel is tender. Strain the soup and keep the pieces of eel warm. Blend the flour with a little milk and stir into the soup, reheat and boil till the flour thickens the soup. Season carefully, and stir in the cream just at boiling point, reheat without boiling. Add the pieces of eel and serve the soup.

**5-6 helpings**
**Cooking time—about 1 hr.**

## EMPRESS PUDDING

*Pouding à l'Impératrice*

**4 oz. rice**
**2 oz. castor sugar**

**Pinch of salt**
**2 pt. milk**
**2 oz. butter *or* margarine**
**Trimmings of pastry**
**Jam *or* stewed fruit**

Simmer the rice in the milk with a pinch of salt until it is tender. Add the fat and sugar. Line the sides of a pie-dish with the trimmings of pastry. Spread a layer of rice on the bottom of the dish. Cover with jam *or* stewed fruit. Repeat until the dish is full, finishing with a layer of rice. Bake in a moderate oven **(350° F., Gas 4)** until browned.

Serve with custard.

**6–7 helpings**
**Cooking time—½ hr.**

## ENDIVE SALAD

*Salade de Chicorée*

**2 heads of endive**
**French dressing *or* Vinaigrette sauce**

Prepare endive as shredded lettuce. Dress with French dressing and serve at once.

**6 helpings**

## ENGLISH OMELET

Separate the eggs. Add half an egg-shell of water for each egg, to the yolks: beat them with a wooden spoon until creamy. Whisk the whites until they stay in the basin when turned upside down. Gently fold the whites into the yolks. Have the butter ready in the pan as for the French Omelette. Pour in the egg mixture, and cook until it is golden brown on the underside. Then put the pan under the grill and lightly brown the top. Fillings are usually spread over the cooked omelet. Now run a palette knife round the edge of the pan. Fold the omelet over and slip on to a hot dish.

## ENGLISH SALAD or SUMMER SALAD

*Salade à l'Anglaise*

**1 large lettuce**
**½ small cucumber**
**3 tomatoes**
**½ bunch radishes**
**A few spring onions**
**Salad dressing**
**Bunch of watercress *or* box of mustard and cress**
**2 hard-boiled eggs (if liked)**

Reserve the best lettuce leaves and shred the rest. Slice the cucumber thinly, skin and slice the tomatoes, slice the radishes. Leave the onions whole. Mix the shredded lettuce leaves lightly with some of the cucumber, radishes and salad dressing. Line a salad bowl with the lettuce leaves. Pile the mixture in the middle and garnish with small bunches of watercress, sliced tomatoes, radishes, cucumber and hard-boiled egg. Hand the onions separately or arrange on the salad so that they may be avoided if not liked.

**6 helpings**

## EPICUREAN SAUCE

**¼ pt. mayonnaise**
**½ cucumber**
**⅛ pt. aspic jelly *or* ⅛ pt. good stock and ½ level teasp. powdered gelatine**
**1 tablesp. tarragon vinegar**
**⅛ pt. cream**
**1 teasp. anchovy essence**
**1 dessertsp. chopped gherkin**
**1 dessertsp. chopped chutney**
**Salt and pepper**
**Sugar**

Peel, dice and cook the cucumber in a very little salted water. When tender sieve the cucumber. Have the aspic jelly liquid but cool. Mix the cucumber purée, the liquid jelly and vinegar together. Carefully fold the cream into the mayonnaise then fold in the anchovy essence, the gherkins and chutney and lastly the aspic jelly and cucumber mixture. Season and add sugar to taste.

Serve with fish salads or with asparagus or globe artichokes.

## ESCOFFIER SAUCE (MAYONNAISE)

**¼ pt. mayonnaise**
**½ teasp. horseradish cream**
**1 teasp. chopped parsley**
**1 teasp. chopped chervil**

Fold the horseradish cream into the mayonnaise, then the parsley and chervil.

## ESCALLOPS OF VEAL—RUSSIAN STYLE

*Escalopes de Veau à la Russe*

**1¼ lb. fillet of veal cut in 6 slices**
**3 oz. butter *or* fat**
**1 small can mushrooms**
**1½ gills demi-glace sauce**

FORCEMEAT

**3 oz. pork**
**3 oz. beef marrow**
**1 teasp. powdered mixed herbs**
**1–2 oz. potted anchovy paste**
**1 egg yolk**
**Salt and pepper**
**Breadcrumbs**

GARNISH

| | |
|---|---|
| **Parsley** | **Stoned olives** |

Beat the fillets well and fry them in 2 oz. of the fat until lightly browned. Drain off the fat, keeping it for sautéing the mushrooms. Press the escallops between 2 dishes until cold. To make the forcemeat either mince or cut the pork and marrow into very fine small pieces and pound until smooth. Add the herbs, anchovy paste, egg yolk, seasoning and breadcrumbs and rub through a wire sieve. Spread the farce on one side of the scallops, sprinkle with fine crumbs and the remainder of the butter which has been melted. Place in a greased tin and bake for 20 min. in a fairly hot oven (**375° F., Gas 5**). Meanwhile, drain the mushrooms and sauté in the butter. Add the demi-glace sauce, season to taste and simmer very gently for 10 min.

Dish the escallops in a circle on a hot dish and place the ragoût of mushrooms in the centre. Garnish with parsley and stoned olives.

**6 helpings**

## ESCALLOPS OF VEAL—VIENNESE STYLE

*Escalopes de Veau à la Viennoise*

| | |
|---|---|
| **1¼–1½ lb. fillet of veal cut in 6 slices** | **Egg and breadcrumbs** |
| **Salt and pepper** | **Oil *or* butter for frying** |
| **Flour** | **Lemon juice** |

BEURRE NOISETTE

| | |
|---|---|
| **2 oz. butter** | **Cayenne pepper** |
| **Salt and pepper** | |

GARNISH

| | |
|---|---|
| **6 stoned olives** | **1 tablesp. chopped parsley** |
| **6 boned anchovy fillets** | **Crimped slices of lemon** |
| **1 hard-boiled egg** | |

Wipe the meat, season, dip in flour and coat with egg and breadcrumbs. Heat the oil or butter and fry the escallops for about 5 min. until golden brown. Make the beurre noisette by heating the butter in a saucepan until golden brown, then seasoning with salt, pepper and cayenne. Place the escallops slightly overlapping on a hot dish. Sprinkle with lemon juice and pour over the beurre noisette. Garnish with olives wrapped in anchovy fillets. Place the chopped egg white, sieved egg yolk and chopped parsley at either end of the dish.

**6 helpings**

## ESPAGNOLE SAUCE

Spanish Brown sauce

| | |
|---|---|
| **1 onion** | **2 oz. flour** |
| **1 carrot** | **1 pt. brown stock** |
| **2 oz. mushrooms *or* mushroom trimmings** | **Bouquet garni** |
| **2 oz. lean raw ham *or* bacon** | **6 peppercorns** |
| **2 oz. butter *or* dripping** | **1 bay leaf** |
| | **¼ pt. tomato pulp** |
| | **Salt** |
| | **⅛ pt. sherry (optional)** |

Slice the vegetables, chop the ham. Melt the fat and fry the ham for a few minutes and then, very slowly, the vegetables until they are golden brown. Add the flour and continue frying very slowly till all is a rich brown. Add the stock, herbs and spices and stir till the sauce simmers; simmer for ½ hr. Add the tomato pulp and simmer the sauce for a further ½ hr. Wring the sauce through a tammy cloth or rub it through a fine hair or nylon sieve. Season, add the sherry, if used, and reheat the sauce.

## ESSENCES

This term means natural juices of meat and vegetables extracted by simmering in wine and then reducing them until the flavour is concentrated and the liquid slightly thick.

## ESCALOPES OF PARTRIDGE

*Escalopes de Perdreau*

| | |
|---|---|
| **1 partridge** | **½ turnip** |
| **1 hard-boiled egg** | **Bouquet garni** |
| **2 slices bacon** | **½ pt. stock** |
| **1 small onion** | **Potato border** |
| **1 carrot** | **¾ pt. brown sauce** |

STUFFING

| | |
|---|---|
| **4 oz. cold roast partridge** | **2 oz. raw ham *or* bacon** |
| **1 teasp. chopped parsley** | **Pinch of mixed herbs** |
| **1 tablesp. chopped suet** | **Salt and pepper** |
| **1 tablesp. breadcrumbs** | **1 egg** |

Make the stuffing: chop partridge and ham, add suet, parsley, breadcrumbs, herbs, seasoning and egg. Split the whole partridge down the back, remove bones, flatten as much as possible, and season well. Spread half the stuffing on the bird, lay on slices of hard-boiled egg, some bacon cut in strips, then remainder of stuffing, form the bird into a roll and stitch securely with white cotton. Lay sliced vegetables and herbs in a pan with remainder of bacon, almost cover with stock and lay bird, wrapped in buttered paper, on top, cover tightly, simmer 1½–2 hr. Pipe a potato border round a dish, glaze and brown it. When bird is cooked, remove paper and cotton, cut bird in slices, arrange these in the border and pour over the brown sauce.

A variation of this dish is made by substituting veal for partridge in the stuffing, and serving garnished with spinach or mushroom.

**6 helpings**

### EVAPORATED MILK DRESSING

| | |
|---|---|
| **4 tablesp. evaporated milk** | **1 level saltsp. mixed mustard** |
| **1 tablesp. vinegar (wine *or* malt)** | **Good pinch castor sugar** |
| | **1 level saltsp. salt** |

Whisk the milk until thick. Add the vinegar drop by drop, stirring vigorously. Add the flavourings.

### FAGGOTS or "SAVOURY DUCKS"

| | |
|---|---|
| **1 lb. pig's liver *or* fry** | **Salt and pepper** |
| **2 medium-sized onions** | **A pinch of grated nutmeg** |
| **4 oz. fat pork** | **1 egg** |
| **A pinch of thyme** | **Breadcrumbs** |
| **½ teasp. powdered sage** | **A pig's caul** |
| **A pinch of basil** | |

Slice the liver, onions and pork thinly. Put in a saucepan with the thyme, sage, basil, salt, pepper and nutmeg and barely cover with water. Simmer for ½ hr., then strain off the liquid and save for the gravy. Mince the contents of the stewpan finely. Add the beaten egg and sufficient breadcrumbs to make into a fairly firm mixture and mix thoroughly. Form into balls and enclose each one in a piece of caul. Place in a baking-tin, and add a little gravy. Bake in a fairly hot oven (400° F., Gas 6) until nicely browned. Serve with a good thickened gravy. If preferred, the mixture can be pressed into a well greased baking-tin and marked into squares. Cover with caul and cut into squares after cooking.

**6 helpings**

### FAT, TO CLARIFY

To clean fat, put the fat in a saucepan and cover with cold water. Bring slowly to the boil, removing the scum as it rises. Strain into a bowl and leave to cool. When the fat has formed a solid cake, remove from bowl, and scrape off the impurities which will have settled at the bottom of the cake. Finally, put in a pan and heat *slowly* to drive off any water.

### FAT, TO RENDER

Cut the fat into small pieces, put into a saucepan and cover with cold water. Bring to the boil and continue boiling until nearly all the water has evaporated, then cook more slowly, stirring occasionally. When the fat is ready it should be clear, and any piece of skin shrivelled and light brown in colour. Allow to cool slightly before straining through a fine strainer into a clean basin.

Fat may also be rendered in the oven. Cut it into pieces, place in a roasting tin in a warm oven until the fat has melted, and any piece of skin shrivelled. Strain into a clean basin, pressing the pieces of skin and tissue against the strainer to extract all the fat.

Do not have the heat too fierce for either method or the fat will burn and be spoiled.

## FIG PUDDING

*Pouding aux Figues*

| | |
|---|---|
| **8 oz. dried figs** | **4 oz. castor sugar** |
| **4 oz. plain flour** | **Pinch of salt** |
| **4 oz. finely-chopped suet** | **Pinch of ground nutmeg** |
| **4 oz. breadcrumbs** | **1–2 eggs** |
| **1 level teasp. baking-powder** | **1½ gills milk (approx.)** |

Grease a 2 pt. basin. Wash, dry and chop the figs.

Mix the flour, suet, breadcrumbs, baking-powder, sugar, salt, nutmeg and figs. Beat the egg with some of the milk and stir into the mixture. Add milk as necessary to make the mixture of a dropping consistency. Put it in the basin; cover. Steam for 2½ hr.

Serve with a custard or sweet sauce.

**6 helpings**

## FILLETS OF BEEF—BEAUFFREMONT STYLE

*Filets de Bœuf à la Beauffremont*

| | |
|---|---|
| **1½–2 lb. fillet of beef** | **¾ pt. tomato sauce** |
| **Salt and pepper** | **¼ pt. Madeira sauce** |
| **Egg and breadcrumbs** | **Butter *or* fat for frying** |
| **4 oz. macaroni** | **Meat glaze** |
| **White stock** | **2 oz. grated cheese** |

GARNISH

**Shredded truffle *or* chopped parsley**

Cut the fillet into rounds about 1½ in. thick and 2½ in. in diameter. Season well and coat with egg and breadcrumbs. Cook the macaroni in well-flavoured stock until tender—about 20 min. Drain and add to ½ pt. of the tomato sauce. Keep hot. Add the remaining tomato sauce to the Madeira sauce and the glaze and keep hot until required. Fry the fillets in the fat in a sauté pan for 6–8 min.; arrange in a circle on a hot dish and glaze. Add the cheese to the macaroni and pile in the centre of the dish. Garnish; pour the sauce round; serve very hot.

**6 helpings**

## FILLET OF BEEF DAUPHIN

*Filet de Bœuf Dauphin*

| | |
|---|---|
| **1½–2 lb. fillet of beef** | **Dripping** |
| **Salt and pepper** | **Meat glaze** |
| **Larding bacon** | **½ pt. Madeira sauce** |
| **Flour** | **12 potato croquettes** |

Wipe, trim and season the meat. Lard with the strips of bacon and dry, sprinkle with flour and tie into a good shape. Put into a roasting, tin with dripping. Cover with paper and put into a hot oven (**425° F., Gas 7**) for 10 min. then reduce the heat to moderate (**350° F., Gas 4**). Baste and cook until tender allowing 15 min. per lb. and 15 min. over. Baste occasionally while cooking. Remove the paper 15 min. before serving. Place fillet on a hot dish, remove string and brush over with glaze. Garnish with the potato croquettes. Pour away the fat from the roasting-tin and add any of the brown sediment to the sauce; heat and serve separately.

**6 helpings**

## FILLETS OF BEEF—GENOESE STYLE

*Filets de Bœuf à la Génoise*

| | |
|---|---|
| **1½–2 lb. fillet of beef** | **3–4 oz. marrow** |
| **Salt and pepper** | **Meat glaze** |
| **½ lb. potatoes** | **Mashed potatoes** |
| **Butter *or* fat** | **½–¾ pt. Génoise sauce** |

Wipe the meat, cut into ½-in. slices and then into rounds about 2½ in. diameter. Season with salt and pepper. Dice the potatoes, parboil them and then fry in hot fat until nicely browned, or finish cooking in the oven with a little butter. Cut the marrow into rather thin rounds ½ the size of the fillets, blanch and grill them and keep hot until required. Melt 1½ oz. fat in a sauté pan and fry the fillets quickly until nicely browned on both sides, then brush them over with meat glaze. Arrange in a close row on a bed of mashed potatoes and place a round of marrow on each fillet. Pour a little Génoise sauce around and garnish with little heaps of potato sprinkled with finely-chopped parsley. Serve the remainder of the sauce separately.

**6 helpings**

### FILLETS OF BEEF—POMPADOUR STYLE

*Filets de Bœuf à la Pompadour*

**1½–2 lb. fillet of beef**
**Salt and pepper**
**2 large firm tomatoes**
**Butter *or* fat**
**Meat glaze**
**Croûtes of fried bread**
**¾ oz. Maître d'hôtel butter**
**¾ pt. Espagnole sauce**
**Macedoine of vegetables**

Wipe the meat and cut into rather thick round fillets of equal size, and season. Cut an equal number of slices of tomato, season and dot with a little butter and bake. Sauté the fillets in the fat, drain, glaze and serve on the fried croûtes. Place a slice of baked tomato on each fillet and place a pat of Maître d'hôtel butter on each slice of tomato. Pour a little sauce round and garnish with the macedoine of vegetables which have been tossed in butter and seasoned after cooking.

**6 helpings**

### FILLETS OF BEEF—PORTUGUESE STYLE

*Portugaise de Filets de Bœuf*

**1½–2 lb. fillet of beef**
**Oil *or* melted butter**
**Salt and pepper**
**Maître d'hôtel butter**
**Stuffed tomatoes**

Wipe and trim the meat and cut into neat fillets. Beat to flatten slightly and brush with oil or melted butter. Season to taste. Grill, then place on a hot dish. Put a pat of Maître d'hôtel butter on each fillet and serve with baked stuffed tomatoes.

**6 helpings**
**Cooking time—according to taste**

### FILLETS OF BEEF—ROSSINI STYLE

*Filets de Bœuf à la Rossini*

**1½ lb. fillet of beef**
**¼ lb. chickens' livers**
**2 oz. butter *or* fat**
**1 shallot**
**1½ oz. foie gras**
**1 tablesp. brown sauce**
**Salt and pepper**
**1 tablesp. olive oil**
**Meat glaze**
**Croûtes of fried bread**
**Slices of truffle**
**½–¾ pt. demi-glace sauce**

Wipe the beef and cut into rounds 2½ in. diameter and ½ in. thick. Wash, dry and slice the liver. Melt 1 oz. of the fat in a sauté pan and fry the finely-chopped shallot slightly. Add the liver and sauté for a few minutes. Drain off the fat and pound the liver with the foie gras, brown sauce and seasoning until smooth, then pass through a wire sieve. Heat the remainder of the fat with the olive oil and fry the fillets quickly until browned on both sides. Drain and cover one side of each with the liver farce. Brush with meat glaze, place on the fried croûtes and put in the oven to become thoroughly hot. Lay a slice of truffle on the top of each fillet, arrange on a hot dish and serve the demi-glace sauce separately.

**6 helpings**

### FILLETS OF BEEF—VIENNESE STYLE

*Filets de Bœuf à la Viennoise*

**1¼ lb. lean tender beef**
**½ teasp. powdered mixed herbs**
**½ teasp. finely-chopped parsley**
**Salt and pepper**
**Nutmeg**
**Cayenne pepper**
**1 large egg**
**Flour**
**2 large onions**
**2½ oz. butter *or* fat**
**½–¾ pt. Espagnole sauce**

Wipe and trim the meat; mince it finely. Add to it the herbs, parsley, salt, pepper, nutmeg and cayenne. Mix well and bind with beaten egg. Divide the mixture into 6–8 portions, shape into round fillets and dredge lightly with flour. Cut the onions across into slices, reserve 6–8 of the large outer rings for garnish, chop the remainder finely. Heat 1 oz. of the fat in a saucepan and fry the chopped onions lightly. Add 2 tablesp. of the Espagnole sauce, season to taste and simmer for 20 min. Heat the remainder of the fat in a sauté pan and fry the fillets. Dip the outer onion rings into the flour and fry until golden brown. Serve the fillets with a little of the chopped onion on the centre of each. Garnish with the onion rings. Pour some of the sauce around the meat and serve the remainder separately.

**6 helpings**
**Cooking time—about 35 min.**

### FILLETS OF PLAICE WITH LEMON DRESSING

*Filets de Plies au Citron*

**4 fillets of plaice (4 oz. each approx.)**
**Seasoning**
**1 oz. butter *or* margarine**
**Juice of ½ lemon**
**Chopped parsley**

Season the fish. Melt the fat in the grill pan and place the fish skin side uppermost in the pan. Cook for 1 min., then turn with flesh side up and grill steadily until golden brown and cooked, about 5–8 min., depending on thickness of fillets. Remove to a hot serving dish, keep hot. Add the lemon juice to the remaining fat in the pan, reheat and pour over the fish. Sprinkle liberally with chopped parsley.

**4 helpings**

### FILLETS OF SOLE AUX FINES HERBES

*Filets de Soles aux fines Herbes*

**Eight 2 oz. fillets of sole**
**Salt and pepper**
**4 tablesp. fish stock**
**½ pt. white wine sauce**
**1 tablesp. finely-chopped fresh herbs**

Wipe the fillets with a clean, damp cloth, season with salt and pepper and fold them in 3. Place in a greased fireproof dish, add the fish stock, cover, and cook in a fairly hot oven (**375° F., Gas 5**) for 15–20 min. Drain the fillets well and place on a dish, coat with white wine sauce and sprinkle with the finely-chopped fresh herbs.

**4 helpings**

### FILLETS OF SOLE BONNE FEMME

*Filets de Sole à la bonne Femme*

**4 fillets of sole**
**4 oz. mushrooms**
**1 shallot**
**1 teasp. chopped parsley**
**Salt and pepper**
**¼ pt. white wine**
**¼ pt. fish Velouté sauce**
**A little butter**

Wipe the fillets with a clean damp cloth. Put them flat in a shallow pan with the sliced mushrooms, sliced shallot, parsley and seasoning. Add the wine, cover and poach for 10–15 min. Drain the fish from the wine, place on a fireproof dish and keep warm. Boil the wine rapidly until it is reduced by half, then stir it into the hot Velouté sauce and thicken with a little butter. When thoroughly blended pour the sauce over the fillets and place under a hot grill until lightly browned. Serve at once in a border of sliced, steamed potatoes.

**4 helpings**

### FILLETS OF SOLE MEUNIÈRE

*Filets de Sole à la Meunière*

**4 large *or* 8 small fillets of sole**
**A little seasoned flour**
**3 oz. butter**
**1 tablesp. lemon juice**
**1 level tablesp. chopped parsley**
**Lemon "butterflies"**

Dredge the fillets lightly, but thoroughly, with seasoned flour. Heat the butter in a frying-pan and when hot fry the fillets until golden brown and cooked through—about 7 min. Arrange the fillets on a hot dish. Reheat the fat until it is nut brown in colour and then pour it over the fish. Sprinkle the lemon juice and parsley over the fillets, garnish with lemon "butterflies" and serve at once.

**4 helpings**

### FILLETS OF SOLE À LA NORMANDE

*Filets de Soles à la Normande*

**Eight 4 oz. fillets of sole**
**Salt and pepper**
**1 gill white wine**
**1 shallot**
**Butter**
**½ pt. Normandy sauce**

GARNISH

**Poached oysters**
**Cooked mussels**
**Fried button mushrooms**
**Croûtes *or* fleurons**

Wipe the fillets with a damp cloth, fold them in two and place in a buttered sauté-pan or fireproof dish. Season with salt and pepper, moisten with the white wine, sprinkle with finely-chopped shallot, place a few pieces of butter over, cover and cook in a fairly hot oven (**375° F., Gas 5**) for about 10 min. Have the garnish ready, put the fillets on a dish, arrange the oysters, mussels and mushrooms neatly and strain over some of the Normandy sauce made with the liquor in which the oysters were cooked. Garnish the sides with croûtes of bread (buttered slices of French rolls browned in the oven) or with fleurons (little half-moon shapes of puff pastry). Serve the remaining sauce separately in a sauce boat.

NOTE: If smelts are in season, this dish should be garnished with a few fried smelts in addition to the other garnish.

**8 helpings**

## FILLETS OF SOLE WITH MUSHROOMS

*Filets de Sole aux Champignons*

| | |
|---|---|
| **Eight 2 oz. fillets of sole** | **6 oz. button mushrooms** |
| **Salt and pepper** | **1 oz. butter** *or* **margarine** |
| **Lemon juice** | **¾ oz. flour** |
| **2 tablesp. white wine** | **⅛ pt. single cream** |
| **2 tablesp. fish stock** *or* **water** | **1 teasp. chopped parsley** |

Wipe the fillets with a clean damp cloth, season with salt, pepper and lemon juice to taste, then fold them in three. Place in a greased fireproof dish, add the wine and fish stock, cover and cook in a fairly hot oven (**375° F., Gas 5**) for 15–20 min. Cook the mushrooms at the same time, placing them in a covered casserole with a very little water, salt and lemon juice. Shortly before serving make a sauce with the butter or margarine, flour and milk, adding the cooking liquor drained from the mushrooms and sufficient of the fish poaching liquor to give a coating consistency; season to taste and if necessary whisk until smooth. Arrange the well-drained fillets round the outer edge of a flat serving dish and coat with the sauce. Pile the mushrooms in the centre and sprinkle with chopped parsley.

**4 helpings**

## FILLET OF TURBOT DUGLÉRÉ

| | |
|---|---|
| **1¼ lb. fillet of turbotin** | **⅓ pt. fish stock** |
| **2 oz. finely-chopped onions** | **½ glass white wine** |
| | **Juice of ¼ lemon** |
| **1 oz. chopped parsley** | **½ gill cream** |
| **1 lb. fresh tomatoes** | **2 oz. butter** |
| **Salt and pepper** | **½ oz. flour** |

Lightly butter the bottom of a shallow saucepan or tray; sprinkle with the onions and parsley. Place the fillets of turbotin on top, with the diced flesh of the peeled tomatoes sprinkled over the fish. Lightly season; add fish stock, white wine and lemon juice to barely cover. Bring to the boil, cover with a lid or buttered greaseproof paper, and cook gently for 8–10 min. either on the stove or in the oven. Remove fish on to serving dish, and keep in a warm place. Reduce the cooking liquor by boiling to ⅓ of its quantity, add the cream and re-boil. To slightly thicken the sauce, stir in a little of the butter mixed with the flour. Again re-boil. Work into the sauce the remainder of the butter. Correct seasoning of the sauce, if necessary.

Pour over the very hot fish and serve.

NOTE: A turbotin is a young turbot.

**4–5 helpings**

## FILLETS OF VEAL

*Filets de Veau*

| | |
|---|---|
| **1¼–1½ lb. fillet of veal** | **2 teasp. grated lemon rind** |
| **1 egg** | **1 teasp. lemon juice** |
| **½ teasp. finely-chopped parsley** | **Breadcrumbs** |
| **¼ teasp. thyme** | **2 oz. butter** *or* **fat** |
| | **Bacon rolls** |
| | **Mashed potatoes** |

SAUCE

| | |
|---|---|
| **½ oz. flour** | **Salt and pepper** |
| **½ pt. white stock** | **1–2 tablesp. cream (optional)** |
| **½ teasp. lemon juice** | |
| **A little gravy browning** | |

Cut the veal into slices about ½ in. thick, then cut each slice into rounds of about 2¼–2½ in. diameter. Beat with a wooden spoon or rolling-pin. Beat the egg and add to it the parsley, thyme, lemon rind and lemon juice. Soak the fillets in this mixture for about ½ hr. then coat with crumbs. Fry in the hot fat until golden brown on both sides, then reduce heat and cook more slowly for 7–10 min. in all. Drain thoroughly and keep hot together with the fried or grilled bacon rolls. To make the sauce, add the flour to the fat remaining in the pan and fry lightly. Add the stock, stir until it boils, then add the lemon juice, gravy browning and seasoning and simmer for 3 min. Add the cream, if liked. Serve the fillets in a circle on a border of mashed potatoes, pile the bacon rolls in the centre and pour the strained sauce round.

**6 helpings**

## FILLETS OF VEAL—MILAN STYLE

*Filets de Veau à la Milanaise*

| | |
|---|---|
| **1½ lb. fillet of veal** | **1 pt. brown sauce** |
| **2 oz. butter** *or* **fat** | **2 tablesp. sherry (optional)** |
| **3 bacon rashers** | |
| **1 shallot** | **3 oz. spaghetti** |
| **2 large tomatoes** | **12 stoned olives** |
| **Salt and pepper** | |

Wipe, trim, season the meat and cut into

neat pieces. Heat the fat and fry the meat quickly and lightly. Drain off the surplus fat and place the meat in a casserole with the diced bacon, finely-chopped shallot and skinned sliced tomatoes. Season to taste. Bring the sauce to the boil, add the sherry (if used) and pour on to the veal. Cook gently for 1 hr. Cook the spaghetti in boiling salted water for 5 min. Rinse with cold water and add to the casserole for 15 min. before serving. Garnish with stoned heated olives.

**6 helpings**

### FILLETING FISH

*See Fish*

### FILLINGS, SWEET, FOR CAKES, GATEAUX, PIES, ETC.

*See the recipe for the type or flavour of filling desired, e.g. Chocolate Filling, Confectioners' Custard, Lemon Meringue Pie.*

### FISH

Fish must be handled and cooked with care. So it does not figure on our menus as often as it should.

Fish is as rich in protein as meat. Oily fish, such as salmon, herrings, mackerel and sprats, in which the fat is distributed throughout the flesh, provide valuable quantities of Vitamins A and D. Canned fish are often packed in oil, thus adding extra fat, and as the bones are usually sufficiently soft to be eaten, they also provide calcium and phosphorus—both bone- and teeth-building materials.

The cost of different varieties of fish gives little idea of their food value. Herrings, one of the cheapest fish, have a high food value.

The flesh of white fish such as cod, haddock and whiting contain very little fat, most of the oil being stored in the liver. Most varieties of white fish (particularly whiting) are easily digested and so figure largely in the diet of children and invalids.

Fish can be served in many different ways, and provides an economical and wholesome dish.

#### Buying Fish

When about to buy fish, the housewife should not set out with the fixed intention of buying a certain type. She should be guided by the state of the market. The price of fish varies more than that of any other food from day to day, because it is such a perishable article of food, and because one kind may be caught in very large numbers at a given time and will therefore be cheap. Quite often, the housewife will find that a particular kind of fish is scarce and priced far beyond its worth, while another is plentiful and inexpensive.

Smaller, younger fish are to be preferred. A flat fish should be thick in proportion to its size. In buying a slice of fish it is better to choose a thick slice from a small fish than a thin slice from a large one. Avoid cuts of fish with too much bone or waste tissue.

#### Choosing Fish

1. Fish should first of all be fresh. The flesh should be firm not flabby.
2. There should be no stale smell.
3. The gills of most varieties should be bright red.
4. The eyes should be bright and not sunken in the head.
5. A "slimy" skin is a sure sign of freshness, providing it is not a decomposed yellowish slime.

#### Keeping Fish

All fresh fish should be cooked the day it is bought as it quickly loses its freshness and flavour. If fish is put into a refrigerator it must be covered to prevent the fish smell tainting other foods. Quick-frozen fish should be stored in the "freezer" compartment; it can be kept for 48 hr. and once it has thawed out it must not be re-frozen. If you have a deep freezer (0° F.) it can be kept for 2–3 months, 2 months for oily fish and 3 for lean fish.

#### Preparing Fish

Fishmongers are only too glad to prepare fish ready for the housewife to cook, but if for some reason that is impracticable here are the simple ways of doing it.

**To Clean Whole Fish**

Scrape off any scales on both sides of the fish with the back of a knife. Hold the fish by the tail and scrape from the tail towards the head. Rinse often whilst working to remove loose scales.

*Round fish:* With a pair of kitchen scissors or sharp knife slit the belly from just below the head to half-way to the tail, remove and discard the entrails, reserve the roe. Wash well. Rub with a little salt to remove any black tissues. If the head is to be left on take out the eyes, if the head is to be removed cut across behind the gills.

*Flat fish:* Cut off the fins, remove the gills. Cut open the belly which is just under the head, on the dark side, and remove and discard the entrails. Wash with cold water. To remove the head make a semi-circular cut below the head.

**To Skin Whole Flat Fish**

The dark skin of sole is always removed but not necessarily the white. The skin of turbot is usually cut off after filleting.

To skin any fish it must be kept wet. With whole flat fish begin at the tail. Cut the skin across, but do not cut into the flesh, and loosen the skin along the fins on either side with the fingers. Then tear off the skin with the left hand, keeping the thumb of the right hand well pressed over the backbone to prevent the removal of the flesh with the skin.

**To Skin Whole Round Fish**

Cut off a narrow strip of skin over and along the backbone near the tail. Make another cut just below the head and loosen the skin below it with the point of a sharp knife. Dip the fingers in salt to give a better grip and gently pull off the skin, working towards the tail. Keep the thumb of the right hand well pressed over the backbone to prevent the removal of the flesh with the skin. Remove the skin from the other side in the same way.

**Filleting**

A fillet is virtually a whole piece of fish taken from shoulder to tail; if a fillet is cut up then the resulting pieces are, correctly speaking, called "pieces" or "portions". Four fillets are obtained from flat fish and two from round fish.

*Flat Fish:* Place the fish flat on a board or table, and with the point of a sharp, flexible knife cut the flesh from head to tail down the backbone. Next insert the knife in the slit made, and carefully separate the flesh from the bone, keeping the knife pressed lightly against the bone meanwhile. Remove the fillet, turn the fish round, remove the second fillet from tail to head, then turn the fish over and remove the other two fillets in the same way.

*Round Fish:* With a sharp knife slit the fish down the centre back to the bone. Working from head end to tail, cut along the belly, cutting the flesh cleanly from the bones by keeping the knife pressed against the bones. Remove the fillet from the other side in the same way.

**To Skin Fillets**

Place the fillets on a board skin side down. Rub a little salt on the fingers of the left hand, take a firm hold of the tail in the left hand, and with a knife in the right hand, and using a "sawing" movement, peel the flesh away from the skin, working from tail to head.

Always use the skin and bones for making fish stock.

Whole fish can be washed and dried. But portions are best wiped with a clean dry cloth only.

## Cooking Fish

Fish is easily spoiled by over or under-cooking. Test whether it is ready by pressing the thickest part gently. The flesh will lift easily off the bones when the fish is ready. When cooking fillets or cutlets, a white "curd" appearing between the flakes indicates that the fish is cooked.

**Boiling or Poaching**

Strictly, fish should never be boiled. It should only be simmered just below boiling point.

The best way to poach fish is in a fish-kettle—a large pan fitted with a strainer so that the fish can be gently lifted from the pan without breaking. If no fish-kettle is available, tie the fish loosely in clean muslin, and place it on a plate in the bottom of the pan.

Salmon and salmon trout should be put into boiling, salted water, to preserve their colour. Other kinds of fish should be put into warm water because boiling water may break the skin, and cold water destroys the fish's flavour.

Cook fish in only just enough water to cover it. For each pint of water add ½ tablesp. vinegar and 1 level teasp. salt. Lemon juice added to the cooking water when cooking white fish helps to keep its whiteness.

Bring fish to the boil gently. When boiling point is reached, reduce the heat immediately, and allow the fish to simmer gently just below the boil. The time required depends on the thickness of the fish rather than its size. 10–15 min. per lb. is usually enough.

**Frying**

Fish to be fried should be very well dried after wiping, and should be coated to prevent fat soaking into the fish. It may be coated with egg and breadcrumbs, milk or beaten egg and seasoned flour; or if to be fried in deep fat, coated with batter. See also notes on frying.

*Shallow frying* is better for thick slices or steaks, which require longer cooking to ensure that they are cooked through.

There should be enough fat in the pan to come half-way up the fish. Heat the fat, put in the coated fish and fry until golden brown on one side, then turn and brown the other side. Allow 6–8 min. for fillets and 8–12 min. for larger pieces.

*Deep frying* requires a deep frying-pan with a frying basket or deep heavy pan with a perforated spoon to remove the fish from the hot fat. The fat should be very hot, but its temperature must be slightly lower when frying fish fillets than when frying croquettes, rissoles, etc., which are usually composed of cooked fish. When the surface of a small piece of bread immediately hardens and slightly changes its colour on being immersed in the fat, the temperature is correct for raw food or anything thickly coated with batter, but when frying anything of which the exterior only has to be cooked, it is better to have the fat sufficiently hot to brown at once whatever is immersed in it. Heat the fish basket, if used, in the fat, but gently drop the coated fish into the fat—do not place directly on the fish basket or the coating will stick to the wires of the basket.

Do not try to fry too much fish at a time as this reduces the temperature of the fat and the result will be pale, greasy fish.

Anything fried should afterwards be well drained on kitchen paper. Fish is usually garnished with lemon and parsley; croquettes with parsley alone.

**Grilling**—suitable for steaks, cutlets or fillets and small whole fish, e.g. herring, plaice and sole.

This method of cooking is an extremely simple one. The fish should be thoroughly dried, then liberally brushed over with a little oil or melted fat and seasoned with salt and pepper. Score deep gashes across whole fish to allow the heat to penetrate, or the outside may dry up before the fish is cooked.

Heat the grill and grease the grill rack to prevent the fish sticking. Cook the fish rather slowly, turning carefully until done. Allow 7–8 min. for thin fillets and 10–15 min. for steaks and thicker fish.

**Steaming**—suitable for fillets or thin slices.

This is a very favourite and excellent way of cooking fish, as although it is a rather slower process than boiling, the flavour is better preserved, and the danger of the fish being broken is eliminated. If using a steamer a piece of greased greaseproof paper placed in the bottom will facilitate removal of the fish after cooking. Season the prepared fish and sprinkle with lemon juice.

When a small quantity of fish has to be steamed the following method is exceedingly easy and gives excellent results: Place the fish on a well-greased soup plate. Sprinkle lightly with salt, pepper and lemon juice, and cover with a piece of greased greaseproof paper. Place the plate over a saucepan of boiling water (or over the pan of potatoes if serving potatoes with the fish) and cover with another plate or the lid of the saucepan. Steam for 10–25 min., depending on the thickness of the fish. Turn the fish once during cooking. Serve with the fish liquor or a fish sauce made from the liquor.

**Stewing**—suitable for steaks, fillets and small pieces of cod.

In stewing, a gentle simmering in a small quantity of fish stock made from bone and fish trimmings, or in milk and water, until the flesh comes easily away from the bones, is all that is required. This is one of the most economical and tasty ways of cooking fish. Cook slowly. Fish should invariably be stewed in a fireproof glass or an earthenware dish. The liquid in which the fish has been simmered may be flavoured and thickened and used as a sauce.

**Baking**—This is a very satisfactory method of cooking almost any whole round white fish or a middle cut from a large fish, or steaks or fillets.

Place the prepared fish in a well-greased baking-tin or fireproof dish with a very little fat, cover with greased greaseproof paper. Bake in a fairly hot oven (**375° F., Gas 5**). Cooking time will vary according to thickness and weight, but average times are 10–20 min. for fillets, depending on thickness; allow about 10 min. per lb. and 10 min. over for whole fish weighing up to 4 lb.

## FISH CAKES

**1 lb. cooked fish**
**1 oz. butter *or* margarine**
**½ lb. mashed potatoes**
**2 eggs**
**Salt and pepper**
**Breadcrumbs**

Remove skin and bones and chop fish coarsely. Heat the butter in a saucepan, add the fish, potatoes, yolk of 1 egg, salt and pepper. Stir over heat for a few minutes, then turn on to a plate and allow to cool. When cold, shape into round flat cakes, brush over with beaten egg, coat with breadcrumbs and fry in hot fat. The fish may be made into one large cake instead of several small ones, in which case grease a fish mould or flat tin and shape the mixture as much like a fish as possible. Brush over with egg, cover with slightly browned breadcrumbs and bake for about 20 min. in a fairly hot oven (**375° F., Gas 5**).

**3–7 helpings**

## FISH CHOWDER

This American dish is something between a soup and a fish stew.

**2 lb. filleted fresh cod *or* haddock, the head, bones and skin of the fish**
**¾ pt. water**
**Salt and pepper**
**Lemon rind**
**A bunch of herbs**
**1 blade of mace**
**2 onions**
**1 lb. potatoes**
**¼ lb. salt pork**
**1 oz. flour**
**1 pt. milk**
**1 oz. butter**

Skin the filleted fish. Make a fish stock with the water, bones, head and skin of the fish, salt, lemon rind, herbs and mace, simmer gently for ½ hr. Cut the fillets into 2-in. strips, slice the onions thinly and dice the potatoes. Cut the pork in tiny cubes and heat it gently in a deep pan until the fat flows freely. In the pork fat cook the onion without browning for 10 min., then add the potatoes and shake them well in the fat for a few minutes. Sprinkle in the flour. Gradually add the hot, strained stock, then put in the pieces of fish and season the soup. Cook very gently for ½ hr. Heat the milk and butter and add them to the soup when the fish and potatoes are soft. Do not reboil. Serve at once.

**4–6 helpings**
**Cooking time—1¼ hr.**

## FISH CREAM

**3 oz. cooked *or* uncooked white fish (whiting, fresh haddock, cod, all suitable)**
**½ oz. butter**
**½ oz. flour**
**½ gill milk**
**1 egg yolk**
**2 tablesp. cream *or* evaporated milk**
**Salt and pepper**

Chop, mince or pound the fish until very smooth. Heat the butter in a saucepan. Add the flour and cook for 2 min. Gradually add the milk and cook until mixture thickens, stirring well. Add fish, egg yolk, cream and seasoning. Put into a greased basin or mould and steam for 45 min. or cover with buttered paper and bake in a warm oven (**335° F., Gas 3**), for same time. Serve with white sauce.

**1 helping** **Cooking time—50 min.**

## FISH FORCEMEAT

**½ lb. raw white fish without bone or skin**
**1 oz. butter**
**1 oz. flour**
**¼ pt. fish stock *or* milk**
**1–2 eggs**
**Salt and pepper**
**Grated lemon rind**
**Lemon juice**

Melt the butter in a saucepan, stir in the flour then the stock and beat the mixture over heat till it forms a stiff ball. Cool this panada, then beat into it the beaten eggs and seasoning. Flake the fish, removing all small bones. Beat the fish into the egg mixture. Add grated lemon rind and lemon juice to taste.

## FISH MOUSSE

**2 eggs**
**1 lb. canned *or* cooked fish (canned salmon is excellent)**
**½ teacup milk**
**1 teacup breadcrumbs**
**Salt and pepper**
**1 dessertsp. lemon juice**
**1 tablesp. chopped parsley**

Drain the fish, remove the skin and bone and flake. Put the milk and breadcrumbs into a pan and add the juice from the canned fish (or ½ teacup liquid in which the fish was cooked). Put this over a low heat for 5 min., stirring occasionally. Then add the fish, salt and pepper, lemon juice and parsley. Mix, leave to cool slightly.

Separate the eggs; add the lightly beaten yolks to the fish mixture and stir well, beat the whites until stiff and fold them in thoroughly. Pour into a well-greased mould, cover with greaseproof paper and place in a tin of hot water reaching quarter-way up the side of the mould. Bake in a cool oven **(310° F., Gas 2)** for 40–45 min. During the last 10 minutes' cooking have the mould uncovered.

When cold, turn out and serve garnished with hard-boiled egg and cucumber.

**4 generous helpings**
**Cooking time—1 hr. (approx.)**

## FISH AND OYSTER PIE

*Pâté de Poisson et d'Huîtres*

**1 lb. cold cooked fish**
**1 doz. oysters**
**Breadcrumbs *or* puff-pastry**

**Salt and pepper**
**½ teasp. grated nutmeg**
**1 teasp. finely-chopped parsley**
**Melted butter sauce *or* white sauce**

Remove the skin and bones and put a layer of fish in a pie-dish, add a few oysters, with seasoning and chopped parsley. Repeat the layers until dish is quite full. Cover with browned breadcrumbs or puff-pastry. If using puff-pastry, cut it into long strips, lay a strip round the edge of the dish and lay the other strips in lattice pattern over the fish. Pour in some melted butter sauce or a little thin white sauce, and the oyster-liquor, then bake.

**6 helpings**
**Cooking time: If made of cooked fish and browned crumbs—¼ hr.**
**If made of fresh fish and puff-pastry —¾ hr.**

## FISH AND POTATO SOUFFLÉ

**2 oz. mashed potatoes**
**½ oz. butter**
**2 oz. flaked cooked fish**
**1 tablesp. milk *or* cream**
**Salt and pepper**
**Few drops anchovy essence (if desired)**
**1 egg**
**1 extra egg white if possible**

Mix the potato with the butter. Add the fish, cream, seasoning and anchovy essence. Stir in the egg yolk. Fold in the stiffly-beaten egg whites. Put into a greased individual soufflé dish. Bake for 25 min. in the centre of a moderate oven **(350° F., Gas 4).** Serve at once.

**1 generous helping**
**Cooking time—25 min.**

## FISH QUENELLES

**½ oz. butter**
**1 tablesp. milk**
**3 oz. uncooked white fish**

**1 tablesp. breadcrumbs**
**1 egg**
**¼ pt. fish stock *or* milk**

Put the butter and milk into a saucepan; stir in the breadcrumbs. Heat together, then add the beaten egg. Chop and pound the fish until smooth (or put it through mincer). Add to egg mixture; allow to cool. Form mixture into 4 finger shapes. Heat the fish stock *or* milk in a small pan, and poach the quenelles for 10 min. Drain and put on to a hot dish. Serve with white sauce.

**1 good helping** **Cooking time—½ hr.**

## FISH ROE BUTTER

*Beurre d' Œufs ou de Laite*

**Equal quantities of butter and cooked *or* raw, soft *or* hard, fish roe, according to use and taste**
**Salt and pepper**
**Lemon juice**

Pound the fish roe, cream the butter, pound the two together. Add the lemon juice a drop at a time. Season to taste. Sieve.

## FISH SALAD

**Cold cooked fish**
**Salt and pepper**
**⅛ pt. tartare sauce *or* ⅛ pt. mayonnaise sauce**
**1 lettuce**
**1 lemon**

Use any cold cooked fish divided into large flakes. Season it and mix with the tartare sauce and a little shredded lettuce. Decorate a dish with the crisp, inner lettuce leaves and slices of lemon and arrange the fish on the dish.

**4 helpings**

## FISH SAUCE

Make a white sauce carefully using concentrated fish stock. A few drops of lemon juice improve the flavour.

## FISH SOUP—HADDOCK, COD or SKATE

*Soupe au Merluche, Morue ou Raie*

**1½ lb. haddock, cod, skate *or* any available white fish**
**2 large onions**
**1 carrot**
**2 sticks of celery**
**1 teasp. curry powder**
**1½ pt. boiling water**
**A bunch of herbs**
**Salt and pepper**
**½ glass white wine (optional)**
**½ lb. potatoes**
**1 oz. butter**
**1 tablesp. olive oil**
**1 oz. flour**
**¼ pt. milk**
**⅛ pt. cream**

Slice the onions, carrot and celery into thin rounds. Cut the potatoes into thick fingers. Heat the butter and olive oil together in a deep pan and in this toss all the vegetables over gentle heat for 10 min. Add the curry powder and stir the mixture over the heat for a few more minutes. Add the boiling water, the herbs, salt and pepper. Cut the fish into neat pieces and add to the soup. Simmer until the fish is tender. Lift the best pieces of fish from the soup and keep them hot with a little of the liquid. Reduce the remaining liquid for 15 min.—pour it through a sieve and press through the potatoes and scraps of fish. Add the wine, if used, and reheat the soup. Blend the flour and milk, stir this into the soup and boil it. Return the pieces of fish and add the cream to the soup, just at boiling point.

**4–6 helpings**
**Cooking time—¾–1 hr.**

## FISH STOCK FOR SOUPS AND SAUCES

**Bones, skin and heads from fish which have been filleted *or* fish trimmings *or* cod's *or* other fish heads**
**Salt**
**Peppercorns**
**1 onion**
**1 stick of celery**
**1 blade of mace**
**1 bay leaf**
**Bouquet garni**

Wash the fish trimmings and break up the bones. Cover them with cold water, add salt and bring slowly to simmering point. Add the other ingredients and simmer gently for no longer than 40 min. Strain and use the same day, if possible.

NOTE: If cooked for longer than 40 min. the fish stock will taste bitter. Fish stock will not keep and should be made as required.

**Cooking time—50 min. altogether**

## FLAKY PASTRY

*Pâte feuilletée*

For Pies, Tarts and Tartlets

**1 lb. plain flour**
**Cold water to mix**

**Pinch of salt** **½ teasp. lemon juice**
**10 oz. butter *or* butter and lard**

Sift the flour and salt into a basin. Divide the butter into 4 equal portions and lightly rub ¼ of the butter into the flour. (If a mixture of butter and lard is used, blend them together with a round-bladed knife to get an even consistency, before dividing into 4.) Mix to a soft dough with cold water and lemon juice. The dough should be of the same consistency as the butter.

Roll out into an oblong strip, keeping the ends square and place ¼ of the butter in small pieces on the top ⅔ of the pastry. Dredge lightly with flour, fold up the bottom third of pastry on to the fat and fold down the top third. Using the rolling-pin, press the edges lightly together to prevent the air escaping. Half-turn the pastry so that the folded edges are left and right when rolling. With the rolling-pin press ridges in the pastry to distribute the air evenly. Roll out as before. Always roll carefully, do not allow the butter to break through the dough. If possible, allow the pastry to relax in a cool place.

Repeat the process with the other two portions of butter and again allow the pastry to relax. Roll out once more and use as required.

Flaky pastry should be put into a very hot oven **(450° F., Gas 8)** until set, then the heat should be reduced to fairly hot **(375° F., Gas 5)**.

## FLANS

A flan is an open tart or pastry shell containing a savoury or sweet mixture.

### To Line a Flan Ring

To line a 7-in. flan ring, about 4 oz. pastry (i.e. 4 oz. flour plus the other ingredients) will be required. Grease a baking-sheet and the flan ring; place the flan ring on the baking-sheet. Roll the pastry into a circle about 1 in. larger than the flan ring and ⅛ in. thick. Lift the pastry with the rolling-pin to prevent stretching and line the ring carefully with the pastry. Press to fit the bottom and sides so that no air bubbles form underneath the crust. Trim off the surplus pastry with a sharp knife or roll across the top of the ring with the rolling-pin.

### "Baking Blind"

If a flan is to be cooked without filling it must be baked "blind". Prick the bottom of the flan, cover with a piece of greaseproof paper and fill with rice, beans, etc. (this prevents the flan from losing its shape during cooking). Bake according to the kind of pastry. When the pastry is cooked remove the paper and rice, beans, etc., and replace the flan case in the oven for 5 min. to dry the bottom. The rice or beans can be used over and over again—cool, store in a tin and keep them for this purpose.

## FLAVOURINGS AND SPICES

**Allspice:** This is the popular name given to pimento or Jamaica pepper. It is the berry of a tree growing in the West Indies, Mexico and parts of South America. It is called "allspice" because its smell and flavour very closely resembles that of a combination of cloves, cinnamon and nutmeg. It may be used whole or ground.

**Capsicums:** Several varieties of this plant are cultivated in the East and West Indies and in America. The red chilli, which invariably forms part of mixed pickles, is the pod of the capsicum, and chilli vinegar is made by infusing capsicum pods in vinegar until some of their pungency and strength is extracted. From the same source comes cayenne pepper, obtained from the pods and the seeds, which are well dried and then ground to a fine powder. Capsicums owe their stimulating power to an active principle called capsicine, and when used in moderation produce no injurious effects.

**Cayenne:** This is an acrid spice, prepared from several varieties of the Capsicum.

**Cinnamon:** The cinnamon tree is a valuable and beautiful species of the laurel family. When the branches are 3 years old they are stripped of their outer bark, and the inner bark is dried, causing it to shrivel up. The bark is sold in stick and in powdered form. Besides being used extensively for culinary purposes—flavouring cakes, buns and puddings, cinnamon is used as a powerful stimulant.

**Cloves:** This spice is the dried flower buds of the *Caryophyllus aromaticus*, a native tree of the Molucca Islands. They take their name from the Latin word *Clavus*, or the French *clou*, both meaning a nail, which the clove closely resembles. The Ambroyna, or royal clove, is said to be the best, but other kinds, nearly as good, are produced in various parts of the world. The clove contains about 20% of volatile aromatic oil, to which is attributed its peculiar pungent flavour, its other parts being composed of woody fibre, water, gum and resin. They form a well-known spice, and are much used in cookery both in sweet and savoury dishes.

**Curry:** Curry is composed of various condiments and spices, which include cardamom seed, coriander seed, cumin seed, dried cassia leaves, dried chillies, cayenne, ginger, mustard seed, turmeric, cinnamon, mace and cloves. It usually owes its peculiar smell and bright colour to the presence of turmeric, a variety of ginger largely cultivated in the East Indies. Thorough cooking is necessary to develop the full flavour of the various ingredients comprising curry powder.

**Garlic:** This is a pungent, strong-scented bulb, composed of smaller bulbs called "cloves".

**Ginger:** Ginger is the tuber of a perennial plant called *Zingiber officinale*. It is sold in root or ground form. Ginger is much used in culinary operations; grated green ginger is considered by epicures to be an important item in a dish of curry.

**Krona Pepper:** This well-known condiment which we usually call Paprika is made from the Hungarian capsicum pod, etc. It is bright red in colour, with a pleasant flavour, less pungent than cayenne. Consequently it may be regarded as an exceedingly useful combination of flavouring and seasoning ingredients.

**Mace:** Mace is the outer shell or husk of the nutmeg, and naturally resembles it in flavour. Its general qualities are the same as those of nutmeg, producing a pleasant aromatic odour. It is sold in "blade" or ground form.

**Mustard:** There are two varieties of mustard seeds: *Sinapis nigra* (the common), and *Sinapis alba* (the white). Commercial mustard is composed of the seeds of both varieties ground and mixed together. Mustard taken in small quantities is said to stimulate the appetite and aid digestion. The pungency of mustard is not fully developed until moistened with water; its flavour is best when freshly prepared. A pinch of salt added to mixed mustard will prevent it from becoming dry, and will, in some slight degree, preserve its aroma.

**Nutmeg:** Nutmegs are the seeds of the nutmeg tree, a native of the Molucca Islands, but now cultivated in Java, Cayenne, Sumatra and some of the West Indian Islands. There are two kinds of nutmegs—one wild, and long and oval shaped, the other cultivated and nearly round: the husk which surrounds the shell of the nutmeg when growing is known as mace. Nutmeg is largely used as a flavouring: but it should be added sparingly to cereal dishes, for its strong aromatic flavour is disliked by many. It is sold whole or in ground form.

**Paprika:** *See Krona Pepper.*

**Pepper:** This valuable condiment is produced from the seed of the berries of the plant *Piper nigrum.* The same plant produces both white and black pepper. The berries when ripe, are bright in colour, and each contains a single seed of globular form and brownish colour, which changes to nearly black when dried. This is the commercial black pepper, white peppercorns being produced by further treatment, and subjecting them to certain rubbing processes, by which their dark husks are removed. It is sold as whole peppercorns or ground pepper.

Owing to the high cost of peppercorns most of the so-called "pepper" now on the market is a mixture of other highly-flavoured spices.

**Salt:** The importance of salt as a condiment, as an antiseptic, and as food cannot be overestimated. In cookery its uses are apparently contradictory, for it helps to soften certain substances when applied through the medium of cold water, and assists in hardening them when the medium is boiling water. It increases the specific gravity of water, and consequently raises the boiling-point, a matter of considerable importance in boiling rice, when it is necessary to keep the water in a state of ebullition to prevent the rice coalescing. Every other condiment, no matter how desirable, may be dispensed with, or one condiment may be substituted for another, but salt is indispensable, for it makes palatable food that would otherwise be uneatable. Salt, like all other seasonings, must be used with judgment.

It is sold as block or table salt. Block salt is the purer salt and is therefore better for cooking as table salt contains other ingredients to make it run freely.

**Turmeric:** Turmeric is the tuber of the *Curcuma longa*, a branch of the ginger family, extensively cultivated in the East Indies. The tubers are dried and then ground to a fine powder. It is a main component of curry powder, and is responsible for its peculiar odour and characteristic bright yellow colour.

**Vanilla:** Vanilla is the fruit of a tropical orchid plant, the best varieties of which are grown in Mexico. The dried, aromatic sheath-like pod has a delicious fragrance. It is extensively used as a flavouring for cakes, custards, puddings, chocolate, liqueurs, etc.

A vanilla pod should be stored in the sugar jar. It may be used for custard, etc., in a pan of heating milk as an infusion (dried after use and returned to the sugar jar), but if the sugar is flavoured then anything the sugar is used for is also flavoured.

**Vinegar:** The best vinegar is that made from white wine. Ordinary vinegar is chiefly made from malt, cheap wine and cider, by a long process whereby acetic acid is produced. Any of these vinegars may be used to form the base of chilli, tarragon, or eschalot vinegar, the ingredients from which they take their name being steeped in the vinegar until the desired flavour is imparted.

Vinegar serves many useful purposes in cookery: it is an ingredient in many sauces, and helps to soften the fibres of tough meat. Vinegar is also an antiseptic: and taken in small quantities it promotes digestion, by stimulating the digestive organs into greater activity; but if taken to excess, it is highly injurious.

## FLAVOURINGS FOR BREADS

*See White Bread.*

## FLAVOURINGS FOR COLD SWEETS (CREAMS, MOULDS, ETC.)

*See Creamed Rice, Junket, Pancakes, Powdered Grain Moulds, etc.*

## FLAVOURINGS FOR MILK PUDDINGS

*See Milk Puddings*

## FLEMISH SAUCE

**½ pt. white sauce made with ½ fish stock and ½ milk**
**1–2 egg yolks**
**½ teasp. English mustard *or* 1 dessertsp. French mustard**
**Lemon juice**

Stir a little of the cooled sauce into the egg yolks; beat this mixture with the mixed mustard into the sauce, and cook the egg yolk without boiling. Add lemon juice to taste.

Serve with fish.

## FLOATING ISLANDS

**½ pt. milk**
**1½ oz. sugar**
**Vanilla essence**
**1 large egg**

Pour the milk into a frying-pan or very shallow saucepan. Add ½ oz. sugar and a few drops of vanilla essence. Heat just to boiling point. Whisk egg white stiffly and *fold* in the sugar. Drop small spoonfuls on top of the hot milk. Cook for 2 min., turn with a fish slice. Cook for further 1–2 min. until just firm. Lift meringues from milk and drain on a sieve. Strain milk over beaten egg yolk. Cook very slowly until the custard thickens. Pour into dish. Allow to cool. Arrange meringues on top.

**2 small helpings**
**Cooking time—about 30 min.**

## FLOUNDERS

*Carrelets*

**3–4 flounders**
**½ carrot**
**½ turnip**
**1 slice parsnip**
**Water *or* fish stock**
**1 small onion**
**1 small bunch herbs**
**6 peppercorns**
**Salt**
**Parsley**

Cut the carrot, turnip and parsnip into very

fine strips and cook till tender in slightly-salted water or fish stock. Trim the fish and place in a deep sauté-pan, with the onion cut up in slices, the bunch of herbs and peppercorns. Add a little salt and pour on sufficient water to cover the fish well. Bring to the boil and cook gently for about 10 min. Lift out the fish and place in a deep entrée dish, sprinkle over the shredded cooked vegetables and some finely-chopped parsley, add a little of the fish liquor and serve.

**3–4 helpings**

## FLOUR

*See Bread and Bread-Making*

## FOIE GRAS as Hors d'œuvre

Foie gras or goose liver, either in the form of pâté or sausage, is frequently served as hors d'œuvre. A pâté or terrine may be served plain after removing the fat on its surface, or scooped out with a dessertspoon previously dipped in hot water, and then dressed neatly on a dish and garnished with parsley. Foie gras sausage must be cut into thin slices, dished up and similarly garnished. In all cases, foie gras must be served very cold.

## FONDANT ICING

**1 lb. loaf *or* granulated sugar**
**¼ pt. water**
**1½ teasp. glucose *or* a good pinch of cream of tartar**

Dissolve the sugar in the water over a low heat, add the glucose or cream of tartar, bring to the boil quickly, and boil to a temperature of 237° F. Pour on to an oiled or wetted slab, let it cool slightly (if worked when too hot it will grain), and work well with a palette knife, keeping the mass together as much as possible. When the paste is sufficiently cool, knead well with the hands. Wrap in paper and store in an airtight tin.

When required put into a basin over a saucepan containing sufficient hot water to come half-way up the sides of the basin. Stir over a very low heat until icing has the consistency of thick cream. Flavour and colour as required. Allow to cool slightly before using.

FLAVOURINGS

**Chocolate:** Add 3 dessertsp. grated chocolate, *or* 2 dessertsp. cocoa, or to taste.

**Coffee:** Stir in 2 dessertsp. coffee essence or to taste.

## "FONDUE" WITH BREAD STICKS—CHEESE

**1 lb. flour**
**½ teasp. salt**
**½ oz. yeast**
**1 teasp. sugar**
**Warm water**

Sift the flour into a warm bowl with the salt and stand in a warm place. Cream the yeast with the sugar and add this, with warm water, to the flour to form a pliable dough. Knead well with a floured hand and return to the clean warm bowl. Cover with a cloth and stand in a warm place 1 hr. to rise. Turn on to a floured board and knead again. Cut off 1-oz. portions and knead and roll these into long sticks or pencil shapes 3–4 in. long. Place on a greased and floured baking tray and allow to rise ½ hr. in a warm place. Bake at the top of a hot oven (**450° F., Gas 8**) for 10–15 min. until brown and crisp.

Cool on a rack and use immediately they are cool.

"FONDUE" FOR TEENAGERS

**1 oz. butter**
**1 oz. flour**
**½ pt. milk**
**½ lb. hard cheese**
**Seasoning**
**Mustard**

Melt the butter, add the flour and mix well, and cook gently over a low heat. Add the milk, grated cheese and seasoning and stir well to boiling-point. Stand this in a fireproof dish over a low heat, e.g. over a nightlight or spirit stove so that it keeps very hot but does not cook. Serve with the bread sticks arranged in a tall receptacle, e.g. a tumbler or napkin-lined bread basket. The fondue is eaten by dipping the bread sticks into the dish and turning it above the dish to remove the drip, so having about half the bread stick coated with fondue.

## FORCEMEAT

Forcemeat or Farcemeat as it was originally called, derives its name from the French verb *farcie*, to stuff.

The excellence of forcemeat depends on flavouring and seasoning. The flavouring should enhance the flavour of the dish with which the stuffing is to be used, e.g. lemon flavouring with sweet dishes, anchovy flavouring with white fish, etc.

Many forcemeats may be made into balls the size of a walnut and baked, fried or poached to serve with roast, braised or stewed meats. For this purpose the mixture must be bound with egg and should be stiff enough to shape into balls. The balls may be coated with egg and crumbs before frying or baking.

## FORCEMEAT FRITTERS

| | |
|---|---|
| **3 oz. butter *or* margarine** | **Salt and pepper** |
| **8 oz. soft breadcrumbs** | **2 eggs** |
| **1 tablesp. chopped parsley** | **¼ pt. milk** |
| **1 teasp. finely-chopped leek *or* onion** | **Butter *or* oil for frying** |
| **1 teasp. chopped *or* powdered mixed herbs** | **2–3 mushrooms** |
| | **Brown sauce** |
| | **Redcurrant jelly** |

Rub the butter or margarine into the breadcrumbs, add the parsley, leek or onion, herbs and a seasoning of salt and pepper. Stir in the eggs and milk, shape the mixture into fingers and fry them in hot butter or oil. Serve garnished with slices of fried mushroom, and add sauce and redcurrant jelly.

**3–4 helpings**

## FOREIGN COOKERY

Many foreign dishes are included in this book. The recipes for them usually state their country of origin, unless they have been wholly "adopted" into British cookery.

## FRANGIPANE TART

*Tourte à la Frangipane*

| | |
|---|---|
| **Rich short crust pastry using 4 oz. flour, etc.** | **2 oz. butter** |
| **2 oz. sugar** | **1 egg** |
| | **2 oz. ground almonds** |
| | **1 teasp. flour** |

Line a 7-in. flan ring or pie-plate with the pastry. Cream the butter and sugar till thick and white. Add the egg, beating well, and then mix in the ground almonds and flour. Place the mixture in the pastry case and bake in a moderate oven (**350° F., Gas 4**) for 25–30 min.

When cool, dredge with icing sugar.

**6 helpings**

## FRENCH CABBAGE SOUP

| | |
|---|---|
| **2 oz. French *or* runner beans** | **2 pt. vegetable stock *or* water** |
| **½ small cabbage** | **4–6 slices of French bread** |
| **4 small onions** | **Salt and pepper** |
| **2 oz. streaky bacon rashers** | **Grated cheese** |
| **Clove of garlic, if liked** | |

Wash the vegetables, peel the onions and cut the bacon into small pieces. Warm the bacon gradually in a large saucepan until the fat runs freely. Chop the onions fine and cook them in the bacon fat, with garlic (if used) for 10 min., until soft. Add the stock or water and bring it to boiling point. Shred the cabbage and add it to the liquid and simmer for 20 min. String and shred the beans; add them to the soup and simmer for another 20 min. Toast or bake the bread till golden and put one slice into each soup plate or cup. Season the soup and serve it with the toast floating in it. Hand grated cheese separately.

**4–6 helpings** **Cooking time—50–60 min.**

## FRENCH CARROT SALAD

*Carottes Marinées*

| | |
|---|---|
| **1½ lb. young carrots** | **1 dessertsp. French mustard** |

MARINADE

| | |
|---|---|
| **¼ pt. water** | **1 bay leaf** |
| **¼ pt. wine vinegar** | **1 crushed clove of garlic** |
| **¼ pt. white wine** | **Good pinch cayenne pepper** |
| **1 level teasp. salt** | **¼ pt. olive oil** |
| **1 level teasp. sugar** | |
| **Sprig of parsley** | |
| **Sprig of thyme** | |

Mix all the ingredients of the marinade and bring to the boil. Slice thickly or quarter the carrots and cook them in the marinade until just soft. Drain them and strain the liquor. Mix the mustard into the liquor and pour over the carrots. Leave till quite cold. Serve.

NOTE: This salad is improved if prepared the day before it is to be served.

**6 helpings**

## FRENCH COLD MEAT SALAD

*Salade de Viande à la Francaise*

**1½ lb. cold roast *or* boiled meat**
**2 shallots**
**4 anchovy fillets**
**Vinaigrette sauce**
**Gherkins**
**Capers**

Cut the meat into strips, about 2½ in. by 1 in. Chop the shallots and anchovy fillets finely and mix with the meat and Vinaigrette sauce. Cover and leave 2 hr., stirring the mixture occasionally. Pile in a pyramid in a salad bowl and garnish with strips of gherkin and chopped capers.

**6 helpings**

## FRENCH CRUST

*Pâte brisée*

**1 lb. plain flour**
**½ teasp. salt**
**6 oz. butter**
**2 eggs**
**Cold water to mix**

Sift the flour and salt. Lightly rub in the butter. Mix to a smooth firm paste with the eggs and cold water added gradually. Use as required.

## FRENCH DRESSING

**2–3 tablesp. olive oil**
**Pepper and salt**
**1 tablesp. wine vinegar**

Mix the oil and seasoning. Add the vinegar gradually, stirring constantly with a wooden spoon so that an emulsion is formed.

NOTE: A pinch of sugar, a little mustard and one or two drops of Worcester sauce may be added.

Lemon juice may be used in place of vinegar. Where suitable, orange or grapefruit juice may also be used.

A graduated medicine bottle is most useful for making French dressing. The oil and vinegar can be measured accurately without waste, and the dressing vigorously shaken to mix it. It can be stored in the larder or refrigerator, the bottle being well shaken before the dressing is used.

## FRENCH GAME PIE

*Pâté de Gibier*

**1 blackcock, pheasant *or* partridge**
**¾ lb. lean veal**
**¾ lb. lean pork**
**Mixed spice *or* herbs**
**2–3 rashers bacon**
**1 truffle *or* 8 mushrooms**
**Salt and pepper**
**¼ pt. stock *or* water**
**Puff pastry using 8 oz. flour, etc.**

Chop or mince the veal and pork finely; season well with spice *or* herbs, salt and pepper; add finely chopped truffle *or* mushrooms. Cut the bird into neat joints, season the pieces lightly. Put a layer of meat in the bottom of a pie-dish, then some game, bacon and more forcemeat until dish is full. Moisten with ¼ pt. water *or* stock. Cover with puff pastry, glaze and bake in a fairly hot oven (**375°–400° F., Gas 5–6**) 1½–1¾ hr., lowering the heat after 20 min. to (**350°–375° F., Gas 4–5**).

Serve hot or cold.

**6–8 helpings**

## FRENCH HASH

*Hachis de Mouton à la Française*

**1¼ lb. cold shoulder *or* leg of mutton**
**3 oz. Patna rice**
**¾ pt. Espagnole sauce**
**4 oz. stewed prunes**
**6 oz. preserved cherries**
**Paprika**
**Salt**

Boil the rice in plenty of seasoned water for about 20 min. or until tender, then drain and dry well. Cut the meat into neat pieces. Heat the sauce and put in the meat. Simmer very gently for about ¾ hr. Then add the prunes, previously stewed and stoned, and also the cherries and rice. Season carefully with paprika and salt.

**6 helpings**

## FRENCH OMELETTE

**2–3 eggs**
**Salt and pepper**
**½ oz. butter**

Break the eggs into a basin. Add salt and pepper to taste. Beat the eggs with a fork until they are lightly mixed. Heat the butter in the pan and slowly let it get hot, but not so hot that the butter browns. Without drawing the pan off the heat, pour in the egg mixture. It will cover the pan and start cooking at once.

Shake the pan and stir the eggs with a fork away from the side to the middle. Shake again. In about 1 min. the omelette will be soft but no longer runny. Let it stand for 4 or 5 seconds for the bottom to brown slightly. Then remove from the heat.

Using a palette knife, fold the omelette from two sides over the middle. Then slip on to a hot dish, or turn it upside down on to the dish.

This omelette can be eaten plain, or it can be filled. There are two methods of filling; flavouring such as herbs, cheese can be added to the eggs after they are beaten, or added to the omelette just before it is folded.

*Suggested savoury fillings* (quantities given are for 2 egg omelettes)

**Cheese:** Grate 2 oz. hard cheese finely. Add most of it to the mixed eggs, saving a little to top the finished omelette.

**Fines Herbes:** Finely chop 1 tablesp. parsley and a few chives, and add this to the mixed eggs before cooking.

**Onion:** Sauté a large onion in a little butter but do not get it too greasy. When cool, add to the egg mixture, saving a few hot morsels for garnishing the omelette.

**Kidney:** Peel, core and cut 2 lamb's kidneys into smallish pieces, and sauté them in a little butter with a small chopped onion or shallot. Pile this mixture along the centre of the omelette after cooking but before folding.

**Mushroom:** Wash and chop 2 oz. mushrooms, sauté them in a little butter until tender. Put them along the centre of the cooked omelette.

**Shellfish:** Shrimps, prawns, crayfish, lobster or crab, fresh or canned, can be used. Chop if necessary and warm slowly through in a little white sauce (or butter') so they are hot when the omelette is cooked. Then pile the mixture along the centre.

**Spanish:** Make a mixture of chopped ham, tomato, sweet pepper, a few raisins, 1 or 2 mushrooms, and sauté in a little butter or olive oil. Add this to the egg before cooking; serve this omelette flat.

## FRENCH ONION SOUP

**2 oz. fat bacon**
**6 medium-sized onions**
**½ oz. flour**
**Salt and pepper**
**½ teasp. French mustard**
**1½ pt. stock**
**¼ pt. white wine** *or* **cider**
**6 small slices of bread**
**2 oz. cheese: Gruyère** *or* **Parmesan**
**A little butter**

Chop the bacon and heat it gently in a deep pan till the fat runs freely. Slice the onions thinly and fry them slowly in the bacon fat till golden. Add the flour, salt and pepper to taste and continue frying for a few minutes. Stir in the mustard, the stock and the wine or cider. Simmer till the onions are quite soft. Toast the bread, grate the cheese. Butter the toast and spread the slices with grated cheese. Pour the soup into individual fireproof soup-bowls, float a round of toast on each and brown it in a very hot oven or under the grill.

**6 helpings**
**Cooking time—about 1½ hr.**

## FRENCH PANCAKES

*Crêpes à la Française*

**½ pt. milk**
**2 oz. butter** *or* **margarine**
**2 oz. castor sugar**
**2 eggs**
**2 oz. plain flour**
**A little grated lemon rind**
**4 tablesp. jam (approx.)**

Warm the milk. Cream the fat and sugar until soft. Well whisk the eggs and beat them gradually into the creamed fat and sugar. Stir in the flour. Add the warmed milk and lemon rind. Beat well. Leave to stand for ½ hr.

Grease 6 small deep plates *or* large saucers and pour an equal quantity of batter into each. Bake in a fairly hot oven **(400° F., Gas 6)** for about 5–10 min., until the batter rises; then more slowly **(350° F., Gas 4)** for about another 10 min., until firm and brown on top.

Turn a pancake out on to a hot dish, spread quickly with melted jam; lay another pancake on top, and so on until the last pancake is put on top.

Dredge well with castor sugar and serve quickly.

NOTE: This is sometimes known as **Angel Pudding**—*Pouding des Anges*.

**5–6 helpings**

## FRENCH VEGETABLE SOUP

*Croûte au pot maigre*

**2 leeks**
**2 carrots**
**2 sticks of celery**
**½ turnip**
**2 tomatoes**
**Salt**
**¼ small cabbage (if liked)**
**1 oz. beef dripping**
**3 pt. stock *or* vegetable boilings**
**Bunch of fresh herbs**
**2 slices brown bread**
**Grated cheese**

Clean the vegetables. Scald and skin the tomatoes. Cut the roots into ¼-in. dice, or grate them on a coarse grater; slice the leeks in thin rings. Melt the dripping in a large pan and cook the cut-up vegetables gently for 10 min. Cut up the tomatoes and add them to the other vegetables, then add the stock (boiling) and herbs. Simmer till the vegetables are soft, then add the finely-shredded cabbage and cook for another 15 min. Toast or bake the bread till golden, cut it into fingers and add it to the soup just before serving. Season carefully, remove the bunch of herbs and serve the soup with grated cheese, handed separately.

**6 helpings** **Cooking time—about 1 hr.**

## FRESH FRUIT SALAD

*Macédoine de fruits frais*

**1 pt. water *or* fruit juice**
**3 oz. sugar**
**Selection of fruit as liked (*see below*)**
**Juice of 1 lemon**
**1 tablesp. brandy *or* kirsch (optional)**
**2 tablesp. sherry (optional)**

Boil the water and sugar together until reduced to half quantity, but sufficient syrup should be made to cover fruit completely. Prepare the fruit according to kind:

**Apples:** Peel, core, quarter and slice thinly.

**Oranges:** Peel in a similar way to an apple, with a very sharp knife, cutting deeply enough to expose the flesh. Cupping the peeled fruit in the hand, cut the pulp cleanly from each section by loosening the thin skin from both sides. Work over a plate as juice is likely to escape.

**Grapes:** Remove seeds, and skins from black grapes. If black colour is required for contrast, leave a few half-grapes unskinned.

**Apricots, Peaches:** Slit around the natural groove, "unscrew" the two halves, skin, stone and cut each half in two or four.

**Pineapple:** Slice off the top cleanly, just below the leaves, using a sharp, thin knife, cut around the rim of the fruit, cutting down to the base, all round. Withdraw the inner "barrel" of fruit by means of a corkscrew. Cut fruit in slices.

**Cherries:** Remove stones neatly—a fine, sterilized hairpin may be kept for this purpose.

**Strawberries, Raspberries:** Hull carefully.

**Plums:** Halve and stone.

**Bananas:** Slice thinly. This fruit must never be chilled, unless covered, as such treatment causes discoloration.

**Melon:** Cut into slices and, if flesh alone is required, remove with a silver spoon. The melon may be used as a receptacle for fruit salad by cutting off the top, removing the seeds, and the flesh, with a spoon. The melon "cup" is then flavoured with kirsch and set on ice to become chilled, while the flesh is used as an ingredient of the mixed salad to be served in the melon case.

Pour the syrup over the prepared fruit and flavour with lemon juice. Cover the bowl and allow the salad to become quite cold. Stir in the liqueur and wine if used, a few minutes before serving. Serve with cream, custard, ice cream, *or* chopped nuts.

## FRICANDEAU OF VEAL

*Fricandeau de Veau*

**2 lb. piece of fillet veal**
**Larding bacon**
**2 onions**
**2 carrots**
**1 turnip**
**2 sticks of celery**
**1 oz. butter *or* fat**
**1 oz. bacon cut in pieces**
**Stock**
**Bouquet garni**
**2 cloves**
**6 peppercorns**
**Salt and pepper**
**Meat glaze**
**1½ lb. sorrel *or* spinach purée**
**Espagnole sauce**

Trim and wipe the meat and beat with a rolling-pin. Lard the best side closely with strips of larding bacon. Slice the onions thickly, cut the carrots and turnip in blocks, cut up the celery roughly. Melt the fat and fry the bacon and the prepared vegetables. Then lay the meat on top and fry gently for about 15 min. Add stock to cover the vegetables, the bouquet garni, flavourings and seasoning. Cover with greased paper and a lid and cook gently for about 1 hr., adding more stock as necessary. Remove the lid and paper and put into a fairly hot oven (**400° F., Gas 6**) for 15 min. to crisp and brown the lardoons. Brush the meat with glaze, place on a hot dish larded side uppermost on a bed of purée and serve the remainder of the sorrel or spinach separately.

Pour a little Espagnole sauce round the meat, and serve the remainder in a sauceboat. The liquid from the braising tin should be strained, reduced, skimmed to remove all fat and poured round the meat or added to the sauce.

**6 helpings**

## FRICASSÉE OF CHICKEN

*Fricassée de Volaille*

| | |
|---|---|
| **1 boiled *or* 1 lb. can of chicken** | **1 egg** |
| **1 pt. Velouté sauce** | **Salt and pepper** |
| **½ gill cream *or* milk** | **Juice of 1 lemon** |

GARNISH

| | |
|---|---|
| **Chopped parsley** | **Sippets of fried bread, *or* potato border** |

Before chicken is quite cold, cut into joints, remove skin and excess fat. Make sauce, thoroughly heat chicken in it, add cream and egg, stir over a low heat until the sauce thickens (do not boil). Season, add lemon juice.

Arrange chicken in entrée dish, strain sauce over and garnish.

NOTE: If a potato border is used, pipe or fork this into the dish, before arranging the chicken for serving.

**6 helpings**
**Cooking time—20 min. (excluding sauce)**

## FRICASSÉE OF FISH

| | |
|---|---|
| **1 lb. white fish** | **A small piece of mace** |
| **½ pt. milk** | **A pinch of nutmeg** |
| **¼ pt. water** | **1 oz. butter** |
| **Salt and pepper** | **1 oz. flour** |
| **½ bay leaf** | **Lemon juice** |

Divide the fish into pieces about 1½ in. square. Put the milk, water, salt and pepper, bay leaf, mace and nutmeg into a saucepan, and when warm add the fish. Bring to the boil and simmer for 10 min., then remove the bay leaf and mace. Meanwhile knead together the butter and flour, add in small portions to the contents of the saucepan and stir gently until the flour is mixed smoothly with the liquor. Simmer for 10 min., then add lemon juice, season to taste and serve.

**2–3 helpings**

## FRICASSÉE OF LAMB

*Fricassee d'Agneau*

| | |
|---|---|
| **A breast of lamb** | **Salt and pepper** |
| **1 onion** | **1 pt. boiling stock *or* water** |
| **2 oz. butter *or* fat** | **1 oz. flour** |
| **2 bay leaves** | **1 dessertsp. roughly-chopped capers** |
| **2 cloves** | |
| **1 blade of mace** | |
| **6 peppercorns** | |

Prepare the meat and cut into 2-in. squares. Slice the onion, melt the fat, add the onion, bay leaves, cloves, mace, peppercorns, salt, pepper and meat. Cover and cook very gently for about ½ hr. stirring frequently. Add boiling stock or water and simmer for about 1½ hr. or until tender. Mix the flour smoothly with a small quantity of cold water. Gradually add to it, stirring all the time, about ½ pt. of the liquor from the saucepan. To this sauce add the meat, bring to the boil and simmer until tender. Serve on a hot dish within a border of mashed potatoes, sprinkle the capers over the meat.

**4–6 helpings, depending on the quantity of meat**

## FRICASSÉE OF RABBIT

*Fricassée de Lapin*

| | |
|---|---|
| **1 young rabbit** | **1 blade mace** |
| **White stock** | **6 white peppercorns** |
| **2 onions, sliced** | **Salt and pepper** |
| **1 carrot, sliced** | **½ pt. milk (if required)** |
| **½ turnip, sliced** | **2 oz. butter** |
| **2 sticks celery** | **1½ oz. flour** |
| **Bouquet garni** | |

Prepare the rabbit wash and cut into neat joints, place in a saucepan and just cover with stock. Bring to boiling point, add prepared vegetables, herbs, mace, peppercorns and seasoning. Cover tightly, cook gently until rabbit is tender—about 1¼ hr.; add some milk, if necessary. Meanwhile, melt butter, add flour, stir and cook gently without browning, then keep the roux hot. Remove rabbit from pan and keep it hot. Strain ¾ pt. stock from the pan, stir this into the roux and allow to simmer for 10 min. Sieve the vegetables, add to the sauce, correct the seasoning, put rabbit in, re-heat thoroughly, then serve.

**3–4 helpings**

## FRICASSÉE OF TRIPE

| | |
|---|---|
| **1½ lb. dressed tripe** | **1 oz. butter** |
| **Milk** | **1 oz. flour** |
| **Salt and pepper** | **Croûtons of toast** |
| **2 Spanish onions** | |

Wash, blanch and scrape the tripe well. Cut into pieces about 2 in. square, put into a stewpan and cover with equal parts of milk and water. Add the seasoning and diced onions, bring to the boil and simmer gently for 1 hr. Knead the butter and flour smoothly together and add it in small pieces to the contents of the stewpan. Stir until smooth, then continue cooking for another ½ hr.

Serve on a hot dish and garnish with croûtons.

**6 helpings**

## FRIED AUBERGINE

*Aubergines frites*

| | |
|---|---|
| **4 aubergines** | **Salt** |
| **Flour** | **1 finely-chopped onion** |
| **Cayenne pepper** | **Salad oil *or* butter** |

Slice the aubergines about ½ in. thick, lay them out on a flat dish, sprinkle with salt and put on a weight (this hastens the process of removing the moisture). After ½ hr. wipe them with a cloth, then coat them lightly with flour seasoned with cayenne and salt. Fry the onion in the oil or butter until lightly browned, drain and keep the onion hot. Replace the butter in the pan and fry the aubergine until both sides are lightly browned. Drain and dish. Sprinkle the onion on the aubergine; serve with tomato sauce, if liked.

**6 helpings**
**Cooking time—to fry the aubergine, about 15 min.**

## FRIED BEEFSTEAK

*Bifteck frit*

| | |
|---|---|
| **1½ lb. frying beefsteak, 1 in. thick** | **Salt and pepper** |
| | **Fat** |

Wipe the meat, remove and discard any skin, beat lightly and season to taste. Put sufficient fat to barely cover the bottom of a frying-pan. When hot, fry the steak quickly on both sides to seal the surface. Then cook more slowly until cooked to taste.

For a good gravy to serve with the steak, drain any fat from the frying-pan, keeping back the sediment. Add salt and pepper and about 1½ gills of boiling water. Boil up, skim and strain.

**6 helpings**
**Cooking time—about 7–10 min.**

## FRIED BRUSSELS SPROUTS

*Choux de Bruxelles frits*

**1 lb. small, tight Brussels sprouts, cooked**
**Coating batter (double quantity) *or* yeast batter:**

| | |
|---|---|
| **½ oz. margarine** | **¼ lb. flour** |
| **¼ pt. milk** | **¼ oz. yeast** |
| | **¼ teasp. salt** |

Prepare the batter, if using yeast batter: warm the milk to blood heat with the margarine, and cream the yeast with a little of it Add the rest of the milk to the yeast, then add all to the warmed flour and salt. Beat till smooth. Put to rise in a warm place till doubled in size. Cook the sprouts so that they are just tender. Drain well. Dip them in the batter on a skewer and lower each piece carefully into hot, deep fat at 340° F. Turn them during frying as they will float, and when golden brown, 5–7 min., remove from the fat. Drain well and serve garnished with fried parsley.

NOTE: The yeast batter gives a pleasant, very crisp result. Tomato sauce is an excellent accompaniment if the sprout fritters are to be served as a separate course.

**4 helpings**

## FRIED CALVES' BRAINS

*Cervelles de Veau frites*

| | |
|---|---|
| **2 calves' brains** | **Salt** |
| **1 tablesp. vinegar *or* lemon juice** | **1 tablesp. olive oil** |
| | **½ gill tepid water** |
| **1 onion** | **1 egg white** |
| **Pinch of sage** | **Deep fat** |
| **2 oz. flour** | **Parsley** |

Prepare and cook the brains as directed for Calves' Brain Cakes until firm excluding the peppercorns and bay leaf. Strain, dry well and cut the brains into fairly thin slices. Make a batter by sifting the flour and salt and mixing smoothly with the oil and tepid water. Whisk the egg white until stiff and then fold lightly into the batter. Have ready a pan of hot deep fat. Dip each slice of brain into the batter, drain slightly and then drop into the hot fat. Fry until golden brown, turning as necessary. Drain well, place on a hot dish and garnish with parsley.

**6 helpings**

## FRIED CALVES' SWEETBREADS

*Fritot de Ris de Veau*

**2 calves' sweetbreads**
**1 pt. white stock; *or* water with vegetables to flavour**
**Salt and pepper**
**Egg and breadcrumbs**
**Butter *or* deep fat**
**Parsley**

*Method 1*

Prepare and blanch the sweetbreads as directed for Braised Sweetbreads. Place the sweetbreads in a saucepan, with the stock, seasoning if required, and simmer gently for 40 min. Press between 2 plates until cold, then cut into slices. Brush with beaten egg and coat with breadcrumbs. Fry in butter in a shallow pan or in a pan of hot deep fat until golden brown. Drain well and garnish with sprigs of fresh or fried parsley.

*Method 2*

After blanching, boil the sweetbreads in slightly salted water for 10 min. and allow to cool. Cut into ¼ in. thick slices and season. Coat both sides with thick Béchamel sauce (½ pt.). Place in a refrigerator or cool place until the sauce is set. Then fry as before.

*Method 3*

After coating the sweetbreads with thick Béchamel sauce (see above) they may be covered with batter then fried. Drain well, sprinkle with salt and pepper and pile on a hot dish. Garnish with parsley.

**6 helpings**

## FRIED CELERIAC

*Céléri-rave frit*

**3 roots of celeriac**
**Butter *or* margarine**
**Finely-chopped parsley**

Cook the celeriac as in vegetable stock. Drain well and dry in a cloth. Fry in butter *or* margarine until golden brown. Drain and dish hot, sprinkled with finely-chopped parsley.

**6 helpings**
**Cooking time—45 min. to boil, 6–8 min. to fry**

## FRIED CHICKEN CREOLE

**1 young chicken**
**2 onions**
**2 tablesp. oil**
**Pinch of saffron**
**1 tablesp. curry powder**
**Pinch of salt**
**Pinch of chilli pepper**
**Coconut milk**

Joint the chicken. Brown sliced onions in oil. Season with saffron, curry powder, salt and pepper. Fry joints of chicken. Before serving add 1 cup of coconut milk.

**6 small helpings** **Cooking time—20–30 min.**

## FRIED COD'S ROE

*Laitance de Cabillaud, frite*

**1 lb. cod's roe**
**Egg and breadcrumbs**
**Fat for frying**

Poach the roe for 15 min. then drain and cut into slices. When cold, brush over with egg, roll in breadcrumbs and fry until nicely browned, in hot fat.

**3–4 helpings**

## FRIED EGGS

*Œufs à la Poêle*

These are eggs fried on one side only. Melt a little bacon fat or butter in a frying-pan, break the eggs and slip them carefully into the pan. Cook over a gentle heat, basting the eggs with some of the hot fat, until the white is no longer transparent and the yolk is set. Season with pepper and salt.

*Œufs Frits*

Only one egg can be cooked at a time, but each takes less than one minute. Put a teacupful of oil into a small pan so that the egg will actually swim in the oil. Heat until the oil begins to smoke lightly, then maintain this temperature. Break the egg into a cup or saucer and season the yolk with salt and pepper. Slip it quickly into the oil, putting the edge of the cup to the surface of the oil. Dip a smooth wooden spoon into the hot oil, then pull the white over the yolk so as to cover it completely. Then turn the egg over in the oil and leave for a second only. It will then be done.

### FRIED FLOUNDERS

*Carrelets frits*

**Flounders**
**Salt**
**Egg and breadcrumbs**
**Fat for frying**
**Fried parsley**

Clean the fish and 2 hr. before required rub them inside and out with salt, to make them firm. Wash and dry them thoroughly, dip into beaten egg and coat with breadcrumbs. Fry in hot fat. Serve garnished with parsley.

**6 oz.–7 oz. per helping for breakfast; rather less when served in the fish course of a dinner**
**Cooking time—10–15 min. according to size**

### FRIED GRAYLING

*Ombre frit*

**4 small grayling**
**Flour**
**Salt and pepper**
**Egg and breadcrumbs**
**Fat for frying**
**Parsley sauce**

Empty, scale, wash and dry the fish, remove the gills and fins, but leave the heads. Roll in flour seasoned with salt and pepper, coat carefully with egg and breadcrumbs and fry in hot fat until nicely browned. Serve with parsley sauce, or any other sauce preferred.

**4 helpings**
**Cooking time—8–9 min.**

### FRIED HALIBUT

*Flétan frit*

**2 lb. halibut**
**1 tablesp. flour**
**½ teasp. salt**
**⅛ teasp. pepper**
**Egg and breadcrumbs**
**Fat for frying**
**Parsley**

Divide the fish into small thin slices. Mix the flour, salt and pepper together, coat the pieces of fish lightly with the seasoned flour, brush over with beaten egg and toss in breadcrumbs. Fry in a deep pan of hot fat until crisp and lightly-browned, or, if more convenient, in a smaller amount of hot fat in a frying-pan. Serve garnished with crisply-fried parsley. Serve with anchovy or shrimp sauce.

**4–6 helpings**
**Cooking time—6–7 min.**

### FRIED JERUSALEM ARTICHOKES

*Topinambours frits*

**1½ lb. Jerusalem artichokes**
**Coating batter (double quantity)**
**Fried parsley**

Prepare and parboil the artichokes (about 15 min.). Cut them into slices ½ in. thick and season them well. Make the batter, dip in the slices of artichokes and fry in hot fat, at 340° F. until golden brown (5–7 min.), turning them during cooking. Drain well and serve very hot with fried parsley.

**6 helpings**
**Cooking time—15 min. to parboil artichokes**
**5–7 min. to fry them**

### FRIED MUSHROOMS

*Champignons frits*

**1 lb. flap mushrooms**
**Butter *or* margarine *or* bacon fat**
**Salt and pepper**

Wash and peel the mushrooms, trim the stalks. Melt the fat and fry the mushrooms in it for 15 min. Drain and serve hot, seasoned with salt and pepper.

Small rounds *or* squares of bread may be fried in the fat, after removing the mushrooms, and the mushrooms served on the bread.

**6 helpings**
**Cooking time—about 15 min.**

### FRIED MUTTON CUTLETS

*Côtelettes de Mouton frites*

**6 cutlets from the best end of neck**
**Egg and breadcrumbs**
**Deep fat**
**½ pt. tomato sauce**

Trim and flatten the cutlets. Coat with egg and breadcrumbs—clean the bone of crumbs.

Reshape the cutlets with a clean dry knife. Fry in deep fat which is faintly smoking for about 5–10 min. Fry a 1-in. cube of bread, place it in the serving dish and prop the first cutlet on it. Lean the cutlets one against the other. Pour some tomato sauce round and serve the rest in a sauce-boat. Garnish with cooked green peas.

**6 helpings**

### FRIED ONIONS

*Oignons frits*

| | |
|---|---|
| **6 large onions** | **Frying fat** |
| | **Salt and pepper** |

Peel and slice the onions. Heat enough frying fat in a frying-pan to cover the bottom of the pan. Fry the onions slowly until golden brown and quite soft, stirring them occasionally during frying. Drain well, season and serve hot.

**6 helpings** **Cooking time—20 min.**

### FRIED PARSLEY

*Persil frit*

Remove stalks from the parsley, leaving it in sprigs. Wash it, shake well and dry in a cloth for at least 1 hr. before frying. Put into the basket of a deep fat pan. Dip the basket just into the hot fat at 340° F., remove quickly, dip again and remove, then plunge into the fat and leave it in until most of the bubbling has ceased and the parsley is bright green and crisp. Drain very well on absorbent paper. Serve hot with many savoury dishes, particucularly with fish.

NOTE: The high water content of parsley causes hot fat to bubble fiercely and if the parsley is plunged straight into the fat and left there, the fat may come over the top of the pan and cause a fire.

### FRIED PEPPERS

*Piment frit*

| | |
|---|---|
| **4 green peppers** | **Egg and breadcrumbs (if to be fried in deep fat)** |
| **Butter *or* margarine *or* deep fat** | |

Wash the peppers. Parboil in salted water for 5 min. Drain and cut into strips or rings. Remove seeds and inner partitions. Toss in hot butter or margarine in a frying-pan for 5–10 min. *or* dip in egg and breadcrumbs and fry in deep fat (**360° F.**) 5–7 min. Drain well and serve hot.

**4–6 helpings**

### FRIED PERCH

*Perche frite*

| | |
|---|---|
| **4 small perch 6–8 oz. each** | **Flour** |
| | **Egg and breadcrumbs** |
| **Salt and pepper** | **Frying-fat** |

Scale, clean, wash and dry the fish thoroughly. Sprinkle with salt and pepper, dredge well with flour, brush over with beaten egg and coat with breadcrumbs. Fry the fish in hot fat until nicely browned. Drain well, and serve with anchovy, shrimp or melted butter sauce.

**4 helpings**

### FRIED PLAICE

*Plie frite*

| | |
|---|---|
| **Four 4 oz. fillets of plaice** | **A little milk *or* water** |
| | **Egg and breadcrumbs** |
| **1 tablesp. flour** | **Frying-fat** |
| **Salt and pepper** | **Parsley** |

Wipe the fillets with a clean damp cloth. Season the flour with salt and pepper to taste and dip each fillet in it. Beat the egg, mix with a little milk or water and brush over each fillet. Coat the fillets with breadcrumbs, press on firmly and fry in hot fat until nicely browned. Garnish with fresh or fried parsley, and serve plain with cut lemon or with anchovy, shrimp or melted butter sauce.

**4 helpings**

### FRIED or GRILLED PORK CUTLETS or CHOPS

*Côtelettes de Porc panées*

| | |
|---|---|
| **6 bones neck *or* loin of pork** | **Salt and pepper** |
| | **Breadcrumbs** |
| **1 egg** | **1½ oz. butter *or* fat** |
| **1 teasp. powdered sage** | |

Trim the cutlets, removing most of the fat. Beat the egg and add to it the sage, salt and pepper. Brush each cutlet with this and then coat carefully with breadcrumbs. Heat the fat and gently fry, or grill, the cutlets for about 20 min., turning frequently until golden brown.

## FRIED RICE

| | |
|---|---|
| 2 lb. boiled rice | Pinch of pepper |
| 2 onions | 2 oz. cooked pork |
| 2 eggs | 1 tablesp. chopped parsley |
| Oil for frying | 2 tablesp. soya sauce |
| Pinch of salt | |

Chop the onions; beat the eggs. Heat oil in a pan and fry rice. Add onions, pepper and salt and pork. When mixed, make a hole in the centre and put in the eggs. When eggs are semi-cooked, stir in rice from the sides of the pan. Add parsley and soya sauce.

## FRIED SALMON (Jewish recipe)

*Saumon frit*

| | |
|---|---|
| 1½ lb. salmon | Olive oil |

Clean the salmon, then dry with a cloth. Pour the oil into a small but deep pan. Heat, and when it ceases to bubble, put in the salmon and fry gently until completely cooked through. When the salmon is golden brown, reduce the heat to allow the fish to cook more slowly to prevent it becoming darker. When thoroughly cooked, drain and leave to become cold.

Serve on a fish paper, garnished with sprigs of fresh parsley.

**4 helpings**
**Cooking time—about ½ hr.**

## FRIED SALSIFY

*Salsifis frits*

| | |
|---|---|
| 1½ lb. salsify | Fried parsley |
| Coating batter (double quantity), *or* yeast batter | |

Prepare and parboil the salsify (about 15 min.). Cut them into slices ½ in. thick and season them well. Make the batter, dip in the slices of salsify and fry in hot fat, at 340° F., until golden brown (5–7 min.), turning them during cooking. Drain well and serve very hot with fried parsley.

**6 helpings**
**Cooking time—15 min. to parboil salsify, 5–7 min. to fry them**

## FRIED SCAMPI

| | |
|---|---|
| 8 oz. frozen *or* fresh Dublin bay prawns (weight when peeled) | Fat for frying |
| | Tartare sauce |
| | Lemon wedges |

BATTER

| | |
|---|---|
| 2 oz. flour | ½ teacup milk |
| 1 egg | Salt and pepper |

Separate the frozen prawns or dry the fresh prawns. To make the batter sift the flour, add the egg and milk gradually, giving a smooth thick batter. Season well. Dip each prawn in the batter and lower into really hot fat. Cook fairly quickly until golden brown. Drain on crumpled tissue or kitchen paper.

Serve on a hot dish with Tartare sauce and garnish with wedges of lemon or serve with spinach.

## FRIED SKATE WITH TOMATO SAUCE

*Raie frite à la Sauce Tomate*

| | |
|---|---|
| 1½ lb. wing of skate | Fat for frying |
| Egg *or* thin batter and white crumbs for coating | ¼ pt. tomato sauce |

Cut the skate into neat pieces and simmer in salted water for 5 min. Drain and dry, then coat each piece with egg or batter and white breadcrumbs, pressing the coating on firmly with a knife. Fry the skate slowly in hot fat until golden brown, turning once during cooking. Drain the fish well and arrange in the centre of a hot dish. Pour the sauce round and serve at once.

## FRIED SOLE

*Sole frite*

| | |
|---|---|
| 1–2 medium-sized soles | Egg and breadcrumbs |
| Salt and pepper | Deep fat for frying |
| 1 tablesp. flour | |

Wash and skin the soles, cut off the fins, and dry well. Add a liberal seasoning of salt and pepper to the flour. Coat the fish with seasoned flour then brush over with egg, and coat with fine breadcrumbs. Lower the fish carefully into the hot fat and fry until golden-brown.

Soles may also be fried, though less easily, and sometimes less satisfactorily, in a large frying-pan. The oval form is preferable for the purpose; and in frying, care should be taken to cook first the side of the sole intended to be served uppermost, otherwise breadcrumbs that have become detached from the side first fried may adhere to the side next cooked, and spoil its appearance. Drain well on kitchen paper and serve garnished with fried parsley.

**1–2 helpings** **Cooking time—about 10 min.**

### FRIED TOMATOES

*Tomates frites*

**6 large tomatoes**
**Butter *or* margarine *or* bacon fat for frying**
**Salt and pepper**

Wash the tomatoes and cut in halves. Fry in hot fat, turning them once during frying. Season. Serve hot.

**6 helpings**
**Cooking time—about 6 min.**

### FRIED VEGETABLE MARROW

*Courge frite*

**2 very small marrows**
**Coating batter (double quantity), *or* yeast batter, *or* egg and breadcrumbs**

Peel and boil the marrows in salt and water until tender. Drain well. Cut into 1½ in. squares or into strips, remove the seeds. Coat with egg and breadcrumbs *or* dip in batter and fry in deep hot fat at 340° F. Turn them during frying as they will float, and when golden brown remove from the fat. Drain well, serve hot.

**6 helpings**
**Cooking time—to fry, 7 min.**

### FRIED WHITING

*Merlan frit*

**3–4 whiting**
**1 tablesp. flour**
**Salt and pepper**
**Egg and breadcrumbs**
**Deep fat *or* oil for frying**
**Parsley**

Wash, clean and dry the fish. Remove their skins and fasten the tail in the mouth with a small skewer. (The fishmonger will usually do this for you.) Season the flour with salt and pepper and coat the fish with it. Brush them over with egg, coat with breadcrumbs and fry in hot fat until nicely browned. Serve on a fish paper, garnished with sprigs of fresh or crisply-fried parsley.

**3–4 helpings**
**Cooking time—6–7 min.**

### FROZEN FOODS, USE OF

*See Quick-Frozen Foods.*

### FROZEN PEACH CAKE

**2 oz. unsalted butter *or* margarine**
**3 oz. icing sugar**
**1 egg**
**½ can sliced peaches**
**Few drops of almond essence**
**6 individual sponge cakes**
**Angelica**
**Cream**

Line the bottom of an oblong cake-tin 7½ in. by 4 in. with greaseproof paper. Cream together fat and sugar. Separate egg yolk from egg white and beat yolk into creamed fat. Drain peaches, reserve a few for decoration, and chop remainder finely. Add peaches to fat mixture, add almond essence then lightly fold in the egg white. Arrange some sponge cakes on bottom of tin, spread with peach mixture, cover with remaining sponge cakes. Chill until firm, then unmould and decorate with peaches, strips of angelica and piped whipped cream.

### FRUIT CAKE, RICH

*See Rich Cakes, Large, Various.*

### FRUIT FOOL

*Foule de Fruit*

**1½ lb. fruit (approx.),** *see below*
**Sugar according to taste and sweetness of fruit**
**1 pt. thick, pouring custard *or* 1 pt. double cream *or* ½ pt. custard and ½ pt. cream mixed**
**Ratafia biscuits *or* tiny macaroons for decoration**

Prepare the fruit and cook if necessary:

**Gooseberries** and **Damsons** will require about 1 pt. water.

Pink, forced **Rhubarb,** if cooked gently in a wet earthenware *or* oven-glass casserole requires *no* water. Sweeten with brown sugar to produce a rich pink juice.

**Red-** and **Black Currants** require about ¼ pt. water.

## *Fruit Fool for Children*

**Strawberries, Loganberries** and **Raspberries** should be crushed, sprinkled with castor sugar and left overnight.

Rub the softened fruit through a fine nylon sieve. Allow to cool then blend with the cream *or* cold custard; taste and sharpen with a little lemon juice if necessary. Sweeten to taste with castor sugar. Chill and serve with ratafia biscuits arranged carefully on top.

**6 helpings**

### FRUIT FOOL FOR CHILDREN

**½ pt. thick cold semolina *or* rice pudding**
**2 tablesp. castor sugar**
**½ cup fruit pulp**
**1 egg white beaten stiffly**

Beat the semolina with a fork until smooth and then fold in the other ingredients lightly, adding the egg white last. Serve immediately.

### FRUIT IN JELLY

*Macédoine de Fruit à la Gelée*

**1½ pt. very clear lemon jelly *or* wine jelly using white wine instead of sherry and brandy**
**Selected pieces of fruit, e.g. bananas, black and green grapes, tangerines, cherries, apricot, pineapple, etc.**

Scald a metal mould, then rinse it with cold water. Cover the bottom with a thin layer of cool jelly (about $\frac{1}{8}$ in. thick). Avoid the formation of bubbles in the jelly by tilting the mould and placing the jelly in spoonfuls in the bottom. Bubbles will spoil the clear transparency of the jelly when turned out. If they do form, remove with a teaspoon. Leave to set. Cut pieces of fruit to suit the hollows and spaces of the mould, dip each piece into cold liquid jelly and set in place around and on the jelly layer. Leave to set and cover carefully with a layer of clear jelly. Allow to set. Repeat, taking care that each layer of fruit is quite firm before adding a layer of jelly—otherwise the fruit may be "floated" from its position. Fill the mould to the top.

When quite set, turn out and decorate with piped cream *or* chopped clear jelly.

**6 helpings**
**Time (without ice)—3–4 hr.**
**(with ice packed around the mould)—1 hr.**

### FRUIT MOULD

*Fruits moulés*

**1 pt. mixture as for cornflour mould**
**½ lb. stewed fruit**

Put a thick layer of cornflour mixture at the bottom of a mould. When set, place a tumbler in the centre, and fill the space between the two with cornflour mixture. When the mixture is firm, remove the tumbler, fill the cavity with stewed fruit, and cover with a layer of cornflour mixture. When set, turn out, and serve with custard or whipped cream.

NOTE: If liked, Ground Rice Mould can be substituted for cornflour mould.

**5–6 helpings**
**Time—about 2 hr.**

### FRUIT PIE OR TART

*See Sweet Pies or Tarts.*

### FRUIT PUDDING—Quick Method

*Pouding aux Fruits*

**1 pt. sweetened, stewed fresh fruit**
**8 oz. plain flour**
**1 heaped teasp. baking-powder**
**Pinch of salt**
**3 oz. butter *or* margarine**
**3 oz. castor sugar**
**2 eggs**
**Milk to mix**

Grease a pie-dish. Strain the syrup from the fruit and lay the fruit at the bottom of the pie-dish. The syrup can be used for making a sauce to serve with the pudding. (Left-over stewed fruit can be used for this purpose; it is not essential to have the exact amount but there should be enough fruit to cover the pie-dish to a depth of at least ½ in.)

Sift together the flour, baking-powder and salt, and rub in the fat. Add the sugar. Mix to a dropping consistency with the beaten eggs and milk. Spread this mixture over the fruit. Bake in a fairly hot oven (**375° F., Gas 5**) for 40–45 min., until the pudding mixture is cooked through and brown on top.

Dredge well with castor sugar. Serve with fruit- *or* custard-sauce *or* thin cream.

NOTE: If raw fruit is used, prepare it in the usual way. Stew it in as little water as possible, sweeten to taste and let it cool before putting the pudding mixture on top.

**6 helpings**

## FRUIT PUDDING WITH SUET CRUST

*Pouding aux Fruits*

**1–1½ lb. fresh fruit** (*see below*)
**2–3 oz. granulated sugar**

SUET CRUST PASTRY

**½ lb. plain flour**
**1 teasp. baking-powder**
**Pinch of salt**
**3 oz. finely-chopped suet**

Prepare the fruit and mix it with the sugar. Sift the flour and baking-powder, add the suet and salt. Mix with sufficient water to make a soft, but firm, dough. Grease and line a basin (*see below*). Fill to the top with the fruit and sugar and add ¼ gill of cold water. Put on the top crust.

*To boil:* Cover with a well-floured cloth and boil for 2½–3 hr.

*To steam:* Cover with greased paper and steam for 2½–3 hr.

**6 helpings**

NOTE: *To line a basin*—cut off one quarter of the pastry for the top. Roll the remaining pastry ½ in. larger than the top of the basin, drop the pastry into the greased basin, and with the fingers work the pastry evenly up the sides to the top. Roll out the lid to the size of the top of the basin, wet the edges and secure it firmly round the inside of the pastry lining the basin.

SUGGESTED FILLINGS

**Apples**
**Blackberries and apples**
**Blackcurrants**
**Cranberries**
**Damsons**
**Gooseberries**
**Plums**
**Rhubarb**

## FRUIT SAUCE

Fruits suitable are: Damsons, Plums, Raspberries, Redcurrants, Blackberries.

**1 lb. bottled *or* fresh fruit**
**A very little water to stew**
**Sugar to sweeten**
**Lemon juice, if liked**
**1 teasp. (rounded) arrowroot to each ½ pt. purée**

Stew the fruit in the water till soft, sieve it. Sweeten, flavour and thicken the sauce with arrowroot blended with a little cold water or fruit juice.

## FRUIT SPONGE

**1 lb. fresh fruit (e.g. apricots, peaches, gooseberries)**
**Sugar to taste**
**3 oz. butter *or* margarine**
**3 oz. castor sugar**
**2 eggs**
**4 oz. self-raising flour**

Prepare the fruit according to kind. Grease a 1½ pt. pie-dish and arrange the fruit in the bottom. Sprinkle with sugar to taste and add a little water if required. Cream together the fat and 3 oz. sugar. Add the well-whisked eggs gradually, beating well between each addition—if sign of curdling, add some flour. Sift flour and stir lightly into the creamed fat and egg. Spread the sponge mixture over the fruit, and bake in the middle of a moderate oven (**350° F., Gas 4**) for 35–40 min. Serve hot or cold.

NOTE: This can be made with canned fruit if liked, drain the fruit from the juice before arranging in the pie-dish.

## FRUIT or JAM TURNOVERS

**Short crust, flaky, rough puff *or* puff pastry**
**Stewed fruit *or* jam**
**Castor sugar**

Roll the pastry thinly and cut into rounds of about 4 in. diameter. Place some jam *or* fruit in the centre of each round and moisten the edges with cold water. Fold the pastry over and press the edges together. Knock up the edges with the back of a knife and place on a baking-sheet. Brush the top with water, sprinkle with sugar and bake in a fairly hot or hot oven (**400°–425° F., Gas 6–7**)—depending on the type of pastry—for 20 min.

## FRUIT SYRUPS AND VINEGARS

These are used for many different purposes. See the recipe for the type or flavour of syrup required for a particular dish.

### Fruit Syrups and Vinegars, to Sterilize

Use only sound, ripe fruit for this purpose and preferably loaf sugar. The syrup or vinegar when ready must be put into perfectly clean, dry bottles and stored in a cool, dry cellar or cupboard. If it is kept for any considerable time, it should be sterilized. To do this, stand the bottles on a layer of straw in a large pan, without letting them touch each other or the pan sides, with the corks or stoppers loosened; pour warm water into the pan and heat gradually to boiling-point. To prevent touching, the bottles may be wrapped in cloth. After ½ hr. lower the heat gradually and when cool lift out the bottles, wipe them and tighten the cork or stoppers; seal if necessary.

**FRUIT WHIP**

**1 egg white**
**1 oz. castor sugar**
**½ teacup cooked sieved *or* mashed fruit pulp**
**A little colouring if liked**

Whisk the egg white until stiff. Fold in the sugar and whisk again. Fold in the fruit and colouring. Pile on to a fruit dish and serve immediately.

**FRYING**

*See Cooking Methods*

**FRYING FISH**

*See Fish*

**FUDGE**

**1 lb. granulated sugar**
**¼ pt. milk**
**2 oz. butter**
**½ teasp. vanilla essence**

Put sugar and milk in a saucepan and leave to soak for 1 hr. Add the butter, place over gentle heat and stir until sugar is dissolved. Then bring to boil and boil to the "small ball" degree (**237° F.**). Remove from heat, stir in vanilla, cool slightly, then beat until thick. Pour into an oiled tin; cut in squares when cold.

NOTE: Coconut, nuts or ginger may be stirred in while fudge is cooling. **Chocolate fudge:** Add 2 tablesp. cocoa or 2 oz. plain chocolate with the butter.

**FUMETS**

These are the same as essences but made from fish and vegetables instead of meat.

**GALANTINE OF FOWL**

*Galantine de Volaille*

**1 boned fowl**
**Salt and pepper**
**1 lb. sausage meat**
**¼ lb. boiled ham *or* tongue**
**2 hard-boiled eggs**
**2 truffles *or* 6 mushrooms**
**½ oz. pistachio nuts *or* almonds**
**1½ pt. stock (approx.)**
**1 pt. chaudfroid sauce**
**½ pt. aspic jelly**

GARNISH—selection of:

**Pimento**
**Truffle**
**Mushroom**
**Lemon rind**
**Hard-boiled egg**

Bone the fowl neatly, cut down the centre of the back (this may be done before boning, as it makes the process easier), spread it out, and distribute the flesh as evenly as possible, season well. Spread with ½ of sausage meat, arrange narrow strips of ham *or* tongue, slices of egg, chopped truffles *or* mushrooms and chopped, blanched nuts on the sausage, season well, then cover with remainder of sausage. Fold over the back skin and stitch firmly. Wrap bird in clean cloth and fasten securely. Simmer gently in stock 2½ hr.; allow to cool a little in the stock, then press between 2 large boards or plates until quite cold. Unwrap, skin, and wipe free from excess grease.

Coat with chaudfroid sauce, garnish, and mask with aspic jelly.

If preferred the galantine may be brushed with glaze, instead of using chaudfroid sauce, and garnished with aspic jelly.

**8–10 helpings**

**GALANTINE OF PORK**

*Galantine de Porc*

**1½ lb. belly pork (preferably salted)**
**Salt and pepper**
**Gherkins**
**Stock *or* water with 2 onions, 1 carrot and ½ turnip**
**Meat glaze (optional)**
**Parsley (optional)**

## rying Food—
## eep Frying.

Melt enough fat in a deep pan over moderate heat to come half-way up pan. Check correct temp. is 360° F.

Quarter fill the basket with (dried) chipped potatoes and lower gently into hot fat. Fry for approx. 3 min.

3 Remove basket and re-heat fat for a few minutes to higher temp. of 375° F. Replace potatoes and cook until crisp and golden brown.

4 Drain well on crumpled kitchen paper and sprinkle with salt.

5 Serve at once whilst very hot.

6 Cool fat; strain into clean basin keep covered for further use. Wipe pan whilst warm with damp cloth; wash as well if preferred.

1

2

3

4

5

6

## Hare, to dress.

1 With a sharp knife cut off the feet just below the foot joint.

2 Cut carefully through the skin straight down the belly; ease back the skin from the flesh. Work round the body until the flesh is freed from the skin.

3 Push forward each hind leg in turn and work the skin free of flesh. Pull the skin from tail. Holding the skinned hindquarters in the left hand, gently pull the skin over the back and shoulders.

4 Work each foreleg free in turn.

5 If head is to be left on remove skin; otherwise cut off the head.

6 Cut through the skin of the belly.

7 Slit the belly from the chest to the legs and draw out the viscera.

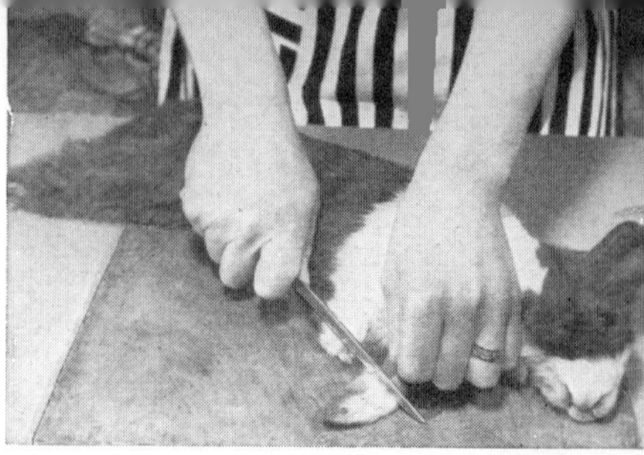

1

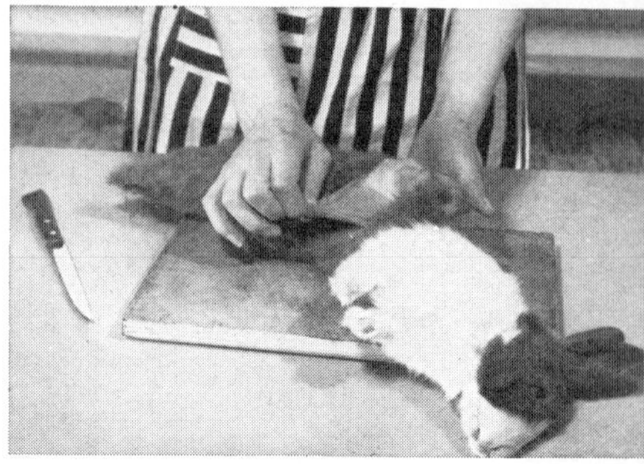

2

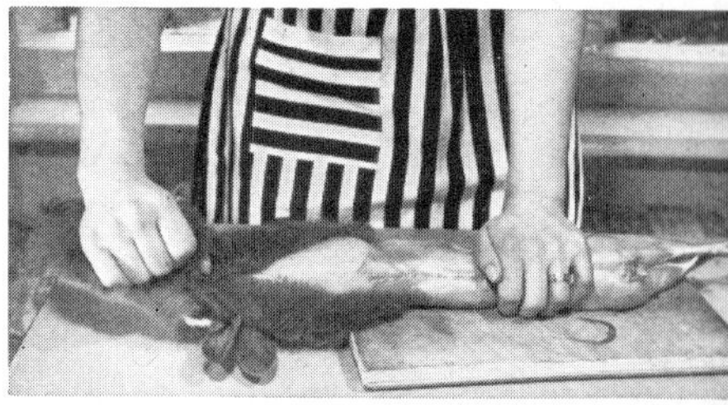

3

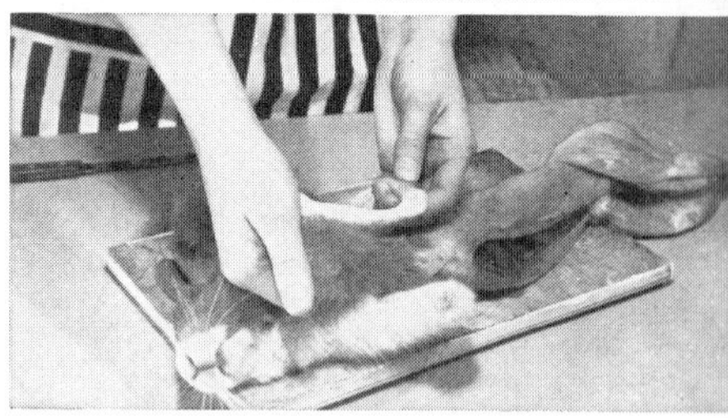

4

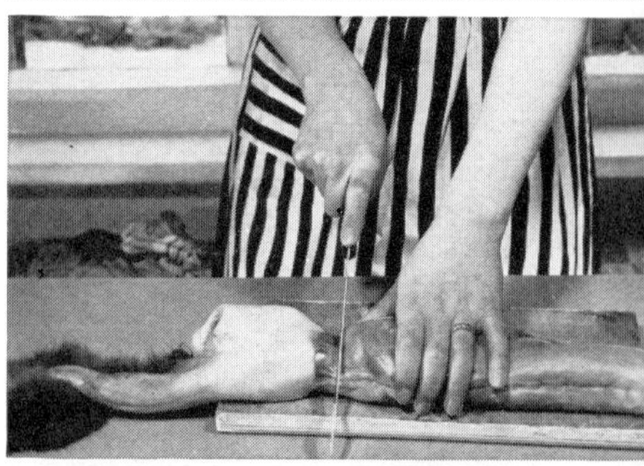

5

6

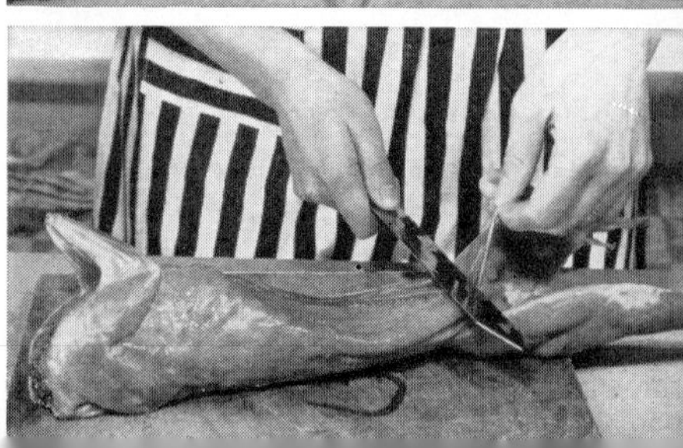

7

Season the inside of the meat well with salt and pepper and arrange thin slicés of gherkin all over it. Roll up tightly and secure with string, then secure tightly in a cloth. Just cover with stock or water and vegetables and simmer gently for about 3 hr. When cooked, press between 2 dishes until cold, then remove the cloth.

The meat may be brushed with glaze and served garnished with parsley.

**6 helpings**

## GALANTINE OF VEAL

*Galantine de Veau*

| | |
|---|---|
| **A small breast of veal** | **Stock *or* water** |
| **1½ lb. sausage meat** | **2 onions** |
| **3 bacon rashers** | **1 turnip** |
| **1–2 hard-boiled eggs** | **1 carrot** |
| **Salt and pepper** | **6 peppercorns** |
| **⅛ teasp. ground mace** | **Meat glaze** |
| **Pinch of grated nutmeg** | **Parsley** |

Bone the veal and flatten out well. Season well and spread on ½ the sausage meat in an even layer. Place narrow strips of bacon and slices of hard-boiled egg on top and sprinkle with the seasoning, mace and nutmeg. Cover with the remainder of the sausage meat and roll up tightly. Wrap in a cloth and tie the ends tightly. Put in a pan of boiling stock or water to which the veal bones, sliced vegetables, peppercorns and seasoning have been added. Cook gently for 3 hr., then remove the cloth, roll up tightly in a clean dry cloth or greaseproof paper and press between 2 dishes until cold. When cold, remove the cloth, brush with liquid glaze and garnish with parsley.

**6 helpings**

## GAME

*See Game Birds, Hares and Rabbits, Venison.*

## GAME BIRDS

Game birds are protected by the law, and they may be killed or sold only during specified months of the year. The following table shows when the various birds are in season.

| *Game* | *In season* |
|---|---|
| Grouse | August 12–December 10 |
| Blackcock | August 20–December 10 |
| Capercailzie | August 20–December 10 |
| Ortolan | November–January |
| Partridge | September 1–February 1 |
| Pheasant | October 1–February 1 |
| Plover | October–February |
| Ptarmigan | September–April |
| Snipe | October–February |
| Wild Duck | August–March |
| Teal | October–February |
| Widgeon | October–February |

NOTE: Some supplies of frozen game are now imported and are available out of season.

### To Choose Game

Young birds are usually much better for the table than old ones, the former being more delicate in flavour and much more tender. The size of the spur, the smoothness of the legs and the tenderness of the pinion are the best guides in choosing a young bird. A bird in good condition should have a thick, firm breast. Choose those which have moist supple feet, and which have not been damaged when shot.

Three of the most popular game birds in this country are:

(1) **Grouse**—a young bird has soft downy feathers on the breast and under the wings, the wings are pointed.

(2) **Partridge**—the grey partridge is considered the best. The young can be distinguished by the fact that the long wing-feather is pointed, not rounded as in older birds.

(3) **Pheasant**—the young bird has short, not very sharp spurs, and a light plumage.

### To Keep Game

Water birds should be eaten as fresh as possible, as their flesh is oily and soon becomes rank.

Most game is kept until putrefaction has begun, but the length of time of keeping varies according to the weather and individual taste. In warm, close weather, game should not be kept as long as in cool or breezy weather.

The game is kept undrawn and unplucked, and should be kept hanging up in a current of air. A good sprinkling of pepper can be applied to the feathers, as it helps to keep flies away. Unless required very "high", it is ready when the tail feathers come out easily when pulled. As soon as the birds are ready, pluck them carefully, so as not to break the skin, draw them if they are to be cooked drawn, and wipe them thoroughly with a damp cloth.

If game has become too "high", it should be washed in salted water containing vinegar, and then rinsed. Fresh powdered charcoal, tied in muslin and left in the crop during cooking, also helps to remove any taint.

**Dressing Game**

The directions given for poultry apply to any bird to be plucked, drawn and trussed for cooking. With smaller birds such as grouse and pigeons great care must be taken as the work is more delicate. One-finger operation is needed for both of these.

Snipe, plover, quails and woodcock are not drawn. They are merely plucked, wiped clean, and are served with the head on.

**Cooking Game**

Young game birds are usually roasted. As there is little fat on game they must be either larded or barded before roasting.

Accompaniments for game birds are usually watercress and/or green salad with French dressing, thin gravy, game chips, bread sauce and browned (fried) breadcrumbs.

## GAME, TO CARVE

*See Carving.*

## GAME PIE

*See French Game Pie.*

## GAME SOUP or HUNTER'S SOUP

*Potage au chasseur*

| | |
|---|---|
| **Carcases and trimmings of 2 partridges *or* equivalent amount of any game** | **½ parsnip** |
| **1 oz. lean bacon** | **1 stick of celery** |
| **1 oz. butter *or* margarine** | **1 oz. flour** |
| **1 onion** | **1 qt. stock** |
| **1 carrot** | **A bunch of herbs** |
| | **1 clove** |
| | **Some neat pieces of breast of bird** |
| | **Salt and pepper** |

Put the pieces of carcase, the trimmings, and the bacon, with the fat in a saucepan and fry them till brown. Remove the game and fry the sliced vegetables till brown. Add the flour and fry it till golden-brown. Stir in the stock, bring to the boil, add the herbs, return the game to the pan and simmer for 1½–2 hr. Meanwhile cut the pieces of breast meat into ¼-in. dice. Strain the soup, in it reheat the diced game, season carefully and serve.

**4–6 helpings**
**Cooking time—about 2 hr.**

## GAME SALAD

*Salade de Gibier*

| | |
|---|---|
| **1 lb. of remains of cold game** | **Mayonnaise sauce** |
| **2 lettuces** | **Cayenne pepper and salt** |
| **1 hard-boiled egg** | **Beetroot** |

Dice the meat. Shred the lettuce finely. Stamp out star-shaped pieces of egg white and beetroot. Mix the meat and chopped egg yolks and remains of whites. Arrange meat, lettuce and mayonnaise in alternate layers in a salad bowl, seasoning each layer, and pile in pyramid shape. Cover the surface with a thin layer of mayonnaise sauce. Garnish with the stars of beetroot and egg white.

**6 helpings**

## GAME SAUCE

*Sauce Gibier*

| | |
|---|---|
| **½ pt. Espagnole sauce** | **4 peppercorns** |
| **Trimmings and carcase of strong-flavoured roast game** | **½ clove** |
| | **Parsley stalks** |
| | **Sprig of thyme** |
| **1 onion** | **1 bay leaf** |
| **2 shallots** | **¼ pt. sherry *or* stock** |
| **1 blade of mace** | |

Break the game carcase into small pieces, chop the onion and shallots. Put the vegetables, game scraps, spices and herbs into a pan with the sherry or stock and simmer very slowly for ½ hr. Strain the liquid into the hot Espagnole sauce and reduce it slightly.

## GARLIC BUTTER

*Beurre d'Ail*

| | |
|---|---|
| **2 oz. butter** | **1 clove of garlic** |

Crush the garlic, pound it with the butter, pass through a fine sieve. Spread in a layer ½ in. thick on a plate, chill.

### GARNISHES

With all the gadgets and equipment now on the market, preparing garnishes is a comparatively simple matter.

One point to remember is that a garnish for a hot dish should be ready before serving time, so that it can be arranged before the dish gets cold. Decorating must be done quickly.

Garnishes for cold dishes should also be applied quickly so that the food does not dry or form a "skin".

Popular garnishes for savoury dishes are:
almonds, aspic jelly, celery curls, croutes and croûtons, gherkin fans, glaze, lemon butterflies, nuts, parsley, potato in a border, radish roses and tomato lilies.

Sweet garnishes include:
candied and crystallized fruits, grated chocolate, cream in various forms, nuts, spun sugar, etc.

For other garnishes, *see Accompaniments for fish, meats, game, poultry, soups, etc.*

### GARNISHES FOR SOUPS

*See Soups.*

### GATEAUX

Gateaux can be served as cold sweets or desserts, or as cakes at special tea or coffee parties.

### "GEFILLTE" FISH

| | |
|---|---|
| **2–2½ lb. fish** | **1 tablesp. chopped parsley** |
| **2–3 onions** | **2 eggs** |
| **1–2 sticks of celery** | **Fresh breadcrumbs** |
| **1 large carrot** | |
| **Salt and pepper** | |

Remove the skin and bones from the fish and put them in a saucepan with 1 onion, the celery and a piece of carrot, pour 1½ pt. water over, season with salt and pepper. Cover and simmer gently for ½ hr., then strain. Put the fish and remaining onion through the mincing machine or chop finely by hand. Add the parsley and beaten eggs to the chopped fish; season with salt and pepper and add sufficient fresh breadcrumbs to bind. With floured hands roll into balls. Slice the carrot thinly, add to the fish stock and bring to the boil; then place in the fish balls, cover and simmer very gently for 1 hr. Lift the balls out carefully on to a serving dish and place a slice of carrot on top of each. Spoon over a little of the fish stock and serve cold, when the stock should have set in a jelly.

NOTE: This dish originated from the East, where salt water fish is in short supply, and was made from pike and carp. But bream, cod, haddock or a mixture can be used.

**5–6 helpings**
**Cooking time—about 1½ hr.**

### GENEVA PUDDING

*Pouding à la Genevoise*

| | |
|---|---|
| **3 oz. rice** | **1 oz. butter** |
| **1½ pt. milk** | **¼ teasp. ground cinnamon** |
| **Pinch of salt** | **3 tablesp. water** |
| **3 oz. sugar** | |
| **2 lb. cooking apples** | |

Wash the rice and let it simmer in the milk with the salt until cooked. Add ½ oz. sugar. While the rice is cooking wipe the apples and chop them roughly; put them in a saucepan with the butter, cinnamon and 3 tablesp. of water. Simmer very gently until tender; then put the mixture through a fine sieve. Add the rest of the sugar (2½ oz.). Well grease a pie-dish with butter and arrange the rice and apple purée in alternate layers, with rice forming the bottom and top layers. Bake in a moderate oven (**350° F., Gas 4**) until brown.

**6 helpings**
**Time—1¼ hr.**

### GENEVA SAUCE

*Sauce Génevoise*

| | |
|---|---|
| **½ pt. brown sauce made with fish stock** | **1 teasp. lemon juice** |
| **2 oz. mushrooms** | **1 teasp. anchovy essence** |
| **½ glass sherry** *or* **Madeira** | |

Wash, peel if necessary, and slice the mushrooms. Add them with the stock when making the brown sauce. After straining the sauce, chop the mushrooms and return them to the sauce. Simmer the wine with the sauce for 10 min. Add the other flavourings.

Serve with fish.

### GENOESE PASTRY

*Génoise*

(Base for small cakes)

**Basic Recipe**

| | |
|---|---|
| **4 oz. flour** | **4 eggs** |
| **Pinch of salt** | **4 oz. castor sugar** |
| | **3 oz. butter** *or* **margarine** |

Sift flour and salt. Beat eggs and sugar in a basin over a pan of hot water till thick. Clarify the fat and fold lightly into egg mixture, then fold in salted flour. Pour into lined Swiss roll tin and bake in a moderate oven (**350° F., Gas 4**). When cold (after 24 hr.) cut and use as desired for small iced cakes, etc.

**Cooking time—30–40 min.**

**Variations**

### CAULIFLOWER CAKES

**Rounds of Genoese pastry 1½ in. in diameter**
**Green colouring**
**Almond paste**
**Apricot glaze**
**Cream (flavoured and sweetened)**

Add a few drops of green colouring to the almond paste and work it well in—roll out paste very thinly. Cut out five circles of almond paste for each cake using 1½-in. cutter. Brush the sides of the cake with apricot glaze, press the pieces of almond paste round so that they overlap slightly, shape top of almond paste pieces slightly. Pipe cream into centre of cakes using a small rose pipe.

**20–24 cakes**

### CONTINENTAL CAKES

*Gâteaux à la Continentale*

**Genoese pastry**
**Butter icing using 1½ oz. butter, etc. flavoured with vanilla and coloured pink**
**Glacé icing using 12 oz. icing sugar**

Cut genoese pastry into rounds 1½ in. in diameter or into diamond shapes 1 in. by 1¾ in. Pile some butter icing on to the top of each cake and smooth off with a knife to shape of cake. Allow icing to harden and stand cakes on wire cooling tray over a large dish. Make glacé icing and coat cakes; the butter icing should just show through. When set decorate by piping lines or spirals of coloured glacé icing on cakes.

**20–26 cakes**

### GENOESE SAUCE

*Sauce Génoise*

| | |
|---|---|
| **½ pt. Espagnole sauce** | **1 clove** |
| **1 onion** | **1 bay leaf** |
| **2 shallots** | **Sprig of thyme** |
| **1 clove of garlic** | **A few parsley stalks** |
| **1 pt. fish stock** | **Sugar to taste** |
| **¼ pt. dry red wine (optional)** | **1 dessertsp. anchovy essence** |
| **Peppercorns** | |

Chop the onion and shallots; crush the garlic. Put the stock into a saucepan with the wine (if used), vegetables, spices and herbs, cover, and cook until reduced to about ¼ pt. Strain this liquid into the hot Espagnole sauce, reheat, add a pinch of sugar, stir in the anchovy essence and serve.

Serve separately with poached fish, or pour over braised fish.

### GERMAN BISCUITS

| | |
|---|---|
| **2 oz. margarine** | **½ level teasp. powdered cinnamon** |
| **1½ oz. sugar** | **¼ level teasp. baking-powder** |
| **¼ egg** | **A little jam** |
| **4 oz. plain flour** | |
| **Pinch of salt** | |

DECORATION

| | |
|---|---|
| **Glacé cherries** | **Glacé icing using 3 oz. icing sugar** |

Cream fat and sugar, add egg. Sift dry ingredients and work into the fat mixture. Mix to a stiff consistency and roll out thinly. Cut into 2–2½-in. rounds and bake in a moderate oven (**350° F., Gas 4**). When cold, put 2 together with jam, coat with the icing and decorate with pieces of cherry or a spot of red colouring.

**12–16 biscuits**
**Cooking time—20 min.**

### GHERKIN SAUCE

*Sauce aux Cornichons*

To ½ pt. brown sauce add 1 tablesp. chopped gherkins, 1 tablesp. gherkin vinegar and sugar to taste.

Serve with meat and poultry entrées or grills.

### GIBLET GRAVY for Poultry

*Jus de Gibier*

| | |
|---|---|
| **1 set of giblets** | **Flour** |
| **1 onion (optional)** | **Salt and pepper** |
| **Cold water to cover** | |

Simmer the giblets very gently in the water with the onion (if liked) for at least 2 hr.—much longer if possible. Drain the fat from the tin in which the bird has been roasted, carefully saving the sediment. Dredge into the thin film of dripping only sufficient flour to absorb it all. Brown this flour until a nut brown colour. Stir in the liquid from the giblets, boil up and season to taste.

### GIBLET PIE

*Pâté aux Abatis à l'Anglaise*

| | |
|---|---|
| **1 set of goose giblets** | **1 lb. rump steak** |
| **1 onion, sliced** | **Puff pastry using 6 oz. flour, etc.** |
| **Bouquet garni** | |
| **Salt and pepper** | **Egg *or* milk for glazing** |

Wash the giblets, put in a saucepan with sliced onion, bouquet garni and seasoning, cover with cold water, simmer gently 1½–2 hr. Slice the steak thinly, and season it. Place alternate layers of steak and giblets in a pie dish (approx. 1½ pt. size) which should be filled, and strain over enough stock to come ¾ of the way up the dish. Cover the pie with puff pastry (allowing the meat to cool first, if possible) and bake in a hot oven (**425°–450° F., Gas 7–8**) until pastry is set—about 20 min.—then lower heat to moderate (**350°–375° F., Gas 4–5**) and continue cooking until meat is tender—about 60 min. more. Fill up the pie with the remainder of the hot stock.

The pie may be glazed with egg *or* milk, about 20 min. before it is ready.

**6 helpings** **Cooking time—1¼–1½ hr.**

### GIBLET SOUP

*Potage aux abatis*

| | |
|---|---|
| **2–3 sets chicken giblets *or* 1 set turkey *or* goose giblets** | **A bunch of herbs** |
| | **1 clove** |
| | **Small blade of mace** |
| | **6 peppercorns** |
| **1 qt. water** | **1 teasp. salt** |
| **1 onion** | **1 oz. flour** |
| **1 carrot** | **1 oz. butter *or* margarine** |
| **1 stick of celery** | |

Prepare the giblets in the usual way then cover them with cold water, bring to simmering point very slowly. Add the whole vegetables, herbs, spice, peppercorns and salt, simmer for 2–3 hr. Strain this stock. In a saucepan, fry the flour in the fat till nut brown without being bitter, stir in the stock, bring to the boil and boil for 5 min. Cut tiny dice from the best pieces of giblets, reheat these in the soup. Season well and serve.

**4–6 helpings**
**Cooking time—2½–3¼ hr.**

### GIBLET STUFFING

| | |
|---|---|
| **Cooked giblets** | **1 teasp. mixed fresh herbs *or* ½ teasp. dried herbs** |
| **1 onion, cooked** | |
| **2–4 oz. breadcrumbs** | |
| **⅛–¼ pt. boiling stock** | **1 tablesp. chopped parsley** |
| **1–2 oz. butter** | |
| **1 egg** | **A little grated lemon rind (if liked)** |
| | **Salt and pepper** |

The giblets are stewed for 1½ hr. or until tender, with the onion. The liquid in which they are cooked makes the gravy for the roast bird. Remove all bones from the neck and the lining of the gizzard and chop or mince the flesh of the giblets. Soak the crumbs in sufficient boiling stock to moisten them. Melt the fat. Beat the egg. Mix all the ingredients together and season the mixture to taste.

Use for chicken or turkey.

### GIGOT DE MOUTON À LA PROVENÇALE

Leg of Mutton à la Provençale

| | |
|---|---|
| **7–8 lb. leg of mutton** | **Thyme** |
| **Lardoons of fat bacon and ham** | **Chopped onions** |
| | **2–3 bay leaves** |
| **A few anchovies** | **Coarse pepper** |
| **Parsley** | **Salt** |
| **Blanched tarragon** | **½ pt. olive oil** |
| **2 cloves of garlic (optional)** | **2 tablesp. vinegar** |

Lift the skin of the leg a little without injuring it, and lard the leg with the lardoons of bacon and ham, some strips of anchovies, and bits of parsley and blanched tarragon and, if liked, a few strips of garlic. Put some thyme, parsley, chopped onions, the bay leaves, coarse pepper and a little salt in an earthenware pot and pour over the olive oil and vinegar. Allow the leg of mutton to lie in this marinade 2–3 hr., turning it frequently. Then take it out, spread over it the herbs, etc., of the marinade, covering them over with the skin. Wrap in buttered paper, and roast in a moderate oven (350° F., Gas 4). Remove the paper, and serve.

**Time—5–6 hr.**

### GINGER BUNS

*See Buns or Cookies*

### GINGER CAKE, RICH

*See Rich Cakes, Large, Various.*

### GINGER PUDDING

*Pouding au Gingembre*

**½ lb. plain flour**
**1 level teasp. ground ginger**
**Pinch of salt**
**1 level teasp. bicarbonate of soda**
**4 oz. finely-chopped suet**
**3 oz. sugar**
**1 tablesp. treacle**
**1 egg**
**Milk to mix**

Grease a 2 pt. basin. Prepare the suet.

Sift the flour, ginger, salt and bicarbonate of soda into a bowl. Add the finely-chopped suet and sugar. Stir in the treacle, beaten egg and sufficient milk to make a soft dropping consistency. Put the mixture into the basin; cover. Steam for 2 hr.

Turn out and serve with syrup sauce.

**6 helpings**

### GINGER SNAPS

**6 oz. self-raising flour**
**Pinch of salt**
**1 level teasp. bicarbonate of soda**
**2 level teasp. ground ginger**
**3–4 oz. sugar**
**2 oz. lard *or* shortening**
**1½ oz. golden syrup**
**1 egg**

NOTE: Take small measure of bicarbonate and ginger.

Sift flour, salt, soda and ginger; add sugar. Melt lard and syrup, cool slightly, then add to dry ingredients; add the egg. Divide into 24 pieces and make into balls, place well apart on greased baking-sheets. Bake in a fairly hot to moderate oven (**375°–350° F., Gas 5–4**) till a good rich brown colour.

**24 Ginger Snaps** **Cooking time—20 min.**

### GINGER SYRUP SAUCE

*Sirop du Gingembre*

**4 oz. brown sugar**
**½ pt. water *or* ¼ pt. syrup from preserved ginger and ¼ pt. water**
**Piece of root ginger**
**Strip of lemon rind**
**1 teasp. arrowroot**
**½ teasp. ground ginger**
**1 teasp. lemon juice**
**1 tablesp. chopped preserved ginger**

Dissolve the sugar in the water, add the root ginger and lemon rind and simmer for 15 min. Blend the arrowroot and ground ginger with a little cold water and the lemon juice, and with this thicken the sauce. Add the preserved ginger and simmer the sauce for 2–3 min.

NOTE: Golden syrup or honey may be used instead of sugar.

### GINGERBREAD

*Pain d'Épice*

**¾ lb. plain flour**
**¼ teasp. salt**
**¼ oz. ground ginger**
**3 oz. sugar**
**3 oz. lard**
**½ lb. black treacle**
**4–6 tablesp. milk**
**1 level teasp. bicarbonate of soda**
**1 egg**

Sift the flour, salt and ginger into a bowl, add the sugar. Put the fat, treacle and most of the milk into a pan and warm them. Dissolve the soda in the rest of the milk. Pour the warm liquid into the flour, add the beaten egg and the dissolved soda and beat well—the mixture should be soft enough to run easily from the spoon. Pour into a greased 7–8-in. tin, or into a bread-tin and bake in a moderate oven (**350°–335° F., Gas 4–3**), reduce heat to the lower temperature after 20 min.

**Cooking time—about 1¼–1½ hr.**

### GINGERBREAD, MOIST

**10 oz. plain flour**
**½ level teasp. bicarbonate of soda**
**¼ teasp. salt**
**4 oz. brown sugar**
**4 oz. sultanas**
**1–2 oz. shredded almonds**
**2 oz. treacle**
**2 oz. golden syrup**

**2 level teasp. ground cinnamon**
**2 level teasp. ground ginger**
**6 oz. butter** *or* **margarine**
**2 eggs**
**Warm milk to mix**

Grease a 7-in. tin and line the bottom with greased greaseproof paper.

Mix sifted flour and soda with other dry ingredients. Cream treacle, syrup and fat together. Add dry ingredients, beaten eggs and enough warm milk to make a stiff consistency. Put into the tin and bake in a moderate oven (**350°–335° F., Gas 4–3**), reduce heat to the lower temperature after 20 min.

**Cooking time—1¼–1½ hr.**

GINGERBREAD PUDDING

*Pouding au Pain d'Épice*

**½ lb. plain flour**
**Pinch of salt**
**1 teasp. baking-powder**
**1 teasp. ground ginger**
**¼ lb. finely-chopped suet**
**½ lb. golden syrup**
**1 egg**
**Milk to mix**

Grease a 2 pt. mould or basin.

Sift together the flour, salt, baking-powder and ginger, and mix with the suet. Slightly warm the syrup, if it is very thick. Beat together the syrup, egg and a little milk. Stir this into the dry ingredients, mixing well. Add more milk, if necessary, to make the mixture of a dropping consistency. Put into a well-greased mould *or* basin; cover. Steam for 2½ hr.

**5–6 helpings**

GINGERBREAD, RICH

**8 oz. plain flour**
**⅛ teasp. salt**
**1–2 level teasp. ground cinnamon**
**1–2 level teasp. mixed spice**
**2 level teasp. ground ginger**
**2 oz. dates** *or* **raisins,** *or* **sultanas**
**1 level teasp. bicarbonate of soda**
**2–4 oz. crystallized ginger**
**2 oz. blanched and chopped almonds**
**4 oz. butter** *or* **margarine**
**4 oz. sugar**
**4 oz. treacle**
**2 eggs**
**A little warm milk, if required**

Grease a 7-in. tin and line the bottom with greased greaseproof paper.

Mix flour and salt and other dry ingredients with prepared fruit, crystallized ginger—cut into pieces, and almonds—chopped roughly. Melt fat, sugar and treacle, add to dry ingredients with beaten eggs. If the mixture seems stiff, add a little warm milk but do not make it too soft. Pour into the tin, and bake in a warm to cool oven (**335°–310° F., Gas 3–2**).

**Cooking time—1¾–2 hr.**

GLACÉ ICING

Glacé icing or water icing (soft icing) is made from sifted icing sugar moistened with warm water to make a thin coating consistency. It is used for icing sponges, sandwich and layer cakes, small cakes, biscuits and petit fours.

**Basic Recipe**

**4 oz. icing sugar**
**1 tablesp. warm water**
**Flavouring**
**Colouring**

If the sugar is lumpy, break up the lumps by rolling the sugar with a rolling-pin before sieving. Sieve the icing sugar and put into a small bowl over hot water. Add the 1 tablesp. warm water gradually. Stir until all the sugar is dissolved and the icing is smooth and warm. Do not allow to get too hot or the icing will lose its gloss. Add the flavouring and the colouring a drop at a time until the required shade is obtained. The icing should be thick enough to coat the back of the spoon; if too thin add more sugar, if too thick add more water. When of the correct consistency, cool slightly, then use at once.

This quantity will coat the top of a 6–8 in. cake.

**Coffee icing:** Add ½ teasp. coffee essence to the basic recipe, omitting ½ teasp. of the water.

**Lemon icing:** Substitute strained lemon juice for all or part of the water in the basic recipe. Add a few drops of colouring.

**Orange icing:** Substitute strained orange juice for all or part of the water in the basic recipe. Add a few drops of colouring.

**To Apply Glacé Icing**

Place cakes on a wire cooling tray over a large flat dish or clean table-top. Petit fours and other small cakes that have to be coated all over are best dipped into the icing on a fork or skewer, then drained. For large cakes the cake top should be fairly level. Brush off any loose crumbs. When the icing is the desired consistency pour quickly into the centre of the cake and allow to run down the sides. Avoid using a knife if possible, but if this is necessary use a palette knife dipped in hot water and dried.

If the top only is to be iced, a smooth flat surface can be easily obtained by pinning a double thickness of greaseproof paper round the sides of the cake so that the paper stands 1 in. higher than the cake. Pour on the icing which will find its own level, and allow to set. When the icing has set remove the paper with the aid of a knife dipped in hot water.

Put any ready-made decorations on to the icing while it is still soft, but piped icing should be added after the surface is dry and firm.

### GLACÉ ICING, ORANGE

*See Orange Boats.*

### TO MAKE GLAZE

Strictly speaking, glaze should be made by reducing 4 quarts of stock to about ¼ pt. As this is extravagant, gelatine is often used.

Demi-glaze is made by reducing stock until it is slightly thick and syrupy.

### GLAZED CARROTS

*Carottes glacées*

**1½ lb. young carrots**
**2 oz. butter**
**3 lumps sugar**
**¼ teasp. salt**
**Good stock**
**Chopped parsley**

Melt the butter in a saucepan, Add the scraped, whole carrots, sugar, salt and enough stock to come half-way up the carrots. Cook gently, without a lid, shaking the pan occasionally until tender. Remove the carrots and keep them hot. Boil the stock rapidly until reduced to rich glaze. Replace the carrots 2 or 3 at a time, turn them until both sides are well coated with glaze. Dish, sprinkle with chopped parsley and serve.

**6 helpings**
**Cooking time—about ¾ hr.**

### GLOBE ARTICHOKES—FRENCH METHOD OF COOKING

*Artichauts aux fines herbes*

**6 globe artichokes**
**Salt**
**1 tablesp. lemon juice**
**A small bunch of savoury herbs**
**Melted butter**

Prepare and cook artichokes as in preceding recipe, but add the bunch of herbs to the cooking water.

Drain the artichokes well and serve with melted butter.

**6 helpings**
**Cooking time—15–45 min.**

### GLOUCESTER SAUCE

**¼ pt. mayonnaise**
**1 tablesp. sour cream *or* yoghourt**
**A little Worcester sauce**
**½ teasp. chopped chives**
**Lemon juice**
**Cayenne pepper**

Fold the cream and sauce into the mayonnaise, add the chives and lemon juice and pepper to taste.

Serve with meat salads.

### GNOCCHI AU GRATIN

**½ pt. water**
**2 oz. butter**
**Salt**
**3 oz. flour *or* 2 oz. semolina**
**2 eggs**
**3 oz. chopped ham**
**3 oz. grated cheese**
**½ pt. Béchamel sauce**
**Paprika pepper**

Put the water, butter and a good pinch of salt into a saucepan over heat. When boiling stir in the flour or semolina, and work vigorously over the heat until the dough leaves the sides of the pan clear. Allow to cool slightly, then beat in the eggs separately, and add the ham and 2 oz. of the cheese. Shape the mixture into quenelles, poach them for about 10 min. in salted boiling water, and drain well. When cool, arrange in a buttered fireproof dish, pour over the Béchamel sauce, sprinkle on the remainder of the cheese, and season well with paprika pepper. Bake in a hot oven (**425° F., Gas 7**) for about 10 min., and serve.

**4–5 helpings**

## GOLDEN BUCK

**4 oz. Cheshire *or* Cheddar cheese**
**½ oz. butter**
**3 tablesp. ale**
**½ teasp. Worcester sauce**
**½ teasp. lemon juice *or* vinegar**
**2 eggs**
**Pinch of celery salt**
**Pinch of cayenne pepper**
**2 large slices buttered toast**

Grate the cheese finely. Put it into a pan with the butter and ale and stir vigorously until creamy. Then add the Worcester sauce, lemon juice or vinegar and the eggs previously beaten. Season to taste with celery salt and cayenne pepper, and continue stirring briskly until the mixture thickens. Trim the toast, and cover with cheese mixture. Garnish with parsley. Serve as hot as possible.

**4 small *or* 2 large helpings**
**Cooking time—10 min.**

## GOLDEN GRILLED COD

**4 cutlets *or* steaks of cod about 1 in. thick**
**1 oz. margarine**
**1–2 oz. grated cheese**
**2 tablesp. milk (optional)**
**Salt and pepper**

Place the prepared fish in a greased fireproof dish and grill quickly for 2–3 min. on one side. Meanwhile soften the margarine and cream the cheese and margarine together, then work in the milk if used and season to taste. Turn the fish over and spread the cheese mixture over the uncooked side and return to the grill. Reduce the heat slightly and cook gently for a further 10–12 min. until the coating is brown and the fish cooked through. Serve at once.

NOTE: Cod fillet can be used instead of cutlets. Allow 1–1¼ lb. and cut into 4 portions before cooking.

**4 helpings**

The topping can be varied as follows:

*Devilled Grill*

**1 oz. margarine**
**1 level teasp. chutney**
**1 level teasp. curry powder**
**1 level teasp. dry mustard**
**1 teasp. anchovy essence (optional)**
**Salt and pepper to taste**

*Surprise Grill*

**1 oz. margarine**
**2 teasp. lemon juice**
**3 level tablesp. grated onion**
**Salt and pepper**

## GOLDEN PUDDING

*Pouding Doré*

**4 oz. marmalade**
**4 oz. plain flour**
**4 oz. breadcrumbs**
**3 oz. finely-chopped suet**
**2 oz. castor sugar**
**1 rounded teasp. baking-powder**
**Pinch of salt**
**2 eggs**
**1 gill milk (approx.)**

Grease a 2 pt. pudding basin. Put 2 oz. marmalade at the base.

Mix together the flour, breadcrumbs, suet, sugar, baking-powder and salt. Beat together the eggs, remaining 2 oz. marmalade and a little of the milk. Stir this into the dry ingredients and, using milk as required, mix to a very soft dropping consistency. Put the mixture into the basin, cover with greased paper. Steam for 1½–2 hr.

Serve with marmalade sauce.

**6 helpings**

## GOOSEBERRY CHARLOTTE

*Charlotte de Groseilles vertes*

**20 savoy fingers**
**1½ pt. gooseberry cream** (p. 140)

DECORATION

**½ pt. clear lemon jelly**
**3 glacé cherries**
**Angelica**

Thinly coat the bottom of a mould with jelly, and, when set, decorate with neatly-cut slices of cherry and leaves of angelica. Both these fruits should be cut thickly as they are translucent and will not show clearly if too thin. Re-coat with a second layer of cold liquid jelly, sufficient only to cover the decoration. When the jelly has set, line the sides of the mould with savoy fingers, having trimmed the ends so that they fit closely on to the jelly. Remove any crumbs from the surface of the jelly with the tip of a dry pastry brush. Pour the gooseberry cream into the lined mould and leave to set. Trim the fingers level with the rim. Turn out and decorate with piped cream.

If preferred, the base of the mould may be lined with sponge fingers.

NOTE: A quicker but less satisfactory method is to pour the gooseberry cream into the mould unlined, and after turning out press trimmed savoy fingers, sugar side outwards, around the sides. Tie a ribbon round to ensure a neat finish.

**6 helpings**

## GOOSEBERRY JAM—GREEN or RED

| | |
|---|---|
| **2¼ lb. gooseberries** | **3 lb. sugar** |
| **¾–1 pt. water** | |

Pick or buy the gooseberries at the green stage, before they have ripened or turned colour. Top and tail and wash them, and put in a pan with the water. Simmer gently until the fruit is soft (this may take ½ hr. or longer). Then add the sugar and stir over a low heat until dissolved. Bring to the boil and boil rapidly until setting point is reached (remove from the heat after 10 min. rapid boiling to test for the set). Skim, pour into dry, warm jars and cover.

NOTE: This is a good jam for beginners, because it is a notoriously good setter. It is specially good served on scones with whipped cream.

GREEN GOOSEBERRY JAM—looks decorative in cakes and biscuits.

Most gooseberry jam turns a reddish colour as it cooks. If preferred gooseberry jam can be kept green by taking the following steps:

1. Choose a variety of gooseberry which is green when ripe, e.g. "Careless", "Green Gem", "Keepsake".
2. Use a copper or brass preserving-pan.
3. Give the jam the shortest possible boil in which it will set once the sugar has been dissolved.

### "MUSCAT FLAVOURED" GOOSEBERRY JAM

For another variation to gooseberry jam, put the flowers from 8 heads of elder flowers in a muslin bag and cook with the gooseberries. Squeeze out the juice and remove the bag before the sugar is added.

## GOOSEBERRY JELLY

*Gelée de Groseilles vertes*

| | |
|---|---|
| **2 lb. gooseberries** | **1½ oz. gelatine** |
| **1 pt. water** | **4 tablesp. cold water** |
| **5–6 oz. sugar** | |

Top and tail gooseberries; wash them. Cook with 1 pt. of water and the sugar until soft. Soak gelatine in 4 tablesp. cold water for 5 min., then heat until dissolved. Rub gooseberries through a fine sieve, and taste for further sweetening. Strain gelatine into the purée and stir well. Pour into a wet mould.

**6 helpings**
**Cooking time—20 min.**
**Setting time—2–3 hr.**

## GOOSEBERRY SAUCE

*Sauce aux Groseilles*

| | |
|---|---|
| **½ lb. green gooseberries** | **Nutmeg** |
| **¼ pt. water** | **Salt and pepper** |
| **½ oz. butter** | **½ teasp. chopped chives (optional)** |
| **1 oz. sugar** | **A few chopped leaves of sorrel (optional)** |
| **Lemon juice** | |

Stew the gooseberries very gently with the water and butter until they are pulpy. Beat them quite smooth or rub them through a hair or nylon sieve. Reheat the sauce, stir in the sugar, add lemon juice and grated nutmeg to taste, season. Stir in the chives and sorrel if used.

Serve with mackerel.

## GOOSEBERRY TART

*Tourte aux Groseilles*

| | |
|---|---|
| **Short crust pastry using 6 oz. flour, etc.** | **1½ lb. gooseberries** |
| | **2 tablesp. water** |
| | **4 oz. demerara sugar** |

Top and tail the gooseberries with a pair of scissors, wash the gooseberries well. Place half of them in a 1½-pt. pie-dish, add the sugar and water and then the remaining gooseberries, piling them high in the centre. Line the edge of the dish with pastry, cover with the remaining pastry and decorate Bake in a fairly hot oven (**400° F., Gas 6**) reducing the heat to moderate (**350° F., Gas 4**) when the pastry is set. Continue cooking till the fruit is tender—about 45 min. altogether.

Dredge with castor sugar and serve.

**6 helpings**

## GOULASH

Goulash

**1½ lb. lean, tender beef *or* veal**
**1 dessertsp. flour**
**¼ teasp. paprika**
**Salt**
**3 oz. butter**
**1 onion**
**½ teasp. caraway seeds**
**1 pt. brown stock**

Trim the meat and cut into cubes of about 1 in. Sift the flour, paprika and salt together on a plate. Chop the onion finely. Put the butter into a heavy pan, heat a little and add the onion, allowing it to cook gently. Dip each piece of meat into the flour mixture and fry with the onions until the meat is browned on all sides and the onions golden. Sprinkle in the remaining flour and the caraway seeds. Pour in the stock. Cover and simmer very gently for 1–1½ hr.

NOTE: Goulash is, of course, originally Hungarian.

**6 helpings**

## GOULASH OF BEEF

*Goulash de Bœuf*

**1½ lb. lean beef**
**2 oz. dripping**
**2 onions**
**1½ oz. flour**
**1 pt. stock**
**¼ pt. red wine (optional)**
**2 tomatoes**
**Salt**
**Paprika**
**Bouquet garni**
**6 diced potatoes**
**2 tablesp. sour cream (optional)**

Wipe and trim the meat, removing any skin and fat. Cut into neat pieces. Heat the fat and sauté the sliced onions with the meat, until the meat is evenly browned. Add the flour and stir until brown. Then add the stock, wine, skinned and diced tomatoes, salt, paprika, and bouquet garni. Stir, bring to the boil. If liked, transfer to a casserole and cook slowly for 1½–2 hr. in the oven, stirring occasionally, or continue cooking in saucepan for the same time. Add the diced potatoes about ½ hr. before the Goulash is ready. They should be cooked but not broken. If liked, 2 tablesp. sour cream may be stirred in before serving.

**6 helpings**

## GRAPE SALAD

*Salade de Raisins*

**1 lb. green grapes**
**French dressing**

Skin, halve and remove pips from the grapes. Place the grapes in a salad bowl and mix lightly with the dressing.

**4–6 helpings**

## GRAPEFRUIT AND CHICORY SALAD

*Salade de Barbe-de-Capucin*

**3 grapefruits**
**3 small heads chicory**
**2 oz. seedless raisins**
**French dressing made with grapefruit juice**
**Fine cress**

Halve the grapefruits and remove the pulp in sections. Remove the partitions from the halved shells. Shred the chicory, reserving some neat rounds for garnish. Mix the grapefruit pulp, raisins and chicory lightly with the dressing. Fill the grapefruit shells with the mixture. Decorate with tiny bunches of cress and rounds of chicory.

**6 helpings**

## GRAPEFRUIT

Select sound, ripe fruit, wipe carefully, cut them in halves. Take out the pips and core and loosen the fruit from the skin. Cut the fruit into suitable small pieces but leave the pieces as if uncut in the halved skin. Sweeten to taste and, if liked, flavour with sherry poured over the fruit.

Serve in glass dishes and decorate with angelica. Keep in the refrigerator or on ice until required, if possible.

## GRAPEFRUIT BASKETS

Remove grapefruit sections as described in previous recipe—mix with diced melon, diced pineapple, pieces of orange and Maraschino cherries but do not make too sweet. Add sugar to taste. Replace in grapefruit halves. Serve in glasses topped with sprigs of mint.

## GRAPEFRUIT MARMALADE

**1½ lb. grapefruit**
**2 lemons**
**3 pt. water**
**3 lb. sugar**

Wash the fruit, cut in half and squeeze out the juice. Remove some of the pith if it is thick, cut it up coarsely and put it with the pips in a muslin bag. Slice the peel finely. Put all the fruit and juice into a bowl, cover with the water and leave overnight. Next day put it all into a preserving-pan and cook gently for 2 hr. or until the peel is soft. Remove the bag of pips, add the sugar, stir until it is dissolved, then boil rapidly until setting point is reached. Pot and cover in the usual way.

**Yield—5 lb.**

## GRAVIES

Gravy is meat essence, usually diluted with a little water stirred in the cooking vessel, as in gravy to serve with roast meat. It can be thickened, if wished, with various agents, according to the custom for the kind of meat being served.

In making gravy, it is a good idea to use the water in which green vegetables have been cooked. The only other permissible addition is a little meat or yeast extract.

## GRAVY—

for any Roast Joint except Pork

*Jus de Viande*

| | |
|---|---|
| **Meat dripping from the roasting tin** | **Water in which vegetables have been boiled *or* stock** |
| **Flour** | **Salt and pepper** |
| **Essences from the joint** | |

Drain the fat from the roasting tin, carefully saving any sediment and meat juices. Dredge into the thin film of dripping sufficient flour to absorb it all. Brown this flour slowly till of a nut brown colour. Stir in water in which green vegetables or potatoes have been cooked, or stock, allowing ½ pt. for 6 persons. Boil the gravy and season it to taste.

To obtain a brown colour without browning the flour add a few drips of gravy browning from the end of a skewer. To improve the flavour add a good meat or yeast extract.

## GRAVY (thickened)

(for a Stuffed Joint or for Roast Pork)

| | |
|---|---|
| **Bones and trimmings from the joint** | **Cold water** |
| | **Salt** |

*To each pint of gravy:*

| | |
|---|---|
| **1 oz. dripping** | **1 oz. flour** |

Make a stock from the bones, allowing at least 2 hr. simmering—much longer if possible (overnight'). Melt the dripping and sprinkle in the flour. Brown the flour slowly until a nut brown colour. Stir in the stock, boil up and season to taste.

## GRAVY for Game

| | |
|---|---|
| **Bones, giblets *or* trimmings of game** | **1 clove** |
| **Cold water to cover** | **6 peppercorns and 1 piece of onion to each pt. of water** |
| **1 bay leaf** | **Salt** |
| **Thyme** | |

Make stock from the above ingredients. Drain all the fat from the roasting-tin and rinse the tin with the game stock, using no flour. Boil the gravy and skim it.

## GRAVY MADE FROM SHIN OF BEEF

| | |
|---|---|
| **½ lb. shin of beef** | **Dripping** |
| **1 pt. water** | **Flour** |
| **½ teasp. salt** | |

Cut the shin of beef across the grain into very thin slices. Soak it in the water with the salt for ½ hr. Bring very slowly to simmering point and simmer very gently for at least 2 hr. Melt the dripping, brown the flour slowly, then stir in the strained liquid from the shin of beef. Boil up and season to taste.

## GRAVY SOUP or SHIN OF BEEF SOUP

*Potage au jus*

| | |
|---|---|
| **1 lb. lean shin of beef** | **1 qt. second stock *or* water** |
| **1 oz. beef dripping** | **1 teasp. salt** |
| **1 onion** | **A bunch of herbs** |
| **1 carrot** | **6 peppercorns** |
| **1 piece of turnip** | **1 oz. flour** |
| **1 stick of celery** | |

Cut the shin of beef in very thin slices across the fibres. Make the dripping smoking hot and in it fry ½ the meat till brown then remove it. Slice the vegetables and fry them till golden brown, then remove them. Put the fried and raw meat and the fried vegetables into a deep pan, cover with the liquid, bring very slowly to boiling point. Add the salt, herbs and peppercorns and simmer very gently for 3–4 hr. Meanwhile fry the flour in the dripping until golden brown. Strain the soup, return to the soup some of the pieces of meat cut very small, and whisk in the browned flour. Whisk till boiling, season and serve. The remainder of the meat may be minced and served with another dish.

**6 helpings**
**Cooking time—4½ hr.**

### GRAVY FOR POULTRY

*See Giblet Gravy.*

### GREEN BUTTER

**4 oz. butter**
**1½ tablesp. finely-chopped, washed parsley**
**Anchovy essence *or* paste**
**1 tablesp. lemon juice**
**Salt and pepper**

Cream the butter, add the parsley, lemon juice, and anchovy essence or paste to taste. Season with salt and pepper and, when thoroughly mixed, use as required.

### GREEN FIG JAM or CONSERVE

**2 lb. figs**
**2 lb. sugar**
**¼ pt. water**
**3 tablesp. lemon juice *or* vinegar**

Wipe and slice the fruit. Boil the sugar, water and lemon juice or vinegar for 10 min. Add the figs to the syrup and boil gently for 1 hr., or until the jam sets when a little is put to cool on a plate. Transfer to hot, dry jars, cover and when cold store in a cool dry place.

### GREEN PEA SOUP

*Purée de Petits Pois*

**1½ lb. green peas in the pod**
**1 onion**
**½ oz. butter**
**1 pt. white stock**
**A few leaves of spinach**
**A sprig of mint**
**A few parsley stalks**
**Cornflour**
**Salt and pepper**
**Sugar to taste**
**Green colouring, if needed**
**⅛ pt. cream *or* ⅛ pt. milk**

Shell the peas, wash ½ the shells, slice the onion. Melt the butter in a deep pan and cook the washed pods and onion very gently for 10 min. Add the stock and bring to boiling point, add the spinach leaves, the peas and the herbs. Simmer only long enough to cook the peas, from 10–20 min. Sieve and measure the soup. For every 1 pt. of soup blend ½ oz. cornflour with a little cold milk, stock or water and stir into the soup. Cook until the soup is thickened, season carefully, add sugar to taste and colouring, if required. If cream is used stir in at boiling point off the heat. A few small cooked peas and a few blobs of cream may be added to the cooked soup.

**4 helpings**
**Cooking time—30 min.**

### GREEN PEA AND PEPPER SALAD

**4 oz. rice**
**Salt**
**1 large *or* 2 small peppers (red *or* green)**
**One 10-oz. carton green peas**

DRESSING

**1 tablesp. oil**
**2 tablesp. vinegar**
**¼ level teasp. salt**
**¼ level teasp. sugar**
**½ level teasp. mustard**
**Shake of pepper**

GARNISH

**Lettuce**
**Tomatoes**
**Watercress**

Cook the rice in plenty of fast boiling, salted water until tender, approximately 12–15 min., then drain and dry well in a cool oven. Meanwhile blanch the peppers then remove pips and pith, and shred finely. Cook the peas according to the directions on the packet, strain and leave until cold. Make up the dressing, then add the rice, peas and peppers, mixing all carefully together.

Arrange the lettuce around the edge of a flat dish and pile the rice mixture in the centre. Decorate with quarters of tomatoes and watercress.

NOTE: This is an ideal salad to serve with chicken or cold skinless pork sausages.

**4–6 helpings**

### GREEN PEAS

*Petits Pois Verts à l'Anglaise*

**2 lb. peas**
**Salt**
**Sprig of mint**
**A little sugar**
**½ oz. butter *or* margarine**

Shell the peas. Have sufficient boiling, salted water to cover the peas. Add the peas, mint and sugar. Simmer gently until soft, from 10–20 min. Drain well. Reheat with butter *or* margarine and serve in a hot vegetable dish.

NOTE: If the peas must be shelled some time before cooking, put them in a basin and cover them closely with washed pea-pods.

**4–6 helpings (according to yield)**
**Cooking time—10–20 min.**

## GREEN PEAS—FRENCH STYLE

*Petits Pois à la Française*

**2–3 lb. green peas (1½ pt. shelled peas)**
**4 very small onions *or* spring onions**
**1 lettuce**
**2 oz. butter *or* margarine**
**2 teasp. sugar**
**Salt and pepper**
**Egg yolk (optional)**

Shell the peas. Peel the onions. Remove the outer leaves of the lettuce, wash the heart, leaving it whole. Put the peas into a thick saucepan, add the lettuce heart, onions and the butter cut into small pieces. Stir in the sugar and a little salt. Cover with the lid and cook over a very low heat, about 1 hr., shaking the pan occasionally. Re-season and serve. The liquid in the pan may be thickened with an egg yolk before serving.

**6 helpings**
**Cooking time—about 1 hr.**

## GREEN TOMATO CHUTNEY

**5 lb. green tomatoes**
**1 lb. onions**
**½ oz. peppercorns**
**1 oz. salt**
**1 lb. sugar**
**1 qt. vinegar**
**½ lb. raisins**
**½ lb. sultanas**

Slice the tomatoes and chop the onions and mix together in a basin with the peppercorns and salt. Allow this to stand overnight. Next day boil up the sugar in the vinegar, then add the raisins (which may be chopped) and the sultanas. Simmer for 5 min., then add the tomatoes and onions, and simmer till thick.

## GREENGAGE JAM

**3 lb. greengages**
**¼–½ pt. water**
**3 lb. sugar**

Remove stalks and put the washed greengages into the pan with the water. Stew slowly until the fruit is well broken down. Ripe fruit or very juicy varieties will need only a small quantity of water and will be cooked in a few minutes. Firmer varieties may take about 20 min. to break down, and will need the larger quantity of water. Add the sugar, stir over a low heat till dissolved, then boil rapidly, removing the stones as they rise to the surface (a stone basket clipped to the side of the pan is useful for holding the stones, and allows any liquid to drip back into the pan). Keep testing for setting point after about 10 min. rapid boiling. Skim, pot and cover.

**Yield—5 lb.**

## GREY MULLET

*Surmulet*

**4 grey mullet**

Clean and scale the fish. If very large, place them in warm salted water; if small, they may be put into hot water and cooked gently for 15–20 min. Serve with anchovy or melted butter sauce.

NOTE: Grey mullet may also be grilled or baked.

**4 helpings**
**Cooking time—15–20 min.**

## GRENADINES OF VEAL

*Grenadins de Veau*

**1½ lb. fillet of veal**
**Strips of larding bacon**
**1 onion**
**1 carrot**
**½ turnip**
**2 sticks of celery**
**2 oz. butter *or* fat**
**Bouquet garni**
**6 peppercorns**
**1 clove**
**1 pt. stock**
**Meat glaze**
**1 oz. flour**
**A border of mashed *or* piped potatoes**
**Peas *or* asparagus tips *or* macedoine of vegetables**

Cut the meat into slices ½ in. thick and cut each slice into rounds about 2 in. diameter (grenadines). Lard them on one side with thin strips of bacon about 1½ in. long. Slice the onion, carrot and turnip, chop the celery. Melt 1 oz. of the fat in a stewpan, put in the bouquet garni, peppercorns, clove and vegetables and fry lightly. Lay the grenadines on top, cover and fry gently for 10 min., then add enough stock to cover the vegetables. Cover the grenadines with greased paper, replace the lid and cook gently for 1 hr., adding the rest of the stock as necessary. Remove the grenadines and place them in the oven to brown and crisp the bacon. Brush with meat glaze. Meanwhile make a brown roux with the remaining fat and the flour. Strain about ¾ pt. of liquid from the stewpan and add to the roux. Stir until boiling then simmer for 5 min. Season to taste. Have ready the mashed or piped potato border on a hot dish. Arrange the grenadines in a circle and fill the centre with peas, asparagus tips or macedoine of vegetables. Pour some of the sauce round and serve the rest separately.

**6 helpings**

### GRILLED BEEFSTEAK

*Bifteck grillé*

**1½ lb. rump *or* fillet steak *or* sirloin**
**Oil *or* butter**
**Salt and pepper**
**Maître d'hôtel butter**

Wipe and cut the meat across the grain into suitable slices. Beat on both sides with a cutlet bat or rolling-pin. Brush with oil or melted butter and sprinkle with salt and pepper. Place under a red-hot grill and grill quickly on both sides to seal the surfaces, thus preventing the juices from escaping. Then grill more slowly until cooked as required, a "rare" steak requires 3–4 min. for each side. Turn frequently using tongs or 2 spoons, never pierce with a fork as this would make holes through which the meat juices would escape.

Serve at once with a pat of Maître d'hôtel butter on the top.

**6 helpings**

### GRILLED BLOATERS

Break off the head, split the back, remove the roe and take out the backbone. Rub over with a little fat, place the fish, inside down, on a grill pan grid. Cook until nicely browned, turn over and cook the back. If preferred place 2 bloaters with the insides together, and cook as above. The roes should be cooked and served with the bloaters.

**Cooking time—7 min.**

### GRILLED BREAST OF MUTTON

*Poitrine d'Agneau grillée*

**A breast of mutton**
**Salt and pepper**

Divide the breast into portions convenient for serving. Remove the surplus fat and skin and season the meat carefully. Grill quickly under a hot grill to seal the surfaces. Then reduce the heat and turn the meat frequently until thoroughly cooked.

Serve with tomato or piquant sauce.

**6–8 helpings**
**Cooking time—15–20 min.**

### GRILLED CHICKEN—WITH MUSHROOM SAUCE

*Poulet grillé aux Champignons*

**1 chicken**
**½ pt. Espagnole sauce**
**1 can button mushrooms**
**Salt and pepper**
**Croûte of fried bread**
**½ lb. lean raw ham**
**Salad oil *or* butter for frying and grilling**

GARNISH

**Ham**
**Mushrooms**

Make Espagnole sauce, add mushrooms to it, correct seasoning and keep the sauce hot. Divide chicken into pieces convenient for serving, brush them with salad oil or oiled butter. Cut a slice of bread to fit the serving dish, fry this until lightly browned. Cut the ham into short strips and fry this. Grill prepared chicken until tender—about 15–20 min.

Pile chicken on the croûte, strain sauce round, and garnish.

**4 helpings**
**Cooking time—about 30 min.**

### GRILLED COD

*See Golden Grilled Cod.*

### GRILLED GRAYLING

*Ombre grillé*

**4 small grayling**
**Salad oil**
**Salt and pepper**
**Lemon**

Empty, scale, wash and thoroughly dry the fish. Brush over with salad oil, sprinkle with salt and pepper and grill on both sides until sufficiently cooked and nicely browned. Serve garnished with quarters of lemon.

**4 helpings**
**Cooking time—about 10 min.**

### GRILLED LAMB CUTLETS

*Côtelettes d'Agneau grillées*

**6–8 cutlets from the best end of neck**
**Salt and pepper**
**Salad oil**

Trim the cutlets to a neat uniform shape. Season with salt and pepper and brush all over with salad oil. Grill, turning 3 or 4 times for about 8 min. Cover the end of each bone with a cutlet frill. Suitable accompaniments are green peas, mashed potatoes, and a good gravy or demi-glace sauce.

**6–8 helpings**
**Cooking time—about 10 min.**

### GRILLED HALIBUT

*Flétan grillé*

**Six 6 oz. slices halibut**
**Oiled butter**
**Salt and pepper**

Brush the fish with oiled butter and sprinkle with salt and pepper. Grill for 10–12 min., turning them 2 or 3 times during the process. Serve with lemon or fish sauce.

**6 helpings**

### GRILLED HERRING WITH MUSTARD SAUCE

*Harengs au Naturel, Sauce Moutarde*

**4 fresh herrings**
**1 onion**
**1 oz. butter**
**½ oz. flour**
**1 teasp. dry mustard**
**⅛ pt. vinegar**

Chop the onion finely and fry in the butter until lightly browned. Put in the flour and mustard, add the vinegar and ¼ pt. water. Stir until boiling and simmer gently for 15 min. Wipe and dry the herrings, remove the heads and score across the back and sides, but avoid cutting the roe. Sprinkle with salt and pepper and grill for 10–15 min. Place on a hot dish and serve the sauce separately.

**3–4 helpings**

### GRILLED KIPPERS

**1–2 kippers per person**
**Butter *or* margarine**

Remove the heads and lay the kippers flat, skin side up, on the grid. Cook for about 3 min. each side, adding a dab of butter or margarine when they are turned over.

Serve alone or on a slice of toast. Alternatively, place a pair of kippers, flesh sides together, and grill under medium heat first on one side then on the other; to serve, separate and top each with a nut of butter.

### GRILLED MUSHROOMS

*Champignons grillés*

**12 flap mushrooms**
**Salt and pepper**
**Butter *or* bacon fat**
**Buttered toast**
**Chopped parsley**
**Lemon juice**

Wash, peel and trim the stalks. Season and brush with melted butter *or* bacon fat. Cook under a hot grill, turning them once. Serve in a hot dish or on rounds of buttered toast, with a sprinkling of chopped parsley and a squeeze of lemon juice.

NOTE: A pinch of very finely-chopped marjoram, sprinkled on each mushroom prior to grilling, imparts an excellent flavour.

**6 helpings**
**Cooking time—10 min. (approx.)**

### GRILLED OX TAIL

*Queues de Bœuf grillées*

**2 ox tails**
**1½ pt. well-flavoured stock**
**Egg and breadcrumbs**
**Oil *or* butter**
**Parsley**
**½ pt. piquant sauce *or* good gravy**

Wash and dry the tails and divide them at the joints. Put into a saucepan with the stock which must be well flavoured, otherwise vegetables and herbs must be added. Simmer gently for 2½ hr., and when tender drain well and put aside until cold. Coat carefully with egg and breadcrumbs, brush with melted butter or oil and grill until brown. Place on a hot dish and garnish with the parsley. Serve with piquant sauce or a good gravy.

**6 helpings**

## Hare or Rabbit—How to Joint.

Before starting the following set of operations the hare or rabbit should be thoroughly washed in salt water.

1 With a sharp knife cut off the side flaps, then the hind legs.

2 Cut off front legs at the joint.

3 Chop the back sharply once or twice (depending on size of the animal), and separate the body into fairly even parts as shown.

4 This photograph shows nine separate joints which can be cut from a hare or rabbit. In foreground are the liver and kidneys.

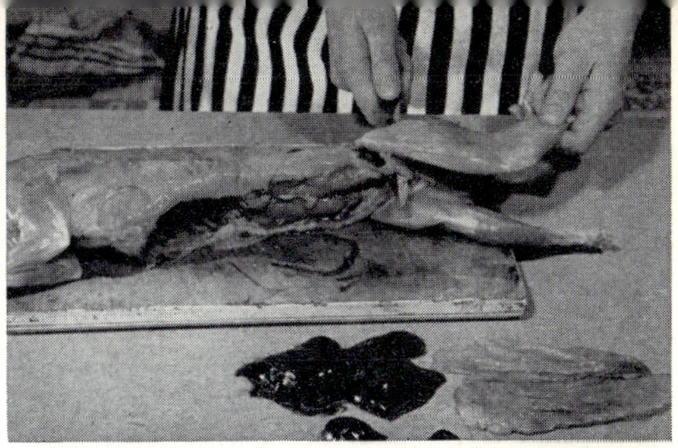

1

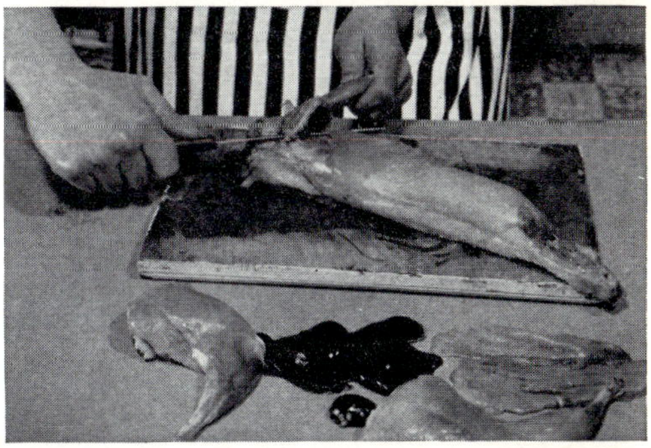

2

3

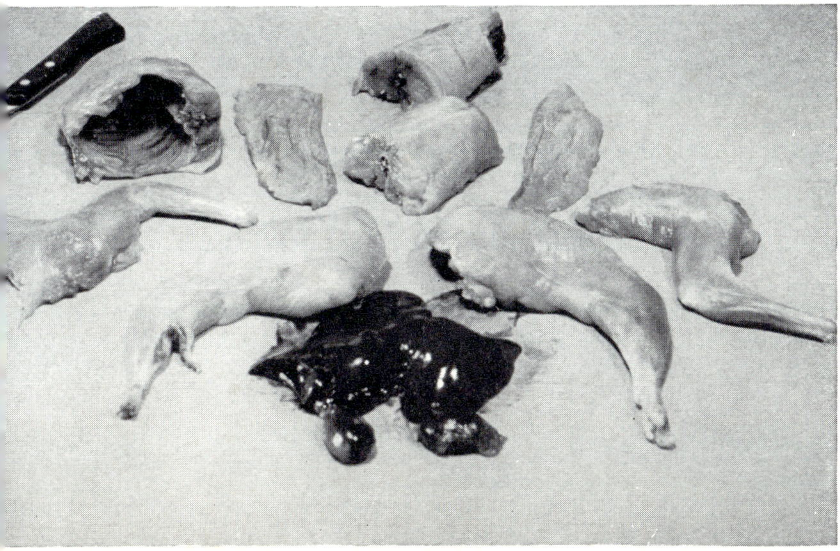

4

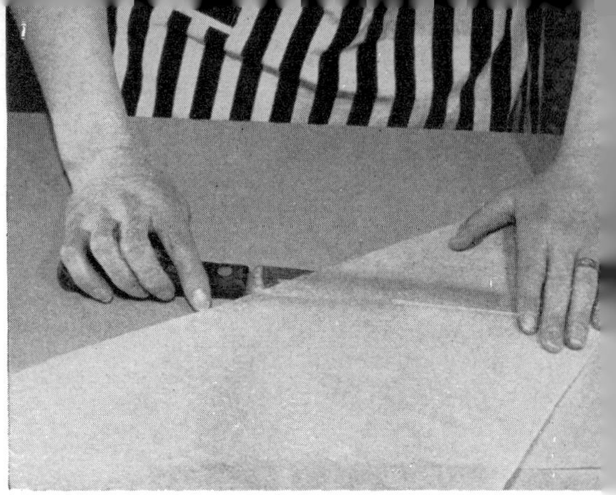

1

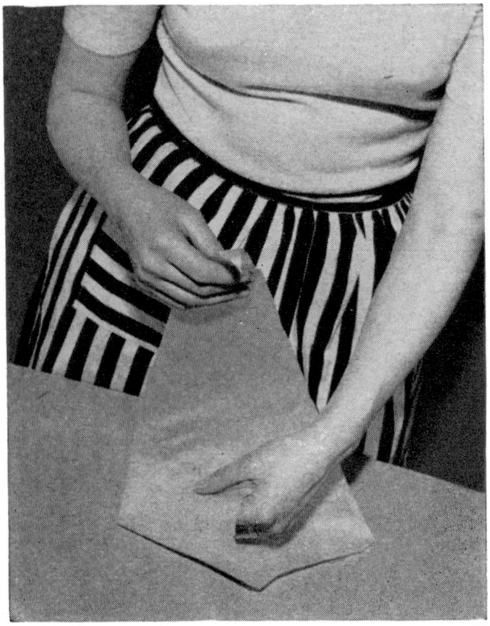

2

Icing Cakes I.

1 Fold an oblong-shaped piece of greaseproof paper in half diagonally and cut along the fold.

2 Using one-half take it by the longest side in the left and right hands. Fold over the left hand.

3 Form into a cone shape and fold over at the top to seal the join.

4 Cut off the pointed end of the cone and slip a forcing pipe into the bag so that the pipe protrudes halfway through the cut point.

3

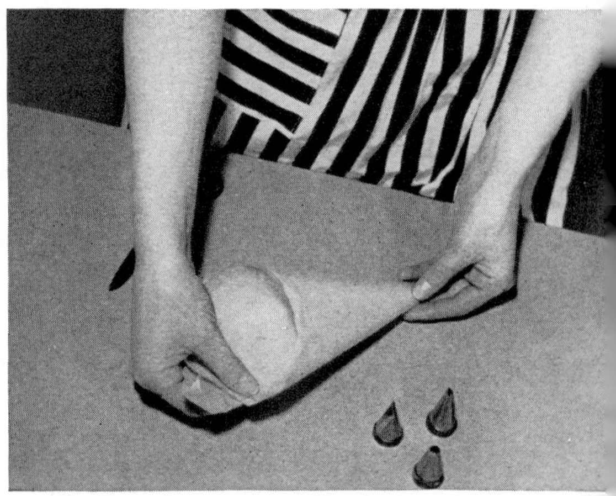

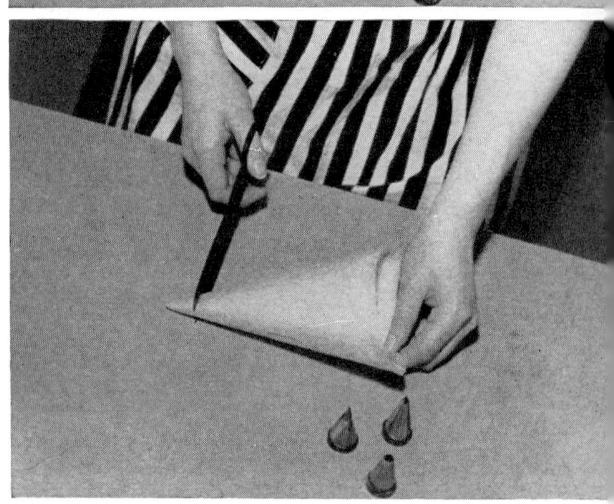

4

Icing Cakes II.

1 Using a pastry brush, brush top and side of cake with apricot glaze. Roll out the almond paste to a round shape about 4 inches wider than the diameter of the cake.

2 Place the cake in the centre of the almond paste with the topside downwards.

3 With the hands work the paste up side of the cake until it is within ½ inch of the top edge (i.e. the bottom of the cake).

4 Using a straight-sided jar roll round the side, holding the cake firm with the other hand and pressing down only very slightly.

5 Take a spoonful of icing and smooth with a palette knife; do the top first then side.

6 Decorate, using a forcing bag and pipe. Draw designs first on greaseproof paper cut to fit top and side of cake. Prick the lines of the design through with a pin. Decorate top, then side, then base.

1

2

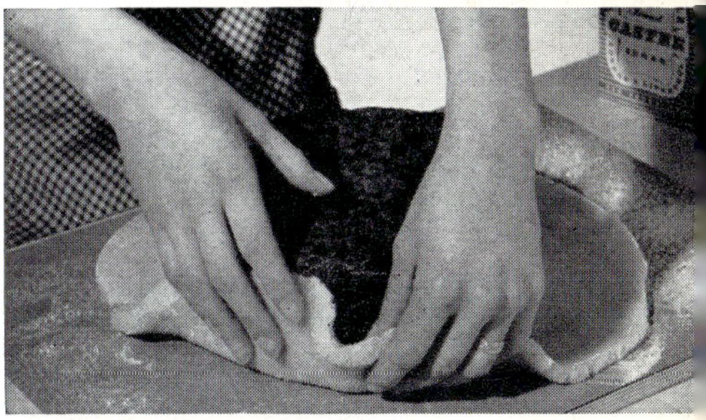

3

4

5

6

Pastry Looks Pretty I
—Decorating Tarts.

A few simple finishing touches like the ones outlined below will soon transform even the plainest tarts and pies into fancy party dishes.

1 With a sharp knife make even cuts about 1 inch apart and 1 inch in depth round the edge of the tart. Damp with a pastry brush and fold alternate pieces down, pressing them only very lightly.

2 Roll out pastry trimmings to a thickness of $\frac{1}{8}$ inch and cut out small circles. Damp the edge of the tart and press cut-outs on edge so that they overlap.

3 Make cuts as in 1. Moisten and fold pieces so that they overlap to give a sunray effect.

4 Decorate the edge with a fork then arrange fleurons (cut with a fluted pastry cutter from pastry scraps) on the filling.

5 Shows three ways of folding an edge after cutting (see 1 above).

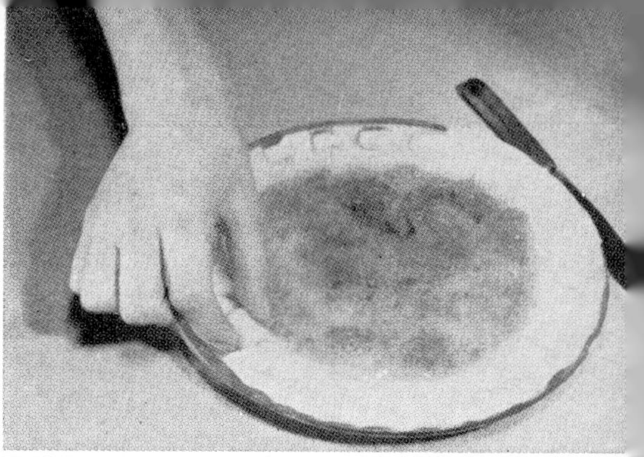

1

2

3

4

5

### GRILLED PARTRIDGE

*Perdreaux grillés*

**A brace of partridge**
**Salt and cayenne pepper**
**2 oz. butter**

GARNISH

**Grilled tomato**
**Mushrooms**

Pluck and draw the birds carefully split in half, wipe the insides thoroughly with a damp cloth. Season with salt and cayenne. Grill about 20 min., turning frequently, and brush with butter just before serving.

Garnish quickly, and serve with mushroom *or* brown sauce.

**4 helpings**

### GRILLED PHEASANT

*Faisan grillé*

**1 pheasant**
**2 oz. butter**
**Salt and cayenne pepper**
**Egg and breadcrumbs**

GARNISH

**Grilled mushroom**
**Tomato**
**Watercress**

Joint the bird, season it, fry in butter until lightly browned, press between 2 plates until cold. Coat with egg and breadcrumbs, grill about 25 min., turning frequently, and brushing with melted butter after the coating has set.

Garnish and serve immediately, piled on a hot dish. Serve with mushroom sauce.

*Alternative sauces*—Madeira, piquant.

**4–5 helpings**

### GRILLED PIGEONS

*Pigeons grillés*

**3 pigeons**
**Salt and pepper**
**2 oz. butter *or* salad oil**

Split pigeons down the back, flatten them with a cutlet-bat (or the back of a large, wet wooden spoon) and skewer them flat. Brush all over the meat with oiled butter *or* salad oil; season. Grill for 20 min., turning frequently, serve very hot.

Serve with 1 pt. tomato *or* mushroom sauce in a sauce-boat.

**6 helpings**

### GRILLED RED MULLET

*Rouget grillé*

**4 small red mullet**
**Salt and pepper**
**Olive oil**
**Parsley**

Scrape the scales from the fish, cut off the fins and remove the eyes, but leave the head and tail on. Gut the fish if necessary and keep the liver. Wash well. Season the inside of each fish and replace the liver. Brush the fish with olive oil and put a little oil in the grill-pan before putting in the fish. Grill quickly for 3 min., then turn the fish over and baste well. Reduce the heat and continue grilling until the mullet are cooked, about a further 15 min. Serve on a hot dish with the remaining oil poured over. Garnish with parsley.

**4 helpings**

### GRILLED SALMON

*Saumon grillé*

**2–3 slices of salmon (middle cut) about ¾ in. thick**
**2 tablesp. olive oil *or* oiled butter (approx.)**
**Salt and pepper**
**1 tablesp. (about 1 oz.) Maître d'Hôtel *or* anchovy butter**
**Parsley**
**Lemon (optional)**

Wipe the fish with a damp cloth, then brush over with oil or oiled butter. Season to taste with salt and pepper and place the slices on a well-greased grill rack. Grill each side for 6–8 min., according to thickness of slices. When done, place the fish on a flat oval dish, spread a little Maître d'Hôtel or anchovy butter over each. Garnish with sprigs of fresh parsley, and if liked with quarters of lemon. Serve hot.

**4–6 helpings**
**Cooking time—about 15 min.**

### GRILLED TENDERLOIN

*Tendrons de Porc*

**6 pork chops from spare rib, tenderloin *or* neck**
**Salt and pepper**
**Sage**
**Marjoram**
**Castor sugar**
**Flour**
**Stock**
**Apple sauce**

Prepare the chops. Sprinkle both sides of the chops with a pinch of salt, pepper, sage, marjoram and castor sugar. Grill carefully until golden brown, turning several times. Keep hot and after pouring away the fat, add flour and stock to make ½ pt. fawn thick gravy. Serve the chops on a hot dish. Serve the gravy and apple sauce separately.

## GRILLED TOMATOES

*Tomates grillées*

**6 large tomatoes**
**Butter *or* bacon fat**
**Salt and pepper**

Prepare as for fried tomatoes. Season and brush with melted fat. Cook under a fairly hot grill, turning them once. Serve hot with bacon, sausages, fish dishes and all grilled meats.

**6 helpings**
**Cooking time—about 10 min.**

## GRILLING

*See Cooking Methods*

## GRILLING FISH

*See Fish*

## GROUSE PIE

*Pâté de Coq de Bruyère*

**2 grouse**
**¾ lb. rump steak**
**2–3 slices of bacon**
**2 hard-boiled eggs**
**Salt and pepper**
**½ pt. good stock**
**Puff pastry using 8 oz. flour, etc.**

Joint the birds and discard vent-end parts of the backs, as these will impart a bitter flavour to the pie. Slice the steak thinly, slice eggs and cut the bacon into strips. Line the bottom of a pie-dish with pieces of seasoned meat, cover with a layer of grouse, add some bacon, egg and seasoning. Repeat until dish is full. Add sufficient stock to ¾ fill the pie-dish, cover with puff pastry and bake 1½–1¾ hr. The first 15 min. of this time, have the oven hot **(425°–450° F., Gas 7–8)** then lower the heat to moderate **(350°–375° F., Gas 4–5)** or cover the pastry with greaseproof paper so that the filling may cook a further 1¼–1½ hr. Glaze the pie ½ hr. before cooking is complete. Simmer the necks and trimmings of the birds in the remaining stock, strain, season and pour into the pie before serving.

Finely-chopped mushrooms, parsley and shallots may be added to the pie, if liked.

**6–8 helpings**
**Cooking time—1¾ hr.**

## HADDOCK CROUSTADES

**1 small dried haddock (smoked)**
**1 oz. butter**
**2 eggs**
**2 tablesp. milk**
**Good pinch of pepper**
**Grating of nutmeg**
**Croustades of bread**
**Bread**
**Butter**
**Cayenne pepper**

Cook the haddock in boiling water until just tender. Flake all the fish away from the bones. Heat the butter in a pan, and when hot add the eggs, beaten with the milk, and pepper, flaked haddock, and nutmeg. Cook very gently until lightly set. Fill croustades of bread—for directions on preparing these see recipe for Sardine Croustades—or put the mixture on to crisp fingers of buttered toast. Garnish with cayenne pepper.

**4 helpings *or* 12 small savouries**
**Cooking time—12 min. (approx.)**

## HAGGIS

**1 sheep's paunch and pluck**
**1 lb. oatmeal**
**1 lb. beef suet**
**2 Spanish onions**
**1 teasp. pepper**
**2 tablesp. salt**
**½ nutmeg, finely-grated**
**Juice of 1 lemon**
**1½ pt. good stock *or* gravy**

Soak the paunch for several hours in salt and water. Then turn it inside out and wash thoroughly several times. Wash the pluck well, just cover the liver with cold water and boil for about 1½ hr. After ¾ hr. add the well-cleaned heart and lights. Chop ½ the liver coarsely and chop the other ½ with the heart and lights, very finely. Mix all together and add the oatmeal, finely-chopped suet, finely-chopped onions, salt, pepper, nutmeg, lemon juice and stock. Press this mixture lightly into the paunch and sew up the opening, allowing space for the oatmeal to swell. (If overfilled, the paunch is likely to burst.) Put the haggis into boiling water and cook gently for about 3 hr. During the first hour prick occasionally and carefully with a needle to allow the steam to escape. Usually no sauce or gravy is served with haggis. If a smaller dish is required use a lamb's paunch and pluck instead of a sheep's.

### HALIBUT PIE

*Pâté de Flétan*

**3 lb. halibut**
**⅓ pt. white sauce**
**1 teasp. anchovy essence**
**Salt and pepper**
**Rough puff *or* puff pastry using 4 oz. flour, etc.**

Add the anchovy essence to the sauce. Wipe and skin the fish, remove the bones and divide fish into 2-in. square pieces. Place in a pie-dish with a good sprinkling of salt and pepper and a little white sauce between each layer. Cover with pastry, bake in a fairly hot oven (**375° F., Gas 5**) for 30–40 min. Serve hot.

**8 helpings**

### HAM

*See Bacon and Ham.*

### HAM CROQUETTES

*Croquettes de Jambon*

**½ lb. cooked ham**
**4 oz. fresh breadcrumbs**
**2 tablesp. mashed potatoes**
**½ egg**
**4 tablesp. white sauce**
**Salt and pepper**
**1 egg**
**Breadcrumbs**
**Deep fat**
**Paprika pepper**
**Parsley**

Mince the ham and mix with the bread-crumbs and potatoes. Place in a small pan and, heating gently, bind with the beaten egg and white sauce. Season well and spread on a plate. Divide into 12 equal portions and leave until cool. Shape into croquettes, coat with egg and breadcrumbs, and fry until golden brown in deep fat. Drain, sprinkle with paprika pepper and garnish with parsley.

Serve with tomato sauce.

**6 helpings**

### HAM CROÛTES

*Croûtes au Jambon*

**2 teasp. chopped shallots *or* onion**
**1 tablesp. cream**
**Pinch of pepper**
**1 oz. butter**
**6 oz. cooked ham**
**2 egg yolks *or* 1 whole egg**
**4 round croûtes of fried bread *or* toast**
**Chopped parsley**

Fry the shallot or onion in the butter until slightly browned, then add the ham and stir over the heat until hot. Put in the egg yolks or egg and cream and season with pepper. Stir until the mixture thickens, then dish on the croûtes and serve sprinkled with parsley.

**6–7 helpings**
**Cooking time—5 min.**

### HAM CUTLETS WITH PINEAPPLE

Take 6 pineapple slices (canned or fresh), cover ham with them when it has baked for 20 min., sprinkle with brown sugar, dot with a little butter and continue baking for about 15 min. or till the pineapple looks glazed.

### HAM AND EGG CROQUETTES

*Croquettes de Jambon*

**6 oz. cooked ham**
**3 hard-boiled eggs**
**1½ oz. butter *or* fat**
**1½ oz. flour**
**1½ gills milk**
**1 teasp. finely-chopped parsley**
**Salt and pepper**
**Egg and fine white breadcrumbs**
**Deep fat**
**Parsley**

Chop the ham and hard-boiled eggs finely. Melt the fat in a saucepan, stir in the flour, add the milk and bring to boil stirring well. Add the ham and eggs, parsley and seasoning. Mix well and turn on to a plate to cool. When cold divide into 12 equal portions and shape into croquettes. Coat evenly with egg and bread-crumbs and fry in deep fat until golden brown. Serve hot, garnished with parsley.

**6 helpings**

### HAM AND EGG FLAN

**Short *or* flaky pastry using 4–6 oz. flour**
**6 oz. thinly-sliced ham**
**3 eggs**
**¾ pt. milk *or* unsweetened evaporated milk**
**Salt and pepper**

Roll out the pastry thinly and line a flan case or sandwich-tin. Dice the ham and put into the flan. Lightly beat the eggs, add the milk, season well and pour on top of the ham.

Bake on middle shelf of a moderate oven **(350° F., Gas 4)** until the pastry is cooked and the filling set.

**6 helpings**
**Cooking time—about 45 min.**

## HAM SAUCE

*Sauce au Jambon*

**½ pt. brown sauce**
**2 oz. lean cooked ham**
**3 shallots *or* 1 tablesp. chopped chives**
**½ oz. butter**
**Juice of ½ lemon**
**Pepper**
**1 tablesp. chopped parsley**

Melt the butter and in it gently cook the onions or chives (chopped finely) for 10 min. Add the ham and heat for a few minutes. Stir in the brown sauce, lemon juice, pepper to taste and when boiling add the parsley.

Serve with fried or grilled meat.

## HAMBURGERS

**1 lb. minced beef**
**½ cup dry breadcrumbs**
**½ cup milk**
**Salt and pepper**
**1 small onion, minced**

Mix together all the ingredients. Form mixture into 6 patties, brown quickly on both sides in hot fat, reduce heat and cook more slowly until done, turning occasionally. Serve between toasted rolls.

## HAM MOUSSE

*Mousse de Jambon Espagnole*

**½ lb. cooked ham**
**Salt and pepper**
**Grated nutmeg**
**½ pt. Espagnole sauce**
**½ oz. gelatine**
**¼ pt. aspic jelly**
**2 tablesp. white stock**
**1 drop of carmine**
**1½ gills cream *or* milk**
**1 tablesp. chopped truffles**
**½ gill pale aspic jelly**

Tie a band of stiff paper round a china soufflé dish of about 5 in. diameter so that it stands about 2 in. higher than the dish.

Pass the ham twice through a mincer and sieve it. Season with salt, pepper and nutmeg. Add the Espagnole sauce which is well coloured and flavoured with tomato. Dissolve the gelatine in the aspic, together with the stock; colour with carmine and add to the ham. Whip the cream very lightly and fold lightly into the mixture. When it is beginning to set creamily, pour into the prepared soufflé case and allow to set. Add the chopped truffle to the pale aspic and pour on the top of the mould, when the jelly is cold, but not set. When set remove paper and serve with green salad.

## HAM ROLLS

**4 thin slices of cooked ham**
**2 oz. cream cheese**
**1–2 tablesp. sweet chutney**
**Crisp lettuce**

Spread each slice of ham on a board, trim off surplus fat. Mix the cream cheese and chutney together, spread over the ham and roll. Put on to lettuce leaves. If wished cut the slices into 1 in. lengths and instead of putting on to lettuce leaves put on small buttered biscuits and garnish with watercress leaves.

**4 helpings *or* 12 small savouries**

## HAM SALAD WITH PINEAPPLE

**½ lb. cooked ham**
**1 small fresh pineapple *or* 1 small can of pineapple**
**Mayonnaise sauce *or* salad dressing**
**Sliced gherkins**

Cut the ham into short strips. Cut the pineapple into small dice. Toss lightly with mayonnaise sauce or salad dressing. Garnish with slices of gherkin.

**4–6 helpings**

## HAM STUFFING or FORCEMEAT

**4 oz. lean ham *or* bacon**
**2 oz. suet *or* margarine**
**4 oz. breadcrumbs**
**1 tablesp. chopped parsley**
**1 teasp. mixed fresh herbs *or* ½ teasp. dried herbs**
**Grated rind of 1 lemon**
**A little grated nutmeg**
**1/16 teasp. powdered allspice**
**1 egg**
**A little milk *or* stock**
**Salt and pepper**

Chop or mince the ham and chop or grate the suet. Mix all the dry ingredients and bind with the egg and stock or milk. Season well.

When the mixture is intended for balls, the consistency should be tested by poaching a small quantity in boiling water.

Use for veal, poultry or hare.

## HARE EN CASSEROLE

*Lièvre en Casserole*

| | |
|---|---|
| **1 hare** | **1½ pt. stock *or* equal quantities stock and stout *or* cider** |
| **3 oz. butter** | **1 oz. flour** |
| **1 onion** | **Veal forcemeat** |
| **3 cloves** | **Fat for frying** |
| **Bouquet garni** | |
| **Salt and pepper** | |

Prepare the hare and cut into pieces convenient for serving. Fry pieces in 2 oz. of the butter until brown then pack closely in a casserole. Slice and fry onion, add to casserole with cloves, bouquet garni, seasoning, stock (*or* equal quantities stock and stout, *or* cider). Cover closely, simmer about 2½ hr., until hare is tender. Knead remaining 1 oz. butter and flour together, divide into small pieces, drop into casserole, about ½ hr. before serving. Shape forcemeat into small balls, fry in hot fat, drain well, add to casserole 5 min. before serving. Remove bouquet garni, correct seasoning.

Serve with redcurrant jelly handed separately.

**6 helpings** **Cooking time—about 3 hr.**

## HARE (COLD) PIE

*Pâté de Lièvre*

| | |
|---|---|
| **½ lb.– ¾ lb. cooked hare** | **Salt and pepper** |
| **½ lb. streaky bacon** | **Worcester sauce** |
| **4 oz. breadcrumbs** | **1 lb. creamed potatoes** |
| **Gravy *or* stock** | **1 oz. butter** |

Cut hare into small pieces; fry and cut up the bacon, mix with hare, breadcrumbs and enough gravy or stock to moisten well. Place a layer of mixture in the bottom of a greased pie-dish; season well; add a little sauce. Cover with a layer of seasoned creamed potato; repeat until all mixture is used, finishing with a layer of potato. Put the butter, cut in small pieces, on the top; brown and heat thoroughly in a hot oven (**425°–450° F., Gas 7–8**). Serve with a good gravy.

**4–5 helpings**
**Cooking time—about 20 min.**

## HARE HARICOT OF

*Haricot de Lièvre*

| | |
|---|---|
| **1 hare** | **Salt and pepper** |
| **1½ oz. butter** | **2 teasp. chopped parsley** |
| **1 small onion** | **½ teasp. thyme** |
| **1 small turnip** | **1½ pt. stock** |
| **1 carrot** | **1 lb. creamed potatoes** |

Wash and joint hare. Melt the butter in a saucepan and fry joints until well browned. Dice the onion, turnip and carrot; add to hare with seasoning, herbs and hot stock. Cover tightly, stew gently 2½–3 hr.; correct seasoning.

Make a border of creamed potatoes on the serving dish, heat it thoroughly; serve the hare in the centre. Serve with redcurrant jelly.

**5–6 helpings**

## HARE HASHED

*Hachis de Lièvre*

| | |
|---|---|
| **Remains of cold roast hare** | **1 glass port, *or* claret, *or* cider (optional)** |
| **¾ pt. brown sauce** | **Salt and pepper** |

Trim hare into neat pieces. Make stock with bones and trimmings and use this instead of wine if liked. Make brown sauce, add wine if used, put in pieces of hare and heat very thoroughly.

Serve with redcurrant jelly handed separately.

## HARE POTTED

*Terrine de Lièvre*

| | |
|---|---|
| **1 hare** | **1 blade mace** |
| **2 rashers of bacon** | **2 bay leaves** |
| **Bouquet garni** | **Salt and cayenne** |
| **3 cloves** | **Stock** |
| **10 peppercorns** | **Clarified butter** |

Prepare hare as in Notes on Trussing Hares , cut into small, neat pieces. Line the base of a saucepan or casserole with bacon, pack the pieces of hare closely on top, add the bouquet garni, cloves, peppercorns, mace, bay leaves, seasoning, and just cover with stock. Cook slowly for about 3 hr., adding more stock as necessary. Remove bones, chop and mince hare and bacon finely, moisten with more stock, season well, put in small pots and cover with clarified butter. The mixture may be sieved if desired.

NOTE: Cold cooked hare may also be potted. Moisten it with good stock or gravy.

## HARE PURÉE

*Purée de lievre*

| | |
|---|---|
| **The bones and inferior pieces of a hare, raw** | **A bunch of herbs** |
| **3 qt. second stock** | **1 bay leaf** |
| **2 oz. lean bacon** | **1 blade of mace** |
| **1 onion** | **Flour** |
| **1 carrot** | **1 glass port** |
| **1½ oz. butter *or* margarine** | **Salt** |
| | **Cayenne pepper** |

Paunch the hare and save the blood; (a few drops of vinegar will prevent clotting.) The best of the flesh and ½ the blood will be used for jugged hare. Break the bones, cover them and the scraps of flesh with the stock and simmer very gently. Fry the bacon, onion and carrot in the butter till brown; add them with the herbs and spices to the simmering stock and simmer for 3–4 hr. Strain, remove the meat from the bones and mince it. Moisten the meat with stock and pass it through a wire sieve. Stir the soup into the purée. For each quart of finished soup blend 1 oz. flour with a little stock or water, add it to the soup, bring to the boil, stirring well. Mix the wine and blood and stir them into the soup; cook them carefully without boiling but until they thicken and the blood does not taste raw. Season carefully.

**6–8 helpings** **Cooking time—3–4 hr.**

## HARE or RABBIT STOCK

| | |
|---|---|
| **Bones of rabbit *or* hare** | **1 onion** |
| **Head, heart and liver** | **1 bay leaf** |
| **"Helmet" and flaps** | **1 blade of mace** |
| **Salt** | **Peppercorns** |

Make as for Brown stock.

## HARE ROAST BARON OF

*Baron de Lièvre rôti*

| | |
|---|---|
| **1 hare** | **¾ pt. brown sauce** |
| **Veal forcemeat** | **1 glass port (optional)** |
| **Larding bacon** | **Redcurrant jelly** |
| **Butter *or* dripping** | |

Prepare the hare, use only the body (the legs, neck and head may be used for soup, potted, or made into a civet with liver Parboil the liver, chop finely, add to veal forcemeat and stuff the hare, sewing it up securely. Carefully remove skin from the back, lard the hare, i.e. insert fine strips of larding bacon see p. 384, then wrap it in greased greaseproof paper. Roast in a fairly hot oven (**375°–400° F., Gas 5–6**) 40–50 min., basting frequently with hot butter or dripping, and remove the paper about 15 min. before cooking is completed. Meanwhile make the sauce and add the wine if used. Remove sewing cotton, dish the hare.

Serve the sauce and jelly separately.

**3 helpings**

## HARE SOUP, THICKENED

*Potage de lièvre*

| | |
|---|---|
| **Bones and trimmings of a hare** | **1½ oz. dripping** |
| **3 pt. second stock *or* water** | **A bunch of herbs** |
| **1 onion** | **1 bay leaf** |
| **1 carrot** | **1½ teasp. salt** |
| **½ turnip** | **8 peppercorns** |
| **Small parsnip** | **1½ oz. flour** |
| **1 stick of celery** | **½ glass port** |

Collect the blood from the hare by piercing the diaphragm. Carefully fillet the meat from the back and legs to be used for Jugged Hare and leave ). The head, flaps and bones of the hare, with the blood may be used for the soup. Split the head, separate the bones, cover them with the cold liquid, add the blood and soak for 1 hr. Fry the sliced vegetables in the dripping then lift them out. Bring the panful of bones and liquid very slowly to simmering point; add the vegetables, herbs, salt and peppercorns and simmer very gently for 3–4 hr. Meanwhile fry the flour till golden brown in the dripping. Strain the soup. Remove from the bones any trimmings of meat, cut these neatly and return them to the soup. Whisk in the fried flour, whisk till boiling, add the port and season the soup.

*See also Hare Purée.*

**8 helpings**
**Cooking time—4½ hr.**

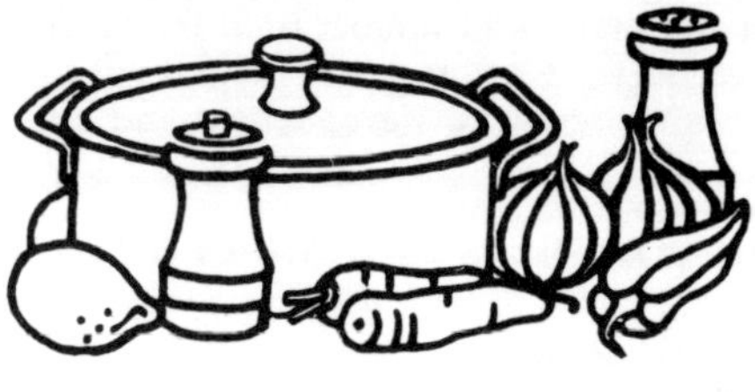

**HARES AND RABBITS**

Hares can be roasted or jugged when young, and make good soup when old. Young ones have smooth sharp claws, a narrow cleft in the lip and soft ears which will tear readily; they have short stumpy necks and long joints. A leveret is a hare up to 1 year old; it will have a small bony knot near the foot, which is absent in a full-grown hare. Hares should be well hung, for 7 or 8 days, in a cool dry place. They should hang, unskinned, by the hind legs, with the head in a tip cup, to catch the blood. Hares are not paunched until required for cooking.

**Skinning hares**: In many respects the dressing of a hare resembles that of poultry. The main difference is that a furry skin has to be removed instead of feathers. This is achieved by first cutting off the feet above the foot joint. The feet can be jointed off with a small thin-bladed knife. Next carefully cut through the skin straight down the belly, taking care not to cut into the meat. Then gently ease back the skin away from the flesh and work round each side until the centre of the hare is completely freed from its skin. Now push forward one hind leg and work the skin free. Repeat with the other and then pull the skin away from the tail. Holding the skinned hindquarters in the left hand, gently pull the skin up the back and over the shoulder, working each foreleg through in turn. The skin must now be eased with a knife from the neck and head. Cut carefully round the base of each ear to free the fur but take care not to cut off the ears, which are left on for cooking.

When free of skin, carefully cut through the skin of the belly from the chest to the legs and draw out the viscera (this is known as paunching). Wipe dry with a clean cloth. The kidneys, found in the back embedded in a little fat, are left in position. The liver and heart are cooked and care should be taken in detaching the greenish gall bladder from the liver.

**Trussing hares:** A hare may be trussed with a needle and string. The desired effect is of the animal crouching prone on the dish. Sew a back leg into each side and also a foreleg (shoulder). Pass a string from front to rear, passing round the neck, and draw tight to cause a small arch in the back.

Rabbits have the same characteristics, when young, as hares. They are paunched, before being hung and they should not be hung for longer than a day. Young ones are suitable for roasting, older ones for stewing, or boiling.

They are dressed as for hares except that the ears and eyes are removed. They may be trussed like a hare. In this case the forelegs are jointed off and sewn back in position. Either rabbit or hare may easily be jointed with a stout-bladed knife which can be tapped through the bones.

Many of the rabbits now on sale are frozen imported animals.

| *Animal* | *Season* |
|---|---|
| Hares . . . . . | September–March |
| Rabbit . . . . . | September–March |

**HARES AND RABBITS, TO CARVE**

*See Carving.*

**HARICOT BEAN AND TOMATO SOUP**

**6 oz. haricot beans**
**1½ pt. water** ***or*** **½ water and ½ stock**
**½ lb. tomatoes**
**1 onion**
**1 carrot**
**1 medium-sized potato**
**½ oz. butter** ***or*** **margarine** ***or*** **bacon fat**
**Salt and pepper**
**A bunch of herbs**
**1 bay leaf**
**1 blade of mace**

Wash the beans and soak them in water overnight. Drain, and put them in a pan with the 1½ pt. water, bring to boil and simmer for 1 hr. Meanwhile slice the tomatoes, onion, carrot and potato. Melt the fat and gently fry the sliced vegetables for 10 min. Add the fried vegetables to the beans with the herbs, bay leaf and mace, and simmer until the beans are quite soft. Remove the herbs, rub soup through a fine wire sieve; reheat and season.

**6 helpings** **Cooking time—2–2½ hr.**

### HARICOT BEANS AND MINCED ONIONS

*Haricots à la Lyonnaise*

| | |
|---|---|
| **½ lb. haricot beans** | **1 oz. butter *or* margarine** |
| **2 medium-sized onions (minced *or* chopped very finely)** | **Seasoning** |
| | **Chopped parsley** |

Cook the beans. Fry the onions slowly in the butter until tender and golden brown. Mix together the onions and beans, season and serve hot sprinkled with parsley.

**6 helpings**
**Cooking time—2–2¼ hr.**

### HARICOT BEANS WITH CHEESE

*Haricots au gratin*

| | |
|---|---|
| **½ lb. haricot beans** | **Cayenne pepper and salt** |
| **1 oz. butter *or* margarine** | **1 tablesp. cream *or* evaporated milk** |
| **1 egg yolk** | **1 tablesp. chopped parsley** |
| **2 oz. grated cheese (preferably Parmesan)** | **Sippets of fried bread** |

Cook the beans. Melt the fat, add all the other ingredients except 1 dessertsp. of the cheese. Shake over the heat till thoroughly hot. Put into a hot, greased fireproof dish, sprinkle with the rest of the cheese and brown quickly under a hot grill.

**4 helpings**
**Cooking time—2½ hr.**

### HARICOT OF VEAL

*Haricot de Veau*

| | |
|---|---|
| **2½ lb. neck of veal** | **1½ pt. stock** |
| **2 onions** | **Salt and pepper** |
| **1½ oz. dripping** | **6 oz. cooked haricot beans** |
| **1½ oz. flour** | |

GARNISH

| | |
|---|---|
| **2 carrots** | **1 turnip** |

Wipe and trim the meat and cut it into pieces convenient for serving. Cut the carrots and turnip into neat dice or strips (these are cooked separately for the garnish). Reserve the trimmings for flavouring. Slice the onion, heat the dripping and fry the meat and onion lightly. Remove to a plate, sprinkle the flour on to the fat and cook slowly until well browned, add the stock, stir until boiling and season to taste. Put in the meat and onion and vegetable trimmings and simmer gently for 1½ hr. Strain the sauce and return to the pan with the cooked haricot beans and simmer for a further 15 min. Lift out the meat, place on a hot dish, pour the sauce over and garnish with the dice or strips of carrot and turnip.

**6 helpings**

### HARICOT MUTTON

*Ragoût de Mouton*

| | |
|---|---|
| **6 small chops from the middle neck *or* 2 lb. scrag end** | **1 large onion** |
| **1 oz. butter *or* good dripping** | **1 oz. flour** |
| | **1½ pt. stock** |
| | **Salt and pepper** |
| | **Bouquet garni** |

GARNISH

| | |
|---|---|
| **2 carrots** | **1 turnip** |

Trim off the skin and surplus fat and cut the meat into small pieces or cutlets. Put the butter or dripping into a saucepan and when smoking, fry the meat quickly and lightly. Remove the meat, chop the onion finely and fry slowly in the same fat without browning. Add the flour and fry slowly until a rich brown. Cool slightly and add the stock, seasoning and bouquet garni. Bring to the boil, put in the meat and simmer gently until tender—about 2 hr. Cut the carrots and turnip into neat dice for garnish. Add the rough trimmings to the meat. Cook the diced carrot and turnip separately in boiling salted water until just tender. Arrange the meat on a hot dish. If necessary rapidly boil the liquid in the saucepan to reduce and then strain over the meat. Garnish with the diced carrot and turnip.

**6 helpings**

### HARICOTS VERTS A LA NIÇOISE

| | |
|---|---|
| **One 10-oz. carton sliced green beans** | **¼ pt. thick fresh tomato purée** |
| **½ oz. butter** | **A little chopped parsley** |
| **Pepper** | |

Cook the beans as directed on the packet and then drain thoroughly. Place the butter in the pan and add the beans, pepper and tomato purée. Toss over a gentle heat until piping hot and serve in a shallow dish sprinkled with chopped parsley.

**3–4 helpings**

## HASHED GOOSE

*Hachis d'Oie*

**Trimmings of roast goose**
**2 onions**
**2 oz. butter**
**1 oz. flour**
**1 pt. stock**
**6 small mushrooms**
**2 cloves**
**1 blade of mace**
**6 allspice**
**Salt and pepper**
**Apple sauce**

GARNISH

**Croûtes of fried bread**

Cut the goose meat into neat pieces. Chop onions finely, put in a saucepan and fry in butter until lightly browned, stir in flour and cook slowly until nut-brown. Stir in stock and boil 10 min. Add goose, mushrooms, and spices wrapped in muslin. Season, simmer gently ¾ hr. Arrange the pieces of meat neatly on a hot dish, remove spices from sauce, correct seasoning and pour over meat.

Garnish; serve sauce separately.

## HASTY PUDDING

**1½ pt. milk**
**2½ oz. sago *or* semolina *or* ground rice**
**1 oz. sugar**

Heat the milk to almost boiling, then sprinkle in the sago, semolina *or* ground rice stirring briskly. Simmer until the grain is cooked and the mixture begins to thicken—about 10–15 min. Add the sugar.

Serve with cream, sugar, jam or treacle.

**6 helpings**

## HERB VINEGAR

**1 pt. malt vinegar**
**2 oz. grated horseradish**
**1 teasp. chopped shallot**
**Rind and juice of ½ lemon**
**2 cloves**
**A sprig each of thyme, basil, savory, marjoram, tarragon**
**1 bay leaf**

Simmer all the ingredients for 20 min. Cool and then strain the vinegar. Bottle when cold.

Use a very little with other vinegar in salad dressings.

## HERBS

Before the nineteenth century, when meat and grain were the principal foods, every garden grew a wide range of herbs to provide flavourings. But when fruit and vegetables became a part of everyday diet and other kinds of food and seasoning could be more easily imported or manufactured, the herb bed lost much of its importance and nowadays contains only a few kinds, of which thyme, mint, sage and parsley are the most general. But there are many others that will add a distinctive and original flavour to your cooking.

Herbs grow well on most types of soil. Cultivation is not difficult and little space is required. One or two bushes of the larger kinds and a short row or small area of 2 to 4 sq. ft. of the smaller ones are generally sufficient.

For convenience in gathering, herbs should be grown along the side of a path or with the beds separated by narrow paths of brick or stone paving. Some kinds can be grown successfully in pots or boxes.

### Storing Herbs

Herbs to be stored for winter use should be harvested when they have made full growth but before the last stages of maturity. The best time is generally when they are coming into flower. Store the dried herbs in air-tight jars in the dark.

### A Selected List of Herbs

**Angelica:** A tall spreading plant growing up to 5 ft. high with hollow stems, large segmented leaves and heads of yellowish-white flowers. Seed should be sown in September and the young plants set out 18 in. to 24 in. apart, preferably in a moist soil and partial shade. If the flower stems are cut off, the plant may last for several years, but it is best treated as a biennial.

**Anise:** A branching plant about 18 in. high with finely-cut leaves and loose heads of yellowish-white flowers. Seed should be sown in April in a sunny position and the seedlings thinned to 9 in. apart.

**Balm:** A perennial shrubby plant about 3 ft. high with yellowish-white flowers and round to oval wrinkled leaves giving a scent of lemons when bruised. Seed should be sown in April or May or old plants may be divided in October.

**Basil** (Sweet)**:** An annual growing up to 2 ft. high with oblong slightly-toothed leaves and white flowers. Seed should be sown in April or May and the seedlings transplanted 9 in. apart.

**Bay:** Although common laurel may be used as a substitute, the true Bay is a shrub which is often seen growing in tubs or clipped to a formal shape. It has shiny dark green leaves, 2 in. to 3 in. long, narrow and pointed, and small whitish-yellow flowers. Propagation is by cuttings taken during the summer. It is not completely hardy but generally succeeds in mild climates, especially if grown in a protected position preferably in full sun.

**Borage:** An annual growing 18 in. high and having hairy stems and egg-shaped leaves. There are two varieties, blue-flowered and white-flowered, both being attractive to bees. Seed should be sown in April or May and the seedlings thinned to 15 in. apart.

**Caraway:** A biennial growing about 18 in. high with slender branching stems, narrow triangular leaves and white flowers. Seed should be sown in autumn or early April and the seedlings thinned to 9 in. apart; the seeds ripen in July.

**Chervil:** This is the garden variety of Wild Parsley and is an annual growing about 18 in. high with slender branching stems, finely-cut leaves and white flowers. Seed should be sown in October or April, preferably in a cool or partially shaded position and the seedlings thinned to 9 in. apart. When required, the leaves should be cut close to the plant in order to encourage fresh shoots.

**Chives:** These plants belong to the same genus as onions and have narrow folded leaves which grow about 9 in. long. Seed may be sown in April, but an easier method is to divide the old clumps and plant in autumn or spring 9 in. apart. In any event the clumps should be lifted and divided every four or five years. Chives make a good edging for other herbs.

**Coriander:** An annual growing about 18 in. high with much-divided leaves and white or pale mauve flowers. Seed should be sown in April and the seedlings thinned to 9 in. apart. The seed ripens about August and should be well dried before being used for flavouring.

**Dill:** An annual growing 2 ft. high with fine leaves and yellowish flowers. Seed should be sown in April and the seedlings thinned to 12 in. apart. The stems should be cut when the lower fruits have matured and dried before the seeds are shaken out.

**Fennel:** A perennial with stout branching stems growing up to 5 ft. high, finely-divided leaves and yellow flowers. Seed should be sown in April and the seedlings transplanted or thinned to 1 ft. apart. Although perennial the stock should be renewed every three or four years.

**Garlic:** The species is closely related to onions and shallots and should be cultivated in a similar way. The bulbs or "cloves" should be planted in February or March in good fertile soil, 9 in. to 12 in. apart with the tips set just below the surface. At the end of the summer when the foliage has died down, the crop should be lifted, dried off and stored in shallow trays or boxes in a cool temperature. Garlic has a strong flavour and should be used sparingly when flavouring soups or stews or including in salads.

**Horseradish:** A perennial with large fleshy roots, long-toothed leaves and white flowers. It is easily propagated by planting pieces of root 4 in. to 6 in. long in March or April. To grow straight roots the soil must be deep, well-cultivated and free from stones, and the plants allowed to grow on for two or three years before being lifted for use. The roots may be planted in trenches, or in holes 15 in. deep made with a dibber, but the best way is to plant in a raised bed made up on a foundation of brick or stone so that the whole bed and crop can be cleared away at lifting time. This method entails having two or three beds and planting up a new one every year, but it avoids any risk of the horseradish getting out of hand and becoming a weed. Because it spreads very easily, it is important to have only small beds which can be kept under control.

**Lavender:** Although not a culinary herb, lavender has its place in a herb garden. It makes an excellent centrepiece or boundary hedge. Propagation is by cuttings about 6 in. long taken during summer and rooted in a sandy compost, preferably in a frame. They should be planted out the following spring in a sunny position 2 ft. apart, or if to form a hedge, 1 ft. apart.

**Marjoram:** Sweet Marjoram is a shrubby branching plant about 18 in. high with egg-shaped leaves and either white or lilac flowers. Pot Marjoram grows about 1 ft. high, has more erect branches, oval leaves and white or occasionally purplish flowers. Both are perennials, but Sweet Marjoram is not hardy and should therefore be regarded as an annual.

**Mint:** Of the many species Spearmint is the most popular. The Broad-leaved or Apple-scented variety is said to have the best flavour but its hairy leaves are often considered objectionable. Propagation is by division of the roots, which should be planted 2 in. deep in autumn or spring. The beds should be renewed every three or four years or earlier if attacked by Mint rust (a common fungus disease causing thick distorted shoots bearing orange cup-like bodies). Peppermint and Pennyroyal are other species of mint which are not suitable for culinary uses but are grown for extraction of oil.

**Parsley:** The plant is a biennial, running to seed in its second year, and in order to keep up a supply of fresh shoots seed should be sown every year—in March or April for the summer supply and in July for winter use. It prefers a fairly rich soil and partial shade. Germination takes a long time, often several weeks.

**Purslane:** An annual growing about 6 in. high with oblong wedge-shaped leaves and yellow flowers. Seed should be sown in March in a sunny position and thinned to 9 in. apart.

**Rosemary:** A hardy evergreen shrub with violet or white flowers and narrow needle-like leaves, dark green above and downy grey beneath. Seed may be sown in April or cuttings about 6 in. long taken in summer. A fairly dry position protected from the wind is required.

**Rue:** A hardy evergreen shrub growing up to 3 ft. high with yellow flowers and leaves 3 in. to 5 in. long. Seeds should be sown in April or cuttings taken in early summer and planted out in a protected position. The leaves, which have a strong acrid flavour, may be used sparingly in fruit cups.

**Sage:** There are two varieties of sage, one having narrow leaves and white flowers and being generally preferred to the other which has large leaves and purple flowers. Seed may be sown in April, cuttings taken in early summer or rooted shoots taken from the old bushes. The plants should be set about 2 ft. apart.

**Savory:** There are two kinds: Summer Savory, an annual growing about 9 in. high is generally regarded as superior to Winter Savory, a perennial growing about 1 ft. high. Both have narrow leaves, downy stems and purplish flowers. Seed should be sown in April and the seedlings thinned to 1 ft. apart. Winter Savory may also be propagated by cuttings or division in April.

**Sorrel:** The best kind is French Sorrel, a perennial growing up to 2 ft. high with yellowish-green arrow-shaped leaves, 3 in. to 4 in. long. Seed should be sown in April in a moist acid soil and the seedlings thinned to 1 ft. apart. The flower stems should be pinched out to encourage the production of the leaves which may be used in salads or for cooking like spinach.

**Southernwood:** A deciduous shrub growing about 2 ft. high, with delicate divided pale-green leaves which give a strong scent when crushed. Seed may be sown in April but it is better to take cuttings about 9 in. long a little earlier.

**Tansy:** A perennial growing up to 3 ft. high with deeply-cut leaves 2 in. to 4 in. long, and yellow flowers borne in flat heads. Propagation is by division of roots in spring, the plants being set out 1 ft. apart.

**Tarragon:** A perennial growing about 3 ft. high with slender shoots, narrow olive green leaves 1 in. to 3 in. long, and greenish flowers. Propagation is by division or cuttings which should be taken in April or May and planted 2 ft. apart, preferably in a fairly dry and sheltered position.

**Thyme:** Of the many species of Thyme two are used for culinary purposes: Garden Thyme, a spreading bush with narrow oblong leaves and lilac flowers, and Lemon Thyme which is closer in growth and has slightly larger leaves and lilac flowers. Seed should be sown or cuttings taken, in April or May, and the plants set 6 in. to 9 in. apart. Thyme makes a good edging plant in a herb garden but after a few years is inclined to get straggly and should then be renewed.

### HERRING ROE TIT-BITS

*Bonnes Bouches de Laitance de Harengs*

**6 large soft herring roes**
**Salt and pepper**
**6 rashers of bacon**
**A little lemon juice**
**12 small rounds of toast *or* fried bread**
**Anchovy paste**
**2–3 small gherkins**

Cut the roes into halves, season lightly with salt and pepper. Divide the rashers of bacon into halves, remove the rinds and wrap each piece of roe in the bacon. Sprinkle lemon juice on the bacon and secure the rolls on a skewer. Cook for about 15 min. in a fairly hot oven (**375° F., Gas 5**) or under a moderately hot grill—reducing the heat after crisping the bacon, to make sure the roes are cooked. Spread the rounds of toast or fried bread with anchovy paste and thin slices of gherkin. Put the roes on top—serve hot or cold.

**12 savouries**
**Cooking time—15 min. in the oven**
**6 min. (approx.) under the grill**

### HERRING ROES—CREAMED

**4 oz. herring roes**
**¼ pt. white sauce**
**Squeeze of lemon juice**
**Seasoning**
**Creamed potatoes**

GARNISH

**Chopped parsley**
**Slice of lemon**
**Little red pepper**

Wash the roes in running cold water; dry. Stir into the sauce, adding lemon juice and seasoning. Simmer for 10 min. Pile on to a bed of creamed potatoes. Garnish with chopped parsley, lemon, and red pepper.

**1 helping** **Cooking time—10 min.**

### HERRING ROLLS

*Paupiettes de Harengs*

**4 salt or rollmop herrings**
**8 anchovy fillets**
**2 hard-boiled eggs**
**1 oz. butter**
**Cayenne pepper**
**Lemon**
**4–6 gherkins**
**1 small beetroot**
**Parsley**

If using salt herrings soak in cold water for several hours, fillet—removing all bones. If using rollmop herrings divide into 2 fillets. Mix chopped anchovy fillets with egg yolks, butter, pepper and little lemon juice. Put on to the herring fillets and roll firmly. Dip each end in finely chopped egg white. Sprinkle with lemon juice. Garnish with slices of lemon, sliced gherkin, diced beetroot and parsley.

**8 savouries**

### HERRINGS AND POTATOES—GERMAN

*Heringskartoffeln*

**3 fresh herrings**
**Salt**
**½ pt. milk**
**2 lb. potatoes**
**1 onion**
**3 oz. butter**
**1 tablesp. breadcrumbs**
**¼ pt. sour cream**

Split, skin, clean and bone the herrings and cut up into small pieces. Sprinkle a little salt on the herrings and put in a dish with the milk and leave for a few hours. Boil the potatoes. Chop the onion and fry in a little of the butter until golden brown. Remove the herrings from the milk and drain. Cut the cooked potatoes into slices. Grease a fireproof dish and arrange in it layers of potatoes, herring and fried onion, finishing with a potato layer. Sprinkle the breadcrumbs on top. Pour over the sour cream and put the rest of the butter in small pieces on top.

Bake in a moderate oven (**350° F., Gas 4**) for 30–45 min.

**6 helpings**

### HERRINGS WITH TOMATOES

*Harengs aux Tomates*

**4 fresh herrings**
**3–4 ripe tomatoes**
**Salt and pepper**
**A few drops of vinegar *or* lemon juice**
**¼ lb. boiled rice**
**½ oz. dripping**

Wipe, fillet and skin the herrings. Cut each fillet in two, crossways, and put a layer of fish in a fireproof dish. Dip the tomatoes into boiling water, skin and cut them into slices. Place a layer of tomato slices over the fish. Sprinkle over enough salt and pepper to season, as well as vinegar or lemon juice to flavour. Cover with the remainder of the fish, then place over the cooked rice, and lastly the remaining slices of tomatoes. Distribute the dripping in little bits on top. Bake in a moderate oven (**350° F., Gas 4**) for about ¾ hr. Serve hot.

**4 helpings**

## HOLLANDAISE SAUCE

See also Mock Hollandaise

| | |
|---|---|
| **2 tablesp. wine vinegar** | **Salt and pepper** |
| **2 egg yolks** | **Lemon juice** |
| **2–4 oz. butter** | |

Boil the vinegar till it is reduced by half; allow to cool. Mix the cool vinegar with the egg yolks in a basin and place this over hot water. Whisk the egg yolks till they begin to thicken, then whisk in the butter gradually until all is absorbed. Season, add lemon juice to taste and serve immediately.

Serve with fish or vegetables.

## HOME-BREWED BEERS

Home brewing requires special knowledge, and the reader should consult a book on the subject. *Home Wine-Making* by Charles Foster (Ward, Lock & Co.) covers the topic thoroughly.

## HOME-MADE WINES AND WINE-MAKING

Home wine-making requires special knowledge, and the reader should consult a book on the subject. *Home Wine-Making* by Charles Foster (Ward, Lock & Co.) covers the topic thoroughly.

## HONEYCOMB MOULD

*Crème Anglaise*

| | |
|---|---|
| **1 pt. milk** | **2 large eggs** |
| **Flavouring: vanilla essence *or* lemon *or* orange rind** | **1 oz. castor sugar** |
| | **½ oz. gelatine** |
| | **4 tablesp. water** |

If orange or lemon rind is being used for flavouring, slowly infuse thinly-cut strips of rind in the milk. Remove the rind and make a custard with the egg yolks, sugar and flavoured milk. If using essence add to the custard after the sugar. Dissolve gelatine in measured water and while still warm stir into the custard. Allow to cool. When just beginning to set, fold in the stiffly-whisked egg whites. Pour into a quart border mould and leave to set.

Turn out and serve with fruit salad piled up in the hollow. Decorate with whipped cream.

**4–6 helpings**

## HORS D'OEUVRE

Strictly, Hors' D'œuvre are dainty "side" dishes designed to stimulate one's appetite before a meal. They are not part of the designed dinner. Today, however, hors d'œuvre can consist of a large variety of cold dishes and salads and may be the only course served before the main course of meat or fish.

(The name Hors D'œuvre is also often given to other kinds of first course, preceding the main one. Thus the "hors d'œuvre" may be an appetizer, grapefruit, melon, smoked salmon—or a hot dish such as individual soufflés or savoury pancakes.)

When a selection of small cold "side" dishes is offered, they can be presented on a large Hors D'œuvre dish which has separate sections for each foodstuff. In this case, each person is left to help himself. If a large dish is not available, the hors d'œuvre can be arranged on individual plates before the meal.

Salads used in hors d'œuvre are usually "dressed" in oil and vinegar or mayonnaise, so there is no need to serve these with them.

A cold hors d'œuvre is an attractive and practical first course for housewives who entertain without domestic help, since it can be prepared and set on the dining-table ahead of time.

## HORSERADISH CREAM (COLD)

*Sauce Raifort Froide*

| | |
|---|---|
| **2 tablesp. grated horseradish** | **Salt and pepper to taste** |
| **1 tablesp. wine vinegar *or* lemon juice** | **Mixed mustard to taste** |
| **2 teasp. castor sugar** | **¼ pt. cream** |

Mix all ingredients except the cream. Half-whip the cream, i.e. until the trail of the whisk just shows on the surface. Lightly fold the horseradish mixture into the cream. Serve the sauce very cold. It may be chilled in a refrigerator and served semi-solid.

Serve with beef.

## HORSERADISH SAUCE HOT

*Sauce de Raifort Chaude*

To ½ pt. white sauce add 1 rounded tablesp. grated horseradish, 1 teasp. vinegar and ½ teasp. sugar.

## HORSERADISH VINEGAR

**1 pt. vinegar**
**2 oz. grated horseradish**
**½ oz. chopped shallot**
**½ teasp. salt**
**1/16 teasp. cayenne**
**1 oz. sugar**

Boil the vinegar; mix together the other ingredients. Pour the boiling vinegar on to the mixture, cover. When cool bottle the mixture and store for 10 days. It may now be used unstrained as horseradish sauce. To store the vinegar, strain, boil it and bottle it in hot, dry sauce bottles. Screw them down at once.

## HOT CROSS BUNS

**1 lb. plain flour**
**½ teasp. salt**
**2 oz. margarine *or* margarine and lard**
**4 oz. sugar**
**1 teasp. mixed spice *or* cinnamon**
**½ oz. yeast**
**1–2 eggs**
**1½–2 gills milk**
**2 oz. currants *or* 2 oz. raisins and peel**
**Short crust pastry**

Mix salt with warmed flour. Rub in fat. Add sugar, spice, creamed yeast, and eggs with the warm milk. Mix to a soft, light dough, beat well and put to rise. When well risen, knead the dough lightly, working in the fruit, and divide into 20–24 pieces. Form into round shapes, flatten slightly and put to prove for 15 min. Cut narrow strips of pastry 1½–2 in. long, brush tops of buns with egg wash *or* milk, place pastry crosses on top and bake in a hot oven (**425° F., Gas 7**).

**20–24 buns** **Cooking time—15–20 min.**

## HOT POT

*Ragoût à l'Anglaise*

**1½ lb. lean beef**
**2 lb. potatoes**
**3 onions**
**3 carrots**
**Salt and pepper**
**Stock *or* water**

Remove any fat and cut the meat into pieces. Cut the onions and carrot into thin slices and the potatoes into thicker slices. Arrange the meat, onion, carrots and potatoes in layers in a casserole and season well. The top layer should be of potatoes neatly arranged. Three-quarters fill the casserole with cold water or stock, adding more later if the dish appears to be dry. Cover and bake in a warm oven (**335° F., Gas 3**) for 2 hr. Uncover ½ hr. before serving to allow the top layer of potatoes to brown. Serve in the casserole.

**6 helpings**

## HOTCH POTCH

**2 lb. neck mutton (scrag and middle neck)**
**2 qt. water**
**Salt and pepper**
**Bunch of fresh herbs**
**1 carrot**
**1 small turnip**
**1 very small cauliflower**
**1 small lettuce**
**6 spring onions**
**¼ pt. young shelled broad beans *or* ¼ lb. runner beans**
**½ pt. shelled peas**
**Chopped parsley**

Wash the mutton, remove all fat and cut the lean meat into small pieces. Put bone and meat into a pan, add the cold water and bring very slowly to simmering point. Add 2 teasp. salt and the herbs, and simmer very gently for ½ hr.

Meanwhile, scrub and peel roots, wash cauliflower and lettuce. Cut the carrot and turnip into ¼-in. dice and the onions into thin rings; add them to the pan and simmer for 1½ hr. Break the cauliflower into small sprigs, shred the lettuce finely and shred the runner beans, if used. Add all these with the shelled beans and peas to the soup and simmer for ½ hr. longer. Season the broth, skim off the fat and remove the bunch of herbs and the bones. Add 1 tablesp. chopped parsley just before serving.

NOTE: The mixture of vegetables may be varied with the season. This soup may well be cooked in a cool oven (**300°–310°F., Gas 1-2**).

**8 helpings as soup; or 4 as a thin stew with extra stock for other soups**
**Cooking time—2½ hr.**

## HOT SWEETS

*See Sweet Dishes.*

ICE CREAM

*See Ice Cream Custard, Ices.*

ICE CREAM CUSTARD

**Basic Recipes**

CUSTARD (1)—Economical

**1 oz. custard powder** **4 oz. castor sugar**
**1 pt. milk**

Blend the custard powder with a little of the milk. Boil remaining milk and pour on to the blended mixture. Return to pan and simmer—stirring continuously. Add sugar; cover, and allow to cool.

CUSTARD (2)

**1 pt. milk** **4 oz. castor sugar**
**3 eggs**

Heat the milk. Beat together eggs and sugar. Add the hot milk stirring continuously. Return to pan and cook without boiling until custard coats the back of a wooden spoon. Strain, cover and cool.

CUSTARD (3)—Rich

**1 pt. milk** **2 eggs**
**8 egg yolks** **4 oz. castor sugar**

Heat the milk. Beat together eggs and sugar until thick and white; add the milk. Cook, without boiling, until it thickens. Strain, cover, and cool.

ICE TO MAKE

If you have a refrigerator and wish to add interest to fruit or alcoholic drinks, colour the water for ice cubes with a little vegetable colouring or make the cubes with diluted fruit juice. Alternatively, half-fill the ice trays with cold water; chill, and when nearly frozen place a cherry, a piece of angelica or shred of orange or lemon rind in each section; chill; almost fill with cold water, and complete the freezing.

ICED SANDWICH CAKE

**1 sandwich cake**

DECORATION

**Butter icing using $1\frac{1}{2}$ oz. butter, etc.**
**Glacé icing using 4 oz. icing sugar**
**2–3 tablesp. sifted, dried, lightly browned, cake-crumbs *or* browned coconut *or* chopped walnuts**

Spread sides of cake evenly with butter icing. Have crumbs in a paper, roll sides of cake in them and press the crumbs into position. Remove any loose crumbs. Mix glacé icing to a stiff coating consistency, pour on to top of cake and spread to edges. Allow to set and trim off any icing which has run down the sides of the cake. Decorate top of cake by piping on butter icing.

ICES

Ices can be divided into two classes, water ices and ice creams.

**Water Ices and Sherbets (Sorbets)**

Water ices are made from the juice of fresh fruit or fruit purée mixed with syrup or fruit syrup. Sherbets (Sorbets) are half-frozen water ices containing egg white or gelatine. They are served at formal banquets in sorbet cups or glasses immediately before the roast to clear the palate, but in private homes they are usually served as a sweet course.

**Ice Creams and Frozen Mousses**

These are sometimes composed almost entirely of cream—sweetened, flavoured and decorated in many ways; but more frequently the so-called "ice cream" consists principally of custard, of varying degrees of richness, with the addition of fruit pulp, almonds, chocolate, coffee, liqueurs and other flavourings. The cream, when used, should be double cream. Evaporated milk can be substituted if properly prepared. (*See Milk.*) Mousses have whipped egg white added.

**Making Ice Cream in a Refrigerator**

To obtain a smooth, evenly-textured ice

cream in a refrigerator, the mixture must be frozen quickly and whisked well. The quicker the freezing the less likelihood there is of ice crystals forming, so set the refrigerator to the coldest point ½ hr. before putting the mixture to freeze, unless instructed otherwise in the recipe. Chill all ingredients and utensils before use.

Prepare the mixture, place it in the ice tray or drawer, and replace the tray in the freezing compartment.

Air acts as a deterrent to crystal formation, so remove the mixture after ½ hr. and whisk well in a chilled bowl. Replace in the tray and put back into the freezing compartment.

**Making Ice Cream in a Freezer**

An ice cream freezer consists of a metal container, in which the ice cream mixture is placed—and an outer container, usually a wooden bucket; the space between the two being packed with alternate layers of crushed ice and salt. Air is incorporated into the mixture by churning.

Most recipes are based on a one quart bucket type mixture; this bucket needs 7 lb. of ice and 2 lb. freezing salt (common salt may be substituted). Broken ice alone is insufficient to freeze or mould the ices.

**Hints on Using a Freezer**

1. Add sugar carefully—too much sugar prevents an ice mixture freezing successfully. Insufficient sugar causes the mixture to freeze hard and rocky.
2. Do not put warm mixtures into the container, and do not fill the container completely. Freezing increases the bulk of the mixture.
3. Raise the lid from time to time and scrape down with a wooden spatula or spoon, the thin coating of ice which will have formed on the side, and mix well with the more liquid contents.
4. Wipe the lid of the container carefully before raising it, so that no salt or salt water gets into the mixture.
5. Churn slowly at first, and more rapidly as the mixture stiffens.
6. If the ice cream is to be served unmoulded it must be frozen stiffly.

**Moulding Ices**

If the mixture is to be moulded it should be removed from the freezer or refrigerator in a semi-solid condition, and then packed into a dry mould or bomb, well shaken, and pressed down into the shape of the mould. The mould should have a tightly-fitting lid, which must be sealed with a thick layer of lard or foil. The mould or bomb is then wrapped in greaseproof paper and buried in broken ice and freezing salt for 1½–2 hr.

To unmould, remove the paper and lard or foil, wipe the mould carefully, dip it into cold water, and turn the ice on to a dish in the same way as a jelly or cream. (*See Unmoulding Jellies and Creams.*)

**ICINGS (BUTTER) FOR BUNS, CAKES, ETC.**

*See Butter Icing.*

**ICINGS FOR CAKES, COLD PUDDINGS ETC.**

*See the recipe for the type or flavouring of icing required, e.g. American Frosting, Glacé Icing, Pineapple Icing.*

**INDIAN FRITTERS**

*Beignets à l'Indienne*

**3 oz. plain flour**
**Pinch of salt**
**Boiling water**
**2 eggs**
**2 egg yolks**
**Frying-fat**
**Jam *or* jelly**

Sift the flour into a basin with a pinch of salt. Stir in a good ½ gill of boiling water and beat to form a very stiff smooth paste. Leave to cool slightly. Beat in the eggs and egg yolks gradually and thoroughly. Have ready the deep fat, just beginning to haze. Half fill a tablespoon with the mixture, put a teaspoonful of jam *or* jelly in the centre and cover with some more of the batter mixture and drop this into the hot fat. Cook until golden brown, about 3 min.; drain well.

Dredge with castor sugar or serve with a sauce made from jam *or* jelly similar to the filling.

**5–6 helpings**
**Cooking time—15–20 min.**

1

2

3

Jam-Making.

1 Wash and dry jars, and put them to warm. Prepare the fruit.

2 Put fruit in pan and add water and acid if called for in recipe. Simmer slowly till skins (if any) are softened. If the water has been added, contents of pan should be boiled down by about $\frac{1}{3}$ before addition of sugar. Stir to dissolve before bringing to boil. Boil rapidly, with a good rolling boil, to setting point. This should take from 1–20 min. according to the kind of jam, size of pan and the quantity of jam being made. Test for setting.

3 After setting point has been reached remove jam from heat. Add pectin if required. Remove any scum from surface of jam with a metal spoon. Allow jam to cool and thicken slightly until fruit ceases to rise, then stir gently to distribute the fruit.

On following page.

4 With a cup or jug fill the jars right to the top. Place on waxed circles immediately, the waxed side to the jam, making sure that there are no air bubbles left between the circles and the jam.

5 Wipe jars with a clean cloth wrung out in hot water. Cover jars with a clean cloth until jam is cold (not warm); then put on outer covers; or put on outer covers at once whilst jam is hot.

STRAWBERRY
STRAWBERRY
STRAWBERRY

## INDIAN MAYONNAISE

**¼ pt. mayonnaise**
**1 clove of garlic**
**½ teasp. curry powder**

Crush the garlic and with it rub the bowl in which the mayonnaise is to be mixed. Add the curry powder to the egg yolks when making the mayonnaise.

## INDIAN PINEAPPLE SALAD

*Salade d'Ananas à l'Indienne*

**1 small pineapple**
**1 sour apple**
**2 heads of celery**
**Mayonnaise sauce**
**Pimento *or* red pepper (capsicum)**

Peel the pineapple and cut into slices. Peel and core the apple, cut into fine shreds, also prepare the celery and cut it into fine strips. Mix these 3 together and add enough mayonnaise sauce to moisten. Place in a glass bowl and garnish the top with thinly cut slices of pimento, and fine sprigs of white celery. Keep the salad as cold as possible.

**6 or more helpings**

## INVALID CONSOMMÉ

**4 oz. lean beef**
**¾ pt. chicken stock *or* stock made from marrow bone**
**Thin slice of onion**
**Small carrot sliced**
**Sprig of parsley**
**1 bay leaf**
**Salt and pepper**
**2 halves of eggshell**

To give additional flavour: ½ teasp. yeast extract and 2 tablesp. sherry *or* squeeze of lemon juice.

Slice the meat thinly or cut into small dice. Put into a pan with stock, onion, carrot, parsley and bay leaf. Season lightly. Bring liquid to the boil, skim if necessary. Lower heat and simmer gently for 1¼ hr. in tightly covered pan so liquid does not evaporate. Strain through double muslin. Return to pan and simmer for further 5 min. with egg shells which should have a little egg white left in them. This assists in clearing tiny particles in soup. Strain again, re-heat with a little seasoning, the yeast extract and sherry or lemon juice. Serve with crisp toast.

**2 helpings**
**Cooking time—1¼ hr. (approx.)**

## INVALID COOKERY

The doctor's instructions must always be followed to the letter.

Where possible, most invalids prefer their meals to be as normal as possible. Unless on a special diet, e.g. a salt- or fat-free diet, most invalids can tolerate plain family cooking. However, they may not be able to eat all ordinary dishes and they may need extra nourishment in a small bulk since they are inactive. Some dishes may have to be specially prepared for them, therefore.

The reader will find notes on some kinds of cookery for invalids in this book, under various headings, e.g. Beverages for Invalids, Fish for Invalids. She will also find recipes well suited for special diets.

If the housewife has a chronic invalid to look after, she will find it worth while to mark the recipes best suited to her needs.

## IRISH RABBIT or RAREBIT

**3 tablesp. milk**
**1 oz. margarine *or* butter**
**4 oz. grated Cheddar *or* Cheshire cheese**
**1 teasp. vinegar**
**1 teasp. mixed mustard**
**Salt and pepper**
**1 dessertsp. chopped gherkin**
**Buttered toast**

Put the milk, butter and cheese into a saucepan, and stir over a LOW heat until the cheese melts and the mixture becomes creamy. Add the vinegar, mustard, a good pinch of salt and pepper and lastly the gherkin. Put on to hot buttered toast and either serve at once, or brown for a few minutes under a hot grill.

**2 helpings *or* 4–5 small savouries**
**Cooking time—8 min. (approx.)**

## IRISH STEW

*Ragoût à l'Irlandaise*

**2 lb. best end of neck**
**1 lb. onions**
**Salt and pepper**
**3 lb. potatoes**
**1½ pt. stock *or* water**
**Parsley**

Cut the meat into neat cutlets and trim off the surplus fat. Arrange in a saucepan layers of the meat, thinly-sliced onions, seasoning and ½ the potatoes cut in slices. Add stock or water just to cover and simmer gently for about 1½ hr. Add the rest of the potatoes—

cut to a uniform size to improve the appearance on top. Cook gently in the steam for about $\frac{3}{4}$ hr. longer. Serve the meat in the centre of a hot dish and arrange the potatoes round the edge.

Pour the liquid over the meat and sprinkle with finely-chopped parsley.

*Alternative method of serving:* Place the meat in the centre of a hot dish. Arrange $\frac{1}{2}$ the potatoes round the edge. Then sieve the liquid—onions and remaining potatoes—and pour over the meat. Sprinkle with chopped parsley.

**6 helpings**

## ITALIAN CREAM

*Crème à l'Italienne*

**1 lemon**
**½ pt. milk**
**3 egg yolks *or* 1 whole egg and 1 yolk**
**2–3 oz. castor sugar**
**½ oz. gelatine**
**½ gill water**
**½ pt. double cream**

Infuse thin strips of lemon rind in the milk. Beat eggs and sugar until liquid and make a thick pouring custard with the flavoured milk, straining back into the pan to cook and thicken. Allow to cool. Soak gelatine in the water for 5 min., then heat to dissolve. Stir juice of lemon gently into the cooled custard, and add the dissolved gelatine, stirring again as it cools. Whip the cream and fold lightly into the custard mixture just before setting.

Pour into a prepared mould and leave to set. If liked the cream may be poured into individual glass dishes, which may be decorated according to personal taste with glacé fruits or chopped nuts.

**6 helpings**
**Setting time—1–2 hr.**

## ITALIAN PUDDING

*Pouding à l'Italienne*

**2 eggs**
**½ oz. castor sugar**
**¾ pt. milk**
**2 oz. cake-crumbs**
**½ lb. stoned dates**
**½ lb. stoned raisins**
**2 oz. finely-chopped mixed peel**
**¼ teasp. ground nutmeg**
**1 lb. cooking apples**

Make a custard by beating together the eggs and sugar and pouring on the warmed milk. Stir in the cake-crumbs. Mix together the dates, raisins, peel and nutmeg. Peel, core and slice the apples thinly. Put the apple slices at the bottom of a well-buttered pie-dish, add the mixed fruit and then cover with the custard mixture. Bake in a warm oven (**335° F., Gas 3**) for $\frac{3}{4}$–1 hr., until firm and set.

Serve hot or cold.

**5–6 helpings**

## ITALIAN RISOTTO

**½ lb. Patna rice**
**2 oz. butter**
**1 small onion, finely chopped**
**½ teasp. saffron**
**Nutmeg**
**1 teasp. salt**
**¼ teasp. pepper**
**Stock**
**1 pt. tomato sauce**
**2 oz. grated Parmesan cheese**

Wash, drain and dry the rice thoroughly in a clean cloth. Heat the butter in a saucepan, put in the onion, and when lightly browned add the rice, and shake the pan over the heat for about 10 min. Then sprinkle in the saffron, a good pinch of nutmeg, salt and pepper. Cover with stock, and cook gently for about 1 hr., adding meanwhile the tomato sauce and as much stock as the rice will absorb, the sauce being added when the rice is about half cooked. Just before serving stir in the cheese.

NOTE: This savoury rice is frequently used for borders instead of plainly-boiled rice or mashed potatoes.

## ITALIAN SAUCE—BROWN

*Sauce Italienne, Brune*

**½ pt. Espagnole sauce**
**4 shallots**
**6 mushrooms**
**1 tablesp. olive oil**
**⅛ pt. stock**
**⅛ pt. white wine (optional)**
**Parsley stalks**
**Sprig of thyme**
**1 bay leaf**
**Salt and pepper**

Chop the shallots and mushrooms and very gently cook them for 10 min. in the olive oil. Add the stock, wine (if used), herbs and spices and simmer gently until reduced by half. Add the Espagnole sauce and cook gently for 20 min. Season and lift out the herbs.

Serve with fish and meat.

## JAM-MAKING

Because utensils and ingredients for jam-making vary so much, even a well-tried jam recipe may give different results from household to household. The recipes in this book have been thoroughly tested, but the yield, for instance, may vary for different cooks.

The fruits from which jam is made vary in their sugar content and in the amount of acid and pectin (a natural gum-like substance) which they contain. All three substances are needed to make jam.

In general, fruits can be divided into three main categories:

(1) Fruits which are easy to make into a well-set jam, e.g. apples, blackcurrants, damsons, gooseberries, plums, redcurrants.

(2) Fruits of medium setting quality, e.g. apricots, blackberries, raspberries and loganberries.

(3) Fruits of poor setting quality, e.g. cherries and strawberries.

If she has any doubt about the pectin quality of her fruit, the cook can perform a simple test on the juice. (*See Jelly-Making*).

But it is generally sufficient to realize that in most recipes pectin is added to medium or poor-setting fruits (*a*) by adding another fruit which contains plenty of pectin (e.g. blackberry and *apple* jam, *gooseberry* and strawberry), or (*b*) by adding a commercial pectin (e.g. whole strawberry jam), or (*c*) by adding fruit juice rich in pectin, e.g. redcurrant, apple, gooseberry or lemon juice. Fruits deficient in pectin are generally those which are also deficient in acid. Fortunately (*a*) and (*c*) above both help to add acid to the recipe.

### Choice of Fruit for Jams

Choose firm-ripe fruit. Alternatively, use a mixture of just ripe and slightly under-ripe fruits. Never use over-ripe fruit or the jam will not set. There is one exception to the above notes: gooseberries should be hard and under-ripe.

### Choice of a Preserving Pan

*Choose a pan which is large enough. It should not be more than half-full when the fruit and sugar are in because they must boil together without risk of boiling over. A pressure pan must never be more than half filled when ready for pressure-cooking jams.*

Use a preserving-pan, or a pan of aluminium, stainless steel or unchipped enamel (it should be unchipped, otherwise the jam may stick and burn, or the iron may spoil its colour). Copper or brass preserving pans can be used—so long as any metal polish used for cleaning is thoroughly removed—but jam made in these pans may contain less vitamin C. Do not use iron or zinc pans—the fruit acid attacks the metal, and the colour and flavour of the jam will be spoiled.

To prevent jam sticking and to help to avoid scum, the inside of the pan can be rubbed before use with glycerine or with a small piece of butter or margarine.

### Testing for Setting Point

There are several tests for setting point including the simple methods given below. Unless otherwise stated in the recipe, jams are usually tested when high frothing ceases and boiling becomes noisy, with heavy plopping bubbles. If the jam is not set then, continue testing at frequent intervals.

1. *Cold Plate Test*

Remove the pan from the heat (otherwise setting point may be missed while this test is being made). Spoon a little jam on to a cold plate or saucer, and allow it to cool. If setting point has been reached, the surface will set and will wrinkle when pushed with the finger.

2. *Temperature Test*

For this an accurate thermometer marked in degrees up to and above 220° F. is required.

Put the thermometer in hot water before and after use. Stir the jam thoroughly so that it is all of an even temperature. Put the thermometer into the jam, holding it well in. Provided a reliable recipe which gives sufficient acid and sugar is being used, a good set should be obtained when the jam reaches 220° F. Occasionally a temperature of 221° F. or 222° F. will give better results.

3. *Flake Test*

Dip a clean wooden spoon into the jam, remove it and twirl it around until the jam on it has cooled slightly. Then tilt the spoon to allow the jam to drop from it; if it has been boiled sufficiently, the jam will partially set on the spoon and the drops will run together to form flakes which will fall cleanly and sharply.

4. *Volume Test*

In a good recipe it is generally reckoned that 5 lb. of jam should be obtained for every 3 lb. of sugar used. To test the volume of the jam:

(*a*) Before use, fill a 1 lb. jar with water five times; pour the water into the preserving pan. See that the pan is perfectly level.

(*b*) Carefully hold the handle of a wooden spoon upright in the centre of the pan, and mark on it the level of the water. Then empty the pan and make the jam.

(*c*) When the jam is to be tested, remove it from the heat so that the bubbling will subside, then hold upright in it the handle of the wooden spoon. A good setting jam should be obtained when the level has been boiled down to the mark on the spoon handle. (It follows that, when making 10 lb. of jam, the level of 10 filled jam jars should be marked on the spoon.)

*If you intend to put jam pot covers on when jam is cold, cover the hot jars with a clean cloth keeping the cloth from the jam with a spoon.*

## JAM SAUCE

**4 good tablesp. jam**
**½ pt. water**
**Sugar**
**Lemon juice**
**1 heaped teasp. arrowroot**
**Colouring, if needed**

Boil the jam and water together, add sugar and lemon juice to taste, and thicken with the arrowroot blended with a little cold water. Strain the sauce if the jam has pips. Colour if necessary.

## JAM TARTLETS

*Tartelettes à la Confiture*

**Short crust *or* rich short crust, flaky *or* rough puff pastry using 4 oz. flour, etc.**
**3–4 tablesp. jam**

Roll pastry out thinly, cut into rounds with fluted cutter (a little larger than patty tin to allow for depth of tin). Line the tins with the pastry and press in well with the fingers. About half-fill with jam and bake in a hot oven (**425° F., Gas 7**).

**10–12 tartlets**
**Cooking time—15 min.**

## JAP CAKES

**2 egg whites**
**4 oz. castor sugar**
**4 oz. ground almonds**
**A few drops almond essence**
**Glacé icing**
**Butter icing using 1½ oz. butter, etc., flavoured with coffee**

Grease and flour a small baking-tray. Whisk egg whites—not too stiffly. Whisk in ½ of the castor sugar, then fold in ground almonds, essence and remaining sugar, lightly. Spread the mixture evenly over the prepared tray. Bake in a moderate oven (**350° F., Gas 4**) until almost set, then cut at once into rounds 1½ in. in diameter, return them to the oven with the trimmings, until quite firm, and place on a cooling tray. Allow trimmings to continue cooking till a good golden colour and when cold crush with a rolling-pin and pass through a fine sieve. Sandwich rounds together in pairs with butter icing, spread top and sides smoothly with butter icing and coat with the sieved crumbs.

Re-shape the cakes, using a knife, and decorate the top of each with a little pink glacé icing dropped in the centre.

**12–14 cakes**
**Cooking time—20–30 min.**

## JELLIED EELS

*Anguilles en Gelée*

Live eels are usually purchased. The fishmonger will prepare them for you, but if you prefer to do it at home, this is the method: Prepare by half-severing the head and slitting down the stomach. Scrape away the gut, etc., and cut off with the head. Cut into 2-in.

lengths. Put in a pan with sufficient water to just cover, boil for about ½ hr., turn into a bowl and leave to set. If the liquor does not look thick enough, add a little gelatine, but normally it will "jell" on its own.

## JELLIED OYSTERS

*Huîtres en Gelée*

| | |
|---|---|
| **6 oysters (natives if possible)** | **1 gill aspic jelly** |
| | **Lemon** |
| | **Parsley** |

Open the oysters and beard them. Put them on a plate or pie-dish to marinade in semi-liquid aspic, well flavoured with oyster liquor, lemon juice and chopped parsley. Clean the lower (deep) shell of each oyster, put in ½ teasp. of aspic jelly: place a marinaded oyster on top, and pour over a little aspic to mask it nicely. Keep cold until required, then dish up. Garnish with slices of lemon and parsley, and serve.

This should be made some time before wanted.

**6 helpings.—If this is the only hors d'œuvre allow 4–6 to each person**

## JELLIES AS SWEET DISHES

*See Cleared Jellies.*

## JELLY WITH CREAM

*Gelée à la Crème*

| | |
|---|---|
| **1 pt. red wine jelly (clear)** | **¼ oz. angelica** |
| | **¼ oz. glacé cherries** |
| **½ oz. gelatine** | **¼ oz. preserved ginger** |
| **½ pt. double cream** | **¼ oz. apricots** |

Set a 1 in. layer of jelly in the bottom of a quart mould. Stand a tumbler in the middle and pour the remaining jelly around it. Weight the tumbler with cold water if necessary. Leave to set firmly. Dissolve gelatine by heating it gently in 2–3 tablesp. water, cool and add gradually to the whipped cream. Shred the fruits and stir into the cream. Remove the tumbler from the jelly by filling it for a minute with warm water. Fill the cavity with the cream and leave to set.

Turn out on to a silver dish, if possible, and decorate with chopped jelly.

**4 helpings**

## JELLY-MAKING (PRESERVES)

### Important Points

1. Use fresh fruit, not over-ripe.
2. Simmer gently in water (the amount varies with the recipe) till the fruit is tender and thoroughly broken down (usually about ¾–1 hour). *If in any doubt about its setting properties, test for pectin at this stage*, as a good set depends upon the amount of acid, pectin and sugar present.

*Test for pectin*

After the fruit has cooked till tender, squeeze from it a teaspoon of juice. Place to cool in a cup or glass. Then add 3 teaspoons methylated spirits. Shake gently and leave 1 minute. If there is plenty of pectin in the fruit, a transparent jelly-like lump will form. If there is only a moderate amount of pectin there may be two or three lumps, not very firm. If there is insufficient pectin, the lump will break into many small pieces and the fruit should be simmered for a little longer before another pectin test is made. It is a waste of effort to strain the juice and attempt to make jelly if there is only a poor amount of pectin. It is preferable to mix with another fruit which is known to be a good setter (e.g. apple—*see Blackberry and Apple Jelly*).

3. After cooking, strain the fruit through a jelly bag, first scalding the bag by pouring boiling water through it. Hang the bag on a special frame, or suspend it from the legs of an upturned stool *or* chair with a basin below to catch the drips.
4. Never hurry the straining of the juice by squeezing the bag—this tends to make the jelly cloudy. Some people leave to drip overnight, but do not leave the juice too long before completing the jelly—certainly not more than 24 hours. Fruit which is very rich in pectin can be extracted twice. The two juices can be mixed together, or two grades of jelly can be made, one from the first and another from the second extraction.
5. Measure the juice into a preserving-pan. Bring to the boil. Add the sugar. Strained juice rich in pectin needs 1 lb. sugar to each pint of juice. Juice with only a fair pectin content needs only ¾ lb. sugar to each pint.

A thick, sticky juice is almost certain to contain plenty of pectin, but many people prefer to be sure by using the Pectin Test above.

6. After dissolving the sugar, boil rapidly till setting point is reached (about 10 minutes—test by any of the methods for Jam).

7. Skim, removing the last traces of scum from the surface with the torn edge of a piece of kitchen paper. Pour into warm jars (1 lb. size or smaller) at once, before jelly has time to begin setting in the pan. Put on waxed circles (waxed side down) immediately. Cover hot or cold. Do not tilt the jars until the jelly has set. Store in a cool, dry, dark place.

NOTE: *Exact yield of jelly from each recipe cannot be given because of varying losses in straining the juice, but usually* 10 *lb. of jelly can be made from each* 6 *lb. sugar used.*

### JELLY MOULDS, TO LINE

*See Cleared Jellies.*

### JUGGED HARE OR RABBIT

*Civet de Lièvre à l'Anglaise*

| | |
|---|---|
| **1 hare** | **1 tablesp. lemon juice** |
| **3 oz. butter** | **12 peppercorns** |
| **Salt and pepper** | **Bouquet garni** |
| **1 onion** | **1½ pt. stock** |
| **4 cloves** | **1 oz. flour** |
| **1 glass port *or* claret (optional)** | **Veal forcemeat** |
| | **Fat for frying** |

Prepare hare as in Notes on Trussing Hares, and cut into neat small pieces. Heat 2 oz. of the butter, fry the pieces of hare in it until brown. Put hare in a casserole with salt, onion stuck with cloves, half the wine (if used), lemon juice, peppercorns, bouquet garni and hot stock. Place a tight lid on the casserole, cook in a moderate oven **(350° F., Gas 4)** about 3 hr. Knead flour and remaining butter together, stir into the stock about ½ hr. before serving. Add remaining wine and season to taste. Make forcemeat, form into small balls and fry. Gently heat blood from hare, stir into gravy, allow to thicken.

Serve hare piled on a hot dish, strain sauce over, arrange forcemeat balls round dish. Serve with redcurrant jelly handed separately.

**5–6 helpings**

### JUGGED PIGEONS

*Civet de Pigeons*

| | |
|---|---|
| **3 pigeons** | **Salt and pepper** |
| **3 oz. butter** | **1 oz. flour** |
| **1 onion** | **1 glass port *or* claret (optional)** |
| **1 pt. good beef stock** | |

GARNISH

**Balls of fried veal forcemeat**

Truss pigeons as for roasting and fry them until well-browned in 2 oz. of the butter. Place birds in a casserole. Brown sliced onion in butter, and add to the pigeons, together with stock and seasoning. Cover and cook in a moderate oven **(350° F., Gas 4)** for 1¾ hr. Knead together the flour and remaining 1 oz. butter and drop in small pieces into the stock; continue cooking ½ hr, adding wine if used, half-way through this period.

Serve pigeons with the sauce poured over, garnished with forcemeat balls.

**6 helpings**

### JUNKET

*Lait caille*

| | |
|---|---|
| **2 pt. fresh milk** | **2 teasp. rennet** |
| **2 teasp. castor sugar** | **Flavouring** (*see below*) |

Warm the milk to blood heat and stir in the sugar until dissolved. Add the rennet, stir and pour at once into serving dishes. Put in a warm place to set.

Serve with cream, if liked.

**6 helpings**

FLAVOURINGS

**Coffee:** Add to milk, coffee essence to flavour, and decorate finished junket with chopped nuts.

**Chocolate:** Add 2–3 oz. plain chocolate, grated and dissolved in a little of the measured milk.

**Rum:** Add rum to taste.

**Vanilla, almond, raspberry,** etc.: Add a few drops of essence.

NOTE: When using rennet in liquid or powder form, the manufacturer's instructions should be followed carefully to ensure the desired result.

## KAISERSCHMARREN—AUSTRIAN

Emperor's Pancakes

| | |
|---|---|
| **4 level tablesp. flour** | **¼ pt. milk** |
| **4 eggs** | **2 oz. lard** |
| **Pinch of salt** | **Castor sugar** |

Put the flour into a bowl, sifting it well. Separate the egg yolks from the whites. Make a well in the centre of the flour and put in the egg yolks and salt. Gradually stir the flour into the egg yolks and add the milk from time to time until the batter is perfectly smooth and free from lumps. Beat well and set aside for about ½ hr. Whisk the egg whites to a stiff snow. Beat the batter again, and with a metal spoon fold in the egg whites. Heat a little lard in a frying-pan and put in half the mixture and fry until light brown on the bottom. Cut the pancake into 2 or 4 and turn the pieces over and fry light brown on the other side. Cut all the pancake up into small pieces and continue frying until golden brown. Dredge some castor sugar on to a sheet of greaseproof paper and turn out the pancake on to it. Shake well until all the pieces are covered with sugar, put on a hot dish in the oven and continue in the same way with the remaining mixture. Before serving, dredge all again with plenty of castor sugar.

**6 helpings**

## KARTOFFEL KNÖDEL

*Austrian Potato Balls*

| | |
|---|---|
| **1 lb. potatoes** | **A little flour** |
| **1 oz. butter** | **1 egg** |
| **Salt** | **Breadcrumbs** |
| **2 egg yolks** | |

Boil and mash the potatoes. Beat in the butter and add a little salt. Beat in the egg yolks. Form the mixture into balls. Beat the whole egg. Dust the balls with flour, paint with beaten egg, roll in breadcrumbs. Fry in deep hot fat until golden brown. Drain and serve.

**6 helpings**

## KEBABS

| | |
|---|---|
| **6 neat pieces mutton from the leg** | **6 small mushrooms** |
| **3 sheep's kidneys** | **6 small tomatoes** |
| **6 small bacon rashers** | **Oil *or* melted butter** |
| **6 small sausages** | **12 bay leaves** |

Trim the meat into neat even-shaped pieces. Skin the kidneys, remove the cores and cut the kidneys in halves. Soak in cold water for 5 min. Curl the bacon into rolls, prick the sausages and peel the mushrooms. Brush them all (including tomatoes) with oil or butter and thread on to 6 skewers with a bay leaf at each end. Grill for 10–15 min., turning as required. Serve on their skewers and if liked on a bed of risotto (rice cooked in stock in a casserole until stock is absorbed).

**6 helpings**

## KEBABS, CURRIED

*An old South African Dish.* *Sosaties*

| | |
|---|---|
| **1 small leg of mutton** | **6 lemon *or* orange leaves** |
| **1 tablesp. sugar** | **3 onions** |
| **½ pt. milk** | **2 oz. butter** |
| **¼ pt. vinegar *or* juice of 3 lemons** | **2 oz. curry powder** |
| | **Salt** |

Cut the meat into slices about ½ in. thick, place them in an earthenware vessel, add the sugar, milk, vinegar or lemon juice, and the lemon or orange leaves (coarsely chopped). Dice the onions and fry them in the butter, sprinkle in the curry powder, and add the whole to the contents of the earthenware vessel. Stir in a liberal seasoning of salt, leave it at least for 12 hr. (preferably 2–3 days), and when wanted place fat and lean pieces of meat alternately on skewers, sprinkle with salt, and grill under the grill. The liquor in which the meat soaked should be strained, heated, and served as gravy.

**12 helpings**
**Cooking time—to grill the meat, about 20 min.**

## KEDGEREE

| | |
|---|---|
| **1 lb. cold fish (smoked haddock is generally preferred)** | **2 hard-boiled eggs** |
| **¼ lb. rice** | **2 oz. butter** |
| | **Salt and pepper** |
| | **Cayenne pepper** |

Boil and dry the rice. Divide the fish into small flakes. Cut the whites of the eggs into slices and sieve the yolks. Melt the butter in a saucepan, add to it the fish, rice, egg whites, salt, pepper and cayenne and stir until hot. Turn the mixture on to a hot dish. Press into the shape of a pyramid with a fork, decorate with egg yolk and serve as hot as possible.

**5–6 helpings**

**Cooking time—40–50 min.**

### KIDNEY AND BACON CROÛTES

*Rognons et Bacon sur Croûtes*

| | |
|---|---|
| **3 sheep's kidneys** | **6 eggs** |
| **3 bacon rashers** | **6 large croûtes of bread** |
| **4 oz. mushrooms** | **2 oz. butter *or* fat** |
| **3 skinned tomatoes** | **Paprika** |
| **Salt and pepper** | |

Skin the kidneys, remove the cores and soak in cold water for 5 min. Chop the kidneys and bacon. Fry the bacon until crisp and keep hot. Fry the chopped mushrooms and kidney for 5 min. in the bacon fat. Halve and grill the tomatoes and season carefully with salt and pepper. Poach the eggs. Fry croûtes of bread in the fat until golden on both sides, and keep hot in the oven. Reheat the bacon in the fat and add the kidneys and mushrooms. Correct the seasoning and spread equally on the croûtes. Place an egg on each one and dredge with paprika pepper. Garnish each with ½ tomato. Serve at once.

**6 helpings**

### KIDNEY HOT POT

*Ragoût de Rognons à l'Anglaise*

| | |
|---|---|
| **1 lb. ox kidney** | **Salt and pepper** |
| **¼ lb. lean bacon rashers** | **Stock** |
| **2 large onions** | **1½ lb. potatoes** |
| **3 tomatoes** | **Bacon fat** |
| **3 oz. mushrooms** | **Parsley** |

Soak the kidney in tepid salt water for 15 min. Wash well, skin if necessary, remove the core and any fat and cut the kidney into slices about ¼ in. thick. Cut the bacon into pieces and the onions, tomatoes and mushrooms into slices. Put alternate slices of kidney, bacon, onion, tomatoes and mushrooms in a casserole, seasoning each layer. Three-quarters fill the casserole with stock and cover the top with a thick layer of sliced potatoes. Place some bacon rinds on top. Cover and cook in a moderate oven (**350° F., Gas 4**) for 2½ hr. Remove the lid and bacon rinds ½ hr. before serving. Dot the top with small pieces of bacon fat and allow the potatoes to brown. Sprinkle with finely-chopped parsley.

**6 helpings**

### KIDNEY PURÉE

*Purée de Rognons*

| | |
|---|---|
| **½ lb. ox kidney** | **1 qt. second stock** |
| **1 oz. dripping** | **A bunch of herbs** |
| **1 onion** | **1 bay leaf** |
| **1 carrot** | **1 blade of mace** |
| **1 stick of celery** | **6 peppercorns** |
| **1 small turnip** | **Salt** |
| **1 oz. flour** | |

Skin and wash the kidney; cut it in small pieces, removing the core. Melt the fat in a saucepan and when the fat hazes, lightly fry the kidney till just brown. Remove kidney and fry the vegetables, sliced. When the vegetables begin to brown, add the flour and carefully brown it without allowing it to become bitter. Add the stock and the pieces of kidney, herbs and spices, bring to simmering point and simmer for 3 hr. Remove herbs and spices, strain the soup, keep a few pieces of kidney for garnish, pass the rest through a wire sieve. Stir the soup into the purée and reheat it. Season carefully.

**4–6 helpings** **Cooking time—3½ hr.**

### KIDNEY SOUP, THICKENED

*Potage aux rognons*

| | |
|---|---|
| **1 lb. ox kidney** | **1 teasp. salt** |
| **1 oz. dripping** | **A bunch of herbs** |
| **1 carrot** | **1 bay leaf** |
| **1 onion** | **6 peppercorns** |
| **½ turnip** | **1 blade of mace** |
| **1 stick of celery** | **1 oz. flour** |
| **1 qt. bone stock *or* water** | |

Cut the kidney in very thin slices. Make the

dripping hot and in it fry $\frac{1}{2}$ the meat till brown, then remove it. Slice the vegetables and fry them till golden brown; remove them. Put the fried and raw meat and the fried vegetables into a deep pan, cover with the liquid, bring very slowly to boiling point. Add the salt, herbs, spice and peppercorns and simmer very gently for 2–3 hr. Meanwhile fry the flour in the dripping until golden brown. Strain the soup, return to the soup the finely-chopped kidney and whisk in the browned flour. Whisk till boiling, season and serve the soup.

**4–6 helpings**
**Cooking time—2½–3 hr.**

### KIDNEY TOAST—MADRAS STYLE

*Croûtes de Rognons à la Madras*

**2 sheep's kidneys**
**Salt and pepper**
**Cayenne pepper**
**¼ teasp. grated lemon rind**
**1 egg**
**Breadcrumbs**
**Butter**
**4 small rounds of buttered toast**
**Curry paste**

Skin the kidneys, cut them in half lengthwise, run small skewers through them to keep them flat, and season with salt and pepper, and a few grains of cayenne. Mix the lemon rind and a little salt and pepper with the egg, dip the kidneys in, roll them in breadcrumbs. Fry in hot butter, cooking the cut side first. Trim the toast to a size a little larger than half a kidney, spread with a thin layer of curry paste. Dish the kidneys on the toast and serve as hot as possible.

**2 helpings**

### KOHL-RABI

This is a vegetable which resembles turnip in flavour, but is grown much more easily and should be eaten soon after it is taken from the ground as its flavour is spoilt by storing.

It may be served in any way suitable for Turnips, but as its characteristic flavour is in and near the skin, it should, where possible, be cooked in the skin.

### LAMB

The colour of good, fresh lamb meat should be cherry red. But there is a lot of difference in the colour of fresh and imported lamb due to freezing.

Lamb fat should be creamy white. Brittle white fat indicates age, and a yellow tinge is usually accompanied by a strong "muttony" smell.

The skeletal structure of lamb and mutton are like that of the bullock, and the cutting into sides and quarters follows the same pattern.

The **leg** (1) or hind limb is leaner, tougher and drier than the **shoulder** (2). It is also dearer. Both contain about the same amount of bone and both are suitable for roasting.

(3) The **chump**, which is equivalent to the rump of beef, (4), the **loin** and the **best end neck** (5) are all used for chops and all equally suitable for frying. There is little to choose in tenderness, but it is generally considered that the best end provides the sweetest eating, and the loin the most tender chops.

(6) The **middle neck** and **scrag** (7) are both used for stewing, but in the case of the middle neck it is possible to cut two or three chops from the end remote from the scrag which are suitable for frying or grilling.

(8) The **breast** may be either roasted or boiled. If roasted with stuffing to which no fat has been added much of the lamb fat is absorbed, providing a more palatable dish.

Three distinct types of lamb **chop** are available, chump, cut from the leg end of the loin, loin chops proper and best end neck chops. Best end chops are often served as cutlets or **noisettes**. They are prepared by removing the chine bone (back bone) and trimming away some of the meat at the rib end. Cutlets should be carefully beaten so that the meat is uniform in thickness. Best end neck may also be served as a **crown roast.** This is a double neck, i.e. the adjoining pieces from each side of the lamb cut so that it can be formed into a ring. The ends of the bones are trimmed as in the case of cutlets.

### LAMB CHOPS WITH MUSHROOMS

*Côtelettes d'Agneau aux champignons*

| | |
|---|---|
| **6 lamb chops** | **1 oz. flour** |
| **1 oz. butter *or* fat** | **½ pt. brown stock** |
| **½ lb. mushrooms** | **Salt and pepper** |

Melt the butter *or* fat in a frying-pan. Fry the prepared chops and mushrooms, remove them as they are cooked and keep hot. This will take about 20 min. When all are removed, mix the flour with the fat and brown. Add the stock and seasoning and stir until boiling. Then replace the chops and mushrooms and heat thoroughly for about 15 min. Dish neatly. Serve with creamed potatoes and peas. Serve the gravy separately.

**6 helpings**
**Cooking time—about 40 min.**

### LAMB CUTLETS EN PAPILOTTES

*Côtelettes d'Agneau en Papilottes*

| | |
|---|---|
| **6 lamb cutlets** | **1 dessertsp. chopped parsley** |
| **A few slices cooked ham** | **Salt and pepper** |
| **Salad oil *or* butter** | **Grated rind of ½ lemon** |
| **1 onion** | |
| **1 dessertsp. chopped mushrooms** | |

Prepare and trim the cutlets neatly. Cut 12 small rounds of ham just large enough to cover the round part of the cutlet. Melt a little fat in a pan and fry the finely-chopped onion until tender. Add the mushroom, parsley, salt, pepper and a little grated lemon rind. Mix well and then cool. Prepare 6 heart-shaped pieces of strong white paper large enough to hold the cutlets. Grease them well with oil or butter. Place a slice of ham on one half of each paper with a little of the chopped mixture on top. Lay the cutlet on the mixture, with more of the mixture on top and place a round of ham over that. Fold over the paper and twist the edges well together. Lay the prepared cutlets in a greased baking-tin and cook for 30 min. in a fairly hot oven (**375° F., Gas 5**). Serve in the papers on a hot dish. A little good sauce may be served separately.

**6 helpings**
**Cooking time—about 30 min.**

### LAMB PIE

*Pâté d'Agneau*

| | |
|---|---|
| **2 lb. loin, neck *or* breast of lamb** | **Stock *or* water** |
| **Salt and pepper** | **Short crust *or* puff pastry using 6 oz. flour, etc.** |
| **1–2 sheep's kidneys** | |

Remove the fat and bones from the meat. Boil the bones for gravy. Cut the meat into neat pieces ready for serving and put in a pie-dish, sprinkling each layer with salt and pepper, and add a few thin slices of kidney. Half-fill the dish with stock or water. Cover with pastry and bake in a moderate oven (**350° F., Gas 4**) for 1½–2 hr., until the meat is tender. Strain and season the gravy made from the bones and pour into the pie just before serving.

**6 helpings**

### LAMB'S FRY

| | |
|---|---|
| **1½ lb. lamb's fry** | **2 tablesp. cooked macaroni** |
| **1 small onion** | **3 oz. butter *or* fat** |
| **1 small carrot** | **1 oz. flour** |
| **Bouquet garni** | **1 teasp. finely-chopped parsley** |
| **Salt and pepper** | **6 thin bacon rashers** |
| **1 teasp. lemon juice** | |
| **Egg and breadcrumbs** | |

Wash the fry, put into a saucepan with the thinly-sliced onion and carrot, bouquet garni and cold water to cover. Simmer slowly for about 1 hr. Put the meat and gravy into a basin and when cold strain off the gravy and divide the meat into 2 portions. Cut half in thin slices and season with salt and pepper, sprinkle over the lemon juice, coat with egg and breadcrumbs and put aside. Dice the rest of the meat and cut the macaroni into small pieces. Melt 1 oz. fat in the saucepan, stir in the flour, cook for 3 min., then pour in about ½ pt. of the strained liquid. Stir until boiling. Season to taste and add diced meat, macaroni and parsley. Cover and keep hot without boiling. Form the bacon into rolls, fix on skewers and grill or bake until crisp. Heat the remaining 2 oz. fat in a frying-pan and cook the coated slices of fry quickly on both sides until brown. Drain well. The contents of the saucepan should be piled in the centre of a dish. Arrange the fried slices of meat round the base and garnish with bacon.

**6 helpings**

## LANCASHIRE HOT POT

**2 lb. best end of neck**
**2 lb. potatoes**
**3 sheep's kidneys**
**1 large onion**
**Salt and pepper**
**Stock**
**1 oz. butter *or* margarine**
**½ pt. good gravy**

Divide the meat into neat cutlets. Trim off the skin and most of the fat. Grease a fireproof baking-dish and put in a layer of sliced potatoes. Arrange the cutlets on top, slightly overlapping each other, and cover with slices of kidneys and slices of onion. Season well. Add the remainder of the potatoes. The top layer should be of small potatoes cut in halves, uniformly arranged to give a neat appearance to the dish. Pour down the side of the dish about ½ pt. hot stock seasoned with salt and pepper. Brush the top layer of potatoes with warmed fat and cover with greased greaseproof paper. Bake for about 2 hr. in a moderate oven (**350° F., Gas 4**). Then remove the paper to allow the potatoes to become crisp and brown, cooking for a further 20 min. When ready to serve, pour some gravy down the sides of the dish and serve the rest in a gravy-boat. Serve the hot pot in the dish in which it is cooked.

**6 helpings**

## LARDY JOHNS

**8 oz. plain flour**
**Pinch of salt**
**4 oz. lard**
**4 teasp. sugar**
**1 oz. currants**
**3 level teasp. baking-powder**
**Cold water *or* milk to mix**

Sift flour and salt and rub in the lard. Add the other dry ingredients and mix to a fairly soft dough with the milk or water. Roll out ¾ in. thick, score on top and cut into 2-in. squares, brush with egg wash. Place on a greased baking-sheet and bake in a hot oven (**450°–425° F., Gas 8–7**).

**10–12 scones**
**Cooking time—10 min.**

## LEEK BROTH

*Bouillon de Poireaux*

**1 qt. broth from sheep's head *or* bone stock**
**1 tablesp. medium *or* coarse oatmeal**
**Salt and pepper**
**6 large leeks**

Have the cooked broth free from fat and at boiling point. Stir in the oatmeal and add salt to taste. Shred the leeks finely. Add the leeks to the broth and simmer them gently till quite soft. Season to taste, and serve while hot.

**4–6 helpings**
**Cooking time—50 min.**

## LEEK SOUP

*Potage aux Poireaux*

**1 lb. thick white leeks**
**¾ lb. potatoes**
**½ oz. butter *or* margarine**
**1 pt. stock *or* water**
**½ pt. milk**
**Salt and pepper**
**⅛ pt. cream (optional)**
**1 egg yolk (optional)**

Proceed as for broth, add seasoning. The potatoes provide sufficient starch thickening. The leeks should be cut into ½-in. lengths to make sieving easier.

**4–5 helpings**
**Cooking time—¾–1 hr.**

## LEG OF BEEF STEW

*Ragoût de Jarret de Bœuf*

**1½ lb. leg *or* shin of beef**
**2 tablesp. vinegar**
**Bouquet garni**
**2 small onions**
**2 small carrots**
**1 small turnip**
**Salt and pepper**

Wipe and bone the meat and cut into neat pieces. Remove any fat and skin. Put the meat into a casserole with the vinegar and leave for about 1 hr., turning 2 or 3 times. Add the bouquet garni, vegetables, seasoning, about 1 pt. water and bones. Cover closely and stew in a warm oven (**335° F., Gas 3**) for 2½–3 hr. When tender remove bones and bouquet garni and serve hot with freshly cooked vegetables.

**6 helpings**

## LEG OF LAMB—FRENCH STYLE

*Gigot d'Agneau à la Française*

| | |
|---|---|
| **A small leg of lamb (boned)** | **1 teasp. chopped parsley** |
| **1 carrot** | **1 clove of bruised garlic** |
| **1 onion** | **Salt and pepper** |
| **1 shallot** | **2 oz. good dripping** |

Slice the carrot, and onion and finely chop the shallot. Mix together the parsley, shallot, garlic, salt and pepper, and then sprinkle the mixture on the inner surface of the meat. Bind into a good shape. Place in a covered baking-tin with the dripping, onion and carrot. Season well with salt and pepper. Bake for 20 min. in a fairly hot oven **(400° F., Gas 6)**, then reduce heat to moderate **(350° F., Gas 4)** for the remainder of the time, allowing 20 min. per lb. and 20 min. over. For the last 10 min. remove the covering and allow the meat to brown and become crisp.

Serve on a hot dish with gravy made from the bones and the sediment in the baking tin.

**6–8 helpings**

## LEMON BUNS

*See Buns or Cookies*

## LEMON CAKE, RICH

*See Rich Cakes, Large, Various.*

## LEMON CHEESECAKES

*Tartelettes à la Frangipane au Citron*

| | |
|---|---|
| **Short crust pastry using 12 oz. flour, etc.** | **3 lemons** |
| **1 lb. loaf sugar** | **3 eggs** |
| **4 oz. butter** | **Finely-shredded candied peel** |

Line about 30 patty tins with the pastry. Put the sugar, butter, juice of 3 lemons and the grated rind of 2 lemons in a pan and stir till the sugar is dissolved. Add the beaten eggs and stir over a gentle heat until the mixture becomes thick. Allow to cool then ¾ fill the patty tins with the mixture. Place a few strips of candied peel on top and bake in a fairly hot oven **(400° F., Gas 6)** for about 20 min.

NOTE: The above filling (lemon curd), if closely covered and stored in a cool, dry place, will keep for several weeks and may be used as required.

**30 cheesecakes**

## LEMON CURD

| | |
|---|---|
| **3 eggs** | **Rind and juice of 2 lemons** |
| **3 oz. butter** | |
| **8 oz. sugar** | |

Whisk the eggs and put into a basin with the butter, sugar, finely-grated lemon rind and the juice. Place the basin over a pan of boiling water, stir until the mixture is thick and smooth. Pour into clean, warm jars and cover.

## LEMON CURD JELLY

*Gelée au Citron*

| | |
|---|---|
| **3 large lemons** | **1 oz. gelatine (light-weight)** |
| **1½ pt. milk** | **4 tablesp. water** |
| **7–8 oz. sugar** | |

Wash lemons and remove rind in thin strips from two of them. Infuse rind in the milk with the sugar until the latter is dissolved. Soak the gelatine in the water and, when soft, stir into the warm milk. Do not allow the milk with gelatine to boil or curdling may occur. Strain into a bowl and allow to cool to blood-heat. Stir in the strained juice of three lemons and mould. Turn out when set.

NOTE: If curdling should occur, whisk vigorouly before moulding and a fine, spongy texture will be formed.

**6 helpings**
**Cooking time—½ hr.**
**Setting time—2 hr.**

## LEMON DELICIOUS PUDDING

| | |
|---|---|
| **1 oz. butter** | **2 lemons *or* oranges** |
| **2 oz. castor sugar** | **2 eggs** |
| **1 oz. flour** | **½ pt. milk** |

Cream together the butter and sugar, add the sifted flour, grated rind and juice of fruit, egg yolks and the milk. Lastly fold in the stiffly whisked egg whites. Transfer into a greased pie-dish, stand it in a baking-dish of water and bake in a cool oven (**310° F., Gas 2**) for ¾ hr.

Serve hot with unwhipped cream.

**4 helpings**

## LEMON AND GINGER MARMALADE

| | |
|---|---|
| **1½ lb. lemons** | **3 lb. sugar** |
| **3 pt. water** | **8 oz. crystallized ginger** |
| **2 oz. root ginger** | |

Wash and peel the lemons in quarters, cut the peel in fine shreds and place in a large bowl. Cut the fruit finely, putting aside the pips and coarse tissue. Put the fruit with the cut peel and cover with 2½ pt. water. Put the pips and coarse tissue into a basin with ½ pt. water. Soak for 24 hr.

Drain the liquid from the pips and tissue and place in a preserving-pan with the rest of the fruit and liquid. Tie the tissue, pips and root ginger in a muslin bag and add to the pan. Bring to the boil, reduce the heat and simmer gently for 1¼–1½ hr. and until reduced by ⅓. Remove muslin bag. Add the sugar and finely-chopped crystallized ginger and place over low heat, stirring until sugar has dissolved. Bring to the boil and boil rapidly until setting point is reached, approx. 20 min. Cool 5–10 min. Pot into clean jars. Cover and label.

**Yield—5 lb.**

## LEMON ICE CREAM

*Glace à la Crème aux Citrons*

| | |
|---|---|
| **8 egg yolks** | **Juice of 2 lemons** |
| **½ lb. castor sugar** | **½ pt. cream** |

Set the refrigerator at coldest temperature. Beat the egg yolks until very thick. Add the sugar and beat again. Stir in the lemon juice. Add the half-whipped cream carefully. Pour into the tray and freeze ½ hr. Remove, stir and continue freezing for another 1½ hr.

**6–8 helpings**

## LEMON JELLY

*Gelée au Citron*

| | |
|---|---|
| **4 lemons** | **1 in. cinnamon stick** |
| **Sherry (optional)** | **1¾–2 oz. gelatine** |
| **1½ pt. water** | **Shells and whites of 2 eggs** |
| **6 oz. sugar** | |
| **4 cloves** | |

Scald a large pan, whisk and metal jelly-mould. Wash lemons and cut thin strips of rind, avoiding white pith. Extract juice and measure. Make up to ½ pt. with water *or* sherry, but if the latter is to be used, do not add until just before clearing the jelly. Put the 1½ pt. water, ½ pt. juice, rinds, sugar, flavourings and gelatine into the scalded pan and infuse, with a lid on, over gentle heat until sugar and gelatine are dissolved. Do not let the infusion become hot. Wash egg-shells and crush. Lightly whisk the whites until liquid and add, with shells, to the infusion. Heat steadily, whisking constantly, until a good head of foam is produced, and the contents of the pan become hot, but not quite boiling. Strain through the egg white crust and add sherry if used, to the jelly as it goes through the filter.

**6 helpings**
**Time—1–1½ hr.**

## LEMON MERINGUE PIE WITH PLAIN PASTRY SHELL

PLAIN PASTRY

| | |
|---|---|
| **½ lb. plain flour** | **1–2 oz. butter** *or* **margarine** |
| **Pinch of salt** | |
| **2 oz. lard** | |

FILLING

| | |
|---|---|
| **2 eggs** | **2 oz. castor sugar** |
| **1 large can sweetened condensed milk** | **2 level teasp. cream of tartar** |
| **1 lemon** | |

Sift together flour and salt. Rub fat into flour until the mixture is like breadcrumbs. Add enough cold water to form a stiff dough. Roll out and line a deep 9-in. pie-plate or flan ring. Bake "blind" in a very hot oven (**450° F., Gas 8**) for about 15 min.

To make the filling: separate the egg yolks from the whites. Beat egg yolks until thick and lemon coloured. Fold in condensed milk, lemon rind juice and cream of tartar. Pour into baked pie-shell. Spread with meringue made from the egg whites and the sugar. Decorate with cherries and angelica. Bake in a cool oven (**200° F., Gas ½**).

## LEMON PUDDING (1)

*Pouding au citron*

| | |
|---|---|
| **2 oz. plain flour** | **8 oz. breadcrumbs** |

## *Lemon Pudding*

| | |
|---|---|
| **Pinch of salt** | **Rind and juice of 2 lemons** |
| **1 teasp. baking-powder** | **2 eggs** |
| **4 oz. sugar** | **1½ gills milk (approx.)** |
| **4 oz. finely-chopped suet** | |

Grease a 1½ pt. basin. Grate the lemon rind. Sift the flour, salt and baking-powder, and add the sugar, suet, breadcrumbs and lemon rind. Stir in the well-beaten eggs and lemon juice adding milk as required to make the mixture of a dropping consistency. Put into the basin; cover. Steam for about 2 hr. Serve with custard-, cornflour-, or melted-butter-sauce.

**6–7 helpings**

### LEMON PUDDING (2)

| | |
|---|---|
| **6 oz. flour** | **2 oz. sugar** |
| **Pinch of salt** | **Juice and rind of 1 lemon** |
| **1 rounded teasp. baking-powder** | **1 egg** |
| **2 oz. butter *or* margarine** | **Milk to mix** |

Grease a 1½ pt. pudding basin. Sift together the flour, salt and baking-powder. Rub in the fat and add the sugar and grated lemon rind. Mix to a soft dropping consistency with the beaten egg, lemon juice and milk. Put the pudding into the greased basin and cover with a piece of greased paper. Steam for 1½–2 hr.

**4–6 helpings**

### LEMON PUDDING—BAKED

*Pouding au Citron*

| | |
|---|---|
| **2 oz. butter *or* margarine** | **Rind and juice of 1½ lemons** |
| **4 oz. castor sugar** | **6 oz. plain flour** |
| **3 eggs** | **½ pt. milk** |

Grease a 2 pt. pie-dish.

Cream together the butter and sugar until soft. Beat in the egg yolks. Add the grated lemon rind and the sifted flour. Stir in the milk and lemon juice. Fold in the stiffly-whisked egg whites. Pour the mixture into the buttered pie-dish. Bake in a moderate oven (**350° F., Gas 4**) for 45 min., until firm and brown.

**4 helpings**

### LEMON SAUCE

*Sauce Citron*

| | |
|---|---|
| **½ pt. milk** | **Rind of 1 lemon** |
| **½ oz. cornflour *or* custard powder** | **Sugar *or* golden syrup** |
| | **Juice of ½ lemon** |

Blend the cornflour with a little cold milk. Boil the rest of the milk with the thinly cut lemon rind. Strain the boiling milk on to the blended cornflour and stir well. Rinse the pan and return the sauce to it. Just bring to boil for custard powder, boil 3 min for cornflour, then add the lemon rind, sugar or golden syrup to taste, stir in the lemon juice.

### LEMON SLICES AS A GARNISH

*To Crimp Lemon Slices:* Cut thin slices of a lemon, and cut the slices in half. With a pair of scissors, snip "V"-shaped cuts in the rind at regular intervals.

### LEMON SOUFFLÉ

*Soufflé au Citron*

| | |
|---|---|
| **Butter** | **Finely-grated rind of 1½ lemons** |
| **1½ oz. plain flour** | **1½ oz. castor sugar** |
| **⅜ pt. milk** | **2 teasp. lemon juice** |
| **5 egg yolks** | **6 egg whites** |

Butter and prepare a soufflé mould with paper . Melt 1½ oz. butter, stir in the flour and cook for a few minutes. Add the milk gradually, beating well, and continue cooking until the mixture thickens. Leave it to cool. Beat in the yolks one at a time. Stir in the lemon rind, sugar and lemon juice. Stiffly whisk the egg whites and fold them into the mixture. Pour into the mould, cover with a buttered paper. Steam for 50–60 min. until firm on top.

**6 helpings**

### LEMON SAUCE—SAVOURY

| | |
|---|---|
| **½ pt. white sauce made with chicken *or* fish stock, *or* milk and stock** | **1–2 tablesp. cream (optional)** |
| **1 lemon** | **1 tablesp. chopped parsley (optional)** |
| | **½ teasp. sugar (optional)** |

Peel the rind from the lemon very thinly and simmer it in the milk or stock for 10 min. Strain the liquid and with it make the white sauce. Carefully stir the juice of the lemon and then the cream into the hot sauce but do not boil it again. Sweeten if liked.

Serve with fish, chicken or rabbit.

LEMON SHERBET (SORBET)

*Sorbet au Citron*

| | |
|---|---|
| **1 pt. water** | **½ pt. lemon juice** |
| **8 oz. loaf sugar** | **2 egg whites** |

Dissolve the sugar in the water. Boil it for 10 min., strain and cool. Add the lemon juice and the stiffly beaten egg whites. Freeze and serve at once.

**6 helpings**
**Time—1½ hr.**

LEMON SYRUP

| | |
|---|---|
| **2 lb. loaf sugar** | **A few drops of lemon essence** |
| **2 pt. water** | |
| **1 oz. citric acid** | |

Boil the sugar and water together for 15 min., put the liquid into a basin, and leave to get cold. Beat the citric acid to a powder, mix with it the lemon essence, then add to the syrup, mix well, and bottle for use. Two tablesp. of the syrup are sufficient for a tumbler of cold water, and will be found a very refreshing summer drink.

LEMON WATER ICE

*Glace aux Citrons*

| | |
|---|---|
| **6 lemons** | **1½ pt. syrup** |
| **2 oranges** | |

Thinly peel the fruit and place the rind in a basin. Add the hot syrup, cover and cool. Add the juice of the lemons and oranges. Strain, chill and freeze.

**6 helpings**
**Time—1½ hr.**

LEMON WHIP

*Gelée au Citron fouettée*

| | |
|---|---|
| **One 1 pt. lemon jelly tablet** | **¾ pt. water** |
| **Sugar if necessary** | **1 tablesp. lemon juice** |

Melt the jelly tablet in ¼ pt. water. Stir in ½ pt. cold water and strained lemon juice. Sweeten if necessary. When cool, whisk briskly until a thick foam is produced. When the whisk leaves a trail in the foam, pile quickly into a glass dish.

**6 helpings** **Time—½ hr.**

LENTIL SOUP

*Purée de Lentilles*

Make as for Butter Bean Purée , substituting red Egyptian or brown lentils, and including carrot with the flavouring vegetables.

**Cooking time—Egyptian lentils 1½ hr.**
**Brown lentils 2½ hr.**

LETTUCE SALAD

*Salade de laitue*

Lettuce, of the cabbage or cos variety, prepared correctly and dressed with a French dressing *or* Vinaigrette Sauce, provides the finest of all salads.

*To prepare lettuce* 1. Cut off the stump of the lettuce and discard the coarse outer leaves only. 2. Separate all the leaves and wash them leaf by leaf under running water if possible, otherwise in several waters in a basin. 3. Put into a salad shaker or a clean tea-towel and swing them to shake out the water. 4. Leave to drain. 5. If possible put into a covered box *or* into a casserole with a lid in the refrigerator for at least ½ hr. before dressing them for table.

The salads in which lettuce is used as a foundation, are so numerous that it is unnecessary to name them all here.

*See also note under Bacon and Potato Salad.*

LINZERTORTE

Linzer Tart

| | |
|---|---|
| **5 oz. butter** | **¼ lb. finely-chopped almonds** |
| **2 eggs** | **Juice and rind of ½ lemon** |
| **5 oz. castor sugar** | **5 oz. sifted flour** |
| **Pinch of powdered cloves** | **6 oz. raspberries *or* redcurrants, well sugared *or* raspberry *or* redcurrant jam** |
| **Pinch of ground cinnamon** | |

Beat the butter until white and creamy. Beat together one egg and one egg white and add slowly to the butter together with the sugar, cloves, cinnamon, almonds, lemon juice and grated lemon rind. Sift in the flour and work into a dough. Grease a 9-in. tart or flan tin and put the dough in, about $\frac{1}{4}$ in. thick, without raising the edge. Form the rest of the dough into long strips or into a number of small leaf shapes cut out with a knife. Paint the edge of the tart with the remaining egg yolk and stick a piece of pastry round it to form an edge, or using the leaves, stick them overlapping all round the edge of the tart. Spread the sugared raspberries or jam in the centre of the tart and cover them with a lattice of the long strips of pastry, sticking them at the edges with egg yolk or, if leaves are being used, form a lattice by putting 4 leaves together at right-angles in groups over the pastry. Paint the lattice and edge of the tart with egg yolk and bake about 45 min. in a hot oven **(425° F., Gas 7)**. Cover with greaseproof paper if tart gets too brown.

**6 helpings**

## LIQUEURS

*See Table Wines and Liqueurs.*

## LIVER AND BACON

*Foie et Bacon*

**1 lb. sheep's liver**
**½ lb. bacon rashers**
**Seasoned flour**
**¾ pt. stock**

Remove the rind and rust from the bacon. Wash the liver in cold water and remove any tubes or blood vessels. Dry the liver and, if necessary, cut in slices $\frac{1}{2}$ in.–$\frac{3}{4}$ in. thick. Dip each slice of liver in seasoned flour. Fry the slices of bacon and remove to a hot dish and keep hot until required. Fry the liver in the fat from the bacon lightly and quickly so that it is browned on both sides without hardening or overcooking. Remove to the hot dish, placing the bacon neatly on top. Drain off all but about 1 dessertsp. of fat, add about $\frac{3}{4}$ oz. flour and stir until browned. Add about $\frac{3}{4}$ pt. stock. Boil and season to taste. Strain round the liver.

Calves' liver may be used equally well.

**6 helpings**
**Cooking time—about 10 min.**

## LIVER DUMPLINGS—GERMAN

*Leberkloesse*

**Boiling stock *or* salted water**
**2 slices of bread**
**A little milk**
**1 lb. calf's liver**
**1 small onion**
**Rind of ½ lemon grated**
**Salt and pepper**
**Nutmeg**
**1 teasp. chopped parsley**
**2 tablesp. flour**
**2 eggs**
**2 oz. melted butter**

Put the stock on to boil. Put the bread to moisten in the milk. Wash, dry, remove skin and finely chop the liver. Squeeze bread as dry as possible and add to liver. Finely chop the onion and add with the lemon rind, salt, pepper, a little grated nutmeg, the chopped parsley and the flour to the liver and bread; mix all well together. Beat the eggs and mix with other ingredients. With 2 dessertspoons form the mixture into rather small oval shapes (quenelles) and drop one by one into the boiling stock. Simmer for 15 min. Remove and serve with melted butter poured over.

NOTE: It is advisable to test the first dumpling before forming the others. If it crumbles, add a little more flour to the rest of the mixture. It is a mistake to have the mixture too stiff—it should be of a dropping consistency and not possible to form the quenelles with the hands.

**6 helpings**

## LIVER PÂTÉ

**1 lb. calf's *or* pig's liver *or* the livers from poultry**
**4 oz. very lean ham *or* bacon**
**1 small onion**
**3 oz. butter**
**Seasoning**
**Pinch of mixed herbs**
**A few gherkins (optional)**
**1–2 hard-boiled eggs (optional)**
**A little cream (optional)**
**Extra butter**

Cut the liver, ham and onion into small pieces. Heat the butter in a pan and cook the liver, ham and onion for about 6 min.—no longer. Put through a very fine mincer twice to give a very smooth mixture. Add the seasoning, herbs and chopped gherkins or chopped hard-boiled eggs too if wished. For a very soft pâté also add a little cream. Put into a dish and cook for about $\frac{1}{2}$ hr. in a moderate oven **(350° F., Gas 4)**, covering with buttered paper and standing in a dish of cold water to prevent the mixture becoming dry. When the pâté is cooked, cover with a layer of melted butter.

Serve cut in slices on a bed of crisp lettuce and accompanied with hot toast and butter.

**4–6 helpings**

### LIVER PURÉE (SOUP)

*Purée de foie de veau, de boeuf, d'Agneau*

| | |
|---|---|
| **½ lb. calf's, ox, or lamb's liver** | **1 qt. stock** |
| **1 carrot** | **1 blade of mace** |
| **1 onion** | **¼ teasp. yeast *or* meat extract** |
| **1 oz. butter *or* margarine** | **Salt and pepper** |
| **1 oz. flour** | **2 tomatoes** |
| | **Lemon juice** |

Slice the carrot and onion, put the slices in a saucepan and fry them in the fat until beginning to brown; add the flour and brown it. Stir in the stock, bring to boil, stirring well. Add the mace, yeast or meat extract and salt and simmer the soup for 1 hr. Scald, skin and cut up the tomatoes and add. Simmer for another ½ hr. Pass the soup through a nylon sieve, pressing through all the tomato. Mince the liver or chop it finely and whisk it into the soup with the lemon juice. Simmer the soup until the liver just loses its red colour. Season.

**4–6 helpings** **Cooking time—1¼ hr.**

### LIVER SAUSAGES

*Saucissons de Foie de Veau*

| | |
|---|---|
| **1 lb. calf's liver** | **1 heaped teasp. salt** |
| **¾ lb. fat bacon** | **¼ teasp. pepper** |
| **½ lb. breadcrumbs** | **Good pinch of dry mustard** |
| **1 teasp. finely-chopped parsley** | **2 eggs** |
| **¼ teasp. powdered thyme** | **Milk** |
| **¼ teasp. finely-grated lemon rind** | **Sausage skins** |
| **¼ teasp. grated nutmeg** | **Frying fat** |
| | **Fried bread *or* mashed potato** |

Prepare the liver, chop it very finely and mix it together with the finely-chopped bacon. Add the breadcrumbs and rest of the dry ingredients and mix thoroughly. Stir in the eggs and add a little milk if necessary. Press the mixture into the skins, leaving room for the bread to swell. Put aside for 5–6 hr. Before cooking, prick well, then fry in hot fat until well browned, frying the bread in the same fat. Serve on fried bread, toast or mashed potatoes.

If preferred, the sausages may be shaped and floured instead of being put into skins, in which case the mixture should be a little less moist.

**5–6 helpings**

### LOBSTER COCKTAIL

As for Prawn Cocktail, but use a small lobster instead of the prawns.

Garnish with the tiny lobster claws.

### LOBSTER CROÛTES

*Croûtes de Homard à la Diable*

| | |
|---|---|
| **1 small lobster (cooked)** | **Pinch of pepper** |
| **1 tablesp. breadcrumbs** | **½–1 teasp. mixed mustard** |
| **1 oz. butter** | **Grating of nutmeg** |
| **1–2 teasp. vinegar** | **Pinch of curry powder** |
| **Pinch of cayenne pepper** | **8–10 rounds of toast *or* fried bread** |
| | **Lemon juice** |

Remove the flesh of the lobster from the body and claws, mix with the crumbs, butter, 1 teasp. vinegar and all the seasonings. Beat well to give a smooth mixture, and if necessary add the rest of the vinegar. Put on to the rounds of toast or fried bread, squeeze over a little lemon juice and garnish with cayenne pepper.

NOTE: If wished a slightly larger quantity of breadcrumbs may be used to give a more economical mixture—add a very little milk as well as vinegar to moisten.

Canned lobster could be substituted in this dish.

**8–10 small savouries**

### LOBSTER MAYONNAISE

*Mayonnaise de Homard*

| | |
|---|---|
| **1 boiled lobster** | **Salad** |
| **Mayonnaise** | |

Lobster Mayonnaise may be served in any of the following ways:

(*a*) Serve as dressed lobster in the shell but with mayonnaise instead of oil and vinegar.

(*b*) Cut the lobster in half lengthways, scoop out the meat from the body, mix with a little mayonnaise and return. Carefully remove the meat from the tail, slice and return to the shell, arranging it in overlapping slices with the red part uppermost. Serve on a bed of salad, garnished with the claws. Serve mayonnaise separately.

(*c*) Remove all the meat from the shell and claws. Arrange on a bed of salad, either cut into slices or roughly flaked and coat with mayonnaise.

The coral can be used, sieved, as a garnish or for making butter.

### LOBSTER MORNAY

*Homard Mornay*

**2 small boiled lobsters**
**½ pt. cheese sauce**
**2–3 tablesp. grated cheese**

Cut the lobsters in half lengthwise. Remove the meat from the tail and cut into slices, keeping the knife on the slant. Place a little of the sauce at the bottom of each shell and arrange the meat on top, overlapping the slices slightly. Pour a little sauce over the top and sprinkle with grated cheese. Brown in a hot oven (**450° F., Gas 8**) for about 10 min.

**4 helpings**

### LOBSTER SALAD (1)

*Salade de Homard*

**1 large cooked lobster**
**1 endive**
**1 lettuce**
**½ pt. mayonnaise sauce**
**Salt and pepper**
**2 hard-boiled eggs**
**12 stoned olives**
**3–4 gherkins**
**1 teasp. capers**
**12 anchovy fillets**
**½ bunch watercress**

Remove all the meat from the lobster and cut into neat pieces. Break the endive into tufts, shred the lettuce coarsely. Arrange the lobster and salad in layers with a little mayonnaise and seasoning. Coat with mayonnaise. Decorate with slices of hard-boiled egg, olives, gherkins, capers, anchovy fillets, the small inner lettuce leaves and watercress.

**6 helpings**

### LOBSTER SALAD (2) (served in the shell)

*Salade de Homard en Coquille*

**1 cooked lobster**
**Salt and pepper**
**⅛ pt. tartare sauce** *or* **⅛ pt. mayonnaise sauce**
**1 lettuce**
**1 lemon**

Split the lobster, remove all the meat. Cut the meat into small dice, season it and mix with the tartare sauce and a little shredded lettuce. Fill the cleaned, trimmed lobster shells with the mixture. Decorate a dish with the crisp, inner lettuce leaves and slices of lemon and arrange the shells on the dish.

**4 helpings**

### LOBSTER SAUCE

**½ pt. Béchamel sauce**
**2 oz. finely-chopped lobster**
**½ oz. butter**

Mix ingredients together, season and add a little paprika, if wished.

### LOBSTER THERMIDOR

*Homard Thermidor*

**2 small boiled lobsters**
**1 shallot**
**1 wine glass white wine**
**1½ oz. butter**
**¼ pt. Béchamel sauce**
**1 level teasp. mixed mustard**
**Pinch of cayenne pepper**
**A little grated cheese**

Cut the lobsters in half lengthwise and remove the stomach and the intestinal cord. Remove the meat from the shell and cut into slices, keeping the knife on the slant. Chop the shallot very finely. Put the white wine in a small saucepan and cook the shallot until it is tender and the wine reduced to half. Meanwhile, melt the butter and heat the meat very carefully in this. Add the shallot and wine mixture to the lobster meat with the sauce, mustard and pepper, mix and return to the shells. Sprinkle with grated cheese and brown under a hot grill.

**4 helpings**

### LOBSTERS

Lobsters can be obtained all the year round,

but are scarce from December to March. They are cheapest during the summer months. Lobsters are usually bought already boiled, but live lobsters can be obtained to order if a few days' notice is given to the fishmonger. Choose one of medium size and heavy in weight, it is illegal to sell lobsters less than 9 inches in length, or to offer "berried" or "spawny" fish, i.e. when the coral is visible outside the shell. If fresh, the tail of a cooked lobster will be stiff, and if gently raised, will return with a spring. The narrowness of the back part of the tail and the stiffness of the two uppermost fins (swimmerettes) in the tail distinguish the cock lobster from the hen.

### TO BOIL LOBSTERS

There are two methods of boiling lobsters, each method having points in its favour.

*Method 1*: Wash the lobster well before boiling, tie the claws securely. Have ready a saucepan of boiling water, salted in the proportion of ¼ lb. salt to 1 gallon water. Throw the lobster head first into the water (this instantly destroys life), keep it boiling for 20–45 min., according to size, and skim well. Allow 20 min.–½ hr. for small lobsters and ½–¾ hr. for large lobsters. If boiled too long the meat becomes thready, and if not done enough, the coral is not red. Rub the shells over with a little salad oil to brighten the colour.

*Method 2*: Put the lobsters into warm water, bring the water gradually to the boil and boil as above. This is believed by many to be a more humane method of killing, as the lobster is lulled to sleep and does not realise it is being killed.

### TO PREPARE A LOBSTER

Wipe the lobster well with a clean damp cloth and twist off claws and legs. Place lobster on a board parallel to the edge with back uppermost and head to left. Cut along the centre of back, from junction of head with body to tail, using a sharp, stainless knife. Reverse so that tail is to left and cut along head; the stomach, which lies just behind the mouth, is not cut until last. Remove intestinal cord, remove stomach and coral (if any) and keep for garnish. Meat may be left in shell or removed and used as required. Knock off the tips of the claws with the back of a knife and drain away any water. Tap sharply round broadest part of each claw and shell should fall apart. Cut cartilage between pincers, open pincers and meat can be removed in one piece. Remove meat from smaller joints of claws.

Remove the skin and any superfluous fat and place the meat in a deep earthenware dish. Slice the onion, and mix with the vinegar, cloves, sage, peppercorns, salt, herbs and berries. Soak the meat in this marinade for 4–5 days, turning daily. Then put the meat and marinade in a baking-dish—do *not* use a baking-tin. Add ½ pt. boiling water and cook very gently in a moderate oven **(350° F., Gas 4)**, basting frequently. Allow 25 min. per lb. and 25 min. over. When cooked, strain the gravy and pour a little over the meat. Serve the rest separately.

## LOIN OF PORK—GERMAN STYLE

*Longe de Porc à l'Allemande*

| | |
|---|---|
| **1 loin of pork** | **24 peppercorns** |
| **1 large Spanish onion** | **1 tablesp. salt** |
| **½ pt. malt vinegar** | **A pinch of thyme** *or* **other herbs** |
| **6 cloves** | **10 juniper berries** |
| **10 fresh sage leaves** | |

Remove the skin and any superfluous fat and place the meat in a deep earthenware dish. Slice the onion, and mix with the vinegar, cloves, sage, peppercorns, salt, herbs and berries. Soak the meat in this marinade for 4–5 days, turning daily. Then put the meat and marinade in a baking-dish—do *not* use a baking-tin. Add ½ pt. boiling water and cook very gently in a moderate oven **(350° F., Gas 4)**, basting frequently. Allow 25 min. per lb. and 25 min. over. When cooked, strain the gravy and pour a little over the meat. Serve the rest separately.

## LONDON BUNS

*See Buns or Cookies*

LUNCH CAKE

**8 oz. plain flour**
**⅛ teasp. salt**
**3 oz. butter *or* lard and margarine**
**4 oz. sugar**
**½ level teasp. cream of tartar**
**Small ¼ teasp. ground cloves**
**1 level teasp. bicarbonate of soda**
**¾ teasp. ground cinnamon**
**¾ teasp. mixed spice**
**3 oz. currants**
**2 oz. raisins**
**1½ oz. shredded peel**
**2 eggs**
**Milk to mix**

Sift flour and salt; rub the fat into the flour. Add other dry ingredients to flour. Beat eggs and add with milk to make a dropping consistency. Place in a greased 7-in. tin and bake in the middle of a fairly hot oven (**375° F., Gas 5**) for 15 min., then reduce heat to moderate (**350° F., Gas 4**).

**Cooking time—1½ hr.**

LYONNAISE POTATOES

*Pommes de terre Lyonnaise*

**2 lb. potatoes**
**½ lb. onions**
**3 oz. butter *or* margarine**
**Chopped parsley**
**Salt and pepper**

Cook the potatoes in their skins until nearly soft. Peel and slice thinly. Slice the onions thinly across and cook them slowly in the butter in a frying-pan until just golden coloured. Remove the onions and keep them hot. Toss the potatoes in the fat as for Sauté Potatoes. Add the onions to them and mix. Season well with salt and pepper. Serve in a hot dish and sprinkle with chopped parsley.

**6 helpings**
**Cooking time—to fry, 15 min.**

MACARONI AND CHEESE À L'ITALIENNE

*Macaroni à l'Italienne*

**2 oz. macaroni**
**8 oz. grated cheese**
**4 oz. finely-chopped suet**
**Salt and pepper**
**2 eggs**
**½ pt. tomato *or* white sauce**

Break the macaroni into short lengths, put it into boiling water and cook until tender. Mix together the cheese, suet and macaroni and season to taste. Add the eggs and beat well, then turn the mixture into a buttered mould or basin. Steam for about 1¼ hr. and serve with the sauce poured round.

**3–4 helpings**

MACARONI AU GRATIN

**4 oz. macaroni**
**1 pt. white sauce**
**4 oz. grated cheese**
**Salt and pepper**
**Brown breadcrumbs**
**Butter**

Break the macaroni into pieces about 1½ in. long, put them into rapidly-boiling salted water and boil for about 20 min., or until the macaroni is tender. (If not required for immediate use, cover the macaroni with cold water to prevent the pieces sticking together.) Cover the bottom of a well-buttered baking-dish with white sauce, sprinkle liberally with cheese, seasoning to taste, and add a layer of macaroni. Repeat the layers, cover the last layer of macaroni thickly with sauce, sprinkle the surface lightly with breadcrumbs and add a few small pieces of butter. Bake in a hot oven (**425° F., Gas 7**) for about 20 min., then serve in the dish in which it is cooked.

**6–7 helpings**

MACARONI À LA NAPOLITAINE

**½ lb. macaroni**
**½ shallot, finely-chopped**
**1 oz. butter**
**¼ pt. Béchamel sauce**
**¼ pt. tomato sauce**
**1 tablesp. finely-chopped ham *or* tongue**
**2 oz. grated cheese**
**Salt and pepper**
**Fried croûtons**

Break the macaroni into short pieces, put them into rapidly-boiling salted water, and cook until tender. Fry the shallot in the butter without browning, add the Béchamel and tomato sauces, ham or tongue, macaroni and cheese. Season to taste and stir over the heat until thoroughly hot. Serve heaped on a hot dish with the croûtons arranged round the base.

**4–5 helpings**

## MACARONI PUDDING

*Macaroni au lait*

**4 oz. macaroni**
**Salt**
**1½ pt. milk**
**2 oz. sugar**
**Grated rind of 1 lemon**
**1½ oz. butter *or* margarine**
**1–3 eggs**

Break the macaroni into ½-in. lengths and throw into boiling salted water. Cook for 10 min. until just tender. Strain the macaroni and put it into the saucepan with the milk and simmer until quite soft. Cool slightly. Add the sugar, lemon rind and butter. Separate the eggs and stir in the beaten yolks, stir for a few minutes but do not let it boil. Whip the egg whites stiffly and fold lightly into the mixture. Remove the lemon rind. Pour into a buttered pie-dish and cook until brown in a moderate oven (**350° F., Gas 4**)—about 20–30 min.

**6 helpings**

## MACARONI SOUP

*Potage au pâte d'Italie*

**1 qt. good stock**
**¾ oz. flour**
**¾ oz. butter *or* margarine**
**1½ oz. macaroni**
**1 teasp. yeast *or* meat extract**
**Salt and pepper**
**A little powdered mace *or* nutmeg**
**2 tablesp. grated cheese (optional)**

Boil the stock. Knead the flour and fat together. Cook the macaroni in a little of the stock until quite tender—about 20 min., then cut it into ¼-in. lengths. Whisk the kneaded flour and fat into the boiling soup, whisk until it thickens. Add the meat or yeast extract and dissolve it, season carefully, add the mace or nutmeg. Add the cooked macaroni and serve the soup. Grated cheese may be handed separately.

**4–6 helpings**
**Cooking time—30 min.**

## MACAROONS

*Macarons*

**2 egg whites**
**4 oz. castor sugar**
**3 oz. ground almonds**
**1 teasp. rice flour**
**½ teasp. vanilla essence**
**Rice paper *or* greaseproof paper**
**Shredded almonds for top**

Beat egg whites stiffly in a large bowl. Mix the sugar, almonds and rice flour together and fold into the beaten whites, add vanilla essence. Place the rice paper or greaseproof paper on a baking-sheet. Put the mixture into a large bag with a ½–1-in. plain pipe and pipe on to the rice paper in rounds about 1½ in. diameter. Decorate with the shredded almonds and bake in a moderate oven (**350° F., Gas 4**).

**20 macaroons**
**Cooking time—20–30 min.**

## MACKEREL MAYONNAISE

*Mayonnaise de Maquereaux*

**2 large mackerel**
**Mayonnaise**
**Sprigs of tarragon, chervil *or* parsley**

GARNISH

**Tomato lilies**
**Watercress**

Clean and fillet the fish, and poach gently for about 15 min. in salted water. Drain and allow to cool. To serve, arrange on a flat dish and coat each fillet with mayonnaise. Decorate with sprigs of tarragon, chervil or parsley and garnish with tomato lilies and watercress.

## MADEIRA CAKE, RICH

*See Rich Cakes, Large, Various.*

## MADEIRA PUDDING

*Pouding au Madère*

**6 oz. bread, cut into ¼-in. dice**
**3 oz. castor sugar**
**1 teasp. grated lemon rind**
**¾ pt. milk**
**3 eggs**
**1 wineglass sherry *or* Madeira (optional)**

Mix together in a basin the bread, sugar and lemon rind. Heat the milk to about blood heat and pour it on to the well-beaten eggs. Add the sherry *or* Madeira, if used, and pour this over the bread, sugar and lemon rind mixture. Leave to soak for 15–20 min. Pour into a well-buttered mould or basin, cover and steam very gently for 2 hr.

Serve with custard, wine or jam sauce.

**5–6 helpings**

## MADEIRA SAUCE

*Sauce Madère*

**½ pt. demi-glace sauce**
**⅛ pt. Madeira wine**
**1 teasp. meat glaze *or* good beef extract**
**Salt and pepper**

Simmer the sauce, wine and extract (if used) together until well reduced. Season to taste, put in the meat glaze (if used), stir until dissolved; strain and use as required.

Serve with meat, poultry and game.

## MAIDS OF HONOUR

*Dâmes d'Honneur*

**Puff pastry, using 4 oz. flour, etc.**
**4 oz. ground almonds**
**2 oz. castor sugar**
**1 egg**
**½ oz. flour**
**2 tablesp. cream**
**1 tablesp. orange-flower water**

Roll out the pastry thinly and line 12 patty tins. Mix the ground almonds and sugar together, add the beaten egg and mix in the flour, cream and orange-flower water. Put a little mixture in each patty tin and bake in a fairly hot oven (**400° F., Gas 6**) till set and golden brown.

**10–12 tartlets**
**Cooking time—25–30 min.**

## MAÎTRE D'HÔTEL BUTTER

**2 teasp. finely-chopped parsley**
**½ teasp. chopped chervil and tarragon (optional)**
**2 oz. butter**
**1 teasp. lemon juice**
**Salt and pepper**

Scald the parsley, chervil and tarragon, if used, in boiling water and dry in a cloth before chopping. Cream the butter, mix in the herbs gradually, add the lemon juice a drop at a time, season to taste. Do not sieve but spread on a plate and chill until firm.

## MALT BREAD

**1 lb. self-raising flour**
**2 level teasp. bicarbonate of soda**
**4 tablesp. golden syrup**
**4 tablesp. malt extract**
**½ pt. milk**
**2 eggs**
**2 teacups sultanas *or* raisins**

Sift the flour and soda into a bowl. Melt syrup and malt in a pan with the milk and add with beaten eggs to the flour; lastly add the fruit. Pour into greased tins (cake- or bread-tins) and bake in a fairly hot oven (**400°–375° F., Gas 6–5**).

**2 medium loaves** **Cooking time—40–50 min.**

## MARGARINE

At one time, margarine was made entirely from the fat of animals. Nowadays, vegetable fats are largely used.

In many ways, margarine today is vastly superior to that of earlier days. The manufacturing processes have improved and the product is clean and wholesome. The proportion of fat is the same as the average specimen of butter and the keeping quality is superior. Margarine is absorbed almost as completely as butter, the difference being only 2%.

In recent years, the flavour of most margarines has been greatly improved. Some manufacturers add about 10% butter to improve the flavour and texture still further.

## MARMALADE-MAKING

This is very like jam-making, and nearly all the same rules apply. As in jam-making, the fruit is first simmered gently (usually in an open pan) until it is soft. During this long, slow cooking, the jellying substance (pectin) is brought into solution. After this process, sugar is added and stirred over a gentle heat until dissolved. Then the marmalade is boiled rapidly until setting point is reached. The tests for setting are the same as in jam-making.

The essential differences between making marmalade and jam are:

(*a*) The peel of citrus fruit takes longer to soften than the fruit used for jams.

(*b*) Because most of the pectin is present in the pips and the pith of citrus fruits, these are important ingredients of marmalade recipes. The pips and pith should *not* be discarded but should be tied loosely in muslin and cooked with the fruit until the pectin has been extracted. If the muslin bag is tied to the handle of the pan, it can easily be removed before adding the sugar.

**Further Points to Note for Marmalade-Making**

1. All citrus fruits should be just ripe, and must be used as soon as possible. It is advisable, if possible, to order the fruit in advance and to ask the greengrocer to tell you as soon as it comes into his shop.

2. It is not usually easy for the layman to distinguish between the true Seville orange and other imported bitter oranges. Sevilles are considered to have a superior flavour, but ordinary bitter oranges can replace them in most recipes.

3. If a recipe tells you to peel the citrus fruit, try soaking the fruit in boiling water first for 1–2 min. This helps the skin to peel off easily.

4. It is necessary to use a very sharp stainless knife to cut the peel into shreds. Remember that the peel swells slightly during cooking. If large quantities of marmalade are made, it may be worth while buying a special machine which cuts the peel swiftly and easily.

Many recipes recommend soaking the peel, etc., for 24–48 hr. to soften it before cooking. If time is limited, this is not essential. But if the soaking is omitted, it may be necessary to cook a little longer to make sure that the peel is sufficiently softened.

The sugar should not be added until the pulp is considerably reduced and the peel disintegrates when squeezed (about 1½–2 hr.). If this is faithfully observed, setting point is generally reached after about 15–20 min. rapid boiling.

**To Pot and Cover Marmalade**

Always remove the scum from marmalade as soon as setting point is reached. Use a metal spoon.

To prevent the peel rising to the top of the pots, leave the skimmed marmalade to cool undisturbed in the pan until a thin skin begins to form on the surface. Then stir it to distribute the peel. Do this gently to avoid air bubbles, and do not stir clear jelly marmalade.

Pour into the pots, using a small jug or cup to pour easily.

Waxed discs should be placed on the marmalade immediately, taking care to avoid air bubbles under the disc. Some recipes advise putting on the outer cover when the marmalade is quite cold. Alternatively, the outer covers can be put on while the marmalade is still very hot. But do not put them on when it is only warm, as the warm marmalade would make moisture condense on the underside of the cover and the heat from the marmalade would not be sufficient to dry it. Moulds grow readily in this damp atmosphere.

## MARMALADE—USING A PRESSURE COOKER

To soften citrus peel for marmalade is a lengthy process. The cooking time (usually 1½–2 hr.) can be shortened to 7–10 min. if a pressure cooker is used. The preliminary cooking to soften the peel is done in the closed pan. The sugar is then added and the cooking finished in the open pan.

Note that some kinds of pressure cooker will not make more than 5 lb. marmalade at one time. The pressure cooker must not be more than half filled when ready for pressure cooking.

## MARMALADE PUDDING

*Pouding à la Confiture d'Oranges*

| | |
|---|---|
| **4 tablesp. marmalade** | **1 oz. sugar** |
| **1 oz. butter** *or* **margarine** | **½ pt. breadcrumbs** |
| | **3 eggs** |
| **1 pt. milk** | **2–4 oz. castor sugar** |

Butter a 2 pt. pie-dish and cover the bottom of the dish with a layer of marmalade. Heat together the butter, milk and 1 oz. sugar. Add the breadcrumbs and leave to stand for about 10 min. Beat together 1 whole egg and 2 egg yolks and stir well into the breadcrumb mixture. Pour half the breadcrumb mixture into the dish; add another layer of marmalade, and put the remainder of the breadcrumb mixture on top. Bake in a moderate oven (**350° F.,**

**Gas 4)** until the mixture is set. Whip the egg whites stiffly, fold in the 2–4 oz. castor sugar and pile on top of the pudding. Dredge well with castor sugar. Bake in a very cool oven **(290° F., Gas 1)** for about 20–30 min. until the meringue is fawn and crisp.

**Cooking time—1 hr.** **5–6 helpings**

## MARMALADE SAUCE

**4 tablesp. stiff marmalade**
**⅛ pt. white wine**

Heat the marmalade and wine together.

## MAPLE SYRUP TARTS

**Short crust pastry using 4 oz. flour, etc.**
**4 tablesp. butter *or* margarine**
**6 tablesp. flour**
**1½ cups maple syrup**
**½ cup hot water**
**Chopped nuts**

Line 8 tart-tins with pastry and bake them at **(400° F., Gas 6)**. Allow to cool. Melt the fat in a pan, blend in the flour, stir over a low heat until smooth. Remove from heat and stir in gradually the maple syrup and water. Return pan to heat, bring to boil and cook, stirring constantly, until thick. Allow to cool, then pour into pastry cases; chill. Decorate with chopped nuts before serving.

**8 tarts**

## MARROW AND GINGER PRESERVE

**4 lb. marrow (weighed after preparation)**
**3 lb. sugar**
**2 oz. root ginger**
**3 tablesp. lemon juice**

Peel the marrow and cut into cubes, removing the seeds. Place the cubes in a colander over a pan of boiling water, put the pan lid on top of the marrow and steam until just cooked and tender. Place in a basin, cover with the sugar and leave overnight. Next day, bruise the root ginger (bang it with a hammer or weight) and tie it in muslin. Put the bag of ginger into a preserving pan with the marrow and lemon juice. Cook slowly for about 1 hr. until the marrow is clear and transparent. This jam does not give a firm set, so do not hopefully go on cooking it. Stop cooking when the correct yield (5 lb.) is obtained.

When reasonably thick, marrow should be transparent and the syrup thick. Remove the bag of ginger just before the end. Pour into dry, warm jars and cover.

**Yield—5 lb.**

## MARROW TOAST

**Marrow from 2 beef bones**
**Buttered toast**
**Salt and pepper**

Soak the marrow in tepid water for about 2 hr. About 15 min. before the dish is needed, cut the marrow into small pieces, put into cold water, bring rapidly to the boil, add a good pinch of salt and cook for 1 min. only. Drain the marrow thoroughly then put on to the hot buttered toast, season well. Either cook for several minutes in a hot oven, until the marrow is well melted, or put under a hot grill—taking care the marrow does not dry. Serve at once. When **savoury marrow** is preferred sprinkle with chopped parsley, chopped chives and lemon juice before serving.

**6–7 helpings** **Cooking time—20 min. (approx.)**

## MARYLAND FRIED CHICKEN

**1 young chicken (3 lb.)**
**2 eggs**
**4 tablesp. water**
**Salt and pepper**
**6 oz. flour**
**6 oz. breadcrumbs**
**6 oz. pork fat**

Cut chicken in pieces for serving. Wash and dry. Beat the eggs slightly, dilute with the water. Season the pieces of chicken with salt and pepper, roll in flour, dip in the egg liquid, and roll in breadcrumbs. Sauté in pork fat in frying-pan until browned. Cover and place in a moderate oven **(350° F., Gas 4)** for ½–¾ hr. Serve with cream gravy.

**6 helpings**

## MARZIPAN CHESTNUTS

**½ lb. chestnuts**
**2 oz. ground almonds *or* cashews**
**2 oz. soft brown sugar**
**1 oz. soya flour**
**Juice of ½ lemon**
**Almond essence**

Pour boiling water over the chestnuts, then peel. Cook the chestnuts gently; do not let them break. Meanwhile make marzipan by mixing all the dry ingredients together. Work with a wooden spoon into a stiff paste with lemon juice and 2 drops of almond essence. Cut the chestnuts into halves, cover with marzipan.

## MASHED JERUSALEM ARTICHOKES

*Purée de Topinambours*

**2 lb. Jerusalem artichokes**
**Lemon juice *or* white vinegar**
**1 oz. butter *or* margarine**
**2 tablesp. milk**
**Salt and pepper**
**Chopped parsley**

Prepare and cook as in Boiled Jerusalem Artichokes until soft Drain well and shake the pan over a low heat to dry the artichokes slightly. Mash with a fork or potato-masher or rub through a nylon sieve. Heat the butter or margarine in the pan and beat in the purée. Stir over heat until thoroughly hot. Season well. Serve in a hot vegetable dish and sprinkle with chopped parsley.

NOTE: To $\frac{2}{3}$ artichoke purée may be added $\frac{1}{3}$ potato *or* carrot purée.

**5–6 helpings**
**Cooking time—30–35 min.**

## MASHED PARSNIPS

*Purée de Panais*

**2 lb. parsnips**
**1 oz. butter *or* margarine**
**2 tablesp. milk**
**Salt and pepper**
**Chopped parsley**

Prepare the parsnips and cook them.

After cooking the vegetables, drain off any liquid left in the pan and reserve it for a soup or gravy. Mash with a fork or rub through a nylon sieve. Heat the butter or margarine in a pan and beat in the purée, add the milk, stir over heat until thoroughly hot. Season well. Serve in a hot vegetable dish and sprinkle with chopped parsley.

**6 helpings**
**Cooking time—35–50 min.**

## MASHED POTATOES

*Purée de Pommes de terre*

**2 lb. potatoes**
**1 oz. butter *or* margarine**
**Chopped parsley**
**A little milk**
**Salt and pepper**
**Grated nutmeg**

Prepare and cook potatoes as for Boiled Potatoes. Pass them through a wire sieve, *or* through a potato masher, *or* mash with a fork or the end of a rolling-pin. Melt the fat (in one corner of the pan if the potatoes have been mashed in the pan itself) and beat in the potatoes. Add milk gradually and beat well until the mixture is thoroughly hot, and smooth. Season well and add a little grated nutmeg. Serve in a hot dish. Sprinkle with chopped parsley.

NOTE: If mashed potatoes are to be served with sausages, use a little of the sausage fat instead of butter *or* margarine.

Successful mashed potato depends upon the use of a floury type of potato, thorough drying of potatoes after the water has been strained off them, and the thorough mashing of the potatoes before fat and milk are added.

**6 helpings**
**Cooking time—30–45 min.**

## MASHED POTATOES—FRENCH STYLE

*Purée de Pommes de terre à la Pernollet*

**2 lb. potatoes**
**1 oz. butter *or* margarine**
**Milk**
**Salt and pepper**
**Chopped parsley**

Peel potatoes and slice them. Put into a pan, add fat and cover with cold milk. Cook very gently. As soon as they are tender, mash them in the pan. Season and beat well. Serve in a hot dish. Sprinkle with chopped parsley.

NOTE: This is an excellent method for cooking potatoes.

**6 helpings**
**Cooking time—25–30 min.**

## MASHED TURNIPS

*Purée de Navets*

**2 lb. turnips**
**1 oz. butter *or* margarine**
**2 tablesp. milk**
**Salt and pepper**
**Chopped parsley**

Prepare the turnips and cook them as in Turnips—Conservatively Cooked. Drain off any liquid left in the pan and reserve it for a soup or gravy. Mash turnips with a fork or rub through a nylon sieve. Heat the butter or margarine in a pan and beat in the purée, add the milk. Stir over heat until thoroughly hot. Season well. Serve in a hot vegetable dish and sprinkle with chopped parsley.

**6 helpings**
**Cooking time—35–50 min.**

### MASHED VEGETABLE MARROW

*Purée de Courge*

**2 young marrows**
**1 oz. butter *or* margarine**
**2 tablesp. milk *or* cream**
**Salt and pepper**
**Chopped parsley**

Prepare the marrows and cook them as in Vegetable Marrow

Drain off liquid left in the pan and reserve it for a soup or gravy. Mash marrows with a fork or masher, or rub through a nylon sieve. Heat the fat in the pan and beat in the purée. Add the milk *or* cream. Stir over heat until thoroughly hot. Season well. Serve in a hot dish and sprinkle with chopped parsley.

**6 helpings**
**Cooking time—about 30 min.**

### MATELOTE SAUCE

*Sauce Matelote*

**½ pt. Espagnole sauce**
**1 onion**
**1 carrot**
**4 mushrooms *or* mushroom trimmings**
**¼ pt. fish stock**
**⅛ pt. red wine**
**A bunch of herbs**
**4 peppercorns**
**Lemon juice**
**Salt and pepper**
**¾ oz. butter**

Chop the onion, carrot and mushrooms. Simmer the stock and wine with the vegetables, herbs and peppercorns until reduced by half. Add the Espagnole sauce and simmer for 10 min. Strain the sauce, add the lemon juice, salt and pepper to taste, and reheat. Whisk in the butter, just at boiling point; serve at once.

Serve with poached or braised fish.

### MATZO MEAL NOODLES

**2 eggs**
**½ teasp. salt**
**2 tablesp. water**
**2 tablesp. fine matzo meal**
**Fat for frying**

Beat eggs lightly with the salt, then add the water and the meal and mix thoroughly. Melt a little cooking fat in a small frying-pan and pour in sufficient of the mixture just to cover the bottom. When lightly browned on one side, turn and cook the other. Turn on to greaseproof paper and cook remaining batter in the same way. Roll up each pancake and cut across about ¼ in. wide. Drop into boiling clear soup and simmer for 2–3 min.

**5–6 helpings**

### MAYONNAISE OR MAYONNAISE SAUCE

**1–2 egg yolks (new laid)**
**Salt and pepper**
**Mustard**
**¼–½ pt. best olive oil**
**Mixed vinegars to taste—4 parts wine vinegar *or* lemon juice, 2 parts tarragon and 1 part chilli vinegar**

The eggs and oil should be at the same temperature and that not too cold. In summer it is easier to make a good mayonnaise beginning with 2 egg yolks.

Remove every trace of egg white from the yolks. Put the yolks in a thick basin which will stand steady in spite of vigorous beating. Add to the egg yolks the pepper, salt and mustard to taste. Drop by drop add the olive oil, beating or whisking vigorously all the time. As the mayonnaise thickens the olive oil can be poured in a thin, steady stream but whisking must never slacken. When the mixture is really thick a few drops of vinegar or lemon juice stirred in will thin it again. Continue whisking in the oil, alternately with a little vinegar until the whole amount is added.

To store the mayonnaise cover it with damp muslin and store in a cool larder or refrigerator.

To use after storing, whisk it again and add a drop or two more vinegar.

If the mayonnaise should curdle, break fresh egg yolk and beat into this the curdled mixture just as the oil was added originally.

### MAYONNAISE—COOKED

**1 teasp. castor sugar**
**1 teasp. salt**
**1 level teasp. dry mustard**
**Good pinch pepper**
**1 tablesp. salad oil**
**3 egg yolks**
**⅛ pt. vinegar (1 teasp. to be tarragon)**
**½ pt. milk *or* single cream**

Mix the sugar, salt, mustard and pepper. Stir in the oil then the well-beaten egg yolks.

Add the vinegar gradually and lastly the milk or cream. Cook in the top of a double saucepan, or in a basin placed in a saucepan containing sufficient boiling water to come halfway up the basin, stirring it all the time until the mixture thickens like custard. Re-season when cold.

NOTE: This salad dressing will keep well if put in a cool larder or in the refrigerator.

## MEAT

Judged in terms of money alone, meat is one of the most expensive foods. Yet valued as calories per penny or in terms of body-building value per ounce consumed, it is among the cheapest.

It would be perfectly feasible for a housewife to give her family a different meat dish on each day of the year. Although after ten months or so her ingenuity might be a little taxed, she would find after 365 days that the average cost of her meat dishes would be less than the common round of "roast, fried, meat pudding or pie".

The busy housewife who combines running a home with an outside job would also find that many dishes once considered expensive in terms of time and cooking heat consumed can in fact cost less than the ones mentioned above. An oven-prepared stew can be prepared and cooked in less working time than fried rump steak, because, once in the oven, it can be left completely unattended, and it is almost impossible to over-cook it. A fried dish requires the cook's presence all the time.

To understand the problems of meat buying one must realise that the Second World War completely changed the face of the meat trade. Flat price increases levelled out many differences which used to exist between prime and cheaper cuts of meat.

Again, many more women went out to work, and have gone on doing so. Young housewives, too, do many more leisure activities outside the home than their mothers did. Overall, modern women are less inclined or less able to spend much time cooking meat than their mothers.

Dealing generally with the meat animals, we may say that at an early age they consist mainly of lean meat and unhardened or gristly bone. This may be confirmed easily by bending a rib bone from a lamb, readily obtained from a best-end chop, and the rib bone from a sheep, that is, from a mutton chop. The meat from such animals, veal, spring lamb and sucking pig, is of a light colour, is tender and has little flavour. When cooked, it often needs flavouring in the form of stuffings or sauces.

As an animal grows older the bone tends to harden and the growth of muscle increases. There become evident light deposits of fat internally and upon the surface of the carcase. The ratio of meat to bone changes considerably. Examples of such carcases are large veal calves, especially Dutch calves, lamb and small pork pigs. The flesh of such animals is, however, lacking in flavour and may be dry when cooked.

In the accepted British sense of the term, quality is not found in meat until the animal has reached maturity. At this stage fat has been laid down internally and on the surface of the carcase, that is, under the skin of the animal, and has begun to be deposited within the muscular structure itself. In the cut surface of muscle from such a beast the intramuscular fat or marbling fat as it is called, shows up as creamy white flecks and streaks among the muscle fibres. In the well-finished mature animal this marbling will be found in all the muscles with the exception of the hardest worked hind and fore leg muscles.

Such fat deposits are a virtual guarantee of the tenderness of the joint. During cooking they baste the muscle internally where it can never be reached by outside basting, ensuring that the meat will be moist whether eaten hot or cold. The final effect is to add considerably to the flavour.

As the animal ages, the muscle develops more flavour. This flavour is considered by some people to be too "strong". An example is the full-flavoured lean flesh of hill mutton.

Given the principle that the less a muscle works, the more tender it will be, it can be seen that a fat animal is more likely to be tender than a lean animal of the same age. Since it is not economic to market animals which have been fed past the calf stage, but which have not yet reached the greatest muscular growth, most lean meat that reaches the market has been over-exercised in relation to its feeding. The meat is less desirable from the point of view of quality.

One other factor applies to all meat but is difficult to describe. Meat of good quality should feel slightly moist and slippery to the touch. This is of little help before buying as it is undesirable that the customer should handle meat. It can however, influence the type of cooking method used. In the trade such meat is described as being silky to the touch, and if a comparison is made between the feel of say, silk and cotton material it will give some idea of what the butcher expresses when he uses the term.

The hardest working muscles are those which the animal uses for walking, that is the hind leg and the fore shin. Those which do the least work are the psoas muscles or undercut which runs along under the loin bones, and the muscles of the middle back, the sirloin and forerib. Between these two extremes are found the muscles of buttock (more tender than the leg but less tender than the loin) and the muscles of the forequarter, constantly exercised during feeding and therefore slightly less tender than the buttock.

When little connective tissue is found in meat it may safely be roasted, grilled or fried. Connective tissue can only be made tender by a boiling action, that is by the combined action of heat and moisture, by which it is turned into gelatine. The grades of meat between the two extremes will need a greater or lesser amount of moisture present according to the amount of connective tissue they contain.

## Cooking Meat

Palatability is important in all food and of supreme importance in meat. There is today a tendency to look at food as so many calories to be administered so many times per day. This is a viewpoint hardly consistent with civilized living. The discriminating housewife appreciates the importance of the correct cooking of the proper cut of meat.

Two factors influence the final cooked product: the first is the temperature; the second is the time. Meat may be brought to any given temperature by a number of means: by radiant heat (grilling or broiling), by hot air (roasting or baking), by hot water (casseroling, boiling, stewing and braising) or by contact with hot metal and fat (frying).

All cooking methods tend to overlap. For example roasting will usually take place with some moisture in the oven if only from the joint. "Boiling" and stewing although often differentiated are really the same process applied to large and small pieces of meat.

Joints for roasting should always enter the oven so that the cut faces of the meat are exposed to direct heat. A rib, cooked on the bone, should be prepared by the butcher so that it will stand upright. A rolled piece of beef should be slightly flattened on one side so that it will stand erect. If the outside covering of fat varies in thickness, the thickest part should go to the top of the oven.

First weigh the meat in order to calculate the cooking time. There are three well-known methods of roasting meat:

**Method 1** 'Sear' or brown the meat in a very hot oven (**450° F., Gas 8**) for 15–20 min., then reduce heat and finish cooking in a fairly hot oven (**375° F., Gas 5**); see time-table below.

**Method 2** Cook the meat in a fairly hot oven (**375° F., Gas 5**) for the whole time. To produce a juicy joint cover the roasting tin with a lid of aluminium foil, although the outside browns less well than when the meat is cooked uncovered.

**Method 3** Cook the meat in a warm–moderate oven (**335°–350° F., Gas 3–4**). This method, known as slow roasting, is suitable for cuts of cheaper, poorer quality meat.

The following timetable gives the approximate cooking times for pieces of meat. These are not precise, however, since the form and thickness of the meat and its age and condition make the cooking time vary. A square solid piece of meat does not cook as quickly as a thin one (e.g. a shoulder of lamb) of equal weight.

Beef (without bone)
- Methods 1 and 2—20 min. per lb. plus 10 min.
- Method 3—20 min. per lb. plus 30 min.

Beef (with bone)
- Methods 1 and 2—15 min. per lb. plus 15 min.
- Method 3—20 min. per lb. plus 20 min.

Mutton
- Methods 1 and 2—20–25 min. per lb. plus 20 min.
- Method 3—30–35 min. per lb. plus 30 min.

Lamb
- Methods 1 and 2—20 min. per lb. plus 20 min.
- Method 3—30 min. per lb. plus 30 min.

Pork (thick cut)
- Methods 1 and 2—25–30 min. per lb. plus 25–30 min.
- Method 3—40 min. per lb. plus 40 min.

Veal
- Methods 1 and 2—25 min. per lb. plus 25 min.
- Method 3—35 min. per lb. plus 35 min.

### Imported Meat

**Frozen:** Up to and sometimes beyond the point of retail sale frozen meat is solid and needs thawing before it can be successfully cooked. The freezing naturally produces ice crystals within the muscle tissue and damages it. On thawing the meat "drips" and so loses some of its goodness. The amount of damage done by the ice formation depends to a large extent on the rate of freezing. Smaller carcases fare better than large and for this reason frozen lamb suffers much less damage than frozen beef. In cooking either lamb or beef in the oven, basting is essential to replace as far as possible the flavour lost by the tendency to "drip". A hot oven is needed as with other meat to seal the outside, but in this case it is especially necessary to prevent loss of nutritive value.

**Chilled:** Meat is termed "chilled" when it has been kept as near as possible to freezing point without freezing (and hence ice formation) taking place. Occasionally, its fat has a slight odour. This can be masked by seeing that the fat is well salted before roasting. Salting also helps to make sure that the outside of the joint is well crisped.

### Offals

The word "offal" is often connected with waste or rubbish so it is perhaps an unfortunate term for the parts of an animal which, properly cooked, yield the finest flavour and nourishment. The best known offal is undoubtedly liver.

**Liver:** We tend to prefer liver from the lamb, calf, pig and ox in that order. Liver is the only offal which smells better than it tastes. The smell of liver and bacon while cooking is one reason why this dish is so popular.

**Ox tail:** Properly cooked this is a delicacy and, in terms of edible meat obtained on cooking, is proportionately expensive. Ox tail should be cooked until the meat just leaves the bone. Longer cooking extracts a glue-like substance from the bones which merely makes the gravy sticky without improving its already high food value. It also spoils its flavour. Oxtail should be brightly coloured and should carry a reasonable quantity of creamy white fat.

**Hearts:** Those of the pig, calf and lamb may be roasted, Being a hard, tightly packed muscle with little fat to leaven the flavour they are best served (and cooked) with a herb-flavoured stuffing. If ready prepared stuffings are used it is an advantage to "lard" the mixture with a little fat before placing in the heart. Ox hearts are only fit for braising but, carefully cooked, make a flavourful, nutritious and economical dish.

**Sweetbreads:** Butchers often speak of two sweetbreads. In fact "they" are one gland, the thymus, which in young animals consists of two portions, one known as the throat bread and the other the heart bread. As an animal matures, both parts tend to grow smaller and only in oxen does a useable part of the heart bread persist into adult life. Sweetbreads should be used very fresh. The heart sweetbread of the calf is firm, white, broad and rather thick. It is most suitable for serving whole. The throat sweetbread is longer, less compact and dark in colour and is more suitable for cutting into pieces. The pancreas or stomach bread is often called a sweetbread but is a very different organ with a very different though not unpleasant flavour.

**Kidneys:** These have a marked flavour, and are useful for flavouring steak pies and puddings. For grilling, lambs' kidneys are usually used. Pig and calf kidneys can be fried. Ox-kidney should only be used for stewed or braised dishes.

**Tongues:** Tongues used to be considered a great delicacy. Although they can be consumed either fresh or salted, they are usually eaten after brining. The most commonly sold is salt, boiled ox-tongue. It is an excellent dish if not overcooked, when it becomes dry and "chaffy" to eat. Tongues from sheep, pigs and calves can be similarly treated and as they are small can be used as a kitchen "experiment" at very little cost.

**Feet:** Today it is uncommon for the feet of cattle to be stewed into "cow-heel". But ox, cows' or calves' feet can provide an excellent base for aspic jellies. For the connoisseur they provide fine pickings. Pigs' feet or pettitoes are a delicacy but must be eaten with the teeth and fingers. Like other feet they are boiled, but if they have been dry salted they should first be soaked overnight and washed for an hour or so under the tap to remove excess salt.

**Tripe:** This again is a connoisseur's dish. Most generally cooked are three of the four stomachs of the ox. That from the sheep is also popular in Scotland. Cooked in milk with onions and flavoured lightly with salted butter it is a dish fit for a king's table and a gourmet's palate.

**Head:** The use of head meats varies with the animal. From the ox the best known meat is ox cheek. This needs prolonged cooking but has an excellent flavour. The equivalent from the pig is the Bath chap, which is the cheek meat salted and boiled. The most flavourful use for this is to thinly slice it and fry it as a flavour garnish for breakfast or lunch dishes. In summer it is pleasant eaten cold. Sheep's heads are generally cooked by boiling, either fresh or salted after they have been split in half. The meat is stripped from the bones and a brawn of fine flavour produced from the meat and the rendered stock. From all heads, brains are obtainable. A little-flavoured dish, they may be boiled and fried.

**Suet:** This is the hard internal fat of the sheep and ox. Calves have little internal fat and pig's fat is oily and of little use in cooking. Lamb or sheep suet is hard, white and usually carries too much flavour to be useful to the cook. Beef suet however is excellent. Its slow melting makes it invaluable in pudding crusts and in fruit puddings.

**Lites:** These are the lungs of the animal and although perfectly edible they are usually set aside for consumption by domestic pets. Their food value is not great and their sale today in retail shops quite small.

**Melts (milts):** The spleen. It can be roasted or stewed for stock.

**Skirt:** Skirts are properly called offals because they are trimmed from many carcases before sale. There are 3 kinds. (*a*) Thick or goose skirt, found in the hind quarter. Although rather "chewy" it can be fried, or makes a good stew. It also makes excellent puddings. (*b*) Thin skirt, the muscular part of the diaphragm. It is usually stewed, and like goose skirt has a fine flavour. (*c*) Body skirt. The pillars of the diaphragm. It may be fried but will not be very tender. Like the other two, it makes excellent puddings, and has the best flavour of the three.

Skirts are only sold from the ox, those from smaller animals being attached to the relevant parts when they are sold.

**Udder:** The mammary gland of the cow. A fine flavoured food, it has fallen into disuse. It should be salted, smoked and fried, and is then difficult to tell from ham.

**Bones:** A point often forgotten is that using bones is pointless on a small scale. To boil bones occasionally is a waste of time. To cook them regularly, and keep a bone stock-pot going, is a great economy for a large household.

A separate stock of veal bones makes the best of all bases for jellies and aspics.

**Other edible offals:** Tripe is not acceptable to many people, yet it is a good food. Many parts of the stomach of pigs and sheep are, in fact, easily eaten by most of us in the form of sausage skins.

A wise housewife produces in her own oven one other important offal, namely rendered fat or dripping. This is an excellent food. Where much dripping is needed, the following plan can be used. Buy from the butcher some clean pieces of beef fat. Render these in a pan, together with a few fat pieces of bacon until the *greaves* or residue is crisp. When set, the fat (which must have been strained off) will be excellent dripping. (If intended for making pastry, the bacon should be omitted).

For other comments on meat, *see Beef, Lamb and Mutton, Pork, Ham and Bacon, Veal. See also Carving.*

### MEAT CROQUETTES

**½ lb. cold, cooked beef *or* mutton**
**½ oz. fat**
**½ oz. flour**
**1 gill stock *or* gravy**
**Salt and pepper**
**1 teasp. chopped parsley**
**1 teasp. of any savoury sauce**
**Egg and breadcrumbs**
**Deep fat**
**Fresh *or* fried parsley**

Remove all the fat, skin and gristle from the meat and mince or chop the meat finely. Melt the ½ oz. fat in a saucepan, add the flour and cook for a few minutes. Add the stock, stir and bring to the boil; cook for 3 min. Add the meat, salt, pepper, chopped parsley and sauce, and stir over heat for 2–3 min. Then turn the mixture on to a plate, smooth over and mark into 6–8 equal-sized sections. Allow to become quite cold and firm before forming into 6–8 croquettes. Coat well with egg and breadcrumbs and press the coating firmly on. Fry in hot, deep fat until crisp and a good brown colour, then drain well. Serve piled on a hot dish garnished with fresh or fried parsley.

**6 helpings**

### MEAT DISHES FOR INVALIDS

Avoid giving invalids fatty or rich meats. They are difficult for inactive people to digest.

Keep in mind foods such as liver, tripe and sweetbreads, for they have high food value. Concentrate on ways of cooking these and other meats which are attractive to look at. A few green herbs such as parsley often make an otherwise dull dish look appealing.

*See Invalid Cookery and various recipes.*

### MELBA SAUCE

To make Melba sauce pass the required quantity of fresh raspberries through a nylon sieve and sweeten with icing sugar. The sauce is not cooked.

Use as required.

### MELBOURNE PANCAKES

**4 oz. plain flour**
**Pinch of salt**
**1 egg yolk**
**¼ pt. sour milk**
**1 dessertsp. butter (melted)**
**¼ level teasp. bicarbonate of soda**
**1 dessertsp. hot water**
**Lard for frying**
**½ pt. ripe fruit mashed and sweetened**
**½ oz. castor sugar**

Sift the flour and salt into a bowl. Add the egg yolk and beat in with some of the flour. Add the milk gradually and beat to a smooth batter. Stand covered for ½ hr. Add the butter and bicarbonate of soda dissolved in the hot water. Melt a small amount of lard in a pan and cook pancakes in usual way. For each person sandwich 3 pancakes with a layer of fruit between.

Sprinkle with castor sugar and serve.

**4 helpings**

### MELON

There are various kinds of melon served as hors d'œuvres, the cantaloup and rock melon being the most favoured. They must not be over-ripe, and should be served as fresh as possible and above all, very cold.

During the summer put crushed ice round the dish on which the slices of melon are served. Serve with powdered ginger and castor sugar.

### MELON CANTALOUP AU MARASQUIN

**1 *or* more cantaloup *or* rock melons**
**Maraschino liqueur**

Cut the fruit in half, and put it into a glass

bowl or deep dish, place it on another (flat) dish surrounded with crushed ice. Pour about 1 tablesp. of Maraschino liqueur in each half melon, then serve as hors d'œuvres with castor sugar.

If small melons are used allow ½ per person but otherwise slice in the usual way.

### MELON SALAD

*Salade de Mélon*

**¼ of a medium-sized melon**
**Salt and pepper**
**Paprika pepper**
**1 teasp. castor sugar**
**Lemon juice**
**1 bunch watercress**
**French dressing**
**Mayonnaise sauce**
**Lemon**
**Cucumber**

Cut the peeled melon into fine shreds. Mix lightly with seasoning, a pinch of paprika pepper, sugar, and a little lemon juice. Cover. If possible, leave on ice. Toss the watercress in French dressing. Pile the melon in a salad bowl, cover with mayonnaise. Decorate with thin slices of lemon and cucumber. Surround with a border of the watercress.

**6 helpings**

### MELTED BUTTER SAUCE

*Sauce au Beurre*

To ½ pt. white sauce (which may be savoury or sweet) made with milk or water, add flavouring as desired. Whisk an extra ounce of butter into the sauce just below boiling point, a small pat at a time.

Serve with fish, poultry, rabbit and certain vegetables.

### MELTING MOMENTS

**2 oz. lard *or* other all-purpose shortening**
**2 oz. margarine**
**3 oz. sugar**
**½ egg**
**½ teasp. vanilla essence**
**5 oz. self-raising flour**
**Cornflakes**

Cream fat and sugar and beat in egg. Add flavouring, stir in the sifted flour and with wet hands make into balls the size of marbles and roll in crushed cornflakes. Bake in a fairly hot to moderate oven (**375°–350° F., Gas 5–4**).

**24 biscuits**
**Cooking time—15 min.**

### MERINGUE

**4 egg whites**
**½ lb. castor sugar *or* 4 oz. granulated sugar and 4 oz. castor sugar**

Make sure that the egg whites are fresh and contain no trace of yolk, or grease. Break down with a whisk to an even-textured liquid by tapping lightly for a few moments. Whisk evenly and continuously until a firm, stiff, close-textured foam is obtained. Add the granulated sugar, *or* half the castor sugar if all castor is being used, one tablespoonful at a time, whisking the foam stiffly between each tablespoonful. Add the rest of the sugar, folding it in lightly with a metal spoon. Force through a ⅜ in. pipe into small rounds, *or* form into egg-shapes with two spoons, dipped in cold water, and place on strips of oiled kitchen paper on baking sheets. Dredge well with castor sugar and dry in a very cool oven (**290° F., Gas 1**), placed low to avoid discolouring and reduce to **265° F., Gas ½** after 1 hr. If a pure white meringue is required, *very* slow drying is essential, and this may be achieved (if cooking by gas) by leaving the oven door slightly ajar and regulating the oven temperature by turning the gas tap very low, as the regulator will not be operating while the door is open. Drying will take very much longer, even overnight, but the meringue cases will be quite crisp throughout, and will store most successfully for weeks in an airtight tin.

**About 12 meringue shells**
**Cooking time—4–12 hr.**

NOTE: Meringue for decorating fruit dishes may be required less sweet than this recipe, in which case half the sugar is whisked into the stiff foam. The mixture is then piled on the pudding *or* flan, dusted lightly with castor sugar and baked in a cool oven (**290° F., Gas 1**) for about 30–40 min.

### MERINGUE BATON

SHORTBREAD

**3 oz. flour**
**½ oz. sugar**
**2 oz. butter *or* margarine**
**Jam**

MERINGUE

| | |
|---|---|
| **2 egg whites** | **4 oz. castor sugar** |

Sift the flour, add the sugar, knead it into the fat. Roll out ¼ in. thick and cut into fingers 3 in. by 1 in. Prick well and cook in a moderate oven (**350° F., Gas 4**).

Whisk egg whites stiffly and gradually whisk in the castor sugar. Spread biscuits with a very little jam, pipe meringue on top using a vegetable pipe and dredge with sugar. Finish in a slow oven (**310° F., Gas 2**) until meringue is crisp and light fawn.

**8 batons**
**Cooking time—40 min.**

## MERINGUE GÂTEAU

| | |
|---|---|
| **6 egg whites** | **Juice of 1 lemon** |
| **12 oz. castor sugar** | **Castor sugar** |
| **1½ lb. strawberries** | **¼–½ pt. double cream** |

Make the meringue (stiffly). Put into a plain forcing pipe (½ in.) and pipe a round base, working from the centre outwards, 6 in. in diameter. Build up the sides to a height of 1½ in. Pipe the remaining meringue into small shell shapes. Bake in a very cool oven (**265° F., Gas ½**); then cool.

Prepare strawberries, sprinkle with lemon juice and castor sugar and allow to stand until meringue case is ready. Reserve a few choice fruits for decoration; place the rest in the meringue case. Cover with the whipped cream. Decorate with meringue shells and strawberries.

NOTE: The meringue case, if completely dried by gentle cooking, will remain firm if kept in an airtight tin. It cannot retain its crispness for long after the inclusion of fruit and cream. Do not put in a refrigerator.

**6 helpings**

VARIATIONS: Use ice cream *or* fresh fruits *or* custard creams for the filling.

## MERINGUES

| | |
|---|---|
| **2 egg whites** | **¼ pt. sweetened and flavoured cream** |
| **Pinch of salt** | |
| **4 oz. castor sugar** | |

Place egg whites and salt in a clean dry bowl and whisk until whites stand up in points. Beat in 2–3 teasp. of sugar, then lightly fold in remainder. Using a bag and plain vegetable pipe, force the mixture in shell shapes on to greaseproof paper on a baking-sheet. Alternatively, use 2 dessertsp. to shape oval meringues, dip the spoons in cold water. Dredge with castor sugar and bake in a very cool oven (**265° F., Gas ½**). When meringues are firm, loosen from paper and press-in the soft centre; return to oven till dry and crisp. When cool, sandwich 2 meringue shells together with whipped cream. Decorate with glacé cherries and angelica.

**12 shells *or* 6 doubles** **Cooking time—3–4 hr.**

## MEUNIÈRE BUTTER or NOISETTE BUTTER

| | |
|---|---|
| **Butter** | **Lemon juice** |

Heat the required amount of butter till it just turns golden-fawn, add a dash of lemon juice. Use hot.

## MIGNONS OF BEEF—BOURGEOISE STYLE

*Mignons de Bœuf à la Bourgeoise*

| | |
|---|---|
| **1½ lb. fillet of beef** | **½ pt. brown sauce** |
| **3 large carrots** | **2 tablesp. tomato purée** |
| **24 button onions** | **Salt and pepper** |
| **2 medium-sized turnips** | **Butter *or* fat** |
| **Stock** | |

Wipe the meat and cut into neat 2-in. pieces or small round fillets. Prepare the carrots, onions and turnips and cook them in strong stock until about half cooked. Place the brown sauce in a saucepan, add the tomato purée, boil up and season to taste. Fry the mignons of meat in hot fat for about 6 min., drain and place in one large casserole or individual casseroles. Cover the mignons with vegetables, add the sauce and cook gently on the cooker or in the oven for 20 min. If preferred the fat may be drained from the mignons when cooked and the sauce and vegetables added to the pan and cooked on the stove. In this case, serve the mignons on a hot dish, pour the sauce over and arrange the vegetables in heaps around the meat.

**6 helpings**

## MIGNONS OF BEEF—MILANAISE STYLE

*Mignons de Bœuf à la Milanaise*

| | |
|---|---|
| **1½–2 lb. fillet of beef** | **½ bruised clove of garlic** |
| **4 oz. macaroni** | |

## *Milanise Souffle*

| | |
|---|---|
| **Butter *or* fat** | **2–4 oz. chopped mushrooms** |
| **2 oz. shredded ham *or* tongue** | **Salt and pepper** |
| **1 finely-chopped shallot** | **½–¾ pt. brown sauce** |
| | **1 oz. Parmesan cheese** |

Break the macaroni into pieces ½ in. long and drop them into rapidly boiling salt water and cook for 20 min. or until tender. Pour off the hot water and cover with cold to prevent sticking. Wipe the meat, cut into small round fillets and trim them neatly. Fry quickly in hot butter or fat for 5–6 min. turning them once. Drain and keep hot. Add the ham or tongue, shallot, garlic, mushrooms and seasoning, and toss over heat for a few minutes. Strain off any surplus fat, add the brown sauce and stir until boiling. Next add the macaroni, simmer gently for 10 min., then add the cheese. Place the mignons in 6 individual casseroles, cover with sauce and cook gently for 15–20 min. on the stove or in a warm oven (**335° F., Gas 3**). Serve in the casseroles.

### MILANAISE SOUFFLÉ

*Soufflé à la Milanaise*

| | |
|---|---|
| **2 lemons** | **½ oz. gelatine** |
| **3–4 eggs, according to size** | **¼ pt. water** |
| **5 oz. castor sugar** | **½ pt. double cream** |

DECORATION

**Chopped pistachio nuts**

Wash lemons, dry, and grate rind finely. Whisk the egg yolks, sugar, rind and lemon juice over hot water until thick and creamy, then remove bowl from the hot water and continue whisking until cool. Soften the gelatine in the ¼ pt. water, and heat to dissolve. Half-whip the cream. Whisk the egg whites very stiffly. Add the gelatine, steaming hot, in a thin stream, to the egg mixture, and stir in. Fold in the cream and the stiffly-whipped whites. Fold the mixture very lightly until setting is imminent—the mixture pulls against the spoon. Pour into the soufflé dish and leave to set. Remove the paper band by coaxing it away from the mixture with a knife dipped in hot water. Decorate the sides with chopped, blanched pistachio nuts, and the top with piped cream, if liked.

**6 helpings**
**Setting time—2 hr.**

### MILK

Milk has often been described as the only substance created by Nature solely for use as a food. Its value, especially for children, is unquestioned.

Cow's milk is the kind most widely known and used in this country, so it is the kind dealt with here.

A cow's milk is of course intended for young calves. A young calf is not exactly like a young human being because their needs vary. So cow's milk is not a perfect food for human beings. For instance, milk contains very little iron, and its Vitamin C content is gradually destroyed soon after leaving the cow. However, cow's milk is just about the *best* single food for human beings.

Since milk is our principal source of calcium, authorities recommend a daily intake of 1 pint for adults, 1–1½ pints for children, and 1½ pints or more for teenagers.

Besides its nutritional qualities, milk contains a number of harmless bacteria. These include the bacteria which bring about souring. Besides these harmless bacteria, milk can also house dangerously destructive bacteria. So it is essential to take great care to make sure that all milk is pure and clean.

Both harmless and harmful bacteria thrive in warm conditions although destroyed by heat treatment. Milk should therefore be kept cool. Pasteurized milk has been heat treated, to make it "safe". But the housewife may be wise to boil unpasteurized milk in hot weather.

#### Grades of Milk

There are a number of grades of milk and their retail prices are fixed by the Government. The designation depends on two factors—the butterfat content and the hygienic quality. The former must be at least 3% for most grades.

**Pasteurized Milk** has been heated in order to destroy all harmful germs without affecting the flavour. This is the most usual grade supplied.

**Homogenized Milk** has been heat-treated and processed so as to break up the fat into such tiny particles that they do not rise to the top to form a cream-line. It has a richer, creamier taste all the way through and is very good for milk puddings.

**Sterilized Milk** is simply homogenized milk which has been bottled and heat-treated at a higher temperature to ensure that it will keep (while still sealed) for at least seven days.

**T.T. Milk** comes from cows of any breed which have passed the tuberculin test. It is of good hygienic quality.

**Buttermilk** is the by-product from the churning of sour cream into butter. It is usually pasteurized and has a similar "solids not fat" content to that of whole milk. Its fat content however is between 0·1 and 1·5%.

**Skim Milk** is milk from which the cream has been removed—thus reducing its butterfat content to somewhere in the region of 0·1%.

**Kosher** *or* **Kedassiah Milk** is specially prepared in accordance with Jewish practice.

**Evaporated Milk** is milk from which approximately ½ the water has been removed by heat. After evaporation it is homogenized, canned and sterilized.

**Condensed Milk** is also heat-treated to remove much of the water but sugar is added so that the finished product contains about 42% sugar. This acts as a preservative and it is not necessary to apply heat-treatment after canning.

**Dried Milk** has been so treated that practically all the moisture (about 95–98%) has been removed and the milk becomes a powder. It may be made from whole or skimmed milk. It will keep for a much longer time but, once it has been opened, care should be taken to see that the lid is always replaced. After reconstitution, evaporated, condensed and dried milks require the same care as fresh milk.

**Yoghourt and Smetana** are what is known as "cultured" milk. They are slightly tart in flavour, and make an excellent dessert either plain or flavoured with fruit.

**Care of Milk in the Home**

Never let milk stay outside. Its quality is soon affected if it is left in a warm, sunny spot Put it in a refrigerator or a cool place as soon as possible after is it delivered. If you have no refrigerator, it is a good idea to stand the bottles in a basin of cold water, covered with a damp piece of muslin.

Milk should be kept in the dark because sunlight destroys some of its important vitamins and tends to spoil its flavour. It should also be kept covered because an open bottle or jug soon picks up dust and germs and because milk has a tendency to absorb flavours and odours from other food.

The best place to keep milk is in the bottle but, once it has been poured into a glass or jug for table use, it should not be returned to the bottle. One day's milk should not be mixed with milk from the day before and milk jugs should have wide tops so that they are easy to clean.

It is not often realized that it is illegal to use milk bottles for anything but milk. They belong to the dairy and should be rinsed in cold water as soon as they are empty and put out for collection by the milkman.

**Use of Milk**

Milk in any form is very easily digested.

Apart from this, one of the chief values of milk is in the infinite number of ways in which it can be used and served by the cook. Furthermore, there is no waste because every drop can be utilized in both sweet and savoury dishes as well as for drinking purposes.

## MILK BREAD

**Basic Recipe**

| | |
|---|---|
| **1 lb. plain flour** | **2 oz. lard** *or* **margarine** |
| **1 teasp. salt** | **½ pt. warm milk (approx.)** |
| **½ oz. yeast** | |
| **½ teasp. sugar** | **1 egg (optional)** |

Mix the salt with the warmed flour, cream the yeast with the sugar. Rub fat into flour and mix with the yeast, milk and egg if used, to a fairly soft, light dough. Beat until mixture is smooth and leaves the sides of the basin clean. **Allow to stand in a warm place till twice its** original size. Proceed as for White Bread or see following recipe.

**Variations**

**Bread Plait**

**1 lb. plain flour, etc., as for Milk Bread**

Roll risen dough into two strips, each 10 in. long by 5 in. or 6 in. wide. Cut each strip almost to the top in three even-sized pieces and plait them as if plaiting hair. Damp and seal the ends neatly but firmly and place on a greased baking-sheet. Allow to prove 10–15 min. Brush with egg wash and place in a hot oven (**450° F., Gas 8**). Bake 20–30 min., reducing heat after first 10 min. to **400° F., Gas 6** or **375° F., Gas 5.**

**2 loaves**
**Cooking time—20–30 min.**

## MILK CHOCOLATE SOUFFLÉ

*Soufflé au Chocolat*

| | |
|---|---|
| **2 eggs** | **2 oz. milk chocolate** |
| **2 oz. sugar** | **½ oz. gelatine** |
| **12 tablesp. evaporated milk** | **4 tablesp. warm water** |

DECORATION

**Whipped cream**

Put the yolks of the eggs and sugar in a double saucepan, and whisk until thick and creamy. Whip the evaporated milk until thick, and add to the eggs and sugar. Melt the chocolate over very gentle heat, add to the egg and sugar mixture. Put the gelatine in the warm water and heat to dissolve; then stir it into the chocolate mixture. Whip up the egg-whites stiffly and stir into the chocolate mixture. Put into the prepared soufflé case. When set, remove the paper carefully, and decorate the top with cream.

**6 helpings**
**Setting time—2 hr.**

## MILK JELLY

| | |
|---|---|
| **½ pt. milk** | **1 level dessertsp. powdered gelatine** |
| **Thinly-cut rind of ½ lemon** | **½ gill water** |
| **1 oz. sugar** | |

Simmer milk with the lemon rind and sugar for a few minutes, then cool. Soften gelatine in 1 tablesp. cold water. Add rest of water (*boiling*). Stir until gelatine is dissolved then cool slightly. Strain milk over gelatine. Stir until dissolved. Pour into 2 sundae glasses or rinsed moulds and allow to set.

This method entirely prevents milk curdling.

**2 individual jellies**
**Cooking time—5 min. (approx.)**

## MILK PUDDINGS

Milk puddings are sweets made with a starch, sugar and milk. Eggs are sometimes added, and some suitable flavouring such as grated orange or lemon rind, grated nutmeg, ground cinnamon or flavouring essences. Bay leaf, orange or lemon rind can be infused in the milk, but they are removed before serving unless the rind is finely grated. If a vanilla pod is available, it can be stored in a jar of sugar and the flavoured sugar can be used as required.

*Skimmed and dried milk* can be used for making milk puddings, and ½–1 oz. butter or suet added to each pint of milk will make up the deficiency of fat. If *sweetened condensed milk* is used the amount of sugar in the recipe should be decreased accordingly. *Evaporated* and *condensed milks* should be made up to the equivalent of fresh milk by following the directions on the tin.

The addition of egg to a milk pudding increases its nutritive value and the pudding is made much lighter if the whites are whisked before being added. Egg must not be added until the grain is fully cooked or the prolonged cooking needed to cook the grain will overcook the eggs and make them curdle. Baking for about 30 min. in a warm oven (**335° F., Gas 3**) is usually long enough to cook the eggs and brown the top of a one pint pudding.

A boiled or baked milk pudding will just flow over the plate when served. This is achieved by using the correct quantities of ingredients, and by long, slow cooking. Slow cooking prevents too much evaporation. Extra milk can sometimes be added, if the mixture becomes too thick.

### Steamed Milk Puddings

Boiling and baking are the commonest methods by which milk puddings are made. But they can also be steamed and unmoulded, provided they contain at least two eggs to each pint of liquid, as well as the farinaceous ingredient. The basin or mould must be well greased and covered.

### General Hints on Making Milk Puddings

1. Avoid using a thin saucepan. Rinse out the pan with cold water before using, *or* grease it with butter to lessen risk of burning.
2. Puddings cooked in a saucepan must be stirred well from the bottom of the pan and only just allowed to simmer.
3. If a double saucepan is used, little attention is required, but the pudding will take longer to cook.
4. A pinch of salt added to all puddings improves the flavour.
5. Finely-shredded suet, *or* flakes of butter *or* margarine, put on top of baked puddings improves the flavour and also increases the fat content.
6. Grease the pie-dish to facilitate cleaning afterwards.
7. In puddings where eggs are included, the mixture must be cooled slightly before the egg yolks are added.
8. For instructions for making meringue *see Meringues.*

### Flavourings

**Ground cinnamon:** Sprinkle on top of large grain puddings *or* mix with any type of milk pudding.

**Nutmeg:** Grate on top of large grain milk puddings and baked puddings.

**Lemon** *or* **orange rind:** Cut thin strips of lemon *or* orange rind, avoiding white pith. Add at commencement of cooking and remove before serving.

**Lemon** *or* **orange rind (grated):** Add to milk pudding just before serving.

**Dried fruit:** Sultanas, seedless and stoned raisins, chopped dates and finely-chopped candied peel can be added to all puddings at commencement of cooking.

**Essences:** Add to small- and powdered-grain puddings at the end of boiling.

**Cocoa:** Blend first with a little of the milk; then add to the rest of the milk. Extra sugar may be required.

**Chocolate:** Grate plain chocolate and dissolve in a little warm milk, add to rest of milk.

## MILK SHAKES

**1 pt. milk**
**2 scoops ice cream**
**2 teasp. flavouring; fruit syrup *or* coffee essence**

*Method 1.*

Stir the flavouring into the milk; add the ice cream just before serving.

*Method 2.*

Mix together all the ingredients; chill. Remove from refrigerator, beat thoroughly and serve whilst still frothing.

**2 glasses.**

## MILK SOUP WITH ONION

**1 Spanish onion *or* 3 medium-sized onions**
**¾ oz. butter *or* other fat**
**¾ oz. flour *or* rice**
**1 pt. milk**
**1 bay leaf**
**1 clove**
**1 blade of mace**
**A little grated lemon rind**
**Salt and pepper**
**2 tablesp. sherry (optional)**

Melt the fat in a deep pan and cook the finely-chopped onion gently for 10 min. Sprinkle and stir in the flour, add the milk and boil. Add the spices and lemon rind; simmer till the onion is just tender. Season and add sherry (if used) before serving.

NOTE: If rice is used add it instead of the flour and cook it in the soup.

**4 helpings**
**Cooking time—about ¾ hr.**

## MILLE-FEUILLE GÂTEAU

**Puff pastry using ½–¾ lb. flour, etc.**
**2–3 tablesp. jam—strawberry *or* raspberry *or* apricot**
**½ pt. double cream *or* custard cream as used for vanilla cream**
**4 oz. icing sugar for glacé icing**

DECORATION, selection of:

**Glacé cherries**
**Shredded almonds**
**Grated chocolate**
**Pistachio nuts**
**Walnuts**
**Candied fruits**

Roll out pastry ⅛ in. thick and cut into 7–8 rounds with a cake tin *or* plate. Rinse baking sheets with cold water, place pastry on damp surface, prick well. Bake in a very hot oven **(450° F., Gas 8)**—about 6 in. from the top —for 10 min. approximately, until golden brown and crisp. Lift off carefully and cool on a rack. Spread thinly with jam and whipped cream; place layer upon layer, without pressure. Ice the top with thick glacé icing. Decorate with chosen fruits *or* nuts.

**6 helpings**

VARIATIONS: Fresh *or* canned fruits, such as pineapple, apricots, mandarin oranges, guavas, may be used. Chop and mix with the cream filling, reserving choice pieces for top decoration.

## MINCE PIES

**Short crust, rich short crust, flaky, rough puff *or* puff pastry using 6 oz. flour, etc.**
**10–12 oz. mincemeat**
**Castor *or* icing sugar**

Roll the pastry out to about ⅛ in. thickness. Cut half of it into rounds of about 2½ in. diameter and reserve these for lids. (Use a plain cutter for flaky, rough puff or puff pastry.) Cut the remaining pastry into rounds of about 3 in. diameter and line some patty tins. Place some mincemeat in the tins, brush the edge of the pastry with water and place a lid on top of each. Press the edges well together; if a plain cutter has been used knock up the edges. Brush the tops with water and sprinkle with sugar. Make a hole or 2 small cuts in the top of each. Bake in a hot oven **(450°–425° F., Gas 8–7)** depending on the type of pastry, for 25–30 min.

Dredge tops with castor sugar *or* icing sugar. Serve hot or cold.

**8–10 pies**

## MINCEMEAT

**1 lb. cooking apples (prepared weight) finely chopped**
**1 lb. currants, cleaned and picked**
**1 lb. beef suet, finely chopped**
**1 lb. large raisins, stoned and quartered**
**½ lb. sultanas, halved**
**1 lb. demerara sugar**
**2 oz. almonds, blanched and finely chopped**
**½ gill rum**
**2 oz. each candied lemon, orange and citron peel, all finely chopped**
**Grated rind and juice of 2 large lemons**
**½ nutmeg, finely grated**
**¼ level teasp. each ground cloves and cinnamon**
**⅛ teasp. each ground mace and ginger**
**½ level teasp. salt**
**¼ pt. brandy**

Mix all the prepared ingredients together, stirring well, and cover closely in clean dry jars. Keep for 2 or 3 weeks to allow to mellow before using.

## MINT JELLY

**3 lb. green apples**
**1⅛ pt. water**
**A small bunch of fresh mint**
**1⅛ pt. vinegar**
**Sugar**
**3 level tablesp. chopped mint**
**A few drops of green colouring**

Wash the apples, cut in quarters and place in a preserving-pan with the water and the bunch of mint. Simmer until the apples are soft and pulpy, then add the vinegar and boil for 5 min. Strain overnight through a cloth, measure the juice and to each pint, allow 1 lb. sugar. Put the juice and sugar into the pan and bring to the boil, stirring until the sugar is dissolved. Boil rapidly until setting point is nearly reached, add the chopped mint and colouring, then boil until setting point is reached. Pour into hot jars and cover immediately with waxed discs. When quite cold, tie down with parchment or transparent covers, label and store.

## MINCED BEEF AND POACHED EGGS

*Emince de Bœuf aux Œufs poches*

**½ lb. under-done roast beef**
**½ oz. butter**
**1 small onion**
**½ oz. flour**
**¼ pt. gravy *or* stock**
**½ teasp. mushroom ketchup, Worcester sauce *or* vinegar**
**Salt and pepper**
**2 eggs**
**Toast**

Mince or cut the meat into dice. Melt the butter in a saucepan and fry the finely-chopped onion until lightly browned. Sprinkle in the flour and brown slightly, then add the gravy or stock and boil for 2–3 min. Add the meat, ketchup, sauce or vinegar, season with salt and pepper, and keep hot without boiling for 10–15 min. Meanwhile poach the eggs and cut the toast into small triangles. Turn the mince on to a hot dish, place the eggs on top and place the pieces of toast round the base.

**2 helpings**

### MINESTRONE ALLA CASALINGA

Minestrone

**2 slices unsmoked bacon**
**1 clove garlic (optional)**
**1 oz. butter**
**1 small onion**
**3 oz. butter *or* haricot beans (previously soaked for at least 12 hr.)**
**12 sticks of celery**
**2 oz. French beans**
**1 large carrot**
**3 potatoes**
**3 pt. water *or* stock**
**1 bay leaf**
**Salt**
**½ small white cabbage**
**2 oz. rice *or* cut macaroni**
**Grated Parmesan cheese**

Chop the bacon and crush the garlic; put into a saucepan with the butter, add the chopped onion and fry together lightly. Next add all the other vegetables (except cabbage) cut up small and toss them in the saucepan, add water or stock, bay leaf and salt to taste. Bring to the boil; add shredded cabbage, simmer for 1 hr., add the rice *or* macaroni, cook until tender. Serve hot with grated Parmesan cheese.

### MINESTRONE—ITALIAN

**¼ lb. haricot beans**
**3 pt. water**
**2 onions**
**1–2 cloves of garlic**
**1 oz. lean bacon scraps**
**2 tablesp. olive oil**
**A bunch of herbs**
**2 large tomatoes**
**1 glass red wine**
**2 carrots**
**1 small turnip**
**2 sticks of celery**
**2 small potatoes**
**½ small cabbage**
**2 oz. macaroni *or* fancy shapes of Italian paste**
**Salt and pepper**
**Grated cheese**

Soak the beans overnight in ½ pt. of the water. Slice the onions, crush the garlic, chop the bacon. Heat the oil in a deep pan and fry the onions very gently for 10 min. Add the garlic, bacon, herbs, cut-up tomatoes and the wine. Reduce this mixture by rapid boiling for 5 min. Add the haricot beans and all

the water and simmer for 2 hr. Dice the carrots, turnip and celery and add them to the soup; simmer for a further ½ hr. Add the potatoes, diced, and simmer for another ½ hr. Add the shredded cabbage and the macaroni and simmer for a final 10–15 min. Season the soup, stir into it a little grated cheese and serve the rest separately.

NOTE: Different mixtures of vegetables may be used when they are in season.

**6 helpings**
**Cooking time—3½ hr.**

### MINIATURE ROUND OF BEEF

**1 large rib of beef**
**1 gallon water**
**2 lb. coarse salt**
**½ oz. saltpetre**
**6 oz. brown sugar**
**12 peppercorns**
**A bunch of mixed herbs**
**2–3 onions**
**Vegetable trimmings**

GARNISH

**Diced carrot and turnip**

Boil the water, salt, saltpetre and sugar together for ½ hr., skimming when necessary, then allow to become cold. Bone the meat, rub well with salt, roll up lightly and tie securely with string. Place in the cold brine and leave for 6 days, turning each day. Then drain well and wash in cold water. Place in a pan, cover with cold water, add the herbs and peppercorns and bring slowly to the boil. Boil for 5 min. Skim, add the onions and vegetable trimmings and simmer for the required time, allowing 25 min. per lb. and 25 min. over. When ready, place on a hot dish, remove the string and skewer if necessary. Serve, garnished with diced vegetables.

### MINT SAUCE

*Sauce à la Menthe*

**3 heaped tablesp.**
**2 tablesp. boiling water**

**finely-chopped mint**
**A pinch of salt**
**2 teasp. sugar**
**¼ pt. vinegar**

The mint should be young and freshly gathered if possible. Wash well, pick the leaves from the stalks and chop the leaves finely.

Mix the mint, salt and sugar in the sauce-boat. Pour on to them the boiling water and leave the mixture to cool. Add the vinegar and if possible leave the sauce for 1 hr. to infuse the flavour of mint into the vinegar.

Serve with roast lamb.

## MIROTON OF BEEF

*Miroton de Bœuf*

**1¼–1½ lb. cold roast beef**
**2 Spanish onions**
**1½ oz. butter *or* fat**
**Bouquet garni**
**1 pt. good brown sauce**
**1 teasp. vinegar**
**Salt and pepper**
**Browned breadcrumbs**

GARNISH

**Croûtons of fried bread *or* cooked vegetables**

Cut the meat into thin slices. Coarsely chop the onions. Melt the fat in a saucepan and fry the onions with the bouquet garni until brown. Then add the brown sauce, vinegar and seasoning to taste. Simmer gently for ½ hr., stirring and skimming occasionally, then pass the sauce through a fine strainer. Cover the bottom of the serving dish with sauce, place the slices of meat in neat layers on top, cover with sauce and sprinkle with browned bread-crumbs. Heat in a fairly hot oven (**375° F., Gas 5**) for 15 min. Serve garnished with croûtons of fried bread, or heaps of diced vegetables, sprigs of cauliflower or peas.

**6 helpings**

## MIXED PICKLE

Make a selection of available vegetables. Any of the following are suitable: small cucumbers, cauliflower, small onions, French beans. Prepare the vegetables: only the onions need be peeled, the rest should merely be cut into suitably sized pieces.

Put all into a large bowl, sprinkle with salt, and leave for 24 hr. Drain thoroughly and pack into jars. Cover with cold spiced vinegar, seal, and leave for at least a month before using.

## MIXED VEGETABLE SALAD (using cooked summer vegetables)

**3 large new potatoes**
**3 new turnips**
**½ pt. shelled peas**
**½ bunch new carrots**
**1 tablesp. chopped parsley**
**1 teasp. chopped mint**
**Salad dressing**

Cook the vegetables and slice the carrots, potatoes and young turnips. Save some of each vegetable for garnish and toss the rest in the salad dressing with the herbs. Put the mixture in a suitable dish and garnish with the remainder. Baste with a little French dressing.

**4–6 helpings**

## MIXED VEGETABLE SALAD (using cooked winter vegetables)

*Salade de Légumes à la Jardinère*

**1 cauliflower**
**2 large carrots**
**1 parsnip *or* 2 turnips**
**1 cooked beetroot**
**1 small can of peas**
**Salad dressing**
**Watercress *or* fine cress**
**A little French dressing**

Steam the cauliflower, carrots, parsnip or turnips. Divide the cauliflower into sprigs. Dice the carrots, parsnip or turnip, and beet-root, or cut into neat rounds with a cutter. Rinse and drain the peas. Mix all trimmings and uneven pieces of vegetable lightly with salad dressing—include some of the peas. Put this mixture into a dish, preferably oblong in shape. Cover with lines of each vegetable, very neatly arranged and with suitable colours adjoining. Garnish the edges with watercress or fine cress. Baste the surface with French dressing.

**6 helpings**

## MIXED VEGETABLES—COOKED FOR FOOD VALUE

**1½ lb. mixed vegetables:**
*In winter:* **parsnip, turnip, carrot, leek, cauliflower**
*In summer:* **new carrots, new turnips, broad beans, peas, spring onions, tomato**

**1 oz. butter *or* margarine**
**½–1 gill boiling water**
**Salt and pepper**
**Chopped parsley**

Prepare all the vegetables. Cut the winter

vegetables into thin slices, cutting the slices in halves or quarters when large. Break the cauliflower into sprigs. Leave most of the summer vegetables whole, cutting the carrots in thick slices, if not really small, trimming the spring onions rather short and cutting the tomatoes into wedges. Melt the fat in a saucepan. Add the vegetables to it at intervals, starting with the ones which take the longest time to cook. Put the lid on the pan after each addition and toss the vegetables in the fat. (Do not add the tomatoes to the summer vegetables until 5 min. before serving.) Add the liquid and the salt (use very little water with the summer vegetables), and simmer gently until the vegetables are tender. Serve hot, sprinkled with chopped parsley.

## MIXED VEGETABLES WITH CHEESE

*Légumes au gratin*

**1 lb. cooked mixed vegetables**
**¾ pt. cheese sauce**
**1 heaped tablesp. dry grated Cheddar cheese *or* 1 dessertsp. dry grated Cheddar cheese *and* 1 dessertsp. grated Parmesan cheese**

After cooking the vegetables drain off any cooking liquor. Make the cheese sauce, using up the cooking liquor. Coat the vegetables with the sauce, sprinkle with grated cheese and immediately brown under a hot grill or in the top of a hot oven.

NOTE: If the mixture of vegetables is stirred into enough thick cheese sauce to bind it, it can be used as a very pleasant vegetarian stuffing for peppers, marrow and potatoes.

**6 helpings**
**Cooking time—about 1 hr.**

## MIXED VEGETABLES—CURRIED

*Légumes en Kari*

**Conservatively cooked vegetables,**
**¾ pt. curry sauce**
**6 oz. boiled, dry, Patna rice**

After cooking the vegetables, drain off any cooking liquor. Make the curry sauce, using up the vegetable liquor, and let it simmer for at least 2 hr. Reheat the cooked vegetables carefully in it. Flavour carefully. Serve with a separate dish of hot, dry rice and any of the usual accompaniments for curry.

**6 helpings**
**Cooking time—about 3 hr.**

## MOCHA FILLING

**½ oz. cornflour**
**1 gill milk**
**1 oz. loaf sugar**
**½ oz. butter**
**1 teasp. coffee essence**
**A few drops of vanilla essence**
**1 egg**

Blend the cornflour in a little cold milk. Put the remaining milk and sugar in a saucepan and bring to boiling-point. Pour the boiling milk on to the blended cornflour, stirring all the time, return the mixture to the saucepan and boil for 3 min. Add the butter and flavourings and lastly the beaten egg. Stir till the mixture thickens then allow to cool.

## MOCK CREAM

**½ oz. cornflour**
**¼ pt. milk**
**1 oz. margarine**
**1 oz. sugar**
**A few drops of vanilla essence**

Blend the cornflour with a little of the milk, and put the rest of the milk on to boil. Pour the boiling milk on to the blended cornflour, stirring well. Return mixture to pan and cook for 2–3 min. Cool. Cream together the margarine and sugar. Gradually beat the cornflour mixture into the creamed fat a little at a time, beat well. Stir in the vanilla essence.

## MOCK CREAM or EGG WHITE CREAM (suitable for fat free diet)

**1 egg white**
**1 level dessertsp. warmed golden syrup *or* clear honey**

Whisk egg white until very firm. Gradually whisk in the warmed syrup or honey. Serve cold.

**2–3 helpings**

## MOCK TURTLE SOUP

*Potage de tortue fausse*

**½ calf's head**
**2 oz. lean bacon**
**1 onion**
**1 bay leaf**
**A bunch of herbs**
**2 qt. water**

1 carrot
1 stick of celery
3 cloves
1 blade of mace
6 peppercorns
2 teasp. salt
Flour *or* cornflour
Salt and pepper
Lemon juice
Sherry (optional)

Simmer the head with bacon, vegetables and flavouring in the water with the salt for 3–4 hr. Strain the soup. Cut some of the meat from the head into ½-in. dice. To each quart of soup blend 1 oz. flour or cornflour with a little milk or water and with it thicken the broth, season, add lemon juice to taste and ½ glass sherry, if liked. Return the pieces of meat to the soup and reheat them.

**8–12 helpings**
**Cooking time—4¼ hr.**

## MOULES MARINIÈRES

**3½ pt. mussels**
**1 shallot, chopped finely**
**5–6 stalks of parsley**
**⅓ of a bay leaf**
**Sprig of thyme**
**Pinch of pepper**
**¼ pt. dry white wine (½ water and ½ dry cider can be used)**
**1 oz. butter**
**Chopped parsley**

Open the mussels by the French method. Strain the liquid through muslin, to remove any traces of sand, then return the liquid to the pan with the butter and boil rapidly until reduced by half. Meanwhile, remove the beards from the mussels, and return the mussels to their half shell, discard empty shells, Arrange in soup plates, pour the reduced liquor over the mussels and sprinkle with chopped parsley.

## MONTPELIER BUTTER

*Beurre Montpelier*

**½ bunch watercress**
**2 oz. butter**
**Salt and pepper**

Wash the watercress and dry it thoroughly. Chop very finely and squeeze it in a piece of muslin to dry still further. Cream the butter and knead in the watercress until it is sufficiently green. Add salt and pepper to taste and use as required.

## MORNAY SAUCE

**½ pt. Béchamel sauce**
**1 egg yolk**
**¾ oz. Gruyère *or* Cheddar cheese**
**¾ oz. Parmesan cheese**
**⅛ pt. cream (optional)**
**Cayenne pepper**

*For a fish dish:*
**¼ pt. fish stock reduced to 2 tablesp. *or* 2 tablesp. fish fumet**

Add the egg yolk mixed with a little cooled sauce to the Béchamel sauce well below boiling point. Cook the egg yolk without boiling it. Stir in the grated cheese and the cream, season and serve the sauce at once. If fish fumet is used add it hot, before the cream.

Serve with fish or vegetables.

## MOUSSELINE SAUCE—SWEET

**1 egg**
**1 egg yolk**
**1½ oz. castor sugar**
**⅛ pt. cream**
**1 tablesp. sherry *or* fruit juice**

Separate the egg white from the yolk and whip it to a stiff froth. Put all the other ingredients into a basin placed over a pan of hot water and whisk until creamy and thick. Fold the egg white into the hot sauce. Serve at once.

## MOUSSES

"Mousse" is a French word, meaning "froth" or "foam". Whether savoury or sweet, hot or cold or frozen, a mousse is always light and creamy.

## MULLET-FRIED À LA MEUNIÈRE

*Mulet frit à la Meunière*

**4 mullet**
**Seasoned flour**
**Butter**
**Lemon juice**
**Parsley**

Prepare the fish then coat with seasoned flour. Fry them gently in the melted butter, turning until cooked on either side, about 12–15 min. Arrange on a hot flat dish, sprinkle with lemon juice and chopped parsley. Add a large nut of fresh butter to the pan, heat until nut brown in colour then pour over the fish and serve.

**4 helpings**

## MULLIGATAWNY SOUP

*Potage à l'Indienne*

**1 lb. lean mutton *or***
**1 qt. bone stock *or***

**rabbit *or* stewing veal *or* shin of beef *or* ox tail**
**1 onion**
**1 small cooking apple**
**1 oz. butter *or* margarine**
**½ oz. curry powder**
**1 oz. flour**
**water**
**Salt**
**1 carrot**
**½ small parsnip**
**A bunch of herbs**
**Lemon juice**
**¼ teasp. black treacle**
**2 oz. boiled rice**

Cut the meat in small pieces. Chop finely the onion and the apple. Heat the butter in a deep pan and in it quickly fry the onion, then the curry powder. Add the apple and cook it gently for a few minutes, then stir in the flour. Add the liquid, meat and salt, and bring slowly to simmering point, stirring all the time. Add the other vegetables, the herbs tied in muslin and a few drops of lemon juice. Simmer until the meat is very tender. This will take between 2 hr. for rabbit to 4 hr. for shin of beef. Taste the soup and add more lemon juice or add black treacle to obtain a flavour that is neither predominatingly sweet nor acid. Strain the soup, cut some of the meat in neat cubes and reheat them in the soup. Boil, drain and partly dry the rice as for curry and hand it with the soup.

NOTE: The amount of curry powder may be varied to taste; the quantity given is for a mild-flavoured soup.

**4–6 helpings**
**Cooking time—from 2–4 hr. according to the meat used.**

## MULLIGATAWNY SOUP

*See Consommé à L'Indienne.*

## MUSTARD, TO MIX

**Mustard is usually prepared for use by simply mixing it smoothly with cold water.**

## MUSHROOM CREAM SOUP

*Crème aux Champignons*

**½ lb. mushrooms**
**1 onion**
**1 clove of garlic**
**2 oz. butter**
**¾ pt. water *or* white stock**
**A little yeast *or* meat extract**
**¾ pt. milk**
**1 oz. flour**
**Salt and pepper**
**¼ pt. cream (optional)**
**1 egg yolk (optional)**

Proceed as for Vegetable Purée. Cook the whole mushrooms till tender then chopping them and returning them to the soup before thickening it.

**6 helpings**
**Cooking time—30–45 min.**

## MUSHROOM PUDDING

**Short crust pastry**
**½ lb. mushrooms**
**Salt and pepper**
**1 oz. vegetarian cooking fat**

Grease a pudding basin and line it with pastry. Wash the mushrooms, peel if necessary, chop them if very big and put into the lined basin, sprinkling each layer with salt and pepper. Add the fat cut into pieces, moisten with water. Put on the pastry lid, cover with greaseproof paper if to be steamed, or with a floured pudding cloth if to be boiled.

**4 helpings**
**Cooking time—1½ hr. (approx.)**

## MUSHROOM SALAD

*Salade de Champignons*

**1 lb. mushrooms**
**1 onion, finely chopped**
**Salad oil**
**Vinegar *or* lemon juice**
**Salt and pepper**

Prepare the mushrooms and leave whole, if small; if large, cut in quarters. Fry the onion gently in the oil until cooked. Drain it. Fry the mushrooms in the same oil. Pour the contents of the pan into a salad dish. Add the onion, seasoning, and about 1 tablesp. vinegar or lemon juice. Serve when cold.

**6 helpings**

## MUSHROOM SAUCE—BROWN

*Sauce aux Champignons*

**½ pt. brown sauce**
**2–4 oz. mushrooms**

Fry the mushroom stalks with the other vegetables when making the brown sauce Season). Add the mushroom skins and the sliced mushrooms with the stock when making the sauce, and simmer them for ½ hr. Strain the sauce, lift out and chop the mushrooms and return them to the sauce.

NOTE: This sauce may also be made with Espagnole sauce foundation

## MUSHROOM SAUCE—WHITE

*Sauce aux Champignons*

**½ pt. white sauce**
**2–4 oz. mushrooms**
**½–1 oz. butter**

Cook the thinly sliced mushrooms very gently in the butter for 15–20 min. Stir the mushrooms with the butter and their juice into the hot sauce.

Serve with fish and meat entrées, poultry etc.

## MUSHROOMS WITH CHEESE

*Champignons au gratin*

**18–24 flap mushrooms**
**Salt and pepper**
**1 tablesp. finely-chopped chives**
**1 tablesp. finely-chopped parsley**
**1 tablesp. fresh breadcrumbs**
**2 tablesp. grated Parmesan cheese**
**½ oz. butter**

Wash, peel, stem the mushrooms. Grease a baking-dish and put in the mushrooms, gills uppermost. Season. Sprinkle with the parsley and chives, then with the breadcrumbs and cheese mixed. Lastly sprinkle with the melted butter. Bake for 25 min. in a fairly hot oven **(375° F., Gas 5).**

**6 helpings**
**Cooking time—25 min.**

## MUSHROOMS—PRINCESS

**12 small mushrooms**
**2 oz. butter**
**3 oz. demi-sel *or* cream cheese**
**Paprika pepper**
**12 rounds of toast *or* fried bread *or* 4 larger slices of toast**

Cook the mushrooms in the butter, removing the stalks before cooking, but using these as well. Drain thoroughly and cool. Pipe a rosette of the soft cheese in the centre of each mushroom. Dust with paprika pepper and put the stalk into position. Serve on toast or fried bread.

NOTE: If preferred the mushrooms could be cooked in a little water and vinegar.

**4 helpings *or* 12 savouries**
**Cooking time—5 min.**

## MUSHROOM STUFFING

**4 oz. mushrooms**
**1 oz. bacon**
**4 oz. breadcrumbs**
**½ oz. butter**
**Salt and pepper**
**Nutmeg**
**1 egg**

Skin and chop the mushrooms (including the stalks). Chop the bacon. Fry the bacon for a few minutes then add the mushrooms and fry them very slowly for 5 min. Mix all the ingredients and season to taste.

Use for pigeons and other small birds, for fish or vegetables.

## MUSHROOMS STEWED WITH WINE

**1 lb. button mushrooms**
**6 rashers of streaky bacon**
**1 teasp. finely-chopped chives**
**1 teasp. finely-chopped parsley**
**Salt and pepper**
**White wine *or* cider**
**Flour**

Wash and peel the mushrooms, trim the stalks. Cut up the bacon into small pieces and cook in a saucepan 15 min. Add the mushrooms, chives and parsley and a little salt. Moisten with white wine or cider, dredge lightly with flour and stew very gently until the sauce is quite thick. Re-season.

**6 helpings**
**Cooking time—40 min. (approx.)**

## MUSSEL SOUP

*Soupe aux Moules*

**1 qt. mussels**
**¼ pt. white wine**
**Lemon juice**
**1½ pt. fish stock**
**1 oz. butter**
**¾ oz. flour**
**Salt and pepper**
**Chopped parsley**
**1 egg yolk**
**⅛ pt. cream**

Wash and scrub the mussels; put them into a pan with the wine, lemon juice and ½ pt. of fish stock. Heat them in the liquid until they open. Strain the liquid through muslin into the remaining 1 pt. stock. Shell the mussels and remove the beards. Melt the butter in a deep pan, stir in the flour, then the fish stock. Bring to boiling point, boil till the flour thickens. Season the soup carefully; add the chopped parsley. Mix the egg yolk and cream and add them and the mussels to the soup, just below boiling point. Cook the egg without allowing it to boil.

NOTE: Other shell fish may be treated in the same way.

**4–6 helpings**
**Cooking time—25–30 min.**

### MUSSELS *Moules*

Mussels are bought while still alive and their shells should be tightly shut. Discard any that do not shut immediately when given a sharp tap, as they are probably dead. Mussels are in season from September to March. They can be served cold with vinegar or hot in soups, sauces or pies.

#### TO PREPARE MUSSELS

Allow 1–1½ pt. mussels per person. Scrape and clean the shells thoroughly in several lots of cold water. Mussels are not opened with a knife like oysters, but open themselves during cooking. The only part of a mussel which needs to be removed is the breathing apparatus which is found in the form of a black strip known as the "beard". This is removed after the shells have been opened.

#### TO OPEN

There are two simple methods of opening mussels:

*English method*—For a small quantity of 1–2 pt., place the mussels (after cleaning) in a rinsed wide pan and cover them closely with a folded damp teacloth. Heat quickly, shaking the pan at intervals, and at the end of 5–7 min. the shells will open. Remove from the heat promptly as overcooking toughens them.

*French method*—To 3½ pt. of cleaned mussels in a wide pan, add 1 shallot, finely chopped, 5–6 stalks of parsley, a sprig of parsley, a sprig of thyme, ⅓ of a bay leaf, a pinch of pepper and ¼ pt. dry white wine (½ water and ½ dry cider could be used). Cover the pan tightly and cook over a sharp heat for 5–6 min. shaking the pan from time to time. Remove from the heat as soon as the shells open.

### MUSSELS, TO COOK *Moules*

**1 qt. mussels**
**1 oz. butter**
**½ oz. flour**
**2 egg yolks**
**1 tablesp. vinegar**
**1 teasp. chopped parsley**
**Salt and pepper**

Open the mussels by the English method. Take them out of the shells and strain the liquor into a basin. Carefully remove the beards. Melt the butter, add the flour and cook for 3–4 min., then pour in the mussel liquor and stir until boiling. Cool slightly, then add the egg yolks, vinegar, and parsley, season to taste and stir over a low heat until the egg yolks thicken. Put in the mussels to re-heat and serve in the sauce.

**2–3 helpings** **Cooking time—about ½ hr.**

### MUSTARD SAUCE *Sauce Moutarde*

**½ pt. sauce made with meat *or* fish stock, milk *or* milk and stock**
**1 teasp. dry English mustard *or* 1 tablesp. French mustard**
**1 teasp. tarragon vinegar**
**1 teasp. sugar**
**½–1 oz. butter**

Mix the dry mustard with the vinegar. Whisk the mixed mustard and sugar into the hot sauce. Whisk the butter into the sauce just below boiling point, adding it a small pat at a time.

Serve with boiled beef, herring or mackerel.

### MUTTON BROTH *Bouillon de Mouton*

**1½ lb. neck of mutton *or* 1 lb. knuckle of mutton**
**1 qt. water**
**1 teasp. salt and pepper**
**1 tablesp. pearl barley**
**1 carrot**
**1 onion *or* leek**
**1 small turnip**
**1 stick of celery**
**Chopped parsley**

Wash the meat and remove all fat. Put the meat with the bones, water and salt into a stew pan and bring very slowly to simmering point. Blanch the barley by covering it with cold water in a small pan, bringing it just to boiling point, straining and rinsing it. Add barley to the pan and simmer all for 2 hr. Lift meat from broth, remove bones, cut meat into ¼-in. cubes and return to broth. If possible, let the broth cool and remove the fat from the top; otherwise skim very thoroughly and draw pieces of absorbent paper over the top till it is free from fat. Scrub, peel and cut the vegetables into ¼ in. dice. Add them to the simmering broth and cook for 1 hr. longer.

Season the broth to taste and add 1 tablesp. chopped parsley before serving.

**4–6 helpings**
**Cooking time—3 hr.**

## MUTTON CUTLETS—ITALIAN STYLE

*Côtelettes de Mouton à l'Italienne*

| | |
|---|---|
| **6 cutlets from the best end of neck** | **½ teasp. finely-chopped shallot** |
| **2–3 tablesp. salad oil** | **1 teasp. chopped parsley** |
| **1 tablesp. lemon juice** | **¼ teasp. finely-grated lemon rind** |
| **1 teasp. finely-chopped mixed herbs** | **A pinch of mace** |
| **Salt and pepper** | **1 egg** |
| **3–4 tablesp. bread-crumbs** | **Fat for frying** |
| **1 tablesp. finely-chopped mushrooms** | **⅓ pt. Italian sauce** |

Mix the salad oil, lemon juice, herbs and a little salt and pepper together. Pour this mixture over the cutlets and let them remain in it for 1 hr., turning 2 or 3 times. Mix together the breadcrumbs, chopped mushroom, shallot, parsley, lemon rind and mace, season with salt and pepper. Drain the cutlets, brush with beaten egg and carefully coat with the bread-crumb mixture. Fry in hot fat until brown on both sides. Serve with Italian sauce.

**6 helpings**
**Cooking time—6–10 min.**

## MUTTON PIES—CUMBERLAND STYLE

| | |
|---|---|
| **12 oz. minced mutton** | **1 dessertsp. chopped parsley** |
| **Short-crust pastry using 12 oz. flour, etc.** | **A pinch of thyme** |
| **1 onion** | **Salt and pepper** |
| **4 oz. mushrooms** | **A little good stock** |
| | **Egg *or* milk** |

Chop and lightly fry the onion. Line 12 small round tins or small saucers with ½ the pastry. Mix together the minced mutton, chopped onion, chopped mushrooms, parsley, thyme and seasoning. Divide the mixture between the tins. Add to each a little stock to moisten. Cover with lids made from the rest of the pastry. Brush with egg or milk and bake in a moderate oven (**350° F., Gas 4**) for about 30–45 min.

**6 helpings**

## MUTTON PIE—PEMBROKESHIRE STYLE

| | |
|---|---|
| **Hot water crust pastry using 1 lb. flour, etc.** | **¼ lb. sugar** |
| **1 lb. minced mutton** | **Salt and pepper** |
| **¼ lb. currants** | **Stock** |
| | **Egg *or* milk for glazing** |

When the pastry is cool enough to handle make into a large pie case or several small ones, keeping back ¼ of the pastry for the lid. Arrange the filling in layers of mutton, currants, sugar, salt and pepper and moisten with stock. Cover with the pastry lid. Bake in a fairly hot oven (**400° F., Gas 6**) for 10 min. then reduce heat to moderate (**350° F., Gas 4**) for the remainder of the time—about 1¼ hr. in all. Brush with egg or milk about 15 min before cooking is complete. Fill with stock and serve hot.

**6 helpings**

## MUTTON AND POTATO PIE

*Pâté de Mouton à l'Anglaise*

| | |
|---|---|
| **2 lb. cold cooked lean mutton** | **2 onions** |
| **2 lb. potatoes** | **Salt and pepper** |
| | **¾ pt. gravy** |

Cut the meat into neat thin pieces. Make the gravy from the meat trimmings. Parboil and slice the potatoes and onions. Line a pie-dish with slices of potato and cover with layers of meat, onions and potatoes, seasoning each layer. Repeat in layers, until all the ingredients are used, the top layer should consist of potato. Add the gravy, cover with greaseproof paper and bake in a moderate oven (**350° F., Gas 4**) for 1 hr. For the last 15 min. remove the greaseproof paper to allow the potatoes to brown.

**6 helpings**

## NAVARIN OF LAMB

| | |
|---|---|
| **1 large breast *or* boned neck of lamb** | **Bouquet garni** |
| **A good pinch of sugar** | **8–10 small onions** |
| **1 large tablesp. flour** | **8–10 small potatoes** |
| **½ lb. skinned tomatoes** | **One A1* can peas** |
| **1 crushed clove of garlic** | **One A1 can small whole carrots** |
| **Salt and pepper** | **Chopped parsley** |

Cut the lamb into about 2½ oz. pieces and gently fry them in some of the fat trimmed off them. Transfer to a casserole. Pour off the fat. Sprinkle the sugar into the pan and heat until it becomes a deep gold. Work in the flour and then the chopped tomatoes (seeds discarded), then stir in enough hot water to make a sauce to cover the meat. Pour over the meat. Add the crushed garlic, a little pepper and salt and the bouquet garni. Cover, cook for a further ½–¾ hr. Add the drained peas and carrots and heat through. Sprinkle with parsley and serve.

* *See* Chart of Can Sizes.

## NEAPOLITAN CAKES

| | |
|---|---|
| **4 oz. plain flour** | **4 oz. sugar** |
| **Pinch of salt** | **4 oz. ground almonds** |
| **4 oz. butter or margarine** | **1 egg** |
| | **Apricot jam** |

DECORATION

| | |
|---|---|
| **A few glacé cherries** | **Glacé icing using 6–8 oz. icing sugar** |

Sift flour and salt and rub in the fat. Add the sugar and ground almonds and mix to a stiff paste with the egg. Roll the paste a good ⅛ in. thick and cut into rounds with a 2½-in. or 3-in. cutter. Bake on a greased baking-sheet in a fairly hot oven (**375° F., Gas 5**) till golden brown. When cold, spread half of the rounds with jam and place the other rounds evenly on top. Ice the top with glacé icing and place half a cherry in centre of each cake.

**12 cakes**
**Cooking time—20 min.**

## NEAPOLITAN JELLY

*Gelée napolitaine*

| | |
|---|---|
| **1½ pt. wine jelly** | **Sap-green colouring** |
| **Carmine colouring** | **¼ pt. double cream** |

Divide jelly into 3, colouring ⅓ red and ⅓ green and leaving ⅓ plain. Mould in layers of equal thickness, alternating the colours, allowing each layer to set before adding another. Turn out and decorate with piped, whipped cream.

**6 helpings**
**Time (without ice)—2–3 hr. according to weather**
**(with ice packed round mould)—¾ hr.**

## NEAPOLITAN MOULD

*Gâteau napolitain*

| | |
|---|---|
| **3 oz. cornflour** | **Colourings: sap green, carmine** |
| **2 pt. milk** | **Flavourings: almond, raspberry and coffee essences** |
| **½–1 oz. butter** | |
| **2 oz. sugar** | |

Blend cornflour and make as for cornflour mould. Whilst cornflour is cooking warm 2 basins. Sweeten cornflour mixture to taste. Pour ⅓ quickly into a heated basin, colour pale pink and flavour with raspberry essence. Stir quickly and pour into a wetted mould. Pour ½ the remaining cornflour mixture into a heated basin, colour pale green and flavour with almond essence. Stir quickly and pour on the top of the set pink mixture. (This should be done lightly and slowly, pouring around the sides of the mould so that the second layer puts no great weight on the surface of the first). Flavour the remaining ⅓ of the mixture with coffee essence and pour on to the set green mixture, taking care, as before, not to pour too heavily. Leave to set and turn out when cold.

**6 helpings**
**Cooking time—20 min. Setting time—2 hr.**

### NESSELRODE PUDDING

*Pouding Glace à la Nesselrode*

**2 dozen chestnuts**
**½ pt. milk**
**4 egg yolks**
**½ pt. cream**
**6 oz. castor sugar**
**Vanilla essence**
**2 oz. glacé cherries**

Parboil, shell, and skin the chestnuts. Simmer them in ¼ pt. milk until tender. Rub through a fine sieve. Heat remaining ¼ pt. milk until almost boiling, add the beaten egg yolks and cook, stirring continuously until it thickens without boiling. Add the chestnut purée and sugar. Cool. Add ½ of the half-whipped cream and vanilla. Freeze until nearly set, then stir in the chopped cherries and the remainder of the cream stiffly-whipped. Freeze until set, stirring frequently. Press into a mould, seal with lard, wrap in paper and bury in ice and salt until required.

**6 helpings**
**Time—3 hr.**

### NOUILLE or NOODLE PASTE (also called Ribbon Macaroni)

*Pâte à Nouilles*

**1 lb. flour**
**1½ oz. butter**
**3 egg yolks** *or* **2 small whole eggs**
**Salt**
**A little milk** *or* **water**

Sift the flour into a basin, make a well in the centre, and put in the butter, eggs and a good pinch of salt. Mix thoroughly and add a little milk or water if necessary, but the paste should be rather stiff. Knead well for about 15 min., or until the paste is perfectly smooth and elastic, then use as required.

**8 helpings**

### NOUILLES AND EGGS

*Œufs aux Nouilles*

**½ lb. nouille paste**
**½ lb. mushrooms**
**Butter**
**4 hard-boiled eggs**
**Pepper and nutmeg**
**2–3 tablesp. grated cheese**
**¼ pt. white sauce**

Let the nouille paste stand for at least 1 hr. before rolling out as thinly as possible. Cut it into long strips 2–3 in. wide, place them on top of each other and cut them into filaments not more than ⅛ in. wide. Shake them well in a little flour to separate and slightly coat them. Put them into rapidly-boiling salted water, boil for 10 min., drain well, then toss them over heat in a little butter. Prepare the mushrooms and cook them for 8–10 min. in hot butter. Cut the eggs into slices. Place a layer of nouilles in the bottom of a well-buttered fireproof dish, season with pepper and a little nutmeg and sprinkle thickly with cheese. Cover with slices of egg, add seasoning, then another layer of nouilles and finally the mushrooms. Spread the white sauce over the surface, sprinkle well with cheese, add a few small pieces of butter and bake in a hot oven (**425° F., Gas 7**) for 10–15 min. Serve in the dish in which it was baked.

**6–7 helpings**

### NEW POTATOES—BOILED

*Pommes de terre nouvelles bouillies*

**2 lb. new potatoes, even-sized**
**Salt and pepper**
**Mint**
**1 oz. butter** *or* **margarine**
**Parsley**

Where possible dig the potatoes just before cooking. Scrub with a stiff brush. (This should be sufficient to remove the skin. If the potatoes are not freshly dug, scrape them to remove skins.) Rinse. Cook as for old potatoes but with mint in the water. When dried, add fat, chopped parsley and chopped mint to the saucepan. Toss the potatoes gently in the fat. Serve hot.

New potatoes are in season from May to July.

**4–6 helpings**
**Cooking time—15–30 min. according to size and freshness**

### NEWMARKET PUDDING

**2 eggs**
**3 oz. sugar**
**½ pt. milk**
**5 individual sponge cakes**
**2 oz. finely-chopped peel**
**2 oz. muscatel raisins (halved)**
**1 oz. currants**
**3 tablesp. redcurrant jelly**

1

Pastry in the Making I
—Flaky Pastry.

1 If a mixture of butter and lard is being used, first blend the two together with a round-bladed knife.

2 Sift the flour and salt into a bowl. Divide fat into four equal portions.

3 Lightly rub quarter of the fat into the flour. Next mix to a soft dough with cold water and lemon juice.

4 Roll dough out into an oblong shape.

5 Place quarter of the fat in small pieces on the top $\frac{2}{3}$ of the pastry.

6 Fold the bottom third of the pastry up and the top third downwards.

7 With the rolling pin, press edges lightly together, make a half turn, and press ridges in the pastry to distribute air evenly. Allow dough to relax. Roll out and repeat with the other two portions of fat.

7

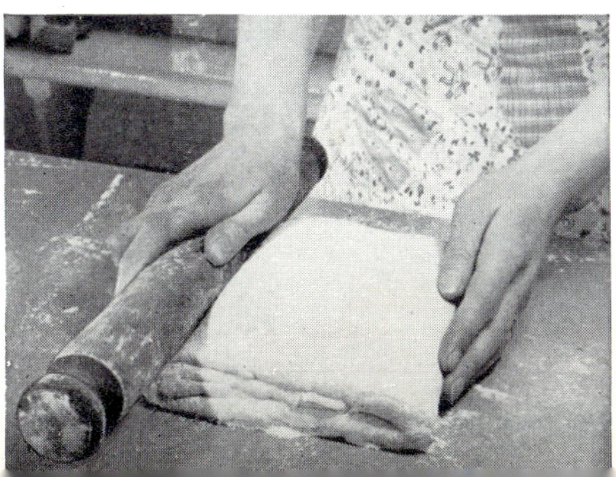

2

3

4

5

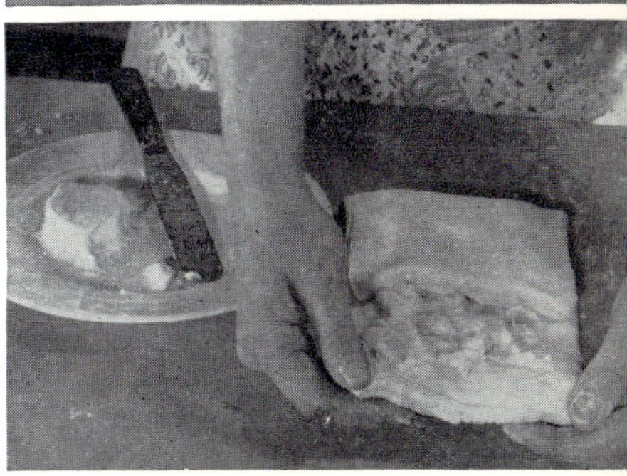

6

1

## Pastry in the Making II —Puff Pastry.

1 Sift the flour and salt into a bowl, then well rub in about 2 oz. of butter.

2 Add the lemon juice to the flour and mix to a smooth dough with cold wate

2

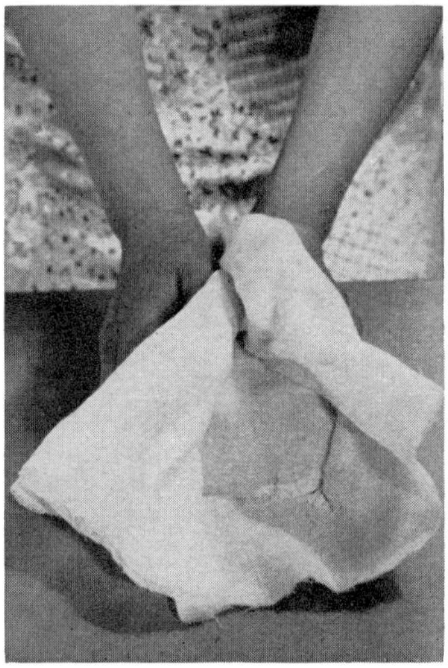
3

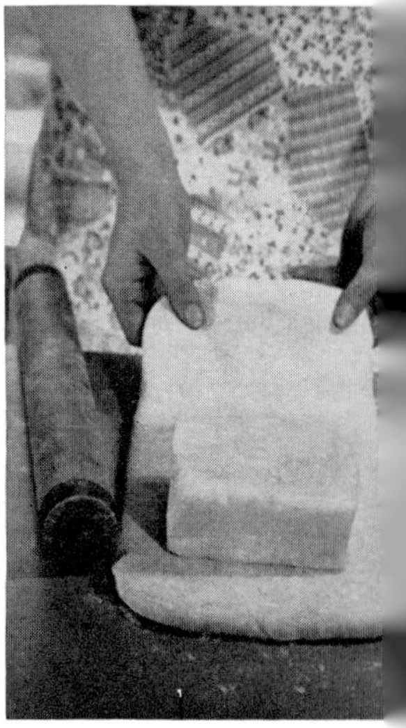
4

3 Press the remaining butter in a floured cloth to remove all the surplus moisture.

4 Knead the dough well. Roll it into a strip large enough to enclose the butter. Place the butter on one half of the pastr

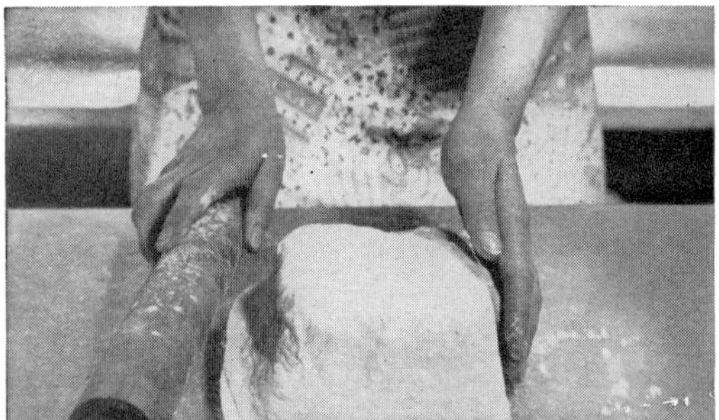
5

6

5 Fold the other half over, press the two edges together firmly with a rolling pin.

6 Roll into a strip three times the original length, but the same width. Fold the bottom $\frac{1}{3}$ up and the top $\frac{1}{3}$ down, press th edges together and give the pastry a half-turn. Roll and fold seven times, leaving the pastry in a cool place for about 15 minutes between each rolling.

Beat together the eggs and sugar and stir in the milk. Slice the sponge cakes and place them in layers alternately with a mixture of peel, raisins and currants. Pour in the custard, cover with greased paper and steam gently for 1–1¼ hr., until set. Warm the redcurrant jelly, turn out the pudding and coat with the jelly just before serving.

**5–6 helpings**
**Cooking time—1–1¼ hr.**

## NORFOLK DUMPLINGS

*Boulettes Norfolk, bouillies*

**Boiling water**
**Salt**

BREAD DOUGH

**8 oz. plain flour**
**½ teasp. salt**
**½ oz. yeast**
**Small pinch of sugar**
**½ oz. lard**
**¼ pt. warm water (approx.)**

Make the dough: sift the flour and salt into a basin. Cream the yeast with the sugar and add the warm water and the melted fat. Mix to an elastic dough. Knead well until smooth, cover with a cloth, and set in a warm place to rise to double its size. Knead again until there are no large holes in the dough when cut.

Roll into small balls. Leave in a warm place to rise slightly. Drop into gently boiling salted water. Simmer for 6–7 min. Strain.

Serve with one of the following: jam, treacle, golden syrup, *or* butter and sugar.

**8 helpings**

## NORMANDY SAUCE

*Sauce Normande*

**½ pt. Velouté sauce made with fish stock**
**1 egg yolk**
**½–1 oz. butter**
**Lemon juice to taste**

The Velouté sauce should be made with fish stock containing liquor from oysters or mussels to give the correct flavour. Heat the sauce—in a double boiler, if possible. Stir in the egg yolk and cook without boiling, till the egg yolk thickens. Whisk in the butter, a small pat at a time. Add a few drops of lemon juice. Use at once.

Serve with sole or other white fish.

## NUDELSUPPE

Noodle Soup

**4 oz. flour**
**2 egg yolks**
**Pinch of salt**
**1 qt. brown stock**
**Chopped chives *or* grated nutmeg**

Mix the flour, egg yolks and salt into a stiff dough, kneading well for at least 15 min. Set aside in a cool place for ½ hr. Roll out as thinly as possible and cut into long "ribbons". Put on top of each other and cut into matchstick lengths. Spread on greaseproof paper to dry a little. Bring the stock to the boil, drop in the noodles gradually so that they do not stick together. Simmer for 10 min. Serve with chopped chives sprinkled on top or a little grated nutmeg.

## NUT BUNS

*See Buns or Cookies*

## NUT FRICASSÉE

**3 oz. cashew nuts *or* pine kernels**
**1 oz. butter *or* vegetarian margarine**
**2 sticks of celery**
**1 medium-sized onion**
**2 oz. flour**
**1 pt. milk**
**Salt**
**2–3 tablesp. cream**
**Cooked spinach *or* green peas**
**Cooked carrot**

Melt the butter in a saucepan, cut up the celery and onion into small pieces and fry in the butter for a few minutes, but do not allow to brown. Stir in the flour, add the milk, continue stirring until it simmers, add the nuts (whole) and salt to taste and cook very gently, with the lid on, for 15 min., then add the cream. Make a border with the spinach or peas on a hot dish, pour the fricassée in the centre and garnish with the cooked carrot cut up in the shape of matches and serve.

**3–4 helpings**

## *Oat Cakes—Rich*

### OATCAKES—Rich

*Biscuits de Farine d'Avoine*

**3 oz. plain flour**
**1/2 teasp. salt**
**2 level teasp. bicarbonate of soda**
**2 level teasp. cream of tartar**
**1 lb. oatmeal**
**1 oz. sugar**
**4 oz. butter and lard *or* margarine and lard**
**Milk**

Sift the flour, salt, soda and cream of tartar; add the oatmeal and sugar and rub in the fat. Add the milk, and mix to a stiff but not hard dough. Dust the baking-board with a mixture of flour and oatmeal, and roll out thinly. Rub the surface with oatmeal and cut out with a 3½-4-in. cutter *or* cut into triangles. Place on a baking-sheet and cook in a warm to cool oven (**335°-310° F., Gas 3-2**).

**About 40 oatcakes—depending on size**
**Cooking time—20-30 min.**

### OATMEAL PUDDING

*Pouding d'Avoine*

**1½ oz. fine oatmeal**
**½ oz. plain flour**
**1½ pt. milk**
**1-2 eggs**
**¼-½ teasp. salt**

Blend the oatmeal and flour to a smooth paste with some of the milk. Put the rest of the milk on to boil. Add the blended mixture carefully, stirring well. Cook gently for 5 min. Cool slightly. Stir in the well-beaten egg(s). Add salt to taste. Pour into a buttered pie-dish. Bake gently in a moderate oven (**350° F., Gas 4**) for about 20 min.

Serve with cream and sugar, or golden syrup.

**4 helpings** **Time—40 min.**

### OEUFS À LA NEIGE

Snow Eggs

**4 eggs**
**12 oz. castor sugar**
**1½ pt. milk**
**1 vanilla pod *or* a few drops of vanilla essence**

Separate the egg yolks from the egg whites and beat the whites until very stiff. Fold in 8 oz. of sugar with a wooden spatula. Place the milk in a shallow saucepan with the vanilla pod or vanilla essence and 1 oz. of sugar; bring to the boil. Mould the egg whites and sugar into egg shapes with 2 tablespoons and put into the simmering milk. Cook slowly for 8-10 min. until firm, turning from time to time. Remove from milk and drain on a cloth. Place in a glass dish. Mix the egg yolks with the remainder of the sugar and slowly pour on to them the milk, stirring with a spoon. Replace the mixture in the saucepan and cook gently until the sauce lightly thickens (i.e. coats the back of the spoon). Do not boil or the sauce will curdle. Pour the sauce through a strainer and coat the cooked snow eggs with it. Serve as a cold sweet.

**6 helpings**

### OFFALS

*See Meat.*

### OKRA AND AUBERGINE

**24 fresh okras**
**1 aubergine**
**2 tomatoes**
**1 oz. butter *or* margarine**
**1 finely-chopped onion**
**Salt and pepper**
**1 tablesp. finely-chopped parsley**

Wash and slice the okras. Peel the aubergine, remove seeds, if necessary, and slice in pieces similar in size to the pieces of okra. Peel and slice the tomatoes. Melt the butter in a saucepan. Add okras, aubergine, tomatoes, onion and a little salt. Stew till tender—about 35 min.—stirring frequently. Stir in the parsley, season carefully and serve.

**6 helpings**
**Cooking time—about 35 min.**

**OLD DUTCH MELK TERT** Milk Flan

**Puff pastry using 4 oz. flour etc.**
**1 stick of cinnamon**
**¼ pt. milk**
**½ oz. butter**
**½ oz. flour**
**1 oz. sugar**
**1 egg**
**½ teasp. ground cinnamon**

Line a 7-in. flan ring or plate with pastry Prick the bottom, cover with greased paper and fill up with old beans or rice. Bake in a hot oven (**425° F., Gas 7**) for 10–15 min. Remove paper and filling. Simmer cinnamon stick in the milk and strain. Make a white sauce with the butter, flour and milk. Cool slightly, add ½ the sugar and egg, lightly beaten. Turn into pastry case. Mix the ground cinnamon with rest of the sugar. Sprinkle this over the tart and brown in the oven.

**4–5 helpings**

**OLIVES**

Both Spanish and French olives are suitable for hors d'œuvres, the Spanish being considered better. Choose them large and firm and a nice green colour. Toss in a little oil and vinegar if wished but this is not essential. Those left over from a meal should be rebottled at once otherwise they will turn black.

**OLIVES À LA MADRAS**

**12 Spanish olives**
**1 oz. butter**
**1 tablesp. anchovy paste**
**2 hard-boiled eggs**
**1 teasp. chutney**
**Cayenne pepper**
**12 rounds fried bread *or* crisp biscuits**
**12 anchovy fillets**
**Parsley**

Stone the olives. Mix together the butter, anchovy paste, yolks of the eggs, chutney and seasoning. Spread a little of the purée on each croûte, and put a stoned olive filled with the rest of the mixture on each. Decorate with chopped egg white. Curl an anchovy fillet round the base of each olive, garnish with parsley.

**12 savouries**

**OMELETS**

There are two types of omelet: the French, which is flat and generally served folded into three, and the English which is fluffy and more like a soufflé.

The essentials in making either type are a thick, clean and dry omelet pan of the right size, i.e. 6–7 in. diameter for a 2 or 3 egg omelet; butter; eggs; and seasoning.

For recipes for sweet omelets, use one of alternate basic recipes, and fill with fruit purée, jam or a liqueur-flavoured sweet butter.

For savoury omelets, use one of the two basic types, and fill or stuff the omelet before folding with a small amount of grated cheese, cooked meat or fish, with a little creamy sauce if liked.

**ONION SALAD**

*Salade d'Oignons*

**3 large mild onions**
**3 firm tomatoes**
**French dressing *or* Vinaigrette sauce**

Parboil the onions and leave to cool. Slice them as finely as possible. Arrange in a dish with slices of peeled tomatoes. Pour over the French dressing or vinaigrette sauce.

**6 helpings**

**ONION SAUCE—BROWN**

*Sauce Miroton*

**½ pt. brown sauce using 2 medium-sized onions (chopped) and omitting the carrot**
**Nutmeg**
**Salt and pepper**
**1 teasp. wine vinegar**
**½ teasp. French *or* mixed mustard**

Make the sauce in the usual way. Do not strain it. Add nutmeg, vinegar and mustard at the end of cooking. Season to taste.

**ONION SAUCE—WHITE**

*Sauce aux Oignons*

To ½ pt. white sauce made from ½ milk and ½ liquor in which onions were boiled, add 2 chopped, cooked onions and a few drops of lemon juice.

Serve with mutton, rabbit or tripe.

**ONION SOUP**

*Purée aux Oignons*

**3 large Spanish onions (about 2 lb.)**
**1 oz. butter *or* margarine *or* dripping**
**1 clove**
**1 bay leaf**
**1 blade of mace**
**Flour to thicken**
**Salt and pepper**

## Onions—Italian Style

| | |
|---|---|
| **1 qt. white stock** ***or*** **1 pt. stock and 1 pt. milk** | **¼ pt. milk** ***or*** **cream** |

Peel and slice the onions. Melt the fat in a deep pan and lightly fry the onions for 10 min., cook slowly to prevent the onions colouring. Boil the stock, add it to the onions with the spices, and simmer until the onions are tender. Rub through a fine sieve, return the purée to the pan and add milk if used. To each 1 pt. of soup allow ½ oz. flour, blend the flour with a little cold milk, water or stock and stir into the soup. Cook until the soup thickens, season to taste. If cream is used, add it to the soup before serving.

NOTE: For Brown Onion soup use brown stock and brown the onions very slowly in the fat (about 20 min.) before adding the stock.

**6 helpings**
**Cooking time—1–1½ hr.**

### ONIONS—ITALIAN STYLE

*Oignons à l'Italienne*

| | |
|---|---|
| **1½ lb. button onions** | **2 cloves** |
| **Salt** | **4 white peppercorns** |
| **2 tablesp. olive oil** | **2 tablesp. wine vinegar** |
| **2 bay leaves** | **1 tablesp. sugar** |

Choose small onions equal in size. Cook gently in boiling, salted water, in their skins. When tender, drain and peel them. Heat the oil, add bay leaves, cloves, peppercorns. Shake these in the oil for a few minutes. Add the onions and simmer very gently for about 5 min. Stir in the vinegar and sugar and continue cooking until the liquid is reduced to a syrup. Serve hot.

**6 helpings Cooking time—altogether 45 min.**

### OPEN SANDWICHES

Use ¼-in. thick slices of white or brown bread, cut into fancy shapes, triangles, diamonds, hearts, etc. Spread with creamed butter and any of the party sandwich fillings. Garnish with stuffed olives, slices of hard-boiled egg, small pieces of tomato, watercress, piped cream cheese, etc. The appeal of these sandwiches, of course, lies in the artistic way in which the garnish is arranged; the sandwiches should look colourful and tempting.

### OPEN TARTS

In Britain, these are usually sweet, and may be used as sweet dishes or desserts, or may be eaten with afternoon tea instead of cakes.

They are usually baked in fireproof glass or enamel plates.

The tarts may be filled with jam, syrup, treacle, custard, fruit etc. For a 7-in. plate about 4 oz. of pastry will be required.

Knead the dough into a round shape then roll into a round about ⅛ in. thick and a little larger than the plate. Fold the pastry over the rolling-pin and gently lift it on to the plate. Smooth it over carefully with the fingers so that no air is trapped between the pastry and the plate—but take care that the pastry is not stretched in the process, as it will only shrink back later.

If the tart is being baked without a filling prick the base well or bake it "blind". When baking stand the plate on a baking-sheet.

The tart may be given a lattice top or the edge may be decorated with fancy shapes.

*See Flans, Pastry-Making, Sweet Pies and Tarts, etc.*

### ORANGE BOATS

*Tartelettes aux Oranges*

PASTRY

| | |
|---|---|
| **6 oz. plain flour** | **3 oz. butter** |
| **Pinch of salt** | **1 egg yolk** |
| **½ oz. ground almonds** | **Water to mix** |

FILLING

| | |
|---|---|
| **3 oz. ground almonds** | **Grated rind of 1 orange** |
| **4 oz. castor sugar** | **1 egg white** |

ORANGE GLACÉ ICING

**2 oz. icing sugar mixed with 1½ tablesp. orange juice and water**

Sift flour and salt, add the ½ oz. ground almonds and rub in the butter. Mix to a stiff paste with egg and water, roll out thinly and line greased boat-shaped moulds.

Mix the 3 oz. almonds, sugar and orange rind and fold into the stiffly beaten egg white. Two-thirds fill the lined tins and bake in a fairly hot oven **(375°–350° F., Gas 5–4)**. When cold put a little glacé icing down the centre of each.

**20 cakes**
**Cooking time—20–30 min.**

## ORANGE CAKE

*Gâteau à l'Orange*

**6 oz. butter *or* margarine**
**6 oz. castor sugar**
**3 eggs**
**8 oz. plain flour**
**¼ teasp. salt**
**1½ level teasp. baking-powder**
**1 orange**

Line a 7-in. cake-tin with greaseproof paper buttered. Cream the fat and sugar till white; add the beaten eggs gradually, beating well between each addition. Sift flour, salt and baking-powder and add with the grated rind and juice of the orange to the creamed fat; mix well. Place in the cake-tin and bake in a moderate oven (**350° F., Gas 4**) for 1–1¼ hr.

## ORANGE CUSTARD

*Crème à l'Orange*

**4 oranges**
**1½ pt. boiling water**
**4 oz. granulated sugar**
**3 eggs**

DECORATION

**¼ pt. cream**
**Candied orange peel**

Wash oranges and cut off thin strips of outer rind avoiding white pith. Put rind, water and sugar into a bowl and leave to stand, covered, for 2 hr. After 2 hr. strain into a saucepan, heat through and pour gradually over the well-beaten eggs, stirring all the time. Strain the mixture back into the rinsed pan and heat again to thicken and cook the eggs. Do not allow the custard to boil or curdling will occur. Whisk *or* stir during cooking. Allow to cool, stir in the strained juice of the oranges and pour into custard glasses. When quite cold (*or* chilled in refrigerator) pile whipped cream on top. Decorate with fine strips of candied orange peel.

**6 helpings**
**Time—3 hr.**

## ORANGE CUSTARD JELLY

*Gelée d'Orange à la Crème*

**5 oranges**
**4 oz. sugar**
**¾ oz. gelatine**
**2 eggs**

Wash oranges and cut rind from 2 in thin strips. Strain orange juice and make up to 1½ pt. with water. Add rind, sugar and gelatine and heat gently until dissolved. Allow to cool and add well-beaten eggs. Cook again to thicken but do not boil. Strain into a wet 2-pt. mould. Turn out when set.

**6 helpings**
**Cooking time—about 45 min.**
**Setting time—2 hr.**

## ORANGE ICE CREAM

*Glace à la Crème d'Orange*

**3 oranges**
**2 oz. loaf sugar**
**1½ pt. custard**
**Saffron yellow colouring**
**Carmine colouring**

Remove the outer, yellow skin of the oranges by rubbing them with lumps of sugar. Dissolve the sugar in 1 tablesp. of hot water. Mix with the strained juice of oranges. Stir into the custard and add the colourings until the desired shade is obtained. Chill and freeze.

**6–8 helpings**
**Time—45 min.**

## ORANGE PUDDING

**Short crust pastry using 5–6 oz. flour, etc.**
**4 oranges**
**½ pt. milk**
**3 oz. sugar**
**3 oz. cake-crumbs *or* sponge cakes**
**Pinch of grated nutmeg**
**2 eggs**

Line the sides of a 2-pt. pie-dish with the pastry. Thinly cut the rind from one orange and infuse this in the milk for about 20 min. then remove it. Add to the milk, the sugar, cake-crumbs, nutmeg and well beaten eggs and lastly the juice of all the oranges. Pour into the lined pie-dish and bake in a fairly hot oven (**375° F., Gas 5**) until the pastry is cooked and the mixture is set; about 30–35 min.

## ORANGE SANDWICH CAKE

**1 large sandwich cake**
**Orange-flavoured butter icing**
**Crystallized orange slices**

Cut cake through centre and spread with orange-flavoured butter icing, sandwich together again. Spread the top of the cake with icing, smooth with a knife and decorate with slices of crystallized orange.

NOTE: A more pronounced flavour may be obtained by adding the finely-grated rind of 1 orange when mixing the cake.

Lemon may be substituted for orange if liked.

### ORANGE SALAD

*Salade d'oranges*

**4 sweet oranges**
**½ teasp. castor sugar**
**1 tablesp. French dressing**
**Chopped tarragon and chervil *or* chopped mint**

Peel the oranges thickly with a saw-edged knife, so that all pith is removed. Cut out the natural orange sections. Place in a salad bowl, sprinkle with sugar. Pour the dressing over and sprinkle with tarragon and chervil, if obtainable, or with chopped mint.

**4–6 helpings**

### ORANGE SAUCE—SAVOURY

*Sauce au Jus d'Orange*

**½ pt. Espagnole sauce**
**½ orange**
**½ lemon**
**⅓ pt. red wine (optional)**
**2 tablesp. redcurrant jelly**
**Salt**
**Cayenne pepper**
**Pinch of sugar**

Remove the outer orange rind without the pith, and cut it in neat, thin strips. Cover the orange rind with a little cold water; stew till just tender; then strain. Squeeze the orange and lemon juice into the sauce, add the orange rind. Reheat, add the wine (if used), the redcurrant jelly, season with salt, pepper and sugar to taste.

Serve with roast duck, goose or wild duck.

### ORANGE SOUFFLÉ — COLD

*Soufflé à l'Orange*

**3–4 eggs according to size**
**Orange colouring**
**½ oz. gelatine**
**4 oz. castor sugar**
**3 oranges**
**Rind of ½ lemon**
**4 tablesp. water**
**½ pt. double cream**

DECORATION

**Pistachio nuts**

Proceed as for Milanaise Soufflé using oranges in place of lemons. A little orange colouring may be necessary.

Decorate with chopped, blanched pistachio nuts.

**6 helpings** **Setting time—2 hr.**

### ORANGE SOUFFLÉ —HOT

*Soufflé à l'Orange*

**Butter**
**1½ oz. plain flour**
**⅜ pt. milk**
**5 egg yolks**
**Finely-grated rind of 1½ oranges**
**Juice of ½ orange**
**1½ oz. castor sugar**
**6 egg whites**

Butter and prepare a soufflé tin with paper. Melt 1½ oz. butter, stir in the flour and cook for a few minutes. Add the milk gradually, beating well. Continue cooking until the mixture thickens. Leave it to cool, then beat in the yolks one at a time. Stir in the orange rind, juice and sugar. Stiffly whisk the egg whites and fold these into the mixture. Pour the mixture into the mould; cover with a buttered paper. Steam for 50–60 min. until firm on top.

Serve immediately.

**5–6 helpings**

### ORANGE WHIP (1)

*Gelée d'Oranges fouettée*

**One 1 pt. orange jelly tablet**
**Water and orange juice to make ¾ pt.**

Proceed as for Lemon Whip.

### ORANGE WHIP (2)

**¾ pt. strained orange juice**
**½ oz. gelatine**
**Castor sugar to taste**

Proceed as for Blackcurrant Whip.

### OX CHEEK MOULD

*Tête de Bœuf en gelée*

**1 lb. cooked ox cheek**
**¼ lb. cooked tongue *or* ham *or* bacon**
**2 hard-boiled eggs**
**Grated rind of ½ lemon**
**¼ teasp. powdered mixed herbs**
**Salt and pepper**

**1 teasp. finely-chopped parsley**
**¼–½ oz. gelatine**
**½ pt. stock**

Cut the cheek and tongue, ham or bacon into small pieces. Slice the eggs and arrange some of them in a pattern on the bottom and sides of a plain mould or basin. Mix the parsley, lemon rind, herbs, salt and pepper together. Cover the bottom of the decorated mould with a thick layer of ox cheek and place a thin layer of tongue on top. Add a few slices of egg, sprinkle with the flavouring mixture and repeat layers until the mould is full. Dissolve the gelatine in the stock, pour the warm stock into the mould. Cover with greased paper and bake steadily in a fairly hot oven (**375° F., Gas 5**) for 1¼ hr. Pour in the remainder of the hot stock and when cold turn out and garnish with parsley.

**6 helpings**

## OX LIVER SAVOURY

*Foie de Bœuf à la Française*

**1½ lb. ox liver**
**Flour**
**Veal forcemeat**
**¼ lb. thin bacon rashers**
**Stock**
**1 oz. flour**
**Salt and pepper**

Wash the liver thoroughly in tepid water, cut out any tubes and dry thoroughly. Cut into slices about ¼ in. thick and coat lightly with flour. Spread each slice with a thin layer of forcemeat and cover with bacon. Put into a large baking-tin, cover with a slice of bacon and pour in stock to ½ cover the liver. Cover with a greased paper and cook in a moderate oven (**350° F., Gas 4**) for about 1½–2 hr. Add more stock as necessary. Arrange the liver on a hot dish and keep hot. Mix the 1 oz. flour to a smooth paste with a little cold stock, add ¼ pt. boiling stock or water, pour into the tin and boil up. If too thick, add more stock or water, season if necessary and strain round the liver.

**6 helpings**

## OX KIDNEY WITH ITALIAN SAUCE

*Rognon de Bœuf à l'Italienne*

**1½ lb. ox kidney**
**1 pt. stock**
**2 oz. seasoned flour**
**2 oz. beef dripping**
**1 small onion**
**1½ oz. butter *or* fat**
**12 mushrooms**
**2 tablesp. sherry (optional)**
**Salt and pepper**

Prepare the kidney as directed in the preceding recipe, cutting into ½-in. slices. Coat the kidney well with seasoned flour. Heat the dripping in a sauté pan and fry the kidney quickly on both sides and then more slowly for 20 min. Finely chop the onion, fry, at the same time keeping the sauté pan covered. In a stewpan, melt the fat and add the rest of the flour and cook (stirring) until a nut brown colour. Add the stock, gradually at first, stir until it boils then simmer for 5 min. Drain the kidney from the fat, place in the sauce and simmer for about ¾ hr. Add the sliced mushrooms, sherry (if used), extra seasoning if liked, and simmer for a further 15 min. Serve hot garnished with green peas.

**6 helpings**

## OXFORD JOHN

**1¼ lb. leg of mutton**
**Salt and pepper**
**1 tablesp. finely-chopped ham *or* bacon**
**1 teasp. finely-chopped parsley**
**1 teasp. finely-chopped onion**
**½ teasp. powdered mixed herbs**
**2 oz. butter *or* margarine**
**¾ oz. flour**
**½ pt. good stock**
**1 teasp. lemon juice**

Cut the meat into neat thin rounds about 4 in. in diameter and season with salt and pepper. Mix together the ham or bacon, parsley, onion, herbs and a little salt and pepper; spread the mixture on one side of the meat and pile the slices one above the other. Leave for 1 hr. Then separate and fry each slice lightly and quickly in hot fat. Remove and keep hot. Sprinkle the flour into the pan, brown well and add the stock. Stir until boiling—season, add the lemon juice and replace the meat. Cook for another 10 min. just below simmering point.

Serve hot.

**6 helpings**

### OXTAIL SOUP

*Potage de Queue de Bœuf*

**1 ox tail**
**1 oz. beef dripping**
**1 onion**
**1 carrot**
**1 piece of turnip**
**1 stick of celery**
**1 qt. water *or* bone stock**
**1 teasp. salt**
**A bunch of herbs**
**6 peppercorns**
**1 oz. flour**

Cleanse the ox tail, remove outside fat and joint the tail. Make the dripping hot and in it fry ½ the meat till brown, then remove it. Slice the vegetables and fry them till golden brown, then remove them. Put the fried and raw meat and the fried vegetables into a deep pan, cover with the liquid, bring very slowly to boiling point. Add the salt, herbs and peppercorns and simmer very gently for 3–4 hr. Meanwhile fry the flour in the dripping until golden brown. Strain the soup, return to the soup some of the thinner pieces of meat and small rounds of carrot. Whisk in the browned flour. Whisk till boiling, season and serve. The thicker pieces of meat may be served as stewed ox tail.

**6 helpings**
**Cooking time—4½ hr.**

### OYSTERS

*Huîtres*

Oysters have the best reputation of the bivalve shellfish, for flavour and digestibility, and are for that reason given to invalids. They are in season from September to April, and can be served raw or baked, stewed, or in sauces, pies, etc. Oysters should be opened as near as possible to the time of eating. Do not try to open them yourself unless you are an expert: ask your fishmonger either to loosen the shell for you or to open them completely and put the oyster with its liquor in the deep shell.

English oysters are in season from September to the end of April and the best oysters to obtain to eat "*au naturel*" are the natives from Whitstable or Colchester—although during the close season in this country Continental oysters are imported.

All the oysters need, after being opened, is to be placed on the upper shell with a little of the liquor; they are then arranged on a dish, garnished with sprigs of fresh parsley, and, if possible, surrounded with ice. Thin slices of buttered brown bread, and quarters of lemon are handed round at the same time; also cayenne pepper and vinegar.

### OYSTERS IN CASES

*Huîtres en Caisses à la Diable*

**10–12 small *or* 8 large oysters**
**½ gill white sauce**
**2 oz. grated cheese**
**Salt and cayenne pepper**
**1 oz. butter (approx.)**
**1 tablesp. breadcrumbs**
**Lemon**

Beard the oysters and cut each into 4 pieces. Strain the liquid into the white sauce, then mix with the oysters, ½ the cheese and a good pinch of cayenne pepper and salt. Grease 4 individual scallop shells or small dishes and put in the oyster mixture. Mix the remainder of the cheese with the breadcrumbs, spread over the top of the oyster mixture, cover with tiny knobs of butter. Bake for about 10 min. only, in a hot oven **(425° F., Gas 7)**, until crisp and brown on top and very hot. Garnish with wedges of lemon.

**4 helpings**
**Cooking time—10 min.**

### OYSTERS AU NATUREL

*Huîtres au Naturel*

Serve the oysters *as soon after opening as possible* in the deep shell in their own liquor. With "hinges" to centre, arrange 4 to 6 oysters on individual plates.

Serve with brown bread and butter and lemon wedges.

### OYSTERS À LA MARINIÈRE

*Huîtres à la Marinière*

**18 sauce oysters**
**½ glass Chablis *or* cider**
**1 tablesp. chopped parsley**
**1 tablesp. chopped shallots**
**1 oz. fresh breadcrumbs**
**Salt and pepper**
**1 oz. butter**
**Lemon juice**

Beard the oysters and put the oysters with their liquor in a basin, pour the wine over and allow to stand for about 1 hr. Mix the parsley, shallots and breadcrumbs, and season to taste with salt and pepper. Arrange the oysters in a buttered fireproof dish, pour over a little of the liquor and wine and cover with the breadcrumb mixture. Place the remaining butter in small pieces on top. Bake in a fairly hot oven (**375° F., Gas 5**) for about 15 min. Squeeze a little lemon juice on top and serve in the dish.

**5–6 helpings**

### OYSTER SAUCE

| | |
|---|---|
| **1 doz. oysters** | **1 oz. butter** |
| **1 blade mace** | **¾ oz. flour** |
| **Small piece lemon rind** | **Lemon juice** |
| **½ pt. milk** | **Salt** |

Beard the oysters, and place beards, oyster liquor, mace and lemon rind in a small saucepan. Boil for 5 min. Strain liquor off and add it to the milk. Make a white sauce with butter, flour and the milk and liquor mixture. Season with lemon juice and salt. Scald oysters by holding in boiling water 5 seconds. Drain oysters and add them to the sauce.

### OYSTER TIT-BITS

*Bonnes Bouches aux Huîtres*

| | |
|---|---|
| **9 small oysters** | **3 small rashers of bacon** |
| **1 oz. butter** | **Lemon juice** |
| **9 round croûtes of bread** | **Cayenne pepper** |
| **Anchovy paste** | **Watercress** |

Beard the oysters and place between 2 plates with their own liquid and the butter. Warm thoroughly in the oven, or over a saucepan of boiling water. Spread the croûtes of bread—which can be toasted or fried if wished—with anchovy paste. Cut each rasher of bacon into 3 pieces, grill or fry, put on the croûtes of bread and top with a hot oyster. Sprinkle with lemon juice and cayenne pepper, and garnish with watercress.

Can be served cold, but nicer hot.

**9 small savouries**
**Cooking time—12–15 min. (approx.)**

### PACIFIC PRAWNS

These make an unusual hors d'œuvre. If they are not already boiled when bought, put into cold water, bring to the boil and simmer for not more than 8 min. They have a slightly sweet flavour but are not very interesting plain, they need to be served with a sauce or fried. See Scampi.

### PAELLA

| | |
|---|---|
| **1 chicken** | **Artichoke hearts** |
| **2 lobsters** | **3 tomatoes** |
| **12 crayfish** | **1 green pimento** |
| **Oil for frying** | **Salt and pepper** |
| **2 cloves of garlic** | **Pinch of saffron** |
| **½ lb. rice** | |

Cut the chicken into small joints. Prepare and cut up the lobsters into fairly large pieces, prepare the crayfish. Heat the oil in a deep pan and put in the chicken, frying gently. Pound the garlic and add to the chicken, which by now should be partially cooked. Put in the lobster, crayfish and uncooked rice and stir well. When the rice has absorbed the surplus oil add a little water and continue cooking, adding water each time it is absorbed by the rice, and stirring the contents of the pan. Meanwhile, prepare and add the artichoke hearts, slice the tomatoes, discard pips and add to the mixture. Cut the pimento into thin strips and add. Add salt, pepper and saffron. Continue stirring and cooking until the whole mixture is cooked, then serve very hot.

NOTE: It is obvious that there can be many varieties of this dish, but the essential characteristics are the rice, chicken and some sort of shellfish.

**6 helpings**
**Time—1¼ hr.**

## PANADA TO MAKE

**Put ½ pt. water, 1 oz. butter and a good pinch of salt into a small pan. When boiling, gradually stir in 4 oz. sifted flour and work vigorously with a wooden spoon over heat until the panada leaves the sides of the pan clear. Spread on a plate, and when cool, use as directed.**

**Panada is used to bind together ingredients which possess no adhesive properties themselves.**

## PANCAKES

*Crêpes*

**Batter as for Batter Pudding**
**A little cooking fat**
**Lemon**
**Castor sugar**

Prepare the batter. Leave to stand for ½ hr. then pour into a jug. Use a small clean frying pan or omelette pan.

If the pan is new or has been washed frequently, melt in it about ½ oz. cooking fat; heat until it is smoking hot, twisting the pan so that the sides are coated with fat. Pour away all the fat and wipe the pan clean with a soft cloth or pieces of kitchen paper, otherwise the pancakes may stick.

Put about ¼ oz. of cooking fat into the cleaned frying pan and heat until it is just beginning to smoke. Quickly pour in enough batter to coat thinly the bottom of the pan, tilting the pan to make sure that the batter runs over evenly. Move the frying pan over a quick heat until the pancake is set and browned underneath. Make sure that the pancake is loose at the sides and either toss or turn with a broad bladed knife or fish slice. Brown on the other side and turn on to a sugared paper. Sprinkle with sugar and lemon juice, roll up and keep hot while cooking the rest.

Serve dredged with castor sugar and pieces of cut lemon.

**6 helpings**

NOTE: Other flavourings such as jam, orange, tangerine or brandy may be used, as follows:

**Jam pancakes**—*Crêpes de Confiture:* Spread with jam before rolling up.

**Orange pancakes**—*Crêpes d'Orange:* Make the pancakes but sprinkle with orange juice and serve with pieces of cut orange.

**Tangerine pancakes**—*Crêpes d'Orange de Tanger:* Add grated tangerine rind to the batter. Sprinkle with tangerine juice before rolling up.

With **brandy filling**: Cream together 2 oz. butter and 1 oz. castor sugar until soft. Work in 1 tablesp. brandy and 1 teasp. lemon juice. Spread the pancakes with this mixture. Roll up and put immediately into the serving dish.

## PAPRIKA SAUCE

**½ pt. Velouté sauce**
**1 small red pimento *or* sweet pepper, fresh *or* canned**
**Paprika pepper to taste**
**2 tablesp.–⅛ pt. cream**

Shred the pimento into neat, equal-length strips. If raw pimento is used it may be necessary to simmer it for 10 min. and to remove the skin before shredding it. Add paprika pepper to the sauce to give it a pink colour and desired flavour. Carefully reheat the pimento strips in the sauce. Stir in the cream when the sauce is below boiling point.

Serve with veal or beef.

## PARSLEY AS A GARNISH

*To chop parsley:* If parsley is chopped by the following method, it is bright green in colour, retains most of its Vitamin C and is chopped quickly, without leaving a stain on the chopping board. (1) Hold a bunch of parsley by the stalks and plunge the leaves into boiling water. Leave for 1 min. in the water. (2) Shake the parsley well and wring it tightly in the corner of a cloth. (3) Cut off the stalks and chop the parsley.

## PARSLEY SAUCE

*Sauce de Persil*

**½ pt. white sauce made with stock, fish stock *or* water**
**1 heaped tablesp. finely-chopped parsley**
**1 oz. butter**

Add the chopped parsley to the boiling sauce, then whisk in the butter, a small pat at a time, at just below boiling point.

Serve with fish, white meat or vegetables.

### PARSNIPS—COOKED FOR FOOD VALUE

| | |
|---|---|
| **2 lb. parsnips** | **½ teasp. salt** |
| **1 oz. butter** *or* **margarine** | **1 gill boiling water** |
| | **Chopped parsley** |

Scrub and scrape the parsnips and slice them thinly. Fat steam the parsnips for 10 min., i.e. shake them in the melted fat, well below frying temperature with the lid on the pan until the fat is absorbed. Add the boiling water and the salt, and simmer gently until the parsnips are tender.

Serve hot with the small amount of liquid remaining, and garnish with chopped parsley.

**6 helpings** **Cooking time—30–45 min.**

### PARTRIDGE PIE

*Pâté de Perdreau*

| | |
|---|---|
| **1 partridge** | **2 mushrooms** |
| **1 oz. butter** | **1 small shallot** |
| **½ lb. veal** | **1 tablesp. chopped parsley** |
| **Salt and pepper** | **½ pt. stock** |
| **2 rashers bacon** | **Puff pastry using 8 oz. flour, etc.** |
| **1 hard-boiled egg** | |

Pluck, draw, singe and wipe bird with a damp cloth, joint it neatly. Fry joints in butter until lightly browned. Slice veal thinly, lay pieces in the bottom of a pie-dish, season well, lay pieces of partridge on top, interspersed with bacon and sections of hard-boiled egg. Sprinkle on roughly-chopped mushrooms, shallot, finely-chopped parsley, ¾ fill dish with stock. Cover dish with puff pastry, bake 1¼–1½ hr. Put in a hot oven (**425°–450° F., Gas 7–8**) for 15 min., then reduce heat to moderately hot (**350°–375° F., Gas 4–5**) for remainder of time. Glaze the pie with egg 15 min. before cooking is complete.

Fill up with hot seasoned stock before serving.

**4 helpings**

### PARTY DISHES

Modern parties are so diverse that almost any everyday dish can be adapted for use at some kind of party. Special dishes for parties are either dishes which are more elaborate than everyday ones, or are snacks and similar dishes used at parties where knives and forks are not supplied.

### PARTY DISHES FOR YOUNG TEENAGERS

*See Children's Food*

### PARTY FOOD FOR CHILDREN

*See Children's Food and various recipes for large and small cakes, biscuits, etc.*

### PARTY SANDWICHES

Bread for party sandwiches must be cut very thin, and the crusts be removed; amusing and unusual shapes can be cut with pastry or biscuit cutters. Attractive results can be achieved by alternating 3 thinly-cut slices of white and brown bread when making up the sandwiches, before cutting them into fingers, triangles or squares.

*To make rolled sandwiches:* Take single slices of thinly-cut bread and butter, remove the crusts; spread with a savoury butter or with creamed butter and the selected filling, then roll up lightly, skewer with a cocktail stick and chill. Remove the sticks before serving.

*To make horn shapes:* Use thinly-cut slices of bread preferably 24 hours old, remove the crusts, trim as shown in diag. opposite. Spread the bread with a creamed filling or savoury butter, then roll into cones. Hold in shape with a cocktail stick and chill. Remove sticks before serving and decorate to taste.

Savoury party sandwiches may be decorated with parsley, cress, fancily-cut shapes of hard boiled egg, tomato, pickled gherkin, stuffed olives, etc., or swirls and rosettes of piped savoury butters. Sweet-filled sandwiches can be garnished with glacé cherry, angelica, halved grapes, etc.

*See Savoury Fillings for Sandwiches, Sweet Fillings for Sandwiches, etc.*

## PASTA

*See Cereals, Pasta.*

## PASTRY WITHOUT BUTTER

**1 lb. flour**
**1 teasp. baking-powder**
**A small wineglass salad oil**

Sift the flour and baking-powder. Add, drop by drop, the oil and sufficient cold water to produce a dough of the correct consistency for rolling. Fold it over and roll it out 2–3 times, place on a baking-sheet and bake immediately.

## PASTRY CASES

Vol-au-Vent shapes or cornet shapes—filled with savoury mixtures are excellent for buffet parties. They can be served hot or cold. If the mixture is being put into the cold pastry cases make sure it is quite cold. If on the other hand it is being put into hot pastry cases heat the filling and the pastry separately, and put together at the last minute, so that the filling does not make the pastry soft.

Directions for making vol-au-vent shapes and cornet shapes are given in the Pastry section.

### SUGGESTED FILLINGS

Quantities given are enough to fill 12 medium sized vol-au-vent cases or about 16 cornet cases (allowing a liberal amount of filling).

### Chicken

**½ pt. thick sauce made with ½ pt. milk and ½ chicken stock**
**¾–1 lb. diced cooked chicken (approx.)**
**Seasoning**

Mix together well, and if possible add just 1 tablesp. cream.

### Mushroom

**¾ lb. mushrooms**
**2 oz. butter *or* margarine**
**2½ gills milk**
**1½ oz. flour**
**Seasoning**
**Cayenne pepper**

Chop the mushrooms into small pieces and toss in the hot butter for a few minutes. Add ½ pt. of milk and cook gently for about 10 min. Blend the flour with the other ½ gill milk, add to the mushroom mixture. Season well and boil until smooth and thick. Stir as the mixture cools. If wished add 1 tablesp. thick cream. Dust with cayenne pepper when the cases are filled.

### Sardine

**1 small can of sardines**
**1 tablesp. white *or* tomato sauce**
**Salt and pepper**
**Few drops of lemon juice**
**2 teasp. grated Parmesan cheese *or* 1 tablesp. grated Cheddar cheese**

Remove the bones and mash the sardines. Mix with the white or tomato sauce (if using white sauce, add a few drops of anchovy essence). Season, blend with a few drops of lemon juice and the cheese.

### Savoury Egg

**5 eggs**
**3 tablesp. cream *or* mayonnaise**
**1 oz. butter**
**Seasoning**
**2 oz. finely-diced lean tongue**

Beat the eggs and cream or mayonnaise together. Heat the butter, add the eggs, season well and cook gently until commencing to thicken. If serving the mixture hot add the diced tongue—but if serving cold do not add this until the eggs are cold. Take care the mixture does not become too stiff—if it appears rather dry beat in more cream or mayonnaise.

### Shell Fish

**½ pt. thick sauce—made with ½ milk and ½ stock made by simmering prawn *or* lobster shells**
**1 large flaked lobster *or* about 1¼ pt. picked prawns**
**2 tablesp. thick mayonnaise**
**Seasoning**

Mix well together, and if wished add 1–2 chopped gherkins and capers. Garnish with whole prawns.

## PASTRY-MAKING

The aim in pastry-making is to make the pastry as light as possible. Success in doing this depends on the amount of cold air incorporated into the mixture during the making. The cold air expands on heating, making the pastry light.

When making puff, flaky or rough puff pastry, the air is incorporated in the pastry in thin layers, while in short crust and suet pastry the air fills the cavities all through the pastry. Self-raising flour is only suitable for suet crust pastry and plain short crust pastry, and should not be used for rich pastries.

Butter, or butter and lard in equal quantities, should be used for pastry-making if possible, although margarine can be substituted.

When the amount of fat is less than ½ the amount of flour a little baking-powder (1 level teasp. to ½ lb. flour) can be added.

**General Hints**

1. Keep everything for pastry-making cool.
2. Work in a cool place and if possible, on a marble slab or enamelled surface.
3. Always sift the flour.
4. When rubbing the fat into the flour use the finger-tips, and lift the hands up from the bowl so that air is caught as the flour falls back into the bowl.
5. Use freshly-drawn cold water for mixing and mix with a round bladed knife. Too much water makes the pastry hard.
6. Lemon juice tends to make pastry lighter.
7. Handle pastry as little and as lightly as possible. Work quickly.
8. Allow pastry to stand for a short time in a cool place after making, particularly in hot weather.
9. Roll pastry lightly, quickly and evenly with short strokes, lifting the rolling-pin between each stroke. Do not roll off the edge of the pastry or the air will be pressed out.
10. Always roll away from oneself and never from side to side.
11. Use very little flour for rolling out and remove any surplus flour with a pastry brush.
12. Use the rolled side of the pastry for the outside.
13. When making puff, flaky or rough puff pastry allow the pastry to relax, if possible, for 15 min. between every two rollings.
14. Most pastries are baked in a fairly hot oven, but the richer the pastry the hotter the oven required for cooking. A high temperature is necessary to expand the air or gas, thus making the pastry light. The starch grains swell with the moisture thereby enabling the fat globules to intermingle more easily with the starch. Unless the heat is sufficiently great to act upon the flour in this way, the melted fat runs out and leaves the pastry less rich, and also, probably, heavy and tough.

NOTE: Hot Water Crust, Choux Pastry and Genoese Pastry are exceptions to these rules.

**To Glaze Pastry**

Meat pies, patties, sausage-rolls, etc., are usually brushed over with well-beaten egg before, or during baking. When a deeper tone is desired the yolk alone is used, or if the egg white is being used in the preparation of a dish, a little milk may be added to the egg yolk to increase the quantity.

Fruit tarts, puffs, etc., may be brushed lightly with cold water, and dredged with castor sugar before baking. If a thin coating of icing is desired, they can be brushed over with well-beaten egg white and well dredged with castor sugar, when nearly baked.

**To Keep Pastry**

Pastry not intended for immediate use should be folded in greaseproof paper and kept in a refrigerator or cool place.

**To Line the Sides of a Pie-Dish**

For a 1½-pt. pie-dish 4 oz. pastry will be required (i.e. 4 oz. flour etc.).

Wet the pie-dish with cold water. Roll out the pastry thinly, cut a strip 3–4 in. wide and lay it round the sides of the dish so that it lies slightly over the outer rim (to allow for shrinkage during baking). Press the pastry well on to the pie-dish, joining the strip neatly by wetting the edges with cold water and pressing firmly together. Wet the rim of pastry and decorate the edge.

## PÂTE SUCRÉE

**8 oz. plain flour**
**Pinch of salt**
**5 oz. butter**
**2 oz. sugar**
**1 egg yolk**
**Cold water to mix**

Sift together the flour and salt. Cut the butter into small pieces and rub it lightly into the flour using the finger tips. Add the sugar and mix with egg yolk and sufficient cold water to make a stiff paste.

Use as required.

NOTE. In warm weather only a very small quantity of water will be required.

## PATRIOTIC CAKE

*Gâteau Patriotique*

**10 oz. plain flour**
**⅛ teasp. salt**
**4 oz. butter *or* margarine**
**6 oz. sugar**
**1 level teasp. bicarbonate of soda**
**2 level teasp. cream of tartar**
**2 eggs**
**1½ gills milk *or* enough to mix to a thick batter**

GLAZE

**2 tablesp. milk**
**1 tablesp. sugar**

DECORATION

**Dessicated coconut *or* crushed cornflakes**

Grease a dripping-tin and line the bottom with greaseproof paper.

Sift flour and salt and rub in the fat. Add the other dry ingredients and mix to a very thick batter with the eggs and milk. Pour into the tin and bake in the top middle of a fairly hot oven (**375° F., Gas 5**) for 15 min. then reduce heat to **350° F., Gas 4,** till firm and well browned.

Boil together the milk and sugar for the glaze for 2 min.; brush the top of the cake with this and sprinkle with coconut or cornflakes.

NOTE: The cake may be spread with glacé icing.

**Cooking time—about 40 min.**

## PAVLOVA CAKE

**3 egg whites**
**6 oz. castor sugar**
**½ teasp. vanilla essence**
**½ teasp. cornflour**
**½ teasp. vinegar**

Beat the egg whites until stiff. Continue beating, gradually adding the sugar. Beat until sugar is dissolved and at this stage the mixture should be very stiff and standing well in peaks. Fold in vanilla, cornflour and vinegar. Spread mixture in a 6–8 in. circle on greaseproof paper on a baking-sheet, making the sides higher than the centre to form a shell to hold filling. Or pipe small shapes for the sides. Place in a cool oven (**310° F., Gas 2**) for 1–1¼ hr.

The pavlova should be crisp and very lightly tinted on the surface yet remain soft and of the consistency of marshmallow in the centre. Cool and remove very carefully on to a flat cake-tray or board. Fill and serve cut in wedges.

FILLING

1. Pile ½ pt. whipped and flavoured cream into the pavlova shell and on top of this arrange a selection of fruit: pineapple; strawberries or other berry fruits; cherries; apricots; mandarins; passion fruit; grapes; fresh or canned peaches, etc., according to taste and season. Finally decorate with angelica, maraschino cherries or almonds as desired.

2. Mash or slice 4–6 bananas. Mix a few tablespoonfuls of sherry or brandy into the mashed bananas, or, place the slices in a basin and cover with sherry or brandy. Allow to stand for 1 hr.

Strain off liquid if bananas are sliced, then fold fruit into ½ pt. whipped and sweetened cream, with a cupful of halved fresh or maraschino cherries. (If the sherry or brandy is inclined to liquify the cream add 1 teasp. dissolved gelatine). Pile into pavlova shell and sprinkle surface generously with shredded chocolate and chopped nuts or toasted coconut.

## PEA SOUP

*Purée de Pois Secs*

As for Butter Bean Purée, using dried, whole or split peas and adding a sprig of mint or a little dried mint.

**Cooking time—2 hr. (after 12 hr. soaking)**

## PEA PURÉE

*Purée de pois*

**¾ lb. green *or* yellow split peas**
**2 carrots**
**2 cloves**

4 oz. fat bacon
2 small onions
Bunch of herbs
Salt and pepper

Soak the peas overnight. Cut up the bacon and put it into a saucepan with the peas, sliced onions and carrots, bunch of herbs, and enough cold, salted water to cover. Simmer gently until the peas are tender, 2–2½ hr. Drain off liquid, but reserve it. Rub ingredients through a sieve. Reheat with a little of the cooking liquid added, if necessary, to give a fairly thick purée. Season and serve.

NOTE: Pea purée is excellent with grilled or fried sausages, *or* bacon *or* bacon and eggs.

**6 helpings**
**Cooking time—about 3 hr.**

## PEA SOUP (YELLOW)

**1 lb. dried yellow peas**
**2 lb. slightly salted pork**
**1 celeriac**
**2 leeks**
**Thyme**
**Potatoes**

Put the peas to soak overnight. Next morning cook in 3 pt. water. Simmer the pork separately with a bunch of herbs, consisting of celeriac, leeks and thyme. Boil the potatoes. When the pork is tender, take it out and keep it warm. Meanwhile press the peas through a sieve and mix with the stock, from which all fat has been removed. Cut the potatoes and vegetables in pieces and put in the soup-tureen, pour over the soup. The pork is served with the soup.

**6 helpings**

## PEACH CONDÉ

*Pêche Condé*

**1 pt. cold rice mould**
**⅛ pt. double cream *or* cream and custard**
**1 small can peaches**
**1 level teasp. arrowroot**

Stir the cream into the cold rice mould to produce a soft, creamy consistency. Pour into serving dishes. Drain the fruit from the juice and arrange attractively on top of the rice. Make up the fruit juice to ¼ pt. with water. Blend the arrowroot with the fruit juice and boil until clear. Pour carefully over the fruit. Finish by decorating with whipped cream.

NOTE: Apricots or pineapple may be substituted for peaches.

**4 helpings**

## PETITS FOURS (1)

**2 egg whites**
**4 oz. ground almonds**
**2 oz. castor sugar**
**A few drops almond essence**
**Rice paper**

DECORATION

**Glacé cherries**
**Angelica**

Whisk egg whites very stiffly and fold in mixed almonds and sugar very lightly, with the almond essence. Place the mixture in a forcing bag fitted with a large rose vegetable pipe and force it on to rice paper in rosettes or oblongs. Decorate with small pieces of cherry and angelica and bake in a moderate to warm oven (350°–335° F., Gas 4–3) till golden brown.

**20–30 petits fours** **Cooking time—20–30 min.**

## PETITS FOURS (2)

**Genoese pastry**
**Apricot marmalade *or* glaze**
**Butter icing and cake-crumbs**
**Almond paste**
**Glacé icing *or* royal icing**

Cut neat shapes of genoese pastry squares, rings, triangles, etc. Using apricot marmalade fasten a small piece of almond paste *or* some butter icing mixed with cake-crumbs and flavoured with vanilla, kirsch, rum, etc., neatly on top of each piece of genoese. Coat with glacé or royal icing and decorate with fine piping, scrolls, etc.

## PEANUT BUTTER BREAD

**1 lb. self-raising flour**
**Pinch of salt**
**6 oz. peanut butter**
**8 oz. sugar**
**1 egg**
**1 cup milk**

Sift flour and salt. Cream butter and sugar. Add beaten egg and milk alternately with sifted flour. Put into a greased tin and bake in a fairly hot oven (375° F., Gas 5).

**Cooking time—½–¾ hr.**

### PEANUT SOUP

**1 lb. peanuts**
**1 onion**
**2 sticks of celery**
**2 cups white stock**
**2 oz. margarine**
**1 oz. flour**
**2 cups milk**
**Pinch of salt**
**Pinch of cayenne pepper**

Mince the peanuts. Cook slowly with chopped onion and chopped celery in stock. In another saucepan melt the margarine and add the flour. Stir till smooth; add milk. Combine the mixtures. Season with salt and pepper. Cook for 5 min. Rub through strainer. Serve hot.

**6 helpings**
**Cooking time—15 min.**

### PEARS FILLED WITH NUT AND DATE SALAD

**3 ripe dessert *or* canned pears**
**1 small crisp lettuce**
**4 oz. chopped dates**
**2 oz. chopped walnuts**
**Chopped parsley**
**French dressing *or* salad dressing**

Peel and halve the pears. Remove the cores with a sharp teaspoon, then scoop out a little of the pulp of the pears to leave a hollow for the filling. Shred a few lettuce leaves very finely and mix with dates, walnuts, chopped parsley and finely diced pear pulp and French dressing *or* salad dressing. Place the halved pears on small crisp lettuce leaves on individual plates. Pile the mixture on each piece of pear.

NOTE: If fresh pears are used, squeeze lemon juice over them to prevent discoloration.

**6 helpings**

### PEASE PUDDING

*Pouding aux pois à l'Anglaise*

**1½ pt. split peas**
**1 small onion**
**Small bunch of herbs**
**2 oz. butter *or* margarine**
**2 eggs**
**Salt and pepper**

Soak the peas overnight, remove any discoloured ones. Rinse and cover with cold, salted water. Bring slowly to boiling point in the water, to which has been added the onion (whole) and the bunch of herbs. Simmer very slowly until tender—2–2½ hr. Drain well and rub through a sieve. Add the butter, cut in small pieces, the beaten eggs, pepper and salt. Beat well until the ingredients are well incorporated. Tie tightly in a floured cloth and simmer in water for an hour. Turn out and serve very hot.

NOTE: Pease pudding is served with hot pickled pork.

**6 helpings**
**Cooking time—about 3½ hr.**

### PECTIN STOCK

(To add to fruit deficient in pectin when making jams.)

Prepare apples, redcurrants or gooseberries, cook and strain through a scalded jelly bag as for jelly making. Bring the juice to the boil but do not add any sugar. Pour into hot preserving jars, sterilize in a pan of hot water, raised to boiling-point and boiled for 5 min.

### PEPERONATA

**1 large onion**
**2 tablesp. olive oil**
**1 large yellow pepper**
**2 large green peppers**
**1 large red pepper**
**1 teacup crushed and peeled tomatoes**
**Salt**

Slice the onion finely and fry lightly in the warm olive oil. Add the peppers—well washed, dried and cut into pieces—the crushed tomatoes. Add salt to taste, cover and cook slowly, stirring frequently to prevent burning.

### PEPPER POT

**2 lb. pork**
**1 lb. beef**
**1 small chicken**
**2 fresh peppers**
**1 sprig thyme**
**1 teasp. salt**
**3–4 tablesp. cassareep**

Cut pork into pieces and fry. Put into an earthenware casserole. Add the chopped beef and chicken cut into pieces. Remove seeds from peppers. Add peppers chopped with thyme and salt. Cover with water and add the cassareep. Stew slowly. Cooked meats can be added each day with additional water and cassareep. If cooked daily the meat does not deteriorate.

**Cooking time—4 hr. (approx.)**

1

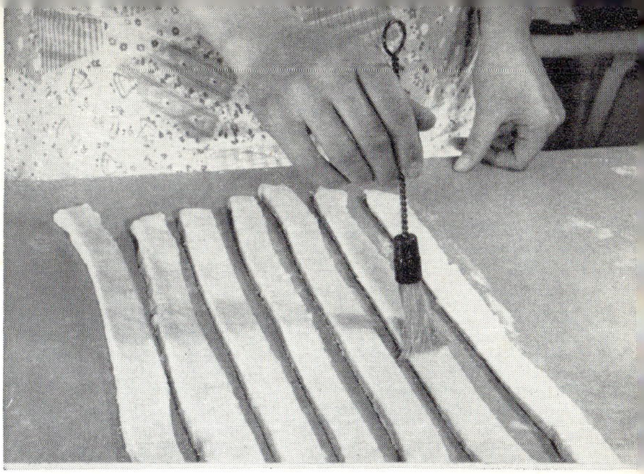

2

3

4

5

**Pastry Looks Pretty II**
**—Making Pastry Cones.**

1 Roll out the pastry to about $\frac{1}{8}$ inch thickness and cut into strips $\frac{1}{2}$ inch wide and 12–13 inches long.

2 Damp the strips lightly with water.

3 Wind round the horn cases, starting from point at the base and working upwards. The moist surface should be kept on the outside.

4 Finish with overlap on the underside of the tin and trim neatly.

5 Allow to stand for about 1 hour. Brush over the surface of the cones with milk or egg and milk.

**Pastry Looks Pretty III —Decorative Pie Rose.**

**1 Roll out left-overs of pastry into a thin round shape, and cut it with a knife into quarters.**

**2 Arrange pieces one on top of the other, overlapping at angles.**

**3 Put the thumb into the centre of the pastry and push into a tube.**

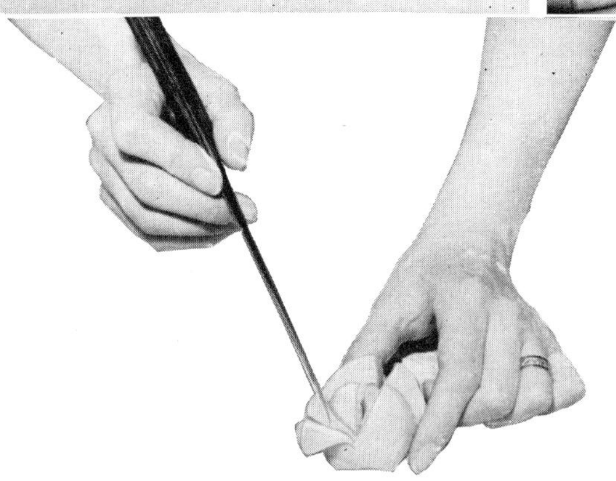

**4 Cut off the uneven ends, and at the rounded end make two cuts a right angles forming a cross. Open the pastry to form petals.**

## PICCALILLI

| | |
|---|---|
| **2 lb. mixed vegetables** | **½ lb. granulated sugar** |
| **2 oz. cooking salt** | **2 oz. mustard** |
| **1 pt. vinegar** | **½ oz. turmeric** |
| **15 chillies** | **2 level tablesp. cornflour** |

Cut into small pieces a variety of vegetables such as cauliflower, cucumber, shallots and young kidney beans, weighing about 2 lb. in all when prepared. Place in a large earthenware bowl and sprinkle with the cooking salt. Leave to stand for 24 hr. and then drain well. Boil the vinegar and chillies for 2 min., allow to stand for ½ hr. and then strain the vinegar.

Mix together the sugar, mustard, turmeric and cornflour. Blend with a little of the cooled vinegar, bring the remainder of the vinegar back to the boil, pour over the blend, return to the saucepan and boil for 3 min. Remove from the heat and fold in the strained vegetables. Pack into prepared jars and cover at once with vinegar-proof covers.

## PICKLED MACKEREL

*Maquereaux marinés*

| | |
|---|---|
| **2–3 small mackerel** | **Allspice** |
| **Salt and pepper** | **12 peppercorns** |
| **2 bay leaves** | **½ pt. vinegar** |

Clean and wash the fish and take out the roes. Place the mackerel in a fireproof dish with the roes (mackerel are best in that part of the season when the roes are not full grown). Sprinkle well with salt and pepper, add the bay leaves, allspice, peppercorns, vinegar and about ¼ pt. of water. Cover with a greased paper and bake in a cool oven (**310° F., Gas 2**) for nearly 1 hr.

Leave them in the liquor until required.

**2–3 helpings**

## PICKLED NASTURTIUM SEEDS

Nasturtium seeds when pickled are a good substitute for capers, and can add variety to salad dressings. As a straight pickle they are rather too small to be popular on the table, but go well in clear mixed pickles.

Gather seeds whilst still green on a dry day

and steep in brine (½ lb. salt to 3 pt. water) for 24 hr. Pack in small jars, warm in the oven for 10 min. and cover with hot spiced vinegar. It is best to use a hot spice mixture for these, and a few leaves of tarragon, if available, are pleasing.

The only important thing to remember is to use small jars or bottles, so that they are consumed at once when opened.

## PICKLED ONIONS

Use small even-sized pickling onions. Peel with a stainless knife and drop them into a basin of salted water until all have been peeled. Remove from water and allow to drain thoroughly before packing into jars or bottles. Cover with cold spiced vinegar and keep for at least 1 month before using.

## PICKLED SALMON—SWEDISH
**(for Smørgåsbord)**

| | |
|---|---|
| **4 lb. fresh salmon (middle cut)** | **1 tablesp. sugar** |
| **3 tablesp. salt** | **1 teasp. white pepper** |
| | **1 large bunch dill** |

Scrape off all the blood and dry the salmon with a clean cloth, but do not scale it. Cut it in ½ along the bone and carefully remove this, at the same time removing small bones. Put the ½ of salmon, skin downwards, into a deep bowl. Mix salt, sugar and pepper and sprinkle this mixture on the meaty side of the salmon. Cover the surface with small bunches of dill. Put in the other ½ of the salmon, skin upwards and so that the thick end lies on top of the thin end below. Put the rest of the dill on the sides and put on a slight pressure. Leave the salmon "buried" till the next day. Then the salmon may be served cut into thick portions or into thin slices. Serve it with a dressing made of French mustard, dill, sugar, pepper, vinegar and oil (half and half).

### PICKLED WALNUTS

Use walnuts whose shells have not begun to form. Prick well with a silver fork; if the shell can be felt, do not use the walnut. The shell begins to form opposite the stalk, about ¼ in. from the end.

Cover with a brine (1 lb. salt to 1 gal. water) and leave to soak for about 6 days. Drain, make fresh brine, and leave to soak for a further 7 days.

Drain, and spread in a single layer on dishes, leaving them exposed to the air, preferably in sunshine, until they blacken (1–2 days). Pack into jars and cover with hot spiced vinegar. Tie down when cold and leave for at least a month before using.

NOTE: To help to prevent stained hands, wear gloves when handling the walnuts.

### PICKLES, SPICED VINEGAR FOR

*See Spiced Vinegar for Pickles.*

### PICNIC or PACKED LUNCH SANDWICHES

For picnic or packed lunch sandwiches use brown or white bread which is 24 hours old to facilitate cutting. Cut even slices or use fresh sliced bread, small baps, barm cakes, tea cakes or rolls.

**Fillings**

1. A slice of Cheddar or Cheshire cheese, topped with thin slices of tomato and chopped fresh mint.
2. A slice of boiled ham with tomato sauce or chutney.
3. Scrambled egg sprinkled with chopped parsley.
4. Chopped hard-boiled egg mixed with anchovies.
5. Thin slices of skinned tomatoes, seasoned and sprinkled with lemon juice or vinegar to taste.
6. Minced cooked chicken and ham, moistened with mayonnaise if liked, sprinkled with watercress.
7. Thin slices of cold roast beef, topped with slices of tomato and cucumber, or a thin layer of horseradish sauce.
8. Smoked cod's roe, sprinkled with lemon juice and topped with slices of cucumber.
9. Flaked cold, cooked white fish, mixed with mayonnaise and chopped parsley.
10. Minced turkey or chicken, mixed with peanut butter and a little ordinary butter.
11. Cooked veal or lean pork with sliced pickled gherkins.

### PICNIC SALAD

**1 lb. cooked haddock**
**1 medium sized carrot**
**1 level tablesp. chopped parsley**
**1 level tablesp. chopped chives**
**3 tablesp. French dressing**
**Lettuce leaves**

Remove all skin and bone and flake the fish. Grate the carrot and add with the parsley and chives to the fish. Toss all together with the French dressing and serve on crisp lettuce leaves, as one salad or as individual portions.

**4 helpings**

### PIES AND TARTS

*See Flans, Open Tarts, Pastry-Making, Savoury Pies and Tarts, Sweet Pies and Tarts. Also recipes for the type or flavour required.*

### PIGEON PIE

*Pâté de Pigeon*

**2 pigeons**
**½ lb. rump steak**
**¼ lb. ham *or* bacon**
**¾ pt. good stock**
**2 hard-boiled eggs**
**Salt and pepper**
**Puff pastry using 8 oz. flour, etc.**
**Egg *or* milk to glaze**

Remove the feet from the pigeons and split each bird in two. Cut the steak in small thin slices, cut the bacon in strips and slice the eggs. Put all ingredients in layers in a pie-dish, seasoning the layers well, and seasoning each half-bird, ¾ fill the dish with stock. Cover pie with puff pastry, glaze, and cook in a hot oven (**425°–450° F., Gas 7–8**) until pastry is risen and set, then lower heat to moderate (**350°–375° F., Gas 4–5**) and bake for 1 hr. more. Cut the toes off the feet, and scald the latter.

Before serving the pie, fill it with the remainder of the hot seasoned stock and fix the feet in an upright position in the hole previously made in the pastry.

**6 helpings**

### PIPERADE BASQUE

| | |
|---|---|
| **6 eggs** | **Salt** |
| **2 red peppers** | **Olive oil** |
| **2 green peppers** | **Pinch of sugar** |
| **1½ lb. tomatoes** | **Black pepper** |
| **1 clove garlic** | **Croûtons** |

Cut the peppers in half, remove the seeds and pith, chop finely and plunge into boiling salted water. Simmer for about 10 min. Reserve 3 tomatoes, skin and quarter the rest. Crush garlic with a pinch of salt and add to 4 tablesp. olive oil in a sauté pan. Heat, add the strained peppers and cook slowly for 3–4 min. Then add the quartered tomatoes, salt and pepper, and sugar. Cover pan and simmer for 15 min. Skin and slice the 3 tomatoes and fry gently in oil. When the pepper mixture is mushy, beat the eggs lightly and add to the pan. Cook, stirring constantly, over a low heat, then pile on a dish and serve with the sliced tomatoes and croûtons arranged around.

**8 helpings** **Cooking time—40 min. (approx.)**

### PETITS POIS À LA FRANÇAISE

Peas—French Style

| | |
|---|---|
| **1 qt. fresh peas (small)** | **3 oz. butter** |
| **1 small globe lettuce** | **1 oz. granulated sugar** |
| **18 spring onions** | **Salt and pepper** |
| **1 sprig of parsley** | **¼ pt. water** |
| **1 sprig of chervil** | |

In a saucepan place the peas, shredded heart of lettuce, spring onions, parsley and chervil sprigs tied together, ½ the butter and all the sugar; season. Thoroughly mix together and allow to stand for a while; then moisten with the water. Bring to the boil and simmer steadily, with the lid on, until cooked, about 35–40 min. Remove the parsley and chervil and stir into the peas—off the heat—the remainder of the butter. This will slightly thicken the cooking liquor of the peas. Do not re-boil.

**6–8 helpings**

### PIZZA ALLA NAPOLETANA

| | |
|---|---|
| **Flaky unsweetened very short pastry *or* bread dough using 4 oz. flour, etc.** | **½ lb. Bel Paese *or* Mozzarella cheese** |
| | **6 anchovy fillets** |
| | **4 tablesp. olive oil** |
| **2 oz. black olives** | **1 teasp. oregano** |
| **Tomatoes** | **1 clove of garlic** |

Well-grease a flat 7-in. tart-tin with olive oil and line with a thin layer of the pastry. Stone the olives and cut the flesh into small pieces. Cover pastry completely with alternate rows of pieces of olive, pieces of tomato, cheese also cut into small pieces and anchovies cut into strips. Pour over the olive oil, sprinkle with the oregano and finely-chopped garlic. Or pulp the tomatoes, add olive oil, oregano and garlic and spread over pastry. Arrange anchovy fillets like the spokes of a wheel with an olive between. Sprinkle with grated cheese. Bake in a fairly hot oven (**375° F., Gas 5**) for about 25 min.

**2–3 helpings**

### PIG'S CHEEK

| | |
|---|---|
| **A pig's cheek** | **Browned breadcrumbs** |

If the cheek has been cured and dried, soak it for 5–6 hr., if not, wash well in several waters. Cover the meat with warm water and simmer gently for 2½ hr. Then remove the cheek, strip off the skin and cover the cheek thickly with lightly browned crumbs. Bake for about ½ hr. in a moderate oven (**350° F., Gas 4**). Serve hot or cold. Baking the meat is not essential and can be omitted if liked.

**3–4 helpings**

### PINEAPPLE AND CREAM CHEESE SALAD

| | |
|---|---|
| **Lettuce leaves** | **Parsley** |
| **1 slice pineapple** | **Gherkin** |
| **1 oz. cream cheese** | **Chilli** |
| **Thousand Island dressing** | |

Arrange a bed of lettuce leaves on a dish. Place a slice of pineapple in the centre. Pile cream cheese on pineapple. Pour Thousand Island dressing over cheese. Garnish with parsley, gherkin and chilli.

THOUSAND ISLAND DRESSING

**1 cup mayonnaise**
**1 tablesp. finely-chopped parsley**
**1 tablesp. finely-chopped capers**
**1 tablesp. finely-chopped olives**
**1 tablesp. finely-chopped pickles**
**Lemon juice**
**Tomato juice**

Stir gradually into the mayonnaise, the parsley, capers, olives and pickles. Reduce to a thin pouring consistency with lemon and tomato juice

## PINEAPPLE SOUFFLÉ

*Soufflé à l'Ananas*

**1½ oz. butter**
**1½ oz. plain flour**
**⅜ pt. milk**
**4½ egg yolks**
**1½ oz. castor sugar**
**A few drops of vanilla essence**
**3 oz. preserved pineapple**
**6 egg whites**
**Angelica (optional)**

Well butter and prepare a soufflé tin or mould. If liked, the bottom can be decorated with angelica and pineapple. Melt 1½ oz. butter, stir in the flour and cook very slowly for a few minutes. Add the milk gradually, beating all the time, continue cooking for a minute longer. Let the mixture cool slightly. Beat in the egg yolks one at a time then add the sugar, vanilla essence and diced pineapple. Stiffly whisk the egg whites and fold them lightly into the mixture. Pour the mixture into the prepared soufflé tin; cover with a buttered paper. Steam gently for 45–60 min. until firm on the top.

Unmould and serve immediately, with pineapple sauce.

NOTE: If canned pineapple is used, drain the fruit well and substitute half the milk with pineapple juice.

**5–6 helpings**

## PINEAPPLE FRITTERS

*Beignets d'Ananas*

**Coating batter**
**2 cans small pineapple rings**
**Fat for frying**
**Castor sugar**

Make the batter. Drain the pineapple well. Dip each ring into batter and then using a skewer, lower the ring into the deep fat which should be just hazing. Cook until crisp and nicely browned. Drain; dredge with castor sugar and serve at once.

If liked, serve with pineapple sauce made from the syrup.

**Allow 2 fritters for each helping**

## PINEAPPLE SALAD

*Salade d'Ananas*

**1 small pineapple**
**1 celery heart**
**Mayonnaise sauce dressing *or* salad**
**Thin slices of lemon**

Peel and core the pineapple and cut into fine shreds. Cut the celery into small shreds and mix it with the pineapple. Toss in sufficient salad dressing or mayonnaise to moisten and season it. Serve ice cold, garnished with lemon.

**4–6 helpings**

## PINEAPPLE WHIP

*Gelée d'Ananas fouettée*

**One 1 pt. pineapple jelly tablet**
**½ pt. canned pineapple juice**
**¼ pt. water**
**Sugar if necessary**

Proceed as for Lemon Whip.

## PINEAPPLE WATER ICE

*Glace à l'eau d'Ananas*

**½ pt. canned pineapple juice**
**1 pt. syrup**
**2 tablesp. lemon juice**

Thoroughly mix all ingredients. Chill and freeze.

**6 helpings**
**Time—1½–2 hr.**

## PINEAPPLE ICING

**1 pt. water**
**12 oz. loaf sugar**
**3 drops pineapple essence**

Put the water and sugar into a strong pan. Allow to dissolve, then bring to boiling-point; skim well. Boil quickly without stirring until a pale brown colour and the syrup threads like caramel. Add the pineapple essence.

## PINEAPPLE HAM SLICES

**12 oz. cooked ham**
**1 teasp. mixed mustard**
**1 tablesp. mayonnaise**
**3 tablesp. sherry, cider *or* pineapple juice**
**6 slices of pineapple**
**4 gherkins (optional)**

Mince the ham and mix with the mustard, mayonnaise and sherry, cider or juice. Drain the pineapple slices and cover neatly with ham mixture. Place in a greased fireproof dish or meat-tin and bake in a moderate oven. (**350° F., Gas 4**) for 10–15 min. Serve garnished with slices of gherkin if liked.

**6 helpings**

## PIQUANT SAUCE

*Sauce Piquante*

**½ pt. brown sauce**
**1 onion *or* 2 shallots**
**1 oz. mushrooms**
**1 bay leaf**
**1 blade of mace**
**2 tablesp. vinegar**
**1 tablesp. halved capers**
**1 tablesp. chopped gherkins**
**1 dessertsp. mushroom ketchup**
**½ teasp. sugar (optional)**

Finely chop the onion or shallots, chop the mushrooms coarsely. Simmer the onion or shallots, the bay leaf and mace in the vinegar for 10 min. Add this mixture and the chopped mushrooms to the brown sauce and simmer till the mushrooms are soft. Add all the other ingredients. Do not strain the sauce but lift out bay leaf and mace.

Serve with pork, mutton or vegetables.

NOTE: This sauce may also be made with Espagnole foundation.

## PISTACHIO CREAM

*Crème aux Pistaches*

**4 oz. pistachio nuts**
**¼ oz. gelatine**
**4 tablesp. water**
**2 oz. castor sugar**
**1 pt. double cream**
**Sap-green colouring**

Blanch, skin and finely chop the pistachio nuts. Soak gelatine in the water, heat to dissolve. Add sugar and stir until dissolved. Whip the cream, fold in the liquid gelatine and chopped nuts, and colour pale green, adding the colouring a drop at a time. Pour into a prepared mould and leave to set.

**6 helpings**
**Setting time—1–2 hr.**

## PLAICE MORNAY

*Plie Mornay*

**Four 4 oz. fillets of plaice**

SAUCE

**1 oz. butter *or* margarine**
**1 rounded tablesp. flour**
**Salt and pepper**
**½ pt. milk and fish stock mixed**
**2 tablesp. grated cheese**
**Mustard**
**Grated nutmeg**

Fold the fillets in half and steam between 2 plates. Meanwhile make the sauce by melting the fat in a small saucepan, adding the flour, a pinch of salt and pepper, and cooking for 2–3 min. without browning. Remove from heat and stir in the liquid gradually, mixing well to prevent lumpiness. Bring to the boil, still stirring, and cook for 5 min. Add most of the cheese and season with mustard and nutmeg. Arrange the cooked fish in a shallow fireproof dish, coat with sauce and sprinkle with the remaining cheese. Place under a hot grill until golden brown.

Serve with grilled half tomatoes and mashed potatoes.

**4 helpings**

## PLUM JAM

**3 lb. plums**
**3 lb. sugar**
**¼–¾ pt. water (¼ pt. for ripe, juicy dessert plums, ¾ pt. for cooking varieties)**

Proceed as for Greengage Jam and cover. If desired, a few of the raw plums may be stoned; crack the stones, remove the kernels, blanch them by dipping in boiling water and add the halved kernels to the pan.

**Yield—approx. 5 lb.**

## PLAIN BUNS AND CAKES

Fat is added to these buns and cakes by rubbing or melting.

**Foundation Proportions**

| | |
|---|---|
| **Base** | —1 lb. flour |
| | —½–1 teasp. salt |
| **Shortening** | —4–8 oz. fat. |
| **Sweetening** | —4–8 oz. sugar |

| | | |
|---|---|---|
| **Raising Agents** | —2–4 teasp. baking-powder | |
| | —1 teasp. bicarbonate of soda and 2 teasp. cream of tartar | |
| | —1 teasp. bicarbonate of soda and 1–2 tablesp. vinegar | |
| | —1–2 teasp. bicarbonate of soda without cream of tartar for brown cakes and ginger-breads | |
| | —2–4 eggs | |
| **Flavouring, etc.** | —4–16 oz. fruit | |
| | —1–2 rounded teasp. mixed spice *or* cinnamon *or* ginger | |
| | —Grated rind of 2–3 lemons *or* oranges | |
| | —3–4 oz. desiccated coconut | |
| | —1 teasp. vanilla *or* lemon *or* almond essence | |
| **Liquid** | —Milk *or* water to mix to required consistency. | |

It is best to line the bottom of all cake-tins with paper to ensure that the cakes will not stick.

### POACHED EGGS

*Œufs pochés*

To poach well, eggs must be fresh. They should be broken into a cup or saucer and then slipped into boiling salted water to which 1 tablesp. vinegar has been added. The water will cease to boil when the eggs are added: do not let it boil again. An average egg will take about 3 min. to poach: it is ready when the white has enveloped the yolk and may be touched without breaking. Remove with a perforated spoon.

If you like poached eggs round in shape, boil them for ½ min. before breaking into the poaching pan.

### POACHED EGGS WITH TOMATO SAUCE

*Œufs pochés à la Tomate*

**6 eggs**
**4 oz. rice**
**½ pt. stock**
**1 oz. butter**
**Salt and pepper**
**¼ pt. tomato sauce**

Wash and drain the rice, add it to the boiling stock. When cooked and the stock has been absorbed, stir in the butter and season to taste. Poach the eggs and trim them neatly. Arrange rice lightly on a hot dish, place the eggs on it, pour the hot sauce around and serve.

**6 helpings**
**Cooking time—30 min. (approx.)**

### POACHED SALMON TROUT

Clean the fish, removing the gills, intestines and eyes but leaving on the head and tail. If a fish kettle with drainer is not available, cradle the fish in muslin and cook in a large saucepan or preserving pan. Lower the fish into simmering, lightly salted water (1 teasp. per qt.) and poach, allowing 10 min. per lb. and 10 min. over. As soon as cooked, lift carefully from the water and drain. To serve cold, cool a little and then neatly remove the skin from one side. When serving hot skinning is optional.

*To serve hot:* Arrange on a flat dish, garnish with sliced cucumber, parsley, lemon and new potatoes. Serve with melted butter or Hollandaise sauce.

*To serve cold:* 1. Serve quite plain, garnished with salad and accompanied by mayonnaise.
2. Glaze the cold fish with aspic jelly made with the liquor in which the fish was cooked, garnish with chopped aspic, stuffed tomatoes and sliced cucumber.

### POACHED TURBOT

*Turbot poché*

**1 chicken turbot *or* a cut 1½–2 lb. in weight**
**Lemon**
**Salt**

Wipe the fish thoroughly and trim the fins. Make an incision down the middle of the back, to lessen the possibility of the skin cracking; and rub the white side of the fish with a cut lemon to retain its whiteness. Have ready a pan containing sufficient warm water to cover the fish, add salt to taste, put in the fish, bring gradually to near boiling-point, then simmer very gently for 15–20 min. Drain the fish and dish up neatly.

Garnish with lobster coral, parsley and cut lemon, and serve with Hollandaise, anchovy, shrimp *or* lobster sauce.

**5–6 helpings**

## POACHING

*See Cooking Methods*

## POACHING FISH

*See Fish*

## POLENTA AND CHEESE

| | |
|---|---|
| **Cold maize-meal porridge** | **Salt** |
| **Grated cheese** | **Cayenne pepper** |
| | **Butter *or* oil** |

Cut the cold polenta into square or oblong pieces about ¾ in. thick. Arrange them on a flat dish, or a pie-dish, in layers, with grated cheese between and over the top. Season to taste. Dab a few pieces of butter over and bake till brown in a fairly hot oven (**375° F., Gas 5**).

## POLISH BEETROOT

*Betterave à la Polonaise*

| | |
|---|---|
| **2 lb. cooked, peeled beetroots** | **1 dessertsp. finely-grated horseradish *or* 1 dessertsp. bottled horse-radish sauce** |
| **1 small onion—finely chopped** | **Salt and pepper** |
| **½ oz. margarine** | **A little sugar, if necessary** |
| **½ oz. flour** | **Chopped parsley** |
| **½ bottle of yoghourt** | |

Grate the beetroot. Melt the fat and fry the onion in it, carefully and thoroughly. Stir in the flour, add the yoghourt and bring to the boil. Add the beetroot and horseradish and heat thoroughly. Season carefully, adding a little more yoghourt if the flavour is too sweet, or a little sugar if too sharp. Serve very hot and decorate with lines of parsley.

This is a very pleasant way of serving beetroot as a hot vegetable and is a very quick dish if cooked beetroots are purchased or available.

**6 helpings**
**Cooking time—15 min.**

## POLISH CABBAGE

*Choux à la Polonaise*

| | |
|---|---|
| **1 lb. cabbage heart** | **Salt and pepper** |
| **1 oz. bacon** | **¼ pt. boiling water** |
| **½ oz. bacon fat** | **1 cooking apple *or* 2 tomatoes** |
| **1 small onion, finely-chopped** | **1 dessertsp. flour** |

Cut the bacon into small pieces and fry lightly in a saucepan, with the bacon fat. Add the onion and fry it. Shred the cabbage finely and add to the bacon and onion, stirring it well. Add boiling water and a little salt and simmer gently until the cabbage is almost soft. Add the apple, chopped, or the skinned and cut up tomatoes and cook until the cabbage is quite soft. Stir in the flour and boil for 2–3 min. until the flour is cooked. Dish very hot.

**4–6 helpings**
**Cooking time—45 min. (approx.)**

## POLISH CAULIFLOWER

*Choufleur à la Polonaise*

| | |
|---|---|
| **1 large cauliflower** | **2 hard-boiled eggs** |
| **Salt** | **2 oz. fine stale bread-crumbs** |
| **1½ oz. butter** | |

Cook and drain the cauliflower. Heat the butter in a pan until just browning. Stir in the finely chopped hard-boiled eggs, then the crumbs. Mix well. Dish the cauliflower and pour the crumb mixture over it. Serve immediately.

**6 helpings**
**Cooking time—35–40 min.**

## POLISH FRITTERS

*Beignets à la Polonaise*

| | |
|---|---|
| **6 pancakes** | **1 egg** |
| **Apricot marmalade** | **Fat for frying** |

2 oz. breadcrumbs
4 oz. finely-crushed macaroons
Castor sugar
Ground cinnamon

Make the pancakes. Spread each one with apricot marmalade and roll up firmly. Trim off the ends and cut each pancake across in half. Mix together the breadcrumbs and macaroons. Coat each piece of pancake with egg; roll in the crumb mixture and fry in hot fat until nicely brown. Drain well.

Sprinkle with castor sugar and cinnamon and serve.

**6 helpings**

## POLISH SALAD

*Salade à la Polonaise*

½ lb. small cooked potatoes
¾ lb. cold roast meat *or* poultry
6 gherkins
3 pickled mushrooms
1 small raw onion
3 sprigs pickled cauliflower
1 hard-boiled egg
Salad dressing *or* sour cream *or* yoghourt
Salt and pepper
1 lettuce
1 dessertsp. chopped parsley

Cook the potatoes in their skins and leave till cold before peeling them. Cut meat into small pieces. Slice the gherkins and mushrooms, chop the onion, cauliflower and hard-boiled egg. Mix all together with salad dressing and seasoning. Arrange in a salad bowl with a border of crisp lettuce leaves. Sprinkle with chopped parsley.

**4–6 helpings**

## POLLO ALLA CACCIATORA

*Italian Chicken with Tomatoes*

1 small roasting chicken
Salt and pepper
A little flour
2 oz. butter
1 tablesp. olive oil
2 rashers lean bacon
A few small onions
1 clove of garlic (optional)
1 glass dry white wine
4 tablesp. crushed and peeled tomatoes
3 oz. mushrooms
Tomato paste
1 bay leaf
Stock

Cut the chicken into small pieces, season well with salt and pepper; coat with flour and brown in a large frying-pan in 1 oz. of butter and the olive oil. Cut the bacon into small pieces and with the onions and crushed garlic, brown all in a saucepan with the rest of butter. Add the browned chicken and wine. Cook all fairly quickly to allow wine to reduce. Add the tomatoes, peeled and sliced mushrooms, tomato paste, bay leaf, and moisten with a little stock. Bring to the boil, lower heat and cook gently until tender.

## POMIDORI RIPIENI ALLA SICILIANA

Stuffed Tomatoes, Sicilian fashion

12 large tomatoes
1 onion
1 glass olive oil
4 anchovies
1 tablesp. finely-chopped parsley
1 tablesp. capers
2–3 tablesp. breadcrumbs
Salt and pepper
Nutmeg
Breadcrumbs fried in olive oil

Cut off the top of the tomatoes and remove the seeds, leave the tomatoes upside down on a plate. Chop the onion very finely, place it in a saucepan with the olive oil and leave to cook very slowly without letting it brown too much, then remove from heat. Meanwhile chop the anchovies, parsley, and capers very finely and add to the onion with the breadcrumbs, salt, pepper and a little nutmeg. Mix well together and fill the tomato skins with the mixture. Sprinkle over each of them ½ tablesp. breadcrumbs which have been previously fried in olive oil. Grease a baking-tin with oil and place the tomatoes in it, pour a little more oil on them and bake in a moderate oven **(350° F., Gas 4)** for about ½ hr.

**5–6 helpings** **Cooking time—45 min.**

## POMMES DE TERRE SAVOYARDE

Potatoes Savoyarde

2 lb. potatoes
Salt and pepper
Nutmeg
3 oz. grated Gruyère cheese
1 very small clove of garlic
⅔ pt. white stock (approx.)
1½ oz. butter

Cut the potatoes into thin slices, approx. ⅙ in. thick. Place in a basin. Season with salt, pepper and a little nutmeg. Add most of the cheese and thoroughly mix together. Butter well, and lightly rub with garlic, an earthenware or fireproof dish. Place in the potatoes and cheese and barely cover with white stock. Sprinkle with the remainder of the cheese and small pieces of butter. Wipe round the sides of the dish and place it in a fairly hot oven **(375° F., Gas 5)** for approximately 40–50 min. Serve the potatoes in the dish in which they are cooked.

**6 helpings**

## PORK

More and more people realize today that the development of cold storage makes it perfectly safe to eat pork at any time of year.

Unlike beef and lamb, the whole of a pig's carcase is suitable for roasting, and all except the loin can be boiled, especially if first salted.

The appearance of the **leg** (1) and **loin** (2) are well known. They may be either baked, the leg boiled or in the case of cutlets and chops, fried.

(7) The **belly**, comparable to the streak in bacon, is usually salted and boiled. It is perfectly suitable for roasting and if bought in the form of thin strips or rashers may be grilled.

(3) The **spare rib** of the pig is almost a parallel cut to the middle neck of lamb. It is a moist eating tender joint, equally pleasant whether roasted or grilled.

From immediately above the spare rib is lifted the **blade-bone** (4). A parallel joint to this, the blade half shoulder, may also be found in lamb. The bladebone is a roasting joint and is especially tasty if the bone is removed and the resulting space filled with stuffing. When skewered and tied with string it may be carved as easily as beef roast.

A joint which is much neglected today is (5) the **hand** and **spring** of pork. This constitutes the foreleg of the animal and in bone structure is akin to the knuckle half shoulder of lamb. Although a large joint for the smaller family to buy it is extremely cheap and economical to use. The knuckle portion is best removed and set aside in strong salt water for two or three days ready for boiling. The remainder can be roasted and if suitably boned and rolled it is an easy joint to carve.

In London and the South of England the pig carcase is the only one delivered to shops with (6) the **head** attached. The effect is that, on the whole, a specialized offal butcher is usually the only one to stock sheeps' heads and ox cheek, together with tongues and brains. However, every butcher who sells pork will have the head. It contains a considerable amount of meat in addition to the tongue and the brain. The large pieces of cheek meat provides the Bath chap when salted and boiled. Cold slices of this are delicious fried. The remainder of the head may be boiled when it is easily removed from the bones, and used for brawn.

General quality considerations applying to beef and lamb are applicable to pork. The flesh should be a pale pink colour. Whenever there is a dark red tinge to the flesh the pork should be avoided. The fat should be white and firm to the touch. It should never be greyish in colour. Occasionally pork may be found with small black spots in the fat, particularly in the belly. This is due to a carry-over of black pigment from the skin of black or brown pigs. It is in no way harmful.

## PORK CHEESE

**1 lb. cold roast pork**
**1 dessertsp. finely-chopped parsley**
**¼ teasp. powdered sage**
**¼ teasp. mixed herbs**
**½ teasp. grated lemon rind**
**⅛ teasp. grated nutmeg**
**Salt and pepper**
**½ pt. good jellied stock**

Cut the pork into neat dice removing the fat according to taste. Add the parsley, sage, herbs, lemon rind, nutmeg, salt and pepper to the meat and mix well together. Press tightly into a mould and fill up with hot jellied stock. Bake for about 1½ hr. in a moderate oven **(350° F., Gas 4)**. Leave until cold and then unmould. Garnish with parsley.

**6 helpings**

## PORK CUTLETS

*Côtelettes de Porc*

**6 pork cutlets**
**1 teasp. vinegar**

| | |
|---|---|
| **2 tablesp. salad oil** | **Salt and pepper** |
| **½ teasp. powdered sage** | |

Trim the cutlets neatly. Make a marinade with the oil, sage, vinegar, salt and pepper and pour over the cutlets. Leave to soak for 1 hr., turning frequently. Drain, then grill or fry until cooked as desired.

**6 helpings**
**Cooking time—about 20 min.**

### PORK PIE

*Pâté de Porc*

| | |
|---|---|
| **1 lb. lean pork** | **1 small onion** |
| **Powdered herbs** | **½ gill water *or* stock** |
| **Salt and pepper** | **Hot water crust pastry using 8 oz. flour etc.** |

Cut the meat into neat small dice and season to taste with herbs, salt and pepper. Place the bones, finely-chopped onion, salt and pepper in a saucepan with the water or stock and simmer for 2 hr., so that the gravy when cold will form a firm jelly. Mould the pastry with the hands or line a pie mould. Put in the filling, add some stock and cover with pastry lid. (The remainder of the stock should be reheated and added after the pie is baked and still hot.) 3 or 4 folds of greased greaseproof paper should be fastened round the pie to preserve its shape and prevent it becoming too brown. Brush the top of the pie with egg, or milk, and make a hole in the centre. Bake in a hot oven (**425° F., Gas 7**) at first and reduce heat as soon as pastry is set to moderate (**350° F., Gas 4**) for about 1½ hr. Remove the greaseproof paper or mould for the last ½ hr. and brush the sides with egg or milk.

NOTE: If preferred, small individual pies may be made. Cook for about 1 hr.

**6 helpings**

### PORK RISSOLES

*Rissoles de Porc*

| | |
|---|---|
| **1 lb. cooked lean pork** | **Pinch of sage** |
| **3 tablesp. dried bread-crumbs** | **Pinch of marjoram** |
| | **1 egg** |
| **1½ teasp. salt** | **Milk** |
| **½ teasp. pepper** | **2 oz. dripping** |
| **2 tablesp. chopped fried onions** | |

SAUCE

| | |
|---|---|
| **2 sticks of celery** | **1½ tablesp. flour** |
| **2 tomatoes** | **½ pt. good stock** |
| **1 small onion** | **Salt and pepper** |

Mince the pork; mix well with the bread-crumbs, salt, pepper, 2 tablesp. onion, sage and marjoram. Bind together with the egg and add sufficient milk to hold the mixture together. Divide into 12 even portions and shape in flour on a board. Melt a little dripping in a frying-pan, fry the rissoles until golden brown, then keep them hot. Chop the celery; skin and chop the tomatoes for the sauce and fry in the same fat. Add the flour and mix well. Stir in the ½ pt. stock, season to taste. Bring to the boil, then pour round rissoles.

**6 helpings**

### PORT WINE SAUCE

*Sauce au Vin d'Oporto*

| | |
|---|---|
| **1 tablesp. redcurrant jelly** | **¼ pt. good mutton *or* venison gravy** |
| | **⅛ pt. port wine** |

Heat all the ingredients together until the jelly is melted.

Serve with roast mutton or venison.

### PORTERHOUSE STEAK

*Entrecôte Double*

| | |
|---|---|
| **1 steak about 1½ in. thick cut from the thick end of sirloin: allow 4–6 oz. steak per person** | **Salt and pepper** |
| | **Melted butter *or* oil** |

Season and brush the steak over on both sides with melted butter or oil. If possible leave oiled for 1 hr. before cooking. Grill and serve plain or with Maître d'hôtel butter, button onions fried in butter and small stuffed tomatoes or horseradish sauce.

**Cooking time—about 10 min.**

### POT ROASTING

*See Cooking Methods*

### POTAGE À LA CRÉCY

Carrot Soup

**10 fresh carrots**
**1 onion**
**1 leek**
**3 oz. butter *or* 2 oz. dripping**
**3 pt. boiling stock *or* water**
**A few rinds of bacon**
**Sugar**
**Salt and pepper**
**Fried croûtons**

Prepare the vegetables and cut them into small pieces. Melt the butter or fat in a stewpan, put in the vegetables, cover with a close-fitting lid and cook gently for 1 hr. Add the boiling stock or water and the bacon-rinds, and continue the gentle cooking until the vegetables are reduced to a pulp. Pass through a sieve, then add sugar, salt and pepper to taste, re-heat and serve. The croûtons should be served separately.

**4–5 helpings**

### POTAGE SOUBISE BRUN

Brown Onion Soup

**4 medium-sized onions**
**A few pieces of stale bread**
**2 oz. butter *or* 1½ oz. good dripping**
**1 qt. water *or* brown stock**
**A few rinds of bacon**
**Salt and pepper**

Peel and dice the onions; cut the bread into small pieces. Melt the fat in a large saucepan, put in the onions, cover closely, and let them cook very slowly for 1 hr. Pour the water or stock over the onions when they are sufficiently cooked. Add the bacon rinds, bread and a little pepper, cover and cook gently for 1 hr., then press through a fine sieve. Replace the soup in the saucepan; if too thin, let it boil rapidly until sufficiently reduced; or if too thick, add a little more stock.

Reheat, season to taste and serve whilst hot.

**4–5 helpings**

### POT-AU-FEU

(2 dishes, a broth and a meat dish)

**2 lb. brisket, topside *or* boned, top ribs of beef**
**½ lb. broken beef bones**
**2 turnips**
**1 small parsnip**
**2 leeks**
**4 onions stuck with one clove each**
**2 teasp. salt**
**2 qt. water**
**Bunch of fresh herbs—parsley stalks, chervil, thyme, garlic, bay leaf**
**4 carrots**
**6 peppercorns**
**¼ cabbage**
**2 tomatoes**
**Potatoes (optional)**
**6 toasted slices of French roll**

Wipe the meat with a damp cloth and remove some of the outside fat if this is excessive, tie the meat into shape. Wash the bones. Put meat and bones in a large strong pan, add the salt and the cold water, and soak for ½ hr. Bring very slowly to simmering point, add the herbs and simmer very gently for 1 hr.

Meanwhile, scrub and peel the root vegetables; keep the onions whole but cut the others into large pieces and add these to the broth after the first hour's simmering. Put on the lid but leave it slightly tilted to allow steam to escape, and simmer very gently for another 2½ hr. Soak, wash and finely shred the cabbage, scald and skin the tomatoes and cut them into small pieces. Add these to the broth and, if liked, sufficient medium-sized peeled potatoes to serve with the meat. Continue gentle simmering for ½ hr.

To serve: strain the broth through a colander, return it to the pan and keep it hot. Dish the meat with the potatoes, some of the large pieces of vegetable round it and a little of the broth to moisten; keep this covered and hot. Remove the bones and herbs from the broth, cut 1 tablesp. of ¼-in. cubes from the carrot, leek, parsnip and turnip and add these to 1 qt. of the broth and reheat. Serve the broth with the toasted bread floating in it. There will be some broth left to use as stock, and the bones can be reboiled for stock.

**Broth—6 helpings**
**A meat dish—6 helpings**
**Stock—about 1½ pt.**
**Cooking time—4 hr.**

### POTATO BALLS or CROQUETTES

*Croquettes de Pommes de terre*

**1 lb. cooked potatoes**
**1 oz. butter *or* margarine**
**2 egg yolks *or* 1 whole egg**
**Optional: 1 teasp. chopped parsley *or* 2 tablesp. dry grated cheddar cheese *or* 2 tablesp. grated**

**Salt and pepper** **Parmesan cheese**
**Egg and breadcrumbs**
**Deep fat**

Put the potatoes through a sieve and mash in a saucepan with the fat, beaten egg, and parsley or cheese if used. Season well. Form into small balls or into rolls. Coat twice with egg and crumbs. Fry in hot deep fat at 380° F., for 4–5 min. Drain well and serve immediately.

**6 helpings**

## POTATO BORDER TO MAKE

*White border:* Allow 3 medium-sized potatoes for a border. Boil or steam the potatoes, then sieve them. Add 1 raw egg yolk, ½ oz. butter, season to taste and beat well over heat. When smooth and creamy, allow to cool sufficiently to handle, then shape mixture into a long, narrow roll, using as little flour as possible. Arrange the roll on the serving dish in a ring or oval form, re-heat in the oven and use. Alternatively put the potato mixture into a forcing bag and pipe a round or oval shaped border.

*Brown border:* Prepare a border as directed above, place on a greased baking-sheet, brush over with beaten egg, bake until nicely browned, then transfer to a hot dish.

## POTATO CHIPS and POTATO STRAWS

*Pommes de terre frites à l'Anglaise*
and *Pommes de terre en Allumettes*

**6 medium-sized potatoes** **Deep fat**
**Salt**

Scrub and rinse the potatoes. Peel them thinly. For chips—cut into sticks about 2 in. long and ½ in. wide and thick. For straws—cut into strips the size of a wooden match. Drop them into cold water as they are cut. Rinse and drain and dry in a clean cloth. Put them into the frying-basket and lower them gently into hot deep fat at 360° F. (Keep the heat fairly high as the potatoes will have cooled the fat.) When the potatoes are soft but *not* brown—about 3 min. for chips and 1 min. for straws—lift out the basket and heat the fat to 375° F. Put back the basket and leave in the fat until the potatoes are crisp and golden brown—about 3 min. for chips and 2 min. for straws.

Drain on absorbent paper, sprinkle with salt and serve immediately.

NOTE: If potato chips or straws are to be served with fried fish or any other fried dish, the second frying of the potatoes to brown and crisp them should be done after the fish, etc., is fried. In this way the potatoes will be sent to table in their best condition.

**6 helpings**
**Cooking time—for chips, about 6 min.**
**for straws, about 3 min.**

## POTATO CRISPS

**6 egg-sized, waxy potatoes** **Deep fat**
**Salt**

Scrub and rinse the potatoes but do not peel unless the skins are very tough and blemished. Slice very thinly with a sharp knife or on a potato slicer bought for the purpose. Drop them into cold water as they are cut. Drain and rinse and dry well between the folds of a clean cloth. Sprinkle gradually into hot deep fat, at 320° F., and fry till golden and crisp. Remove from the fat as they brown and drain on absorbent paper. Keep them hot while frying the rest. Sprinkle with salt.

They can be kept in an air-tight tin for some time and be reheated when necessary.

NOTE: To the professional cook or chef these are known as "chips". They are served with grills and with poultry and game but may also be served with many meat and fish dishes.

**6 helpings**
**Cooking time—3–4 min.**

## POTATO, ONION AND CHEESE SAVOURY

**½ oz. fat**
**4 oz. finely-chopped onion**
**2 oz. grated cheese**
**2 tablesp. chopped parsley**
**6–8 oz. mashed potatoes**
**Salt and pepper**

Melt the fat in a saucepan and fry the onion till golden brown. Add most of the cheese, all the parsley and mashed potatoes, and season to taste. Stir over the heat until the mixture is well mixed and warmed through. Then put into a fireproof dish, sprinkle the remaining cheese on top and brown under the grill. If liked the mixture can be divided between 4 slices of toast, the cheese sprinkled over and browned under the grill.

**4 helpings**

## POTATO PUFFS

*Pommes de terre soufflées*

**9 medium-sized potatoes**
**Deep fat**
**Salt**

Scrub, peel and rinse the potatoes. Cut them lengthwise into slices about $\frac{3}{16}$ in. thick. Trim into ovals and drop into cold water. Rinse and drain. Dry in a clean cloth. Put the potato slices into the frying-basket and lower them gently into hot, deep fat at 320° F. Cook until just soft but not coloured. Lift out the basket. Reheat the fat to 350° F., put in the basket and fry until the potatoes begin to brown. Lift out again and heat the fat to 380° F. Fry the potatoes a third time till golden brown. Drain carefully, sprinkle with salt and dish.

**6 helpings**
**Cooking time—about 25 min.**

## POTATO SALAD (1)

*Salade de Pommes de Terre*

**6 large new potatoes *or* waxy old potatoes**
**French dressing *or* Vinaigrette sauce**
**2 heaped tablesp. chopped parsley**
**1 teasp. chopped mint**
**1 teasp. chopped chives *or* spring onion**
**Salt and pepper**

Cook the potatoes until just soft, in their skins. Peel and cut into dice whilst still hot. Mix while hot with the dressing and the herbs and a little seasoning. Serve cold.

**6 helpings**

## POTATO SALAD (2)

**6 large, new potatoes *or* waxy old potatoes**
**½ pt. salad dressing**
**1 tablesp. chopped parsley**
**Salt and pepper**

**2 finely-chopped spring onions *or* 1 heaped teasp. finely-chopped chives**
**Radishes *or* tomatoes**
**Fine cress**

Prepare potato salad as in preceding recipe. Garnish with overlapping rounds of radish or wedges of tomato from which the pips have been removed, and tiny bunches of fine cress.

**6 helpings**

## POTATO SOUFFLÉ

*Soufflé de Pommes de terre*

**1 lb. cooked floury potatoes**
**Salt and pepper**
**Grated nutmeg**
**1 oz. butter**
**3 eggs**
**¼ pt. cream**

Put the potatoes through a sieve. Mix them, in a basin, with the salt, pepper and nutmeg. Melt the butter and add to the potatoes, then add the beaten egg yolks and the cream. Whisk the whites stiffly and fold lightly into the mixture. Pour into a greased pie-dish or china or fireproof soufflé case. Bake in a moderate oven (**350° F., Gas 4**) for 30 min.

**4 helpings**

## POTATO SOUP

**2 lb. potatoes**
**2 onions *or* the white of 2 leeks**
**2 sticks of celery**
**2 oz. dripping, bacon fat *or* margarine**
**1 qt. white stock *or* water**
**A bunch of herbs**
**¼ pt. milk**
**Salt and pepper**
**Grated nutmeg**

Proceed as for Vegetable Purée. Heat No added starch thickening is needed.

**4–6 helpings**
**Cooking time—¾–1 hr.**

## POTATOES—BAKED IN FAT

*Pommes de terre rôties*

**2 lb. even-sized potatoes**
**Salt and pepper**
**Dripping**

Peel the potatoes and cut in halves or even in quarters if very large. Parboil and strain off the water and dry the potatoes over a low heat. Put into hot dripping in a roasting-tin, or in the tin containing the roast joint. Roll the potatoes in the fat and cook till tender and brown.

**Cooking time—to parboil, 10 min.; to bake, 1 hr. (approx.)**

## KARTOFFEL MIT KÄSE

Cheese Potatoes

**2 lb. cold cooked potatoes**
**4 tablesp. grated cheese**
**Salt and pepper**
**1 tablesp. chopped parsley**
**1 tablesp. finely-chopped onion**
**3 eggs**
**1 pt. milk**
**1 tablesp. brown bread-crumbs**

Slice the potatoes. Grease a fireproof dish and arrange a layer of potatoes at the bottom. Sprinkle with some of the grated cheese, salt, pepper, a little of the chopped parsley and onion. Beat the eggs and stir in the milk and pour a little of this over the potatoes in the dish. Continue with these layers, finishing with cheese and the brown breadcrumbs. Bake in a moderate oven **(350° F., Gas 4)** for about ½ hr. If not well browned on top, place under a grill before serving.

**6 helpings**

## PARISIAN POTATOES

*Pommes de terre Parisienne*

**2 lb. potatoes**
**2–3 oz. butter *or* margarine**
**Salt**

Scrub, rinse and peel the potatoes. Using a round vegetable scoop, scoop small balls from the potatoes. Boil them until nearly tender and drain them well. Heat the butter in a frying-pan or sauté pan and fry the potatoes in it, tossing them all the time until they are brown. Season and serve.

**6 helpings**
**Cooking time—to fry, about 10 min.**

## POTTED CHICKEN

*Terrine de Volaille*

**Trimmings of cold roast chicken**
**3 oz. cooked ham**
**Salt and pepper**
**Nutmeg**
**2 oz. butter**
**Clarified butter**

Mince chicken and ham very finely, season well, add pinch of nutmeg, and work in butter gradually, making the mixture as smooth as possible. Press paste into small pots, cover contents with clarified butter.

## POTTED GAME

*Terrine de Gibier*

**Cooked game**
**Butter *or* stock *or* gravy**
**Salt and pepper**
**Cayenne pepper**
**Clarified butter**

Remove skin and bone from game, chop or mince meat very finely. Pound until smooth, gradually adding strong game stock *or* gravy *or* oiled butter, until mixture is moist. Season well.

Press into small pots, cover with clarified butter.

*Use as a savoury spread, or in pastry cases.*

## POT PIE OF VEAL

*Pâté de veau et pommes de terre*

**1¼ lb. lean veal**
**½ lb. pickled pork**
**Salt and pepper**
**Stock**
**1 lb. potatoes**
**Puff *or* rough puff pastry using 6 oz. flour, etc.**

Cut the meat into pieces convenient for serving and cut the pork into thin small slices. Place the meat and pork in layers in a large pie-dish, seasoning each layer well with salt and pepper, and fill the dish ¾ full with stock. Cover with a lid and cook in a moderate oven **(350° F., Gas 4)** for 1½ hr. Meanwhile parboil the potatoes and cut in thick slices. After cooking for 1½ hr., allow the meat to cool slightly. Add more stock if necessary, place the potatoes on top, cover with pastry and make a hole in the top. Bake in a very hot oven **(450° F., Gas 8)** until the pastry is set, reduce heat and cook more slowly for the remainder of the time, making 40–50 min. altogether. Add more hot stock through the hole in the top.

Garnish with parsley and serve.

**6 helpings**

## POTTED LOBSTER

*Terrine de Homard*

| | |
|---|---|
| **2 boiled lobsters** | **Cayenne pepper** |
| **2 oz. butter** | **¼ pt. cream** |
| **Salt and pepper** | **Clarified butter** |

Pick the meat from the shells, chop finely and put into a saucepan with the butter and seasoning. Cook slowly for 20 min. Add the cream, stir, and cook gently until the mixture has the consistency of a smooth and fairly thick paste. Rub through a fine sieve, press into pots, and when cold cover with clarified butter. It will keep for several days in a refrigerator.

## POTTED CRAB

*Terrine de Crabe*

| | |
|---|---|
| **2 crabs** | **Powdered mace** |
| **Salt** | **About 4 oz. clarified butter** |
| **Cayenne pepper** | |

Pick the crab meat from the shells, mix with salt, cayenne and mace to taste, rub through a fine sieve. Press into small pots, cover with melted butter and bake in a moderate oven (**350° F., Gas 4**) for ½ hr. When cold, cover each pot with clarified butter.

## POTTED HAM

*Terrine de Jambon*

| | |
|---|---|
| **2 lb. lean ham** | **¼ teasp. grated nutmeg** |
| **½ lb. fat ham** | **⅛ teasp. cayenne pepper** |
| **¼ teasp. ground mace** | **Clarified butter** |
| **¼ teasp. pepper** | |

Pass the ham through a mincing machine 2 or 3 times or chop very finely. Then pound well and rub through a fine sieve. Add gradually the mace, pepper, nutmeg and cayenne and mix well together. Put into a well greased pie-dish, and cover with greased greaseproof paper. Bake in a moderate oven (**350° F., Gas 4**) for about ¾ hr. When cooked, press into small pots and cover with clarified butter.

**Cooking time—about ¾ hr.**

## POTTED OX TONGUE

*Terrine de Langue de Bœuf*

| | |
|---|---|
| **1 cooked ox tongue** | **Cloves** |
| **3 oz. clarified butter to each 1 lb. of tongue** | **Nutmeg** |
| **Powdered mace** | **Cayenne pepper** |
| | **Salt and pepper** |
| | **Extra clarified butter** |

Chop the tongue finely, then pound it well. Add gradually the clarified butter in the proportion stated above and the flavourings and seasoning to taste. When the mixture is reduced to a moist smooth paste, rub through a fine sieve, press into pots and cover with melted clarified butter.

## POTTED PRAWNS or SHRIMPS

*Terrine de Crevettes*

| | |
|---|---|
| **1 qt. fresh prawns** *or* **shrimps** | **Ground mace** *or* **nutmeg** |
| **¼ lb. fresh butter** | **A little salt** |
| **Cayenne pepper** | **Clarified butter** |

The fish should be perfectly fresh and as large as possible. Boil, then shell and divide them slightly. Pound to a paste with the butter and seasoning. Rub through a fine sieve, press into small pots, cover with clarified butter, and when cold tie down closely.

**Cooking time—8 min.**

## POTTED SHRIMPS

| | |
|---|---|
| **1 pt. shrimps—measure when picked** | **Pinch of salt** |
| **2–3 oz. butter** | **Grating of nutmeg** |
| **Good pinch of cayenne pepper** | **Lettuce** |
| | **Lemon** |

Heat the butter and turn the shrimps in this until they are well coated, but do not cook them. Add the seasonings and nutmeg. Pour into small moulds or dishes and leave until the butter is set. Turn out on to a bed of crisp lettuce and garnish with lemon.

Serve with cayenne pepper and crisp toast.

## POULTRY

### Chickens

The flesh of young chickens is the most delicate and easily digested of all meats. This makes it especially suitable for children and invalids.

Few birds undergo so great a change with regard to the quality of their flesh as the domestic fowl. When quite young, cocks and hens are equally tender, but as chickens grow older the flesh of the cock is the first to toughen, and a free-range cock over a year old is fit only for conversion into soup. A hen of the same age still makes a substantial and palatable dish.

Birds of all sizes may now be obtained all the year round. The youngest birds may be called Baby Chicks, Spring Chickens or Squabs (French—*poussins*, *petits poulets*). These are usually grilled or fried, and have a delicate flavour.

The birds likely to be the most popular in the average household are cockerels, roasting chickens and fowls, and capons (French—*poulets de grain*, *poulets reine*, *poulardes*, *chapons*). These may be cooked in a number of ways, two of the most popular being roasting and braising.

Older birds used for boiling may also be an economical purchase for the housewife (French—*poules*).

As a rule small-boned birds are an economical purchase; they should be plump.

When fresh, poultry should be free from any tainted smell, the eyes clear and not sunken, the feet limp and pliable. The legs should be soft and smooth, and the breast-bone and wing-tips pliable.

The signs of an old fowl are stiff, horny-looking feet, long spurs, dark-coloured and hairy thighs, stiff beak and hard bones.

**Capons and Poulardes:** The male fowl, the capon (chapon), and the female bird, the poularde, are both, by treatment while young, made incapable of generating, with the result that their size is increased, and they become fatter than ordinary fowls. The flesh of these birds does not toughen with age, and even when three years old they may be as tender as chicken—with a delicate flavour. The flavour of the poularde is considered more delicate than that of the capon (chapon), but the latter is the larger bird. They may be boiled, braised, roasted or otherwise prepared, according to the directions given for cooking chickens and fowls.

**Turkeys:** These when young have smooth black legs and short spurs. The eyes of a fresh bird are bright and not sunken. Choose one which has a broad, plump breast and white flesh, the best being from seven to nine months old. The flesh of the hen is usually more tender than the cock.

An old bird has pale or reddish, rough legs, and long spurs.

**Ducks:** When young these usually have yellow feet and bills. The under-bill should be so soft that it will bend back easily, and the webbing of the feet should be soft; the breast should be meaty. (French: duck—*canard*: duckling—*caneton*.)

**Geese:** The signs of freshness in a goose are the same as those in a duck. A gosling or green goose is one up to four months old.

### Dressing Poultry

**Plucking:** The removal of the feathers some time after the bird has been killed is a slow business. If a strong hook firmly fixed to a wall is available, plucking can be facilitated by tying the two feet of the bird together with strong string, and hanging the bird over the hook. Draw out one wing and pull out the under feathers, taking a few at a time. Work towards the breast and then down to the tail. Repeat on the other side. Only half the neck need be plucked, for the half remaining towards the head is cut off. The flight feathers (large quilled feathers at the ends of the wings) need hard pulling to remove and are best snapped away from the direction of growth. Small hairs may be singed away with a taper: burnt feathers, however, will impart an unpleasant flavour to the bird.

**Drawing:** Half way along the neck, cut a ring round the outer skin and cut off the head. Slip the knife under the skin and cut back towards the body. Holding the neck in a dry cloth, pull the skin loose. At the base of the neck cut through the meat and then, still holding the neck in a dry cloth, twist firmly round until it is detached from the body. (Keep the neck for stock.) Push the index finger into the crop cavity to loosen the crop and gizzard.

Turn the bird around and with a sharp knife cut the skin on the leg, place over a board or table edge and snap the bone. Grasp the foot in one hand and the thigh of the bird in the other and pull off the foot with the tendons. There should be seven tendons.

To remove the viscera make a slit of about two to three inches, above the vent, taking care not to cut into the rectal end of the gut. Insert the first two fingers of the right hand, knuckles upwards and gently draw out the "innards". Several attempts may have to be made by a novice before he can withdraw all the organs at once. But it can be done. When they are free, trim the end of the intestines and the vent away. Separate the liver from the gall bladder.

The lungs, which are bright red, lie close to the ribs. They are best removed by wrapping the index finger in a dry cloth and pushing in turn down from the back bone and out along each rib.

Burn the inedible waste, i.e. head, intestines, lungs, crop, feet, container of grit from the gizzard, etc., immediately. Keep the giblets, i.e. the neck, gizzard, liver and heart, away from the bird so that its flesh will not be discoloured.

Wipe the inside of the bird with a dry cloth. Do not wet it by washing unless the bird is to be cooked immediately.

**Trussing:** The object of trussing a bird is only to ensure that it looks attractive when cooked. Poultry can be cooked just as well untrussed or semi-trussed as fully trussed.

The easiest way to truss any bird is with a needle similar in size to a packing needle. When the bird is clean, lay it down with the breast uppermost and away from you. Thread the needle, and pass it through the left leg just above the thigh bone and near to the joint between the thigh and leg bone. (When the leg is folded down against the bird these two bones form a "V" shape with the apex of the "V" pointing towards the front of the bird.) Pass the needle on through the body, out the other side, and through the other leg joint. The legs should be pushed tight against the body during this operation.

The string should now be passing through the body and the leg joints. Leaving sufficient on either side, turn the bird breast downwards and carry the string through the elbow joint of the wing on each side, then twist the end of the wing under the neck of the bird to hold the neck flap of skin. The two ends may now be drawn together not too tightly and tied off. (The expert trusser will perform the whole of this job by threading and running the string with the needle. In the way described above it is easier to discover where the strings should pass.) It now only remains to tie down the legs. This may simply be done by looping the string over the end of the drum sticks and drawing them together, tying off round the tail end of the "parson's nose". To make this operation easier a slit may be cut in the flesh above the original vent cut and the "parson's nose" pushed through. The legs may also be tied down, using the needle on each leg end in turn. The packing needle and string can also usefully be used to repair any tears that have occurred during plucking or drawing. When trussed the skin should be as complete as possible in order to prevent the loss of fat from the birds during cooking, so resulting in over dryness and an unpalatable meat.

**Boning poultry and game:** Birds are invariably plucked and singed before boning, but not drawn. The crop, however, should be removed, the wings and legs cut off at the first joint, and the tendons of the legs carefully drawn at the same time. To bone the bird, use a small sharp knife, and first remove the merry-thought at the neck. Cut the skin down the centre of the back and raise the flesh carefully on either side, sever the wing joints, and continue to detach the flesh, keeping the blade of the knife close to the bone. When the legs are reached, dislocate the joints, cut the connecting tendons, but leave both wings and legs intact until the breast and backbones have been removed, together with the viscera. Turn the body completely inside out; take the thigh bones of one of the legs in the left hand and strip the flesh downwards. Repeat this until all the small bones are removed. The bird may then be turned right side out again, when it will be found completely boned and should be quite whole.

Both large and small birds may be boned in this way. They are then stuffed, re-shaped and trussed, or rolled into galantines.

**Accompaniments to Poultry**

Whilst the choice of accompaniment to a particular dish is largely a personal one depending on individual taste, we list below the usual British accompaniments to the following dishes:

**Roast Chicken:** Thin brown gravy, bread sauce, bacon rolls, green salad, game chips, watercress to garnish, veal forcemeat stuffing.

**Roast Duck:** Thickened gravy, sage and onion stuffing, apple-, cranberry- *or* orange-sauce, watercress to garnish.

**Roast Wild Duck:** Port wine- *or* orange-sauce *or* orange salad.

**Roast Turkey:** Thickened gravy, veal- *or* chestnut-stuffing, sausage-meat stuffing, bacon rolls, grilled sausages, bread- *or* cranberry-sauce.

**Roast Goose:** Thickened gravy, sage and onion stuffing, apple-sauce.

**General Hints**

(*a*) Chicken is stuffed at the neck-end, duck and goose are stuffed from the vent-end, turkey is stuffed with veal- *or* chestnut-stuffing in the crop and with sausage-meat-stuffing in the body.

(*b*) Chickens and game birds may be roasted for a while at the beginning of the cooking time, on the breast. This will make the breast-meat more moist. It should not be done with duck or goose. All birds should be roasted on a trivet, not resting in the tin in basting fat.

(*c*) Sufficient garnish should be served with each dish to provide some with each portion served. When dishes are to be served hot, the garnish must be ready in advance and arranged quickly. If the process takes time, the serving dish may be placed in a shallow tin of hot water to ensure that the food is served very hot.

(*d*) Frozen chickens or chicken portions can be utilized in many of the following recipes.

(*e*) The use of metal foils for cooking can be recommended (1) to ensure a tight-fitting lid when stewing or braising, (2) to wrap birds during roasting when a covered roaster is not available or proves too small. Before cooking is completed the foil should be turned back from the breast and legs of the bird to allow the skin to become crisp and brown.

(*f*) If a good stock is not available it may be produced quickly by using one of the reliable makes of consommé soup-mix now on the market.

(*g*) When the method of cooking is in a casserole or by stewing, some dry cider or dry wine may be substituted for some of the stock.

## POULTRY, TO CARVE

*See Carving.*

## POULTRY FOR INVALIDS

*See Invalid Cookery, Meat for Invalids, Poultry.*

## POULTRY HOT-POT

*Hochepot de Volaille*

| | |
|---|---|
| **1 boiling fowl** | **½ pt. stock *or* water** |
| **3 rashers of bacon** | **½ oz. butter** |
| **Salt and pepper** | **½ oz. flour** |
| **Nutmeg** | **2 teasp. chopped parsley** |
| **2 shallots** | |

Place the giblets from the fowl in the bottom of a casserole. Joint the fowl, remove skin and put joints into casserole, adding bacon (cut in strips), salt, pepper, nutmeg, sliced shallots and the hot stock (*or* water). Cover tightly, cook in a fairly hot oven (**375°–400° F., Gas 5–6**) for about 2 hr. Knead together butter and flour and add in small pieces to the hot-pot. Add parsley and cook for another ½ hr. Correct seasoning and serve.

This may be served with plain boiled Patna rice.

**6 helpings**

## POURING CUSTARDS

*See Custard and Custard Mixtures.*

## POWDERED GRAIN MOULDS (Cornflour, Tapioca)

For a basic recipe, *see Cornflour Mould.*

## PRAWNS

*Crevettes*

Prawns are available all the year. They are usually sold cooked, and can be served cold, fried, or in soups, sauces and in made-up dishes.

### TO BOIL FRESHLY-CAUGHT PRAWNS

Cooked prawns should be very red and have no spawn when cooked; much depends on their freshness and the way in which they are cooked. Wash well, then put into boiling salted water and keep them boiling for about 7–8 min. They are ready when they begin to change colour, do not overboil or they will become tasteless and indigestible.

### TO SHELL PRAWNS

To shell prawns, take the head between the right-hand thumb and second finger, take the tip of the tail between the left thumb and forefinger; with the nail on the right fore-finger raise the shell at the knee or angle, pinch the tail and the shell will come apart, leaving the prawn attached to the head.

Prawns make an excellent hors d'oeuvre—either by themselves or with a selection of other small savouries.

The large Mediterranean prawns should be served in their shells, garnished with lettuce and lemon slices. Put finger bowls on the table in this case.

If preferred shell the prawns, arrange on crisp lettuce, garnished with lemon. Serve with brown bread and butter and cayenne pepper.

**Shrimps** can be served in the same way.

## PRAWN COCKTAIL

**Heart of a small lettuce**
**½ pt. picked prawns**
**½ gill mayonnaise**
**1 tablesp. tomato purée *or* tomato ketchup**
**1 teasp. chilli vinegar—if available**
**1 teasp. tarragon vinegar**
**Good pinch of salt**
**Good pinch of cayenne pepper**
**Lemon**

Wash and dry the lettuce very well—pick out the tiny leaves and break into very small pieces. Arrange in cocktail glasses. Put the prawns on top. Mix the mayonnaise with the tomato ketchup or purée—to obtain this rub one large tomato through a fine sieve. Add the vinegars and seasoning. Put over the prawns and garnish with a piece of lemon and a dusting of cayenne pepper.

Serve very cold.

**4 helpings**

## PREPARING FISH

*See Fish*

## PRESERVED MUSHROOMS WITH BROWN SAUCE

**1 small can *or* bottle of mushrooms**
**Stock**
**1 oz. butter *or* margarine**
**1 oz. flour**
**1 tablesp. sherry (optional)**
**Salt and pepper**

Strain the liquor from the can *or* bottle, and add to it sufficient stock to make up to ½ pt. Fry the butter and flour together until well-browned, add the liquor and stir till the mixture boils. Add sherry and mushrooms and heat thoroughly. Season and serve.

**4–5 helpings**
**Cooking time—about 30 min.**

## PRESERVED MUSHROOMS WITH CREAM SAUCE

**1 small can *or* bottle of mushrooms**
**Milk**
**1 oz. butter *or* margarine**
**1 oz. flour**
**2 tablesp. cream**
**Salt and pepper**

Strain the liquor from the can *or* bottle, and add to it sufficient milk to make up to ½ pt. Heat the fat in a saucepan, add the flour, stir and cook for a few minutes without browning, then put in the mushroom liquor. Add the mushrooms, and when really hot stir in the cream. Season and serve.

**4–5 helpings**
**Cooking time—about 20 min.**

## PRESERVES

These are a valuable way of providing food energy. They include Bottled and Canned

Fruits, Meats, Poultry and Vegetables, Candied and Crystallized Fruits, Chutneys, Pickles and Sauces, Jams, Jellies and Marmalades, Dried and Salted foods, Syrups and Vinegars.

### PRESERVING EGGS

*See Eggs*

### PRESSED BEEF

*Bœuf pressé*

**Salt brisket of beef**
**1 onion**
**1 carrot**
**½ turnip**
**Bouquet garni**
**10 peppercorns**
**Meat glaze**

Weigh the meat. Wash it well, or if very salt soak for about 1 hr. in cold water. Put into cold water and bring slowly to boiling point. Skim well. Cut the prepared vegetables into large pieces, add to the meat with the bouquet garni and peppercorns, and simmer gently, allowing 25 min. per lb. and 25 min. over. Take the meat out, remove the bones and press between 2 boards or dishes until cold. Then brush over with meat glaze.

### PRESSED VEAL

*Galantine de Veau*

**A breast of veal**
**Salt and pepper**
**1 large onion**
**A few sticks of celery *or* ¼ teasp. celery seeds**
**1 carrot**
**½ turnip**
**Bouquet garni**
**10 peppercorns**

Wipe the meat and remove the skin, bones and gristle. Trim the meat neatly, season well, roll up tightly and tie with string. Slice the onion, celery, carrot and turnip and put into a saucepan with the bones and trimmings, bouquet garni, peppercorns and salt and put the meat on top. Add water to the depth of the vegetables. Cover the meat with greased paper, put on the lid and cook gently for 3 hr., basting occasionally. When the meat is tender, place it between 2 dishes or boards with weights on top, until quite cold. Strain the stock and on the following day boil rapidly until reduced to a glaze. Add colouring if liked. Trim the meat and brush it over with the glaze.

### PRESSURE COOKERY

Pressure cookery is specialized, and the reader interested in it should refer to *Mrs Beeton's Cookery and Household Management* where the topic is treated in some detail.

### PRINCE ALBERT PUDDING

**1 lb. prunes**
**1 pt. water**
**A few strips of lemon rind**
**1 oz. brown sugar**
**4 oz. butter *or* margarine**
**4 oz. castor sugar**
**2 eggs**
**Rind of ½ lemon**
**1½ oz. rice flour**
**4 oz. brown breadcrumbs**

SAUCE

**1 teasp. arrowroot**
**½ pt. prune syrup**
**½ oz. granulated sugar**
**Juice of ½ lemon**
**Cochineal**

Wash and soak the prunes in the water overnight. Stew them with the strips of lemon rind and brown sugar until soft. Strain them (reserving the liquid for the sauce) and remove the stones.

Line a dry mould or basin completely with the prunes, as follows: halve each prune; dip in clarified butter *or* margarine, and press skin-side against the mould. Chop any prunes left over.

Cream the butter and castor sugar together. Separate the eggs; beat in the yolks. Add the grated lemon rind, chopped prunes, rice flour and brown breadcrumbs. Fold in the stiffly-whisked egg whites. Turn mixture into the mould; cover. Steam gently for 1¾ hr.

Meanwhile make the sauce; blend the arrowroot with some of the prune syrup. Boil the remainder of the syrup and pour over the blended arrowroot; return to pan and simmer for 3 min. Add the sugar and juice of ½ lemon and colour pink with a few drops of cochineal.

Turn out the pudding and coat with the sauce.

**6 helpings**

### PRINCESS CAKES

**7 oz. butter *or* margarine**
**1–2 oz. castor sugar**
**Grated rind of ½ orange**
**Orange butter icing**

**8 oz. self-raising flour**
**Pinch of salt**
**Chocolate glacé icing**

Beat fat and sugar till very creamy and soft, stir in the sifted flour and salt. Stir in thc orange rind. Using a vegetable star pipe, pipe out the mixture in 3½-4 in. lengths on greased baking-sheets. Bake in a moderate oven (375°–350° F., Gas 5–4), then sandwich 2 together with butter icing and dip the ends in chocolate glacé icing.

NOTE: ½ an egg may be added to the creamed fat and sugar.

**16–20 cakes** **Cooking time—15–20 min.**

## PRINCESS TRIFLES

**One 10-oz. carton raspberries (just thawed)**
**4 trifle sponge cakes**
**1 tablesp. orange liqueur *or* to taste**
**¼ pt. double cream**
**2 meringue shells**
**Angelica**

Crumble the sponge cakes and divide between 4 shallow glasses. Strain the syrup from the raspberries and flavour to taste with the orange liqueur. Pour over the sponge in each glass, add a layer of raspberries and leave to soak in. *Just before serving* whisk the cream until slightly stiff and fold in the roughly crumbled meringues. Completely cover the soaked sponge with this cream and stud thickly with the remaining whole raspberries. Decorate with angelica leaves.

## PRUNE MOULD

*Pruneaux moulés*

**1 lb. prunes**
**1½ pt. water**
**1 lemon**
**3 oz. sugar**
**1 in. cinnamon stick**
**¾ oz. gelatine**
**Carmine colouring**

Wash prunes, and soak overnight in the measured water. Cook with thinly cut strips of lemon rind, sugar and cinnamon until quite soft. Remove lemon rind, remove stones and chop prunes to a pulp. Soak the gelatine in 2 tablesp. cold water for a few minutes, then heat until dissolved. Add to the prune mixture and flavour with lemon juice. Colour if necessary. If liked, the kernels may be removed from the prune stones, shredded and addeu.

Stir thoroughly and pour into a wet mould. When set, unmould and serve with thin custard.

**6 helpings**
**Setting time—2 hr.**

## PRUNE SAUCE

**½ lb. prunes**
**½ pt. water**
**1 strip of lemon rind**
**1 oz. sugar**
**Pinch of ground cinnamon**
**1 tablesp. rum *or* brandy (optional)**
**Lemon juice**

Soak the prunes overnight in the water. Stew them with the lemon rind till quite soft. Rub them through a hair, nylon or fine wire sieve. Add the other ingredients to taste.

Serve with roast pork, goose, venison or mutton. It is also good with some hot puddings.

## PUDDINGS

The baked, boiled or steamed pudding made with a pastry or butter crust is used largely in British cookery. In mediaeval times, savoury puddings or herbs or meat (often with fruit and honey added) were commonly served in every course of a main meal. Puddings as a "sweet course" did not come in until the use of sugar became widespread. Today, however, most puddings are sweet, treacle pudding, ginger pudding and Spotted Dick being examples. Some savoury puddings such as steak and kidney pudding are still widely served; and of course Yorkshire Pudding is a traditional British accompaniment for roast beef.

Sweet puddings are made basically from flour, breadcrumbs or cake-crumbs, fat, sugar, eggs and a raising agent. By using breadcrumbs or cake-crumbs and flour instead of all flour in suet mixtures, a lighter pudding is obtained. A good pinch of salt is added for each ½ lb. of flour used.

When the proportion of baking-powder to flour is 1 teasp. to ½ lb., self-raising flour is a satisfactory alternative.

The fat is worked into the mixture in various ways, as follows:

(*a*) **Chopped-in Method (Suet)**

Either beet or mutton suet can be used, although beef suet is generally preferred as mutton suet sometimes has too strong a flavour. Shredded packet suet is, of course, ready for use and requires no further chopping.

To prepare suet remove the skin and fibrous tissue from it. Sprinkle the suet liberally with some of the measured flour or breadcrumbs. Shred or cut it down in flakes: then chop it finely. (A quick and easy method of chopping is to use a cook's knife. The handle, held in the right hand, is raised and lowered quickly, while the point of the knife is held down on the board by the thumb and first finger of the left hand.) Add more measured flour if the suet becomes sticky. Mix all the other dry ingredients with the suet. Stir in the eggs and sufficient milk to obtain the consistency required by the recipe.

(*b*) **Rubbed-in Method**

Sift the flour, salt and raising agent into a mixing bowl. Cut the fat (generally butter or margarine) into small pieces. With the tips of the fingers, rub the fat into the flour, lifting it above the bowl so that, in falling back between the fingers, the mixture become aerated. Continue this until all the lumps of fat have been worked down and the mixture resembles breadcrumbs. Add the rest of the dry ingredients. Stir in the beaten eggs and liquid, according to the recipe.

(*c*) **Creaming Method**

This method is used for richer puddings, where the amount of fat is often too great to be rubbed in, or where flour is not used in the recipe. Castor sugar should be used, as the small crystals are more easily dissolved.

Work the fat and sugar well together until the mixture is light coloured and creamy. Add any essences at this stage.

Add the beaten egg a little at a time, beating well between each addition so that the mixture remains smooth. Curdling of the mixture may occur if the egg is added too quickly or if the egg used has come direct from the refrigerator. Sift in the flour, salt and baking-powder. Stir in lightly, and add the rest of the ingredients.

(*d*) **Creaming of Yolks and Sugar Method**

Each egg should be broken separately in a saucer or cup so that if there is one bad egg it does not spoil the others. Put the yolks into a basin with the sugar. Whisk until light in colour and frothy. Stir in the other ingredients lightly, according to the recipe.

(*e*)

**Consistency of Mixtures**

A *dropping consistency* is reached when the mixture will just drop off a spoon when it is shaken lightly. For a *soft dropping consistency* the mixture should drop easily from the spoon. For a *slack consistency* the mixture should fall easily from the spoon.

**Steamed and Boiled Puddings, General Hints**

The mould or basin in which a pudding is cooked should be well-greased with fresh butter, clarified butter *or* margarine, *or* cooking fat. Always prepare the mould or basin and the covering *before* the pudding is mixed.

(*a*) **Steamed Puddings**

1. Have the steamer ready before the pudding is mixed. There should be plenty of boiling water in the steamer. If a steamer is not available, the pudding can be *partly steamed*, by standing it on an old plate, saucer or pastry cutter (to prevent direct contact with the source of heat) in a saucepan, with just enough water to reach half-way up the mould or basin. Put a tightly-fitting lid on the saucepan and simmer gently. If the water boils away, add more *boiling* water to replace it.
2. Where gentle steaming is indicated in the recipe, the water below the steamer should only simmer.

3. The basin or mould should not be more than three-quarters full.
4. Always cover the pudding with greased paper before putting a lid or cover on it. This paper acts as a waterproof cover against condensing steam. Use a piece of strong paper such as greaseproof, grease it well and place it greased side down on the basin. Turn the edges under and twist them securely below the rim of the basin.
5. After taking the pudding out of the steamer, leave it for a minute or two, to allow it time to shrink slightly from the sides of the mould or basin, before turning it out.
6. If puddings are steamed in a pressure cooker, follow the manufacturer's instructions regarding time and pressure.

(*b*) **Boiled Puddings**

1. The pudding can be boiled in a basin covered with a cloth *or* in a cloth only.
2. The cloth should be clean and well floured before use. Lay the cloth over the top of the basin and tie it with string under the rim, using a loop knot which can be easily untied. Gather the four corners of the cloth up on top and either tie them together or pin them with a safety pin. Roly-poly types of puddings are rolled in the floured cloth, forming a sausage-shape, and tied loosely at either end, to allow room for the pudding to swell.
3. The water must be boiling rapidly when the pudding is put in and then should simmer gently.
4. The water must completely cover the pudding and be deep enough to float those boiled in cloths; otherwise a plate or saucer must be placed at the bottom of the pan.
5. As the water boils away, *boiling water* must be added.
6. The pudding should be allowed to stand a minute or two before being turned out in order that some of the steam may escape, causing the pudding to shrink and thus be less liable to break.

(*c*) **Christmas Puddings**

After the first boiling, the cloth should be taken off and a clean, dry, well-floured cloth tied on to the pudding. Cover or wrap in greaseproof paper and store in a cool larder. Give at least another $1\frac{1}{2}$ hours' boiling before serving.

## PUDDINGS FOR INVALIDS

Most milk puddings are suitable for an invalid, if these recipes are planned to look attractive, to be easily prepared and to give the most nourishment.

In *most* cases a certain amount of fruit is essential, so do not disregard the importance of fresh fruit and particularly citrus fruits in an invalid diet.

## PUDDINGS USING PASTRY

*See Pastry-Making, and various recipes for savoury and sweet puddings, e.g. Beefsteak Pudding, Spotted Dick.*

## PUFF PASTRY

*Feuilletage*

For Pies, Tarts, Tartlets, Bouchées, Vol-au-Vents, Patties, etc.

| | |
|---|---|
| **1 lb. plain flour** | **1 teasp. lemon juice** |
| **Pinch of salt** | **⅓ pt. cold water (approx.)** |
| **1 lb. butter** | |

Sift the flour and salt and rub in about 2 oz. of butter. Press the remaining butter firmly in a floured cloth to remove the moisture, and shape into a flat cake. Add the lemon juice to the flour and mix to a smooth dough with cold water. The consistency of the dough must be the same as that of the butter. Knead the dough well and roll it out into a strip a little wider than the butter and rather more than twice its length. Place the butter on one half of the pastry, fold the other half over and press the edges together with the rolling-pin to form a neat parcel. Leave in a cool place for 15 min. to allow the butter to harden.

## *Pumpkin Pie*

Roll out into a long strip 3 times the original length but the original width, keeping the corners square and the sides straight to ensure an even thickness when the pastry is folded. Do not let the butter break through the dough. Fold the bottom third up and the top third down, press the edges together with a rolling-pin and half turn the pastry so that the folded edges are on the right and left. Roll and fold again and lay aside in a cool place for 15 min. Repeat this process until the pastry has been rolled out 6 times. The rolling should be done as evenly as possible and the pastry kept in a long narrow shape which, when folded, forms a square. Roll out as required and leave in a cool place before cooking.

Bake in a very hot oven (**450° F., Gas 8**)—the oven door should not be opened until the pastry has risen and become partially baked, as a current of cold air may cause the pastry to collapse.

### PUMPKIN PIE

**½ pt. pumpkin (cooked and sieved)**
**¼ teasp. ground ginger**
**¼ teasp. nutmeg**
**Good pinch of cinnamon**
**3 eggs**
**2 tablesp. brandy**
**¼ pt. milk (approx.)**
**4 oz. castor sugar (approx.)**
**Short crust pastry using 8 oz. flour, etc.**

Put the pumpkin in a mixing-bowl. Stir in the spices, the well beaten eggs, the brandy and sufficient milk to give a consistency of thick batter. Sweeten to taste. Turn into a deep 9-in. pie-plate lined with pastry. Cover with pastry. Bake in a fairly hot oven (**375° F., Gas 5**) about 45 min. Serve hot.

NOTE: Pumpkins should be peeled, sliced and the seeds removed before boiling in slightly salted water until tender.

**5–6 helpings**

### PUNCH

**1 large lemon**
**2–3 oz. loaf sugar**
**Pinch of ground cinnamon**
**Pinch of grated nutmeg**
**Pinch of cloves**
**½ pt. brandy**
**½ pt. rum**
**1 pt. boiling water**

Remove the rind of the lemon by rubbing it with some of the sugar. Put all the sugar, the cinnamon, nutmeg, cloves, brandy, rum and boiling water into a stewpan, heat gently on the side of the stove, but do not let it boil. Strain the lemon juice into a punch bowl, add the hot liquid, serve at once.

### PUNCHES AND HOT DRINKS

Punches are alcoholic drinks. Some may seem expensive to prepare, but they can be skipped by the frugal. In any case, the cost of most punches can be controlled by the amount of hot water used.

Orange or lemon rind must be cut wafer-thin, avoiding the white pith. More flavour is obtained if the rind is bruised before putting it into the drink.

QUEEN MAB'S PUDDING

*Pouding de la Reine Mab*

**1 pt. milk**
**3 eggs**
**3 oz. castor sugar**
**Vanilla essence**
**½ oz. gelatine**
**4 tablesp. water**
**2 oz. glacé cherries**
**1 oz. citron peel**
**¼ pt. double cream**

Make a custard with the milk, eggs and sugar, and flavour with vanilla. Soak gelatine in the water for 5 min., then heat until dissolved. Stir into the custard. Cut cherries in halves and shred the peel. Stir into the custard and lastly fold in the cream, whipped to a consistency similar to that of the cool custard. Just before setting, pour into a prepared mould. Turn out when set.

**6 helpings**
**Setting time—1–2 hr.**

QUEEN'S PUDDING

*Pouding à la Reine*

**¼ lb. biscuit-** *or* **cake-crumbs**
**1 pt. milk**
**2 oz. sugar**
**2 eggs**
**Vanilla essence**
**6–9 apricot halves (preserved, i.e canned** *or* **bottled)**
**Glacé cherries for decoration**

APRICOT SAUCE

**½ pt. apricot syrup**
**Sugar to taste**
**1 tablesp. kirsch** *or* **rum**

Rub the biscuit- or cake-crumbs through a fine sieve. Heat the milk, add the crumbs, leave to stand for 10–15 min. until soft; then beat until smooth. Beat in the sugar and eggs. Flavour with vanilla essence. Grease a plain mould or basin with butter, line the base with a round of greased paper and sprinkle with castor sugar. Pour in the mixture and cover with paper. Stand the mould in a tin of hot water, and bake in a warm oven (**335° F., Gas 3**) until the mixture is firm to the touch; about ¾ hr.

Meanwhile make the apricot sauce by boiling the apricot syrup with sugar added to taste until it is slightly reduced, then add the rum *or* kirsch.

When the pudding is set in the middle, leave it to stand a few minutes and then carefully unmould on to a dish. Tear off the paper, arrange apricot halves round the dish, decorate pudding with cherries, and pour round it the apricot sauce.

**6 helpings**

QUENELLES TO MAKE

Use 2 dessertspoons. Dip one spoon into boiling water, shake off the surplus water, then fill it with quenelle mixture. Press the mixture from the sides and shape it into an oval shape with a knife dipped in hot water. Dip the second spoon into hot water and scoop the mixture carefully from the first spoon into the second, and place the quenelle in the pan.

QUENELLES OF VEAL

**3 oz. fillet of veal**
**½ oz. butter**
**½ oz. flour**
**1½ gills stock**
**1 egg yolk**
**Salt and pepper**

Mince or chop meat finely. Heat butter in a saucepan; stir in flour, cook for 2–3 min. Gradually add ½ gill stock and cook until thick. Stir in egg yolk, veal and seasoning. Remove from pan and form into finger shapes. Put rest of stock in pan, bring to boil. Poach the fingers or quenelles for 10–15 min. in hot stock. Serve with white sauce made partly of remaining stock.

**1 helping**

QUICK BREADS

These are breads and rolls made without yeast. *See Bread and Bread-Making, Gingerbreads, Scones, etc.*

QUICK FREEZING

This is a specialized art. The reader interested in it should therefore refer to a specialized book on the subject, or to *Mrs Beeton's Cookery and Household Management* (1960 edition) where it is treated in some detail.

**QUICK-FROZEN FOODS**

Quick-frozen foods are now an important factor in modern housekeeping. Garden vegetables, sea-fresh fillets of fish, fruit and poultry are all available independent of the seasons, without any waste or need for preparation. What you buy, you can eat, and the time saved can be devoted to "finishing touches".

Quick-frozen food can be kept for up to 36 hours in the ice-making compartment of a refrigerator. However, (although below freezing-point) it is only a "shallow" freezing place, and foods cannot be kept in it indefinitely.

If a refrigerator is not available, most quick-frozen foods will keep for up to 24 hours in a cool place. Some people take the precaution of wrapping such foods, in their cartons, in newspaper.

Generally, once quick-frozen foods are thawed, they should be eaten as soon as possible. *Under no circumstances should they be refrozen.*

For maximum flavour and food value, quick-frozen vegetables should be cooked as soon after purchase as possible, preferably while still frozen. The cooking time required is only a fraction of the time needed for cooking market-bought vegetables, so the instructions on the cartons should be carefully followed, Quick-frozen vegetables *must not be over-cooked.*

Quick-frozen fish fillets, on the other hand, should be partially thawed before cooking—at least enough to separate the fillets. Thawing is best done naturally by leaving the unopened carton at room temperature for 2–3 hours, but if it is necessary to speed up the operation, place the unopened carton under running cold water. The only time when complete thawing is necessary is when the fish is to be fried in deep fat. Fish still frozen reduces the temperature of the fat greatly and suddenly, and can cause severe spluttering. Cooking times vary with the thickness of the fish and the degree of thaw, but average times for *partially thawed* fish are as follows: to fry—8–15 minutes; to grill—8–16 minutes; to bake—15–30 min.; to steam—8–20 min.

Quick-frozen fruits need no preparation other than thawing, and they are packaged with a natural sweetening of cane sugar or syrup. Always thaw in the unopened carton and as slowly as possible; 3–4 hours at room temperature is an average time to allow for this. These fruits are at their best if served as soon as they are completely thawed, as they will still be slightly chilled. The most popular way of eating them is in their natural state with either cream or ice cream. They can, however, be used for flans, tarts, and shortcakes, in jellies, fruit creams, salads, or in any of the numerous ways in which unfrozen fruits are used. One 10 oz. carton of fruit will fill a 7-in flan case or 6 large tartlet cases.

Quick-frozen chickens, too, should be partially thawed—sufficiently to remove the giblets before cooking. They are ready then for roasting, frying or grilling, according to individual taste, and all the familiar chicken recipes can be adapted for their use. Cooking times depend on the recipe selected.

**QUINCE SAUCE**

| | |
|---|---|
| **½ lb. quinces** | **Sugar** |
| **½ pt. water *or* water in which carrots have been cooked** | **Ground clove** |
| **Ground nutmeg** | **Lemon juice** |
| | **⅛ pt. red wine (optional)** |

Stew the quinces very gently in the water until pulpy. Beat them quite smooth or rub them through a hair or nylon sieve. Reheat the sauce, add nutmeg, sugar, clove and lemon juice to taste. Stir in the red wine if used.

**QUINCE JELLY**

| | |
|---|---|
| **Quinces** | **Sugar** |
| **Water** | |

Wipe fruit carefully. Do not peel but cut into quarters and put into the preserving pan with sufficient cold water to cover. Bring slowly to the boil and simmer gently until the quinces are quite tender. Strain through a scalded jelly bag—do not squeeze or the jelly will not be clear. Add 1 lb. of sugar to each pint of juice and boil till setting point is reached.

## RABBIT—AMERICAN STYLE

*Lapin à l'Americaine*

**1 rabbit**
**2 oz. dripping**
**Stock**
**1½ oz. butter**
**1 oz. flour**
**¼ pt. tomato purée**
**Salt and pepper**
**Castor sugar**
**1 teasp. lemon juice**

Wash and dry the rabbit thoroughly. Divide into neat joints. Heat the dripping in a saucepan, fry the pieces of rabbit until well browned, drain away any surplus fat, add sufficient stock to just cover the rabbit, cover with a closely-fitting lid and cook until tender, about 1–1¼ hr. Meanwhile, melt the butter in another saucepan, stir in the flour, and cook gently until the roux is nut-brown, then stir in the tomato purée. When ready, remove rabbit and keep it hot. Strain and stir ¾ pt. of the stock into the blended flour, butter and purée, stir until boiling, season, add a pinch of sugar and lemon juice. Put the rabbit in the sauce, make thoroughly hot, serve as quickly as possible.

**3–4 helpings**

## RABBIT BROTH

*Bouillon de Lapin*

**1 rabbit**
**½ lb. streaky bacon *or* pickled pork**
**3 pt. water**
**Bunch of herbs—parsley stalks, thyme, marjoram, bay leaf**
**A strip of lemon rind**
**4 peppercorns**
**1 clove**
**1 small piece blade mace**
**2 onions *or* leeks**
**1 carrot**
**1 very small turnip**
**1 stick of celery**
**1 tablesp. rice**
**½ teasp. salt**
**1 teasp. lemon juice**
**Chopped parsley**

Soak the rabbit in salt water for ½ hr., then rinse it well, or blanch it by covering with cold water in a saucepan (with a lid), bringing to boiling point and rinsing. The best pieces of meat may be filleted from back and legs to be used for another dish, or the jointed rabbit may be cooked in the broth and served with a sauce made from ½ pt. of the broth.

Split the head, divide the backbone in sections, cut off the flaps and keep them, discard the internal organs unless their rather strong flavour is liked, and have the rabbit neatly jointed or the bones separated into small units. Put the bones and as much of the meat as is to be used into a strong pan; scrape and wash bacon or pork and add it whole, with rind, to the pan; cover all with the cold water and bring very slowly to simmering point. Add the bunch of herbs, the lemon rind, the peppercorns, clove and mace and simmer very gently for 1 hr. Meanwhile cut the vegetables into ¼-in. dice, blanch the rice and add these to the broth at the end of the hour. Simmer for a further 1½ hr. If the rabbit joints are being cooked in the broth, remove them to serve separately. If only bones have been used, drain the broth through a colander or metal sieve. Return the broth to the pan and keep it hot. Remove bones, herbs, rind and spices and cut small any scraps of meat that cling to the bones; return these pieces of meat to the pan. Cut the bacon into ½-in. cubes and return it to the broth. Reheat; season carefully, being cautious not to over-salt it if the bacon is already salt; add the lemon juice and parsley.

**6 helpings**
**Cooking time—2½ hr.**

## RABBIT EN CASSEROLE

*Lapin en Casserole*

**1 large rabbit**
**Strips of fat bacon (optional)**
**2 oz. butter**
**2 onions**
**2 slices lean bacon**
**Salt and pepper**
**1 oz. flour**
**1 pt. stock**
**Bouquet garni**

Wash and joint the rabbit. If desired, lard the joints with strips of fat bacon ( and suet ). Heat the butter in a casserole and brown in it the rabbit, sliced onions and lean bacon (diced). When well-browned, add salt and pepper; sprinkle in flour, and when this has browned, stir in stock. Bring to boiling point, add bouquet garni. Cover tightly and cook slowly in a moderate oven (**350° F., Gas 4**) for 2–2½ hr. Remove bouquet garni and correct seasoning.

Serve from the casserole.

**4–5 helpings**

## RABBIT PIE

*Pâté de Lapin*

| | |
|---|---|
| **1 rabbit** | **½ pt. stock** |
| **½ lb. beef steak** | **Puff pastry using 8 oz. flour, etc.** |
| **½ lb. bacon *or* pickled pork** | **Egg for glazing** |
| **Salt and pepper** | |

Wash, dry, and joint the rabbit, dice the beef and bacon *or* pork. Place these ingredients in layers in a pie-dish, season well, ¾ fill dish with stock. Cover with pastry. Bake 1¾–2 hr. in a hot oven (**425°–450° F., Gas 7–8**) for 15 min., and in a moderate oven (**350° F., Gas 4**) for the remainder of the time. Glaze with egg 20 min. before pie is cooked. Add remainder of seasoned stock and serve hot or cold. If the pie is required cold, forcemeat balls and sliced hard-boiled egg will be an improvement.

**6–8 helpings** **Cooking time—1¾–2 hr.**

## RABBIT PIE—ROMAN

| | |
|---|---|
| **1 cooked rabbit** | **2 hard-boiled eggs** |
| **Short crust pastry using 12 oz. flour, etc.** | **2 shallots** |
| | **4 mushrooms** |
| | **Salt and pepper** |
| **1½ oz. cooked macaroni** | **¼ pt. gravy *or* stock** |
| | **Egg *or* milk for glazing** |

Make pastry, line an 8-in. greased round cake tin with ⅔ of it. Put a layer of chopped cooked macaroni on the pastry, add the flesh of a cooked rabbit (cut into small pieces) and the hard-boiled eggs (cut in sections). Chop and fry the shallots and mushrooms; add these to the pie, season well, moisten with gravy or stock in which the rabbit has been cooked. Cover with remainder of pastry, make a hole in the lid, glaze, bake in a fairly hot oven (**375°–400° F., Gas 5–6**) 30–40 min.

Serve hot with extra gravy *or* stock.

**6 helpings**

## RABBIT SOUP—WHITE

*Potage blanc de lapin*

| | |
|---|---|
| **1 rabbit** | **1 blade of mace** |
| **3 pt. bone stock *or* water** | **¼ lb. lean bacon *or* pickled pork** |
| **2 onions stuck with 2 cloves** | **1½ oz. flour** |
| | **¼ pt. milk *or* ½ gill milk and ½ gill cream** |
| **1 small turnip** | |
| **2 sticks of celery** | |
| **A bunch of herbs** | **Salt and pepper** |
| **1 bay leaf** | **Lemon juice** |

Cleanse and joint the rabbit; blanch it. Make a broth with the rabbit, the liquid, the vegetables (cut into dice) and spices.

Strain broth, cut some neat ½-in. dice of rabbit and lean bacon or pork (the rest of the meat can be used for a fricassée, etc.). Blend the flour with cold milk and stir this into the broth; boil till the soup is thickened. Season and add lemon juice to taste. If cream is used add it to the boiling soup, off the heat, and serve at once.

NOTE: The internal organs of rabbit, having a strong flavour may be used or omitted as liked.

**6–8 helpings**
**Cooking time—2½–3 hr.**

## RABBIT STEW—RICH

*Gibelotte de Lapin*

| | |
|---|---|
| **1 rabbit** | **1 pt. good stock** |
| **4 oz. streaky bacon** | **Bouquet garni** |
| **18 button onions** | **2 cloves** |
| **2 oz. butter** | **Salt and pepper** |
| **1½ oz. flour** | **1 glass claret (optional)** |

Wash, dry and joint the rabbit, put the liver aside. Dice the bacon, peel the onions. Melt the butter in a large saucepan, fry onions and bacon until brown, then lift out. Fry rabbit lightly, sprinkle in flour and continue frying until well browned. Replace onions and bacon, add hot stock, bouquet garni, cloves and seasoning, cover tightly and stew gently until rabbit is tender—about 1¼ hr. About 15 min. before serving, add claret if used, put in liver (washed and cut into small pieces) and finish cooking.

Pile the rabbit on a hot dish, strain the sauce over and garnish with bacon dice and onions.

**3–4 helpings**
**Cooking time—about 2 hr.**

## RABBIT—WITH SPANISH ONIONS

*Lapin aux Oignons d'Espagne*

| | |
|---|---|
| **1 large rabbit** | **½ oz. flour** |
| **4 *or* 5 Spanish onions** | **Salt and pepper** |
| **¼ lb. ham *or* bacon** | |

Wash the rabbit, and cut into pieces convenient for serving. Slice onions; dice ham *or* bacon. Line the base and sides of a casserole with onion slices. Put in a layer of rabbit, some ham *or* bacon, sprinkle with seasoned flour, cover with slices of onion. Repeat the layers until all the ingredients are used. Add 2 tablesp. cold water. Cover with a tightly-fitting lid, cook in a moderate oven **(350° F., Gas 4)** for about 2–2½ hr. Correct the seasoning.

Serve very hot.

**4–5 helpings**
**Cooking time—2–2½ hr.**

## RADISH ROSES AS A GARNISH

Cut off the roots of the radishes, make 4–6 cuts down almost to the base, taking care not to cut right through, thus cutting the radishes in pieces. Put into cold water, preferably iced, and leave until the radishes open like roses.

## RADISHES AS A GARNISH

*Radis*

Choose small, round and firm radishes of a light red and white colour. Trim and wash them in plenty of water. Dish up in little glass dishes. Keep in a refrigerator if possible until ready to serve.

## RAGOÛT OF BEEF

| | |
|---|---|
| **1½ lb. cold under-done roast beef** | **1 pt. stock** |
| **2 onions** | **Salt and pepper** |
| **2 oz. fat** | **1 tablesp. mushroom ketchup *or* vinegar** |
| **1½ oz. flour** | |

Cut the meat into neat slices. Chop the onions coarsely. Melt the fat in a saucepan, add the onions and fry until brown. Sprinkle in the flour, stir and cook slowly until well browned. Add the stock, stir and bring to the boil. Season to taste, add the carrot and turnip trimmings from the garnish, mushroom ketchup or vinegar, and simmer for 15 min. Put in the slices of meat and heat thoroughly without boiling for about 1 hr. When nearly ready, cook the diced vegetables. Place the meat on a hot dish and pour the strained sauce over it.

**6 helpings**

## RAGOÛT OF FOWL

*Ragoût de Volaille*

| | |
|---|---|
| **1 fowl** | **1½ oz. flour** |
| **2½ oz. butter** | **1¼ pt. stock** |
| **1 onion** | **¼ lb. ham *or* bacon** |
| **Salt and pepper** | |

Joint fowl and trim, heat the butter in a saucepan, fry the joints in this until lightly browned; remove and keep them hot. Fry the sliced onion lightly, sprinkle in the flour, and brown this slowly; add the stock, stir until boiling, season carefully. Replace the joints in the sauce, add diced ham *or* bacon, cover with a tightly-fitting lid and cook gently until fowl is tender—2–2½ hr. Correct the seasoning, serve with the sauce strained over.

**5–6 helpings**

## RAGOÛT OF RABBIT

*Ragoût de Lapin*

| | |
|---|---|
| **1 rabbit** | **1 pt. stock** |
| **4 oz. streaky bacon** | **Salt and pepper** |
| **2 oz. butter** | **1 carrot** |
| **1 onion** | **½ small turnip** |
| **1½ oz. flour** | **6 peppercorns** |

GARNISH
**Macédoine of vegetables**

Wash, dry and joint the rabbit; dice the bacon. Heat the butter in a saucepan, fry rabbit in it until well browned; remove rabbit and keep hot. Fry diced onion, put in flour, stir and fry until well browned. Add boiling stock; boil for 10 min. Return rabbit to pan, add seasoning, diced carrot and turnip, bacon and peppercorns. Cover tightly. Stew gently until rabbit is tender—about 2 hr. Correct seasoning.

Serve rabbit on a hot dish with sauce strained over. Garnish at either end with macédoine of vegetable.

**3–4 servings**

## RAGOÛT OF VEAL

*Ragoût de Veau*

| | |
|---|---|
| **2½ lb. neck, breast *or* knuckle of veal** | **Hot water** |
| **1½ oz. dripping** | **Salt and pepper** |
| **1 onion** | **1½ oz. butter *or* fat** |
| | **1½ oz. flour** |

GARNISH

| | |
|---|---|
| **2 carrots** | **Chopped parsley** |
| **2 turnips** | **Bacon rolls** |

Cut the meat into pieces convenient for serving. Heat the dripping in a saucepan, fry the meat until lightly browned, then remove it. Fry the sliced onion for a few minutes, then drain off the surplus fat. Return the meat to the saucepan, cover with hot water and add seasoning. Cover with a lid and cook slowly until a pale brown colour. Meanwhile dice the vegetables for the garnish and add the trimmings to the meat. Cook the diced vegetables separately, strain then toss in a little butter. Add the chopped parsley and keep hot. When pale brown, remove the meat and keep hot. Strain the liquid in the saucepan and make up to ¾ pt. with water, if necessary. Add to it the blended fat and flour and cook and stir for 4 min. Season to taste, return the meat and simmer gently for ½ hr. Garnish with grilled bacon rolls and the diced vegetables.

**6 helpings**

## RAISED PIE

*Pâté de Gibier*

| | |
|---|---|
| **½ lb. game** | **Veal forcemeat** |
| **½ lb. pork** | **½ pt. good stock (approx.)** |
| **½ lb. veal** | |
| **Salt and pepper** | **Egg to glaze** |

HOT WATER CRUST PASTRY

| | |
|---|---|
| **½ lb. flour** | **¼ pt. water *or* milk and water** |
| **Pinch of salt** | **3 oz. lard** |

Remove skin and bones from the game, cut into small pieces, mix with pork and veal (also cut finely); season well.

Prepare and mould pastry: sift flour and salt into a warm basin. Put the milk and water (or water) and lard to boil, then pour into middle of flour and mix well with wooden spoon until cooler. Knead with the hands until smooth, keep warm throughout or the moulding may be extremely difficult—but avoid overheating. Cut off ¼, roll to shape for the lid. Raise remainder with the hands to a round or oval shape.

When the lower part of the pie has been raised to the required shape and thinness, line it with veal forcemeat to support the lower part of the pie. Line the sides with forcemeat, put in the prepared meat, cover with a thin layer of forcemeat, add some stock and put on the cover. Fasten 3 or 4 folds of greased, grease-proof paper round the pie to preserve its shape and prevent it becoming too brown. Brush the top of the pie with egg and make a hole in the centre. Bake in a hot oven **(425° F., Gas 7)** and reduce heat to moderate **(350° F., Gas 4)** as soon as pastry is set.

The pie may be baked in a tin (choose one with a loose base), if desired. Prepare and bake the pie, removing it from the tin and glazing top and sides with egg about 30 min. before cooking is complete. If the pie is required cold, return to the tin when cooked and leave it until cold—this prevents the pastry from becoming hard.

**6 helpings**
**Cooking time—about 2 hr.**

## RAISED PIE CRUST *or* HOT WATER CRUST PASTRY

For Pork, Veal and Ham or Raised Game Pies

| | |
|---|---|
| **10 oz. plain flour** | **3 oz. lard** |
| **½ teasp. salt** | **¼ pt. milk *or* water** |

Sift the flour and salt into a warm bowl, make a well in the centre, and keep in a warm place. Heat the lard and milk *or* water together gently until boiling then add them to the flour, mixing well with a wooden spoon, until cool enough to knead with the hands. Knead thoroughly, use as required. Leave covered for ½ hr.

Throughout the processes of mixing, kneading and moulding, the pastry must be kept warm, otherwise moulding will be extremely difficult. On the other hand, if the pastry is too warm it will be so soft and pliable that it cannot retain its shape, or support its own weight.

Bake in a hot oven **(425° F., Gas 7)**, reduce

heat to moderate (350° F., Gas 4) as soon as pastry is set.

TO RAISE A PIE

The pastry must be raised or moulded whilst still warm. Reserve ¼ for the lid and leave in the bowl in a warm place covered with a cloth. Roll out the remainder to about ¼ in. thickness in a round or oval shape as preferred. Gently mould the pie with the hands; if this proves too difficult mould it over a jam jar. Grease and flour the jar, invert it, place the pastry over and mould the pastry round the sides, taking care not to stretch the pastry and ensuring that the sides and base are of an even thickness. Leave to cool.

When cold, remove the pastry case from the jar, put in the filling. Roll the ¼ of pastry reserved for the lid, damp the rim of the case, put on the lid and press edges firmly together.

Three or four folds of greased paper should be pinned round the pie to preserve its shape during baking and to prevent it becoming too brown.

NOTE: If the pie is raised without using a jar, when the lower part of the pie has been raised to the required shape and thinness, moulding can be facilitated by pressing in firmly some of the filling to support the lower part of the pie. If liked the pie can be baked in a pie mould, cake-tin or a small loaf-tin; grease well before lining with the pastry.

## RAISING AGENTS

*See Bread and Bread-Making.*

## RASPBERRY BUNS

*See Buns or Cookies*

## RASPBERRY ICE CREAM

*Glace à la Crème de Framboises*

**1 small can raspberries**
**¼ pt. cream**
**¼ pt. custard (2)**
**2 oz. castor sugar**

Drain the raspberries and pass through a nylon sieve. (Purée and juice together should measure ½ pt.) Mix with custard and then add the half-whipped cream. Add the sugar, and a little colouring if necessary. Chill and freeze.

**6 helpings**

## RASPBERRY JAM—Quick Method

This jam does not set very firmly, but it has a delicious fresh flavour. Do not wash the raspberries unless absolutely necessary; if they have to be washed, drain very thoroughly.

**2½ lb. raspberries**
**3 lb. granulated sugar**

Bring the fruit gently to the boil, then boil rapidly for 5 min. Remove from the heat, add the warmed sugar and stir well over a low heat until all the sugar has dissolved. Bring to the boil and boil rapidly *for 1 min.* Skim quickly, pour the jam at once into dry, warm jars and cover.

**Yield—5 lb.**

## RASPBERRY PUDDING

*Pouding de Framboises*

**1 lb. raspberries**
**3 oz. granulated sugar**
**4 oz. butter** *or* **margarine**
**4 oz. castor sugar**
**2 eggs**
**6 oz. plain flour**
**1 rounded teasp. baking-powder**
**2–4 tablesp. milk (approx.)**

Grease a pie-dish. Put the cleaned and washed raspberries, with the granulated sugar, in the bottom of the dish.

Cream together in a mixing bowl the butter and castor sugar. Beat in the eggs gradually. Stir in the sifted flour and baking-powder, adding milk to make an easy dropping consistency. Spread this mixture over the fruit. Bake in a moderate oven (350° F., Gas 4) until the pudding is cooked and nicely browned—about 1–1¼ hr.

Well dredge with castor sugar before serving.

Serve with cream *or* custard sauce.

**6 helpings**

### RASPBERRY SOUFFLÉ

*Soufflé aux Framboises*

As for Milanaise Soufflé using raspberry purée (made from fresh raspberries) instead of rind and juice of lemons; colour suitably.

### RASPBERRY SOUFFLÉ

*Soufflé aux Framboises*

**½ lb. ripe raspberries**
**2 oz. cornflour**
**2 oz. castor sugar**
**⅛ pt. cream**
**3 eggs**
**2 oz. cake- *or* bread-crumbs**

Butter a soufflé dish. Pass the raspberries through a fine nylon sieve. Mix together the cornflour, sugar and raspberry pulp to a smooth consistency. Add the cream. Separate the eggs, beat the egg yolks into the mixture and add the cake-crumbs. Stiffly whisk the egg whites and fold them into the mixture. Turn the mixture into the soufflé dish and bake in a fairly hot oven **(400° F., Gas 6)** for 25–30 min.

**4 helpings**

### RASPBERRY WHIP (1)

*Gelée de Framboise fouettée*

**One 1 pt. raspberry jelly tablet**
**½ pt. raspberry juice**
**¼ pt. water**
**Sugar if necessary**

Proceed as for Lemon Whip

### RASPBERRY WHIP (2)

**¾ pt. strained raspberry juice**
**½ oz. gelatine**
**Sugar to taste**

Proceed as for Blackcurrant Whip

### RATAFIA BISCUITS

**1½ egg whites**
**1 oz. butter**
**6 oz. castor sugar**
**4 oz. ground almonds**
**Rice paper *or* greaseproof paper**

Beat the egg whites stiffly in a large bowl. Cream the butter and sugar. Add the ground almonds and mix well together. Fold into the egg whites and mix to a smooth paste. When the mixture begins to get stiff put it into a large bag with a plain pipe. Place the rice paper or greaseproof paper on a baking-sheet and pipe small drops about 2 in. apart. Bake in a moderate oven **(350° F., Gas 4)**.

**24–30 ratafias** **Cooking time—about 15 min.**

### RAVIGOTE SAUCE—HOT

**½ pt. Velouté sauce**
**1 tablesp. Ravigote butter**
**1 tablesp. wine vinegar**
**Nutmeg**
**Sugar**
**Salt and pepper**

RAVIGOTE BUTTER

**1 heaped tablesp. of a mixture of picked parsley, chervil leaves, chopped shallot, tarragon leaves, chopped chives, crushed garlic**
**½ oz. butter**

To make the Ravigote butter, scald the herbs, shallot and garlic in a little boiling water; drain them and wring dry in muslin. Pound the herbs and butter together, then rub through a fine sieve. Heat the Velouté sauce, add to it the vinegar, nutmeg, sugar and seasoning. Whisk the Ravigote butter into the sauce, adding a small pat at a time, keeping the sauce almost at boiling point but not allowing it to boil. Serve the sauce at once.

### RAVIOLI AL SUGO

Ravioli with Sauce

**6 tablesp. plain flour**
**3 eggs**
**¼ teasp. salt**
**½ calf's brain**
**½ small onion**
**1 oz. butter**
**2 rashers lean bacon**
**A little cooked chicken *or* meat**
**1 bay leaf**
**2 tablesp. cooked, chopped spinach**
**Salt and pepper**
**2 tablesp. stock**
**Parmesan cheese to taste**

With the flour, 2 of the eggs and ¼ teasp. salt make a firm dough, put on a floured board and knead well until smooth. Cover with a cloth and let it stand to dry a little. Cut in ½ and roll into 2 thin sheets.

Make the filling: wash and remove all blood from brain in cold water, drain and dry, slice the onion and fry it in the butter, add bacon, brain, chicken, bay leaf, spinach, salt, pepper and stock, and cook gently for about 30 min. Remove the bay leaf and pass the mixture through a fine mincer, place it in a basin, add the yolk from the 3rd egg, cheese, and mix into a thick paste.

Damp the sheets of dough with the remain-

## Pastry in the Making III
## —Short Crust Pastry.

2

1

1 Ensure all utensils are cold. Sift flour and salt into a bow

2 With a sharp knife cut, or use a grater to shred in the fat.

3 Rub in the fat with the finger tips until the mixture looks like fine breadcrumbs. Lift the hands up from the bowl so that the air is entrapped as the flour falls back into the bowl.

3

4

5

6

Using a knife, mix to a stiff dough with only necessary amount of freshly-drawn cold water.

Gather the mixture together leaving the bowl clean. Dough should feel damp but not sticky.

On a floured surface, press the dough lightly with the fingers into rough shape required.

Pie-Making
—A Raised Pie.

1 Pour the boiling lard and water or milk on to the sifted flour and salt, mixing well with a wooden spoon or a palette knife.

2 When the mixture is cool enough, knead it thoroughly with the hands.

3 Cut off $\frac{1}{4}$ of the dough and keep covered in warm place till needed.

4 Roll out the remaining dough to a round and line greased tin, working the dough up the sides of tin.

5 Roll the chopped meat in seasoned flour, put half into lined tin with the shelled eggs, fill with the remaining meat. Damp edge of the pastry lining the tin and cover with the remaining rolled-out pastry.

6 When the pie is baked fill up with stock poured through a funnel made of clean greaseproof paper.

1

2

3

4

5

6

ing egg white (beaten). Drop ½ teaspoonfuls of stuffing about 1 in. apart on one sheet. Cover with other sheet of dough. Press well together and around each heap of filling, and cut into 1 in. squares. Edges should again be sealed between finger and thumb, so that ravioli will not open while cooking. Boil for about 20 min. in a large saucepan of boiling water. Drain well, serve with tomato sauce and sprinkle grated Parmesan cheese on top.

## RÉCHAUFFÉ OF LAMB

*Réchauffé d'Agneau*

**1½ lb. cold cooked lamb**
**1 small onion**
**¾ oz. butter *or* margarine**
**½ oz. flour**
**¾ pt. gravy *or* stock**
**1 tablesp. mushroom ketchup**
**Salt and pepper**
**Mashed potatoes *or* boiled rice**
**Sippets of toast**

Cut the meat into neat dice and boil the bones and trimmings for stock. Finely chop the onion, melt the fat in a saucepan and fry the onion lightly. Add the flour and brown. Stir in the stock, add the ketchup and season to taste. Simmer for 10 min. Put in the meat and bring to simmering point. Keep just below simmering for about ½ hr.

Serve the meat surrounded by a border of mashed potatoes or boiled rice and garnished with sippets of toast.

**6 helpings**

## RECHAUFFÉS

Every housewife is sometimes faced with left-over food. With a little skill and ingenuity, she can turn it into a palatable dish for another meal. A number of recipes in this book can be used to make such reheated dishes.

## RED CABBAGE WITH APPLES

*Choux aux Pommes*

**1 small red cabbage**
**1 oz. margarine**
**1 onion chopped very fine**
**2 cooking apples**
**1 tablesp. golden syrup**
**Juice of ½ lemon**
**2 tablesp. vinegar**
**Salt**

Melt the fat. Add the onion and fry gently until light brown. Add cabbage finely shredded, peeled and sliced apples, and syrup. Cook over very gentle heat for 10 min., shaking pan frequently. Add lemon juice, vinegar and salt and simmer covered, 1–1½ hr. Stir occasionally. Season and serve.

**6 helpings**
**Cooking time—1½–2 hr.**

## RED CABBAGE AND APPLE SALAD

*Salade de chou rouge*

**½ small red cabbage**
**3 dessert apples**
**French dressing (with mustard)**
**Fine cress**

Shred the red cabbage very finely. Shred the peeled, cored apples in equally fine shreds. Mix lightly with the dressing and serve in a salad bowl with tiny bunches of fine cress.

**6 helpings**

## RED CABBAGE WITH CHEESE

*Choux au fromage*

**1 small red cabbage**
**¼ pt. boiling water**
**1 teasp. quince jelly**
**4 oz. grated cheese**
**2 teasp. vinegar**
**Salt and pepper**

Soak, wash and slice the cabbage thinly. Boil gently in the water with the jelly and a little salt added. Add the cheese and vinegar and mix well. Season and serve hot.

**6 helpings**
**Cooking time—¾–1 hr.**

## RED CABBAGE—SCANDINAVIAN STYLE

**1 red cabbage**
**Vinegar**
**2 oz. butter *or* margarine**
**Redcurrant jelly**
**Sugar**
**Salt**

Cut the cabbage into thin slices and sprinkle a little vinegar on it. Melt the butter in a pan, add the cabbage and cook gently for 3 hr., stirring frequently. When nearly done, add a little redcurrant jelly, sugar and salt to taste. Do not cook it in a iron pot. Serve hot. Red cabbage is best if prepared the day before eating and re-heated.

**6 helpings**

## RED HERRINGS

*Harengs Saurs*

**Red herrings**
**Milk *or* water**
**Oil**
**Vinegar**
**Egg yolk and gherkins *or* diced boiled potatoes**

Cover the herrings with boiled water and after several minutes, drain. Soak in milk or water for 1 hr. Skin and fillet, then cut into pieces and dress with oil and vinegar. The herrings can be garnished with sieved egg yolk and chopped gherkins. Alternatively mix the herring pieces with diced boiled potatoes and dress the whole with oil and vinegar.

## RED MULLET À LA NIÇOISE

*Rouget à la Niçoise*

**4 small red mullet**
**Salt and pepper**
**Olive oil for frying**

SAUCE

**2 shallots**
**1 clove of garlic**
**1 tablesp. olive oil**
**1 lb. ripe tomatoes**
**Salt and pepper**

GARNISH

**Anchovy fillets**
**A few stoned olives**

Prepare the fish and season the insides with salt and pepper. Grill or fry the fish in olive oil, turning to cook and brown evenly on both sides. Meanwhile make the sauce: chop the shallots, crush the garlic and fry for several minutes in the oil. Peel and roughly chop the tomatoes, add to the shallots and cook rapidly until reduced to a thick sauce consistency; season to taste. Place the fish in a shallow dish, pour the hot sauce over and leave to get cold.

Serve garnished with olives and with a lattice pattern of thin strips of anchovy.

**4 helpings**

## REDCURRANT JELLY—RICH

**6 lb. large, juicy redcurrants *or* redcurrants and whitecurrants mixed**
**Sugar**

Remove the leaves and only the larger stems. Place the cleaned fruit in the preserving-pan, without any water, and heat very gently until the currants are softened and well cooked (about ¾ hr.). Mash, then strain the pulp through a scalded jelly bag, leaving it to drip undisturbed. Measure the juice into the cleaned pan. Add 1¼ lb. of sugar to each pint of juice. Bring to the boil, stirring constantly, and boil, without stirring, for 1 min. Swiftly skim the jelly and immediately pour it into the warmed jars, before it has a chance to set in the pan.

## REDCURRANT SAUCE

*Sauce aux Groseilles Rouges*

**¼ lb. redcurrant jelly**
**⅛ pt. port *or* other red wine**

Heat the two ingredients together gently until the jelly is melted.

Serve with game, venison *or* as a sweet sauce with puddings.

## REGENCY SAUCE

**½ pt. Normandy sauce**
**1 dessertsp. shredded truffle**
**1 tablesp. shredded cooked mushroom**
**1 tablesp. liquor in which the mushrooms were cooked**
**White wine to taste**

Blend all the other ingredients with the hot Normandy sauce. Serve with fish.

To serve with chicken or veal use Suprême sauce instead of Normandy sauce.

## RÉMOULADE SAUCE

**¼ pt. mayonnaise**
**1 teasp. French mustard**
**A few drops of anchovy essence**
**1 dessertsp. mixed chopped: gherkins, capers, parsley, tarragon, chervil**

Stir the mustard, essence and herbs into the mayonnaise.

## RICE, TO COOK

**Boiled—Long Grained**

**½ lb. rice**
**2 cups water**

Wash rice and drain off water. Boil 2 cups of fresh water. Add rice and boil hard for 5 min. Reduce heat, cover and cook for 20 min.

**Boiled—Oval Grained**

| | |
|---|---|
| **½ lb. rice** | **2 cups water** |

Wash rice and drain off water. Boil 2 cups of fresh water. Add rice. Boil for 30 min.

**Steamed—Long and Oval Grained**

| | |
|---|---|
| **½ lb. rice** | **2 cups water** |

Wash rice and drain off water. Add 2 cups of fresh water to rice and boil for 3 min. Drain. Steam rice for 30 min.

## RICE, POLISH STYLE

*Riz à la Polonaise*

| | |
|---|---|
| **4 oz. Patna rice** | **Salt and pepper** |
| **1¼ pt. stock (approx.)** | **Cayenne pepper** |
| **1½ oz. butter** | **1 tablesp. grated Parmesan cheese** |
| **4 small mild onions** | **Finely-chopped parsley** |
| **2 tablesp. finely-shredded cooked ham** | |

Pick over, wash, blanch and drain the rice, replace it in the pan, cover with stock and simmer gently until tender, adding more stock as that in the pan boils away. When the rice is nearly ready heat the butter in a saucepan, put in the onions thinly sliced, fry for a few minutes without browning, then add the ham and the rice. Season to taste, as soon as the rice is sufficiently dry stir in the cheese, let it cook for 2–3 min., then pile on a hot dish, sprinkle with parsley and serve.

**3–4 helpings**

## RICE PUDDING, COLD

*See Whole Rice Mould.*

## RICE PUDDING, HOT

*See Milk Puddings*

## RICE SALAD

| | |
|---|---|
| **3 oz. Patna rice** | **Small red *or* green pepper (capsicum)** |
| **1–2 tablesp. olive oil** | **2–3 gherkins** |
| **1–2 tablesp. vinegar** | **Seasoning** |
| **½ teacup cooked peas** | **1 teasp. chopped chives *or* onion** |
| **½ teacup cooked diced carrots** | **Watercress** |

Cook the rice in boiling salted water, drain and mix with the oil and vinegar while still hot. The smaller quantity of oil and vinegar gives a fairly dry salad. Add the peas, carrots, finely-chopped uncooked red or green pepper, chopped gherkins, seasoning and chives or onion. Put into a dish and garnish with watercress.

**5–6 helpings**
**Cooking time—12 min. (approx.)**

## RICH CAKES, LARGE

In these cakes, the fat is usually creamed with the sugar.

### Foundation Proportions

| | |
|---|---|
| **Base** | —1 lb. plain flour |
| | —¼ teasp. salt |
| **Shortening** | —½–1 lb. fat |
| **Sweetening** | —½–1 lb. sugar |
| **Raising agents** | —2–4 level teasp. baking-powder (less as the number of eggs is increased). Self-raising flour may be used alone or with 1 teasp. baking-powder for small rich cakes and sandwich cakes. |
| | —4–12 eggs |
| **Fruit** | —½–3 lb. |
| **Other flavours** | —grated rind 3–4 oranges *or* lemons |
| | —1–2 teasp. vanilla essence |
| | —3 oz. cocoa (flour reduced by 1 oz.) |
| | —3 tablesp. coffee essence, etc. |
| **Liquid** | —milk or water to mix to required consistency. The more "melting ingredients", e.g. fat, sugar, etc., the stiffer the consistency. |

## RICH CAKE

### Basic Recipe

| | |
|---|---|
| **6 oz. butter *or* margarine** | **⅛ teasp. salt** |
| **6 oz. sugar** | **1½–2 level teasp. baking-powder** |
| **3 eggs** | **Milk *or* water to mix** |
| **8 oz. plain flour** | |

Line a 7-in. cake-tin with greaseproof paper Cream the butter and sugar till white, whisk eggs and add to the fat a little at a time, beating well between each addition. If mixture shows signs of curdling, add a little flour. Sift the flour and salt. Add the flour to the mixture, stirring in lightly with the baking-powder. (The eggs may be added whole and the egg and flour may be added alternately for a close-textured cake, e.g. fruit cake.) Add milk or water to make a fairly soft consistency. Turn into the cake-tin and bake in a moderate oven **(350° F., Gas 4).**

**Cooking time—1¼–1½ hr.**

### Variations of Basic Recipe

**Cherry Cake**

*Gâteau aux Cerises*

Add 4 oz. chopped glacé cherries when adding the flour.

**Cornflour Cake**

*Gâteau à la Crème de maïs*

Use 6 oz. cornflour and 2 oz. flour in the basic mixture. Dredge top of the cake with castor sugar before baking. The tin may be prepared by greasing and dusting with equal quantities of sugar and flour.

**Fruit Cake**

*Gâteau anglais*

Add 6–8 oz. sultanas, currants, raisins or dates to basic mixture. For fruit cake add eggs and flour alternately. Stir in fruit mixed with some of the flour *after* eggs have been added.

**Ginger Cake**

*Gâteau au Gingembre*

Sift ½ teasp. ground ginger with the flour, add 2–4 oz. coarsely chopped crystallized ginger with the flour.

**Ground Rice Cake**

*Gâteau de Riz*

Use 6 oz. flour and 2 oz. ground rice in basic mixture.

**Lemon Cake**

*Gâteau au Citron*

Add the grated rind of 2 lemons with the flour. The cake may be iced when cold with lemon glacé icing.

**Madeira Cake**

*Gâteau de Savoie*

Add the grated rind of 1 lemon with the flour. Place 2 strips of citron peel on top of the cake when mixture has begun to set (after about 30 min.).

## RICH CAKES, SMALL

The following is a suitable mixture for small cakes. It can be varied in many ways.

### Basic Recipe

**2 oz. butter *or* margarine**
**2 oz. castor sugar**
**1 egg**
**3 oz. self-raising flour *or* 3 oz. plain flour and 1 level teasp. baking-powder**
**Pinch of salt**
**Water *or* milk as required**

Beat the fat and sugar until creamy and white. Whisk the egg and add gradually; beat well between each addition. Sift together the flour, salt and baking-powder. Gently stir flour, etc., into creamed fat; add milk *or* water to make a soft dropping consistency (water is considered best). Half-fill greased bun tins with the mixture and bake in a fairly hot to moderate oven **(375°–350° F., Gas 5–4).**

NOTE: This mixture may be baked in paper cases and decorated with glacé icing or cherries.

**10–12 cakes**
**Cooking time—15–20 min.**

### Variations of Basic Recipe

**Cherry Cakes**

Add 1–2 oz. coarsely chopped glacé cherries with the flour.

**Chocolate Cakes**

Sift ½ oz. cocoa with the flour, and add a few drops of vanilla essence with the water or milk. The cakes may be iced with chocolate glacé icing.

**Coconut Cakes**

Add ½ oz. coconut with the flour and add ¼ teasp. vanilla essence with the milk or water.

**Lemon Cakes**

Add the grated rind of 1 lemon with the flour, and ice with lemon glacé icing.

**Madeleines**

Bake the basic mixture in greased dariole moulds. Turn out when baked; cool. Spread all round top and side with warmed apricot jam. Roll in desiccated coconut, decorate with ½ glacé cherry.

**Nut Cakes**

Add 1–2 oz. coarsely chopped walnuts, almonds, etc., with the flour.

**Queen Cakes**

Add 1–2 oz. currants *or* sultanas with the flour or a few currants may be placed in the bottom of each queen cake tin and the mixture placed on top.

## RICH SHORT CRUST PASTRY

For Pies, Tarts, etc.

| | |
|---|---|
| **1 lb. plain flour** | **2 teasp. castor sugar** |
| **Pinch of salt** | **2 egg yolks** |
| **10–12 oz. butter** | **Cold water to mix** |

Sift the flour and salt together. Cut the butter into small pieces and rub it lightly into the flour using the finger tips. Add the sugar and mix to a stiff paste with the egg yolks and 1 tablesp. cold water, using more water if necessary. Use as required.

## RISSOLETTES OF VEAL

*Rissolettes de Veau*

| | |
|---|---|
| **½ lb. cold cooked veal** | **Salt and pepper** |
| **4 oz. lean cooked ham *or* tongue** | **Short crust *or* rough puff pastry, using 8 oz. flour, etc.** |
| **¾ oz. fat** | **Egg and breadcrumbs *or* crushed vermicelli** |
| **¾ oz. flour** | **Deep fat** |
| **1½ gills stock** | **Parsley** |
| **1 teasp. finely-grated lemon rind** | |
| **Pinch of mace** | |

Chop the veal and ham or tongue very finely. Melt the fat, add the flour and cook lightly. Add the stock and stir and cook until thick and smooth. Add the lemon rind, mace and minced meats, season well and stir over a low heat until thoroughly mixed. Then turn on to a plate and leave to cool. Roll out the pastry wafer thin and cut into rounds of 1½–2 in. diameter. Place a little meat on each round, moisten the edges and fold over in half-moon shapes. Press the edges well to seal. Brush with beaten egg and toss in breadcrumbs or vermicelli. Fry in hot deep fat until golden brown, then drain well. Garnish with sprigs of fresh or fried parsley.

**6 helpings**
**Cooking time—about 10 min.**

## ROAST BEEF

*Bœuf rôti*

| | |
|---|---|
| **Joint of beef suitable for roasting** | **Beef dripping (allow 1 oz. per lb. of meat)** |
| **Salt and pepper** | |

Weigh meat to be able to calculate cooking time. Wipe with a damp cloth. Place joint in a roasting-tin, season and add dripping.

Put roasting-tin into a very hot oven (**450° F., Gas 8**) for 10–15 min. to brown or "sear" the meat. Then reduce heat to fairly hot (**375° F., Gas 5**) and baste every 20 min. for the first ½ of the cooking time and afterwards every 30 min. Allow 20 min. per lb. and another 10 min. over for solid joints, i.e. joints without bone; and 15 min. per lb. and 15 min. over for thick joints, i.e. joints with bone.

Remove on to a hot dish when cooked, remove string and skewer with a metal skewer if necessary. Keep hot. Drain off fat from tin and make gravy from sediment in the tin.

## ROAST CAPERCAILZIE

*Coq de Bruyère rôti*

**1 capercailzie**
**¼ lb. beef steak**
**1 or 2 slices bacon**
**Fat for basting**

GARNISH

**Watercress**
**French dressing**

Prepare the bird season , place the steak inside it, and truss. (The steak improves the flavour, and may afterwards be used in the preparation of a cold meat dish.) Cover the bird with bacon, roast in a fairly hot oven (**375°–425° F., Gas 5–7**) for about 1 hr., basting if necessary. Remove bacon about 15 min. before bird is cooked, baste, dredge with flour, baste and return to oven. This "frothing" will give a brown, crisp skin.

Serve (without the steak) garnished with watercress tossed in French dressing, and with gravy, bread sauce and fried breadcrumbs served separately.

**6 helpings** **Cooking time—1 hr.**

## ROAST CHICKEN

**1 roasting chicken**
**Salt and pepper**
**2–3 rashers of bacon**
**½ pt. stock**
**Fat for basting**

GARNISH

**Bunches of clean watercress**

Truss chicken for roasting, season lightly and cover with bacon. Roast on a trivet in the roasting tin in a fairly hot oven (**375°–400° F., Gas 5–6**) until tender 1–1½ hr. Baste frequently. The chicken may be roasted on the breast for a little while at the beginning, this will make the breast-meat more moist. (Prick the thigh to test for tenderness—if there is any trace of blood the chicken is not cooked.) The bacon may be removed 10–15 min. before serving, to allow the breast to brown. When the chicken is cooked place on a hot meat dish, remove trussing string, and keep hot. Make the gravy: pour excess fat from roasting tin but retain sediment; pour in stock, boil 2–3 min. Season to taste, strain into a hot sauce-boat.

Have ready the watercress washed, drained and lightly seasoned, garnish the chicken; serve with the gravy and bread sauce.

## ROAST CHICKEN—FRENCH STYLE

*Poulet rôti à la française*

**1 roasting chicken**
**1 oz. butter**
**1 small onion**
**1 carrot**
**2 or 3 rashers of bacon**
**Salt and pepper**
**1½ gill stock**

GARNISH

**Watercress**

Truss chicken for roasting, spread the breast thickly with butter. Slice vegetables, place in roasting tin with bacon and the washed liver and heart of the bird; fry gently. Place bird on mirepoix of seasoned vegetables roast in hot oven (**425° F., Gas 7**) until tender, 1–1½ hr., covering the breast with buttered paper if it browns too quickly; baste if necessary. Remove trussing string, keep chicken hot. Drain fat from roasting tin, add stock, boil 2–3 min., season and strain into gravy-boat.

Garnish; serve with gravy and bread sauce.

**5–6 helpings**

## ROAST CHICKEN (Quick)

**1 roasting chicken**
**Salt and pepper**
**2 rashers of streaky bacon**
**Fat for basting**

Joint the chicken, season the pieces, lay them in a roasting tin with the bacon (cut into small pieces) over. Bake in a fairly hot oven (**375°–400° F., Gas 5–6**) for about 40 min., basting when necessary. Should the chicken look too dry, cover with a buttered paper. Make the gravy as for Roast Chicken.

**5–6 helpings**

## ROAST DUCK

*Canard rôti*

**1 duck**
**Fat for basting**
**Sage and onion stuffing**
**½ oz. flour**
**½ pt. stock**
**Salt and pepper**
**Apple sauce**

Fill duck with sage and onion stuffing, truss for roasting. Baste well with hot fat, roast in a fairly hot oven (**375°–400° F., Gas 5–6**) 1–1½ hr. basting frequently. Keep duck hot, pour fat from roasting tin, sprinkle in flour and brown it. Stir in stock, simmer 3–4 min., season and strain. Remove trussing strings from duck.

Serve gravy and apple sauce separately.

**4–5 helpings** **Cooking time—1½ hr.**

### ROAST DUCK—WITH ORANGE

*Canard rôti à l'Orange*

**1 duck**
**Fat for basting**
**1 large orange**
**1 tablesp. brandy** *or* **red wine**

Truss and roast duck in a fairly hot oven (**375°–400° F., Gas 5–6**) for 1–1¼ hr., until tender, basting if necessary. Meanwhile, stand the orange in a pan of boiling water for about 3 min., remove skin, cut orange into sections, soak these in brandy *or* wine. Remove all white pith from the skin, cut the latter into thin strips, boil in a little water for about 5 min., drain. Heat the orange sections gently in the brandy. Remove trussing strings from duck.

Serve with strips of rind and hot orange sections as a garnish.

**4–5 helpings**

### ROAST FILLET OF BEEF

*Filet de Bœuf rôti*

**1½–2 lb. fillet of beef**
**Meat glaze**
**½ pt. demi-glace sauce**

MARINADE

**2 tablesp. olive oil**
**1 tablesp. lemon juice** *or* **vinegar**
**1 teasp. chopped onion**
**1 teasp. chopped parsley**
**A good pinch of powdered herbs**
**A pinch of ground cloves**
**Salt and pepper**

Wipe, trim and tie the meat into a good shape, place on a dish and pour over the marinade. Allow to soak in the marinade for 2–3 hr., turning and basting frequently. Drain off ½ the liquid and fold the remainder with the meat in a thick sheet of well-greased greaseproof paper or aluminium foil, fastening all ends securely. Roast for 1 hr. and remove the paper to allow the meat to brown. Place on a hot dish and brush with meat glaze. If liked a little sauce may be poured round the dish, the rest being served separately. Serve with horseradish sauce.

**6 helpings**

### ROAST FOWL—GERMAN STYLE

*Poulet rôti aux Marrons*

**1 fowl**
**1 lb. chestnuts**
**Veal forcemeat**
**Basting fat**
**1 oz. butter**
**1 oz. flour**
**1 pt. stock**
**Salt and pepper**

GARNISH

**Slices of lemon**
**1 lb. fried sausages**

Make a slit in the chestnut skins, put them into boiling water and cook for 15 min. Remove both skins, and bake until tender. Stuff the body of the bird with chestnuts, retaining about 1 dozen. Stuff the crop with veal forcemeat. Truss the bird lightly, and roast in a fairly hot oven (**375°–400° F., Gas 5–6**) until tender—1½–2 hr., basting frequently. Melt butter, add flour and brown slightly; add stock, stir until boiling, season to taste; add remaining chestnuts and simmer 15 min. Remove trussing strings.

Serve bird with sausages and garnished with lemon. Serve the sauce separately.

**5–6 helpings** **Cooking time—about 2 hr.**

### ROAST FOWL—STUFFED

*Poulet farci, rôti*

**1 roasting fowl**
**Veal forcemeat**
**Salt and pepper**
**Fat for basting**

GARNISH

**Bacon rolls**
**Watercress**

Make the forcemeat rather moist, and press lightly into the bird, rounding it under the skin. Any extra may be formed into small balls, coated with egg and breadcrumbs and baked or fried. A good flavour is imparted if the bird is stuffed some hours before cooking. Truss the bird, roast it in a fairly hot oven (**375°–400° F., Gas 5–6**) until tender (test the thigh of the bird with a thin skewer for tenderness), about 1½–2 hr. Remove trussing string.

Garnish bird and serve with gravy and bread sauce.

**5–6 helpings**

### ROAST GREEN GOOSE OR GOSLING

*Oison rôti*

Geese are called green until about 4 months old—they are not stuffed usually.

## *Roast Goose*

**1 green goose**
**2 oz. butter**
**Salt and pepper**

GARNISH

**Watercress**

Prepare the goose, mix together the butter, salt and pepper, and place this in the body. Truss the bird, and cook in a moderate oven **(350°–375° F., Gas 4–5)** for about 1 hr., basting with fat if necessary. Dish the bird. Garnish with the watercress.

Brown gravy and gooseberry jelly, or gooseberry sauce may be served, if desired.

**5–6 helpings**

### ROAST GOOSE

*Oie rôtie*

**1 goose**
**Sage and onion stuffing**
**Fat for basting**
**Flour**

Prepare the goose, make the stuffing and insert this in the body of the bird. Truss the goose season , and prick the skin of the breast. Roast bird in a fairly hot oven **(375°–400° F., Gas 5–6)** 2½ hr.—until tender. When almost cooked, dredge breast with flour, baste with some of the hot fat and finish cooking. Remove trussing string; dish the bird.

Serve with apple sauce and beef gravy handed separately.

Gravy made from goose giblets is very rich, but may be served instead of beef gravy, if desired.

**8–10 helpings**

### ROAST GROUSE

*Coq de Bruyère rôti*

**A brace of grouse**
**8 oz. rump steak *or* 2 oz. butter**
**Salt and pepper**
**2 rashers of bacon**
**Flour**
**2 croûtes fried bread or toast**

Prepare the birds ( prick), insert a piece of seasoned steak or butter into the body of each; truss for roasting. (If steak is used it can afterwards be used for a cold meat dish, it is inserted to flavour the birds and is not meant to be served with them.) Cover the breast of the birds with bacon, roast in a fairly hot oven **(375°–400° F., Gas 5–6)** until tender—about 30 min. Baste if necessary. When almost cooked, remove bacon, baste, dredge with flour, baste again and return to oven. Toast or fry the bread and place pieces in the baking-tin beneath the birds after 15 min. cooking, so that they will absorb any liquid which comes from the birds.

Dish birds on the croûtes of bread, and serve with gravy, bread sauce and fried breadcrumbs.

**5–6 helpings**
**Cooking time—about 30 min.**

### ROAST GUINEA FOWL

*Pintade rôtie*

**1 guinea fowl**
**2 oz. butter**
**Salt and pepper**
**2 slices fat bacon**

GARNISH

**Watercress**
**French dressing**

Prepare the bird neatly, mix the butter and seasoning, place in body of bird. Truss the bird, lay slices of bacon over the breast, and roast in a moderately hot oven **(350°–375° F., Gas 4–5)** 1–1½ hr., basting frequently. When the bird is almost cooked, "froth" the breast, i.e. dredge with flour, baste and finish cooking. Wash and dry watercress, toss lightly in French salad dressing . Remove trussing strings from bird and garnish.

Serve with browned crumbs, bread sauce, and Espagnole sauce.

**4–5 helpings**

### ROAST HARE

*Lièvre rôti*

**1 hare**
**Veal forcemeat**
**Fat bacon**
**Milk**
**2 oz. butter**
**1 teasp. chopped shallot**
**½ teasp. chopped parsley**
**Pinch of thyme**
**1½ oz. flour**
**¾ pt. stock**
**1 glass port (optional)**
**Salt and pepper**
**Redcurrant jelly**

Skin, draw and truss the hare. Stuff , reserving the liver. After inserting the forcemeat, sew up the hare, cover with bacon, bake in a fairly hot oven **(375°–400° F., Gas 5–6)** 1½–2 hr. until tender, basting frequently with milk, and a little butter, if liked. Meanwhile, remove gall-bladder from liver, wash the liver, put into cold water, bring to the boil and boil for 5 min., chop very finely. Melt the butter, add the liver, shallot, parsley and thyme. Fry for 10 min. Lift the liver mixture from the butter, put in the flour, brown the roux. Stir in the stock (*or* milk used for basting), bring to boiling point; add the liver mixture, season, simmer for 10 min.; add wine if used. Remove bacon from hare, dredge with flour, baste and allow to brown. Remove trussing strings and cotton.

Serve on a hot dish. Serve the liver sauce and redcurrant jelly separately.

**5–6 helpings**

### ROAST HAUNCH OF VENISON

*Quartier de Chevreuil rôti*

| | |
|---|---|
| **A haunch of venison** | **Flour** |
| **Clarified butter *or* dripping** | **Brown sauce *or* gravy** |
| | **Redcurrant jelly** |

Saw off knuckle-bone, brush joint well with clarified butter *or* dripping and wrap in well-greased paper. Make a stiff paste of flour and water, put it over the joint, cover with another well-greased paper and tie securely with string. Roast the joint in a moderate oven (**350° F., Gas 4**) for 3–4 hr. and baste frequently. After 2½ hr., remove paste and papers, dredge lightly with flour, baste well with hot butter until the joint acquires a good brown colour.

Serve as hot as possible. Serve gravy *or* sauce and redcurrant jelly separately.

**12 (or more) helpings**
**Cooking time—allow 25 min. per lb.**

### ROAST NECK OF VENISON

*Carré de Venaison rôtie*

Let the neck remain attached to the shoulder until required for use, so as to preserve the appearance of both joints.

Remove the chine bone and short bones. Fold the flap under and fasten in a neat shape. Cook according to instructions given in Roast Haunch of Venison.

### ROAST OX LIVER

*Foie de Bœuf rôtie*

| | |
|---|---|
| **1–1½ lb. ox liver** | **Seasoned flour** |
| **¼ lb. fat bacon** | **Parsley** |
| **Stock *or* water** | |

Wash the liver in tepid salt water, remove any skin and tubes and cut the liver in slices. Place in a deep baking-tin or dish. Lay the rashers of bacon on top and add enough stock or water to ½ cover the liver. Bake gently for 1½–2 hr., basting well and dredging frequently with seasoned flour. Dish neatly and strain the gravy round. Garnish with parsley.

NOTE: The bacon may be cut into dice and served as a garnish, in which case it must be kept covered with 2–3 thicknesses of greaseproof paper while cooking, or it will become too crisp.

### ROAST PARTRIDGE

*Perdreau rôti*

| | |
|---|---|
| **1 partridge** | **Butter *or* dripping** |
| **1 rasher of bacon** | **Toast *or* fried bread** |

Pluck, draw and truss bird as for roasting a chicken. Cover breast with bacon, roast in a fairly hot oven (**375°–400° F., Gas 5–6**) about 30 min., basting frequently with butter *or* dripping. (A piece of seasoned butter may be put in the body of the bird if liked.) 10 min. before serving, remove bacon, baste, dredge with flour, baste and return to oven to complete cooking. Remove trussing string.

Dish bird on croûte of bread. Serve with brown gravy, bread sauce.

**4 helpings**

### ROAST PIGEON

*Pigeon rôti*

| | |
|---|---|
| **3 pigeons** | **Lemon juice** |
| **3 oz. butter** | **1 rasher fat bacon** |
| **Salt and pepper** | **3 croûtes of fried bread** |

GARNISH

| | |
|---|---|
| **Watercress** | **French dressing** |

Wipe the birds with a damp cloth, insert in each 1 oz. butter mixed with lemon juice and seasoning. Truss each and cover with a piece of bacon. Roast pigeons in a fairly hot oven (**375°–400° F., Gas 5–6**) until tender, 20–30 min., basting if necessary. Remove bacon 10 min. before cooking is completed to allow birds to brown. Remove trussing strings, replace bacon.

## *Roast Pheasant*

Serve each bird on a croûte of fried bread, garnish with washed watercress tossed in French dressing and serve with Espagnole, tomato *or* piquant sauce

**6 helpings**

### ROAST PHEASANT

*Faison rôti*

| | |
|---|---|
| **1 pheasant** | **1 slice bacon *or* strips of larding bacon** |
| **¼ lb. beef steak** | **Butter *or* dripping** |

GARNISH

| | |
|---|---|
| **Watercress** | **French dressing** |

Pluck and draw the bird and trim but leave the head on. Insert the steak in the body of the bird (this improves the flavour and keeps the bird moist, but is not intended to be eaten with it, the steak can be used for a cold meat dish later). Truss the pheasant as for a roasting chicken. Cover the breast with strips of bacon, *or* lard it with the prepared larding bacon and dry Roast bird in a moderate oven **(350° F., Gas 4)** until tender, 40–50 min., basting when necessary. When bird is almost cooked, "froth" the breast Remove trussing string.

Garnish with watercress tossed in French dressing and serve with brown gravy, bread sauce and fried breadcrumbs.

If preferred, the head may be removed and the bird ornamented with the best tail feathers before serving. The feathers should be washed, baked until dry in a cool oven, and stuck fanwise into the vent-end of the cooked bird.

**4–5 helpings**
**Cooking time—40–50 min.**

### ROAST SUCKING PIG

*Cochon de lait rôti*

| | |
|---|---|
| **A sucking pig not more than 3 weeks old** | **Butter *or* salad oil** |
| **Sage and onion stuffing** | **Thick cream (optional)** |

Stuff the pig with the forcemeat, then sew up the opening with fine string. Brush the entire surface of the pig with salad oil or warmed butter and wrap in several folds of well-greased greaseproof paper. Draw the legs well back and tie in a good shape. Roast in a moderate oven **(350° F., Gas 4)**, according to size, allowing 25 min. per lb. and 25 min. over. Baste well and about ½ hr. before serving, remove the paper and brush with salad oil or thick cream to improve the colour and crisp the surface. Before serving, cut off the head and split the pig down centre back. Lay the 2 halves on a dish—divide the head and place ½ at each end of the dish.

Usual accompaniments are brown sauce, apple sauce, and sometimes hot currants. The currants should be washed and scalded the day before to make them plump, and then dried.

**9–10 helpings**

### ROAST TEAL

*Sarcelle rôtie*

| | |
|---|---|
| **Teal** | **Butter for basting** |
| **Bigarade sauce** | |

GARNISH

| | |
|---|---|
| **Watercress** | **Sections of lemon** |

Pluck, draw and truss birds for roasting (neatly). Brush them with melted butter, roast in a fairly hot oven **(375°–400° F., Gas 5–6)** 25–30 min., basting frequently.

Serve on a hot dish; garnish. Serve the Bigarade sauce separately.

**1 helping is a half or a whole bird, according to size**

### ROAST TURKEY

| | |
|---|---|
| **1 turkey** | **2–3 rashers streaky bacon** |
| **1–2 lb. sausage meat** | |
| **1 lb. veal forcemeat** | **Fat for basting** |

Stuff crop of bird with veal forcemeat and put seasoned sausage meat inside body of bird. Truss the bird for roasting. Lay bacon rashers over the breast, roast in a pre-heated hot oven **(425° F., Gas 7)** for 15–20 min. then reduce heat to moderate **(350° F., Gas 4)**, basting frequently. The cooking time will vary according to the size and quality of the bird—as a general guide, allow 15 min. per lb. for a turkey under 14 lb. weight, and 12 min. per lb. if over 14 lb. About 20 min. before serving remove the bacon to allow the breast to brown. Remove trussing string; serve on a hot dish.

Serve with gravy, sausages and bread sauce if liked, or cranberry sauce.

## ROAST TURKEY—WITH CHESTNUTS

*Dinde farcie aux Marrons*

**1 turkey**
**2 lb. chestnuts**
**½ pt. stock**
**2 oz. butter**
**1 egg**
**Salt and pepper**
**Cream *or* milk**
**1–1½ lb. sausage meat *or* 1 lb. veal forcemeat**
**2–3 slices bacon**
**Fat for basting**

Slit the skins of the chestnuts, cook in boiling water for 15 min., then remove skins. Now stew chestnuts in stock for 1 hr.—drain and chop or sieve them. Add melted butter, egg, seasoning and sufficient cream *or* milk to moisten the stuffing. Fill the crop of the bird with the chestnut stuffing, and the body of the bird with seasoned sausage meat. Truss the bird for roasting. Cover the bird with bacon, roast in a moderate oven (**350° F., Gas 4**) until tender (allow 15 min. per lb. for a turkey weighing under 14 lb., and 12 min. per lb. for a turkey over 14 lb.). Baste well. Remove bacon towards end of cooking to allow the breast to brown. Remove trussing string, dish. Serve gravy separately.

NOTE: If the turkey is large the breast meat may dry up in a small oven before the legs and thighs are cooked. Either remove legs before roasting and cook separately, or take turkey from oven when breast is ready and cook the legs according to any suitable recipe, for use at another meal.

## ROAST WIGEON or WIDGEON

*Canard siffleur rôti*

**1 wigeon**
**Butter for basting**

SAUCE

**1 pt. Espagnole sauce**
**1 glass port *or* claret (optional)**
**Juice of 1 lemon**
**Juice of 1 orange**
**Salt and pepper**
**Castor sugar**

GARNISH

**Watercress**
**Sections of lemon**

Truss bird for roasting. Baste well with hot butter, roast in a fairly hot oven (**375°–400° F., Gas 5–6**) about 20–30 min. according to size and age of bird. Baste well. "Froth" the bird

before serving

Meanwhile, heat sauce, add the wine (if used), fruit juices, a pinch of sugar and seasoning to taste. Re-heat thoroughly.

Garnish and serve. Serve sauce separately.

**2–3 helpings**

## ROAST WILD DUCK

*Canard Sauvage rôti*

**1 wild duck**
**Butter for basting**

Pluck and draw the bird, cut off the head. Cut off the toes, scald and scrape the feet, truss the bird with the feet twisted underneath the body. If the fishy taste is disliked, cover a deep roasting-tin to a depth of ½ in. with boiling water, add 1 tablesp. salt, put in the bird and bake it for 10 min., basting frequently with the salt water. Drain, sprinkle lightly with flour, baste well with hot butter and roast in a moderate oven (**350° F., Gas 4**) for 20–30 min., basting frequently. The birds should always be served rather underdone, or the flavour is lost. The breast meat has much the best flavour.

Serve with Bigarade or Port Wine sauce and orange salad.

ORANGE SALAD: Allow the oranges to stand in boiling water for a few minutes, peel them and remove all pith. Cut fruit into thin slices, removing pips. Sprinkle slices with a little sugar and French dressing, to which a little brandy may be added if liked.

**3 helpings**

## ROASTING

*See Cooking Methods*

### ROCK BUNS

*See Buns or Cookies*

### ROES ON TOAST

| | |
|---|---|
| **¾ lb. herring roes** | **1 bacon rasher** |
| **Seasoned flour** | **4 rounds of toast** |

Wash and dry the roes, dip in seasoned flour and fry in a little hot fat. Chop the bacon and add it to the roes when they are almost cooked.

Serve piled on rounds of buttered toast.

**4 helpings**

### ROLLED BEEF

*Roulade de Bœuf*

| | |
|---|---|
| **2 lb. fillet of beef** | **½ teasp. powdered allspice** |
| **1 gill port (optional)** | **Redcurrant jelly** |
| **1 gill vinegar** | **Brown *or* piquant sauce *or* a good gravy** |
| **4–6 oz. savoury forcemeat** | |

Wipe and trim the meat. Pour the wine (if used) and vinegar over the meat and let it stand for 2 days, baste frequently and turn once or twice. Then drain well, flatten slightly and cover with the forcemeat. Roll up tightly and tie securely. Place in a baking-dish, add the allspice to the liquid in which the meat was soaked and pour over the meat. Cook in a moderate oven **(350° F., Gas 4)** for about ¾ hr., basting frequently. Remove the strings and serve with a good gravy or brown or piquant sauce and redcurrant jelly.

**6 helpings**

### ROLLMOP HERRINGS

These make a most economical hors d'œuvre by themselves, and add flavour to a mixed hors d'œuvres.

| | |
|---|---|
| **6 large herrings** | **2 bay leaves** |
| **2 oz. kitchen salt** | **4–6 small gherkins** |
| **1 pt. water** | **Chillies** |
| **1 pt. malt vinegar** | **1 tablesp. pickling spice** |
| **2 large onions** | |

Clean, bone and fillet the herrings. Mix the salt and water together and put the herrings to soak in this for 2 hr. Lift out of the brine, drain and put into a shallow dish, covering with the vinegar and leaving for several hours. Shred the onions finely. Drain the herring fillets, reserving the vinegar, put 1 tablesp. of onion on to each fillet and roll firmly. Secure with small wooden cocktail sticks if possible. Put into jars with bay leaves, gherkins and chillies (use 1 per jar). Pour the vinegar from the dish into a saucepan and boil for a few minutes with the pickling spice. Cool and strain over the herrings. Cover the jars and store in a cool place. They will keep for 2–3 weeks prepared in this way. Note that the herrings are NOT cooked for this dish.

**6–12 helpings—or fillets can be divided into halves for part of a mixed hors d'œuvres**

### ROLLS

*See Bread and Bread-Making.*

### ROSE HIP SYRUP

| | |
|---|---|
| **6 pt. water** | **2 lb. preserving sugar** |
| **3 lb. ripe, wild, rose hips** | |

Boil 4 pt. of the water. Mince the hips coarsely and put immediately into the boiling water. Heat until the water boils again, skim off the scum as it rises and boil for a few minutes. Then allow to cool for about 15 min. Pass the pulp through fine linen or muslin twice to ensure that all the hairs are removed. Put the liquid obtained to one side. Boil the pulp again with the remaining 2 pt. water, leave to cool for 15 min., and strain twice as before. Return both extracted liquids to the pan and boil until the juice is reduced to about 3 pt. Sweeten, stirring well. Pour into warmed bottles, seal; store in a dark cupboard until required.

### ROLY POLY

*Roulade*

| | |
|---|---|
| **12 oz. plain flour** | **Pinch of salt** |
| **2 rounded teasp. baking-powder** | **Water to mix** |
| **6 oz. finely-chopped suet** | **Jam** |

Sift the flour and baking-powder, add the suet and salt. Mix with sufficient water to make a soft, but firm, dough. Roll it into a rectangle about ¼ in. thick. Spread with jam almost to the edge. Damp the edges and roll up lightly. Seal the edges. Wrap the pudding in a scalded well-floured cloth; tie up the ends. Put into fast boiling water. Simmer for 2–2½ hr.

**6 helpings**

## ROQUEFORT STUFFING FOR SAVOURIES

*See Savouries (Appetizers).*

## ROUGH PUFF PASTRY

**½ lb. plain flour**
**Pinch of salt**
**6 oz. butter *or* butter and lard**
**½ teasp. lemon juice**
**Cold water to mix**

Sift the flour and salt. Add the butter cut up into pieces the size of a walnut and mix lightly with the flour. Make a well in the centre, put in the lemon juice and gradually add sufficient water to mix to an elastic dough. Roll into a long strip, keeping the corners square, fold into three. With the rolling-pin seal the edges and give the pastry a half-turn, so that the folded edges are on the right and left. Repeat until the pastry has been rolled and folded 4 times, if possible leaving for 15 min. in a cool place between the second and third rollings.

Use as required. Bake in a very hot oven **(450° F., Gas 8).**

## ROYAL ICING

*Glace Royal*

**1 lb. icing sugar (approx.)**
**2 egg whites**
**1 teasp. lemon juice**

If the sugar is lumpy, roll with a rolling-pin before sieving. Put the egg whites into a bowl, beat slightly with a wooden spoon. Add 2 tablesp. sieved sugar and beat again. Gradually add the remainder of the sugar, beating well until a thick, smooth consistency and a good white colour are obtained. Add the lemon juice and beat again.

NOTE: If a softer icing is required 1 teasp. glycerine may be stirred in after the sugar; this prevents the icing becoming brittle and facilitates cutting.

If the icing is not to be used immediately, cover the bowl with a damp cloth to keep the icing soft.

Some cooks add 1 or 2 drops of confectioner's blue to make the icing white, but if the eggs are fresh and the icing is sufficiently well beaten, no blue colouring is necessary.

### To Ice a Cake with Royal Icing

NOTE: These quantities are sufficient to coat a cake of 8 in. diameter.

Place the cake already covered with almond paste on a cake-board or inverted plate. Place the cake-board on a turntable if available.

#### AMOUNTS REQUIRED

*First coating:* Royal icing, using 1¼ lb. icing sugar, etc., mixed to a stiff consistency.

*Second coating:* ¾–1 lb. icing sugar, etc., consistency to coat the back of a spoon.

*Decorative piping:* ½ lb. icing sugar, etc., mixed to a stiff consistency, i.e. that will stand up in points when the back of the spoon is drawn away from the side of the bowl.

#### TO APPLY FIRST COATING

With a tablespoon take enough icing to cover the top, and place it in the centre of the cake. Spread evenly over top, smoothing the surface with a hot, wet palette knife (shake or dry the knife after dipping it in hot water as too much water softens the icing). Take up small portions of the icing with the end of the palette knife blade, spread it smoothly round the side until the cake is completely covered and the surface smooth.

Allow to set for a few days before applying the second coat. Whilst the icing is drying and as soon as it is hard enough, place a thin sheet of paper lightly over the top to protect it from dust.

#### TO APPLY SECOND COATING

Mix icing to a thin coating consistency and pour over the cake. Prick any bubbles with a fine skewer or pin; allow to firm before decorating.

#### TO DECORATE THE CAKE WITH PIPED ICING

Cut pieces of greaseproof paper the same sizes as the top and sides of the cake. Sketch on to these the patterns to be used for the decoration. Pin papers firmly into position on cake and prick pattern through. Mix icing to a stiff consistency and pipe design on to cake, starting at centre and working outwards, and finishing with the sides and the base.

*Using a forcing bag:* Decorative icing can be piped from a forcing bag and pipe. Fold an oblong of greaseproof paper in half diagonally and cut along the fold. Form one half into a smooth cone-shaped bag . Cut off the pointed end of the cone and slip a forcing pipe into the bag so that it protrudes halfway through the cut point. Make a bag for each pipe to be used. Fill the bags ⅔ full with icing and fold over the top edges. Holding the pipe between the first and second fingers force the icing through the pipe by exerting pressure with the thumbs on the top of the bag.

*Icing syringes* are made of metal or plastic and can be bought in sets complete with decorative pipes and a turntable. If coloured icings are being used the syringe must be washed before filling with another colour.

All pipes must be kept clean. Always keep the bowl containing the icing covered with a damp cloth whilst decorating, to prevent the icing drying out.

The beginner should practise on an upturned cake tin or plate before starting on the cake, and the icing may be removed if scraped off immediately and returned to the covered bowl.

For Christmas cakes other decorations may be made with coloured marzipan, e.g. holly, mistletoe, etc., and the smooth icing surface roughened into points with a palette knife to form "snow drifts". For this one coat only is needed.

## RUM BUTTER

**4 oz. butter**
**8 oz. soft brown sugar**
**1 sherryglass rum**

Beat the butter to a cream and beat in the sugar. When light and creamy, add the rum gradually. Transfer to a serving dish and chill thoroughly before using.

## RUM CREAM

*Crème au Rhum*

**1 bay leaf**
**½ pt. milk**
**3 egg yolks *or* 1 whole egg and 1 yolk**
**2–3 oz. castor sugar**
**½ oz. gelatine**
**4 tablesp. water**
**1 wineglass of rum**
**½ pt. double cream**

Infuse the bay leaf in the milk for 20 min. Beat eggs and sugar until liquid and make a thick pouring custard with the flavoured milk, straining back into the pan to cook and thicken. Allow to cool. Soak gelatine in the water for 5 min., then heat to dissolve. Stir the dissolved gelatine into the cooled custard. Stir in the rum. Whip the cream and fold lightly into the custard mixture just before setting. Pour into a prepared mould, or into glass dishes.

**6 helpings**
**Setting time—1–2 hr.**

## RUM TODDY

**1 lump sugar**
**Jigger of rum (1½ oz.)**
**Boiling water**
**Slice of lemon**
**2 cloves**

Put the sugar and rum in a tumbler with boiling water. Add a slice of lemon and the cloves.

## RUSSIAN SALAD

**1 small cauliflower**
**¼ pt. peas**
**¼ pt. vegetables (carrot, turnip, French beans)**
**3 potatoes**
**1 small cooked beetroot**
**2 tomatoes**
**Aspic jelly**
**2 oz. diced ham *or* tongue**
**2 oz. cooked fish (shrimps, prawns, lobster)**
**2 oz. smoked salmon (optional)**
**3 gherkins**
**1 dessertsp. capers**
**A few lettuce leaves**
**Mayonnaise sauce dressing *or* salad**
**1 hard-boiled egg (white only)**
**6 stoned olives**
**6 anchovy fillets**

*Method 1.* Prepare and cook all the vegetables (or use canned or bottled vegetables). Drain them well. Divide the cauliflower into small sprigs, dice all the other vegetables except the peas. Skin and slice the tomatoes. Line a border mould with aspic jelly and decorate it with a little of the diced vegetables. Set layers of vegetables, meat, fish and pickles alternately with jelly in the mould; do not use all the vegetables. When set, turn out. Toss shredded lettuce and remaining vegetables in mayonnaise or salad dressing and pile in the centre of the mould. Decorate with egg white, olives and anchovy fillets.

*Method 2* (without aspic jelly). Put layers of vegetables, meat and fish in a salad bowl, season with salt and pepper and a pinch of castor sugar and cover each layer with mayonnaise sauce. Arrange in pyramid form. Cover lightly with mayonnaise. Decorate with beetroot, diced egg white, olives, capers, anchovies and shredded salmon. Or arrange as on plate 63, serve mayonnaise separately.

NOTE: Meat may be omitted from a Russian Salad.

**6 helpings**

## RUSSIAN STEAKS

*Biftecks à la Russe*

**3/4 lb. tender steak**
**3/4 lb. fillet of veal**
**1 finely-chopped shallot**
**2 teasp. finely-chopped parsley**
**Salt and pepper**
**2 egg yolks**
**Flour for dredging**
**Egg and breadcrumbs**
**Oil *or* dripping**
**Tomato sauce *or* 1 tablesp. yoghourt *or* sour cream (optional)**

Wipe and trim the meats, removing all fat and skin. Mince the meats finely and mix well with the shallot, parsley, seasoning and egg yolks. Spread on a wet plate and leave in a cold place to become firm. Divide into 12 equal portions and form into flat cakes, using a little flour. Coat with egg and crumbs and fry in hot deep fat or oil until cooked and a good brown colour. Drain well and place in a pyramid on a hot dish. Pour a little tomato sauce over them and serve the rest separately. A tablesp. of yoghourt or sour cream may be added to the sauce. Garnish with peas.

**6 helpings**

## SAFFRON CAKE

**Small 1/2 oz. yeast**
**1/2 pt. warm water**
**1 lb. plain flour**
**1/2 teasp. salt**
**6–8 oz. margarine**
**4 oz. sugar**
**2 eggs**
**A good pinch of saffron (infuse the saffron with 1/8 pt. of the warm water)**
**4–6 oz. currants and raisins**

Cream the yeast and add the warm water to it. Stir into it enough sifted flour to make a nice soft dough. Knead it well and leave to rise in a warm place. When well risen, take the remaining flour and salt, and rub the fat into it; add the sugar, eggs and fermented dough, together with the strained saffron liquor. Knead this well and work in the currants, and stoned raisins. Put the dough into two greased ½ lb. cake-tins and leave to rise well. Bake in a fairly hot to moderate oven **(400°–350° F., Gas 6–4)** for 1–1½ hr.

**2 cakes**

## SAGE AND ONION SAUCE

*Sauce au Sauge*

**1/2 pt. brown sauce**
**2 onions**
**1 oz. butter *or* pork *or* goose dripping**
**1/2 teasp. chopped fresh sage**
**1 tablesp. fresh crumbs**

The onions may either be boiled till tender and then chopped, or chopped fine and cooked very gently till quite tender, but not brown, in the fat. Add onion, sage and crumbs to the brown sauce and cook it gently for a further 10 min.

Serve with pork, goose or duck.

## SAGE AND ONION STUFFING

**1/4 lb. onions**
**4 young sage leaves *or***
**2 oz. breadcrumbs**
**1 oz. butter**

| | |
|---|---|
| **½ teasp. powdered sage** | **Salt and pepper** |
| | **½ egg (optional)** |

Slice the onions thickly, parboil them 10 min. in very little water. Scald the sage leaves. Chop the onions and sage. Mash and work all the ingredients together and season to taste.

Use for pork, goose or duck.

## SAGO PUDDING, HOT

*See Milk Puddings*

## ST. CLOUD PUDDING

*Pouding Froid à la St. Cloud*

| | |
|---|---|
| **½ oz. butter** | **1 pt. strong, clear coffee *or* coffee essence in water** |
| **2 oz. almonds** | **2 tablesp. double cream** |
| **Stale sponge cake** | **3 tablesp. apricot jam** |
| **2–3 eggs according to size** | |
| **2 oz. castor sugar** | |

DECORATION

| | |
|---|---|
| **Glacé cherries** | **Angelica** |

Thickly butter a 1½ pt. soufflé tin. Blanch, shred and bake the almonds golden brown gently ). Sprinkle liberally over the buttered surface of the tin. Three quarters fill the tin with crumbled cake and the remainder of the almonds. Beat the eggs and sugar to a liquid, warm the coffee and pour over the egg liquid. Stir, add the cream and strain into the prepared tin. Cover with a buttered paper and steam very gently for about 1½–2 hr. Cool slightly, then turn out and leave to go cold. Heat the apricot jam with a little water (2 tablesp.) and when cool strain over the pudding.

Decorate with rings of cherry and angelica.

**6–7 helpings**

## SALAD DRESSING (with foundation of Béchamel Sauce)

This is an excellent salad dressing, very smooth in texture, of excellent flavour and and good keeping qualities. It is the best dressing to use for a potato salad.

| | |
|---|---|
| **1 egg *or* 2 yolks** | **1 tablesp. tarragon vinegar** |
| **½ pt. Béchamel sauce (made with all milk)** | **Salt and pepper** |
| **2 tablesp. wine *or* malt vinegar** | **A little castor sugar** |

Beat the egg or egg yolks. Cool the Béchamel sauce until the hand can be placed in comfort on the bottom of the pan. Stir in the egg and cook without boiling. Wring through muslin and when cooled a little, stir in the vinegars gradually and the seasoning and sugar. Leave until quite cold, then taste and reseason if necessary.

## SALAD DRESSING (with foundation of custard)

| | |
|---|---|
| **½ pt. milk** | **3 tablesp. vinegar** |
| **½ oz. custard powder (an unflavoured one if possible)** | **A little castor sugar** |
| **½ oz. margarine** | **Salt and pepper** |
| | **1 level teasp. mixed mustard** |

Make the custard, putting the margarine in the pan with the milk at the beginning. Cool the custard, stirring it from time to time to prevent the formation of a skin. When cool stir in the vinegar, sugar, mustard and seasoning. When cold, correct the seasoning.

NOTE: This salad dressing will keep for several days in a cool place.

## SALADS

Originally, a salad consisted of uncooked, edible leaves of various plants but today the name is also applied to mixtures of cooked vegetables, herbs, fruits, meat and fish. Although lettuce usually forms the foundation of our salads, most other edible vegetables and plants can be used.

On the Continent mixtures of cold, cooked vegetables are made into tempting salads. Cooked peas, beans, carrots, cauliflower sprigs and parsnips can be made into very pleasing salads, with the addition of watercress or fine cress and chopped parsley to add Vitamin C and green colour.

In France a salad is composed of one vegetable only; the French cook will on no account mix two or more vegetables or salad plants. Dressed with oil, wine vinegar and seasoning the delicate flavour of the individual plant is fully appreciated.

Poultry being Dressed I.

1

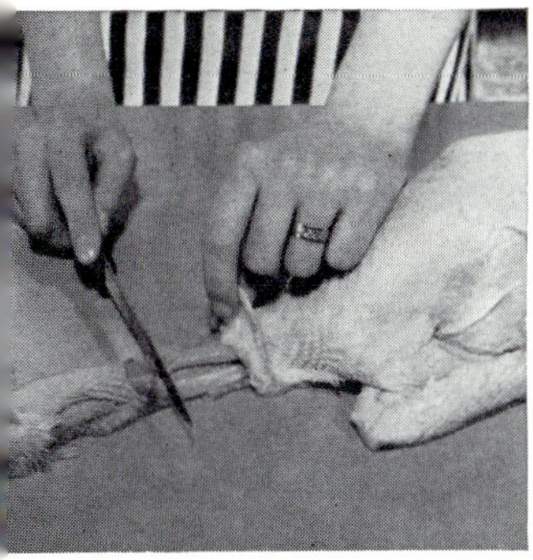

2

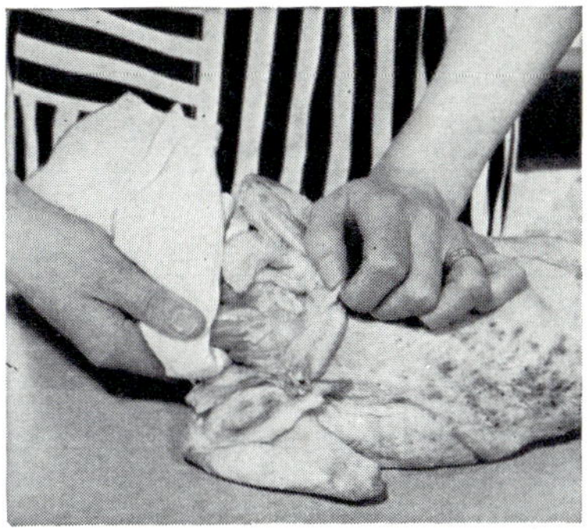

1 Halfway along the neck of the plucked chicken, cut a ring round outer skin and pull or cut off the head—the latter is perhaps the best way.

2 Holding the neck with a dry cloth, pull the skin loose. Twist the neck round until it is detached from the body. Push index finger into crop cavity to loosen crop and gizzard.

3 With a knife cut the skin on the leg, place the leg over the table edge and snap the bone.

4 Pull off the foot together with the tendons.

5 Make a slit of from 2 to 3 inches above the vent to enable the viscera to be removed.

6 Insert the first two fingers of the right hand.

7 Draw out intestines—with knuckles upwards.

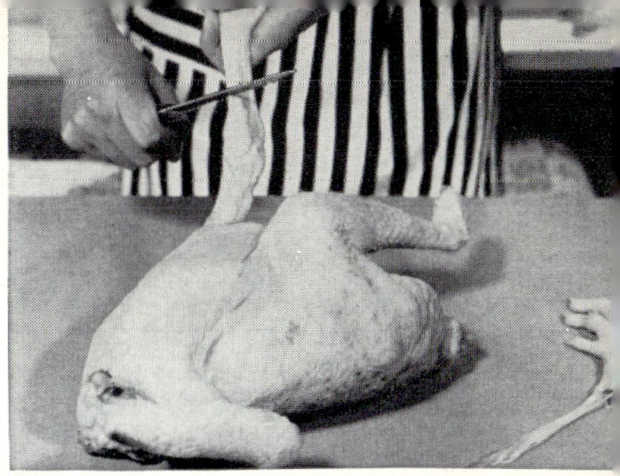

3

4

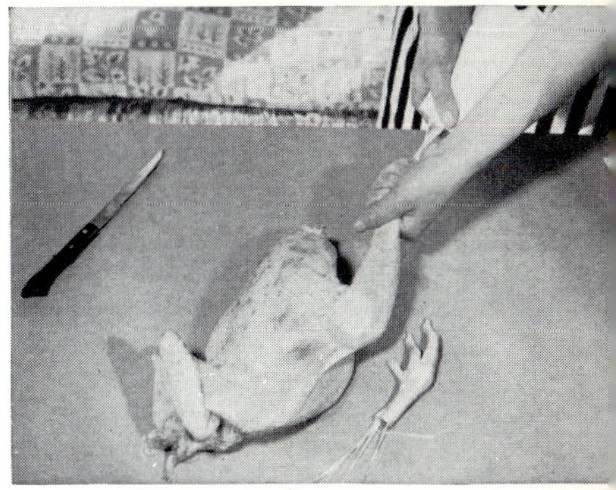

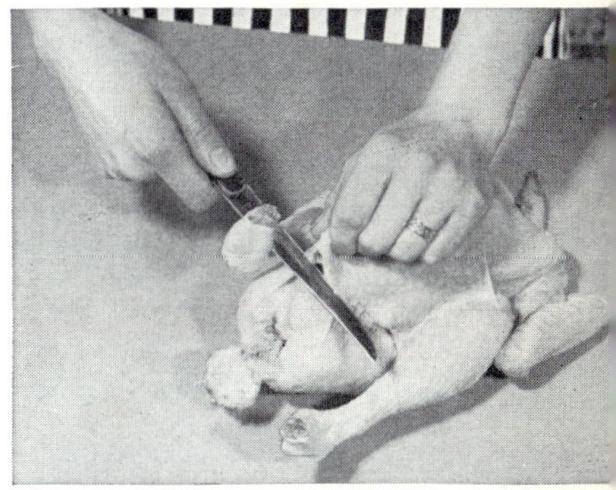

5

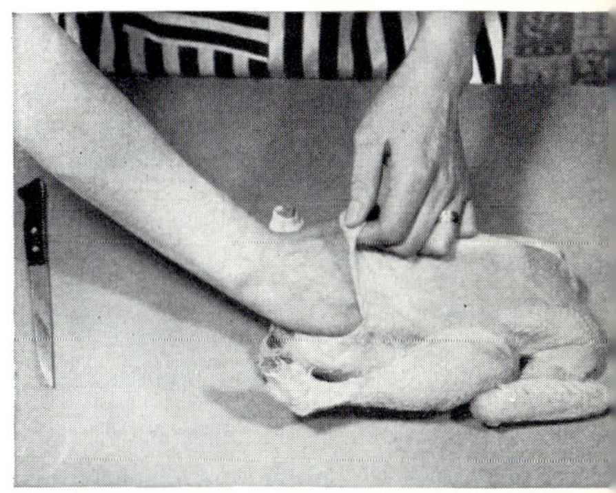

6

7

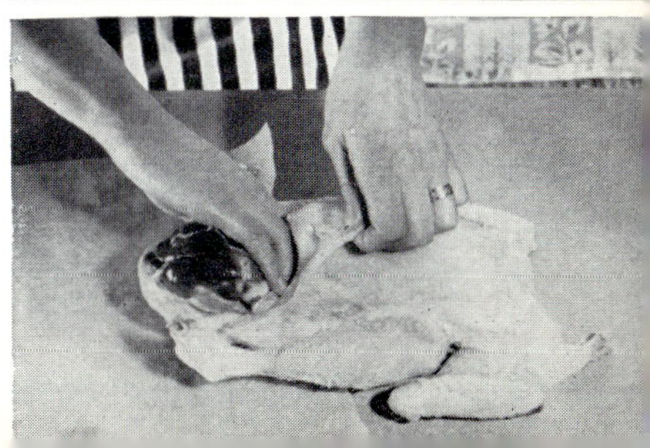

Poultry being Dressed II.

8 Trim the end of the intestines and vent away with a sharp knife.

9 Separate the liver from the gall bladder. Do not break the latter.

10 Skin the meaty outside of the crop from the gritty contents. Remove and discard the lungs.

11 Wipe the inside with a dry cloth.

12 Pass a threaded needle through the left leg just above thigh bone; pass through body, and through other leg joint. Turn breast downwards, carry string through the elbow joint of the wing on each side, twist end of wing under the neck of the bird to hold the neck flap of the skin. Draw the two ends together and tie up.

13 Cut a slit in the flesh above the original vent-cut and push parson's nose through. Loop the strings over the ends of the drum sticks, draw together and tie off round tail end of parson's nose.

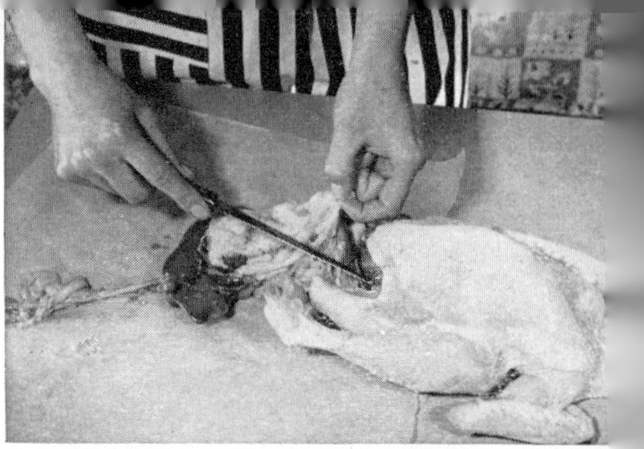
8

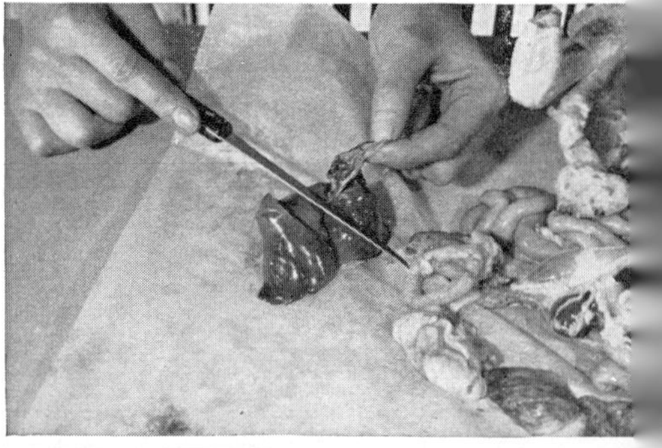
9

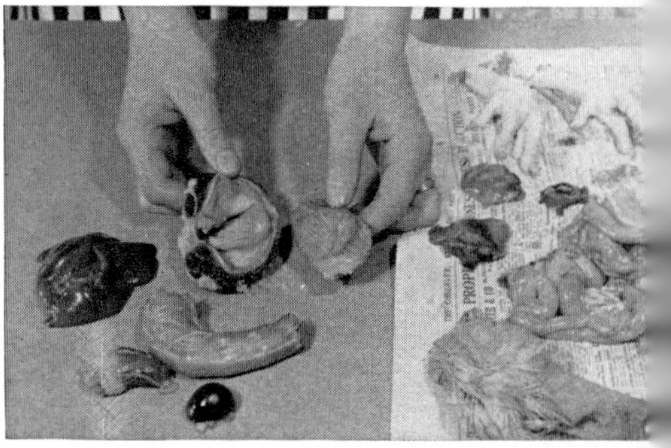
10

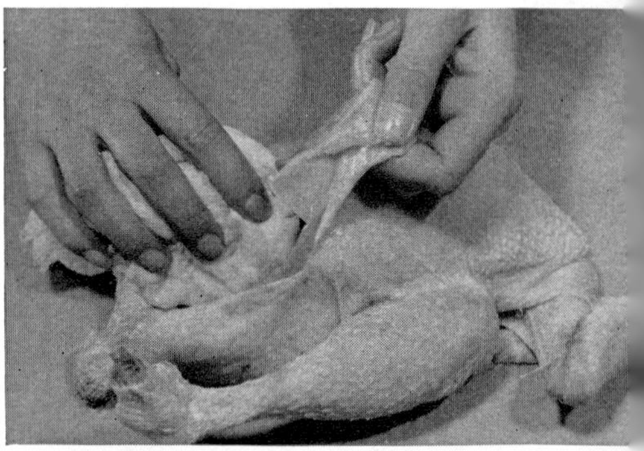
11

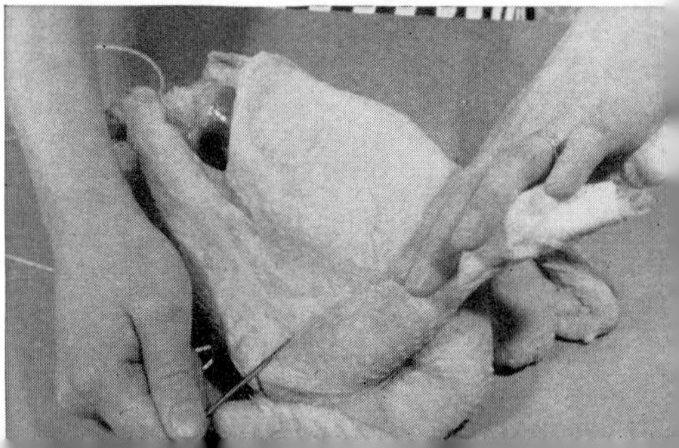
12

13

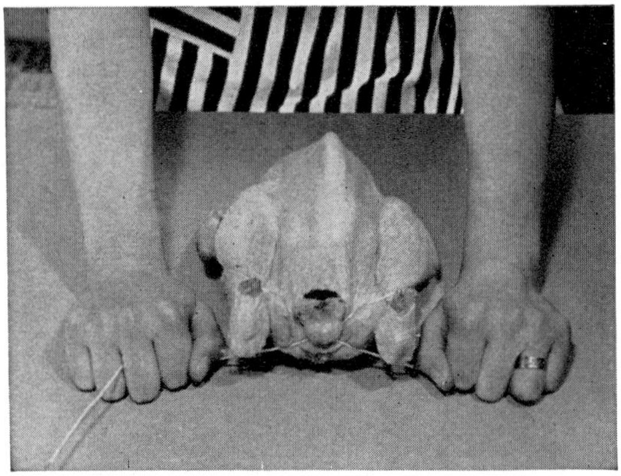

In America fruits of all kinds are mixed with vegetables so that it is sometimes a little difficult to decide whether the salad is part of a savoury or sweet course. Fruits such as grapefruit, orange, pineapple, grapes, used in moderation, provide a most refreshing addition to a vegetable salad. Dried fruits such as raisins, chopped dates or figs are also pleasing.

To ensure success in making salad, all vegetables and fruits must be in perfect condition. Leafy salad plants should be young, crisp and freshly gathered. They must be properly washed in several waters or under running water. As much water should be removed as possible, after washing, by shaking the plants in a salad shaker or colander, allowing them to drain well and then drying in a clean cloth held by the corners. If possible they should be put into a covered container in the refrigerator to crisp them before use. Lettuce leaves, which need to be mixed into a salad should be cut with a stainless knife or torn with the fingers.

Vegetables which are usually eaten cooked should be very finely divided when used for a salad, or they may be indigestible. Carrots and young turnips should be grated. Cabbage should be finely chopped. Cauliflower should be broken into tiny sprigs.

Salads are usually mixed with a dressing just before they are served. The dressing often adds considerably to their flavour and food value.

Salads of fruit used as cold sweet dishes are often called compôtes, except when several mixed fruits are used. This mixture is always called Fruit Salad.

## SALLY LUNN

**½ lb. plain flour**
**¼ teasp. salt**
**1½ oz. margarine**
**½ teasp. sugar**
**½ oz. yeast**
**1 egg**
**1 gill warm milk (approx.)**

Mix flour and salt, rub in the fat. Cream yeast with sugar, add to it the egg and milk and make a very soft dough with the flour, beat well. Put mixture in greased Sally Lunn rings on tins—2 small *or* 1 large—and allow to rise till well up the tin. Bake in a fairly hot oven (425°–400° F., Gas 7–6) for 20–30 min.

**2 small *or* 1 large Sally Lunn**

## SALMI OF WILD DUCK

*Canards sauvages en Salmis*

**Cold roast duck**
**1 small onion**
**2 or 3 sprigs thyme**
**1 bay leaf**
**1½ oz. butter**
**1 oz. flour**
**1 pt. stock**
**1 teasp. orange juice**
**1 teasp. lemon juice**
**1 glass port *or* claret (optional)**
**Salt and cayenne pepper**
**Thin strips of orange rind**

GARNISH

**Orange *or* lemon sections**

Cut the remains of 2 cold roast wild ducks into neat pieces. Place bones, trimmings, onion, thyme and bay leaf into a pan with 1 pt. stock *or* water and simmer at least 1½ hr. Meanwhile, melt butter in a saucepan, stir in flour and brown roux very slowly. Stir in the strained stock, stir until boiling, boil 5 min. Add duck, fruit juices, wine (if used), orange rind and seasoning to taste. Allow to become thoroughly hot but do not boil again.

Serve garnished with sections of orange or lemon.

TO PREPARE ORANGE OR LEMON SECTIONS: Scrub fruit, cut into 4, 6 or 8 sections, lengthways; cut off any white pith or skin from the inner edge so that the juice may be pressed out of the fruit easily.

A salmi may be made from any cold cooked game, and makes an excellent dish if the sauce is good. Other garnishes may be used, e.g. croûtes of fried bread *or* fleurons of puff paste, braised olives, button mushrooms *or* truffles.

**Cooking time—about 2 hr.**

## SALMON DARIOLES À LA MOSCOVITE

*Darioles de Saumon à la Moscovite*

**1 lb. cooked salmon (approx.)**
**½ pt. aspic jelly (approx.)**
**1 large truffle**
**Red chillies**
**6 large cooked oysters**
**1 hard-boiled egg**
**½ oz. anchovy paste**
**Pinch of cayenne**
**Salt and pepper**
**Grated nutmeg**
**1 teasp. tarragon vinegar**
**¼ gill cream**
**4 filleted anchovies**
**A few slices of cucumber**

Remove all skin and bone and flake the salmon. Line 6–8 small dariole, bouchée or timbale moulds with a thin layer of aspic jelly, decorate with a few thin slices of truffle, some flakes of salmon and a few strips of red chillies. Set the garnish with a little aspic and put aside to cool. Pound the remainder of the fish together with 6 cooked oysters, the hard-boiled egg and the anchovy paste; season with a pinch of cayenne pepper, salt and a little grated nutmeg. Rub through a fine sieve, add the tarragon vinegar, the cream and about 1 gill of aspic jelly. Mix the ingredients well together and half-fill the moulds. Put in the anchovy fillets and a few slices of truffle, add the rest of the fish mixture. If the mixture does not quite fill the moulds, fill up with aspic jelly, then put the moulds in the refrigerator or stand in a cool place until required. For serving, immerse the moulds in tepid water, turn out the contents quickly and place on a round dish. Garnish with chopped aspic and a few fancily-cut slices of cucumber.

**6 helpings**

## SALMON KEDGEREE

| | |
|---|---|
| **One ½ lb. can of salmon** | **Salt and pepper** |
| **1 oz. butter** | **Grated nutmeg** |
| **4 oz. well-boiled rice** | **Finely-chopped parsley** |

Divide the fish into rather large flakes. Melt the butter in a saucepan, put in the rice, make thoroughly hot, season to taste, and add the fish. Stir very gently over the heat for 3–4 min., then serve piled on a hot dish. Sprinkle with parsley.

NOTE: 1–2 hard-boiled eggs coarsely chopped are sometimes added to the above ingredients.

**4–5 helpings**

## SALMON MAYONNAISE

*Mayonnaise de Saumon*

| | |
|---|---|
| **Cold boiled salmon** | **Beetroot** |
| **Lettuce** | **Gherkins** |
| **Mayonnaise sauce** | **Capers** |
| **Aspic jelly (optional)** | **Boned anchovies** |
| **Cucumber** | **Hard-boiled eggs** |

A mayonnaise of salmon may consist of a large centre-cut, a thick slice, or the remains of cold salmon cut into pieces convenient for serving. Arrange a bed of shredded lettuce in the bottom of a salad bowl. Remove the skin and bone from the fish. Flake the fish and place on the lettuce. Mask the fish completely with thick mayonnaise sauce. The sauce may be made stiffer by adding a little liquid, but nearly cold, aspic jelly. When obtainable, a little endive should be mixed with the lettuce, for although the somewhat bitter flavour of this salad plant is disliked by many, its delicate, feathery leaves greatly improve the appearance of a dish. Garnish with the suggested ingredients or many other garnishings, in addition to those given above, may be used; tarragon and chervil leaves and fancily-cut thin slices of truffle are particularly effective when used to decorate the surface of Mayonnaise sauce.

**Allow 5–6 oz. salmon per helping**

## SALSIFY SALAD

*Salade de Salsifis*

| | |
|---|---|
| **1½ lb. cooked salsify** | **Mayonnaise sauce** |

Cut the salsify into 2-in. lengths. Pile in a salad bowl and coat with mayonnaise sauce or salad dressing.

**6 helpings**

## SAND CAKE

*Gâteau sablé*

| | |
|---|---|
| **4 oz. butter *or* margarine** | **½ oz. ground rice** |
| **Grated rind of 1 lemon** | **Pinch of salt** |
| **4 oz. castor sugar** | **½ level teasp. baking-powder** |
| **2 large eggs** | **Ratafia crumbs (optional)** |
| **4 oz. cornflour** | |

Grease a border mould or 6 in. cake-tin and if liked, coat with ratafia biscuit crumbs *or* with equal quantities of castor sugar and flour.

Cream the fat with the lemon rind; add the sugar and cream again. Beat the eggs and add them gradually, beating well between each addition. Sift together the cornflour, ground rice, salt and baking-powder. Add the flour lightly to the creamed fat, ⅓ at a time, and put the mixture into the mould. Bake in a moderate oven (**350°–335° F., Gas 4–3**).

**Cooking time—about 1 hr.**

SANDRINGHAM RABBIT

*Lapin, Sandringham*

**1 rabbit**
**Salt and pepper**
**2 large tomatoes**
**1 teasp. grated lemon rind**
**2 oz. breadcrumbs**
**1 teasp. chopped parsley**
**½ teasp. thyme**
**1 small shallot**
**2 oz. suet**
**1 egg**
**1 rasher of bacon**
**Fat for basting**
**Tomato *or* brown sauce**

GARNISH

**Bacon rolls**

Wash rabbit, season it well. Skin and finely chop tomatoes, mix with lemon rind, breadcrumbs, parsley, thyme, chopped shallot and suet. Mix with a small egg. Stuff the rabbit with this mixture, truss it and lay the bacon over the back. Roast the rabbit 50–60 min. in a fairly hot oven **(375°–400° F., Gas 5–6)** basting if required. Remove bacon about 10 min. before serving. Remove trussing strings.

Serve rabbit garnished with grilled bacon rolls. Serve sauce separately.

**3–4 helpings**

SANDWICH BUNS

*See Bridge Rolls.*

SANDWICH CAKE

**3 oz. butter *or* margarine**
**4 oz. sugar**
**2 eggs**
**5 oz. plain flour**
**1 level teasp. baking-powder**
**Pinch of salt**

Cream fat and sugar well; add egg yolks and continue beating. Sift flour, baking-powder and salt and stir into the mixture. Fold in the stiffly-whisked egg whites; add a little tepid water if necessary to make the mixture "easy". Place in a prepared 7-in. sandwich cake-tin and bake in a moderate oven **(350° F., Gas 4)**.

NOTE: Self-raising flour may be used with satisfactory results, in which case no baking-powder is required.

**Cooking time—30–40 min.**

SANDWICH CAKE, LARGE

**3 oz. butter *or* margarine**
**4½ oz. plain flour**
**Pinch of salt**
**4½ oz. sugar**
**3 eggs**
**2 level teasp. baking-powder**

As for Victoria sandwich cake (below) using an 8-in. sandwich cake-tin. Bake in a moderate oven **(350° F., Gas 4)**.

**Cooking time—50–60 min.**

SANDWICH CAKES

These differ from true sponge cakes because they contain fat. A sponge cake is usually fatless.

In making sandwich or layer cakes, grease the tin and line its base with greaseproof or silicone-treated paper.

SANDWICHES

The term "sandwich" has a much wider meaning today than when it was first introduced by the Earl of Sandwich, and applied only to slices of meat placed between bread and butter. We have now "Open" or Continental sandwiches, Club or Two-decker sandwiches, Toasted sandwiches and attractively-shaped Party sandwiches. Their fillings are now immensely varied, savoury or sweet, minced, or shredded and mixed with various butters, sauces and seasonings.

Making sandwiches requires little skill, just plenty of imagination and an eye for colour.

For sandwiches the bread should be fresh but not too new; French rolls, Vienna rolls, wholemeal or milk bread make an interesting change from ordinary loaves. Creamed butter is more easily spread than ordinary butter. When ordinary butter is used it should first be beaten to a cream (add 1 teasp. hot water to ½ lb. butter) to facilitate spreading. Savoury butters give piquancy and variety to other fillings, and can be used alone for rolled sandwiches.

Sandwiches simplify entertaining, for they can be prepared well in advance and can be served buffet-style, leaving the hostess free to mix with her guests. If prepared some time before required, sandwiches keep fresh and moist if wrapped in greaseproof paper and then in a damp cloth, or if put into a polythene bag, or wrapped in waxed paper or aluminium foil, and kept in the refrigerator or a cool place. Sandwiches with different fillings should be wrapped separately to prevent the flavours mixing.

*See also Party Sandwiches, Picnic Sandwiches.*

### SARDINE AND EGG FINGERS

*Canapés d'Œufs et Sardines*

| | |
|---|---|
| **8–10 sardines** | **1 tablesp. chopped gherkin** |
| **2 hard-boiled eggs** | **Cayenne pepper** |
| **Bread** | **Anchovy essence** |
| **Butter *or* fat** | |

Lift the sardines out of the tin, and drain them well. Rub the yolks of the eggs through a fine sieve, or mash them, and chop the whites finely. Cut thin slices of stale bread into fingers, fry in clarified butter or fat, and drain well. Chop the gherkin finely. Add a pinch of cayenne pepper and a few drops anchovy essence to a little butter, mix well and spread it on the fingers. Put a sardine on each. Decorate in 3 sections—covering the centre lightly with the chopped gherkin, one end with egg white and the other end with the egg yolk.

**8–10 savouries**

### SANDWICHES FOR PARTIES

*See Party Sandwiches.*

### SARDINE CROUSTADES

*Croustades de Sardines*

| | |
|---|---|
| **3 large slices of stale bread (approx.)** | **Few drops of lemon juice** |
| **Butter *or* fat for frying** | **2 teasp. grated Parmesan cheese *or* 1 tablesp. Cheddar cheese** |
| **1 small can of sardines** | **Watercress** |
| **1 tablesp. white *or* tomato sauce** | |
| **Salt and pepper** | |

Cut slices of stale bread about $\frac{3}{4}$ in. in thickness, stamp out 8–10 rounds or oval shapes of about 2 in. diameter. With a smaller cutter make an inner circle or oval about $\frac{1}{3}$ in. from the outer edge of the croustade. Fry these bread shapes in hot fat until lightly browned, drain, then with the point of a small knife lift out the inner ring, remove any moist crumb—and if wished place the cases in a moderate oven for a short time to crisp the inside. Cool before using. Mash the sardines—removing bones first—mix with the white or tomato sauce; if using white sauce add a few drops of anchovy essence. Season, blend with a few drops of lemon juice and the cheese. Put into the crisp cases and garnish with watercress.

**10 savouries**
**Cooking time—5 min.**

### SARDINE EGGS

*Sardines aux Œufs*

| | |
|---|---|
| **4 sardines** | **1 dessertsp. coarsely-chopped pickled gherkin** |
| **4 hard-boiled eggs** | **Watercress** |
| **1 teasp. anchovy essence** | **A little oil and vinegar** |
| **2 tablesp. white sauce** | |
| **Cayenne pepper** | |

Cut the eggs across in halves, trim off the extreme end of each to enable them to stand firmly and carefully remove the yolks. Skin and bone the sardines, chop them coarsely, and pound them together with the egg yolks till smooth. Add the anchovy essence and the white sauce gradually until a moist paste is obtained, then season to taste. Add the gherkin to the mixture, put it into the egg white cases, garnish with watercress seasoned with oil and vinegar and serve.

**8 savouries**

### SARDINES IN ASPIC

*Sardines en Gelée*

| | |
|---|---|
| **8 sardines** | **½ pt. aspic jelly** |
| **2 oz. very thinly sliced tongue *or* smoked salmon** | **2 tomatoes** |
| | **Sliced cucumber** |
| | **Sliced beetroot** |

Roll up each sardine in a thin slice of cooked tongue or smoked salmon. Place them in a shallow dish containing a layer of previously set aspic jelly, pour over sufficient half-set aspic to cover the sardine rolls and allow to set. Cut out the shapes as neatly as possible and arrange them on a dish. Garnish the dish with slices of tomatoes, cucumber and beetroot.

**8 savouries**

### SAUCE ANGLAISE

| | |
|---|---|
| **2 egg yolks** | **½ pt. milk** |

**2 oz. castor sugar** **Vanilla pod** *or* **essence**

Place the egg yolks and sugar with a little of the cold milk in a basin; mix thoroughly. Put remainder of milk on to boil with the vanilla pod (if used). Remove vanilla pod, gently pour the milk on to the eggs and sugar, mixing well. Return all to the saucepan, add vanilla essence (if used) and slowly cook until the sauce lightly thickens on the back of a wooden spoon. *Do not boil.* Strain and serve.

## SAUCES

The French joke, now more than a hundred years old, that the English "are a nation of only one sauce", is as true or untrue now as it ever was. Even today, a sauce is more often than not bought ready-made and poured out of a bottle on to hot or cold meat and fish alike. This is a really bad habit because it makes food monotonous, which is just what sauces are intended to prevent.

In the days before refrigeration, when meat and fish could not always be obtained fresh, it was frequently necessary to disguise "tainted" or "high" flavours in these foods, and sauces were therefore often hot, vinegary and highly spiced. Nevertheless, many traditional sauces of British cookery are dietetically and gastronomically excellent by modern standards. Mint sauce with lamb, apple sauce with pork, and horseradish sauce with beef all provide delightful contrasts without overpowering the flavour of the meats. Moreover the acids they contain make the digestion of the meat proteins easier.

Good modern British cookery tries to conserve as much of the natural quality and flavour of food as possible. A sauce should enhance but should never overpower or disguise the flavour of the food with which it is served.

There is such a wide choice of sauces that there is plenty of scope for variety and originality in the sauce one chooses to serve with any food. But these sauces are all based on a few simple foundation sauces.

These are:

1. English Foundation Sauce; White Sauce
2. English Foundation Sauce; Brown Sauce

3. Sauces made from jams, jellies, fruit or vegetable juices with eggs, wine, stock or starch and flavourings.
4. French White Sauce, or Béchamel Sauce
5. French Brown Sauce, or Espagnole Sauce
6. French Fawn Sauce, or Velouté Sauce
7. Mayonnaise and derived sauces, made with egg and seasoned liquids to which oil or butter is added
8. Sweet sauces, to serve with hot and cold puddings and other desserts (often custard-based sauces)
9 Store sauces, which are really vinegars, to keep in the store-cupboard.

For further information on sauces, *see Stock for Soups and Sauces, Gravies and various recipes in the book.*

## SAUERBRATEN

"Sour Roast"

| | |
|---|---|
| **3 lb. fillet of beef** | **3 rashers fat bacon** |
| **1 lemon** | **1 onion** |
| **2 bay leaves** | **1 tablesp. flour** |
| **6 cloves** | **1 oz. loaf sugar** |
| **4 peppercorns** | **¼ pt. sour cream** *or* **sour milk** |
| **Salt** | **Juice of ½ lemon** |
| **½ pt. vinegar** | |
| **2 oz. butter** | |

Skewer beef to a good shape; place in a bowl. Into a saucepan put enough water to cover the beef in the bowl. Slice the lemon. Add to the water the lemon slices, bay leaves, cloves, peppercorns and salt and bring to the boil. Add the vinegar and allow to cool. When cold, pour the liquid over the beef and leave to stand for several hours—all night if convenient. Remove the meat and dry it—retain the liquid. Put the butter in a large, heavy saucepan and heat. Put in the bacon, onion (sliced) and meat and fry, turning the meat on all sides until it is a rich brown. Add the flour and fry until brown. From the liquid in which the meat was standing, take ½ pt., also the bay leaves and cloves, and add it to the meat in the saucepan and bring to the boil. Remove the pan to a moderate oven **(350° F., Gas 4)** (if a long-handled pan, transfer all to covered ovenware dish), see that it is tightly covered, and cook gently for 1½ hr. Put the sugar with a few drops of water in a saucepan and cook slowly until a deep brown colour. Add the sour cream to the sugar and stir. Take up the meat and keep hot. Strain the liquid formed in cooking and add it to the sugar and cream. Add the lemon juice, bring to the boil, and serve with the beef.

**6–8 helpings**

### SAUERKRAUT SOUP

*Purée de Chou Croûte*

**1 lb. sauerkraut (or medium-sized can)**
**1 qt. stock *or* water**
**½ lb. potatoes**
**A few scraps of fat bacon and bacon rinds**
**1 oz. mushrooms *or* left-over mushroom stalks and peelings from another dish**
**1 bay leaf**
**1 blade of mace**
**Salt and pepper**
**A pinch of sugar**
**2 sausages—preferably Frankfurter**
**⅛ pt. cream (optional)**
**Grated cheese**

Boil the stock, and add to it the sauerkraut, sliced potatoes, bacon, mushrooms, spices and salt. Simmer for ¾ hr. or until the sauerkraut is quite soft. Rub through a sieve. Reheat, adding the sugar and seasoning and the sausages cut into ¼-in. thick rounds. Simmer the soup 15–20 min. until the sausage is cooked. Add the cream if liked. Sprinkle cheese on top or serve separately.

**6 helpings** **Cooking time—1 hr. 20 min.**

### SAUSAGE ROLLS

**Rough puff pastry using 4 oz. flour, etc.**
**½ lb. sausages**
**Egg yolk to glaze**

Roll out the pastry and cut into 8 even-sized squares. Skin the sausages. Divide the sausage meat into 8 portions and make each piece into a roll the same length as the pastry. Place the sausage meat on the pastry, wet the edge and fold over leaving the ends open. Knock up the edges with the back of a knife. Make three incisions on top. Brush over with beaten egg and place on a baking-sheet. Bake in a hot oven **(425° F., Gas 7)** until the pastry is well risen and brown. Reduce the heat and continue baking till the pastry is cooked.

NOTE: Small sausage rolls can be quickly made by rolling the pastry into an oblong. Form the sausage meat into long rolls the length of the pastry, place the meat on the pastry then divide the pastry into strips wide enough to encircle the meat. Damp one edge of each strip, fold over and press together firmly. Cut into rolls of the desired length, finish as above.

**8 sausage rolls**
**Cooking time—about ½ hr.**

### SAUSAGE STUFFING—HOME-MADE

**½ lb. lean pork**
**2 oz. breadcrumbs**
**½ teasp. mixed fresh herbs *or* ¼ teasp. dried herbs**
**2 small sage leaves**
**Salt and pepper**
**Grated nutmeg to taste**
**The liver of the bird to be stuffed**
**Stock**

Mince the pork. Chop the liver. Mix all the ingredients, using enough stock to bind the mixture. Season to taste.

Use for turkey or chicken.

NOTE: A good bought pork sausage meat mixed with the liver of the bird makes a quick stuffing for poultry.

### SAUSAGE TOAD IN THE HOLE

**4 oz. plain flour**
**¼ teasp. salt**
**1 egg**
**½ pt. milk *or* milk and water**
**1 lb. sausages**
**1 tablesp. cooking fat**

Make a batter with the flour, salt, egg and milk, and leave to stand for ½ hr. Heat the fat in a Yorkshire pudding-tin, skin the sausages, put the sausages in the hot fat, pour the batter over and bake in a hot oven **(425° F., Gas 7)** for about 30 min.

## SAUTÉED SHEEP'S KIDNEYS

*Rognons sautés*

| | |
|---|---|
| **2 sheep's *or* 1 pork kidney** | **½ teasp. finely-chopped parsley** |
| **1 shallot *or* small onion** | **Salt and pepper** |
| **1 oz. butter** | **3–4 tablesp. good brown sauce** |

Skin the kidneys, cut them across into very thin slices and remove the core. Chop the shallot or onion finely. Heat the butter and fry the shallot until golden brown, then put in the kidney and parsley. Season with salt and pepper, and toss over heat for 5–6 min. Add the brown sauce, mix it well with the kidneys and when thoroughly hot, serve.

If liked, garnish with 2 tablesp. each finely-shredded carrot, turnip and onion cooked separately.

**2 helpings**

## SAUTÉED OR TOSSED POTATOES

*Pommes de terre sautées*

| | |
|---|---|
| **6 medium-sized potatoes (waxy ones)** | **1–2 oz. butter or margarine** |
| | **Seasoning** |

Cook the potatoes, preferably in their skins, until only just soft. Let them dry thoroughly then peel and slice them ¼-in. thick. Heat the fat in a frying-pan and put in the potatoes. Season them with salt and pepper. Toss in the fat until they are light brown and have absorbed all the fat.

Serve at once.

**4–6 helpings**

## SAUTÉING

*See Cooking Methods.*

## SAVARIN

| | |
|---|---|
| **4 oz. plain flour** | **1 egg** |
| **Pinch of salt** | **¼ oz. sugar** |
| **¼ oz. yeast** | **1½ oz. butter** |
| **¼ gill warm water** | |

RUM SAUCE

| | |
|---|---|
| **3 oz. loaf sugar** | **1–2 tablesp. rum** |
| **¼ pt. water** | **Juice of ½ lemon** |

DECORATION

| | |
|---|---|
| **Apricot jam** | **Blanched almonds, browned** |

Sift the flour and salt into a basin and put it to warm. Cream the yeast with the tepid water. Make a well in the centre of the flour and pour in the yeast mixture. Sprinkle over the top with a little of the flour from the side of the bowl. Leave to prove for 10–15 min. in a warm place. Add the egg gradually, beating well to a smooth elastic dough, using a little more tepid water if necessary. Knead well. Put the dough back into the basin and press down, sprinkle the sugar on the top and put on the butter in small pieces. Cover with a damp cloth and leave in a warm place to double its size. Beat well again until all the sugar and butter is absorbed. Grease a border mould and fill it ⅓ of the way up with the mixture.

Leave to prove in a warm place until the mixture just reaches the top of the mould. Then bake in a fairly hot oven **(400° F., Gas 6)** for about 20 min.

Make the sauce: boil the water and sugar steadily for about 10 min. Add the rum and the lemon juice.

Turn the savarin out on to a hot dish, prick with a needle or hat pin and soak well in the sauce. Coat with hot sieved apricot jam and decorate with spikes of almonds etc. Serve with the rest of the sauce poured round

**4 helpings**

## SAVOURIES

These may be used as the last course served at a dinner, after (or instead of) the sweet course and before the dessert and coffee; or they may be used as a first course instead of hors d'œuvre and soup. Savoury dishes used in this way are sometimes called Appetizers or "Starters", and they may be light or quite solid. If they are substantial, they can also be used as main course dishes for supper or high tea. Some savouries, however, are small and light enough to serve as snacks at cocktail parties, to accompany drinks.

## SAVOURIES (APPETIZERS)

### —with Celery Bases

Use only crisp, tender, white stalks cut about 1½ in. long.

EGG STUFFING

To 1 chopped hard-boiled egg add 2 tablesp. mayonnaise seasoned with salt and pepper. Sprinkle with chopped parsley. Fill celery pieces.

ROQUEFORT STUFFING

To 4 oz. Roquefort cheese add 1 tablesp. Worcester sauce, 1 tablesp. mayonnaise, salt and pepper. Blend and fill celery pieces.

## SAVOURIES—with Bread Bases

Cut bread into desired shapes. Sauté one side in a small amount of butter over low heat. Place in a moderate oven (**350° F., Gas 4**) for 10 min.

SAVOURY BUTTERS

(1) To 6 oz. fresh butter add 3 oz. sieved pimentoes and a dash of cayenne pepper. Spread over bases. Decorate with chopped green olives.

(2) To 6 oz. fresh butter add 1 teasp. paprika. Flavour with a few drops of white wine. Spread over bases. Decorate with leaves of watercress.

(3) To 6 oz. fresh butter add 3 tablesp. horseradish and 1 teasp. lemon juice. Spread over bases. Decorate with a little lemon rind grated.

*See also Savoury Butters, General Method.*

## SAVOURIES—with Pastry Bases

PASTRY BASE

**12 oz. plain flour**
**Salt**
**6 oz. butter**
**6 oz. cream cheese**
**1 tablesp. cold water**

Sift together flour and salt. Rub in the butter and cheese; add water and mix to a dough. Roll out and cut into rounds or oblongs. Bake in a very hot oven (**450° F., Gas 8**).

**Cooking time—10 min.**

(Dough can be kept in refrigerator for several days and used a little at a time.)

CHEESE ONION SPREAD

To 1 oz. cream cheese add 1 dessertsp. minced onion and season with salt. Add cream to moisten. Spread on bases. Sprinkle with paprika.

EGG BUTTER

To 2 hard-boiled egg yolks finely-mashed add ½ teasp. lemon juice and a few drops of tabasco sauce. Season with salt and cayenne pepper. Spread on bases.

## SAVOURY BATTER

**4 oz. flour**
**1 egg**
**½ pt. milk**
**Salt and pepper**
**4 tablesp. finely-chopped beef *or* mutton**
**1 teasp. finely-chopped parsley**
**½ teasp. mixed herbs**

Mix the flour, egg, milk, salt and pepper into a smooth batter, let it stand for ½ hr. Then add the meat, parsley and herbs. Melt a little dripping in a Yorkshire pudding-tin, pour in the batter, and bake in a fairly hot oven (**375° F., Gas 5**) until set.

**2–3 helpings**
**Cooking time—20–30 min.**

## SAVOURY BUTTERS

*Beurres Composés*

*General Method:*

Roughly chop the ingredients to be mixed with butter. Crush and pound the additions. Pound the butter and additions together. Usually the compound butter is sieved and chilled.

NOTE: Herbs are best scalded in boiling water and dried in a cloth before being chopped and pounded.

*Uses of Savoury Butters:*

1. Used in place of sauce, e.g. Maître d'hôtel butter, with any grill.
2. As a thickening and flavouring combined, e.g. Lobster Butter in Cardinal Sauce.

## SAVOURY FILLINGS FOR OMELETS, ETC.

*See French Omelette.*

SAVOURY FILLINGS FOR SANDWICHES

**Savoury fillings**

1. Anchovies mixed with hard-boiled egg yolk, cheese and butter, with a sprinkling of cayenne. Spread the bread with curry butter.
2. Canned tuna fish mixed with salad cream and chopped parsley, with a dash of cayenne.
3. Canned salmon, mashed with lemon juice and chopped chives, spread on a bed of cucumber slices.
4. Minced cooked smoked haddock, seasoned and mixed to a smooth paste with butter and anchovy paste.
5. Very thin slices of cooked chicken and ham, seasoned and placed between bread spread with curry butter.
6. Very finely shredded celery, moistened slightly with canned or double cream, seasoned to taste.
7. Finely-grated cheese, mixed to a smooth paste with a little seasoning, anchovy essence or paste, and butter.
8. A layer of finely-chopped gherkin, olives and capers, mixed with mayonnaise sauce, covered with a layer of cream cheese.
9. Mashed sardines, a little lemon juice and seasoning, mixed to a smooth paste with butter.
10. Sardines mashed with an equal amount of grated cheese until smooth; seasoned to taste, with a little lemon juice or vinegar added and sufficient cream or milk to moisten.
11. Minced cooked chicken and ham or tongue, combined with cream cheese and egg yolk, seasoned and moistened with oil.
12. Finely-shredded lettuce and watercress, seasoned with salt and mixed with mayonnaise.
13. Thin slices of Gruyère cheese on slices of bread and butter, spread with French mustard, seasoned with pepper.

SAVOURY FILLINGS FOR STUFFED VEGETABLES

*See Stuffed Cucumbers, Stuffed Globe Artichokes, etc.*

SAVOURY FILLINGS FOR VOLS-AU-VENT, ETC.

*See Pastry Cases.*

SAVOURY FRITTERS

**Cold meat**
**Mashed potatoes**
**Salt and pepper**
**Milk**
**Coating batter *or* egg and breadcrumbs**
**Frying-fat**

This dish can be varied in many ways: thin slices of veal and ham put together; underdone beef seasoned with ketchup or Worcester sauce; mutton with slices of tomato, etc. Whatever meat is used, it must be cut into rounds of $1\frac{1}{2}$–$1\frac{3}{4}$ in. diameter. Season the potatoes liberally with salt and pepper, and stir over heat, adding a little milk gradually until moist enough to be easily spread. Cover both sides of the meat with potato, smoothing it with a hot wet knife. Dip in batter or coat with egg and breadcrumbs and fry in hot fat.

SAVOURY JELLY

**1 pt. tomato juice**
**Lemon juice *or* vinegar**
**Seasoning**
**A little sugar**
**1 oz. gelatine**
**2 hard-boiled eggs**
**4 oz. ham**

Flavour the tomato juice with a few drops of lemon juice or vinegar. Add seasoning and sugar. Dissolve gelatine in a little juice and add to the rest of the liquid. Pour a little liquid in the bottom of a mould or individual moulds, arrange some slices of hard-boiled egg in this and allow to set. Chop or mince the ham and mix with the rest of the chopped-up egg and jelly, fill up the mould and place in the refrigerator to set. Turn out and serve with salad and mayonnaise.

SAVOURY LOIN OF PORK

*Longe de Porc farcie*

**3 lb. loin of pork**
**½ teasp. powdered sage**
**1 saltsp. dry mustard**
**1 tablesp. finely-chopped onion**
**½ teasp. salt**
**¼ saltsp. pepper**
**Apple sauce**
**Brown gravy**

Score the pork with narrow lines. Mix the onion with the sage, salt, mustard and pepper and rub the mixture well into the meat. Wrap the joint in greased greaseproof paper and roast in a covered tin in a hot oven (**425° F., Gas 7**) for 10 min. and then reduce heat to moderate (**350° F., Gas 4**) for the remainder of the time. Allow 25 min. per lb. and 25 min. over. About ½ hr. before serving, remove the paper and lid and continue cooking to crisp the crackling. Serve the apple sauce and gravy separately.

**6 helpings**

### SAVOURY OMELETS

*See Omelets.*

### SAVOURY PANCAKES (1)

| | |
|---|---|
| **Batter as for Batter Pudding** | **4 bacon rashers** |
| | **Dripping** |

Whilst the batter is standing for ½ hr., remove the rind from the bacon, cut the bacon into small pieces and fry gently. Remove from frying-pan and stir into the batter. Put a little dripping into the frying-pan and heat until smoking hot. Quickly pour in enough batter to coat the bottom of the pan evenly. Cook until brown underneath, turn and brown on the other side.

Serve immediately.

**4 helpings**

### SAVOURY PANCAKES (2)

| | |
|---|---|
| **1 small onion** | **2 tablesp. milk** |
| **2 oz. cheese** | **Salt and pepper** |
| **½ oz. butter** *or* **margarine** | **Batter as for Batter Pudding** |

Grate the onion and cheese. Put into a saucepan, add the butter or margarine and stir in the milk. Season to taste. Heat gently until thoroughly hot.

Make the pancakes, spread with the hot filling and roll up. Serve immediately.

**4 helpings**

### SAVOURY PIES AND TARTS

In Britain, these consist of one or two pastry layers with cheese, meat, fish, a vegetable, eggs or a mixture of these as "filling". Pies usually have a pastry crust on top. Double-crust pies have a pastry shell underneath as well.

In the United States, almost any dish in a pastry shell is called a *pie*. In France, it may be called a *tourte*, a *quiche*, a *gougère* or *flan*.

### SAVOURY RICE ROLLS

*Croquettes de Riz*

| | |
|---|---|
| **4 tablesp. rice** | **Salt and pepper** |
| **1 tablesp. finely-chopped onion** | **1 qt. milk** |
| **1 bay leaf** | **1 oz. butter** |
| **½ teasp. finely-powdered herbs** | **2 eggs** |
| | **Egg and breadcrumbs** |
| | **Fat for frying** |

Pick over, wash and drain the rice. Place in a pan with the onion, bay leaf, herbs, salt and pepper, and milk, and simmer until the milk is absorbed and the rice tender. When ready, stir in the butter and 2 slightly-beaten eggs, reduce the heat and continue stirring for a few minutes to allow the eggs to become partially cooked, then turn the rice on to a plate to cool. Before it is quite cold, divide it into small portions and shape them into rolls. Coat them carefully with egg and breadcrumbs, fry in hot fat until golden-brown and use as required.

### SAVOURY RISSOLES

| | |
|---|---|
| **6 tablesp. mashed potato** | **Salt and pepper** |
| **2 tablesp. breadcrumbs** | **2 egg yolks** |
| **1 dessertsp. finely-chopped parsley** | **Egg and breadcrumbs** |
| **1 teasp. finely-chopped onion** | **Butter** *or* **frying-fat** |

Mix the potato, breadcrumbs, parsley, onion and a liberal seasoning of salt and pepper well together, and moisten with the egg yolks, adding a little milk if the mixture appears at all dry. Form into round flat cakes, coat with egg and breadcrumbs and fry in hot butter or fat until nicely browned.

**2–3 helpings**

### SAVOURY SANDWICH LOAF

| | |
|---|---|
| **1 day-old loaf** | **Salt and pepper** |
| **Butter** *or* **margarine** | **6 tablesp. crushed sardines** |
| **6 tablesp. lean cooked ham (minced)** | **1 small tomato** |
| **Mayonnaise** | **2 green olives** |
| **6–8 oz. cream cheese** | **Green colouring (optional)** |
| **2 hard-boiled eggs** | |

Remove crusts from loaf and cut loaf lengthwise in five equal slices. Butter each slice and spread the lower one with the ham mixed with enough mayonnaise to make an easy spreading consistency. Spread the next slice with 2 oz. cream cheese and place on top of the ham slice. Spread the third slice with crushed eggs, seasoned and mixed to a spreading consistency with mayonnaise; place on top of the cheese slice. Spread the fourth slice with sardines, place on top of the egg slice. Put the fifth slice on top, so that it has the form of the original loaf. Soften the remaining cream cheese with a little milk if necessary, colour if liked, and coat the top and sides of the loaf.

Decorate with slices of tomato and olives. The loaf can be wrapped in damp greaseproof paper and a cloth and stored in the refrigerator until required.

## SAVOY AND APPLE SAVOURY

**1 savoy cabbage**
**2 apples**
**3 medium-sized leeks**
**Curry sauce**

Wash and quarter the cabbage. Steam for about 20 min., then cool and cut into thick slices. Place a layer of cabbage in the bottom of a greased fireproof casserole, then add a layer of thinly sliced apple. Wash and cut the leeks lengthwise into four and place a layer on top of the apple. Cover with cabbage and pour over the curry sauce. Cover the casserole and cook in a fairly hot oven (**400° F., Gas 6**) for 30 min.

## SAVOY FINGERS

*Biscuits à la Cuiller de Savoie*

**5 oz. plain flour**
**1 oz. cornflour**
**Pinch of salt**
**4 eggs**
**5 oz. sugar**

Sift together flour, cornflour and salt. Beat the whites of the eggs stiffly, add the sugar and beat well again. Stir in the beaten yolks and fold in the sifted flour. Place the mixture into a bag with a plain ½-in. pipe and pipe on to a greased baking-sheet in 3-in. lengths. Dust the biscuits with castor sugar. Bake in a moderate oven (**350° F., Gas 4**).

NOTE: These biscuits are particularly useful for making such sweets as Charlotte Russe

**28 fingers** **Cooking time—10–20 min.**

## SAVOY PUDDING

*Pouding de Savoie*

**8 oz. stale savoy** *or* **sponge cake**
**2 oz. finely chopped mixed peel**
**1½ gill milk**
**2 oz. warmed butter**
**1 wineglass sherry** *or* **Marsala (optional)**
**4½ oz. castor sugar**
**3 eggs**

Pass the cake through a fine wire sieve. Add the peel, milk, warmed butter, wine and 1½ oz. of the sugar. Separate the eggs and add the yolks to the mixture. Beat well and pour the mixture into a buttered pie-dish. Bake in a moderate oven (**350° F., Gas 4**) until the pudding is set—about ¾ hr. Stiffly whisk the egg whites, stir in the remaining 3 oz. of sugar lightly, and pile on top of the pudding. Bake in a very cool oven (**265°–290° F., Gas ½–1**) to set and colour the meringue, about ½ hr.

**5–6 helpings**

## SCALOPPINE ALLA MILANESE

**Thin slices of veal**
**Salt and pepper**
**Flour**
**Egg and fresh breadcrumbs**
**Olive oil and butter for frying**
**Lemon**
**Watercress**

Cut some thin slices of veal (from the leg), season, and coat with flour, egg and fresh breadcrumbs. Fry in a mixture of olive oil and butter until a nice golden brown. Serve on a hot dish with quarters of lemon, garnished with watercress.

At the last minute pour hot foaming butter over the top.

**Cooking time—30 min. (approx.)**

## SCALLOPED SALMON

**1 can of salmon**
**Butter**
**Breadcrumbs**
**1–2 tablesp. white sauce**
**Grated cheese**
**Salt and pepper**

Divide the salmon into rather large flakes. Butter some scallop shells thickly and sprinkle lightly with breadcrumbs. Nearly fill them with salmon, add a little sauce and cover with breadcrumbs. Sprinkle lightly with cheese, season with salt and pepper, then add 2–3 small pieces of butter. Bake in a moderate oven (**350° F., Gas 4**) until nicely browned.

## SCALLOPS

Scallops are usually opened by the fishmonger and displayed in their flat shells. If the scallops are to be served in their shells ask the fishmonger for the *deep* shells. If however it is necessary to open escallops they should be put over a gentle heat to allow the shells to open. When they have opened, remove from the shells, trim away the beard and remove the black parts. Wash the scallops well, drain and dry. Wash and dry the shells; keep the deep shells for serving dishes.

Scallops are in season from November to March. They can be served baked, fried, poached or grilled.

## SCALLOPS AU GRATIN

**6 scallops**
**5 tablesp. dry cider *or* dry white wine**
**2 oz. mushrooms *or* 1 small onion**
**1 oz. margarine**
**¾ oz. flour**
**6 tablesp. top of milk**
**Seasoning**
**A little finely-grated cheese *or* browned breadcrumbs**
**Creamed potatoes (optional)**

Put the prepared scallops in a small pan with the cider or white wine. Simmer until tender, approximately 6–8 min.—do not allow to boil. Meanwhile chop the mushrooms or onion finely. Melt the margarine in another small saucepan and fry the mushrooms or onion. When soft add the flour and cook for 2–3 min. Stir in the liquid from the escallops, and the milk. Stir and boil for a few minutes, then season to taste. Cut the scallops into pieces and add to the contents of the saucepan. Put the mixture into 4 deep scallops shells. Sprinkle with grated cheese or breadcrumbs, and if liked, pipe a border of creamed potatoes round the edge and brown lightly under the grill.

Serve at once.

**4 helpings**

## SCALLOPS AND MUSHROOMS

*Coquilles St. Jacques aux Champignons*

**6 scallops**
**1–2 tablesp. white sauce**
**Milk**
**Salt and pepper**
**6 large flat mushrooms**
**1 oz. butter**

Put the prepared scallops in a saucepan with just sufficient milk to cover, add a little salt and pepper and simmer gently for about 15 min. Drain well, reserve the orange roe for garnish and chop the white parts, moisten with a little white sauce and season to taste. While the scallops are cooking remove the stalks of the mushrooms. Peel the tops of the mushrooms and fry in hot butter. Place an equal portion of the white part of the scallops on each mushroom and garnish with the orange roe.

Serve hot.

**3–6 helpings, depending on size of scallops**

## SCALLOPS IN SHELLS

**1½ doz. small scallops**
**1 oz. butter**
**1 cup fresh breadcrumbs**
**Cayenne pepper**
**A little chopped parsley**
**A little lemon juice**
**Salt and pepper**
**1 gill white sauce**

Prepare the scallops and 6 shells. Butter the shells and sprinkle in a few breadcrumbs. Put 3 scallops in each and season with cayenne, chopped parsley and a drop or two of lemon juice. Mix a little pepper and salt with the remaining breadcrumbs. Cover the scallops with white sauce, sprinkle with breadcrumbs, place bits of butter on top and bake for about 20 min. in a fairly hot oven (**375° F., Gas 5**).

**6 helpings**

## SCALLOPS IN WHITE SAUCE

*Coquilles St. Jacques à la Sauce blanche*

**18 scallops**
**Milk**
**1 small onion**
**1 clove**
**½ bay leaf**
**Salt**
**¾ pt. white sauce**
**A little butter *or* 1 tablesp. cream**
**Cayenne pepper**
**Nutmeg**

Wash the scallops and put them in a saucepan, with sufficient milk and water to cover. Add the onion, peeled and stuck with the clove, bay leaf and a pinch of salt, and simmer for 15 min. Take up, drain, put into the hot white sauce to finish cooking. Add butter.

## SCAMPI

These large prawns have become a very popular hors d'œuvres. If you wish to buy fresh prawns then ask the fishmonger for Dublin Bay prawns, shell them and cook as individual recipes. If preferred, packets of quick frozen Scampi can be bought; these are uncooked, and need cooking as individual recipes. The ordinary boiled prawns are NOT suitable for these recipes.

## SCAMPI MEUNIÈRE

| | |
|---|---|
| **8 oz. frozen *or* fresh Dublin Bay prawns (weight when peeled)** | **2–3 oz. butter** |
| | **Seasoning** |
| | **Lemon juice** |

Separate the frozen prawns. Heat the butter and cook the prawns steadily for about 5 min. only. Lift on to a hot dish. Add seasoning and lemon juice to the hot butter and cook gently until brown. Take care not to overcook the butter and turn it too dark. Pour over the prawns and garnish with lemon and parsley.

Serve with brown bread and butter.

**2–3 helpings**

## SCANDINAVIAN TEA RING

| | |
|---|---|
| **6 oz. plain flour** | **Small ½ oz. yeast** |
| **¼ teasp. salt** | **½–¾ gill warm milk** |
| **½ oz. sugar** | **½–1 egg** |

FILLING

| | |
|---|---|
| **1 oz. ground almonds** | **Hot water to mix to a spreading consistency** |
| **1 oz. castor sugar** | |

ICING

| | |
|---|---|
| **3 oz. sifted icing sugar** | **Warm water to mix** |

DECORATION

**½ oz. blanched and chopped almonds**

Mix flour and salt; add most of the sugar. Cream yeast with remainder of sugar, add warm milk and egg and mix with flour to a light but workable dough. Put dough to rise and when well risen roll out in an oblong shape. Spread with almond mixture; damp edges with water and roll up. Form into a ring or horseshoe shape; prove 10–15 min. Bake in a hot oven (**425° F., Gas 7**), reducing the heat after 10 min. to fairly hot (**375° F., Gas 5**). When cold, spread with icing and sprinkle with chopped almonds.

**Cooking time—20–30 min.**

## SCONES

Even an otherwise good cook sometimes finds considerable difficulty in producing really light, well-shaped scones. As in pastry-making, the "light hand" is important to good results. However, success can be achieved by following the simple rules given below.

### Important Points in Scone-Making

1. If the basic proportions are correct they can be varied in many different ways—see suggestions.
2. It is essential to be accurate with proportions, e.g. too much soda will ruin the scones.
3. Whereas yeast mixtures are kept warm, scones etc. made with other raising agents should be kept as *cool* as possible. The cold air expands with the heat and so helps to make the scones lighter.
4. The best utensil for mixing scones is a round-bladed knife; it gets well down to the bottom of the bowl and can be used for mixing without *pressing* on the mixture.
5. The most important rule is to add *all* the liquid *at once* and mix lightly to a spongy dough.

   Scones should be handled as little and as lightly as possible.
7. Scones should be cooked quickly—10 minutes in a hot oven for small scones and 15 minutes for a round of 4 or 6.
8. Oven scones should be cooled on a cooling tray to keep the outside crisp. Girdle

scones are best cooled in a tea towel to keep the skin soft.

NOTE: From experiment it has been found that better results are obtained if the scones are allowed to stand (after cutting out) for 10 minutes before cooking. This applies especially to scones raised with bicarbonate of soda and cream of tartar.

### Girdle Scones

It is not economically sound to heat an oven just to make a few scones for tea. When they are wanted, a girdle will be found very useful. Even a strong frying-pan will do, and many cooks use an electric hot-plate. There are also non-grease girdle plates on the market, which are pleasant to use and give good results.

The plain oven scone recipe can be used for girdle cookery, but one must remember that there is only contact heat compared with the radiated heat and convection currents in an oven. So the dough must be rolled out more thinly than for oven scones.

A good method of greasing a girdle is to tie a piece of suet (hard fat) in muslin and rub the heated surface with this; it lasts for a considerable time, as suet has a high melting-point. When a girdle is hot the greased surface should show a *faint* haze rising from it. Another method of testing a hot girdle is to sprinkle on a little flour—if the flour browns within a few seconds the girdle is ready for use.

### Basic Recipe

**1 lb. plain flour**
**½ teasp. salt**
**2–3 oz. lard *or* margarine**

*and*

**2 level teasp. bicarbonate of soda and 4½ level teasp. cream of tartar with ½ pt. fresh milk**

*or*

**2 level teasp. bicarbonate of soda and 2 level teasp. cream of tartar with ½ pt. sour *or* butter milk**

*or*

**4–6 level teasp. baking-powder with ½ pt. fresh milk**

Sift flour and salt and lightly rub in the fat; sift in the raising agents and mix well. Add

*all the milk at once* and mix *lightly* to a *spongy* dough. Knead very lightly to make the dough smooth and roll out ½–¾ in. thick. Cut out with a 2-in. cutter, brush with egg *or* milk, if desired, and bake in a hot oven (**425°–450° F., Gas 7–8**). The dough may be divided into 4 and each piece formed into a round cake and marked into 6 with a knife.

**24–30 scones**
**Cooking time—about 10 min.**

### Variations of Basic Recipe

**Cheese Scones**

Add 4–6 oz. grated cheese to above proportions. Cut out in fingers shapes or squares.

**Cheese Whirls**

Add 4–6 oz. grated cheese to the basic recipe.

Roll out dough into oblong shape. Spread with cheese and roll up like a Swiss Roll. Cut into slices and lay on greased baking-sheets with the cut side uppermost. Brush with milk or egg. If any cheese is left over, sprinkle it on and bake the whirls in a hot oven (**425°–450° F., Gas 7–8**).

**20–24 scones**
**Cooking time—10–15 min.**

**Fruit Scones**

Add 2 oz. sugar and 2-4 oz. fruit (currants, sultanas, etc.) to the basic recipe.

**Girdle Scones**

*Galettes*

Add 2–3 oz. currants; roll out ¼ in. thick, cut into 2½ in. rounds or triangles; cook on both sides on a moderately hot girdle about 5 min. till nicely brown and edges dry. Cool in a towel.

**Nut Scones**

Add 2–4 oz. chopped nuts to the basic or to the wholemeal recipe.

**Sweet Scones**

Add 2 oz. sugar and, if liked, 1 egg.

**Treacle Scones**

Add 1 oz. sugar, 1 teasp. ground cinnamon, 1 teasp. mixed spice, 2 tablesp. black treacle. Put the treacle in with $\frac{2}{3}$ of the milk, then add the rest as required.

**Wholemeal Nut Scones**

Use half wholemeal flour and half plain flour, add 2–4 oz. chopped nuts.

**Wholemeal Scones**

Use half wholemeal flour and half plain flour.

## SCOTCH COLLOPS

**1½ lb. good stewing steak**
**2 oz. butter *or* fat**
**2 teasp. finely-chopped onion *or* shallot**
**2 teasp. flour**
**½ pt. stock**
**Salt and pepper**
**Gravy browning**
**Mushroom ketchup**
**Sippets of fried *or* toasted bread**
**Parsley**

Cut the meat into small neat dice. Heat the fat in a stewpan and fry the onion or shallot lightly. Add the flour and cook for about 5 min., stirring all the time. Add the stock, seasoning, a little brown colouring, and the meat. Bring slowly up to the boil, add the mushroom ketchup and simmer very slowly for 1 hr., or until tender. Season if necessary and place on a hot dish. Arrange sippets of bread around the dish and garnish with chopped parsley.

**6 helpings**

## SCOTCH EGGS

*Œufs Écossaises*

**3 hard-boiled eggs**
**½ lb. sausage meat**
**Egg and breadcrumbs**
**Frying fat**

Shell the eggs and cover each egg with sausage meat. If liked, a little finely-chopped onion can be mixed with the sausage meat before using. Coat carefully with beaten egg and breadcrumbs, fry in hot fat until nicely browned. Cut each egg in half. Scotch eggs can be served either hot or cold.

**3 helpings**
**Cooking time—40 min. (approx.)**

## SCOTCH RABBIT

*Lapin Écossais*

**1 rabbit**
**¼ lb. pork *or* bacon**
**1 cabbage**
**Salt and pepper**
**2 tomatoes**
**1 small onion**
**Bouquet garni**
**½ pt. stock (approx.)**

Wash the rabbit, cut the flesh from the bones (the bones can be used to make stock). Mix flesh with chopped pork *or* bacon. Separate and wash cabbage leaves; blanch and season them. Line a saucepan with some of the cabbage, put in the meat, chopped tomato and onion, seasoning and bouquet garni. Cover closely with more cabbage leaves (an extra piece of bacon may be put on top if liked); add the hot stock, cover tightly, and simmer for about 2½ hr. Correct seasoning, remove bouquet garni and serve.

Kale may be used instead of cabbage.

**4 helpings**

## SCOTCH WOODCOCK (1)

**Toast**
**Butter**
**Anchovy paste**
**½ gill milk (*or* for special occasions use ½ milk and ½ cream)**
**2 eggs**
**Salt and pepper**

Cut the toast into 2-in. squares, butter, then spread with anchovy paste. Heat the milk and beaten eggs together, season well with salt and pepper. Stir over a very low heat until thickened, then pour on to the hot toast. Serve at once.

**6-8 small savouries**
**Cooking time—6 min. (approx.)**

## SCOTCH WOODCOCK (2)

This is the recipe most used today for this savoury dish.

| | |
|---|---|
| **4 slices of toast** | **Good pinch of salt** |
| **Butter** | **Good pinch of pepper** |
| **4 eggs** | **1 small can anchovy fillets** |
| **2 tablesp. milk** | |

Cover the hot toast with butter and keep warm. Beat the eggs with the milk and seasoning. Put a good knob of butter (about 1 oz.) into a saucepan, heat gently, then add the eggs and milk. Cook gently until the mixture thickens. Spread on toast and garnish with anchovy fillets—arranged in a lattice design.

**4 helpings** *or* **8 small savouries**
**Cooking time—6 min. (approx.)**

## SCOTS or "SCOTCH" BROTH

*Bouillon Écossais*

| | |
|---|---|
| **1 lb. scrag neck of mutton** | **2 leeks** |
| **1 teasp. salt** | **1 small turnip** |
| **1 qt. cold water** | **1 stick of celery** |
| **1½ oz. pearl barley** | **Pepper** |
| **2 carrots** | **1 dessertsp. chopped parsley** |

Scrape and wipe the meat, remove outside fat and skin. Cut the lean meat into ½-in. cubes. Put the meat, bones and salt into a pan with the cold water; bring slowly to simmering point. Blanch the barley then drain, and add it to the broth. Simmer very gently 1 hr.

Scrub and peel the vegetables and cut them into ¼-in. dice, except 1 carrot, which is grated and added later. Simmer for a further 2 hr., adding the grated carrot 20 min. before serving. Skim the fat from the surface and remove the bones. Season; add the chopped parsley and serve.

NOTE: To remove fat more completely, *see Mutton Broth.*

**4–6 helpings**
**Cooking time—3 hr.**

## SCOTTISH OATCAKES

| | |
|---|---|
| **8 oz. medium oatmeal** | **1 tablesp. melted dripping** |
| **½ teasp. salt** | **Boiling water** |
| **Pinch of bicarbonate of soda** | |

Mix oatmeal, salt and bicarbonate of soda in a bowl; add melted fat and enough boiling water to make a pliable but not wet dough. Knead well. Sprinkle board with oatmeal and roll mixture out thinly. Cut into 3½-in. rounds or alternatively cut into 6-in. rounds and divide into 4 triangles. Rub with oatmeal to whiten. Cook on *one side* on a moderately hot girdle, then place in oven or before fire to crisp through and till ends curl up.

**12 oatcakes depending on size**

## SCOTS KAIL BROSE or BROTH

*Potage au choux Écossais*

| | |
|---|---|
| **2 lb. shin of beef** *or* **"hough"** *or* **half an ox head** *or* **2 cow heels** | **2 leeks** |
| **2 qt. water** | **2 lb. kail** *or* **1 medium cabbage** |
| **2 teasp. salt** | **2 oz. toasted oatmeal** *or* **2 oz. pearl barley** |
| | **Pepper** |

Have the ox head thoroughly cleaned and blanched, or the cow heels scraped, cleaned and blanched. If shin of beef is used, keep it whole. Put the meat whole into a strong pan, add water, salt and the leeks, cut in 1 in. pieces, bringing slowly to simmering point and simmer gently till the meat is tender 3–4 hr. for shin or cow heel, 2–3 hr. for ox head. If barley is used, blanch it and simmer it in the broth for the last 2 hr. Strip the green from the ribs of the kail or cabbage, shred it finely and simmer it in the broth for 20 min. If oatmeal is added it should be toasted till golden-brown and cooked in the broth for 2–3 min. before serving. To serve, lift out the meat, dice some of the lean and return it to the broth. Season the broth and serve. The remainder of the meat may be used for another dish or served separately with a little of the broth.

NOTE: Scots Kail is the *Pot-au-feu* of Scotland, and like its Continental prototype may have the meat served separately, or in the broth.

**6–8 helpings** **Cooking time—3–4 hr.**

## SCRAG OF MUTTON

| | |
|---|---|
| **Scrag end of neck of mutton** | **Bouquet garni** |
| **2 onions** | **10 peppercorns** |
| **2 carrots** | **Stock** *or* **water** |
| | **Egg and breadcrumbs** |

**½ turnip**
**Bacon rashers**
**2 oz. dripping**

Wash the meat in warm salt water. Slice the onions, carrots and turnip and put in a saucepan. Lay the meat on top, cover with slices of bacon. Add the bouquet garni, peppercorns and enough stock or water to nearly cover the vegetables. Cover with a close-fitting lid and cook gently for 2½ hr. Remove the meat, brush with beaten egg and coat with breadcrumbs. Put in a tin with the hot dripping and cook in a fairly hot oven (**400° F., Gas 6**) for about ½ hr. until nicely browned. Baste occasionally. Serve with brown gravy made from the stock in which the meat was cooked.

**6–8 helpings**

## SCRAMBLED EGGS

*Œufs brouillés*

The secret of serving good scrambled eggs lies in slow cooking over a very low heat (a double saucepan is useful for this), continuous stirring, and immediate service as the eggs go on cooking in their own heat. It is helpful to add a little butter, or cream, when the scrambling is almost finished: this stops the cooking and improves the flavour.

**4 eggs**
**Salt and pepper**
**1 tablesp. butter**
**½ tablesp. butter *or* cream**

Break the eggs into a bowl, add seasonings and beat eggs lightly. Meanwhile melt the 1 tablesp. butter in the bottom of a pan and roll it around. Before it begins to sizzle pour the eggs into the pan. Reduce the heat to very low, and stir the mixture evenly and constantly with a wooden spoon. When almost ready add about ½ tablesp. butter or cream. Remove from the heat as soon as the eggs are set to a soft creamy consistency. Serve immediately.

**2 helpings** **Cooking time—10 min. (approx.)**

## SCRAMBLED EGGS WITH ANCHOVIES

**Toast**
**Butter for toast**
**4 eggs**
**¾ oz. butter**
**Seasoning**
**Small can anchovy fillets**
**Capers**
**1 tablesp. cream**
**½ teasp. anchovy essence**
**Parsley**

Cut the toast into pieces, and spread them thickly with butter. Beat the eggs slightly, then put them with the ¾ oz. butter, cream and anchovy essence into a saucepan and season to taste. Stir over low heat until the mixture thickens, spread it over the pieces of toast, lay strips of anchovy across, forming a lattice, and place a caper in each division. Garnish.

**4 helpings *or* 8 small savouries**
**Cooking time—5 min.**

## SCRAMBLED EGGS WITH GREEN PEA PURÉE

*Œufs à la St. Germaine*

**6 eggs**
**⅓ pt. green pea purée**
**1½ oz. butter**
**1 tablesp. brown *or* white sauce**
**Salt and pepper**
**2 tablesp. milk**
**Finely-chopped parsley**

Make the purée by passing cooked green peas through a fine sieve. Place this in a pan with ½ oz. butter, the sauce and seasoning to taste. Heat through thoroughly. Melt the remainder of the butter in another pan, add the eggs previously beaten, seasoned and mixed with the milk, stir until cooked. Place the purée in 6 individual dishes, fill with the scrambled eggs, sprinkle with parsley and serve.

**6 helpings** **Cooking time—30 min. (approx.)**

## SEA BREAM MAYONNAISE

*Mayonnaise de Brème de Mer*

**1–1½ lb. fillets of sea bream (approx.)**
**A little lemon juice**
**Seasoning**
**¼ pt. mayonnaise**
**1 tablesp. chopped parsley**
**1 hard-boiled egg**
**Lettuce**

Skin the fillets and place in a greased fireproof dish, sprinkle with lemon juice and seasoning. Cover with greaseproof paper and bake in a fairly hot oven (**375° F., Gas 5**) for about 20 min. When cooked, flake with a fork, remove any bones and leave to become cold. Just before serving mix the fish with mayonnaise, parsley and chopped egg and serve on a bed of lettuce.

**4 helpings**

**SEA-FOOD CHOWDER**

**1 smoked haddock (1–1¼ lb.)**
**1–2 sliced onions**
**1 breakfastcup diced raw potatoes**
**2–3 skinned tomatoes**
**1–1½ oz. butter** *or* **margarine**
**1 tablesp. flour**
**3–4 tablesp. cream**
**Salt and pepper**
**½ pt. shelled prawns** *or* **shrimps**
**½ A1 can peas**
**1 dessertsp. freshly-chopped parsley**

Cover the well-washed haddock with cold water, bring slowly to boil then remove and wash again. Skim off scum from the stock. Cook onions in a little of the stock until almost soft. Add potatoes and cook until soft. Cut tomatoes into eighths, discard seeds; simmer in remaining stock. Add tomatoes to other vegetables and cook a little. Meanwhile, free the haddock flesh of skin and bones. Melt the fat, add flour and cook for a few min. without browning. Remove from heat. Slowly stir the strained remaining stock into this roux. Cook gently for a few min., while stirring. Stir in the cream and season to taste. Add the vegetable mixture, then the haddock and prawns or shrimps, reserving a few. Add the drained peas. Heat through but do not boil. Sprinkle in the parsley, turn into a serving dish and garnish with the reserved shellfish.

**4–5 helpings**

**SEA FOOD FLAN**

FLAN CASE (uncooked)

**2 oz. butter** *or* **margarine**
**¼ teasp. salt**
**1 oz. grated cheese**
**4 oz. crushed plain biscuits (Cream Crackers)**

FILLING

**1 dessertsp. gelatine**
**½ small sized can pink salmon** *or* **tuna**
**6 sardines**
**1 gill mayonnaise**
**2 tablesp. tomato ketchup**
**1 teasp. finely-chopped onion**
**1 teasp. finely-chopped parsley**
**Salt and pepper to taste**

To make the flan case: Cream fat, salt and cheese together and knead in the crushed biscuits. Place mixture on a plate and mould it into a greased 7-in. flan ring. Put into refrigerator until firmly set. Remove flan ring.

Dissolve gelatine in 3 tablesp. hot water. Flake the salmon or tuna and sardines (free from bones) and mix together all ingredients for filling. When beginning to set, pour into prepared flan case. Decorate with shrimps, parsley, slices of tomato *or* hard-boiled egg. Serve with salads.

**SEED BUNS**

*See Buns or Cookies*

**SEMOLINA CROQUETTES**

*Croquettes de Semoule*

**1 pt. milk**
**1 oz. butter**
**1 lb. semolina**
**3 egg yolks**
**1 oz. grated Parmesan cheese**
**Salt and pepper**
**Egg and breadcrumbs**
**Fat for frying**

Put the milk and butter into a pan, when boiling stir in the semolina and cook slowly for about 10 min. Then add the 3 egg yolks, cheese and seasoning. Continue the cooking and stirring for a few minutes longer, then spread the mixture on a large dish. When cold, cut into rounds or other shapes, coat them with egg and breadcrumbs and fry in hot fat until nicely browned. Drain well, dish in a pyramid.

**5–6 helpings**

**SEMOLINA MOULD**

*Gâteau de Semoule*

**1 qt. milk**
**4 oz. semolina**
**3 oz. castor sugar**
**Flavouring** (*see below*)

Rinse a thick saucepan, put in the milk and heat to boiling point. Sprinkle in the semolina, stirring continually. Boil gently, stirring all the time, until the grain is quite cooked, and appears transparent when lifted on the back of a spoon (7–8 min.). Add sugar and stir well. Pour quickly into a cold, wet mould.

**6 helpings**
**Cooking time—10 min.**
**Setting time—2 hr.**

FLAVOURINGS

**Lemon** *or* **Orange**: Infuse thin strips of rind

with the milk during heating. Remove before adding the grain.

**Coffee:** Add 1 tablesp. coffee essence, with the sugar.

**Chocolate:** Melt 3 oz. chocolate in the milk, *or* blend 1½ oz. cocoa with some of the milk. Add rum, brandy, sherry *or* vanilla essence.

## SEMOLINA PUDDING

*See Milk Puddings*

## SEVILLE ORANGE MARMALADE

| | |
|---|---|
| **1½ lb. Seville oranges** | **Juice of 1 lemon** |
| **4 pt. water** | **Sugar** |

Wash the fruit and cut it in half. Squeeze out the juice and the pips. Cut the peel into shreds. Tie the pips in a muslin bag and put into a bowl with the orange and lemon juice, water and peel. Soak for 24–48 hr., covered to keep it clean. Transfer to the pan and cook gently until the peel is soft (approx. 1½ hr.). Remove the bag of pips, squeezing it gently. Take the pan from the heat, add 1 lb. sugar to each pint and stir over a medium heat till dissolved. Return pan to heat, bring to the boil, and boil rapidly until setting point is reached.

**Yield: about 6½ lb.**

## SHARP SAUCE—HOT or COLD

*Sauce Piquante*

| | |
|---|---|
| **1 shallot** | **Salt and pepper** |
| **2 hard-boiled egg yolks** | **Sugar to taste** |
| **4 anchovies** | *For a cold sauce:* **¼ pt. thin cream** |
| **½ teasp. mixed mustard** | *For a hot sauce:* **¼ pt. good meat gravy** |
| **2 teasp. vinegar** | |
| **1 teasp. chopped capers** | |

Chop the shallot finely. Crush and pound the hard-boiled egg yolks, anchovies and shallot together. Add the other ingredients to this paste. For a cold sauce, half-whip the cream and fold it carefully into the other ingredients. For a hot sauce, add the gravy (boiling) and reheat the sauce.

Serve with meat, fish or vegetables.

## SHEEP'S HEAD

*Tête de Mouton*

| | |
|---|---|
| **A sheep's head** | **2 onions** |
| **Bouquet garni** | **1 small turnip** |
| **10 peppercorns** | **2 small carrots** |
| **Salt and pepper** | **1 oz. butter *or* fat** |
| **2 tablesp. pearl barley *or* rice** | **1 oz. flour** |
| | **Parsley** |

If necessary, split the head and remove the brains. Wash the head several times, taking care to remove all splintered bones. Scrape the small bones from the nostrils and brush the teeth. Soak in salt water for 30 min. Cover with cold water and bring to the boil. Pour away the water and replace with fresh cold water and add the bouquet garni, peppercorns and salt. Boil up and skim well. Add the barley (blanched) or rice. Cook slowly for about 3 hr. Meanwhile prepare the vegetables and cut into dice; these should be added about 1 hr. before serving. Remove the skin and fibres from the brains with salt and wash in cold water. Tie the brains in muslin and cook with the head for about 15–20 min. Then chop coarsely. Heat the fat in a saucepan and add the flour. Stir over the heat and cook without browning for about 3 min., then add ¾ pt. of liquid in which the head is cooking. Stir until boiling, correct the seasoning and add the brains. Remove the head and take all the flesh from the bones. Skin and slice the tongue. Place the meat neatly on a hot dish. Pour the brain sauce over. If liked, garnish with some of the sliced tongue, vegetables and chopped parsley. Serve the broth separately.

**3 helpings**

## SHEEP'S HEAD BROTH

| | |
|---|---|
| **1 sheep's head split in two** | **1 turnip** |
| **3 qt. water** | **2 carrots** |
| **3 teasp. salt** | **1 tablesp. chopped parsley** |
| **2 oz. pearl barley** | **Pepper** |
| **2 leeks** | |

Remove the brains and soak them in vinegar and water (these may be used for Brain Cakes to be served with Dressed Sheep's Head). Soak the head in salt water for 1 hr. Scrape the small bones and centre cartilage from the nostril and scour with salt. Scrape and scour the teeth. Blanch the head and rinse it thoroughly. Tie the head with string, put it into a large pan with the water and 3 teasp. salt; bring very slowly to boiling point and simmer gently. Blanch the barley and add it to the broth. Cut the leeks, turnip and 1 carrot into ¼-in. dice and add them. Simmer the broth 3–4 hr. Half an hour before serving, grate and add the other carrot. When the head is tender lift it out and serve it as Dressed Sheep's Head with parsley To serve the broth, skim off the fat, add the chopped parsley and season carefully. Some broth may be strained off for stock.

**6–8 helpings, keeping 2–3 pt. of broth for stock**
**Cooking time—3–4 hr.**

## SHEEP'S HEART

*Cœur de Mouton*

| | |
|---|---|
| **1 sheep's heart** | **½ pt. good stock** |
| **Veal forcemeat** | **¾ oz. flour** |
| **2 oz. dripping** | **Salt and pepper** |

Soak the heart for about ½ hr. Wash well in clean water. Cut the pipes from the top, leave the flaps to fasten down and cut the dividing walls of the chambers. Dry thoroughly and fill the heart with forcemeat, fold over the flaps and tie or skewer to keep it in. Heat the dripping in a small meat-tin. Put in the heart, baste well and bake in a cool to moderate oven **(310°–350° F., Gas 2–4)** for 1½ hr. Gentle cooking and frequent basting are necessary to prevent the heart from becoming dry and hard. When cooked, place the heart on a hot dish and keep hot. Drain off most of the fat but keep back any sediment. Blend the flour and stock and add to the sediment to make thickened gravy. Season carefully. Pour a little round the heart and serve the rest in a gravy-boat.

NOTE: Sheep's heart may be stuffed with sage and onion stuffing and cooked in a saucepan on top of the cooker. This must be done very carefully over a very gentle heat.

**6 helpings**

## SHELL FISH AND TOMATO SOUP

| | |
|---|---|
| **1 lb. cooked *or* 1 can of crawfish, crayfish *or* prawns** | **Lemon rind** |
| **2 raw potatoes** | **1 lb. tomatoes *or* 1 medium-sized can** |
| **1½ pt. fish stock** | **1 onion** |
| **A bunch of herbs: fennel *or* tarragon, parsley, basil** | **2 oz. rice** |
| **1 bay leaf** | **¼ pt. white wine *or* cider** |
| **Lemon juice** | **Chopped parsley** |
| | **Paprika pepper** |
| | **½ gill cream** |

Slice the potatoes thickly, and boil them till soft in ½ pt. fish stock with the herbs, lemon juice and a piece of lemon rind. Meanwhile cut up the tomatoes and chop the onion. Cook the tomatoes and onion without any other additions till they are quite soft. Sieve the potatoes and to them add all the stock. Bring the stock and potatoes to the boil, add the rice and cook till quite soft. Sieve the tomatoes and onion and add this purée to the thickened fish stock. Add the wine and the chopped fish and bring the soup to boiling point. Grate in a little lemon rind, add the chopped parsley and season well. Off the heat, stir in the cream.

Serve at once.

**4–6 helpings**
**Cooking time—30 min.**

## SHELL FISH COCKTAIL

| | |
|---|---|
| **4–6 picked shrimps or prawns *or* 6 oz. lobster *or* crawfish meat, diced** | **Shredded lettuce** |

COCKTAIL SAUCE

| | |
|---|---|
| **2 medium-sized ripe tomatoes** | **Salt** |
| **Juice of ½ lemon** | **¼ pt. thin cream *or* evaporated milk** |
| **1 teasp. Worcester sauce** | |

Sieve the tomatoes, add the lemon juice and seasonings and stir in the cream or milk. Mix the shell fish with the sauce. Place shredded lettuce at the bottom of four glasses and pile the shellfish on top. Sprinkle with paprika and serve as an appetizer.

**4 helpings**

## SHEPHERD'S PIE

| | |
|---|---|
| **1 lb. cold cooked beef *or* mutton** | **2 lb. cooked mashed potatoes** |
| **1 small onion** | **Egg *or* milk** |
| **½ pt. gravy** | **Salt and pepper** |

Remove any skin, gristle or bone and cut the meat into small dice. Parboil and finely chop the onion and place in a pie-dish with the meat and the gravy. Season well. Cover with mashed potatoes and smooth and decorate the top to look like pie-crust. Glaze with beaten egg or milk if liked. Bake in a moderate oven (**350° F., Gas 4**) for about ½ hr. until thoroughly warmed and the surface is well browned.

**6 helpings**

## SHERBETS

*See Ices.*

## SHERRY BISCUITS

| | |
|---|---|
| **5 oz. plain flour** | **1 egg** |
| **4 oz. butter** *or* **margarine** | **1 tablesp. sherry** |
| **3 oz. castor sugar** | **Chopped almonds** |

Sift the flour and rub in the fat. Add the sugar and mix stiffly with the egg yolk and sherry. Roll out the dough to ⅛ in. thickness. Prick all over and cut into fancy shapes, using 2–2½-in. cutter. Brush the biscuits with lightly beaten egg white and sprinkle with chopped almonds. Bake in a moderate oven (**350° F., Gas 4**).

**30–32 biscuits** **Cooking time—15–20 min.**

## SHERRY CREAM PIE

| | |
|---|---|
| **½ lb. chocolate biscuits** | **4 oz. margarine** |

FILLING

| | |
|---|---|
| **½ pt. milk** | **Grated nutmeg** |
| **4 oz. sugar** | **3–4 tablesp. sherry** |
| **2 eggs** | **½ pt. cream** |
| **1 dessertsp. gelatine** | |

To make pie shell: crush biscuits finely. Melt margarine and mix with biscuit crumbs. Press firmly on the bottom and round the sides of a greased 10-in. pie-dish. Put into the refrigerator to harden. Meanwhile make the filling. Heat the milk, stir in the sugar and lightly beaten egg yolks. When custard is cooked, allow to cool, add gelatine dissolved in a little cold milk, stir in nutmeg to taste. Add sherry a little at a time to prevent curdling; leave to thicken. Stiffly beat egg whites and fold into thickened custard. Whip the cream and stir in. Turn into pie shell; put in refrigerator until set.

## SHORT CRUST PASTRY

For Pies, Tarts, etc.

| | |
|---|---|
| **½ lb. plain flour** | **2 oz. lard** |
| **Pinch of salt** | **Cold water to mix** |
| **2 oz. butter** | |

Sift together the flour and salt. Rub the butter and lard lightly into the flour using the fingertips. Mix to a stiff paste with cold water. Use as required.

## SHORT CRUST PASTRY—PLAIN

For Pies, Tarts, etc.

| | |
|---|---|
| **½ lb. plain flour** | **1 teasp. baking-powder** |
| **Pinch of salt** | **Cold water to mix** |
| **3 oz. lard, clarified fat** *or* **dripping** | |

Sift the flour and salt. Rub in the fat, add baking-powder and using a knife, mix to a stiff dough with cold water. Use as required.

Bake in a very hot oven (**450° F., Gas 8**), lower later to cook filling.

NOTE: For sweet tarts, 1 tablesp. castor sugar may be added to the above ingredients.

## SHORTBREAD BISCUITS

| | |
|---|---|
| **4 oz. butter** *or* **margarine** | **2 oz. castor sugar** |
| | **8 oz. plain flour** |

Cream fat and sugar and work in the sifted flour with the hand; knead well. Roll out a good ¼ in. thick and cut into fancy shapes or fingers (for fingers a more effective result is obtained if shortbread is rolled from ¼ in. to ½ in. thick). Prick neatly and bake in a moderate–warm oven (**350° –335° F., Gas 4–3**) till pale fawn in colour and crisp. Dredge with castor sugar while still warm.

**16–20 fingers** *or* **24–30 biscuits**
**Cooking time—20–30 min.**

### SHORTBREAD (SCOTTISH)

*Sablé*

| | |
|---|---|
| **8 oz. flour** | **4 oz. butter** |
| **2 oz. castor sugar** | |

Put the flour and sugar in a pile on a pastry-board. Gradually knead the sugared flour into the butter with the hand. It is important not to let the butter become broken up. When a firm dough is formed, roll out and shape into a cake about 1 in. high. Decorate the edges by marking with a fork or fluting with finger and thumb, or make in a shortbread mould, and prick a pattern on top with a fork or skewer. Fasten a narrow band of paper round to keep the cake in shape. Bake in a warm to cool oven (**335°–310° F., Gas 3–2**). Dredge with castor sugar when cooked.

**Cooking time—about 1 hr.**

### SHREWSBURY BISCUITS

**Basic Recipe**

| | |
|---|---|
| **4 oz. butter** *or* **margarine** | **½ level teasp. ground cinnamon** *or* **1 teasp. grated lemon rind** |
| **4 oz. castor sugar** | **Milk as required** |
| **1 small egg** | |
| **8 oz. plain flour** | |

Cream the fat and sugar and beat in the egg. Sift flour with cinnamon, *or* add grated rind, and add to the creamed fat mixture. Mix to a stiff consistency, using milk if required. Roll out fairly thinly and cut out with a 2½-in. cutter. Place on a greased baking-sheet and bake in a moderate oven (**350° F., Gas 4**) till light fawn colour.

**30–32 biscuits** **Cooking time—15–20 min.**

**Variations of Basic Recipe**

### EASTERTIDE BISCUITS

Add ½ level teasp. mixed spice and 2 oz. currants to the basic recipe for Shrewsbury Biscuits. Roll out mixture to ¼ in. thickness and cut into 4-in. rounds. If desired, brush with egg white and dredge with sugar. Bake in a moderate oven (**350° F., Gas 4**) until golden brown.

**12–16 biscuits** **Cooking time—20–30 min.**

### SULTANA, CURRANT or DATE FINGERS

Add 4–6 oz. sultanas or currants or chopped dates to the basic recipe for Shrewsbury Biscuits. Divide mixture into 2 pieces. Roll each into an oblong and spread one with the fruit. Cover with second piece. Roll lightly till about ¼ in. thick, trim edges and decorate top with a knife, cutting diamond shapes. Brush with egg-wash and cut into fingers 1 in. by 3 in. long. Put on a greased baking-sheet and bake in a fairly hot to moderate oven (**375°–350° F., Gas 5–4**) till golden brown.

**24 fingers** **Cooking time—15–20 min.**

### SHRIMP or PRAWN SALAD

*Salade de Crevettes*

| | |
|---|---|
| **1 pt. picked shrimps** | **Slices of cucumber** |
| **2–3 tablesp. mayonnaise sauce** | **Crisp, inner lettuce leaves** |

Mix shrimps lightly with the mayonnaise sauce and pile in a salad bowl. Garnish with shreds of lettuce and cucumber.

**5–6 helpings**

### SHRIMP SAUCE

*Sauce aux Crevettes*

To ½ pt. white sauce made with ½ fish stock and ½ milk, add ¼ pt. picked *or* canned shrimps and a few drops of anchovy essence and lemon juice to taste. Season with cayenne pepper.

Serve with fish.

### SHRIMPS

Shrimps are available all the year. They are usually sold cooked and served cold in soups, sauces, etc.

#### TO BOIL FRESHLY-CAUGHT SHRIMPS

Throw the shrimps into boiling salted water, and keep them boiling for about 5 min. Care should be taken that they are not overboiled, as they then become tasteless and indigestible; they are done when they begin to change colour.

TO SHELL SHRIMPS

Take the head between the right thumb and forefinger and with the left forefinger and thumbnail raise on each side the shell of the tail, pinch the tail, and the shell will at once separate.

SHRIMPS FRIED AND BRAISED

| | |
|---|---|
| **1 lb. shrimps** | **1 tablesp. soya sauce** |
| **3 shallots** | **1 oz. cornflour** |
| **1 clove of garlic** | **Pinch of salt** |
| **1 piece of ginger** | **Pinch of sugar** |
| **Oil for frying** | **Pinch of pepper** |

Peel the shrimps. Chop shallots, garlic and ginger and fry in smoking hot oil for 2 min. Reduce heat, add shrimps and cook for another 2 min. Blend cornflour to a smooth paste with a little cold water, mix with soya sauce and add to shrimps. Add salt, sugar and pepper. Braise for 5 min.

**6 small helpings**

SIMNEL CAKE

*Gâteau de la mi-carême*

**Mixture:** as for Birthday Cake or any other fruit cake.
**Almond paste:** 6 oz. ground almonds, etc.
**Glacé icing:** 2 oz. icing sugar, etc.

Line a 6–7-in. cake-tin with greaseproof paper greased. Cut off about $\frac{1}{3}$ of the almond paste and roll out into a round slightly less than the diameter of the tin to be used. Place $\frac{1}{2}$ the cake mixture in the tin, cover with a round of almond paste and place the remaining cake mixture on top. Bake in a moderate oven (**350° F., Gas 4**) for $\frac{1}{2}$ hr., reduce heat to cool (**310°–290° F., Gas 2–1**) for 2–2$\frac{1}{2}$ hr. Leave for 24 hr. Using about $\frac{1}{2}$ the remaining almond paste, cover the top of the cake. With the remainder, make small balls and place these at even intervals round top edge of the cake. Brush them over with egg wash. Tie a band of greaseproof paper tightly round the top of the cake. Place in a hot oven until balls are nicely browned. When cool, pour glacé icing into the centre of the cake and decorate as required with almond paste eggs, small chicks, etc.

**Cooking time—about 3 hr.**

NOTE: This cake used to be served only on Mother's Day but is now often served on Easter Sunday.

SKATE WITH CAPER SAUCE

*Raie, Sauce aux Câpres*

| | |
|---|---|
| **4 small slices of skate** | **2 bay leaves** |
| **¼ pt. vinegar** | **2–3 sprigs of thyme** |
| **1 tablesp. salt** | **½ pt. caper sauce** |
| **½ teasp. pepper** | |
| **1 sliced onion** | |
| **1 small bunch of parsley** | |

Put all the ingredients except the caper sauce into a saucepan with just sufficient warm water to cover the fish, and simmer for about 15 min. until tender. When the fish is cooked, drain well, put on a hot dish, pour over a little caper sauce and serve the remainder separately.

NOTE: Skate may also be served with onion sauce, or parsley and butter.

**4 helpings**

SKINNING FISH

*See Fish*

SLOW ROASTING

*See Cooking Methods*

SMALL GRAIN MOULDS (Semolina, Ground Rice, Tapioca, small Sago)

For a basic recipe, *see Semolina Mould.*

SMOKED HADDOCKS

*Aiglefins fumés*

Smoked haddocks are best cooked either in the oven or on the top of the cooker in a dish with a little water to create steam, to prevent the surface of the fish becoming hardened. Medium-sized haddocks should be cooked whole, and before serving an incision should be made from head to tail and the backbone removed. The fish should be liberally spread with butter, sprinkled with pepper and served as hot as possible.

### SMOKED HADDOCK SOUFFLÉ

*Soufflé de Merluche fumée*

**1 small cooked smoked haddock**
**1½ oz. butter**
**2 eggs**
**1 egg white**
**Pinch of pepper**
**Cayenne pepper**

Flake the fish while still hot, and when quite smooth beat in most of the butter and the yolks of the eggs. Use the rest of the butter to grease a soufflé dish. Add all the stiffly-beaten egg whites and pepper and cayenne pepper. It should not be necessary to add salt, but it is advisable to taste the mixture, since the saltiness of smoked haddock varies a great deal. Put the mixture into the soufflé dish and bake for approximately 15–20 min. in the centre of a moderate oven (**350° F., Gas 4**).

Serve at once.

NOTE: For a softer texture add 2–3 tablesp. white sauce *or* cream to the haddock before putting in the egg yolks.

An excellent flavour is given to this dish if 1 tablesp. grated Parmesan cheese is added with the egg yolks.

**4–5 helpings**

### SMOKED SALMON

1. Serve this with cayenne pepper, wedges of lemon and thin slices of brown bread and butter.

2. For an unusual hors d'œuvres, serve thin slices of smoked salmon with tiny crisp pastry cases filled with very hot and very creamy spinach.

3. Serve a mixture of smoked salmon and potted shrimp on a bed of crisp lettuce.

### SMOKED SALMON WITH CUCUMBER

**1 large cucumber**
**Olive oil**
**White *or* malt vinegar**
**Chopped parsley**
**Bread**
**Butter**
**4–6 oz. smoked salmon**
**Salt and pepper**
**Mustard and cress**
**Watercress**

Cut the cucumber into 1-in. pieces as near as possible of the same size. Cut the rind so as to form stripes of green and white (crinkled). Scoop out some of the centre and round off the bottom of each to give them the appearance of cups. Chop the pulp scooped out of the centre and put it in a basin with the oil, vinegar and parsley. Stamp out some rounds of bread with a 1½-in. cutter, butter them on one side, cover the buttered side with thin slices of smoked salmon; cut some of the salmon into fine strips and mix with the cucumber pulp; season with salt and pepper. Put the cucumber cups on the prepared rounds of bread, and fill the cavities with the above mixture. Arrange on a dish in the shape of a crown, garnish with mustard and cress and watercress.

**10–12 savouries**

### SMOKED TROUT

This makes a delicious hors d'œuvre. Buy the trout already smoked and remove the bones if possible. Serve with horseradish sauce, lemon, cayenne pepper and brown bread and butter.

### SODA CAKE

**8 oz. plain flour**
**⅛ teasp. salt**
**4 oz. butter *or* margarine**
**4 oz. sugar**
**½ teasp. mixed spice *or* nutmeg**
**2 oz. currants**
**2 oz. sultanas**
**2 oz. raisins**
**2 oz. peel**
**1 level teasp. bicarbonate of soda**
**1 egg**
**1½ gills milk (approx.)**

Sift flour and salt and rub in the fat. Add all the dry ingredients except soda. Slightly beat the egg and dissolve soda in a little milk. Add both to dry ingredients, using enough milk to make a soft dropping consistency. Beat well. Place in a greased 7-in. tin and bake on the middle shelf of a fairly hot oven (**375° F., Gas 5**), reduce heat to **350° F., Gas 4** after 15 min. about 1–1½ hr. in all.

### SOLE À LA PORTUGAISE

**1 medium-sized sole**
**1 oz. butter**
**1 shallot**
**1 teasp. finely-chopped parsley**
**½ teasp. anchovy essence**
**Salt and pepper**
**1 onion**
**2–3 tomatoes**
**1 dessertsp. grated Parmesan cheese**
**1 dessertsp. brown breadcrumbs**
**Extra butter**

Skin the sole and make an incision down the centre as for filleting; raise the flesh from the bone on each side as far as possible. Mix the butter, finely-chopped shallot, parsley and anchovy essence well together, and stuff the mixture inside the sole. Place the fish in a buttered fireproof dish, season. Arrange slices of onion and tomato alternately and overlapping each other, on top of the fish; or if less onion is preferred, surround each slice of tomato with a single ring of onion. Mix together the cheese and breadcrumbs and sprinkle over the fish. Place small pieces of butter on top, cover with a lid or greased paper and bake for about 20 min. in a moderate oven **(350° F., Gas 4)**.

Serve with tomato or brown sauce.

**2 helpings**

### SOLE AU GRATIN

| | |
|---|---|
| **3 fillets** *or* **1 large sole** | **Preserved mushrooms, sliced** |
| **Salt and pepper** | **Italian sauce** |
| **½ glass white wine** | **Brown breadcrumbs** |
| **Lemon juice** | **Butter** |
| **Mushroom liquor** | |
| **1 teasp. chopped parsley** | |

If using a whole sole, skin both sides, cut off the head and fins and make several incisions with a knife across one side of the fish. Place fish on a well-buttered fireproof dish (if using whole fish place cut side uppermost), season with pepper and salt, add the white wine, a few drops of lemon juice, a little mushroom liquor and some chopped parsley. Slice the mushrooms and place in a row down the centre of the fish; cover with a rich Italian sauce. Sprinkle with brown breadcrumbs, dot a few tiny bits of butter on top of the fish and bake in a moderate oven **(350° F., Gas 4)** for 20–30 min., according to size of sole.

**2–3 helpings**

### SOLE BELLE MEUNIÈRE

| | |
|---|---|
| **6–8 oz. sole (1 per person)** | **2 soft herring roes** |
| **1½–2 oz. butter** | **1 small tomato** |
| **Salt and pepper** | **4 button mushrooms** |
| **Flour** | **Juice of ¼ lemon** |
| | **Chopped parsley** |

Clean the sole and remove the dark skin; dry on a cloth. Heat a little of the butter in a frying-pan. Season the sole and dust with flour. Place in the heated butter—white skin side down, and gently cook both sides until light brown—8–10 min. Season and flour the herring roes; cook in the pan with the sole; also cook the seasoned tomato at the same time. Place the sole on a dish, with the tomato on top and soft roes each side. Thinly slice the mushrooms, heat the remainder of the butter in a clean frying-pan, and cook the mushrooms to a nice light brown colour. Sprinkle the sole with lemon juice and pour on to it the mushrooms and butter. Serve immediately, lightly sprinkled with chopped parsley.

### SOMERSETSHIRE PUDDING

| | |
|---|---|
| **3 oz. butter** *or* **margarine** | **¼ teasp. vanilla essence** |
| **3 oz. sugar** | **4 oz. plain flour** |
| **2 eggs** | **1 level teasp. baking-powder** |

Grease 6–7 dariole moulds.

Cream the fat and sugar together. Beat in the eggs and flavouring. Sift in the flour and baking-powder and mix to a soft dropping consistency. Put the mixture into the moulds and bake in a fairly hot oven **(375° F., Gas 5)** until brown and cooked through—about 20 min.

Serve with jam- *or* custard-sauce.

NOTE: These puddings can also be served cold, with the inside scooped out and the cavity filled with jam *or* stewed fruit and whipped cream.

**4 helpings**

### SOPA DE ARROZ

*Spanish Rice Soup*

| | |
|---|---|
| **½ cup frying oil** | **3 onions** |
| **½ lb. rice** | **4 tomatoes** |

1 clove of garlic
1 lb. lean ham
1 qt. meat stock

Heat the oil, put in the uncooked rice and fry until golden brown. Pound a clove of garlic and stir into the rice. Slice the onions and tomatoes. In a deep pan, fry the ham, onions and tomatoes. Add the rice to the ham and stir altogether. Add the stock, cover closely and simmer gently for about 1 hr.

**6 helpings** **Time—1½ hr.**

## SORBETS

*See Ices.*

## SOUFFLÉ MONTELIMAR

**1 level teasp. gelatine**
**½ teacup sliced maraschino cherries and ⅓ teacup juice (bottled cherries will do)**
**¼ pt. milk**
**1 level tablesp. castor sugar**
**12 marshmallows**
**2 eggs**

DECORATION
**Chopped roasted almonds**
**Whipped cream**
**Glacé cherries**
**Angelica**

Dissolve gelatine in cherry juice, add milk, sugar, marshmallows and egg yolks. Cook all together in a double saucepan until mixture is creamy and smooth and marshmallows are dissolved. Remove mixture from heat. Cool to setting point, stir in chopped cherries and lastly fold in stiffly-beaten egg whites. Turn into a soufflé dish or sundae glasses. Decorate with chopped almonds, whipped cream, glacé cherries and angelica.

## SOUFFLÉS

These may be savoury or sweet, served hot or cold. Cold soufflés are very like mousses.

For a basic recipe for a sweet soufflé, see Milanaise Soufflé. For other soufflés, *see the recipe for the flavour desired, e.g. Apricot soufflé, Cheese soufflé.*

## SOUPS

Soup-making is unfortunately neglected in British domestic cookery. To serve soup means, more often than not, to open a can and reheat its contents. Good as canned soups are, they do not—to quote Mrs Beeton herself—"offer the same opportunities of utilizing material that must otherwise be wasted" as fresh ingredients.

### Soup in the Menu

Soup may be the first course in a dinner in which two or more other courses are to follow; or it may be the main course of a simpler meal—a peasant-style lunch, light supper or snack meal. The soup that acts as the forerunner of a meal must be light and stimulate the appetite rather than satisfy it. The soup that forms the main course of a meal should contain a high proportion of solid foods; it may be almost as much a stew as a soup, for example, Scots Broth or the French Pot-au-Feu.

### Soups, Classified

Although there are hundreds of different soups, they can be divided into a few simple categories.

There are two main groups of soups, thin soups and thick soups. These may be subdivided thus: thin soups into broths and clear soups; thick soups into purées and thickened soups and bisques. There are also some unclassifiable or "national" soups.

### Kinds of Soups

**(a) Broths** are the uncleared liquids in which mutton, beef, veal, rabbit, sheep's head or chicken have been cooked. They are not thickened but may have such a large proportion of small pieces of meat, vegetables and pearl barley or rice that they are confused with thick soups.

**(b) Clear Soups** are made from good first stock and if cleared with egg white are known as consommés. Consommés must be sparkling clear; they may vary in colour from pale fawn to deep golden-brown according to the kind of meat used and they are always garnished. They take their distinguishing names from the different garnishes, of which there is an enormous variety.

(c) **Purées** are soups in which the main ingredients are sieved to make them thick. They may also have additional thickening, like thickened soups. Purées are not garnished but are usually served with an accompaniment of croûtons of fried or toasted bread, or some form of rusked bread handed separately.
(d) **Thickened Soups** are thickened by various added ingredients, the chief of which are:

cereal foods, such as flour, cornflour, arrowroot, barley, rice flour, semolina or fine tapioca.
white or brown roux
kneaded butter and flour
egg yolk mixed with milk or cream
cream
blood (little used except for hare soup)

(e) **Bisques** are fish soups.

In French cookery, thickened soups in which the main liquid ingredient is stock in which the flavourings used have been cooked are called Veloutés. When the thickening agent is mixed into a white or Béchamel sauce, and the flavourings are put into this, the soup is called a Crême. In English cookery, however:
(f) **Cream Soup** is any thick soup, whether a purée or a thickened soup, which has had cream added to it.

### Proportions Used in Soup-Making

**Meat:** For first stock and meat purées and broths: 1 lb. meat to 1 quart water.

**Vegetables:** 2 lb. vegetables to 1 quart stock *or* water.

**Pulses:** 4 oz. dry pulse to 1 quart stock *or* water.

**Thickening:** 1 oz. starchy ingredient to 1 quart of finished soup.

Approximately 2 egg yolks and ⅛ pint cream to each quart, but this may vary widely according to personal taste and economy.

2 oz. roux or kneaded butter and flour to each quart.

*See also Stock for Soups and Sauces.*

### Accompaniments for Soups

Accompaniments are usually handed separately.

**Forcemeat Balls** are served with meat purées, notably with hare soup.

**Croûtons of Bread:** Tiny cubes of bread, fried in deep or shallow fat, served hot, golden brown. Or baked croûtons made by buttering a ¼-in. thick slice of bread, cutting it into cubes, arranging these, butter side up, on a tin and baking them in a moderate oven oven till golden and crisp.

**Sippets or Croûtons of Toast:** The toast to be fairly thin, crisp and golden, cut into fingers or tiny cubes.

**Fairy Toast:** Bread cut into very thin slices, baked in a slow oven till golden and very crisp.

**Melba Toast:** Bread toasted golden on both sides, then carefully split into two thicknesses and slowly dried till crisp.

**Pulled Bread:** The inside of a French roll pulled with a fork out of the crust, torn into rough pieces which are then dried in a slow oven until pale golden and very crisp. The crusts cut into fingers and dried make delicious rusks.

**Grated Cheese:** Handed with Minestrone and other mixed vegetable soups.

**Sour Cream:** Handed with Bortsch and with other Polish, Russian or Hungarian soups.

### Clear Soups

For consommé it is essential to use stock made from raw meat, i.e. First Brown Stock; this is cleared by either of the two following methods except where otherwise stated in the recipes. The albumen in the egg whites coagulates at 160° F., and as the hardened particles rise to the surface they carry with them all the insoluble substances with which they come in contact, forming a thick "crust" of foam. The soup is then strained through a finely-woven linen cloth, the foam "crust" covers the bottom of the cloth and acts as a filter.

#### TO CLEAR FIRST BROWN STOCK

| | |
|---|---|
| **1 qt. stock (cold and free from fat)** | **¼ pt. water** |
| **1 small onion, scalded** | **1 egg white** |
| **1 small carrot** | **⅛ teasp. salt** |
| **1 small stick of celery** | **4 peppercorns** |
| **¼ lb. lean shin of beef** | **Small piece of blade mace** |

*Method 1.* Scrub and peel vegetables and rinse them thoroughly. Scrape the lean beef

into fine shreds with a sharp knife, discarding every scrap of fat, soak the beef in the water for ¼ hr. Put all the ingredients into a deep pan with the stock and whisk over moderate heat till almost boiling. Remove the whisk and let the stock boil till the froth rises to the top of the pan, then cover the pan and infuse the contents for ½ hr. Strain very slowly through a dry, finely-woven linen cloth.

**6 helpings (with garnish)**
**Cooking time—about 35 min.**

*Method 2.* Using the recipe above, prepare vegetables, shred and soak the beef as directed, beat the egg white. Put all the ingredients into a pan and bring them very slowly to simmering point. Simmer, without stirring or whisking, very gently for 1 hr. Strain as above.

NOTE: This method gives a better flavour and is almost as clear as the first.

**Cooking time—1 hr.**

## SOUPS FOR INVALIDS

*See Invalid Cookery and the Recipe for the type or flavour of soup desired.*

## SOUR CHERRY SOUP—SCANDINAVIA

**1 lb. morello *or* other acid variety of cherry**
**Pinch of cinnamon**
**1 pt. water**
**To each pint of sieved soup: ½ oz. cornflour, arrowroot *or* minute tapioca**
**3–4 oz. sugar to taste**
**¼ pt. white *or* red wine (optional)**
**A little lemon rind**
**Whipped cream (optional)**

Halve the cherries and crack some of the stones. Put the cherries, stones, cinnamon and water into a pan and simmer till the cherries are soft. Rub the fruit through a hair or nylon sieve. Blend the cornflour with a little wine or water and stir it into the soup. Reboil and stir the soup till it thickens. Sweeten, add the wine (if used) and grated lemon rind. The soup may be served hot or iced.

Whipped cream (served separately) makes a delicious accompaniment.

NOTE: Other suitable fruits are **damsons, cranberries**, white or red **currants, apples** *or* **rosehips.**

**4 helpings**
**Cooking time—about 20 min.**

## SOUR MILK BREAD

**1 lb. plain flour**
**1 teasp. salt**
**1 round *or* 2 level teasp. bicarbonate of soda**
**1 round *or* 2 level teasp. cream of tartar**
**½ pt. sour milk *or* buttermilk (approx.)**
**2 oz. lard may be rubbed in; this makes a better keeping bread**

Sift the flour and salt, and, if required, rub in the fat. Add the soda and tartar, making quite sure that all the lumps are sifted out of the soda. Mix to a light spongy dough with the milk. Divide the dough and form into two round cakes. Place on a greased baking sheet and bake in a hot oven **(450°–425° F., Gas 8–7).**

**2 loaves** **Cooking time—30 min.**

## SOUR–SWEET SAUCE

**2 onions**
**1½ oz. butter *or* margarine**
**1½ oz. flour**
**¾ pt. water *or* stock**
**4 tablesp. vinegar**
**1–2 teasp. any good commercial bottled sauce**
**2 tablesp. sugar**
**1 level teasp. French mustard**
**1 level teasp. yeast *or* meat extract**
**Salt and pepper**

Chop the onions, put into a saucepan and fry them till tender and golden-brown in the butter. Add the flour and brown it a very little. Stir in the liquid, bring to the boil, stirring all the time. Add the other ingredients and simmer the sauce for 15–20 min.

Serve with boiled beef or other meat, fish or vegetables.

## SOUSED FISH

*Poissons marinés*

**1¼ lb. boiled fish *or* other fish left over**
**½ gill fish stock**
**½ gill vinegar**
**A few leaves of fennel (if obtainable)**
**2 bay leaves**
**2 cloves**
**1 dozen peppercorns**
**2 slices of lemon**
**Salt**
**Chopped parsley**

Place the neatest pieces of fish in a deep dish.

Boil up the fish stock with an equal quantity of vinegar, and the herbs, cloves, peppercorns, lemon and seasoning. Pour over the fish, turn fish over gently from time to time so that the seasoning gets thoroughly saturated. Serve in a little of the vinegar liquid—garnished with chopped parsley.

**4 helpings**

## SOUSED HERRINGS

*Harengs marinés*

**8 fresh herrings**
**1 Spanish onion**
**Salt and pepper**
**1 bay leaf**
**1 level dessertsp. mixed pickling spice**
**Vinegar**

Wash and scale the herrings, cut off the heads, split the herrings open and remove the gut and backbone. Put a slice of onion in the centre of each fish, roll up tightly, beginning with the neck. Pack the herrings closely in a pie-dish, sprinkle with salt, pepper, bay leaf and spice, half fill the dish with equal quantities of vinegar and water, and bake in a moderate oven (**350° F., Gas 4**) for 40 min.

Serve cold with salad, or cut up for hors d'œuvres; or eat plain, hot or cold, with bread and butter.

**6 helpings**

## SPAGHETTI ALLA BOLOGNESE

Spaghetti Bolognese

**1 onion**
**1 small carrot**
**1 stick of celery**
**1 clove of garlic (optional)**
**2 tablesp. olive oil**
**1 oz. butter**
**1 bay leaf**
**4 oz. minced raw beef (fillet if possible)**
**1 glass dry Italian wine**
**8 peeled tomatoes**
**2 tablesp. tomato paste**
**Meat extract**
**Seasoning**
**12 oz. spaghetti**
**Grated Parmesan cheese**

Chop the onion, carrot, celery and garlic very finely, place in a small saucepan with the oil, butter and bay leaf, and fry for 5 min., then add the meat, wine, tomatoes and tomato paste, with meat extract and seasoning to taste. Cook slowly for ½ hr. Meanwhile cook the spaghetti in plenty of boiling salted water for 20 min. Drain, put in a hot serving dish and add the sauce, mix well, and serve with grated cheese.

## SPANISH SALAD

**1 large Spanish onion**
**1 cucumber**
**6 firm tomatoes**
**Salt and pepper**
**French dressing**
**2 tablesp. grated Parmesan cheese**
**6 stoned Spanish olives**

Cut the onion into very thin slices. Slice the cucumber finely and the tomato into thicker slices. Arrange in layers, seasoning each layer, and sprinkling it with French dressing and grated cheese. Garnish with stoned olives.

**6 helpings**

## SPICE CAKE

*Gâteau aux Quatre Épices*

**8 oz. plain flour**
**⅛ teasp. salt**
**3 oz. margarine**
**1 teasp. mixed spice**
**3 oz. sugar**
**1½ teasp. baking-powder**
**1 egg**
**1–1½ gills milk** *or* **enough to make a soft dropping consistency**

Grease a 6-in. cake-tin and line the bottom with greaseproof paper.

Sift flour, salt and spice into a bowl, cut in fat with a round-bladed knife, then rub with finger tips till quite fine. Add sugar and baking-powder. Mix with egg and milk to a soft dropping consistency. Put into the cake-tin and bake in a fairly hot oven (**375° F., Gas 5**).

NOTE: Self-raising flour may be used with advantage in the above recipe, in which case omit the baking-powder.

**Cooking time—1¼ hr.**

## SPICED BEEF

*Confit de Viande*

**3–4 lb. pickled beef**
**1 small teasp. black pepper**
**½ teasp. ground ginger**
**A good pinch of powdered cloves**
**A good pinch of powdered nutmeg**
**A good pinch of powdered mace**
**½ pt. stock** *or* **wine and stock**

Drain the beef from the pickle and wash well. Mix together the pepper, ginger, cloves, nutmeg and mace and sprinkle over the entire surface of the meat. Roll and tie the meat securely into a good shape and put in a baking-dish. Pour over the wine and stock. Cover with 2 or 3 thicknesses of greased greaseproof paper and put on the lid. As no more liquid is added it is essential to cover well and to cook very slowly. Cook in the oven for about 2 hr. Then press between 2 boards or dishes until cold.

### SPICED HAM WITH RAISIN SAUCE

| | |
|---|---|
| **1 smoked ham** | **½ cup vinegar** *or* |
| **½ lb. brown sugar** | **rough cider** |
| **Whole cloves** | |

Bake the ham, uncovered, in a very cool oven **(290° F., Gas 1)**. One half hour before meat is done remove rind from ham, cover ham with brown sugar, stick with cloves 1 in. apart and pour vinegar or cider over ham. Continue baking, basting with drippings.

Serve hot with Raisin Sauce. Equally good served cold.

**One 8-lb. ham sufficient for 20 helpings**
**Cooking time—20–30 min. per lb.**

#### RAISIN SAUCE

| | |
|---|---|
| **3 oz. brown sugar** | **1¾ cups boiling water** |
| **1 oz. flour** | **¼ cup vinegar** |
| **½ oz. dry mustard** | **2 oz. seedless raisins** |
| **Pinch of salt and pepper** | **1 oz. butter** |

Mix dry ingredients in the top of a double saucepan and add water and vinegar gradually, stirring all the time. Cook slowly 15–20 min. Add raisins and cook a further 5 min.; then add the butter. Serve hot.

### SPICED LAMB ROLL

*Roulade d'Agneau aux fines herbes*

| | |
|---|---|
| **2 small breasts of lamb** | **1 saltsp. saltpetre** |
| **6 oz. salt** | **1 large onion** |
| **2 teasp. brown sugar** | **¼ teasp. pepper** |

*Method 1.* Boil 2 pt. of water with the salt, sugar and saltpetre until dissolved. When cool put in a deep bowl. Bone and trim the breasts and remove surplus fat. Place skin side down and sprinkle the inside with finely-chopped onion and pepper. Roll tightly, starting from narrow end. Sew up with a darning needle and coarse white cotton. Put in the cold brine with a plate on top to keep the meat under the surface of the brine. Leave for 2 days, in a cool place or refrigerator. Then drain well. Boil in plain water for 2–3 hr. until tender. Drain and press between 2 plates with a weight on top. Leave until cold and serve thinly sliced with salad.

**6 helpings**
**Time—2 days to pickle**
**2–3 hr. to cook**

*Method 2.* The pickling for 2 days can be omitted, if preferred. In which case the meat is seasoned and rolled as above but should then be cooked in water to which the following have been added: any bones and meat trimmings; parsley; and a pinch of herbs, 4 cloves, 10 peppercorns, and a bay leaf tied in muslin. Cooking time as above.

### SPICED PINEAPPLE UPSIDE-DOWN CAKE

| | |
|---|---|
| **4 oz. butter** | **1 lb. self-raising flour** |
| **12 oz. brown sugar** | **1 teasp. cinnamon** |
| **1 large can pineapple slices** | **1 teasp. nutmeg** |
| | **2 eggs** |
| **10 maraschino cherries** | **½ cup milk** |

Melt half of butter in baking-tin; add half of sugar; stir until dissolved. Drain the pineapple slices and arrange in a neat pattern on the caramel coating. Place a cherry in the centre hole of each pineapple slice. Sift together the flour and spices. Beat eggs with remaining brown sugar; add milk and remaining butter, melted; stir into spiced flour. Pour over pineapple in tin. Bake in a moderate oven **(350° F., Gas 4)** for 45–50 min. Remove tin from oven and invert on to serving plate, leave the tin on for a few minutes so that caramel will run down over cake and not stick to tin.

Remove tin and serve cake warm with cream.

#### APRICOT OR PEACH UPSIDE-DOWN CAKE

Use drained, canned apricot or peach halves instead of pineapple slices, flavour with vanilla essence and omit spices.

### SPICED VINEGAR FOR PICKLES

Buy only the best bottled vinegar for pickling; this should have an acetic acid content of at least 5%. It is false economy to buy cheap barrelled vinegar: if—as is often the case—the percentage of acetic acid is too low the pickles will not keep.

For exhibition, white vinegar is often recommended because it shows off the colour and texture of the pickle, but for home use, the flavour of malt vinegar is generally preferred.

To make spiced vinegar, add to 1 qt. of vinegar; $\frac{1}{2}$ oz. cloves, $\frac{1}{2}$ oz. allspice, $\frac{1}{2}$ oz. ginger, $\frac{1}{2}$ oz. cinnamon, $\frac{1}{2}$ oz. white pepper.

NOTE: All the above spices should be whole, not ground. Buy them fresh. If you find this spice too strong, the quantities can be reduced—even halved.

Steep the spices in the unheated vinegar for 1–2 months. Shake the bottle occasionally. Then strain and re-cork the bottle until needed.

*Quick method:* If the spiced vinegar is wanted immediately, put the spices and vinegar into a basin. Cover the basin with a plate and stand it in a sauce-pan of cold water. Bring the water to the boil, remove the pan from the heat, and allow the spices to remain in the warm vinegar for about 2 hr. Keep the plate on top of the basin so that no flavour is lost. Strain the vinegar and it will be ready to use, either cold or hot according to the recipe.

## SPICES

*See Flavourings and Spices.*

## SPINACH—ITALIAN STYLE

*Épinards à l'Italienne*

**2 lb. spinach**
**2 tablesp. olive oil**
**1 clove of garlic**
**Salt and pepper**
**1 oz. sultanas**
**1 oz. pine kernel nuts**

Cook the spinach, press out the water well, and chop the spinach coarsely. Warm the oil in a wide pan. Add the spinach, finely-chopped garlic, salt and pepper. Turn the spinach over and over in the pan to heat it thoroughly without frying it. Add the sultanas, washed in boiling water to make them plump, and the nuts.

Reheat and serve hot.

**4–6 helpings**
**Cooking time—about 30 min.**

## SPINACH WITH POACHED EGGS

*Épinards au œufs pochés*

**Spinach purée**
**6 poached eggs**
**Fleurons of pastry** *or* **crescents of fried bread**

Poach the eggs in as plump a form as possible. Trim the edges and put the trimmings on the bottom of a hot dish. Serve the spinach on top, flattening the surface. Arrange the poached eggs on it, garnish the base with fleurons of pastry *or* crescents of fried bread.

## SPONGE CAKES—SMALL

**3 oz. plain flour**
**Pinch of salt**
**3 eggs**
**3 oz. sugar**
**1 level teasp. baking-powder**
**½ teasp. vanilla essence**

As for Sponge Cake. Put the mixture into oblong sponge cake-tins prepared by greasing and dusting with equal quantities of flour and castor sugar. Half-fill the tins and dredge the tops with castor sugar. Bake in a moderate oven (**350°–335° F., Gas 4–3**) until well risen, firm and a pale fawn colour.

**10–12 cakes** **Cooking time—20 min.**

## SPONGE CAKE

*Gâteau mousseline*

**4 oz. plain flour**
**Pinch of salt**
**3 eggs**
**4½ oz. castor sugar**
**Grated lemon rind**

Grease and dust a 6-in tin with 1 teasp. flour and 1 teasp. castor sugar mixed together. Sift the flour and salt. Beat the eggs and sugar over a pan of hot water till thick and creamy. Fold flour, salt and lemon lightly into the egg and turn the mixture into the tin. Bake in a warm oven (**335° F., Gas 3**). When cold, split the sponge and spread with jam. Dust with icing sugar.

This may be cooked in a border or other mould if to be used as the base of a sweet.

**Cooking time—45 min.**

## SPOTTED DICK

*Pouding aux raisins de Corinthe*

**12 oz. plain flour**
**2 rounded teasp. baking-powder**
**Pinch of salt**
**6 oz. finely-chopped suet**
**4 oz. castor sugar**
**6 oz. currants**
**Milk to mix**

Sift together the flour, baking-powder and salt. Add the suet. sugar and fruit and mix with the milk to a soft dough. Form into a roll and turn on to a well-floured cloth. Roll up the cloth loosely, and tie at both ends, leaving enough room for the pudding to swell. Drop into boiling water and simmer for 2 hr; *or* steam for 2½ hr.

Serve with custard *or* lemon sauce.

**6 helpings**

## SPREADS, SAVOURY

*See Savouries (Appetizers).*

## SPRING BROTH

**12 spring onions**
**4 young carrots**
**1 young, small turnip**
**A few head of "sprue" asparagus**
**¾ oz. butter *or* 2 small tablesp. olive oil**
**½ pt. shelled green peas**
**1 qt. stock, preferably white**
**Salt and pepper**
**2 teasp. chopped parsley**

Cut the onions and carrots into thin rings and the turnip into ¼-in. dice. Remove the tips of the asparagus, to be added later, and cut the stalks into ¼-in. lengths, using only the tender part. Melt the butter and in it cook the vegetables over very gentle heat. Keep the pan covered, shake it vigorously every few minutes and continue cooking without browning for about 10 min. Add the stock, boiling, and simmer all for ½ hr., add the asparagus and cook for a further ¼ hr. Season and add the chopped parsley just before serving.

**4–6 helpings** **Cooking time—55 min.**

## SPUN SUGAR

**1 lb. loaf sugar**
**½ pt. water**
**½ saltsp. cream of tartar**

Dissolve the sugar in the water in a sugar boiler or pan, and boil to the "large crack" degree (**312° F.**). Add the cream of tartar, reduce the heat, repeatedly test the consistency of the syrup with a tablespoon, and use as soon as it runs in a fine thread from the spoon to the pan.

*To spin sugar:* Take in the left hand a large knife previously oiled, hold it in a horizontal position, take a spoonful of syrup and spin the sugar into fine threads by moving the spoon to and fro over the flat blade of the knife.

To spin sugar successfully it must be done in a dry atmosphere, and the worker must avoid standing in a draught.

## SQUARE WALNUT CAKE

*Gâteau carré aux Noix*

**4 oz. butter *or* margarine**
**4 oz. sugar**
**3 eggs**
**5 oz. self-raising flour**
**1 level teasp. baking-powder**
**Pinch of salt**
**1½ oz. chopped walnuts**

FILLING

**3 tablesp. ground almonds**
**1 teasp. vanilla essence**
**1 tablesp. chopped walnuts**
**2–3 tablesp. sieved apricot jam**

DECORATION

**Glacé icing using 10 oz. icing sugar**
**Halved walnuts**
**Glacé cherries**

Grease an 8-in. square sandwich tin and line the bottom with greaseproof paper.

Cream the fat and sugar till light and white, add beaten egg gradually, beating well between each addition. Sift flour, baking-powder and salt and stir into the mixture with the walnuts. Put into the sandwich tin. Bake in a moderate oven (**350° F., Gas 4**).

Beat together all ingredients for the filling. When cake is cold, cut through the middle, spread with the filling and sandwich together again. Ice with white glacé icing; use some of the icing to pipe squares on the top and place a walnut and a glacé cherry alternately in the squares.

NOTE: The sides may be brushed with apricot glaze *or* cream and coated with chopped walnuts, the top only being iced with glacé icing.

**Cooking time—40–50 min.**

## STEAK

*See Beef.*

## STEAK PUDDING

*Pouding de Steak, cuit au Four*

**½ lb. good stewing**
**Dripping**

1

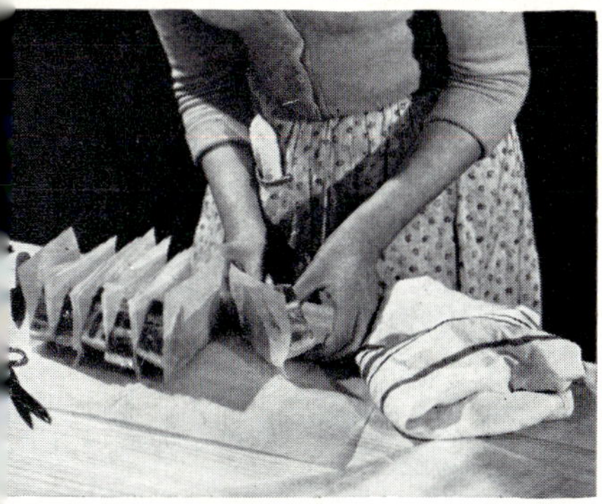

2

3

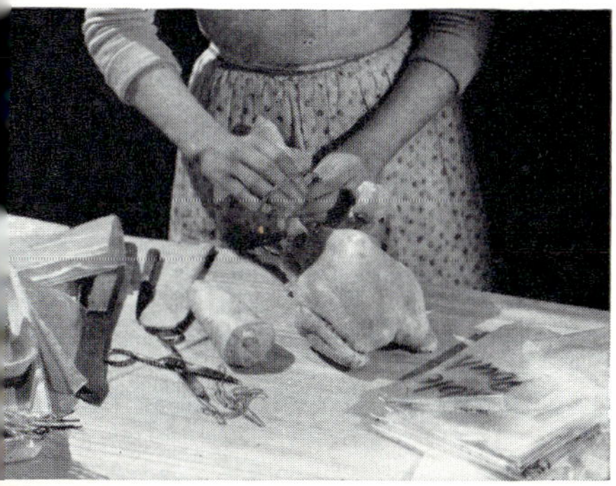

4

5

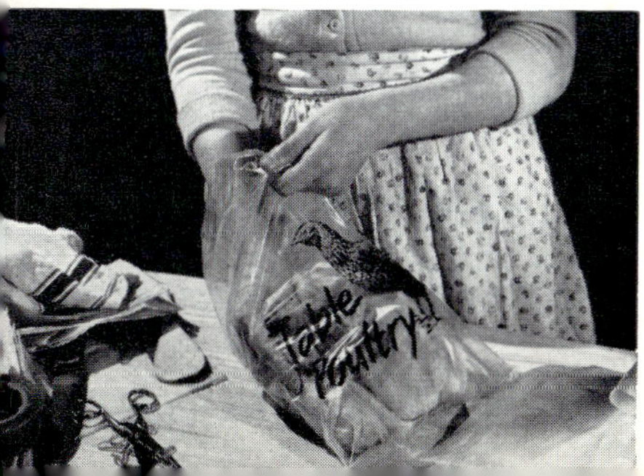

6

7

Quick Freezing.

1 Meat is cut into portions suitable for use. Wrap large pieces of meat in moisture-vapour-proof covers. Turn in the edges and seal with special sealing tape or by heat.

2 Separate small cuts by 2 pieces of greaseproof paper so that number needed can be removed without defrosting rest.

3 After sealing, over-wrap with a mutton cloth or similar wrapping to protect them from damage in the home freezer.

4 Before freezing, prepare poultry ready for cooking. Wrap sharp ends to protect container. Wrap giblets separately.

5 Place the bird in a suitable container, e.g. plastic bag. Place the giblets by the side, expel the air and seal.

6 Blanched and cooled vegetables may be packed in various types of containers—polythene bag, box with grooved lid.

7 Shows how peas blanched, drained and cooled, are placed in a bag, then the air is expelled and the bag sealed.

8 Fruits—in this case strawberries, packed in a polythene bag, covered with syrup, the air expelled and bag sealed.

8

Roast lamb is always a Sunday favourite.

| | |
|---|---|
| **steak** | **6 oz. flour** |
| **½ lb. ox kidney** | **2 eggs** |
| **Salt and pepper** | **¾ pt. milk** *or* **water** |

Cut the steak into finger-shaped pieces. Cut the kidney into thin slices and season well. Fry the steak for a few minutes in the dripping to seal the surface. Mix the flour, eggs and milk or water into a smooth batter and season. Melt about ½ oz. dripping in a casserole or pie-dish and put in ½ the batter and bake until set. Place the steak and the kidney on top of the batter, fill up the dish with the remainder of the batter and bake in a hot oven **(425° F., Gas 7)** for 10 min.; then reduce to moderate **(350° F., Gas 4)** for about 1 hr. until set and well browned. Serve with a good gravy.

**6 helpings**

## STEAMED BATTER PUDDING

| | |
|---|---|
| **1 pt. milk** | **2 eggs** |
| **¼ teasp. salt** | **½ lb. plain flour** |

Prepare the mixture as in previous recipe. Pour it into a well-greased pudding basin. Cover with a greased paper and steam for 2 hr.

Serve with a fruit- or sweet-sauce.

**6 helpings** **Cooking time—2 hr.**

## STEAMED CUSTARDS

*See Custard and Custard Mixtures.*

## STEAMED PUDDINGS

*See Puddings.*

## STEAMING

*See Cooking Methods*

## STEAMING FISH

*See Fish*

## STEWED BREAST OF VEAL

| | |
|---|---|
| **2½ lb. breast of veal** | **12 peppercorns** |
| **2 onions** | **Salt** |
| **2 small carrots** | **1 pt. parsley sauce** *or* |
| **1 small turnip** | **piquant sauce** |

Wipe the meat and place in a pan with as much cold water as will cover it. Bring to the boil and skim. Add the vegetables, cut into dice, peppercorns and salt to taste. Cover with

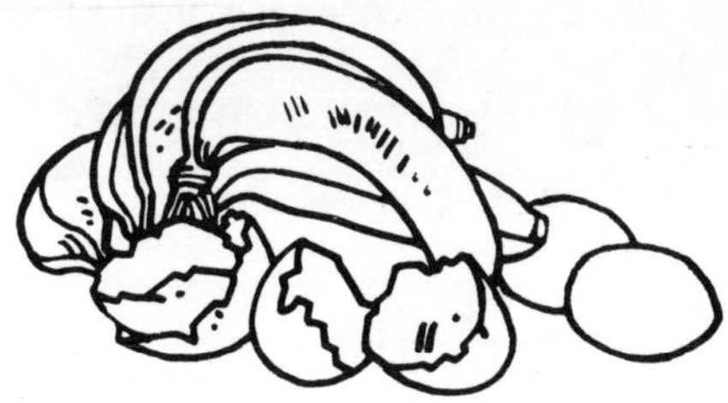

a well fitting lid and simmer gently for 2½–3 hr. Prepare the sauce using some of the veal stock. Place the veal on a hot dish, pour over sufficient sauce to cover the meat and serve the remainder in a sauce-boat.

**6 helpings**

## STEWED BRISKET OF BEEF

*Poitrine de Bœuf à la Bourgeoise*

| | |
|---|---|
| **3 lb. brisket of beef** | **2–3 sticks of celery (optional)** |
| **Vinegar** | |
| **Salt and pepper** | **1 blade of mace** |
| **2 carrots** | **10 peppercorns** |
| **2 onions** | **Bouquet garni** |
| **1 turnip** | **1 oz. butter** *or* **fat** |
| | **1 oz. flour** |

Wipe and trim the meat, rub it over with vinegar and salt and leave for 2–3 hr. Put into a stewpan, barely cover with water, add salt, bring to the boil and skim well. Cover with a well-fitting lid, simmer gently for ½ hr., then add the vegetables cut in large slices, mace, peppercorns and a bouquet garni and cook as slowly as possible for another 1½ hr. Melt the fat in a small saucepan, add the flour and cook slowly, stirring until nut brown. Take out the meat, remove the bones and place the meat on a hot dish; remove the vegetables. Strain the stock and add to the contents of the small saucepan. Season, stir until boiling and boil well for 4 min. Serve the vegetables with the meat and the sauce in a gravy boat.

## STEWED CORN

*Maïs bouilli*

| | |
|---|---|
| **6 ears** *or* **cobs of corn, freshly picked** | **1 oz. flour** |
| | **¾ pt. milk** |
| **1 oz. butter** | **Salt and pepper** |

Prepare the corn.

Place the grains in a saucepan, with sufficient boiling water to cover, and cook gently 15–20 min. Drain well. Make a sauce with the flour, fat and milk. Season well. Stir in the corn and when thoroughly hot, serve.

**6 helpings**

## STEWED or BRAISED DUCK

*Canard en Ragôut*

| | |
|---|---|
| **1 duck** | **1½ oz. butter** |
| **2 onions, sliced** | **1½ oz. flour** |
| **2 sage leaves** | **1 pt. brown stock** |
| **Bouquet garni** | **Salt and pepper** |

Truss duck, roast it in a hot oven (**425°–450° F., Gas 7–8**) for 20 min. Place in a saucepan with herbs and onions, cover tightly and cook slowly for ¾ hr. Melt butter, add flour and brown well, stir in stock, simmer 20 min. and strain. When duck is tender, remove trussing strings. Add sediment from pan to the sauce; season and serve in a sauce-boat.

Some mushrooms may be added to the sauce if desired.

**4–5 helpings**
**Cooking time—about 1¼ hr.**

## STEWED DUCK (Whole)

*Canard à l'Anglaise*

| | |
|---|---|
| **1 duck** | **1 pt. stock** |
| **Fat for basting** | **4 sage leaves** |
| **2 onions** | **2–3 strips lemon-thyme** |
| **2 oz. butter** | **Salt and pepper** |
| **1½ oz. flour** | |

Truss duck, baste with hot fat, cook in a hot oven (**425°–450° F., Gas 7–8**) until well-browned, basting frequently. Slice onions, fry until golden brown in butter, remove them, and brown the flour in the butter. Place duck in a large saucepan, barely cover it with hot stock, add fried onions, sage and lemon-thyme. Cover with a closely-fitting lid, and simmer gently until tender—about ¾ hr. When duck is cooked, strain sauce from pan, and stir ¾ pt. of it into the brown roux; stir until boiling, cook 5 min. and season.

Serve the duck with gravy and 1 pt. green peas, handed separately.

**4–5 helpings**
**Cooking time—1¼–1½ hr.**

## STEWED FOWL—WITH RICE

*Poulet au Riz.*

| | |
|---|---|
| **1 fowl** | **Bouquet garni** |
| **2 onions** | **4 oz. rice** |
| **3–4 sticks of celery** | **Salt and pepper** |
| **2 pt. stock** | |

Slice the vegetables and place a few pieces inside the body of the fowl. Truss the bird for boiling, place in a large saucepan or casserole, add the stock and bring to boiling point. Add remainder of vegetables, and bouquet garni, tied in muslin. Cover closely, and cook very gently for 1 hr., then add well-washed rice and seasoning. Continue cooking gently until fowl and rice are tender—about 2 hr. The rice should absorb nearly all the stock. Dish the fowl, removing strings. Remove vegetables and bouquet garni from the rice, correct the seasoning of this, and serve with the bird.

**5–6 helpings** **Cooking time—about 2–2½ hr.**

## STEWED LAMB

*Ragoût d'Agneau*

| | |
|---|---|
| **1½–2 lb. loin, neck *or* breast** | **2 sprigs of mint** |
| **1 oz. dripping** | **Stock *or* water** |
| **A few young carrots** | **Peas** |
| **1 onion** | **1 oz. flour** |
| **Bouquet garni (parsley, thyme, bay leaf, 6 pepper-corns)** | **Salt and pepper** |

Trim the meat and cut into portions suitable for serving. Heat the dripping in a stewpan and put in the meat, diced vegetables, and the bouquet garni and mint tied in muslin. Cover closely and cook very gently for 10 min., stirring occasionally. Add stock or water just to cover the meat, cover closely and simmer gently until tender (about 2 hr.). About ½ hr. before cooked, add the peas a few at a time so that the temperature is not much reduced. Blend the flour to a smooth paste with a little cold water, add some of the hot liquid from the pan and stir well. Return to the stewpan and stir until boiling. When cooked, remove the herbs, season to taste and serve hot.

**6 helpings**

## STEWED LETTUCE

*Laitue au Jus*

**6 small lettuces**
**1 oz. butter *or* margarine**
**1 oz. flour**
**½ pt. stock**
**1 dessertsp. chopped chives**
**1 bay leaf**
**1 dessertsp. chopped parsley**
**Salt and pepper**

Wash the lettuces well. Plunge into boiling salt water and simmer 2 min. Plunge into cold water, drain. Melt the butter in a saucepan, add the flour, mix well, then add stock and stir until smooth and thick. Add chives, bay leaf, parsley, and a little salt and put in the lettuces. Cook gently for ½ hr., stirring from time to time. Re-season and serve.

**6 helpings**
**Cooking time— ½ hr. (approx.)**

## STEWED MUSHROOMS

*Champignons à la crème*

**1 lb. flap *or* button mushrooms**
**2 oz. butter *or* margarine**
**1 dessertsp. arrowroot**
**¼ pt. stock**
**Lemon juice**
**2 tablesp. cream**
**Salt and pepper**
**Chopped parsley**
**Fleurons of pastry**

Wash and peel the mushrooms, trim the stalks. Melt the butter in a saucepan and fry the mushrooms in it slowly, about 10 min. Blend the arrowroot with the stock. Add to the pan and stir till boiling. Simmer 20–30 min. Add lemon juice and cream and season carefully. Dish and garnish with parsley and fleurons of pastry.

NOTE: This mixture may be used to fill small French rolls.

**6 helpings**
**Cooking time—30–40 min.**

## STEWED ONIONS

*Oignons au jus*

**6 large onions**
**1 pt. brown stock**
**Salt and pepper**
**Small bunch of herbs**

Peel the onions and blanch them. Put them into a pan which will just hold them standing side by side. Add the stock, bunch of herbs, and a little salt and put on the lid of the pan. Simmer gently 1½ hr. Season and serve in a hot dish with the cooking liquid poured round.

**6 helpings**
**Cooking time—about 1½ hr.**

## STEWED OX KIDNEY

*Ragoût de Rognons*

**1½ lb. ox kidney**
**2 oz. seasoned flour**
**2 oz. dripping**
**1 onion**
**1½ pt. water *or* stock**
**3 teasp. tomato *or* mushroom ketchup**
**Border of rice *or* mashed potatoes**
**Green peas**

Prepare the kidney as directed for Kidney Hot Pot. Coat the slices of kidney with seasoned flour. Heat the dripping in a stewpan and fry the kidney until browned on both sides. Chop the onion finely and fry at the same time until lightly browned. Stir in any remaining flour and brown. Add the stock and ketchup and stir until boiling. Cover with a lid and simmer very gently for about 1½–2 hr. If cooked too quickly the kidney will become tough. When ready re-season if necessary and serve on a hot dish with a border of rice or mashed potato. Garnish with green peas.

**6 helpings**

## STEWED OX TAIL

*Queues de Bœuf en Ragoût*

**2 small ox tails**
**2 oz. fat**
**2 onions**
**1½ oz. flour**
**1½ pt. stock *or* water**
**Salt and pepper**
**Bouquet garni**
**Cloves to taste**
**Mace to taste**
**Juice of ½ lemon**

GARNISH

**Croûtons of fried bread**
**Dice *or* Julienne strips of carrot and turnip**

Wash the tails, dry well and remove any superfluous fat. Cut into joints and divide the thick parts in half. Melt the fat in a saucepan, fry the pieces of tail until brown, then remove from the pan. Slice the onions and fry them until light brown, add the flour, mix well and fry slowly until a good brown colour. Add the stock or water, salt, pepper, bouquet garni, cloves and mace and bring to boiling point, stirring all the time. Return the pieces of tail and simmer gently for about 2½–3 hr. Remove the meat and arrange on a hot dish. Add the lemon juice to the sauce, correct the seasoning, strain and pour over the meat. Garnish with croûtons of fried bread and diced or thin strips of cooked carrot and turnip.

**6 helpings**

### STEWED RED CABBAGE

*Choux au Jambon*

| | |
|---|---|
| **1 small red cabbage** | **¼ pt. vinegar** |
| **1 slice of ham** | **Salt and pepper** |
| **½ oz. butter *or* margarine** | **1 tablesp. granulated sugar** |
| **1 pt. stock** | |

Soak, wash and slice the cabbage thinly. Put into a stewpan with the ham (diced), the butter, ½ pt. of stock, and the vinegar. Put on the lid and stew gently 1 hr. When very tender add the rest of the stock, sugar and seasoning. Mix and stir over heat until nearly all the liquor has dried away Serve at once.

This is an excellent dish to serve with sausages.

**6 helpings**
**Cooking time—1¼ hr.**

### STEWED SHEEP'S BRAINS

*Cervelles de Mouton*

| | |
|---|---|
| **3 sheep's brains** | **A small bunch of parsley** |
| **Salt and pepper** | **Stock** |
| **1 tablesp. vinegar** | **Croûtons of fried bread** |
| **3 bacon rashers** | **Matelote sauce** |
| **1 small onion** | **2 teasp. lemon juice** |
| **2 cloves** | |

Remove the skin from the brains with a little salt and soak in cold water for ½ hr. Have ready a saucepan of boiling water. Add the vinegar and some salt. Tie the brains lightly in muslin, and cook in the water for about 15 min., keeping just under boiling-point. Remove the muslin and place the brains in another saucepan with the bacon placed on top. Add the onion, stuck with the cloves, parsley and salt and pepper. Just cover the brains with stock and simmer gently for about 25 min. Have ready croûtons of fried bread and place the brains on them on a hot dish. Put the bacon on top of the brains and cover with matelote sauce to which the lemon juice has been added.

NOTE: Parsley sauce with lemon juice may be served instead of the matelote sauce, in which case a carrot and a bay leaf should be added to the other vegetables in the stock, and the bacon and cloves omitted.

**6 helpings**

### STEWED STEAK

*Ragoût de Steak*

| | |
|---|---|
| **1½ lb. stewing steak** | **1 large onion** |
| **2 large carrots** | **1½ oz. flour** |
| **2 large turnips** | **1½ pt. water *or* stock** |
| **1½ oz. fat** | **Salt and pepper** |

Wipe the meat, cut off any superfluous fat, and cut the meat into neat pieces. Cut the vegetables into dice or julienne strips and keep in water until required. Put the trimmings aside for adding to the stew. Heat the fat in a saucepan and when smoking hot, fry the meat until lightly browned on both sides, then remove from the pan. Slice the onion and fry until lightly coloured. Add the flour, mix well, and cook slowly until a good brown colour. Add the water or stock, the vegetable trimmings and stir until boiling. Season, replace the meat, cover with a tightly fitting lid and simmer gently for about 2–2½ hr. or until tender. Have ready the dice or strips of vegetable which have been cooked in boiling salted water. Arrange the meat in the centre of a hot dish, pour the stock over and garnish with the vegetables.

**6 helpings**

### STEWED or BRAISED TURKEY

*Dinde braisée*

| | |
|---|---|
| **1 small turkey** | **Bouquet garni** |
| **2–4 oz. butter** | **Salt and pepper** |
| **2 onions, sliced** | **Stock** |
| **2 carrots, sliced** | **2 slices streaky bacon** |
| **1 turnip, sliced** | |

Truss bird as for roasting Season . Melt butter in a large pan or roasting tin, and brown turkey in the fat. Remove turkey, place vegetables, bouquet garni and seasoning in pan, adding sufficient stock to almost cover the vegetables. Place turkey on bed of vegetables, lay bacon slices on the breast, cover and cook gently on top of the stove or in a moderate oven (**350° F., Gas 4**) until bird is tender. Remove trussing string, dish bird.

**8 helpings**

## STEWED VENISON

*Ragôut de Venaison*

| | |
|---|---|
| **Shoulder of venison** | **Salt and pepper** |
| **Thin slices of mutton fat** | **1½ pt. stock** |
| | **½ teasp. peppercorns** |
| **1 glass port (optional)** | **½ teasp. allspice** |

If port is used soak the mutton fat in it for 2–3 hr. Bone the venison, flatten with a cutlet-bat, season well, cover with slices of mutton fat. Roll up lightly, tie securely with tape, place in boiling stock together with bones, peppercorns, allspice and the port in which the fat was soaked. Simmer gently 3–3½ hr.

Serve with redcurrant jelly, handed separately.

**10–12 helpings**

## STEWING

*See Cooking Methods*

## STEWING FISH

*See Fish*

## STOCK FOR SOUPS AND SAUCES

This is the liquid which forms the base of a great many soups and sauces. It can be made with meat and vegetables, fish and vegetables or vegetables alone, suitably seasoned. For more detailed information on Stock, *see Bone Stock, Brown Stock and Soups.*

## STORING HERBS

*See Herbs.*

## STRAWBERRY JAM

| | |
|---|---|
| **3½ lb. hulled strawberries** | **Juice of 1 large lemon** |
| | **3 lb. sugar** |

Heat the strawberries and lemon juice gently in the pan, stirring constantly to reduce the volume. Add the sugar, stir till dissolved and boil until setting point is reached. Remove the scum. Leave the jam undisturbed to cool until a skin forms on the surface and the fruit sinks (about 20 min.). Stir gently to distribute the strawberries. Pour into warm, dry jars and cover immediately with waxed discs. Tie down when cold.

**Yield—5 lb.**

## STRAWBERRY SHORTCAKE

*Gâteau de Fraises*

| | |
|---|---|
| **8 oz. plain flour** | **4½ oz. margarine** |
| **⅛ teasp. salt** | **2 oz. sugar** |
| **Pinch of baking-powder** | **1 egg yolk** |
| **½ oz. ground almonds** | |

FILLING

| | |
|---|---|
| **1 pt. strawberries** | **1–2 gills whipped cream** |
| **Sugar to taste** | |

Sift flour, salt and baking-powder and mix with the ground almonds. Cream the fat and sugar and add egg yolk. Work in the flour mixture as for a cake of shortbread. Divide into three pieces and roll into rounds a good ¼ in. thick. Bake in a moderate oven (**350° F., Gas 4**) until golden brown, then allow to become cold. Crush strawberries slightly with sugar to taste and add a little whipped cream. Spread this on to the first round of shortcake, cover with the second round and so on finishing with a layer of strawberries. Pipe whipped cream on top and round edges. Decorate as desired.

**Cooking time—30–40 min.**

NOTE: Self-raising flour may be used if liked.

## STRAWBERRY SOUFFLÉ

*Soufflé de Fraises*

| | |
|---|---|
| **Strawberries to make ¼ pt. pulp** | **3 eggs** |
| | **2 oz. castor sugar** |
| **1½ oz. butter** | **A few drops of cochineal** |
| **2 oz. plain flour** | **½ lb. strawberries, cut into dice** |
| **¼ pt. cream *or* top of milk** | |

Butter a soufflé dish. Reduce strawberries to a ¼ pt. pulp by crushing them with a fork, sweeten to taste. Melt the butter, add the flour and cook for a few minutes. Stir in the milk *or* cream and continue cooking until the mixture thickens. Leave to cool. Beat in the egg yolks. Work in the strawberry pulp and sugar. Add a few drops of colouring if necessary and the ½ lb. diced strawberries. Stiffly whisk the egg whites and fold these into the mixture. Turn into the mould and bake in a fairly hot oven (**400° F., Gas 6**) 35–40 min.

Serve with a fruit syrup or sweet sauce.

**6–7 helpings**

## STRAWBERRY AND TOMATO SALAD

*Salade de fraises et tomates*

**¾ lb. firm strawberries**
**6 tomatoes**
**Salt**
**Paprika pepper**
**Lemon juice**
**Mayonnaise sauce**
**Lettuce heart**
**Thinly-sliced cucumber**

Cut the strawberries into quarters. Skin the tomatoes, cut in halves, remove the seeds and the pulp, then cut them into thin slices. (The tomato pulp may be sieved and used for cocktails, etc.) Season the slices with a little salt and the paprika pepper and sprinkle with lemon juice. Just before serving, mix the strawberries and tomatoes and put into a salad bowl. Add a little mayonnaise, barely to cover the fruit. Place the lettuce heart in the centre of the dish and garnish the base with thinly-sliced cucumber.

**6 helpings**

## STRAWBERRY TORTONI

**One 10-oz. carton whole strawberries (just thawed)**
**3–4 macaroons**
**¼ pt. double cream**
**1 egg white**
**Flavouring of kirsch *or* 1 teasp. lemon juice**

Crumble the macaroons coarsely, strain the syrup from the strawberries. Whip the cream until thick and fold in the stiffly-beaten egg white. Then fold in the kirsch or lemon juice, the syrup from the strawberries and finally the crumbled macaroons. Divide between 4 sundae dishes and stud the top with whole strawberries. This sweet should be prepared not longer than 1 hr. before serving.

## STRAWBERRY WHIP

*Gelée de Fraise fouettée*

**1 pt. strawberry jelly tablet**
**½ pt. strawberry juice**
**¼ pt. water**
**Sugar if necessary**

Proceed as for Lemon Whip.

## STUFFED CABBAGE

*Choux farcis*

**6 large leaves of cabbage**
**4 oz. cooked rice**
**2 teasp. very finely-chopped onion**
**4 oz. fresh minced meat**
**Powdered mace**
**Pepper and salt**
**Worcester sauce**
**Stock**
**Arrowroot**

Wash and boil the cabbage leaves for 5 min. in salt water. Drain. Mix the filling, moistening it with stock and flavouring it carefully. Form into rolls. Remove a little of the coarse vein of the cabbage leaves. Wrap each roll of filling in a cabbage leaf and tie with cotton or secure with a cocktail stick. Place in a saucepan, barely cover with stock, put on lid and simmer very gently 45 min. Lift on to a hot dish and thicken stock by boiling it with blended arrowroot (1 teasp. to ¼ pt. of stock). Season carefully. Pour sauce over cabbage rolls and serve immediately.

**6 helpings**
**Cooking time—about 1 hr. (approx.)**

## STUFFED CUCUMBERS

*Concombres farcis*

**2 large cucumbers**
**1 oz. margarine**
**½ lb. minced cold meat e.g. ham, veal, beef, chicken**
**2 heaped tablesp. fresh breadcrumbs**
**1 tablesp. finely-chopped parsley**
**¼ teasp. mixed herbs**
**1 egg**
**A little stock**
**Seasoning**
**Worcester sauce**
**Croûtes of fried bread**

Wash and peel the cucumbers and cut into 2-in. lengths. Scoop out the centres with a teaspoon. Steam until soft—about 15 min. While the cucumber is cooking, heat the margarine in a saucepan. Stir in the meat, breadcrumbs, parsley and herbs, heat thoroughly, add the beaten egg and enough stock to give a soft stuffing. Season well, adding Worcester sauce for extra flavour, if necessary. Drain the cucumber and put each piece on a croûte of bread. Fill with the hot stuffing, which should be piled up high. Garnish with chopped parsley.

Serve tomato sauce (**thick**) or brown sauce

6 helpings
Cooking time—35 min. approx.

## STUFFED DUCKLING

*Caneton à la Rouennaise*

| | |
|---|---|
| 1 large "Rouen" duckling | 3/4 pt. brown sauce |
| Fat for basting | Sections of 1 large orange |

STUFFING

| | |
|---|---|
| 1 chicken liver | Salt and pepper |
| 1 duckling liver | Nutmeg |
| 1/2 teasp. parsley | 1 oz. butter |
| 1/4 teasp. thyme | 1 egg |
| 3 oz. breadcrumbs | |

Blanch chicken and duckling livers, chop them finely, add herbs, breadcrumbs, melted butter, pinch of nutmeg, salt and pepper, then bind with egg. Stuff duckling with liver mixture; truss, baste well with hot fat, roast in hot oven (**425°–450° F., Gas 7–8**) for ½ hr., basting frequently. Drain off all fat, pour hot brown sauce into baking tin and continue cooking until duckling is tender—about 20 min. Baste frequently with sauce.

Serve on a hot dish. Strain a little sauce round, garnish with orange (heated in a little wine *or* stock, over a pan of hot water), and serve remainder of sauce separately.

4 helpings
Cooking time—1 hr.

## STUFFED FILLET OF PORK

| | |
|---|---|
| 2 lb. fillet of pork | 1 cup of cream |
| 4 oz. prunes | Salt and pepper |
| 2 apples | A little extra butter |
| 2 oz. butter *or* margarine | |

Wash and clean the fillets of skin and fat; cut them down the middle almost all the way. Stone the prunes, peel the apples and cut into pieces. Put the apples and prunes inside the fillets and tie them up like a sausage. Melt and brown the butter in a large saucepan, put the fillets in to brown on all sides. Add ½ a cup of boiling water, ½ a cup of cream and salt and pepper to taste. Cook gently for ½ hr. with lid on. Take out the fillets and remove the string, keep the fillets warm. Add the other ½ of the cream to the pan, whip well, add a little cold

butter. Pour over the fillets. Serve. Fillets can also be stuffed with parsley, if preferred.

6 helpings

## STUFFED GLOBE ARTICHOKES

*Artichauts farcis*

| | |
|---|---|
| 6 globe artichokes (cooked) | 1/2 oz. butter *or* margarine |
| 1 teasp. finely-chopped onion | 3 tablesp. chopped ham |
| 2 tablesp. finely-chopped mushrooms | 1 tablesp. breadcrumbs |
| | Brown sauce *or* egg to bind |
| | Salt and pepper |

Remove the inner leaves and the "chokes" from the artichokes. Fry the onion and mushrooms in the butter, add the other ingredients and sufficient brown sauce or egg to bind. Season the mixture carefully and fill the artichokes with it. Put them into a greased, fireproof dish, cover with greased paper and bake for 10–15 min. in a fairly hot oven (**375° F., Gas 5**) to ensure they are served hot.

6 helpings
Cooking time—1–1¼ hr.

OTHER STUFFINGS:

(1) Cooked, chopped chicken liver, mushrooms, onion, chicken stock.

(2) Hard-boiled egg, lemon juice, spinach purée.

## STUFFED GREEN PEPPERS

| | |
|---|---|
| 4 green peppers | 1 egg |
| 6 oz. diced cooked chicken | Pinch of salt |
| | Pinch of pepper |
| 1/4 cup seedless raisins | 1 teasp. chilli sauce |
| 1 oz. margarine | 2 oz. grated cheese |
| 1 cup cooked rice | |

Cut the peppers in halves lengthwise,

remove seeds and parboil in salted water 5–15 min. Combine chicken, raisins, margarine, rice, egg, seasonings, sauce and cheese. Stuff peppers. Bake in a moderate oven **(350° F., Gas 4).**

**Cooking time—½ hr.**

## STUFFED HAM

*Jambon farci*

**1½–2 lb. slices of ham—about ¼ in. thick**
**6–8 apricots *or* 2 apples**
**3 oz. breadcrumbs**
**Salt and pepper**
**1 egg**
**A little flour**
**1 cup milk**
**½ cup water *or* syrup from canned apricots**

If dried apricots are used, soak overnight and stew until tender before using. Cut the slices of ham in two. Chop the apricots or apples and mix with the breadcrumbs and seasoning and bind lightly with beaten egg. Spread this mixture over half the slices of ham and make into sandwiches. Coat lightly with flour and place in a casserole. Pour over the milk and water, or syrup, and bake in a moderate oven **(350° F., Gas 4)** for 30–40 min. Remove lid of casserole for last 10 min.

**6 helpings**

## STUFFED LAMB'S LIVER

*Foie d'Agneau farci*

**¾ lb. lamb's liver**
**Seasoned flour**
**4–6 oz. bacon**
**½ pt. stock**
**Browned breadcrumbs**
**Parsley**
**1 teasp. Worcester sauce**

STUFFING

**3 oz. breadcrumbs**
**3 teasp. chopped parsley**
**2 teasp. finely-chopped onion**
**Salt and pepper**

Wash the slices of liver, dry, and dip in the seasoned flour. Place in a greased meat-tin or fireproof dish. Mix all the ingredients for the stuffing and spread some on each slice of liver. Arrange pieces of bacon to cover the stuffing. Pour in the stock carefully, cover and cook in a moderate oven **(350° F., Gas 4)** for ½–¾ hr., depending on the thickness of the liver. Serve the slices sprinkled with some browned breadcrumbs and a little chopped parsley. Boil up the stock with a little thickening and add the Worcester sauce. Pour a little round the liver and serve the rest separately.

**6 helpings**

## STUFFED MUSHROOMS

*Champignons farcis*

**6 medium-sized mushrooms**
**½ oz. butter *or* margarine**
**1 small onion finely-chopped**
**1 tablesp. finely-chopped ham**
**1 dessertsp. fresh breadcrumbs**
**1 teasp. grated Parmesan cheese**
**1 teasp. chopped parsley**
**Brown sauce**
**Salt and pepper**
**6 round croûtes fried *or* toasted bread**

Wash, peel and remove stalks from mushrooms. Trim the mushrooms to neat, round shapes with scissors and use the trimmings in the stuffing. Melt the butter in a saucepan, add the onion and mushroom trimmings (finely-chopped) and cook 10 min. Add the other ingredients, with sufficient sauce to bind. Stir till well mixed and hot. Season carefully. Pile on the underside of the prepared mushrooms. Put on to a greased tin, cover with greased paper or metal foil and bake in a fairly hot oven **(375° F., Gas 5)** about 20 min. Serve on the fried or toasted croûtes.

**6 helpings**
**Cooking time—about 30 min.**

## STUFFED AND ROAST LOIN OR SHOULDER OF MUTTON

*Filet ou Epaule de Mouton, farci*

**A loin *or* shoulder of mutton**
**Veal forcemeat *or* sage and onion stuffing**
**Salt and pepper**
**2–3 oz. dripping**

Remove all the bones from the meat. Trim off any skin and surplus fat and flatten the meat with a rolling-pin. Season the meat well with salt and pepper and spread on the forcemeat or stuffing. Roll up and tie securely with string. Melt the dripping in a covered meat-tin, put in the meat and roast in a moderate oven **(350° F., Gas 4)** until tender. Allow 25 min. per lb. and 25 min. over. Baste occasionally. A good gravy or brown sauce may be served with the meat.

## STUFFED ONIONS

*Oignons farcis*

| | |
|---|---|
| **6 large onions** | **1 tablesp. breadcrumbs** |
| **4 tablesp. finely-chopped liver *or* cooked ham *or* any cooked meat** | **½ teasp. finely-chopped fresh sage *or* ½ teasp. dried sage** |
| **1 tablesp. finely-chopped cooked onion** | **Salt and pepper** |
| | **1 egg** |
| | **Butter *or* margarine** |
| | **¾ pt. brown sauce** |

Peel and steam the onions gently until almost soft, about 1 hr. Lift out the centre of each onion with a teaspoon handle. Chop the onion centres and add to the stuffing. Mix the stuffing ingredients with the beaten egg. Season well. Press it firmly into each onion and pile neatly on top. Sprinkle the top of each onion with a little melted butter *or* margarine. Pin a band of stiff, greased paper round each onion to prevent splitting. Put into a greased, fireproof dish and bake 30–40 min. in a moderate oven (**350° F., Gas 4**). Serve with the sauce poured round.

**6 helpings**
**Cooking time—about 1¾ hr.**

## STUFFED OX CHEEK

*Tête de Bœuf farcie*

| | |
|---|---|
| **1 cooked ox cheek** | **Egg and browned breadcrumbs** |
| **4–6 oz. veal forcemeat** | **Fat for basting** |

Prepare and cook the cheek as for Stewed Ox Cheek. When the bones—if left in—can be easily separated from the meat, or when the meat is tender, remove the cheek from the pan. Spread 4–6 oz. veal forcemeat over the cheek, roll up tightly and tie securely with string. Coat thickly with egg and browned breadcrumbs and bake in a moderate oven (**350° F., Gas 4**) for ¾ hr., basting frequently. Serve with a gravy made from the liquid in which the cheek was cooked.

**6 helpings**

## STUFFED PEPPERS

*Piment farci*

| | |
|---|---|
| **6 mall *or* 3 large peppers** | **1 tablesp. breadcrumbs** |
| **Stuffing, *see Stuffed cabbage, Stuffed onions, Stuffed tomatoes, or Stuffed vegetable marrow,*** | **A little melted butter *or* margarine** |

Wash and parboil the peppers as in preceding recipe. Drain, cut in ½ lengthwise and remove seeds. Fill the halved peppers with the stuffing, sprinkle with a few breadcrumbs and a little melted fat. Pack tightly into a greased, fireproof dish and bake for 35 min. in a fairly hot oven (**375° F., Gas 5**).

**6 helpings**
**Cooking time—about 40 min.**

## STUFFED TOMATO SALADS

*Salade de Tomates Farcies*

| | |
|---|---|
| **6 large firm tomatoes** | **Crisp lettuce leaves** |

STUFFING, choice of:

1. **Finely-shredded lettuce leaves; cold cooked asparagus tips; salad dressing *or***
2. **Chopped celery; finely-diced cooked carrot; canned peas; salad dressing *or***
3. **Chopped hard-boiled egg; chopped gherkins; salad dressing *or***
4. **Chopped shrimps *or* prawns; finely-shredded lettuce leaves; salad dressing**

Cut off the tops of the tomatoes, take out the centres and the pulp. Use a little of the pulp with the stuffing. Mix the chosen stuffing and fill the tomatoes. Put back the tops. Garnish with tiny sprigs of parsley or with a suitable ingredient of the filling. Dish on crisp lettuce leaves on individual dishes or plates.

**6 helpings**

## STUFFED TOMATOES

*Tomates farcies*

| | |
|---|---|
| **6 large firm tomatoes** | **1 tablesp. fresh breadcrumbs** |
| **1 teasp. finely-chopped onion** | **½ teasp. chopped parsley** |
| **1 teasp. finely-chopped mushroom** | **Salt and pepper** |
| **½ oz. butter *or* margarine** | **1 teasp. dry grated cheese** |
| **1 heaped tablesp. finely-chopped cooked ham** | **6 rounds of fried *or* toasted bread** |

Wash and dry the tomatoes. Cut a small round from each tomato at the end opposite the stalk. Scoop out the centre with the handle of a teaspoon. Fry the onion and the mushroom in the butter or margarine until cooked. Add the ham, crumbs, parsley and sufficient tomato pulp to bind the mixture. Season well. Fill the tomatoes with the mixture, piling some on top. Bake in a moderate oven (**350° F., Gas 4**) until the tomatoes are soft—about 20 min. Sprinkle the tops with cheese, replace the lids and serve on the fried or toasted bread. Garnish with parsley.

NOTE: For alternative filling see Stuffed Cabbage.

For a vegetarian filling replace the ham and cheese in the above recipe with chopped mushrooms *or* chopped nut meat.

**6 helpings**
**Cooking time—to bake, about 20 min.**

## STUFFED VEGETABLE MARROW

*Courge farcie*

| | |
|---|---|
| **2 small vegetable marrows** | **¾ pt. brown sauce *or* tomato sauce** |

STUFFING

| | |
|---|---|
| **1 small finely-chopped onion** | **1 tablesp. chopped parsley** |
| **½ lb. cooked ham *or* nut meat for vegetarians** | **2 oz. breadcrumbs** |
| | **1 egg** |
| | **Seasoning** |
| **6 mushrooms, chopped** | **1 gill stock (approx.)** |
| **2 oz. butter *or* margarine** | |

COATING

| | |
|---|---|
| **Browned crumbs** | **Melted butter *or* margarine** |

Peel the marrows and cut into halves lengthwise *or* cut into rings, about 2 in. thick. Remove the seeds with a tablespoon and steam the marrow until almost soft. Drain carefully. Fry the chopped mushrooms and onion in the butter until cooked—about 10 min. Add all the other ingredients and bind with the egg and enough stock to make a soft stuffing. Season well. Stuff the marrow halves or rings of marrow with filling. Sprinkle browned crumbs on top, then a little melted butter. Bake in a fairly hot oven (**375° F., Gas 5**). Serve with brown *or* tomato sauce.

**6 helpings**
**Cooking time—about 1 hr.**

## STUFFINGS

These may be hot or cold, savoury or (less often) sweet. They are often used to make meat "go further" or to add fruit to a starchy sweet dish such as pancakes. *See the recipe for the type or flavour of stuffing required. See also Savouries (Appetizers), Forcemeat and similar entries.*

## STUFFINGS FOR SAVOURIES

*See Savouries (Appetizers)*

## SUET CRUST PASTRY

For Meat puddings, Fruit puddings, Jam Roly Poly, Suet Puddings, etc.

| | |
|---|---|
| **3–4 oz. suet** | **1 teasp. baking-powder** |
| **½ lb. plain flour** | |
| **¼ teasp. salt** | **Cold water to mix** |

Chop the suet finely with a little flour or use shredded suet. Sift the flour, salt and baking-powder, and mix in the suet. Mix to a firm dough with cold water. Use as required.

## SUET CRUST PASTRY—RICH

| | |
|---|---|
| **½ lb. plain flour** | **6 oz. suet** |
| **3 oz. breadcrumbs** | **1 teasp. baking-powder** |
| **¼ teasp. salt** | **Cold water to mix** |

Sift the flour and salt and add the breadcrumbs. Chop the suet finely or use shredded suet, add to the flour and breadcrumbs. Add the baking-powder and mix with cold water to a firm dough—soft enough to roll out easily, but not so moist that it sticks to the board and rolling-pin. Use as required.

NOTE: This pastry makes a very light, easily digested pudding but is liable to break if turned out of the basin.

## SUET PUDDING

*Pouding Roulé à l'Anglaise*

| | |
|---|---|
| **12 oz. plain flour** | **4–6 oz. finely-chopped suet** |
| **¼ teasp. salt** | |
| **2 rounded teasp. baking-powder** | **Water to mix** |

Sift the flour, salt and baking-powder. Mix in the suet. Add cold water, stirring gradually until a stiff dough is formed. Shape the dough into a roll. Put the dough into a scalded, well-floured pudding cloth and roll up loosely. Tie the ends securely with string. Put into a saucepan of boiling water and boil gently for 1½–2 hr., adding more boiling water, if necessary, to keep the pudding covered. Serve with jam-, treacle-, fruit- or marmalade-sauce.

Serve with cream, if liked.

**6–7 helpings**

### SULTANA CAKE ECONOMICAL

*Gâteau aux Raisins, Economique*

**8 oz. plain flour**
**⅛ teasp. salt**
**3 oz. beef dripping**
**2 level teasp. cream of tartar**
**1 level teasp. bicarbonate of soda**
**4 oz. moist sugar**
**½ lb. sultanas**
**2 oz. mixed shredded peel**
**1 egg**
**1¼ gills milk (approx.)**

Sift flour and salt and rub in the fat. Mix raising agents thoroughly with the flour and add other dry ingredients. Beat egg and add with milk to make a soft dropping consistency. Place in a greased 7-in. cake-tin and bake in a fairly hot oven **(375° F., Gas 5)**. Reduce heat after 15 min. to moderate **(350° F., Gas 4)**.

**Cooking time—1½ hr.**

### SULTANA PUDDING

*Pouding aux Raisins de Smyrne*

**4 oz. butter *or* margarine**
**½ lb. plain flour**
**Pinch of salt**
**1 heaped teasp. baking-powder**
**4 oz. castor sugar**
**4 oz. sultanas**
**2 eggs**
**Milk to mix**
**A few drops vanilla essence**

Grease a 2 pt. basin. Clean the sultanas. Rub the fat into the sifted flour, salt and baking-powder. Add the sugar and fruit. Mix with beaten egg, milk and vanilla essence to a soft dropping consistency. Put the mixture into the basin; cover. Steam for 1½–2 hr.

Turn out, dredge with sugar, and serve with custard or lemon sauce.

**6 helpings**

### SUMMER PUDDING

**12 individual sponge cakes (approx.)**
**2–4 oz. sugar according to sweetness of fruit**
**1½–2 lb. soft fruit: apples, *or* rhubarb, gooseberries, strawberries, raspberries, redcurrants, *or* black currants, *or* a mixture, as liked**

Choose a 1½ pt. pudding basin *or* charlotte *or* soufflé mould. Cut sponge cakes into inch-wide fingers for lining the sides, and triangles for lining the base. Cook the selected fruit with the least possible amount of water, until pulped; and sweeten to taste. Pour into the lined mould. Cover the top with slices of sponge cake, press down with a small weighted saucer, and leave pudding to become cold. Turn out on to a dish.

Coat with either custard cream, fruit juice thickened to coating consistency with 1 level teasp. arrowroot to ½ pt. juice. Decorate with choice pieces of fruit *or* shredded almonds.

**6 helpings**

### SUPRÊME SAUCE

*Sauce Suprême*

**½ pt. Velouté sauce**
**2 tablesp.–⅛ pt. cream**
**1 egg yolk**
**½–1 oz. butter**
**Nutmeg to taste**
**Lemon juice**
**Salt and pepper**

Heat the Velouté sauce, preferably in a double boiler. Mix the egg yolk and cream, and stir into the sauce, cook without boiling, till the egg yolk thickens. Whisk in the butter, a small pat at a time. Add a pinch of nutmeg, a few drops of lemon juice, season and use the sauce at once.

Serve with any meat, poultry, fish or vegetables.

## SWEDISH RICE

*Riz à la Suèdoise*

**¾ lb. rice**
**Salt**
**1½ lb. cooking apples**
**¾ pt. milk**
**Rind of 1 lemon**
**3 oz. sugar**
**Pinch of ground cinnamon**
**Wineglass of sherry**
**¼ lb. raisins, stoned and roughly chopped**

Wash the rice and throw it into slightly salted boiling water. Boil for 3 min. then strain off the water. Peel, core and thinly slice the apples. Add the milk, lemon rind and the apples to the rice; cook until tender. Remove the lemon rind. Add the sugar, ground cinnamon, wine and prepared raisins. Cook for 3–4 min. longer.

Serve with cream.

**6 helpings**

## SWEDISH SALAD

*Salade à la Suédoise*

**4 oz. cold roast beef**
**1 pickled herring**
**4 oz. cooked potatoes**
**4 oz. cooking apples**
**4 oz. cooked *or* pickled beetroot**
**1 tablesp. chopped gherkin**
**1 tablesp. chopped capers**
**Chopped chervil**
**Chopped tarragon**
**Oil**
**Vinegar**
**1 hard-boiled egg**
**3 anchovy fillets**
**6 bearded oysters (optional)**

Dice the beef, herring, potatoes, apples and beetroot. Mix with the gherkin, capers, herbs and moisten with a little oil and vinegar. Pile in a dish and garnish with hard-boiled egg, anchovy fillets and if liked 6 bearded oysters.

NOTE: This salad is often served with stiffly-beaten sour cream coloured with pickled beetroot juice.

**4–6 helpings**

## SWEET CHEESE, RUSSIAN

*Pashka (an Easter Speciality)*

**4 lb. cream cheese**
**1½ lb. fresh butter**
**1 lb. vanilla castor sugar (close vanilla pod with the sugar in tin for a few days before making)**
**6 eggs**
**1 lb. stoned raisins**
**¼ lb. sultanas**
**¼ lb. chopped cherries**
**Blanched almonds**
**Angelica**

Pass the cream cheese and butter together through a sieve—it must be absolutely smooth and well blended. Put the vanilla sugar into a bowl. Separate the eggs and add the egg yolks to the sugar, beat until white. Stir in the raisins, sultanas and cherries. Add this to the cheese mixture, mixing all thoroughly together. Beat the egg whites to a stiff snow and fold into the mixture. Put into a muslin bag, or if possible, a wicker cheese basket lined with butter muslin or a similar receptacle which will allow any surplus moisture to drain off. Put in a cold place for 24 hr. Unmould and decorate with almonds and angelica—cherries may also be used.

**12 helpings**

## SWEET DISHES

When these are served as a separate course at a meal, Americans call them *desserts* and the French *entremets*. These sweet dishes may be hot, warm or cold, frozen or iced.

Cold sweets include Cereal Moulds, Cakes, Creams and Custards, Fruit prepared in various ways, Gateaux, Ices, Pies and Tarts. Unsalted dessert cheeses are also sometimes used as cold sweets, e.g. Pashka, and so are various mousse and meringue mixtures. *See the various headings for recipe suggestions.*

Hot sweets include Batter puddings, Custards, Flans, Fritters, Fruit prepared in various ways, Milk puddings, Pies and Tarts, baked, boiled and steamed puddings. *See these headings for the various kinds of hot sweets.*

## SWEET DISHES USING PASTRY

These may be cakes, gateaux, sweet pies or tarts, etc. *See Pastry-Making and these headings.*

## SWEET FILLINGS FOR SANDWICHES

1. Bananas mashed with lemon juice and ground almonds and sprinkled with sugar.
2. A layer of cream or cottage cheese, covered with a layer of fresh strawberries or raspberries sprinkled with castor sugar.
3. Softened creamed cheese, mixed with canned crushed pineapple and finely-chopped preserved ginger.
4. Chocolate spread, mixed with chopped walnuts.
5. Chopped pears, dates and walnuts, mixed with golden syrup.
6. Thick slices of banana sprinkled with coarsely-grated chocolate.

## SWEET PIES OR TARTS

These are made of one or two layers of pastry with fruit, jam, nuts, sweet cheese, crumbs or a custard mixture. In Britain, dishes with a pastry crust on top are usually called pies. Tarts usually, although not always, hold the filling in a pastry shell but have no top crust. Double-crust pies or tarts have a shell and a top crust too.

### To Make a Fruit Pie or Tart

A $1\frac{1}{2}$-pt. pie-dish requires about 6 oz. pastry (i.e. 6 oz. flour plus the other ingredients made into pastry) and $1\frac{1}{2}$–2 lb. fruit.

Place $\frac{1}{2}$ the amount of fruit in the dish, sprinkle over the sugar and flavouring (if used) and pile the remaining fruit on top, piling it high in the centre. The sugar should not be sprinkled on top as it would go into the pastry and make it soggy. If the fruit is likely to shrink during cooking or if there is insufficient fruit to fill the dish, place a pie funnel or inverted egg-cup in the centre.

Roll out the pastry a little larger than the pie-dish. Cut off a strip of pastry the width and length of the rim of the dish, wet the edge of the pie-dish with cold water and place the strip on the pie-dish cut edge inwards, without stretching it. Join the strip by wetting the cut ends and pressing them firmly together.

Wet the strip of pastry; lift the remaining pastry with the rolling-pin and place it gently over the dish, taking care not to stretch it. Press the strip and the cover together and trim off the surplus with a sharp knife. Knock up the edge of the pastry with the back of a knife and decorate as desired.

To allow the steam to escape either cut a slit in the centre of the crust before placing pie in the oven (if a pie funnel has been used the slit should come over it); *or* leave a few gaps under the pastry cover at the edge; *or* raise the pastry slightly at one corner immediately after cooking.

### Double Crust Pies or Tarts

Double crust pies or tarts may be made in fireproof glass or enamel plates or dishes.

About 8 oz. pastry (i.e. 8 oz. flour plus the other ingredients made up into pastry) will be required for an 8–9 in. plate.

Divide the dough into 2 portions, form each into a round shape and roll one portion into a round about $\frac{1}{8}$ in. thick and a little larger than the plate. Fold over the rolling-pin and lift on to the plate; smooth to fit the plate without stretching the pastry. Cut off the surplus pastry with a sharp knife or scissors. Put in a layer of filling, sprinkle with sugar if required and cover with another layer of filling. This prevents the sugar getting into the pastry and making it soggy.

Roll the remaining piece of pastry into a round a little larger than the plate. Wet with cold water the edge of the pastry lining the plate; lift on the cover and ease into position without stretching—if stretched it will only shrink back later. Press the 2 edges together firmly, knock up the edge and decorate.

Bake according to the type of pastry, and to ensure that the bottom crust cooks through stand the plate on a baking-sheet.

## SWEET MELTED BUTTER SAUCE

*Sauce au Beurre Sucrée*

To $\frac{1}{2}$ pt. white sauce cooled add 1 oz. butter extra, sweeten to taste and add any sweet flavouring desired.

## SWEET PASTRY FOR TARTLETS

| | |
|---|---|
| **1 lb. plain flour** | **8 oz. castor sugar** |
| **Pinch of salt** | **1 egg** |
| **5 oz. butter** | **Cold water, if necessary** |
| **Rind of 1/2 lemon** | |

Sift the flour and salt. Rub in the butter, add the sugar and finely grated lemon rind and mix to a stiff dough with beaten egg and a little cold water, if necessary.

Use as required.

## SWEET SAUCE—RICH

**4 egg yolks *or* 2 whole eggs**
**4 oz. castor sugar**
**¼ pt. milk**
**Grated rind of 1 orange**
**¼ pt. cream**

Beat the egg yolks or whole eggs with the sugar and milk until well mixed. Add the orange rind and cream and cook over very gentle heat or in a double boiler until the sauce thickens. It must not boil.

## SWEET WINE SAUCE

*Sauce au Vin Sucré*

**⅛ pt. water**
**⅛ pt. sherry**
**2 tablesp. any jam *or* jelly**
**Sugar to taste**
**Lemon juice to taste**

Boil all the ingredients together for 5 min. Rub through a hair or nylon sieve or strain the sauce. Adjust the flavour, reheat if necessary. If liked this sauce may be thickened as Jam sauce

## SWEETBREADS—BOURGEOISE STYLE

*Ris d'Agneau à la Bourgeoise*

**1½ lb. lambs' sweetbreads**
**1 oz. butter *or* fat**
**Good stock**
**Salt and pepper**
**½ pt. good brown sauce**
**2 tablesp. cooked peas**
**2 tablesp. pea-shapes of cooked turnip**
**2 tablesp. pea-shapes of cooked carrot**

Soak the sweetbreads for 2 hr., then blanch and drain them well. Melt the butter in a saucepan and toss the sweetbreads in it. Then barely cover with stock. Season carefully and cook gently for 1 hr. until tender. Prepare ½ pt. brown sauce and keep hot. Cook the vegetables separately until tender but whole and add them to the sauce. Place the sweetbreads in individual casseroles or china cases and add the sauce and vegetables. Serve very hot.

**6 helpings**

## SWEETS, CONFECTIONERY

Strictly, these are sweetmeats. Making confectionery is a specialized branch of cookery, and the reader interested in it should refer to a specialized book on the subject, or to *Mrs Beeton's Cookery and Household Management* where the topic is treated in some detail.

## SWISS CREAM

*Crème à la Suisse*

**¼ lb. ratafia biscuits *or* sponge cake**
**3–4 tablesp. sherry**
**1¼ oz. cornflour**
**1 pt. milk**
**1 lemon**
**2 oz. castor sugar**
**¼–½ pt. double cream**
**2 teasp. chopped *or* grated nuts *or* glacé fruits**

Put the ratafia biscuits or cake in the bottom of a glass dish, or individual dishes, and soak with sherry. Blend the cornflour with sufficient of the milk to make a smooth cream. Heat the remainder of the milk slowly with thin strips of lemon rind. Strain on to the blended cornflour, return to the pan and cook thoroughly but gently for 3–4 min. Stir in the sugar. Allow to cool. Whip the cream slightly and add it and the juice of the lemon gently and gradually to the cool cornflour cream. Re-sweeten if necessary. Pour over the soaked biscuits or cake and leave to go cold.

Decorate with chopped nuts, or tastefully arranged glacé cherries and thinly cut strips of angelica.

**4–6 helpings**
**Cooking time—25 min.**

## SWISS ROLL

*Bûche*

**3 oz. plain flour**
**Pinch of salt**
**1 level teasp. baking-powder**
**3 fresh eggs**
**3 oz. castor sugar**
**¼ teasp. vanilla essence**
**2 tablesp. raspberry jam**

Line and grease a Swiss roll tin.

Sift flour, salt and baking-powder. Beat eggs and sugar in a bowl over a pan of hot water till thick and pale in colour. Do not let the bottom of the bowl touch the water. Lightly fold in flour etc. and add the vanilla essence. Spread on the tin and bake in a hot oven **(425° F., Gas 7)**. Quick cooking is essential to keep the roll moist. Sprinkle castor sugar on to a sheet of kitchen paper, turn the roll on to this and cut half-way through the roll about 1 in. from the bottom end. Spread the roll with warm jam to within ½ in. of edge. Turn in the 1 in. at the bottom to make the initial roll and continue to roll up firmly with the aid of the kitchen paper. Press gently to keep in place. Remove paper and dust with castor sugar. (A very *lightly* damped clean tea cloth may be used instead of paper.)

NOTE: If the edges are very crisp it is advisable to trim them before rolling or the roll may crack.

**Cooking time—7 min.**

## SWISS SALAD

*Salade Suisse*

**3 small cooked potatoes**
**1 cooked carrot**
**½ small cooked beetroot**
**1 small cooking apple**
**2 oz. tongue**
**1 cooked herring**
**Chopped parsley**
**Salad dressing**

Dice the potatoes, carrot, beetroot, apple and tongue. Divide the herring into flakes. Mix all together lightly with chopped parsley and salad dressing. Pile in a salad bowl.

**4–6 helpings**

## SYLLABUB

**4 oz. castor sugar**
**Juice of 1 lemon**
**Finely-grated rind of ½ lemon**
**Pinch of ground cinnamon**
**1 small wineglass sherry *or* Madeira**
**Ratafia essence**
**1 pt. cream**
**10 macaroons**

Mix together the sugar, lemon juice and rind, cinnamon and wine. Add a few drops of essence and stir until the sugar is dissolved. Add the cream and whip to a froth. Arrange the macaroons in the bottom of a deep dish, and as the froth is formed on the syllabub, skim it off and place it on the biscuits, until the whole of the mixture has been reduced to a froth and piled on the biscuits. Chill before serving.

**7–8 helpings**

## SYRUP FOR WATER ICES

**2 lb. loaf sugar**
**1 pt. water**

Place the sugar and water in a strong saucepan. Allow the sugar to dissolve over gentle heat. Do not stir. When the sugar has dissolved, gently boil the mixture for 10 min., or, if a saccharometer is available, it should register 220° F. Remove scum as it rises. Strain, cool and store.

**1 pt. syrup**
**Time—½ hr.**

## SYRUP SPONGE PUDDING

*Pouding de Savoie au Sirop*

**6 oz. plain flour**
**6 oz. breadcrumbs**
**4 oz. finely-chopped suet**
**2 oz. castor sugar**
**1 teasp. ground ginger**
**1 level teasp. bicarbonate of soda**
**Pinch of salt**
**1 egg**
**2 tablesp. golden syrup**
**1 tablesp. treacle**
**Milk to mix**

Grease a basin and, if liked, put an extra tablesp. of golden syrup in the bottom. Mix together the flour, breadcrumbs, suet, sugar, ginger, bicarbonate of soda and salt. Beat the egg with the golden syrup, treacle and a little of the milk. Stir this into the other ingredients, using more milk if required, to mix to a very soft dropping consistency. Put the mixture into the basin; cover with greased paper. Steam for 1½–2 hr.

**6–7 helpings**

## TABLE WINES AND LIQUEURS

Serving wine with a meal enhances the value of the food and often turns an "everyday" meal into an "occasion". Many people think that wine-drinking in the home is an expensive pleasure. However, there are many reasonably priced wines on the market.

### Storing Wine

Most people buy wine as they need it, often only a few hours before it is going to be consumed. This practice has definite disadvantages; (*a*) it is not always possible to obtain the wine that is most wanted, and one has to make do with second best; (*b*) there is insufficient time to acclimatize the wine to room temperature and it is therefore not drunk at its prime; *and* (*c*) you often pay more for a good wine than you need. This is because a good wine bought when it is young and laid down for a number of years may well cost only half what it does when purchased from a merchant at the height of its maturity.

The ideal is, of course, to have a proper cellar. But in these days of flats and small houses, few people can manage this. The word "cellar" is however always used for a stock of wine, however small.

Wine should be kept lying on its side, or the cork will become dry, and allow the entry of air.

The opposite is true in the case of spirits. The action of the spirit may eat into the cork if they touch. The ethers rising from the bottle's contents keep the cork moist enough. Stand spirits upright.

If a special place is available for keeping wine, even if it is only under the stairs, place a simple wine-rack there. One advantage is that it saves the wine from being disturbed whenever a bottle is removed.

Wine should be kept in the dark, as nearly as possible, even if only under a cloth or a sheet of brown paper.

### A Note on Temperature

Wine should be stored at a temperature between 55 and 65° F., but unless you have really fine wines, there is no need to buy a thermometer. 60° F. is the temperature of an average living-room.

Store wine with the label uppermost, so that if the bottles must be moved, they can be relaid in the same position, thus avoiding the serious disturbance of any sediment the wine may contain.

### Decanting Wine

Speaking generally, the only wines one need decant are red wines which "throw" a heavy sediment as they age. Both Clarets and Burgundies do this in varying degrees. Vintage and Crusted Ports throw a very heavy sediment; hence the name of the latter. Unless one has these wines in sufficient quantity to allow them a lengthy period of rest, it is better to let the wine-merchant keep them and decant them as required. If it is preferred to keep them at home, the delicate process of decanting must be fully understood.

The reader will understand this process best by reference to some book such as *Mrs Beeton's Cookery and Household Management* where it is treated in some detail.

### Glasses and Decanters

The plainer the decanter, the better the wine is seen.

The choice of glasses is wide. Hock glasses are the most graceful, and some German specimens are of surpassing beauty. For all wine, the use of tinted glass is deprecated today, unless it is antique.

The types of glass used for Port are well known. Preference should be given to a glass which narrows slightly towards the brim. This keeps the bouquet within bounds, and lets one enjoy it more. An outstanding shape is the one called "tulip-shaped", which is indeed shaped like a tulip.

Salad vegetables are a good basis for Hors D'Oeuvre.

Lobster thermidor.

Sherry glasses are like port glasses.

Champagne glasses are of several kinds. The most widely used is a shallow saucer.

Although the fashion is to drink brandy from a large "balloon" glass, this leads to the escape of some of the brandy's natural strength. Almost any thin glass tapering towards the top makes a suitable glass for a liqueur brandy. The emphasis is on *thin*, for this quality lets the hand's warmth assist the release of the precious bouquet.

The remarks on brandy also apply to the drinking of liqueurs.

### TANGERINE WATER ICE

*Glace aux Tangerines*

| | |
|---|---|
| **2 oz. loaf sugar** | **¼ pt. water** |
| **6 tangerines** | **1 pt. syrup** |
| **2 oranges** | |
| **2 lemons** | |

Rub the sugar on the rind of the tangerines to extract some of the flavour. Place the sugar in a saucepan, add the thinly peeled rind of 1 orange, 1 lemon and the ¼ pt. water. Boil the mixture for 10 min., then add the juice of all the fruit and the syrup. Boil up, strain and cool. Freeze.

**6–8 helpings**
**Time—1½ hr.**

### TAPIOCA CREAM

*Crème au Tapioca*

| | |
|---|---|
| **½ pt. packet red jelly** | **1 bay leaf** |
| **1 tablesp. sherry (optional)** | **2 pt. milk** |
| **1 tablesp. redcurrant *or* crab-apple *or* bramble jelly** | **1½ oz. tapioca** |
| **Rind of ½ lemon** | **2 oz. castor sugar** |
| | **2 egg yolks** |
| | **2 tablesp. double cream** |

Make the jelly to just less than ½ pt., inclusive of sherry (if used) and preserves, and add these when jelly is cool. Pour into a wet border mould and leave to set. Cut thin strips of lemon rind without white pith; infuse in the milk with the bay leaf. When milk boils, remove flavourings and sprinkle in tapioca, stirring continuously. Cook gently 15–20 min. until smooth and soft. Add sugar, cool slightly, and add beaten egg yolks. Re-heat to cook the yolks, but do not boil. Allow to cool, then lightly stir in whipped cream. Pour into the border mould and leave to set.

**6 helpings**
**Cooking time—1 hr.**
**Setting time—2 hr.**

### TAPIOCA CREAM PUDDING—HOT

*Tapioca au lait à la Crème*

| | |
|---|---|
| **2½ oz. tapioca** | **1½ oz. sugar** |
| **1½ pt. milk** | **¼ teasp. almond essence** |
| **Pinch of salt** | **3 eggs** |
| **½ oz. butter** | **3 oz. crushed ratafias** |

Wash and soak the tapioca in the milk with the salt for 1–2 hr. Simmer the tapioca in the milk until cooked. Add the butter, sugar and almond essence. Separate the eggs and add the egg yolks. Pour into a well-buttered pie-dish and bake in a moderate oven (**350° F., Gas 4**) until just set. Stiffly whisk the egg whites and fold in lightly, the crushed ratafias. Pile on top of the tapioca. Reduce the heat of the oven to cool (**290°–310° F., Gas 1–2**) and bake until a pale golden brown on top; about 30 min. **6 helpings**

### TARRAGON BUTTER

| | |
|---|---|
| **2 oz. butter** | **Lemon juice** |
| **1 teasp. chopped tarragon** | |

Scald the tarragon in boiling water and dry in a cloth before chopping. Pound the chopped tarragon with the butter, add lemon juice to taste, pass through a sieve.

### TARRAGON VINEGAR

| | |
|---|---|
| **1 pt. vinegar** | **2 oz. tarragon leaves** |

Bruise the tarragon leaves slightly. Put them into a bottling jar, pour in the vinegar and screw down the cap. Store the vinegar for 6 weeks, then strain and rebottle it. Store in a cool dry place.

NOTE: If using home-grown tarragon, the leaves should be gathered on a dry day about the end of July, just before the plant begins to bloom.

### TARTS AND TARTLETS

*See Pastry-Making, Flans, Open Tarts, Savoury Pies and Tarts, Sweet Pies and Tarts, etc. See also recipe for the type of flavour of filling required, e.g. Apple Tart.*

### TARTARE SAUCE—COLD

**¼ pt. mayonnaise**
**1 teasp. each of chopped gherkin, chopped olives, chopped capers, chopped parsley, chopped chives**
**A little French mustard**
**1 dessertsp. wine vinegar**
**A little dry white wine (optional)**

Mix the chopped ingredients into the mayonnaise, add the mustard. Thin to the required consistency with vinegar and wine.

Serve with fried and grilled fish and meat.

### TARTARE SAUCE—ECONOMICAL (HOT)

*Sauce Tartare*

**½ pt. Béchamel sauce**
**1–2 egg yolks**
**1 tablesp. cream**
**1 heaped teasp. chopped gherkin**
**1 heaped teasp. chopped capers**
**1 dessertsp. chopped parsley**
**Lemon juice *or* wine vinegar**

Mix the egg yolks and cream, stir them into the hot sauce well below boiling point. Cook the egg yolk without boiling it. Add the gherkin, capers and parsley and flavour with lemon juice or vinegar. Serve at once.

Serve with salmon and other fish.

### TEA

The most popular non-alcoholic beverage in Britain is Indian tea. It makes a pleasant drink, and has a refreshing effect.

#### To Make Tea

To make good tea the water must be boiling, and freshly boiled. It is a good plan to empty the kettle and refill it with fresh cold water, and make the tea the moment the water reaches boiling-point.

The tea pot should be warmed before making the tea. The boiling water should be poured on the tea then left to stand for 3–4 min. It should never be allowed to stand for longer.

### TEA CAKES

*Brioches plates*

**1 lb. plain flour**
**1 oz. sugar**
**½ teasp. salt**
**2 oz. lard and margarine**
**½ oz. yeast**
**½ pt. warm milk**
**2–3 oz. currants (if liked)**

Sift warm flour and salt and rub in the fat. Cream the yeast with the sugar, add the warm milk to it and mix with the flour and fruit to a light elastic dough. Put to rise to double its size. Divide risen dough into 4–6 pieces, knead each into a round and roll out to the size of a tea plate. Place on greased baking sheets, prick the top neatly, and allow to prove for 15 min. Bake in a hot oven **(425° F., Gas 7)** for 20–25 min.

If liked the cakes may be brushed with egg and water before baking or rubbed over with margarine after baking.

**4–6 cakes**

### TEA, CHINA

Tea is served all day long in China, in homes, offices and tea-houses.

Tea grows in all parts of China and there are many different kinds. Broadly they fall into two categories: (1) red or black tea, (2) green tea. The first is dried over fire and the second is dried in the sun.

#### GREEN TEAS

**Dragon's Well Tea:** There are various qualities of this tea and the best qualities are expensive. That which is picked before the rain is best and is labelled with the words "Before the rain".

**Cloud Mist Tea:** This tea is the most expensive kind. It is rarely exported as there is only enough for home consumption. It has an exquisite fragrance and is drunk in small cups as one would drink a liqueur. It grows high up on rocks and monkeys are trained to pick the leaves. It is also called "Monkey Pluck".

**Water Nymph Tea, Eyebrows of Longevity, Silver Needles Tea:** These three types of tea come from Kwangtung. They all have good flavour and slight fragrance. They are moderately priced and popular.

#### RED OR BLACK TEAS

**Keemun and Ningchow Teas:** These two types of red or black tea are considered the best of their kind. They are appreciated for smoothness and delicate aroma.

**Jasmine Tea:** Jasmine blossom is added and gives a distinct flavour and beautiful aroma.

**Lei-Chee Tea:** Dried lei-chee fruits are added and give a flavour similar to the fruit.

## TEA SCONES

**8 oz. plain flour**
**1/4 teasp. salt**
**2 oz. margarine**
**2 oz. castor sugar**
**2 level teasp. cream of tartar**
**1 level teasp. bicarbonate of soda**
**2 eggs**
**Water or milk to make a light spongy mixture (average 1/2–3/4 gill)**

Sift the flour and salt and lightly rub in the fat. Add the other dry ingredients and mix with the beaten eggs and water to make a light spongy dough. Roll out ¼ in. thick and cut into rounds. Bake on a greased, fairly hot girdle or in a hot oven (**450°–425° F., Gas 8–7**). If the scones are to be baked in the oven, roll the dough ½ in. thick.

**12–15 scones**
**Cooking time—10 min.**

## TEENAGERS' DISHES FOR PARTIES

*See Children's Food.*

## TENDERLOIN OF BEEF

*Filet de Bœuf*

**A thick piece of well-hung sirloin**
**Olive oil, melted butter *or* fat**
**Salt and pepper**

Wipe the meat and beat it well. Brush both sides with oil or fat and season with salt and pepper. Grill as for grilled beefsteak until golden . Serve immediately with Maître d'hôtel butter and fried potatoes or other accompaniments if preferred.

## TENNIS CAKE

*Gâteau de Tennis*

**4 oz. butter *or* margarine**
**4 oz. castor sugar**
**1 oz. glacé cherries, cut in pieces**
**1 oz. chopped *or* shredded peel**
**5 oz. plain flour**
**Pinch of salt**
**2 eggs**
**3 oz. sultanas**
**1 tablesp. sherry (optional)**
**A little egg white *or* apricot glaze**

DECORATION

**Almond paste using 3 oz. ground almonds, etc.**
**1 tablesp. chopped pistachio nuts *or* green cake-crumbs**
**Royal icing using 1 small egg white, etc.**

Grease a small (1-lb.) loaf-tin. Cream fat and sugar till light. Sift together flour and salt and add eggs and flour alternately to the creamed fat; beat well. Stir in the prepared fruit and sherry if used. Place in the tin and bake in a moderate oven (**350° F., Gas 4**), reduce heat to **335° F., Gas 3** after ½ hr. Turn out, allow to cool and stand 24 hr. Brush over top of the cake with egg white *or* apricot glaze cooled and if cake is not level, build up around edge with almond paste, then cover top only with paste. Keep the surface level and sides sloping. Spread top smoothly with royal icing, sprinkle half the top with chopped pistachio nuts *or* green cake-crumbs. Allow icing to set. Using a small rose or writing pipe, pipe small roses or dots round edge of cake and across division between white and green cake.

**Cooking time—1–1½ hr.**

## THATCHED BROAD BEANS

**One 10-oz. carton broad beans**
**1/2 pt. white sauce (coating consistency)**
**Salt and pepper**
**4 rashers streaky bacon**
**Parsley**

Cook the beans according to the directions on the carton. While the beans are cooking, make the white sauce and when cooked, add the strained beans. Season to taste and turn into a shallow fireproof dish. Cut the bacon into strips and use to "thatch" the top of the beans. Place under a fairly hot grill and grill slowly until the bacon is crisp.

**3–4 helpings**

## TINS FOR CAKES, TO PREPARE

*See Cake-Making.*

**TIPSY CAKE**

*Gâteau au Madère*

**1 sponge cake *or* 8 individual cakes**
**Raspberry jam**
**1 glass Madeira *or* sherry**
**1 pt. cup custard**

DECORATION

**Almonds**
**Angelica**
**Glacé cherries**

Split the cake or cakes and spread half thickly with jam. Sandwich together again and place in a dish. Pour over the wine and allow to soak for 1 hr. Pour over the custard, stick the blanched almonds in like a porcupine, and decorate with cherries and angelica.

**6–7 helpings**

**TOAD-IN-THE-HOLE**

**¾–1 lb. chuck steak**
**¾ pt. batter**
**¾ oz. dripping**
**Salt and pepper**
**A good gravy**

*Method 1.* Remove any excess fat from the meat and cut the meat into small pieces. Heat the dripping in a flat baking-tin until just smoking, pour in ¼ of the batter and bake until set. Add the chopped meat and season well. Pour in the remainder of the batter and put in a hot oven (**450° F., Gas 8**) until it has risen well. Then reduce heat and cook more slowly until ready. Serve with a good gravy.

*Method 2.* Prepare the meat and batter as above. Heat the dripping in a flat baking-tin and heat until just smoking. Add the chopped seasoned meat and cook in the oven for 5 min. Then pour in all the batter and bake as above for about 1 hr. Serve with a good gravy.

**6 helpings**

**TOASTED SANDWICHES**

Toast made from either white or brown bread may be used for toast sandwiches and the sandwiches may be single, double or triple decker (the toast should of course be very thin for double or triple-decker sandwiches). The bread may be toasted on one side only or on both sides; the sandwiches may be eaten hot or cold. Spread the toast with butter and one of the suggested fillings, sandwich together and cut into triangles.

**Fillings**

1. Cooked skinned sausages split lengthwise and covered with a layer of apple sauce.
2. A rasher of fried bacon covered with sautéd mushrooms.
3. A thick slice of fried canned meat, topped with slices of grilled or fried tomato.
4. Cooked skinned sausages split lengthwise and spread with scrambled egg.
5. Lettuce leaf with a slice of Cheddar or Cheshire cheese and slices of tomato on top.

**TODDLERS' PARTY CAKE**

**3 eggs**
**4 oz. sugar**
**4 oz. flour**

Whisk the eggs and sugar until thick. The mixture should be very thick before folding in the flour lightly. Pour the mixture into a lined 7-in. tin and bake in a moderate oven (**350° F., Gas 4**) for 25–35 min. Cool on a wire rack. Cut across twice and fill with sieved raspberry jam. Ice with Marshmallow Icing as below.

MARSHMALLOW ICING—for top and sides of cake

**8 oz. granulated sugar**
**⅛ pt. water**
**Pinch of cream of tartar**
**2 egg whites**
**Colouring (optional)**

Put the sugar and water and cream of tartar into a small saucepan, dissolve and boil to the small ball stage, 237° F. Stir well. Whisk the egg whites very stiffly and add the sugar to these, gradually whisking all the time, adding the colouring at this stage. Continue to whisk until the mixture starts to thicken. Then spread over the cake and add any decorations before the icing sets. If 1 teasp. of the icing is reserved and thinned with 1 or 2 drops water or colouring this may be used to pipe the child's name on the cake.

**TOMATO ASPIC**

**½ oz. gelatine**
**2 tablesp. water**
**½ pt. tomato pulp**
**½ gill aspic**
**1 tablesp. meat glaze**

Soak the gelatine in the water. Put all the

ingredients in a saucepan over heat, stir until boiling, season to taste with salt and a pinch of cayenne pepper. Strain through a cloth or fine sieve.

Use for masking and decorating purposes.

### TOMATO KETCHUP

**6 lb. ripe tomatoes**
**1 pt. vinegar**
**½ lb. sugar**
**1 oz. salt**
**½ teasp. allspice**
**½ teasp. cloves**
**½ teasp. cinnamon**
**½ teasp. cayenne pepper**

Cut the tomatoes into quarters, place them in a preserving-pan with the salt and vinegar and simmer until the tomatoes are quite soft and broken up. Strain the mixture through coarse muslin or a nylon sieve, then return the purée to the preserving-pan and add the sugar. Continue to simmer till the ketchup starts to thicken, and then add the spices a little at a time, stirring thoroughly until the flavour is to taste.

When the ketchup is reasonably thick, fill into hot bottles and seal immediately, or allow it to cool slightly, then fill the bottles and sterilize at 170° F. for 30 min.

Remember it will be thicker when cold than hot, so don't reduce it too far.

### TOMATO LILIES AS A GARNISH

Using a stainless steel knife, make zigzag cuts into the centre of the tomato and pull the two halves apart. Alternatively use a potato peeler to make the zigzag cuts.

### TOMATO MAYONNAISE

**¼ pt. thick mayonnaise**
**⅛ pt. tomato purée, canned *or* fresh, *or* ⅛ pt. cold tomato sauce *or* bottled tomato sauce**

Fold the tomato purée carefully into the mayonnaise.

NOTE: If fresh tomatoes are used some of the juice must be pressed out and kept apart from the firm flesh before sieving.

### TOMATO IN SALADS

For all salads containing sliced tomatoes, the tomatoes should be skinned first. The removal of the pips from the tomatoes is a matter for personal choice.

*To skin tomatoes*

There are 3 methods of skinning tomatoes. The 1st and 2nd methods listed below are excellent where only a few tomatoes have to be skinned. The 3rd method is preferable where a large number of tomatoes have to be skinned.

1. Rub the surface of the tomatoes firmly with the back of a knife. Slit and remove the skin.
2. Impale the tomato on a fork and hold over a low gas flame, turning it in the flame until the skin wrinkles and splits. (A gas taper may be used instead of the gas burner.) Remove the skin and cool the tomato.
3. Cover the tomatoes with boiling water and leave for 1 min. Drain and plunge the tomatoes immediately into cold water. Slit and remove the skins.
   Care must be taken to avoid leaving the tomatoes too long in the boiling water and thus partially cooking them.

### TOMATO AND ONION SALAD

*Salade d'Oignons et Tomates*

**6 tomatoes**
**1 large onion**
**Salad dressing *or* French dressing**

Boil *or* bake the onion until almost tender. When cold chop it finely. Skin and slice the tomatoes, sprinkle the onion over them and add a little salad dressing or French dressing.

NOTE: 1 dessertsp. finely-chopped chives, *or* 3 spring onions, finely chopped may be substituted for the cooked onion.

**6 helpings**

## TOMATO SALAD

*Salade de Tomates*

**6 large firm tomatoes**
**Salt and pepper**
**French dressing**
**Finely-chopped parsley**

Skin and slice the tomatoes. Season lightly. Pour the dressing over the tomatoes. Sprinkle with chopped parsley.

**6 helpings**

## TOMATO SAUCE

**1 onion**
**1 small carrot**
**1 oz. bacon scraps *or* bacon bone *or* rinds**
**½ oz. butter *or* margarine**
**4 medium-sized tomatoes, fresh, bottled *or* canned**
**½ oz. rice flour**
**½ pt. white second stock *or* liquid from canned *or* bottled tomatoes**
**Salt and pepper**
**Lemon juice**
**Sugar**
**Grated nutmeg**

Slice the onion and carrot. Put them into a saucepan with the bacon and fry them in the fat without browning them for 10 min. Slice and add the tomatoes and cook them for 5 min. Sprinkle in the rice flour, add the stock or juice, stir till the sauce boils. Simmer the sauce for 45 min. Rub the sauce through a hair or nylon sieve. Reheat, season and add lemon juice, sugar and nutmeg to taste.

## TOMATO SOUP

*Purée de Tomate*

**1 lb. tomatoes fresh *or* canned**
**1 onion**
**1 carrot**
**½ oz. margarine**
**1 oz. bacon scraps, rind *or* bone**
**1 pt. white stock *or* juice from canned tomatoes**
**Grated nutmeg**
**Lemon juice**
**A bunch of herbs**
**Minute tapioca *or* cornflour**
**Salt and pepper**
**Sugar**
**Red colouring, if needed**

Slice the tomatoes, onion and carrot. If canned tomatoes are used, strain them and make the juice up to 1 pt. with stock. Melt the margarine in a deep pan and lightly fry the sliced vegetables and chopped bacon for 10 min. Boil the stock or tomato juice and add to the vegetables with the nutmeg, lemon juice and herbs and cook for ¾–1 hr. Sieve and thicken the soup with ½ oz. cornflour or minute tapioca to each 1 pt. soup, blended with a little cold milk, stock or water. Stir into the soup, cook till clear, season, add sugar to taste and colouring if needed.

**4 helpings**
**Cooking time—¾–1 hr.**

## TOMATO SOUP—ITALIAN

*Purée de Tomate à l'Italienne*

**1½ lb. ripe tomatoes**
**1 tablesp. olive oil**
**1 pt. stock**
**1 clove of garlic**
**Parsley**
**Basil**
**Marjoram**
**1 tablesp. ground rice**
**Salt and pepper**
**⅛ pt. cream (optional)**
**1 egg yolk (optional)**

Proceed as for Vegetable Purée. Cook for 5 min. only, in stock before sieving. (The tomatoes should be chopped fine to hasten cooking.)

NOTE: If this soup is not thickened it may be served iced. Sprinkle in some finely sieved brown breadcrumbs before chilling.

**4 helpings**
**Cooking time—20 min.**

## TOMATO STUFFING

**1 large ripe tomato**
**½ sweet, red pepper *or* pimento**
**½ clove of garlic**
**2 tablesp. breadcrumbs**
**Salt and pepper**

Scald, skin and chop the tomato. Remove the seeds from the pimento and chop it. Crush and chop the garlic. Mix the ingredients, using enough crumbs to absorb the juice of the tomato. Season to taste.

Use with pigeon or other small birds.

## TOMATES FARCIES À LA PROVENÇALE

Stuffed Tomatoes Provençale

**1 lb. tomatoes**
**Salt and pepper**
**1 teasp. olive oil**
**2 oz. chopped onion *or* shallots**
**1 small clove of garlic**
**1 oz. butter**
**3–4 oz. white breadcrumbs**
**Chopped parsley**

Cut the tomatoes in 2 crosswise. Remove

the pips and juice. Place the halves of tomatoes in a fireproof dish. Lightly season and cook 1–2 min. in the oven. Heat the olive oil in a saucepan, add the finely-chopped onion or shallots and the crushed clove of garlic, and gently cook without colouring (stirring with a wooden spoon). Add the butter and when this has melted add also the white breadcrumbs, chopped parsley and seasoning. Thoroughly mix together, then fill the halves of tomatoes. Place the dish of tomatoes in a hot oven and quickly gratinate (i.e. cook until a crust forms).

### TOURNÉE SAUCE

**½ pt. Velouté sauce**
**6 spring onions—white parts only**
**4 small mushrooms**
**A bunch of herbs**
**Chopped parsley**

Chop the onions and mushrooms and simmer them with the bunch of herbs in the Velouté sauce until they are quite tender. Remove the herbs, add the chopped parsley and serve the sauce.

Serve with meat or fish.

### TOURTIÈRE

**1 lb. lean pork**
**1 large onion**
**½ cup boiling water**
**Salt and pepper**
**1 small chicken**
**1 stick of celery**
**Flaky *or* rough puff pastry using 8 oz. flour, etc.**

Mince or finely chop the pork. Peel and chop the onion; mix with the pork. Put into a pan, add the boiling water and season to taste. Bring to the boil, stirring continuously. Cut chicken into 5–6 pieces and add to pork. Break celery into 3–4 pieces and add to contents of pan. Put lid on pan and simmer slowly until chicken is tender. Remove chicken, cut flesh into large dice. Drain the pork, and mix with the diced chicken. Discard the celery.

Line a 9-in. pie-dish with pastry, put in the meat filling, cover with pastry. Bake in a hot oven (**425° F., Gas 7**).

**Cooking time—1½ hr. to cook chicken**
**½ hr. to bake pie**

### TRANSPARENT ICING

**1 lb. loaf sugar**
**½ gill warm water**
**Lemon juice to flavour**

Put the sugar and water into a strong saucepan, let it dissolve, then bring to the boil and simmer for about 5 min., or until a thick syrup is formed (**230° F.** on a saccharometer), brushing down the sides of the pan with a damp brush to remove the sugar. Stir in the lemon juice, and beat until the icing thickens and becomes opaque, then use as required.

### TRANSPARENT PASTRY

For certain pies

**¾ lb. butter**
**1 lb. plain flour**
**Pinch of salt**
**1 egg**

Remove as much moisture as possible from the butter, using a dry cloth. Melt the butter over a very low heat; allow to cool. When almost cold stir in the sifted flour, salt and beaten egg. Knead lightly until smooth and use as required.

### TREACLE LAYER PUDDING

*Pouding à la Mélasse*

**2 oz. breadcrumbs**
**Rind of 1 lemon**
**½ lb. treacle *or* golden syrup (approx.)**

SUET CRUST PASTRY

**4–6 oz. finely-chopped *or* shredded suet**
**12 oz. plain flour**
**Pinch of salt**
**2 rounded teasp. baking-powder**
**Water to mix**

Sift the flour, salt and baking-powder and mix them with sufficient water to make a soft, but firm, dough. Divide the dough into two equal portions, using one portion to line a 2 pt. basin. From the other portion cut off enough to make the lid; roll out the remainder thinly.

Mix the breadcrumbs and grated lemon rind.

Put a layer of treacle in the basin; sprinkle well with the breadcrumbs. Cover with a round of the thinly-rolled pastry. Moisten the edge of it with water and join securely to the pastry at the side of the basin. Add another layer of treacle, crumbs and pastry; then more treacle and crumbs. Finally cover with the rolled-out top as the last layer of pastry. Cover with greased paper. Steam for 2½ hr.

**6–7 helpings**

### TREACLE TART

| | |
|---|---|
| **Short crust pastry using 6 oz. flour, etc.** | **3 tablesp. golden syrup** |
| | **Lemon juice *or* ginger** |
| | **2 oz. fresh breadcrumbs** |

Slightly warm the syrup, flavour with a pinch of ginger or a little lemon juice, then stir in the breadcrumbs.

Line a 9-in. fireproof plate with the pastry, trim and decorate the edge. Spread over the syrup mixture, decorate with cross strips of pastry, and bake in a fairly hot oven (**400° F., Gas 6**) for about 30 min.

NOTE: If preferred the tart may be baked as a double crust tart, increase the amount of pastry and bake for 50 min. Crushed cornflakes may be substituted for the breadcrumbs if liked.

**6 helpings**

### TRIFLE—TRADITIONAL RECIPE

*Trifle Anglaise*

| | |
|---|---|
| **4 individual sponge cakes** | **1 oz. almonds (blanched and shredded)** |
| **Raspberry *or* strawberry jam** | **½ pt. custard using ½ pt. milk, 1 egg and 1 egg yolk** |
| **6 macaroons** | **¼ pt. double cream** |
| **12 ratafia biscuits** | **1 egg white** |
| **¼ pt. sherry** | **1–2 oz. castor sugar** |
| **Grated rind of ½ lemon** | |

DECORATION

| | |
|---|---|
| **Glacé cherries** | **Angelica** |

Split the sponge cakes into two and spread the lower halves with jam. Replace tops. Arrange in a glass dish and cover with macaroons and ratafias. Soak with sherry, and sprinkle with lemon rind and almonds. Cover with the custard and leave to cool. Whisk the cream, egg white and sugar together until stiff and pile on top of the trifle. Decorate with glacé cherries and angelica.

**6 helpings**

### TRIPE À LA LYONNAISE

*Gras-Double à la Lyonnaise*

| | |
|---|---|
| **1½ lb. cold boiled tripe** | **2 heaped teasp. finely-chopped parsley** |
| **1 large onion** | **3 teasp. vinegar** |
| **3 oz. butter** | **Salt and pepper** |

Cut the tripe into pieces about 2 in. square and slice the onion. Heat the butter in a frying-pan and fry the onion until tender and golden brown. Add the tripe, parsley, vinegar, salt and pepper, and toss in the pan for a few minutes until thoroughly heated. Serve immediately.

**6 helpings** **Cooking time—about 15 min**

### TRIPE AND ONIONS

*Tripes aux Oignons*

| | |
|---|---|
| **1½ lb. tripe** | **2 large onions** |
| **½ pt. milk** | **1 oz. flour** |
| **1 teasp. salt** | **Salt and pepper** |

Blanch the tripe and cut into 3-in squares. Put in a saucepan with the milk, ½ pt. water and the salt; bring to the boil. Peel and slice the onions finely. Add them to the tripe and simmer very slowly for 2 hr. Mix the flour to a smooth paste with a little cold milk and add to the pan. Stir with a wooden spoon until boiling. Simmer for another 10 min., season to taste and serve.

**6 helpings**

### TRUITES AU BLEU

| | |
|---|---|
| **One 6–8 oz. trout** | **Salt** |
| **Vinegar** | **Parsley** |

The essential factor of this famous dish is that the trout should be alive until just before cooking. In continental restaurants they are often kept in a tank from which the customer selects his fish, which is then stunned, cleaned and cooked immediately.

The fish should be stunned, cleaned (gutted) and immediately plunged into a pan of boiling salted water to which a little vinegar has been added. (The fish are not scaled or washed as this would spoil the blue colour.) Draw the pan aside or reduce the heat and poach the fish for about 10–12 min. Drain and serve garnished with parsley and accompanied by melted butter, Hollandaise sauce and small boiled potatoes.

### TUNA SALAD IN GRAPEFRUIT

Allow one grapefruit for two helpings. Cut across in half and remove the pulp. Add to it an equal amount of drained canned peas and half this amount in flaked tuna fish moistened with mayonnaise. Cut out the core and skinny bits of the grapefruit and squeeze their juice into the grapefruit shells. Line the inside of the shells with shredded lettuce, heap the mixture into them and sprinkle with paprika.

### TURKEY SOUP

*Potage de dinde*

**Carcase and trimmings of 1 turkey**
**1 oz. lean bacon**
**1 oz. butter *or* margarine**
**1 onion**
**1 carrot**
**½ parsnip**
**1 stick of celery**
**1 oz. flour**
**1 qt. water to each 1 lb. cooked turkey remains**
**A bunch of herbs**
**1 clove**
**Some neat pieces of breast of bird**
**Salt and pepper**

Put the pieces of carcase, the trimmings, and the bacon, with the fat in a saucepan and fry them till brown. Remove the turkey and fry the sliced vegetables till brown. Add the flour and fry it till golden-brown, stir in the stock, bring to the boil, add the herbs, return the turkey to the pan and simmer for 1½–2 hr. Meanwhile cut the pieces of breast meat into ¼-in. dice. Strain the soup, in it reheat the diced meat, season carefully and serve.

NOTE: Scraps of forcemeat improve the flavour and help to thicken.

**4–6 helpings**
**Cooking time—about 2 hr.**

### TURBOT WITH CREAM SAUCE

*Turbot à la Crème*

**¾ lb. cold cooked turbot (approx.)**
**1½ oz. butter**
**1 oz. flour**
**½ pt. milk**
**1 teasp. lemon juice**
**3 tablesp. cream**
**Pinch of ground mace**
**Salt and pepper**

Remove the bones and skin from the fish, and separate the flesh into large flakes. Melt the butter in a saucepan, add the flour and cook for 3 min. Pour in the milk, stir until it boils and then simmer gently for 10 min. Put in the fish and let it become thoroughly hot, then add the lemon juice, cream and seasoning to taste and serve.

**3–4 helpings**
**Cooking time—about 20 min.**

### TURBOT À L'ITALIENNE

*Turbot à l'Italienne*

**Remains of cold turbot**
**Italian sauce**

Remove the bone and black skin carefully from the fish. Heat the sauce in a flat saucepan and when hot place in the fish to warm through, but do not let it boil. Serve on a hot dish garnished with fried bread croûtons.

**Cooking time—5 min.**

### TURBOT AU GRATIN

*Turbot au Gratin*

**Remains of cold turbot**
**Béchamel *or* other white sauce**
**Seasoning**
**Breadcrumbs**
**Butter**

Divide the flesh of the turbot into small pieces, carefully freeing it from all bone and black skin. Put the fish into a saucepan, moisten with sufficient white sauce to cover well. Season to taste with salt and pepper and let it get thoroughly hot, but do not allow to boil. Arrange the fish and sauce in a baking-dish, cover with white or brown breadcrumbs and place a few very small pieces of butter over the top. Brown in the oven or under the grill.

**Cooking time—altogether ½ hr.**

## TURNIPS —COOKED FOR FOOD VALUE

| | |
|---|---|
| **2 lb. turnips** | **½ teasp. salt** |
| **1 oz. butter *or* margarine** | **½-1 gill boiling water** |
| | **Chopped parsley** |

Scrub and peel the turnips thickly. If large, cut into quarters, then slice thinly (if young turnips, slice the whole turnip). Fat steam the turnips for 10 min., i.e. shake them in the melted fat, well below frying temperature with the lid on the pan until the fat is absorbed. Add the liquid and the salt, and simmer gently until the turnips are tender, 15–30 min. according to age of turnips. Serve hot with the small amount of liquid remaining, and garnished with chopped parsley.

**6 helpings**

## TURNIPS WITH CREAM

*Navets à la crème*

As for Turnips— Cooked for Food Value Stir in 1 tablesp. cream just before serving.

**6 helpings**
**Cooking time—20–35 min.**

## GLAZED TURNIPS

*Navets glacés*

| | |
|---|---|
| **1½ lb. young turnips** | **¼ teasp. salt** |
| **2 oz. butter** | **Good stock** |
| **3 lumps sugar** | **Parsley** |

Melt the butter in a saucepan. Add the scraped, whole turnips, sugar, salt and enough stock to come halfway up the turnips. Cook gently, without a lid, shaking the pan occasionally, until tender. Remove the turnips and keep them hot. Boil the stock rapidly until reduced to a rich glaze. Replace the turnips 2–3 at a time, turn them until both sides are well coated with glaze. Dish, sprinkle with chopped parsley and serve.

**6 helpings**
**Cooking time—about ¾ hr.**

## STUFFED TURNIPS

*Navets farcis*

| | |
|---|---|
| **6 even-sized, young turnips** | **1 tablesp. breadcrumbs** |
| **4 tablesp. finely-chopped liver *or* cooked ham *or* any cooked meat** | **½ teasp. finely-chopped fresh sage *or* ½ teasp. dried sage** |
| **1 tablesp. finely-chopped cooked onion** | **Salt and pepper** |
| | **1 egg** |
| | **Butter *or* margarine** |
| | **¾ pt. brown sauce** |

Peel and steam the turnips gently until almost soft—about 1 hr. Lift out the centre of each turnip with a teaspoon handle. Chop the turnip centres and add to the stuffing. Mix the stuffing ingredients with the beaten egg. Season well. Press the stuffing firmly into each turnip and pile neatly on top. Sprinkle the top of each turnip with a little melted butter *or* margarine. Pin a band of stiff, greased paper round each turnip to prevent splitting. Put into a greased, fireproof dish and bake 30–40 min. in a moderate oven (**350° F., Gas 4**).

Serve with the sauce poured round.

**6 helpings**
**Cooking time—about 1¾ hr.**

## UNMOULDING JELLIES AND CREAMS

The unmoulding of jellies and creams can only be successfully achieved by one single, quick, and total immersion in very hot water. Repeated dipping in water that is not hot enough to loosen the mould instantly will spoil the shape and dislodge any decoration. Charlottes lined with sponge fingers are dipped only to the rim, as any dampening of the sponge would cause the charlotte to collapse.

After total immersion, quickly absorb any surface moisture with a clean cloth, and with one sharp jerk, turn out the mould on to the serving dish by gently sliding the fingers of the supporting hand from underneath the loosened jelly.

Mask the dish surrounding the jelly with piped cream or chopped jelly and rub the dish lightly to remove any spot or mark before serving.

## VANILLA CREAM

*Crème à la Vanille*

| | |
|---|---|
| **3 egg yolks** *or* **1 whole egg and 1 yolk** | **½ oz. gelatine** |
| **2–3 oz. castor sugar** | **4 tablesp. water** |
| **½ pt. milk** | **2 teasp. vanilla essence** |
| | **½ pt. double cream** |

Beat the eggs and sugar until liquid. Heat the milk to almost boiling point and pour over the egg mixture. Strain the egg and milk back into the saucepan, and cook very gently until thick, stirring all the time. Allow to cool. Soak the gelatine in the water for 5 min., then heat to dissolve. Stir the vanilla essence into the cooled custard, and add the dissolved gelatine, stirring again as it cools. Whip the cream and fold lightly into the custard mixture just before setting. Pour into a prepared mould or into glass dishes.

**6 helpings**
**Setting time—1–2 hr.**

## VANILLA CRESCENT BISCUITS—AUSTRIAN

*Vanille Kipferl*

| | |
|---|---|
| **7 oz. butter** | **3 oz. blanched finely-chopped almonds** |
| **2 oz. sugar** | **Vanilla sugar** |
| **8 oz. plain flour** | |

Put the butter and sugar into a bowl and beat until white and creamy. Sift in the flour gradually, add the chopped almonds and work all into a paste. Take small pieces of the paste and roll them with the hand into thin "sausages" about the size of the little finger, making each end slightly thinner. Curve them into the shape of a crescent. Fit a piece of greaseproof paper on to a baking-sheet and lay the crescents on it. Bake in a cool oven **(310° F., Gas 2)** until a pale brown. Dust with vanilla sugar.

## VANILLA ICE CREAM (1)—Economical

*Glace à la Crème de Vanille*

| | |
|---|---|
| **¼ pt. cream** *or* **prepared evaporated milk** | **1 pt. cold custard (1)** |
| | **1 teasp. vanilla essence** |

Half whip the cream *or* evaporated milk. Add the custard and vanilla. Chill and freeze.

**6 helpings** **Time—2½ hr.**

## VANILLA ICE CREAM (2)—Rich

| | |
|---|---|
| **½ pt. cream** | **1 teasp. vanilla** |
| **½ pt. cold custard (2)** | **2 oz. castor sugar** |

Half whip the cream. Add the custard, vanilla and sugar. Chill and freeze.

## VANILLA ICE CREAM (3)

| | |
|---|---|
| **1 pt. milk** | **½ pt. cream** |
| **8 egg yolks** | **1 teasp. vanilla essence** |
| **4 oz. castor sugar** | |

Heat the milk and pour it on to the beaten egg yolks. Strain it back into the saucepan and cook without boiling until it coats the back of a wooden spoon. Add sugar, cover and cool. Half whip the cream and add it to the cooled custard with the vanilla. Pour into the tray and freeze at medium for ½ hr. Beat well and continue to freeze for another 2 hr.

**8 helpings**

## VANILLA SOUFFLÉ

*Soufflé à la Vanille*

| | |
|---|---|
| **1½ oz. butter** | **1½ oz. castor sugar** |
| **1½ oz. plain flour** | **½ teasp. vanilla essence** |
| **⅜ pt. milk** | **5 egg whites** |
| **4 egg yolks** | |

Prepare the soufflé tin according to the method of cooking. If the soufflé is to be baked, butter the mould well, if steamed

Melt the butter, stir in the flour and cook gently for a few minutes without colouring. Add the milk, stir well until smooth. Reheat stirring continuously until the mixture thickens and leaves the sides of the pan. Leave to cool· Beat in the egg yolks, sugar and vanilla essence. Whisk the egg whites stiffly and fold them in lightly. Pour the mixture into the mould or tin and cover. Steam for $\frac{3}{4}$–1 hr. or bake in a fairly hot oven (**375° F., Gas 5**) for 30—35 min.

**6 helpings**

## VEAL

Once the facts about beef, pork and lamb are known little need be added on veal. The carcase is only sparsely fatted in all except the largest calves and even in these there is less fat than on other meat. The flesh is usually described as pink but the colour is usually darker than pork. The cuts follow the same pattern as lamb cutting and are described by the same names. Occasionally the shoulder is called an **oyster of veal** after the fore knuckle has been removed.

The meat from the hind and fore knuckles, equivalent to the shin and leg of beef together with the scrag and middle neck are used for stewing. All the other cuts are suitable for roasting or frying. Due to the absence of fat, veal needs a moist, fat-containing stuffing, or should be served with a sauce. The breast, stuffed and roasted, is probably the most tasty and the most economical cut.

## VEAL BROTH

*Bouillon de Veau*

**1½ lb. knuckle of veal**
**3 pt. water**
**2 teasp. lemon juice**
**1½ teasp. salt**
**1 oz. pearl barley *or* rice**
**1 carrot**
**1 small turnip**
**1 leek**
**1 stick of celery**
**A bunch of herbs: parsley stalks, thyme, bay leaf**
**Strip of lemon rind**
**Peppercorns**
**1 dessertsp. chopped parsley**

Scrape and wash the knuckle, put it into a pan with cold water. Bring slowly to simmering point, add lemon juice and salt. Blanch barley (skim well) and add it to the pan. Simmer gently 2 hr. Scrub and peel the vegetables and cut them in $\frac{1}{4}$-in. dice. Add them to the broth with the herbs (tied in a bundle), lemon rind and spice and simmer for a further 1 hr. before serving. When the meat is quite tender lift it out. Remove the meat from the bones and cut it into $\frac{1}{4}$-in. cubes. Strain the broth through a colander, return it to the pan to keep hot and remove bones, spice and herbs from the vegetables. Return meat and vegetables to the pan, add parsley, season and reheat. Use the bone again for stock.

**4–5 helpings** **Cooking time—3–4 hr.**

## VEAL CAKE or VEAL MOULD

**1 lb. lean fillet of veal**
**½ lb. lean bacon**
**2 hard-boiled eggs**
**2 teasp. finely-chopped parsley**
**2 teasp. finely-grated lemon rind**
**Salt and pepper**
**¾ pt. jellied veal stock**
**¼ oz. gelatine (if required)**
**Parsley *or* salad**

Dice the veal and bacon. Cut the eggs into slices and arrange some of them in a pattern on the bottom of a greased mould. Mix the parsley, lemon rind and seasoning together. Place a thick layer of veal in the mould, cover with a thin layer of bacon, a layer of sliced egg and a layer of the parsley and lemon mixture. Repeat the layers until the mould is full. Pour in the jellied stock, cover with greased greaseproof paper and bake in a moderate oven (**350° F., Gas 4**) for 2–2½ hr. Fill up the mould with extra stock, adding $\frac{1}{4}$ oz. gelatine to $\frac{1}{2}$ pt. stock if the stock is not stiff enough. When cold, turn out the mould and garnish with parsley or salad.

**6 helpings**

## VEAL CUTLETS

*Côtelettes de Veau*

**1½ lb. fillet *or* neck of veal**
**2 eggs *or* 1 egg and milk**
**1 teasp. finely-chopped parsley**
**¼ teasp. powdered thyme**
**½ teasp. finely-grated lemon rind**
**Salt and pepper**
**½ oz. butter**
**Breadcrumbs**
**Butter *or* fat for frying**

GARNISH

**Parsley**
**Slices of lemon**

Cut the meat in slices about $\frac{1}{2}$ in. thick and trim into neat fillets. Beat the eggs, or egg and milk, and mix with the parsley, thyme, lemon rind, seasoning and $\frac{1}{2}$ oz. melted butter. Brush the cutlets with this mixture and coat carefully with breadcrumbs. Fry in hot butter or fat for about 10–15 min. Fry both sides quickly first, then cook more slowly, turning as required, until golden brown. Drain well and place on a hot dish. Garnish with parsley and slices of lemon.

Serve with tomato, demi-glace or piquant sauce, or gravy.

**6 helpings**

## VEAL CUTLETS—MAINTENON STYLE

*Côtelettes de Veau à la Maintenon*

**1½ lb. fillet *or* neck of veal**
**Butter *or* fat**
**1 oz. ham**
**1 shallot**
**1 oz. flour**
**¾ pt. white stock**
**Few strips of lemon rind**
**Salt and pepper**
**Oil *or* butter**

Cut the veal into neat cutlets, allowing 2 per person. Fry until slightly browned in hot fat and put aside. Finely shred the ham and finely chop the shallot. Melt 1 oz. fat in a stewpan, add the ham and shallot and sauté for a few minutes. Add the flour and cook slowly until light brown. Add the stock, lemon rind, seasoning to taste and bring to the boil, stirring constantly. Simmer for 15 min., then add the cutlets and cook very gently just below simmering point until the meat is tender. Test with a skewer. Take out the cutlets, strain the sauce and leave to become cold. Take one sheet of greaseproof paper or aluminium foil per cutlet and cut away the corners. Brush both sides with oil or butter. Place one cutlet on each, cover with sauce and fold and fasten so that the sauce cannot escape. Bake in a fairly hot oven (**375° F., Gas 5**) for 15 min. Serve in the paper cases.

**6 helpings**

## VEAL FORCEMEAT

*See Veal Stuffing.*

## VEAL AND HAM PIE

**2½ lb. neck *or* breast of veal**
**Salt and pepper**
**1½ lb. ham *or* bacon**
**2 hard-boiled eggs**
**Forcemeat balls**
**Puff *or* rough puff pastry**
**Pinch of ground mace**
**Grated rind of 1 lemon**

Cut the meat into 1½ in. square pieces. Put into a fireproof dish or saucepan, season with salt and pepper, cover with cold water, and cook gently either in the oven or on the stove for 2 hr. Meanwhile cut the ham into narrow strips, the eggs into thin slices, make the forcemeat balls, and fry them lightly in a little hot dripping. Roll out the pastry to a suitable thickness and cut a piece to cover the top of the pie-dish. Line the edge of the dish with the trimmings. Allow the meat to cool slightly, then cover the bottom of the pie-dish with meat, add a few strips of bacon and slices of egg. Sprinkle lightly with salt, pepper, mace, lemon rind, then intersperse with forcemeat balls. Repeat until the dish is full then half-fill the dish with gravy. Put on the pastry cover, moisten and press the edges together. Make a hole in the centre of the top, decorate with pastry leaves, brush over with egg, and bake for 45–60 min. in a fairly hot oven (**375° F., Gas 5**). As soon as the pie is baked add a little more well-seasoned gravy through the hole in the top, and when served hot serve with gravy made from the liquor in which the meat was stewed.

**8-10 helpings**

## VEAL KROMESKIES

**6 oz. cooked veal**
**1½ oz. cooked ham**
**¾ oz. butter**
**¾ oz. flour**
**1½ gills white stock**
**1½ tablesp. cream**
**2 tablesp. chopped mushrooms**
**1 teasp. chopped parsley**
**Salt**
**Cayenne pepper**
**Pinch of nutmeg**
**6 bacon rashers**
**French batter**
**Deep fat**
**Parsley for garnish**

Chop the veal and ham very finely. Melt the butter, add the flour, and stir and cook without colouring for 3 min. Add the stock slowly and stir whilst boiling for 5 min. Remove from the heat, cool a little, then add the cream. Add the chopped meats, mushrooms, parsley, salt, cayenne and nutmeg and mix well. Spread evenly on a wet plate and leave to become cold and firm. Divide into 12 portions and roll into cork shapes. Enclose each in half a rasher of bacon and dip into the batter. Fry in hot deep fat until golden brown then drain. Garnish with fried or fresh parsley.

Serve with tomato sauce.

**3 helpings**

## VEAL OLIVES

*Olives de Veau*

| | |
|---|---|
| **1½ lb. fillet of veal** | **1½ oz. butter *or* fat** |
| **8 thin bacon rashers** | **1 pt. brown sauce** |
| **4–6 oz. veal forcemeat** | |

GARNISH

| | |
|---|---|
| **Mashed potatoes** | **Slices of lemon** |
| **Green peas** | **Spinach purée** |

Prepare the veal and cut it into 8 thin slices about 4 in. by 3 in. and season. Place a slice of bacon on each piece of meat and spread with a thin layer of forcemeat. Then roll up tightly and fasten securely with fine string. Heat the fat in a saucepan and fry the rolls (olives) until lightly browned. Pour off the surplus fat and add the hot brown sauce to the olives. Cover and simmer gently for about 1½ hr. When tender, remove the string and place the olives on a bed of mashed potato and pour the sauce over. Garnish with green peas and slices of lemon and serve with spinach purée.

**6 helpings**

## VEAL PUDDING

*Pouding de Veau*

| | |
|---|---|
| **1½–2 lb. veal** | **Salt and pepper** |
| **6 oz. ham, bacon *or* pickled pork** | **1 gill stock** |
| **Suet pastry using 8 oz. flour, etc.** | **Good gravy** |
| | **Parsley** |

Wipe the meat, remove bones and gristle, and cut the meat into rather small neat pieces. Cut the ham, bacon or pork into narrow strips. Line a greased basin thinly with suet pastry, put in alternately, the meat, thin layers of ham and seasoning. Add the stock when the basin is ½ full. Put on a lid of pastry and cover with greased paper. Place the basin in a steamer or in a saucepan containing water to ½ the depth of the basin, replacing it with *boiling* water as it reduces. Steam for 3 hr. and serve in the basin. Garnish with sprigs of parsley and serve with a good gravy.

**6 helpings**

## VEAL À LA ROMAINE

*Poitrine de Veau à la Romaine*

| | |
|---|---|
| **The thick end of a breast of veal (about 2¼ lb.)** | **Bouquet garni** |
| **¾ lb. sausage meat** | **6 peppercorns** |
| **1 large onion** | **Salt and pepper** |
| **1 carrot** | **½ lb. Carolina rice** |
| **½ turnip** | **2 oz. grated cheese** |
| | **Meat glaze** |
| | **Slices of lemon** |

Remove all bones and tendons, trim meat neatly and season well. Spread the sausage meat evenly over the inner surface of the meat, roll up and tie securely with string. Slice the onion, carrot and turnip and place with the bones and trimmings in a stewpan. Add the bouquet garni, peppercorns and salt, add water to cover the vegetables. Place the meat on top and cover with greased paper and a well-fitting lid. Cook very gently for about 2½ hr. Baste occasionally and add more water or stock when necessary. Cook the rice in about 1½ pt. of boiling stock (taken from the pan) until the stock is absorbed, season to taste and stir in the cheese. Place the rice on a hot dish and put the meat on top. Brush the meat with glaze and garnish with slices of lemon.

**6 helpings**

## VEAL STUFFING or FORCEMEAT

| | |
|---|---|
| **4 oz. breadcrumbs** | **Nutmeg** |
| **2 oz. chopped suet *or* margarine** | **Grated rind of ½ lemon** |
| **1 tablesp. chopped parsley** | **Salt and pepper** |
| **½ teasp. chopped mixed herbs** | **1 beaten egg** |

Mix together all the ingredients and season to taste.

Use for veal and poultry, fish or vegetables.

## VEGETABLE CREAM SOUP

*Crème de Légumes*

| | |
|---|---|
| **2 lb. mixed vegetables:** | **A bunch of herbs** |

onions, carrots, turnip, leeks, 1 tomato, 2 medium potatoes
1 oz. butter, margarine *or* dripping
1 qt. stock *or* water
1 teasp. yeast *or* meat extract if water is used
¼ pt. milk
1 oz. flour to each qt. of sieved soup
Salt and pepper
¼ pt. cream (optional)
2 egg yolks (optional)

Proceed as for Vegetable Purée.

**6–8 helpings** **Cooking time—1 hr.**

## VEGETABLE GOOSE

**½ lb. bread soaked in cold water**
**1 onion**
**1 teasp. chopped sage**
**1 oz. butter**
**Salt and pepper**
**4 oz. chopped walnuts**

Squeeze the bread nearly dry and mash it. Mix in the other ingredients, chopped small. Butter a Yorkshire pudding dish, put in the mixture and bake in a fairly hot oven (**375° F., Gas 5**) for about ¾ hr.

**3 helpings**

## VEGETABLE MARROW— COOKED FOR FOOD VALUE

**2 small marrows**
**1 oz. butter *or* margarine**
**½–1 gill boiling water**
**½ teasp. salt**
**¾ pt. white sauce**

Peel the marrows. Cut into halves lengthwise and scrape out the seeds and pith with a tablespoon. Cut into pieces, about 2 in. square. Fat steam the pieces for 10 min., i.e. shake them in the melted fat, well below frying temperature with the lid on the pan until the fat is absorbed. Add the liquid and the salt, and simmer gently until the marrow is tender, about 15 min. Drain well, retaining the cooking liquor for use in making the white sauce. Dish the marrow in a hot dish and coat with the sauce. Serve immediately.

**6 helpings**
**Cooking time—about 25 min.**

## VEGETABLE MARROW SOUP

*Purée de Courge*

**1 lb. marrow after peeling and removing seeds**
**2 onions**
**1 stick of celery**
**1 oz. margarine**
**1 pt. white stock**
**A bunch of herbs**
**1 blade of mace**
**¼ pt. milk**
**Cornflour to thicken**
**Salt and pepper**

Proceed as for Vegetable Purée.

**4–6 helpings** **Cooking time—30 min.**

## VEGETABLE MARROW WITH CHEESE

*Courge au gratin*

**1 mature marrow**
**1 onion *or* clove of garlic**
**4 oz. dry grated cheese**
**1 tablesp. breadcrumbs**
**Salt and pepper**

Peel the marrow, discard seeds, cut into thin slices; steam until tender. Drain well. Rub over a casserole with cut onion *or* garlic. Put in a layer of marrow, season lightly, sprinkle with cheese. Continue in this way, finishing with a good tablesp. of cheese mixed with the breadcrumbs. Bake in a hot oven until brown (**425° F., Gas 7**).

**6 helpings**
**Cooking time—about 1 hr.**

## VEGETABLE PIE

*Pâté aux Légumes*

**½ lb. cooked vegetables**
**Meat extract**
**1 teasp. mixed herbs**
**8 oz. well-cooked haricot beans *or* a small can of nut meat**
**Short pastry using 8 oz. flour, etc. *or* 8 oz. cheese pastry *or* 1½ lb. mashed potatoes**

After cooking the vegetables, stir in the herbs, meat extract, beans, or nut meat cut in small cubes. Put into a pie-dish and cover with pastry *or* mashed potato. (If mashed potato is used, decorate the surface and dot with small pieces of fat). Bake in a fairly hot oven **(400° F., Gas 6)** until the pastry is cooked or the potato browned.

**6 helpings**
**Cooking time—about 40 min. in the oven if pastry is used.**
**about 25 min. in the oven if potato is used.**

## VEGETABLE PURÉE

### Basic Recipe

| | |
|---|---|
| **1 lb. vegetable** | **¼ pt. milk *or* ⅛ pt. milk and ⅛ pt. cream for light-coloured soups** |
| **Flavouring vegetable** | **½ oz. starchy thickening, e.g. flour, cornflour, ground rice, tapioca *or* potato to each pint of sieved soup** |
| **½–1 oz. butter, margarine *or* other suitable fat** | **Salt and pepper** |
| **1 pt. stock—white for white and pale green vegetables; brown for dark-coloured vegetables; *or* water; *or* vegetable boilings** | **Other flavouring *or* colouring if required** |
| **Flavouring herbs (optional)** | |

*For a Cream Soup add:*

**⅛–¼ pt. cream (this may replace some of the milk), sometimes also 1 egg yolk**

Slice or chop the main and flavouring vegetables. Melt the fat in a deep pan and in it cook the vegetables over gentle heat for 10 min. Keep the lid on the pan and shake it vigorously from time to time. Boil the stock, add it to the vegetables with the herbs and other flavouring (if used) and simmer the whole until the vegetables are quite soft. This cooking time should be as short as possible but will vary with the kind and age of the vegetables used. Remove the herbs, rub or press the vegetables through a sieve (wire for soft, pulpy or very firm vegetables; nylon if a very smooth purée is needed). Mix the liquid with the purée and measure the soup. Weigh or measure the thickening in the proportion given above. Blend the starch powder with cold milk, stock or water and stir it into the soup. Cook the soup until the starch is thickened and no longer tastes raw Season carefully to taste.

*For a Cream soup:*

After the starch thickening has been cooked, remove the pan from the heat. Mix the egg yolk and cream together, stir them into the soup, which should be well below boiling point. Stir over gentle heat till the egg yolk thickens, but do not boil. Serve the soup at once; cream and eggs cannot be kept hot. Cream when used alone may be stirred into the soup just at boiling point, as it is removed from the heat. It must not be allowed to boil.

Serve separately with any vegetable purée, fried croûtons of bread, pulled bread, Melba toast or "fairy" toast

## VEGETABLE STOCK FOR SOUPS AND SAUCES

| | |
|---|---|
| **2 large carrots** | **2 qt. boiling water** |
| **½ lb. onions** | **½ teasp. vegetable extract** |
| **3 sticks of celery** | **Bouquet garni** |
| **2 tomatoes** | **1 teasp. salt** |
| **Outer leaves of 1 lettuce *or* ¼ small cabbage** | **½ teasp. peppercorns** |
| **1 oz. butter** | **1 blade of mace** |
| | **1 bay leaf** |

Clean the vegetables in the usual way. Thinly slice the roots, cut up the tomatoes and shred the lettuce or cabbage. Fry the roots gently in the fat until golden brown, add the tomatoes and fry slightly. Add the boiling water, the extract, bouquet garni, salt, peppercorns, mace and bay leaf and simmer for 1 hr. Add the lettuce or cabbage and simmer 20 min. longer. Strain and use as soon as possible.

NOTE: Water in which fresh vegetables or pulses have been boiled should always be utilized for soups, sauces or gravy.

**Quantity—4 pt.** **Cooking time—1½ hr.**

## VEGETABLES

Vegetables are all too often considered by the cook to be the least important part of the meal. The general level of British vegetable growing is high, and vegetables can and should be interesting and pleasant to eat.

Unfortunately, some growers keep vege-

Vegetables are essential to health. Here is a cauliflower, cooked for food value, garnished with bacon rolls.

Try eggs for protein value, as a soufflé, for instance.

tables back until they are large and really past the stage at which they should be eaten. There is no excuse for this, however, in the case of the private gardener, who should supply the housewife with really tender, young vegetables. Small, young peas, carrots, new potatoes and Brussels sprouts, have a flavour entirely different from that of the large, full grown vegetables. They also take much less time to cook, so the housewife can conserve much more of their food value.

### VEGETARIAN COOKERY

Vegetarians can be divided into two classes; the strict vegetarians (known as vegans) who eat no food of animal origin whatsoever; and those who do not eat meat or fish, but will include eggs, milk and milk products in their diet.

For healthy life and growth, one must have an adequate supply of proteins, fats, carbohydrates, mineral matter and vitamins. In a normal mixed diet most protein is obtained from meat, fish, eggs, cheese and milk, so on this score a vegan may be sadly lacking. However, there are vegetable proteins. The chief sources of these are cereals, pulses (lentils, peas and beans) and nuts, and for the health of those who adopt this very restricted form of diet, it is essential that a wide variety of all types of vegetable proteins be included in the dishes. For instance, it is not advisable to use just one variety of nut kernel. Again, the biological value of pulse dishes is improved considerably if some form of cereal and green leaf protein is added to them.

Where the sweet course is concerned, there is no difficulty as most vegetarians (of both categories) prefer fruit in some form or other, and milk, though without animal gelatine. An acceptable substitute for the latter is *agar-agar* which is of vegetable origin.

There are on the market many ready-to-eat savouries in cans; rissole and fritter mixtures available in packets; several savoury spreads and canned vegetarian sausages, which the housewife will find are a great help in preparing a quick vegetarian meal. These can be obtained from Health Food Stores.

Many recipes in this book are suitable for vegetarians, and some are specially designed for them.

### VELOUTÉ SAUCE

French Fawn sauce

**2 oz. butter**
**6 button mushrooms *or* mushroom trimmings**
**12 peppercorns**
**A few parsley stalks**
**2 oz. flour**
**1 pt. good white stock**
**Salt and pepper**
**Lemon juice**
**⅛–¼ pt. cream**

Melt the butter in a saucepan and gently cook the mushrooms, peppercorns and parsley for 10 min. Add the flour and cook for a few minutes without browning it. Stir in the stock, bring the sauce to simmering point and simmer for 1 hr. Wring the sauce through a tammy cloth or damp muslin. Season, add lemon juice, and reheat. Just at boiling point stir in the cream. The mushrooms may be rinsed and used as garnish for the dish.

Serve with chicken, veal, sweetbreads, fish or vegetables.

### VENETIAN SAUCE

**½ pt. white wine sauce**
**6 tablesp. tarragon vinegar**
**2 shallots**
**1 teasp. chopped chervil**
**1 teasp. chopped tarragon**

Reduce the tarragon vinegar with the finely-chopped shallots to ½ its volume, strain it. Add this flavoured vinegar, then the herbs, to the hot white wine sauce.

Serve with chicken, veal *or* fish.

NOTE: This sauce may also be made with Béchamel foundation.

### VENISON

Venison should always be well hung before cooking, and the flavour is further improved if it is marinaded before use. The choicest part of the animal is the haunch, i.e. the leg and loin in one joint, which is usually roasted.

## *Venison Cutlets*

The best end of neck may be boned, rolled and roasted too, but the neck and shoulder are usually made into stews or pies. An abundance of clear, creamy-white fat indicates good quality meat. The flesh of the buck is usually preferred to that of the doe.

Venison should be hung for about 14 days in a cool, dry place but should be inspected carefully every day. It can be rubbed with a mixture of ginger and black pepper to preserve it. To test the meat, run a sharp knife into the flesh near the haunch bone; if it has an unpleasant smell when withdrawn, the meat should be washed with warm milk and water, dried thoroughly and covered with more preserving mixture. The latter should be washed off before the meat is cooked.

### VENISON CUTLETS

*Côtelettes de Venaison*

**6 cutlets of venison**
**3 oz. butter (approx.)**
**1½ pt. good gravy** ***or*** **sauce**
**Salt and pepper**

GARNISH

**Mushrooms**

Cut 6 cutlets from the best end of the neck of venison, trim the bones at the end, flatten and trim cutlets. Brush with melted butter; season. Heat gravy *or* sauce, trim mushrooms (peel them if necessary), brush with melted butter. Grill the cutlets, brushing with more butter if necessary. Grill mushrooms.

Place a dab of butter on each cutlet, serve very hot. Garnish with mushrooms. Serve sauce separately. Alternatively, the mushrooms may be stewed in the sauce.

**6 helpings**
**Cooking time—20–25 min.**

### VENISON, TO CARVE

*See Carving.*

### VERMICELLI CROQUETTES

*Croquettes de Vermicelle au Fromage*

**2 oz. vermicelli**
**¾ pt. milk**
**2 oz. grated cheese**
**1 oz. butter**
**Cayenne pepper**
**Salt and pepper**
**Egg and breadcrumbs** ***or*** **extra vermicelli**
**½ teasp. mixed mustard**
**Parsley**

Break the vermicelli into short pieces; put it into the milk when boiling, and cook until tender. Add the cheese, butter, mustard, a few grains of cayenne and salt and pepper to taste. Stir over heat until well mixed, then spread to about ½ in. thick on a large dish. When cold, cut into circles, ovals or crescents. Dip in beaten egg, coat with breadcrumbs or crushed vermicelli and fry in hot fat until lightly browned. Garnish with fried parsley.

**3–4 helpings**

### VICTORIA BUNS

**10 oz. plain flour**
**¼ teasp. salt**
**3–4 oz. sugar**
**2 small teasp. ground cinnamon**
**⅛ teasp. grated nutmeg**
**1 level teasp. bicarbonate of soda**
**2 teasp. golden syrup**
**2 teasp. treacle**
**4 oz. butter** ***or*** **margarine**
**2 eggs**
**Enough warm milk to make a pouring consistency**

DECORATION

**Blanched almonds**

Grease queen cake or deep patty tins and place a half blanched almond in the bottom of each. Mix all dry ingredients in a bowl, heat the fat, syrup and treacle and add to dry ingredients with the beaten eggs. Add enough warm milk to make a pouring consistency. Half-fill the prepared tins and bake in a moderate oven (**350° F., Gas 4**).

**26–30 buns** **Cooking time—20–30 min.**

### VICTORIA SANDWICH

**4 oz. butter** ***or*** **margarine**
**4 oz. castor sugar**
**2 eggs**
**4 oz. plain flour**
**Pinch of salt**
**1½ level teasp. baking-powder**

Cream fat and sugar very thoroughly. Add well-whisked eggs gradually, beating well between each addition—if sign of curdling, add some flour. Sift flour, salt and baking-powder and stir lightly into the creamed fat and eggs. Mix to a soft dropping consistency, adding a little water if necessary. Place the mixture in a prepared 7-in. sandwich tin and bake in a moderate oven (**350° F., Gas 4**).

**Cooking time—40–45 min.**

## VIENNESE PUDDING

*Pouding à la Viennoise*

**1 oz. almonds**
**½ pt. milk**
**2 eggs**
**3 tablesp. sherry (optional)**
**5 oz. white bread cut into ¼-in. dice**
**2 oz. castor sugar**
**3 oz. sultanas**
**2 oz. finely-chopped candied peel**
**Grated rind of 1 lemon**

CARAMEL

**1 oz. loaf sugar**
**4 tablesp. water**

Blanch, shred and, if liked, the almonds can be browned in a very cool oven . Dredge the loaf sugar into a small saucepan with 4 tablesp. of water and heat gently, stirring well until all the sugar is dissolved, without boiling. Remove the spoon, bring to the boil without stirring until light brown. Remove from the heat and add the milk quickly. Reheat gently until the caramel has dissolved in the milk. Allow to cool, then add the well-beaten eggs and sherry (if used). Meanwhile mix together the bread dice, castor sugar, cleaned sultanas, peel, almonds and lemon rind and pour the custard mixture on to this. Leave to stand for 1 hr. Pour into a well-buttered mould, cover with greased paper and steam for 2 hr. until set.

Turn out and serve with custard or arrowroot sauce.

**6–7 helpings**

## VINAIGRETTE SAUCE

This consists of a simple French dressing to which the following are added:

**1 teasp. finely-chopped gherkin**
**½ teasp. finely-chopped shallot** *or* **chives**
**½ teasp. finely-chopped parsley**
**1 teasp. finely-chopped capers**
**½ teasp. finely-chopped tarragon and chervil (if available)**

## VINEGARS

*See Fruit Syrups and Vinegars, Spiced Vinegar for Pickles, Tarragon Vinegar.*

## VINNOY KREM

Brandy Cream

**1 pt. double cream**
**Nutmeg**
**1 wineglass of brandy**
**Juice of ½ lemon**
**¼ lb. sponge fingers**

Whip the cream adding the brandy gradually, and the lemon juice. Pile into individual glasses. Grate a little nutmeg on top and put into a refrigerator until ready to serve.

Serve with sponge fingers. (Sugar may be beaten into the cream if desired.)

**6 helpings**

## VIOLET WATER ICE

*Glace à l'eau de Violette*

**¼ lb. violet petals**
**1½ pt. syrup**
**3 lemons**

Clean the violet petals. Place them in a bowl and pour over the boiling syrup. Infuse for 10 min. Strain and cool. Add the strained juice of the 3 lemons. Chill and freeze.

**6 helpings**
**Time—2–2½ hr.**

## VITELLO TONNATO

Veal with Tunny Fish

**1 lb. lean veal**
**1 stick of celery**
**1 carrot**
**1 small onion**
**1 bay leaf**
**Salt and pepper**
**4 oz. tunny fish**
**6 anchovy fillets**
**2 tablesp. capers**
**Juice of 1 lemon**
**Olive oil**
**Home-made mayonnaise**

GARNISH

**Sliced lemon**
**4 gherkins**
**A few green olives**
**Capers**

Stew veal with the celery, carrot, onion, bay leaf, salt and pepper, until tender, and allow to cool in its stock. Pass tunny fish, anchovies and capers through a fine sieve, and add lemon juice and enough oil to make a liquid sauce. Blend with 4–5 tablesp. mayonnaise and mix well. Arrange veal in thin slices on a dish, cover with sauce and decorate with sliced lemon, gherkins, olives and a few capers.

## VOLS-AU-VENT

*See Pastry Cases.*

## WALNUT GRAVY

**2 pickled walnuts**
**½ pt. vegetable stock**
**Salt and pepper**
**2 tablesp. walnut ketchup**

Chop the walnuts coarsely. Strain the stock, season to taste, add the walnut ketchup and chopped walnuts and serve. The colour may be improved by the addition of a few drops of caramel.

## WALNUT ICE CREAM

*Glace Crème aux Noix*

**4 oz. walnuts**
**Orange flower water**
**Vanilla essence**
**1½ pt. custard**

Pound the nuts, gradually adding a little orange flower water. Add the vanilla essence to the custard. Chill and freeze; when partially frozen add the walnuts.

**6–8 helpings**
**Time—1–1¼ hr.**

## WALNUT ROAST

**½ lb. milled walnuts**
**½ lb. fresh, wholemeal breadcrumbs**
**Salt and pepper**
**1 large onion**
**2 oz. vegetable margarine**
**¼ teasp. powdered sage**
**6 tablesp. thick gravy**

FILLING

**4 oz. fresh, wholemeal breadcrumbs**
**2 oz. melted margarine**
**½ teasp. thyme**
**2 tablesp. chopped parsley**
**Rind of ½ lemon (grated)**
**Salt and pepper**

Mix the nuts, breadcrumbs and seasoning together. Chop the onion finely and fry until golden brown in the margarine, mix in the powdered sage. Place the onion on top of the nut mixture and pour over the gravy. Mix to a stiff dough and form into a roll. Cut through the centre of the roll lengthwise. Mix together all the ingredients for the filling and spread over one half of the roll, sandwich the two halves together and smooth with a knife. Place on a greased baking-sheet and bake for 30 min.

## WASSAIL BOWL

**1½ gills water**
**2 cloves**
**¼ oz. root ginger**
**½ small nutmeg**
**1 blade of mace**
**2 coriander seeds**
**2 cardamom seeds**
**12 oz. loaf sugar**
**1 lemon**
**2 bottles of sherry**
**3 eggs**
**3 egg yolks**
**6 peeled, cored and roasted apples**

Put the water in an enamel saucepan and heat slowly. Stir in the cloves, ginger, grated nutmeg, mace, coriander and cardamom seeds and boil for 5 min. Rub the sugar on the rind of the lemon to extract the zest and add this to the saucepan. Then carefully stir in the sherry. Break the 3 eggs into a large basin and add the egg yolks, beat well and pour over them, a little at a time, 2½ gills of the hot liquid from the pan—it must not be too hot. Bring the rest of the liquid to near boiling-point and pour it into the basin, stirring vigorously until the mixture is light and frothy. Just before serving, add the roasted apples.

## WATER ICES

*See Ices, Syrup for Water Ices.*

## WATER ICES, SYRUP FOR

*See Ices, Syrup for Water Ices.*

## WATERCRESS SOUP

**½ lb. lean pork**
**3 pt. water**
**½ lb. watercress**
**2 slices of ginger**
**Pinch of salt**

Cut pork into small pieces. Put into a heavy saucepan and add water, watercress and ginger. Pick out watercress 10 min. before soup is cooked. Cut off stems and put leaves back into soup. Add salt.

**Cooking time—40 min.**

## WEDDING CAKE

*Gâteau de Noce*

NOTE: These quantities are sufficient for a 3-tier cake.

**3–3¼ lb. flour**
**¼ teasp. salt**
**3 level teasp. ground cinnamon**
**3 level teasp. ground mace**
**1 nutmeg (grated)**
**1½ teasp. baking-powder**
**3 lb. butter**
**3 lb. castor sugar**
**1½ teasp. parisian essence *or* other gravy browning**
**24 large eggs**
**5½ lb. currants**
**2 lb. sultanas**
**1–1½ lb. glacé cherries**
**1–1¼ lb. mixed chopped peel**
**Rind and juice of 1 lemon**
**½–1 lb. blanched chopped almonds**
**1½ gills rum *or* brandy *or* rum and brandy**

Prepare and line 3 cake-tins (paper), one 12 in. diameter, one 8 in., and one 4 in. diameter.

Sift together flour, salt, spices and baking-powder. Mix together all the fruit with a little of the measured flour. Cream the butter and sugar very well, add browning. Add egg and flour alternately to the creamed fat beating well between each addition. Stir in the prepared fruit, almonds and brandy. Divide ½ of the mixture between the 2 smaller tins, and put the remaining ½ of the mixture in the biggest tin. Tie a thick band of brown paper round the outside of each tin. Smooth the mixture and make a depression in the centre of each cake. Bake the 4-in. cake for 2–3 hr., the 8-in. cake for 3½–4 hr., and the 12-in. cake for 5–6 hr. Put in a cool oven (**310° F., Gas 2**) for the first ½ hr. then reduce heat to very cool (**290°–240° F., Gas 1–½**) for the remainder of the time.

To cover the 4-in. cake with almond paste about 1 lb. ground almonds etc. will be required; 2 lb. ground almonds etc. for the 8-in. cake and 3 lb. ground almonds, etc., for the 12-in. cake.

For the royal icing use 1 lb. sifted icing sugar, etc., for the 4-in. cake, 2 lb. for the 8-in. cake and 3 lb. sugar, etc., for the 12-in. cake.

Transparent icing cooled may be poured over as a last layer, if liked. For the 4-in. cake use 1–1½ lb. loaf sugar, etc., for the 8-in. cake use 3 lb. sugar, etc., and for the 12-in. cake 4 lb. sugar, etc.

Decoration of each cake is then completed upon silver boards (of correct size) covered with a lace d'oyley. The cake is then assembled by placing one cake on top of the other with pillars supporting them. The pillars for the bottom tier should be 3 in. in height and for the top the pillars should be 4 in. high. Place a silver vase containing white flowers and smilax on top.

## WEIGHTS AND MEASURES USED IN COOKERY

*See Appendix.*

## WELLINGTON PUDDING

*Pouding à la Wellington*

**1 oz. granulated sugar for the caramel**
**4 oz. brown bread-crumbs**
**4 oz. plain flour**
**Pinch of salt**
**1 small level teasp. baking-powder**
**4 oz. finely-chopped suet**
**½ teasp. ground cinnamon**
**½ teasp. ground nutmeg**
**4 oz. sultanas**
**1 oz. finely-chopped candied orange peel**
**4 oz. castor sugar**
**3 eggs**
**1 gill milk (approx.)**
**1 small glass Marsala *or* sherry (optional)**

PURÉE

**1 lb. chestnuts**
**Pinch of salt**
**A little milk**
**2 tablesp. cream**
**A few drops of vanilla**
**Sugar to sweeten**

Grease a 1 pt. border mould with butter.

Make the caramel by heating the granulated sugar with a little water until dissolved, then boil rapidly until the syrup is golden brown. Then quickly throw in, all at once, 3 tablesp. of cold water, lower the heat and let the caramel dissolve.

Mix together the breadcrumbs, sifted flour, salt, baking-powder, suet, cinnamon, nutmeg, sultanas, peel and castor sugar. Beat together the eggs, the cooled caramel and a little of the milk. Stir this into the dry ingredients, adding the wine (if used) and using more milk, if necessary, to mix to a soft dropping consistency. Pour into a well-buttered border mould—only ¾ fill it. Cover with greased paper. Steam for 2½–2¾ hr.

Prepare the chestnut purée by cooking the chestnuts for 10 min. in boiling water with a pinch of salt, then skinning them. Put the chestnuts with a little milk in a saucepan; cook until tender. Rub them through a fine sieve; add the cream and vanilla, and sweeten to taste.

Turn out the mould on to a hot dish. Pipe the purée quickly into the centre. Serve with apricot sauce poured round.

**6 helpings**

## WELSH RAREBIT

| | |
|---|---|
| **1 oz. butter** *or* **margarine** | **Few drops of Worcester sauce** |
| **1 level tablesp. flour** | **4–6 oz. grated Cheddar cheese** |
| **5 tablesp. milk;** *or* **3 tablesp. milk and 2 tablesp. ale** *or* **beer** | **Salt and pepper** |
| **1 teasp. mixed mustard** | **4 slices of buttered toast** |

Heat the fat in a pan and stir in the flour. Cook for several minutes, stirring well. Add the milk and stir well over the heat until a smooth thick mixture, then add the ale, mustard, Worcester sauce, cheese and a good pinch of salt and pepper. Do not overcook the mixture otherwise the cheese will become "oily". Spread on the slices of buttered toast and put under a hot grill until golden brown. Serve at once.

NOTE: A larger quantity of Welsh Rarebit mixture can be made and stored in the refrigerator being used as required.

**4 helpings** *or* **8 small savouries**
**Cooking time—10 min. (approx.)**

## WHITE BREAD

### Basic Recipe

| | |
|---|---|
| **3½ lb. white flour** | **1 teasp. sugar** |
| **3½ teasp. salt** | **1¾ pt. warm water** |
| **1 oz. yeast** | |

Grease 3–4 loaf tins and put them to warm. Mix salt and flour well together, cream yeast with the sugar and add to warm water. Make a well in the centre of the flour, pour the liquid into the well and sprinkle on or mix in a little of the flour to form a pool of batter and allow to stand in a warm place for 20 min. Mix to an elastic dough, using more water if required; knead well till the dough leaves the basin clean, and put to rise in a warm place until the dough has doubled its size. Then turn on to a floured board, knead again not too heavily but until there are only small holes in the dough, and put into the prepared tins. Put to prove until the dough is well up the sides of the tin then bake in a hot oven (**425° F., Gas 7**).

**3–4 loaves**
**Cooking time—1 hr.**

### Variations

#### Nut Bread

As for white bread. Add 8 oz. chopped nuts —walnuts, peanuts, etc.

#### Raisin Bread

As for white bread. Add 8 oz. chopped raisins when kneading the dough for the second time.

#### Sultana Bread

As for white bread. Add 8 oz. sultanas when kneading the dough for the second time.

## WHITE CHAUDFROID SAUCE

*Sauce Chaudfroid Blanche*

| | |
|---|---|
| **½ pt. Béchamel sauce** | **1 teasp. wine vinegar** *or* **lemon juice** |
| **¼ pt. aspic jelly** | **1 tablesp. thick cream** |
| **¼ oz. powdered gelatine** | |
| **Salt and pepper** | |

Have the sauce just warm. Heat the jelly over hot water and in it dissolve the gelatine. Cool the jelly until it also is just warm. Fold the jelly into the sauce and season the mixture, add the vinegar or juice. Wring the sauce through muslin, fold in the cream.

Use the sauce for masking fish, poultry or veal served en chaudfroid, using it when cold but liquid.

## WHITE ITALIAN SAUCE

*Sauce Italienne Blanche*

½ pt. Béchamel sauce
2 shallots
2 oz. button mushrooms
½ oz. butter
¼ pt. good stock (veal *or* chicken)
½ glass dry white wine (optional)
Salt and pepper
Lemon juice to taste
1 dessertsp. chopped parsley
2 tablesp. cream

Chop the shallots and mushrooms very fine. Melt the butter and in it cook the mushrooms and shallots very gently for 10 min. Add the sauce, the stock and wine if used. Stir all well together and simmer the sauce steadily until mushrooms are soft and the whole is reduced to a creamy texture. Season, add the lemon juice and chopped parsley and just before serving stir in the cream.

Serve with chicken, fish, etc.

## WHITE SAUCE

*Sauce Blanche*

*For a coating sauce:*

2 oz. butter *or* margarine
2 oz. flour
1 pt. milk *or* fish stock *or* white stock *or* a mixture of stock and milk
Salt and pepper to taste

*For a pouring sauce:*

1½ oz. butter *or* margarine
1½ oz. flour
1 pt. of liquid as for coating sauce
Salt and pepper to taste

(1) *Roux Method*

Melt the fat in a deep saucepan, large enough to hold the amount of liquid with just enough room to spare for beating the sauce. Stir the flour into the fat and over gentle heat allow it to bubble for 2—3 min. On no account allow it to change colour; this is a White Roux. Remove from heat and stir in ½ the liquid. Return to moderate heat and stir the sauce briskly till it thickens, then beat it vigorously for a minute or two. Stir in the rest of the liquid, always adding the last portion with due regard to the required thickness of the sauce. Boil the sauce for 3 min., beating vigorously. Season and use the sauce at once. If a sauce must be kept hot cover it with wet greaseproof paper and a lid and before use beat it again in case skin or lumps should have formed.

A coating sauce should coat the back of the wooden spoon used for stirring, and should only just settle to its own level in the pan.

A pouring sauce should barely mask the spoon, flow freely, and easily settle to its own level in the pan.

**Cooking time—15 min.**

(2) *Kneaded Butter and Flour or Beurre Manié*

Knead the butter and flour, or work them together with a fork or spoon until they are quite smoothly mixed.

Heat the liquid, and when just below boiling point, gradually whisk in the kneaded butter and flour. Whisk the sauce until it boils by which time all the thickening must be smoothly blended into the whole. Season and use.

NOTE: Both White Roux and Beurre Manie may be prepared in advance and stored for weeks, if necessary, in a refrigerator or cold larder. To use: allow 4 oz. to 1 pt. for a coating sauce, 3 oz. to 1 pt. for a pouring sauce.

## WHITE STOCK FOR SOUPS AND SAUCES

2 lb. knuckle of veal
2 qt. cold water
1 teasp. salt
1 dessertsp. white vinegar *or* lemon juice
1 onion
1 stick of celery
½ teasp. white peppercorns
Small strip of lemon rind
1 bay leaf

Make as for Brown Stock.

**Quantity—about 3 pt. Cooking time—at least 3 hr.**

## WHITE WINE SAUCE

*Sauce au Vin Blanc*

½ pt. white stock *or* fish stock
2 oz. butter
1 oz. flour
⅛ pt. white wine
1–2 egg yolks
Juice of ½ lemon
Salt and pepper

Make a white sauce with the stock, ½ the butter and the flour. To this add the wine and simmer it for 10 min. Whisk in the remaining butter just below boiling point, then stir in the egg yolks mixed with lemon juice; season. Thicken the egg yolks without boiling.

Serve with fish or white meat.

### WHITEBAIT

*Blanchailles*

| | |
|---|---|
| **Whitebait** | **Cayenne *or* black pepper** |
| **Ice** | **Salt** |
| **Flour** | **Lemon** |
| **Deep fat for frying** | |

Frying whitebait is a difficult task for inexperienced cooks. The following is a well-tried method which, if carefully followed, never fails to produce satisfactory results. Put the whitebait with a piece of ice in a basin, which must be kept cool. When required for cooking, spread the fish on a cloth to dry, dredge well with flour, place in a wire basket and shake off the superfluous flour. Plunge the basket into a pan of clean, very hot lard and fry rapidly for 3–4 min. Keep moving the basket all the time whilst frying. Lift the basket, shake it to strain off the fat, and turn the fish on to greaseproof paper. Place on a warm dish and repeat until all the whitebait are fried. Season with cayenne or black pepper and fine salt. Serve garnished with quarters of lemon.

**Cooking time—3–4 min.**

### WHITEBAIT FRITTERS

| | |
|---|---|
| **$1\frac{1}{2}$ pt. whitebait (approx.)** | **1 tablesp. butter (melted)** |
| **2 eggs** | **$1\frac{1}{2}$ teasp. baking-powder** |
| **$\frac{1}{3}$ pt. milk** | **Salt and pepper** |
| **5 oz. flour** | |

GARNISH

| | |
|---|---|
| **Parsley** | **Slices of lemon** |

Separate the whites from the yolks of the eggs. Add the milk and the flour alternately to the well-beaten egg yolks and beat the mixture well. Add the melted butter. Stir the baking-powder into the mixture and fold into it the stiffly beaten egg whites.

Put the whitebait into a strainer or colander and wash them carefully. Turn them out on to a clean cloth, moving the whitebait along the cloth until they are free from water. Fold the whitebait lightly into the batter. Season to taste. Drop spoonfuls of batter into hot fat and fry the fritters on both sides until they are golden brown. Drain the fritters on soft paper and serve decorated with parsley and sliced lemon.

### WHOLE GRAIN MOULDS (Rice, large Sago, Tapioca)

For a basic recipe, *see Whole Rice Mould.*

### WHOLE RICE MOULD

*Gâteau de Riz*

| | |
|---|---|
| **6 oz. rice** | **Flavouring** |
| **1 qt. milk** | **$\frac{1}{2}$–1 oz. fresh butter (optional)** |
| **3 oz. castor sugar** | |

Wash the rice and put it with the milk into a double saucepan, or a thick pan standing over a very low heat. Simmer very gently, with the lid on the pan to prevent undue evaporation. Stir occasionally to prevent the rice from settling on the bottom of the pan, and cook until the rice is quite tender and the milk almost absorbed. Sweeten to taste, add flavouring if required, stir in the butter if used. Pour quickly into a cold, wet basin or mould. Turn out when set and serve with stewed, canned, or fresh fruit, jam, jelly, etc.

**6 helpings**
**Cooking time—2–3 hr.** **Setting time—2 hr.**

FLAVOURINGS

**Lemon *or* Orange**: Wash fruit, dry well and grate rind finely; stir into the cooked mixture just before moulding. Alternatively, peel rind in thin strips, avoiding white pith and infuse in mixture during cooking; remove before adding sugar and butter.

**Coffee**: Add coffee essence to taste, with the sugar.

### WHOLEMEAL BREAD

| | |
|---|---|
| **$3\frac{1}{2}$ lb. wholemeal flour** | **1 oz. yeast** |
| **$3\frac{1}{2}$ teasp. salt** | **2 oz. lard** |
| **1 teasp. sugar** | **$1\frac{3}{4}$ pt. warm water** |

Mix salt well with flour and make warm in a large basin. Cream the yeast with the sugar, add the warm water, together with the melted fat, and mix with the flour to an elastic dough. Knead well until smooth, cover with a cloth, to prevent surface evaporation, and set in a warm place to rise to double its size—about 1 hr. When the dough is sufficiently risen it has a honeycombed appearance. The first kneading distributes the yeast and softens the gluten of the flour. Knead the dough a second time to distribute the carbonic acid gas which has formed. Continue kneading until, when the dough is cut, there are no large holes in it, but do not knead too heavily. Divide into the number of loaves required. Place in warmed greased tins, making the top round. Prick and allow to prove or recover for 20 min. or until the dough is well up to the top of the tin. If the dough is over-proved it will collapse and give heavy bread. Bake in top middle of a very hot oven (**450° F., Gas 8**), (to kill the yeast), for 10–15 min. then reduce heat to fairly hot (**375° F., Gas 5**), baking in all about 1 hr. When ready the loaf should have a hollow sound when knocked on the bottom, and should be well risen and nicely browned with a crisp crust.

**4 loaves**
**Cooking time—1 hr.**

## WIENER FLEISCHSNITTE

Vienna Steaks

**1½ lb. lean beef**
**1 teasp. chopped parsley**
**1 teasp. powdered mixed herbs**
**A little nutmeg**
**Salt and pepper**
**2 eggs**
**1 tablesp. flour**
**¼ lb. butter**
**2 onions**

Trim and finely mince the beef. Put into a bowl and add the parsley, herbs, grated nutmeg, salt and pepper. Beat together one whole egg and one egg yolk, and add to the meat. Stir all together, divide into equal portions and form into neat shapes like fillets of beef. Put the flour on a plate and cover each of the "steaks" with a light coating of flour. Heat the butter in a pan and fry the steaks, drain and keep hot. Slice the onions into very fine rings and coat them with flour. Beat the remaining egg white to a stiff snow. Dip each onion ring into egg white and then again into flour and fry in the butter until golden and crisp. Serve the steaks garnished with the onions and accompanied by a brown sauce.

**6 helpings**

## WIENER GUGELHUPF

**¼ lb. butter**
**7 oz. sugar**
**8 oz. sifted flour**
**1 large teasp. baking-**

**powder**
**3 eggs**
**A tumbler of milk**

Cream the butter and sugar together until light and fluffy. Separate the egg yolks from the whites and stir the egg yolks into the creamed butter. Add the milk and stir. Sift in the flour and baking-powder. Beat the egg whites to a stiff snow and fold into the mixture. Put into a 9-in. "gugelhupf mould", previously well greased, and bake in a moderate oven (**350° F., Gas 4**) for about 45 min.

## WIENER SCHNITZEL

**6 fillets of veal about ½ in. thick**
**Salt and pepper**
**1 tablesp. flour**
**1 egg**
**¼ lb. dry breadcrumbs**
**3 oz. butter**
**1 lemon**

See that each fillet is neatly trimmed, lay on a board and beat with a cutlet bat. Sprinkle the fillets with salt and pepper. Put the flour on a plate and lightly coat each fillet. Beat the egg and into it dip each fillet. Coat the fillets with breadcrumbs. Put the butter into a frying-pan and when hot fry the fillets on each side to a rich golden brown. Drain and garnish with lemon.

**6 helpings**

## WINDSOR PUDDING

**1½ oz. rice**
**¾ pt. milk**
**2 lb. cooking apples**
**2 oz. castor sugar**
**Grated rind and juice of ½ lemon**
**3–4 egg whites**

Wash the rice and stew it in the milk until the rice is tender and all the milk has been absorbed. Wipe the apples, cut them roughly and stew them in as little water as possible. When soft, pass them through a fine sieve into a mixing bowl. Stir in the sugar, rice, lemon rind and juice. Whisk the egg whites stiffly and fold them lightly into the mixture. Put into a greased basin; cover. Steam very gently for about 40 min.

Serve with custard sauce made from the egg yolks.

**6 helpings**

## WINE JELLY

*Gelée au Vin*

**4 lemons (¼ pt. juice)**
**½ lb. sugar**
**1½–2 oz. gelatine**
**1 pt. water**
**Whites and shells of 2 eggs**
**¼ pt. brandy**
**½ pt. sherry**

Infuse the thinly cut lemon rinds, sugar and gelatine in the measured water until dissolved. Add lemon juice, whites and crushed shells of the eggs and whisk steadily until boiling-point is almost reached. Remove whisk and boil to the top of the pan. Pour in the brandy and sherry without disturbing the foam "crust". Boil again to the top of the pan. Remove from the heat, cover, and leave to settle for 1 min. Strain through double muslin Cool, remove froth, and mould in scalded individual moulds.

**4–6 helpings**
**Time—1–1½ hr.**

## WINE SAUCE, SWEET

*See Sweet Wine Sauce.*

## WINES

*See Table Wines and Liqueurs.*

NOTE: Choosing, serving and storing wine correctly is a specialized skill. This topic is covered in some detail in *Mrs Beeton's Cookery and Household Management*, and the reader should refer to that book for fuller information.

## WORCESTER SAUCE

**4 shallots**
**1 qt. best brown vinegar**
**6 tablesp. walnut ketchup**
**5 tablesp. anchovy essence**
**4 tablesp. soy**
**½ teasp. cayenne pepper**
**Salt to taste**

Chop the shallots very finely. Put with all the other ingredients into a large bottle, and cork it closely. Shake well 3 or 4 times daily for about 14 days, then strain the sauce into small bottles, cork tightly, and store in a cool, dry place.

## YAMS

*Ignames au naturel*

**Yams** **Salt**

Yams can be cooked in most of the ways suitable for potatoes.

**1 yam for 2 to 3 helpings**
**Cooking time—about 35 min.**

## YEAST BREADS AND ROLLS

*See Bread and Rolls Made with Yeast.*

## YEAST, USE OF

### Important Points to Remember

1. Yeast is a plant organism, and requires warmth, moisture and food for growth. Its growth can be completely stopped by great heat, shrinkage of the yeast buds is caused by bringing it into contact with too much sugar or salt, and of course it does not grow if too cold. This shows quite clearly that in using yeast the flour, liquid and atmosphere should be just warm.
2. Sufficient moisture is vital. A stiff dough will never give a successful result.
3. In most cases, the growth of the yeast is started off by creaming it with a small amount of sugar.
4. There are two ways of using yeast in mixtures: (i) by direct mixing with flour and liquid to make the required dough and (ii) by "setting the sponge"—*see White Bread.* The latter is considered to give a better textured bread.
5. The larger the amount of flour used, the smaller the proportion of yeast needed, e.g. 1 oz. will raise 3½ lb. flour in 1 hour, but it will take ½ oz. to raise 1 lb. flour in the same time. Again, the longer the time which can be given for raising the dough, the less yeast proportionately will be required. Dough is usually "raised" twice.
6. When fruit is added to the dough, it should be put in after the dough has risen for the first time; this prevents it from being squashed by much handling.
7. When dough is rising, cover it with a clean towel, to prevent surface evaporation.
8. A dough which has been raised too long will become overstretched with gas ($CO_2$) and will collapse, giving heavy bread.
9. After kneading the dough for a second time, it *must* be allowed to "prove" or recover from the kneading, because some of the gas will have been knocked out of it. If baked immediately after kneading, the dough will be heavy and probably uneatable.
10. When the yeast has done its work and filled the dough with gas to capacity, it must be killed off by great heat, hence the instruction to bake in a hot oven.

In order to produce carbonic acid gas for "raising" starches, yeast requires warmth, moisture and food. Its action can be retarded by cold, by contact with salt and a high concentration of sugar, and it can be killed entirely by great heat, e.g. too hot water for mixing. One ounce of yeast should raise 1½ lb. of flour in 1 hr.

Compressed yeast can be stored in a refrigerator for a week or two.

Another form of yeast is described as "dry, granular" yeast. This yeast keeps without refrigeration. It can be bought in tins, and instructions for use are stated on the tin or package. The required amount of yeast is mixed with warm water, not *hot* water, and it is allowed to stand without stirring for five minutes. It is stirred however before being added to the flour.

It is important to remember that whatever further liquid is being added to mix the required dough, all the prepared yeast must be put in first.

### Other Raising Agents Used in Baking

**Sour Milk is a raising agent,** especially for steamed breads. It is not widely used otherwise.

**Baking-powder** is a leavening or raising agent produced by the mixing of an acid reacting material, e.g. tartaric acid and sodium bicarbonate—this is generally blended with some starchy material. The ideal baking-powder gives the most gas ($CO_2$) for the least volume and weight of powder. It gives the gas slowly when cold and increasingly in the cooking dough—this means that some doughs Baking-powder is used in the proportion of one to three teaspoonfuls to each pound of flour, depending on the richness of the mixture—usually the plainer the mixture (fewer eggs, less fat) the more baking-powder is required.

**Egg powders** are just coloured baking powders and must not be confused with dried egg.

**Eggs (fresh)** act as raising agents because when beaten they possess the property of holding air which expands on heating.

**Bicarbonate of Soda and Cream of Tartar** (without starchy material as in baking-powders) are used in the making of scones, etc. The proportion used in scones is one teaspoonful bicarbonate of soda and two and a quarter teaspoonfuls cream of tartar to one pound of flour, or equal quantities if sour milk (acid) is used. It is most important to combine the soda with the correct amount of cream of tartar, or the excess soda will affect the colour and taste of the food. The cream of tartar and the bicarbonate of soda only act upon one another in the presence of moisture. So they must be kept dry if they are to retain their strength.

Bicarbonate of soda is used sometimes without the cream of tartar, e.g. in the making of gingerbread or treacle pudding where the resulting dish is required to be brown.

**Self-Raising Flour** may be used for some things; in this case the raising agent has been added to the flour and usually no more is required. Self-raising flour is more expensive than plain flour but it has an appeal for some amateurs because they feel more confident when they use it.

## YELLOW RICE

**½ lb. rice**
**½ lb. stoned raisins**
**1 small teasp. turmeric *or* saffron**
**½ stick cinnamon**
**A little butter**
**Sugar**

Boil all ingredients gently (except butter and sugar) in 1 pt. water, and add more water if necessary. When ready, remove the cinnamon and stir in butter and sugar to taste.

NOTE: In the countryside especially, it is the custom to serve yellow rice with roast chicken, also on festive occasions.

## YORK BISCUITS

**2 oz. lard *or* margarine**
**3 oz. sugar**
**¼ egg**
**4 oz. plain flour**
**1 level teasp. cream of tartar**
**½ level teasp. bicarbonate of soda (good measure)**
**2 level teasp. ground ginger**
**Milk as required**

Cream the fat and sugar, add the egg. Sift the dry ingredients and work into the fat mixture, adding milk as necessary. The consistency should be such that it can be handled; not too soft but not stiff. Make into about 20 balls and place well apart on greased baking-sheets, press very lightly if necessary. Bake in a moderate to warm oven (**350°–335° F., Gas 4–3**) till fawn colour.

**20 biscuits** **Cooking time—20 min.**

## YORKSHIRE PUDDING

*Pouding à la Yorkshire*

**1 pt. batter as for Batter Pudding**
**2 tablesp. dripping**

Prepare and cook as for Batter Pudding but cook the pudding in meat dripping. Start cooking on the top shelf above the meat and finish off below the meat on a lower shelf.

Serve with roast beef.

NOTE: In Yorkshire this pudding is served with gravy, as a separate course, before the meat.

ZABAGLIONE

*Sabayon*

| | |
|---|---|
| **6 egg yolks** | **6 tablesp. castor sugar** |
| **6 tablesp. Madeira, *or* Marsala *or* sherry** | |

Place an oven-glass *or* earthenware bowl over a pan of hot water. Add the ingredients and whisk continuously until the mixture is creamy and retains the impression of the whisk. Pile into glasses and serve immediately with savoy fingers.

**6 glasses** **Time—10–20 min.**

ZAITZA S SMETANE

Hare in Sour Cream

| | |
|---|---|
| **1 large hare** | **Lard** |
| **½ pt. vinegar** | **4 rashers bacon** |
| **1 bay leaf** | **1 pt. milk** |
| **A few peppercorns** | **1 pt. sour cream** |
| **1 large onion** | |

Cut the hare just below the ribs and use the back and hind legs. Put in a bowl with the vinegar and enough water to cover. Add the bay leaf, peppercorns and onion and leave for several hours—or overnight. Remove the hare, dry and cover with lard. Chop the onion and put it with the bay leaf into a roasting tin and add the chopped bacon. Put in the hare and roast in a pre-heated oven. After 10 min. begin to baste the hare with the milk. When tender remove the hare and cut up putting it on to a hot dish. Strain the sauce into a pan and add the sour cream. Bring to the boil and pour over the hare.

Serve with redcurrant jelly.

**6 helpings** **Time—2 hr. (excluding marinade)**

ZEPHIRES OF CHEESE

*Zephires au Parmesan*

| | |
|---|---|
| **1 oz. gelatine** | **¼ pt. cream** |
| **½ gill water** | **Seasoning** |
| **2½ gills milk** | **½ pt. aspic jelly** |
| **2 oz. grated Parmesan cheese** | **Watercress** |
| **2 oz. grated Cheddar cheese** | **Red pepper (capsicum)** |

Dissolve the gelatine in the very hot ½ gill of water, cool slightly, add milk and when quite cold, but not set, stir in all the cheese, lightly whipped cream and seasoning. Turn into individual fluted moulds or 1 large mould, allow to set. Turn out and garnish with chopped set aspic jelly, watercress and strips of red pepper.

**4–5 helpings**

ZUPPA DI FAVE ALLA ROMANA

Broad Bean Soup

| | |
|---|---|
| **1 qt. young shelled broad beans** | **4–5 sage leaves** |
| **Salt** | **2 small onions** |
| **5 oz. ham *or* bacon** | **1 tablesp. tomato extract** |
| **Parsley** | **Slices of toast** |

Boil the broad beans in salted water. While they are cooking, cut into very small pieces the ham or bacon, finely chop the parsley, sage leaves and onions. Put into a saucepan, fry and let them brown a little, then add the tomato extract. After a few minutes add 1½ pt. water. When the broad beans are tender, drain them and add to the soup, cook for another ¼ hr. Place at the bottom of each soup bowl a slice of toast, pour in the soup and serve.

**6 helpings**
**Cooking time—¾ hr. (approx.)**

# APPENDIX

Weights and measures used in cookery
Oven chart
British can sizes
Cookery terms in English, French etc.
Preparation methods
Culinary herbs and their uses
Suggestions for Menus and Diets

Vols-au-vent are easy to make.

1 Roll out the puff pastry to a thickness of about $\frac{3}{4}$ inch. Place a dish on the top of the rolled pastry and mark out the shape.

2 Cut out the shape with a knife. During this operation make sure that the knife cuts cleanly and does not drag or twist the pastry.

3 Place on a wet baking sheet. Mark the inner ring and cut down to about $\frac{1}{2}$ the depth of the pastry.

4 Brush over the marked top of the pastry with the beaten egg mixture.

5 Mark slanting cuts outwards from the inner ring—again taking care not to drag or twist the pastry.

6 When baked remove the inner ring (the lid) and scoop out the soft inside ready to take the filling.

1

2

3

4

5

6

Why not serve a salad as a vegetable?

# WEIGHTS AND MEASURES USED IN COOKERY

### Measuring Cups

The British Standard measuring cup has a capacity of 10 fluid ounces, which is equal to the Imperial ½ pint.

The American and Canadian Standard measuring cup has a capacity of 8 fluid ounces, which is equal to the American ½ pint.

### Measuring Spoons

The British measuring tablespoon has a capacity of $\frac{1}{32}$ of the Imperial pint. Therefore 16 tablespoons equal the Imperial ½ pint. Three British Standard teaspoons equal the capacity of one British Standard tablespoon.

The American and Canadian Standard measuring spoons are slightly smaller in capacity than the British Standard spoons. Three American Standard teaspoons equal one American Standard tablespoon.

*Reproduced from Artistry in Cold Food Preparation published by the General Electric Co. Ltd. of England.*

### Some Handy Measures Used in Baking

Accurate weighing and measuring are vital to successful cooking. Many failures are due to "slapdash" weighing. Remember that the food in the scale pan must just "balance" the weight.

| INGREDIENT | STANDARD MEASURING SPOONS | | | |
|---|---|---|---|---|
| | BRITISH SPOON | | AMERICAN SPOON | |
| | | *Weight* | | *Weight* |
| Sifted flour . . . . | 3 tablespoonfuls | 1 oz. | 4 tablespoonfuls | 1 oz. |
| Granulated, castor or superfine sugar . . . | 2 tablespoonfuls | 1¼ oz. | 2 tablespoonfuls | 1 oz. |
| Sifted icing or confectioner's sugar . | 3 tablespoonfuls | 1 oz. | 4 tablespoonfuls | 1 oz. |
| Margarine or butter . . | 2 tablespoonfuls | 1¼ oz. | 2 tablespoonfuls | 1 oz. |
| Rice, whole . . . . | 2 tablespoonfuls | 1¼ oz. | 2 tablespoonfuls | 1 oz. |
| Cornflour or cornstarch . . . . . . | 2 tablespoonfuls | 1 oz. | 3 tablespoonfuls | 1 oz. |
| Syrup, treacle, molasses, warmed . . | 1 tablespoonful | 1 oz. | 1 tablespoonful | ¾ oz. |
| Granulated or powdered gelatine . . | 4 teaspoonfuls | ½ oz. | 5 teaspoonfuls | ½ oz. |

All weights refer to level spoons. Approximate to the nearest ¼ oz.

The average modern tablespoon is equal in capacity to the British Standard measuring tablespoon and a large teaspoon is equal in capacity to the British Standard measuring teaspoon.

*Spoons.*—A rounded spoon means as much above the level of the spoon as below; for accuracy it is wise to measure in level teaspoons so that 1 rounded teaspoon will be 2 level ones. To talk of a "heaped" spoon is no guide at all, as one person's idea of a "heap" may be quite different from that of another person. Always divide a spoonful by measuring the length of the spoon e.g. ¼ oz. of cornflour will be half a level tablespoon—divided lengthwise.

| INGREDIENT | STANDARD MEASURING CUPS | | | | HOMELY MEASURES (BRITISH) | | | |
|---|---|---|---|---|---|---|---|---|
| | BRITISH CUP | | AMERICAN CUP | | BREAKFAST-CUP | | TEACUP | |
| | | *Weight* | | *Weight* | | *Weight* | | *Weight* |
| Sifted flour . . . | 1 cup | 5 oz. | 1 cup | 4 oz. | 1 cup | 5 oz. | 1 cup | 3 oz. |
| Granulated, castor or superfine sugar. | 1 cup | 9 oz. | 1 cup | 8 oz. | 1 cup | 9 oz. | 1 cup | 6 oz. |
| Sifted icing or confectioner's sugar . . . . | 1 cup | 5 oz. | 1 cup | 4½ oz. | 1 cup | 5 oz. | 1 cup | 3½ oz. |
| Margarine or lard . | 1 cup | 9 oz. | 1 cup | 8 oz. | 1 cup | 9 oz. | 1 cup | 6 oz. |

All weights refer to level cups.

### METRIC EQUIVALENTS

*Weights (Approximate)*

1 oz. = 30 grammes
½ lb. (8 oz.) = 225 grammes
1 lb. (16 oz.) = 453·5 grammes
2·205 lb. = 1 kilogramme

*Fluid (Approximate)*

½ Imperial pint = 2⅕ decilitres
1¾ Imperial pints = 1 litre

### MEASURES OF LENGTH

12 inches (in.) = 1 foot (ft.)
3 feet = 1 yard (yd.)
6 feet = 1 fathom
5½ yards = 1 pole, rod or perch
22 yards = 1 chain = 100 links
10 chains = 1 furlong
8 furlongs = 1 mile = 1,760 yards

### LIQUID MEASURES

2 British Standard tablespoons = ¼ gill
4 British Standard tablespoons = ½ gill
6 British Standard tablespoons = ¾ gill
8 British Standard tablespoons = 1 gill = 5 fluid ounces = ¼ Imperial pint
4 gills = 20 fluid ounces = 1 Imperial pint
2 pints = 1 Imperial quart
4 quarts = 1 Imperial gallon

### DRY MEASURES

2 pints = 1 quart
8 quarts = 1 peck
4 pecks = 1 bushel (bush.)
3 bushels = 1 sack

### AVOIRDUPOIS WEIGHT

27$\frac{11}{32}$ grains = 1 drachm
16 drachms = 1 ounce
16 ounces = 1 pound (lb.)
14 pound = 1 stone

## Oven Chart

The oven settings in the chart below have been used throughout the book. It must be noted however that the temperatures given are *indications* of oven heat conditions and, within limits, the cook can follow these safely; these limits however will vary from make to make and from one size of oven to another. Therefore the housewife must ascertain the individual variation of her oven, which, once found, can always be applied in future. For example, it may be found that a particular oven will need to be operated at a little higher or a little lower figure than that given in the recipe.

<table>
<tr><th>THERMOSTAT SETTING</th><th>APPROXIMATE TEMPERATURE CENTRE OVEN</th><th>HEAT OF OVEN</th><th>THERMOSTAT SETTING</th><th>APPROXIMATE TEMPERATURE CENTRE OVEN</th><th>HEAT OF OVEN</th></tr>
<tr><td>¼</td><td>240°</td><td rowspan="3">Very Cool</td><td>5</td><td>375°</td><td rowspan="2">Fairly Hot</td></tr>
<tr><td>½</td><td>265°</td><td>6</td><td>400°</td></tr>
<tr><td>1</td><td>290°</td><td>7</td><td>425°</td><td>Hot</td></tr>
<tr><td>2</td><td>310°</td><td>Cool</td><td>8</td><td>450°</td><td rowspan="2">Very Hot</td></tr>
<tr><td>3</td><td>335°</td><td>Warm</td><td>9</td><td>470°</td></tr>
<tr><td>4</td><td>350°</td><td>Moderate</td><td></td><td></td><td></td></tr>
</table>

Test for solid fuel or other oven without regulator:

**Hot oven:** (a) A piece of white paper put into the hottest part of the oven (usually the top) should become a good rich brown in 3 min.

(*b*) The hand held in the hottest part of the oven should begin to sting after an 8 or 9 seconds count. Suitable for bread, scones, pastry.

**Fairly hot oven:** The paper becomes light brown in 3 min. Suitable for small rich cakes etc.

**Moderate oven:** The paper becomes yellow. Suitable for cakes of the sandwich type and for starting off large cakes.

**Warm oven:** The paper does not colour.

## Abbreviations

The following abbreviations are used throughout this book. Spoonfuls are *level* spoonfuls unless otherwise stated.

| | |
|---|---|
| sp. | spoonful |
| teasp. | teaspoonful |
| dessertsp. | dessertspoonful |
| tablesp. | tablespoonful |
| oz. | ounce |
| lb. | pound |
| in. | inch |
| min. | minute |
| hr. | hour |
| pt. | pint |
| qt. | quart |
| wineglass | wineglassful |
| liqueurglass | liqueurglassful |

**British Can Sizes**

| NO. | APPROX. NET WEIGHT | USED PRINCIPALLY FOR |
|---|---|---|
| Baby Food Can | 4½ oz. | Strained Fruits and Vegetables |
| 5 oz. | 5 oz. | Baked Beans, Peas |
| 8 oz. | 8 oz. | Meat Puddings, Baked Beans, Spaghetti, Vegetables, Fruit |
| A 1 | 10 oz. | Baked Beans, Soups, Vegetables, Meats, Pilchards |
| E 1 | 14 oz. | Fruits, Vegetables |
| No. 1 Tall Can | 1 lb. | Vegetables, Fruit, Meat, Soups, Pilchards, Milk, Cream, Fruit Juices |
| 1 lb. Flat Can | 1 lb. | Sweet and Meat Puddings, Tongue, Galantine |
| A 2 Can | 1¼ lb. | Fruit and Vegetables, Fruit and Vegetable juices |
| A 2½ Can | 1¾ lb. | Fruit and Vegetables |
| 3 lb. HR. | 3 lb. | Meat Rolls, etc. |
| A 10 Can | 6¾ lb. | Fruit, Vegetables and Tongue |

# COOKERY TERMS IN ENGLISH, FRENCH, ETC.

**Absinthe** (Fr.) Name of an aromatic plant; also of a liqueur prepared from it, used in France and Switzerland as a beverage; occasionally used for flavouring purposes.

**À la carte** (Fr.) A list of dishes with the prices attached to each dish.

**À la—, À la mode de** (Fr.) After the style or fashion of, e.g. *à la Francaise* French style, *à la Reine* in the Queen's style; *à la Russe* Russian style, etc.

**Albumine** (Fr.) **Albumen** (Eng.) Egg white.

**Anglaise, à l'** (Fr.) English style. Usually plain, roast or boiled.

**Apéritif** (Fr.) Drink taken before meals.

**Appetissants** (Fr.) **Appetizers** (Am.) Hors D'oeuvre. Small tit-bits or savouries.

**Aquavit** A potent, colourless Scandinavian liqueur. Often flavoured with caraway seeds.

**Aromates** (Fr.) Aromatic herbs used for flavouring.

**Aspic** (Fr.) A savoury jelly used for garnishing, etc.

**Au bleu** (Fr.) Term applied to fish boiled in salted water, seasoned with vegetables, herbs, and white wine or vinegar.

**Au four** (Fr.) Baked in the oven.

**Au gratin** (Fr.) A term, derived from the French verb *gratiner*, to brown, applied to dishes prepared with sauce and bread-crumbs, baked brown in the oven or under the grill, and served in the dish in which they are baked. The term does not necessarily imply that cheese is an ingredient.

**Au jus** (Fr.) A term for dishes of meat dressed with their juice or gravy.

**Au maigre** (Fr.) Dishes prepared without meat; Lenten dishes.

**Au naturel** (Fr.) Food served without cooking or cooked plainly and simply.

**Baba** (Polish *babka*) A very light yeast cake.

**Bain-marie** (Fr.) The culinary water bath. It is a large open vessel, half filled with hot water, in which saucepans containing sauces, etc., are placed so that their contents are kept nearly at boiling-point without burning or reducing.

**Barbecue** (Fr.) Originally the method of cooking (roasting) an animal whole; to dress and roast whole. Nowadays, especially in the U.S., a social entertainment where the food is cooked outside in the open.

**Bavarois** (Fr.) Bavarian cream. A term applied to creams with a custard or fruit purée base.

**Béchamel** (Fr.) French white sauce. One of the four foundation sauces.

**Beignets** (Fr.) Fritters. Also a kind of pan-cake, fried in deep fat.

**Bisque** (Fr.) Fish soups of a thick, creamy consistency usually made from molluscs or crustaceans.

**Blanquette** (Fr.) A white fricassée or stew, usually made of veal or fowl, with a white sauce enriched with cream or egg yolks.

**Bombay duck** A small East Indian fish, which when salted and cured is eaten as a relish.

**Bombe** (Fr.) An iced pudding which is shaped like a bomb and filled with a rich custard or fruit cream or mousse mixture.

**Bouchées** (Fr.) Literally "a mouthful". Small patties of puff pastry with savoury or sweet fillings.

**Bouillabaisse** (Fr.) A kind of fish stew or soup, very popular in France.

**Bouquet garni** (Fr.) A small bunch of herbs tied together and used to impart a rich flavour to stews, sauces, etc. In its simplest form, a sprig of parsley, thyme and bay leaf. Chervil, chives, celery leaf, basil and tarragon may be added.

**Brioche** (Fr.) A light French yeast cake.

**Canapés** Small shapes of fried bread, toast or pastry on which savouries, etc., are served.

**Caramel** (Fr.) A colouring substance made by boiling sugar.

**Carmine** Crimson, colouring used in confectionery, etc.

**Carte du Jour** (Fr.) The bill of fare for the day.

**Casserole** (Fr.) Originally a copper stewpan,

now a fireproof earthenware or other cooking dish with a lid, used especially for stews. The food is served in the dish.

**Cassolette** (Fr.) A very small case filled with a savoury filling, served as hot hors d'œuvre or savoury. The case may be made from fried bread, pastry, egg and breadcrumbs,

**Caviar** (Fr.) **Caviare** (Eng.) The salted roe of the sturgeon or sterlet fish.

**Cereals** All grains such as rice, wheat, oats, oatmeal, barley and semolina.

**Charlotte** (Fr.) A corruption of the old English word Charlyt, "a dish of custard". Today, a hot or cold sweet made of a casing of sponge cake or bread with a creamy filling.

**Chartreuse** 1. A mixture of fruit, meat or vegetables, served as an entrée. 2. A French liqueur. There are two well known kinds—yellow and green.

**Chaudfroid** (Fr.) 1. A cold entrée. 2. A sauce for masking cold fish, game, etc.

**Chianti** (It.) Wine from the region of the Chianti Mountains, Tuscany, especially a dry red variety; also wine of the same type made elsewhere.

**Chipolata** (It.) Small sausages, Italian in origin. Also dishes which contain them.

**Chowder** (Eng.) A dish of American origin, consisting of boiled pickled pork cut in slices, fried onions, slices of turbot or other fish, and mashed potatoes, all placed alternately in a stewpan, seasoned with spices and herbs, claret and ketchup, and simmered.

**Citronné** (Fr.) Anything which has the taste or flavour of lemon.

**Clam** A bivalve shell-fish, several kinds of which are edible, popular in N. America.

**Cochenille** (Fr.) **Cochineal** (Eng.) A liquid pink colouring substance, used for colouring creams, sauces, icing, etc.

**Cocottes** Small fireproof cooking and serving dishes which hold one portion.

**Compôte** (Fr.) 1. Fruit stewed with sugar. 2. A stew of small birds.

**Condé** Name of an old French family. Several soups, entrées and sweets, of which rice forms an essential part, are styled "a la Condé".

**Condiments** Seasoning spices.

**Cordon Bleu** (Fr.) An ancient culinary distinction bestowed on skilful female cooks in France since the time of Louis XV. It consists of a rosette made of dark blue ribbon.

**Coulibiac** Name of a Russian dish—a kind of fish-cake mixture wrapped up in Brioche paste and baked.

**Court-Bouillon** (Fr.) 1. Name given to meatless liquid in which fish is poached. 2. A highly-seasoned fish stock and stew.

**Crécy, Potage à la** (Fr.) Crécy or carrot soup (Eng.) Dishes named "à la Crécy" are generally connected with carrots in the form of a purée.

**Crêpes** (Fr.) Pancakes.

**Croissants** (Fr.) Crescent-shaped bread rolls.

**Croquettes** (Fr.) Savoury mince of fowl, meat, fish or potatoes mixed with a binding ingredient, and formed into various shapes. They are usually coated with egg and breadcrumbs and fried crisp.

**Croustades** (Fr.) Shapes of fried bread, rice or pastry, in which various mixtures are served.

**Croûtes** Blocks or shapes of fried bread on which salmis, whole birds, etc., are served.

**Croûtons** (Fr.) Sippets of fried bread or toast cut into dice shapes and fried, used for garnishing dishes.

**Cuillères de cuisine** (Fr.) Wooden spoons, the use of which is strongly recommended instead of metal spoons, especially for stirring sauces.

**Cuisine** (Fr.) Kitchen, cookery. *Faire la cuisine*, to cook or to dress foods.

**Culinaire** (Fr.) Anything connected with the kitchen or the art of cooking.

**Curaçao** (Fr.) A liqueur prepared from the yellow part of the rind of a peculiar kind of bitter orange. Used for flavouring jellies, ices, etc.

**Dariole** (Fr.) 1. A small tin mould. 2. A kind of small entrée mixture, composed of a compound of forcemeat or mince, baked or steamed in these small moulds.

**Dhâll** or **Dholl** A kind of pulse much used in India for kedgeree, or as a kind of porridge. In England it is best represented by split peas or lentils.

**Diable** (Fr.) "Devil". Applied to numerous dishes with sharp and hot seasoning.

**Drageés** (Fr.) **Sugar plums** (Eng.) Sweetmeats made of fruits, small pieces of rinds or aromatic roots, or nuts, covered with a coating of sugar icing.

**Dripping** The fat obtained from cooked meat or from rendering down pieces of fat.

**Éclair** (Fr.) Small French pastry cake made from choux pastry filled with cream or custard.

**En casserole** (Fr.) A dish cooked and served in an earthenware or other casserole.

**Entrée** (Fr.) A course of dishes, or corner dish for the first course; the conventional term for hot or cold side dishes. Also defined as dishes generally served with a sauce.

**Entremets** (Fr.) Dainty dishes usually hot and cold sweets.

**Epigrammes** (Fr.) 1. A culinary term for breast of lamb or mutton braised and divided into small portions, egged, crumbed and fried. 2. A dish of alternate cutlets of the neck and breast.

**Escalopes** (Fr.) 1. Thin round steaks of veal called "collops". 2. Thin slices of any kind of meat, usually egged, crumbed and fried.

**Escargot** (Fr.) Edible snail.

**Espagnole** (Fr.) Rich brown sauce, one of the four foundation sauces.

**Farce** (Fr.) Forcemeat or stuffing.

**Farinaceous** Consisting, or made of flour or meal.

**Feuilletage** (Fr.) Puff pastry; leafy, flaky.

**Filet** (Fr.) **Fillet** (Eng.) The under-cut of a loin of beef, mutton, veal, pork and game. Boned breasts of poultry, birds, and the boned sides of fish are also called fillets.

**Fines herbes** (Fr.) A combination of finely-

chopped fresh herbs, such as parsley, tarragon, chervil and other kitchen herbs; mostly used in omelets and sauces.

**Flamber** (Fr.) 1. To singe poultry or game. 2. To cover a pudding or omelet with spirit and set it alight.

**Flan** (Fr.) An open tart.

**Flapjack** A griddle cake.

**Fleurons** (Fr.) Small half-moon shapes of puff pastry, baked, used for garnishing.

**Flummery** (Eng.) Cold sweet dish, mainly of cereals, originally of oatmeal set in a mould and turned out. To be eaten with wine, cider, milk or a compound sauce.

**Foie de veau** (Fr.) Calf's liver.

**Foie gras** (Fr.) Fat goose liver.

**Fondant** (Fr.) 1. A soft kind of icing. 2. Dessert bonbon.

**Fondue** (Fr.) 1. Melted cheese. 2. Melted cheese or savoury sauce.

**Forcemeat** Stuffing.

**Fouetté** (Fr.) Whipped with a whisk.

**Frangipane** A thick custard-style preparation made of eggs, milk, some flour, with lemon peel, rum, brandy, vanilla, etc., to flavour.

**Frappé** (Fr.) Iced. *Frapper*: To place on ice; ice (used when cooling champagne).

**Fricassée** (Fr.) **Fricasséed** A white stew.

**Frit** (Fr.) Fried in shallow or deep fat.

**Frittata** (It.) An Italian dish; a kind of rolled pancake, crumbed and fried in fat.

**Frosting** (Am.) Icing.

**Fumet** (Fr.) The flavour or essence of game, fish or any highly flavoured concentrated substance used to impart a rich flavour to certain dishes.

**Galantine** (Fr.) 1. A dish of white meat, glazed and served cold. 2. A fowl or breast of veal, boned and stuffed with farce, tongue, ham, etc.

**Garnish** The decorations added to a dish to improve its appearance.

**Gâteau** (Fr.) A rich, elaborate, decorated cake.

**Gaufre** (Fr.) A thin biscuit wafer; baked or fried in specially constructed gaufre moulds.

**Gelatine** A manufactured substance for giving solidity to liquids.

**Genièvre** (Fr.) Juniper berry. A blue-black berry, possessing a peculiar aromatic flavour, used as a flavouring condiment, also used in syrups and liqueurs.

**Ghee** An Indian word for clarified butter.

**Glacé** (Fr.) Frozen, iced or glazed.

**Glaze** (Eng.) Stock or gravy reduced to the thickness of jelly; used for glazing meats, etc., to improve their appearance. Used also for strengthening soups and sauces. (Well-made glaze adheres firmly to the meat.)

**Gnocchi** (It.) Dumplings; a light savoury dough, boiled and served with tomato sauce and grated Parmesan cheese. Also fancy-shaped pieces of semolina paste used for garnishing soups and savoury dishes.

**Goulash** Hungarian dish. A rich meat stew.

**Gourmet** (Fr.) An epicure; a judge of good living; one who values and enjoys good eating.

**Grenadin** (Fr.) Small fillets of veal or fowl larded and braised.

**Guinée pepper** (Eng.) **Poivre de guinee** (Fr.) A kind of cayenne pepper prepared from the seeds of the ripe chilli. Also called chilli pepper.

**Gumbo** The American term for okra soup, or other preparations from okra, gumbo being the name by which okra is chiefly known in South America.

**Hominy** (Am.) A farinaceous food made of maize.

**Hors d'œuvre** (Fr.) Small side dishes, served cold, generally before soup, in order to create an appetite. Large hors d'œuvre may be served instead of a main course.

**Icing** or **Glacé** Covering for cakes, etc.

**Irlandaise, à l'** (Fr.) Irish-style. This term is usually applied to dishes containing potatoes in some form.

**Isinglass** Egg preservative.

**Jardinière** (Fr.) 1. A garnish of mixed spring vegetables. 2. Vegetables stewed down in their own sauce.

**Julep** Ancient Arabian name for a cooling drink containing mucilage, opium, etc. An American drink.

**Julienne** (Fr.) Nowadays, usually a garnish of the fine strips of mixed vegetables. 2. A clear soup named after an 18th-century French chef.

**Junket** (Eng.) A dessert made of sweetened and flavoured curds.

**Jus** (Fr.) Juice, broth, gravy. The juice of cooked meats, seasoned, but without any thickening.

**Kebabs, Kebobs, Kabobs** Dish, Middle Eastern in origin; a dish served in Indian and Turkey, consisting of small slices of mutton run on skewers, and either grilled or braised; now term given to any savoury itèms, e.g. tomatoes, sausages, slices of kidney, etc., run on skewers and grilled.

**Kedgeree** An Indian dish of fish and rice, often curried.

**Kirsch** A colourless liqueur distilled from black cherries. It comes from Germany and Switzerland and is often used to flavour trifles and fruits.

**Kromeskis** A Polish word, meaning croquette.

**Liaison** (Fr.) Mixture of egg yolks, cream, etc., used for thickening or binding white soups and sauces.

**Liquor** Any liquid or juice produced by cooking.

**Lyonnaise, à la** (Fr.) Lyonese style. As a garnish it generally signifies that shredded onion (fried) has been introduced.

**Macaroni** (It.) A paste prepared from wheat flour dried in various shapes and forms but usually made into long tubes.

**Macaroons** Sweet biscuits made of almonds, sugar and egg whites.

**Macédoine** (Fr.) 1. A mixture of various vegetables or fruits, cut in even-shaped dice. 2. Also applied to a collection of fruit embedded in jelly and set in a mould, or a fruit salad flavoured with liqueurs and syrup.

**Madeleine** (Fr.) Small cake baked in a dariole or shell mould, often coated with jam and sprinkled with coconut. Also the name of a pear.

**Madère** (Fr.) Madeira wine.

**Maintenon** Name of the Marchioness Françoise d'Aubigné, Louis XIV's favourite and a great patroness of cooks. Several dishes are called "à la Maintenon", usually signifying something grilled in a paper case.

**Maraschino** (Fr.) A delicately flavoured white liqueur, distilled from a species of cherry. Used for flavouring jellies and ices.

**Marinade** (Fr.) A mixture of oil, herbs, wine or vinegar, etc., in which fish or meat is soaked, soused or pickled.

**Marsala** (It.) A sweet wine similar to Madeira.

**Marzipan** (Ger.) Almond paste or icing.

**Mayonnaise** (Fr.) A thick cold sauce made of egg yolks, oil and vinegar. 2. A cold dish made with this.

**Mazarines** (Fr.) Turbans. Forcemeat decorations of fish, poultry or game. Entrées consisting of combined fillets of meat and forcemeat.

**Médallion** (Fr.) Round fillets, meat mixtures, etc. in a round form.

**Medlar** Roundish fruit about $\frac{1}{2}$–1 in. long; reddish-brown in colour. The Japanese Medlar is the Loquat.

**Menu** (Fr.) The bill of fare. Literally, the word means minute detail of courses.

**Meringue** (Fr.) A light pastry, made of egg white and sugar. Used as a topping for a pie or pudding, or filled with creamy fruit purée, etc. as a cold sweet.

**Mignonette Pepper** Coarsely-ground white peppercorns.

**Minute, à la** (Fr.) A surname given to dishes which are hurriedly prepared or anything cooked in the quickest possible way.

**Mirepoix** (Fr.) The foundation bed of mixed vegetables, herbs and bacon on which meat and vegetables are braised; also a mixture of diced carrots, onions, ham sautéed in fat then added to brown soups and sauces for flavouring.

**Miroton** (Fr.) Thin round slices of meat, about 2 in. in diameter, braised, stewed, and dished up in a circle.

**Muscat** (Fr.) **Muscadine** (Eng.) A wine, also the grape producing it.

**Napolitaine, à la** (Fr.) Naples or Neapolitan style.

**Navarin** (Fr.) A stew of mutton or lamb.

**Neat's Foot** The foot of a calf or ox.

**Nepal pepper** A red pepper of the same kind as cayenne and Guinée pepper.

**Noisettes** Neatly trimmed, round or oval shapes of lamb, mutton, or beef not less than $\frac{1}{2}$ in. thick.

**Normande, à la** (Fr.) 1. Normandy style. The application of this name usually implies that the flavour of apple has in some form or other been introduced into the composition of the dish. 2. A dish known as *à la Normande*, used for fish entrées. Made with a mushroom and oyster sauce.

**Nougat** (Fr.) A sweetmeat made with sugar, honey, almonds, pistachios, etc.

**Nouilles** (Fr.) **Noodles** (Eng.) A German preparation *Nudeln*. It consists of a stiff paste made with flour and eggs, rolled out very thinly, cut up in thin strips and boiled, and served as garnish or main dish.

**Noyau** (Fr.) The stone of a fruit; a liqueur flavoured with peach or nectarine kernels.

**Okra** Name of a vegetable extensively used in South America. Used as a vegetable and also for soup.

**Orly** Name given to dishes, usually slices of fish or meat, dipped in rich batter and fried in fat. Served with parsley.

**Pain d'épice** (Fr.) Spiced bread; a kind of gingerbread.

**Panada** Culinary paste of flour and water or soaked bread, used for preparing forcemeat or stuffing.

**Papillotes** (Fr.) Paper cases in which food is cooked and served.

**Paprika** The fleshy fruit of the mild capiscum, grown in the south of Europe, and used as spice for ragoûts or salads, and as a mild pepper.

**Parson's nose** The extreme end portion of the carcass of a bird.

**Passer** (Fr.) **Pass** (Eng.) To pass a sauce, soup, vegetable or meat, means to run it through a tammy-cloth, sieve or strainer.

**Pâte** (Fr.) 1. Pastry. 2. A savoury meat paste or a raised pie.

**Pâté de foie gras** (Fr.) A well-known delicacy prepared from the livers of fat geese.

**Pâté feuilletée** (Fr.) Puff pastry.

**Pâtisserie** (Fr.) 1. A pastry-cook's business. 2. Pastries, or small, rich cakes.

**Perry** (Eng.) Name of a beverage made of pears, similar to cider made of apples.

**Petits Fours** (Fr.) Small fancy cakes highly decorated with fancy icing, crystallized fruits, etc.

**Pilaf, Pillaff, Pillau, Pilaw** Fish or meat with savoury rice, i.e. rice flavoured with spices and cooked in stock.

**Pilcaithly Bannock** A kind of Scottish shortbread.

**Pimiento** A red Spanish pepper pod used in salads, and as garnish.

**Pistaches** (Fr.) **Pistachios** (Eng.) Kernels of the nut of the turpentine tree, used for flavouring and garnishing galantines, sweets, etc.

**Pizza** (It.) Pie or large flat tart spread with tomatoes, cheese and often meat, anchovies, etc.

**Polenta** (It.) A standard Italian dish made of maize or cornflour.

**Pot-au-feu** (Fr.) is an economical and wholesome beef broth. It is the standard dish of all classes in France, and the origin of beef stock.

**Praline** (Fr.) Burnt almond.

**Praliné** (Fr.) Flavoured with burnt almonds.

**Provençale, à la** (Fr.) A surname for certain French dishes, indicating, generally, that garlic or onion and olive oil have been used.

**Pulses** Term used for dried peas, beans, lentils, split peas, etc.

**Pumpernickel** (Ger.) Westphalian brown bread.

**Purée** (Fr.) A smooth pulp; mashed vegetables or fruit; thick soup. The name is also given to meat or fish which is cooked, pounded, then passed through a sieve.

**Quenelles** (Fr.) Forcemeat of different kinds, composed of fish, poultry or meat, eggs, etc., shaped in various forms—balls, ovals, etc., poached, and served as an entrée or garnish to soup, etc.

**Ragoût** (Fr.) A rich stew of meat, highly seasoned.

**Ramequin** (Fr.) **Ramakin** 1. Small tartlets or fondues with cheese. 2. Cocotte.

**Raspings** Very fine crumbs made from baked bread, used with beaten egg to coat foods for frying, and for 'au gratin' dishes.

**Ratafia** 1. A culinary essence of bitter almonds. 2. A special kind of almond biscuit. (The name is also given to a liqueur flavoured with almonds.)

**Réchauffé** (Fr.) Warmed-up food, left-over food re-cooked or re-dressed.

**Rennet** The prepared inner membrane of a calf's, pig's, hare's or fowl's stomach; used for curdling or coagulating milk.

**Rissoles** (Fr.) A mixture of minced fish or

meat, enclosed in pastry half-moon shapes, and fried in deep fat (The name is now often given to meat mixtures which are shaped into rolls and coated with egg and breadcrumbs before frying.)

**Roe** Fish eggs.

**Roulade** (Fr.) Roll, rolling. Rolled meat, cake, etc., cooked.

**Roux** (Fr.) A mixture of equal quantities of fat and flour cooked together and used for thickening soups and sauces. There are 3 kinds—"white", "blond" and "brown", depending on the length of time of the preliminary cooking.

**Royal** Name of an egg custard used for garnishing clear soups. Also the name applied to an icing (glacé royale) made with egg whites and icing sugar, and used for coating and decoration.

**Sabayon** (Fr.) **Zabaglione** (It.) 1. A sauce served with puddings, composed of cream or milk, sugar, white wine and eggs. Also served in glasses as a cold sweet. 2. A savoury sauce.

**Saccharometer** A device for measuring the amount of sugar in a solution, especially a hydrometer with a special scale.

**Salami** (It.) A kind of uncooked sausage that is smoked or air-dried and keeps indefinitely in a dry atmosphere.

**Sally Lunn** (Eng.) Name of a kind of teacake, slightly sweetened and raised with yeast.

**Salmi** or **Salmis** A hash made of half-roasted game.

**Salpicon** A mince of poultry or game with ham, tongue and mushrooms, used for croquettes, rissoles, etc. or for filling bouchées, patty cases, etc.

**Salsify** or **Salsifis** An edible plant; sometimes called oyster-plant.

**Sauerkraut** (Ger.) **Choucroute** (Fr.) Pickled cabbage, cabbage preserved in brine. A national dish of Germany. Served hot with bacon or sausages.

**Sauté-pan, Sautoire** (Fr.) A shallow cooking-pan.

**Sauterne** (Fr.) A French white wine much used in cookery.

**Savarin** A light pudding made from a yeast mixture.

**Seasoned flour** Flour mixed with salt and pepper usually in the proportion of 1 tablesp. flour, 1 teasp. salt and $\frac{1}{2}$ teasp. pepper.

**Sippets** Bread cut into crescents and triangles, then fried, used as a garnish.

**Skewer** A metal or wooden pin used for fastening pieces of meat together, also used for trussing poultry.

**Sorbet** (Fr.) 1. An iced Turkish drink. 2. The name of a water ice with fruit or liqueur flavour, usually served in goblets.

**Soubise** (Fr.) A smooth onion pulp served with various kinds of meat entrées. As a surname to dishes, *à la Soubise* is generally applied when onions enter largely into the composition of a dish.

**Soufflé** (Fr.) A light, fluffy, very lightly-baked or steamed pudding. Also applied to light sweet or savoury creams set with gelatine and served cold, similar to mousses.

**Soy** A dark-brown condiment sauce, originally made in Japan; there are many English relishes in which soy is employed as an ingredient.

**Spaghetti** (It.) An Italian paste made into long tubes, intermediate in size between macaroni and vermicelli.

**Stirabout** Name of an Irish dish similar to Scotch porridge.

**Syllabub** 1. A kind of milk punch flavoured with liqueurs and spices. 2. A cold sweet made from brandy or wine and milk, flavoured and sweetened.

**Table d'Hôte** (Fr.) A general title for a meal of several courses at a fixed price. Table at which meals at an hotel or restaurant are served.

**Tamis** (Fr.) **Tammy** (Eng.) Woollen canvas cloth which is used for straining soups and sauces.

**Tepid** Almost blood heat, the temperature of a mixture of 2 parts cold water and 1 part boiling water.

**Terrapin** South American fresh-water and tidal turtle.

**Timbale** (Fr.) Literally "kettle-drum". A kind of crusted hash baked in a mould.

**Toddy** A punch. The fundamental juice of various palms of the East Indies; a mixture of whisky, sugar and hot water.

**Tournedos** (Fr.) Small fillets of beef served as entrées.

**Tourte** (Fr.) An open tart; also a flat dough case in which ragoûts are served.

**Tutti frutti** (It.) Various kinds of fruits, or fruit ice.

**Vermicelle** (Fr.) **Vermicelli** (It.) Very fine strings of paste, made from a wheat flour dough, forced through cylinders or pipes till it takes a slender, worm-like form, when dried; used in soups, puddings and (crushed) for coating.

**Vitamins** Vital food elements.

**Vol-au-vent** (Fr.) A light round puff-pastry case, filled with delicately flavoured ragoûts of chicken, sweetbread, etc.

**Zabaglione** *See* Sabayon.

**Zéphire** (Fr.) Name of a small oval-shaped forcemeat dumpling, poached and served with a rich sauce; anything shaped in a Zéphire mould.

**Zest** The coloured, oily, outer skin of citrus fruits added to cookery for flavouring. It should be very finely cut, grated, or rubbed off with lumps of sugar.

# PREPARATION METHODS

### TO BARD

To place very thinly cut rashers of fat, green (or plain) bacon on the breasts of poultry and game to prevent them from drying up when roasting, the reason being that the legs take longer to cook. Very thinly cut rashers should be tied on with string and only removed just before completion of cooking, so that the poultry or game can brown. Certain joints of butcher's meats, such as veal and lean beef are barded for roasting. This does not obviate basting from time to time.

### TO BASTE

To pour liquid or melted fat over food during cooking to keep the food moist.

### TO BEAT

To turn cake mixtures, batters, etc., over and over with a circular motion to mix in the maximum amount of air.

### TO BLANCH

Some foods are blanched to improve their colour, others to remove some strong, undesirable flavour, and nuts such as almonds are blanched to facilitate removal of their skins. In all cases, the method is the same: immerse the article to be blanched in a saucepan of cold water (without a lid) bring to the boil, then strain the water off.

### TO BLEND

To mix smoothly. When referring to thickening liquids with flour, it means mixing the flour to a smooth paste with a little cold liquid before adding the hot liquid.

### TO COAT

To cover completely with a thin layer of sauce, icing, etc.

### TO CREAM

To mix fat and sugar with a wooden spoon or with the hand until light and fluffy and white in colour. To mix to the consistency of whipped cream.

### TO DEVIL

To rub a highly-flavoured paste—mustard, cayenne pepper, etc., into the legs of game, poultry, etc., before grilling.

### TO DICE

To cut (food) into small cubes. A simple method is to slice the food first, cut the slices into strips, then holding the strips together, cut into dice by cutting across them.

### TO DOT

To put small bits (e.g. butter) over the surface of food.

### TO DREDGE

To sprinkle lightly with flour or sugar.

### TO FOLD IN

This means the combining of an aerated ingredient with other ingredients so that the air entrapped is retained. It is used when combining sifted flour with other ingredients or to combine two whisked mixtures. Place the ingredient to be folded in, on top of the whisked mixture or other ingredients. With a spoon, cut a line vertically through the centre of the mixture, take the spoon round the half of the bowl, spoon up half the mixture and lay it lightly on the other half, thus trapping the dry ingredient between two layers of whisked mixture. Repeat this process until all the dry ingredient has been folded in.

### TO GLAZE

To brush over the tops of pies, galantines, etc., with some preparation to improve their appearance. Fruit pies and buns are usually brushed over with egg and water, or milk or sugar and water; meat with a glaze made of thickened clear stock.

**TO GRATE**

To rub food into fine shreds on a grater. Food to be grated should be firm.

**TO KNEAD**

To work dough lightly until smooth, using the knuckles. The dough should be brought from the outside into the centre each time.

**TO LARD**

To insert strips of fat bacon into the breasts of poultry, game or into pieces of meat, to prevent them drying up when roasting. The fat bacon should be cut into short pieces about 2 in. long and $\frac{1}{4}$ in. thick, chilled well to harden them and make them firm, then inserted into the bird or meat with a larding needle. The ends should be left protruding, but they can be trimmed with scissors if they look ragged or uneven.

**TO MASK**

To cover with a thin layer—of sauce, icing, etc.

**TO PARBOIL**

To partly-boil. The food is boiled by the normal method, but for only half the normal time, and finished by some other cooking method.

**TO REDUCE**

To boil (mixtures) quickly in an open pan to reduce the amount and thus strengthen the flavour and make a thicker consistency.

**TO RUB IN**

To combine fat and flour for shortcrust pastry, plain cakes, etc. First cut the fat into small pieces with a knife, then using the tips of the fingers, rub the fat into the flour, lifting the fat above the bowl so that, in falling back between the fingers, the mixture becomes aerated. When all the lumps of fat have been worked down the mixture should resemble breadcrumbs.

**TO SCALD**

To heat a liquid to just below boiling-point; to pour boiling water on to an article of food.

**TO SCORE**

To make gashes or cut narrow grooves, to make incisions in the surface of food.

**TO SEAR**

To brown or form a hard surface on meat to seal in the juices by exposing to fierce heat, after which the heat is reduced and cooking continued.

**TO SIEVE**

To rub or pass through a sieve to reduce the food to a fine consistency and to introduce air into the food. The back of the bowl of a wooden spoon is usually used to rub or press most substances through a sieve, but the palm of the hand is better when sieving bread-crumbs. Sieving some purées is not an easy process, but it may be facilitated by moistening the purée with any liquid ingredients included in the recipe.

**TO SIFT**

This is the same as "to sieve".

**TO SIMMER**

To cook as just below boiling-point, only an occasional bubble should rise to the surface when a liquid is simmering.

**TO STEEP**

To soak in liquid, which may be hot or cold.

**TO TAMMY**

To pass sauces or soups through a tammy cloth (a cloth made of fine wool) to produce a smooth, glossy finish.

# CULINARY HERBS AND THEIR USES

| *Herb* | *Part Used* | *Purpose* |
|---|---|---|
| Angelica | Leaf stalks | These can be candied (*see* p. 1080) and used for flavouring and decorating cakes and fruit |
| | Midribs | As a vegetable |
| Anise | Leaves | Flavouring soups and sweets |
| | Seeds | Flavouring drinks |
| Balm | Leaves | Flavouring soups, stews, sauces and dressings |
| Basil | Leaves | In salads or for flavouring soups and sauces |
| Bay | Leaves | Flavouring stock, sauces, puddings and custard |
| Borage | Leaves | In salads |
| | Leaves and shoots | Flavouring fruit cups and other drinks |
| Caraway | Seeds | Flavouring cakes, soups and sauces |
| Chervil | Leaves | As a garnish, in salads or for flavouring soups, entrées and sauces |
| Chives | Leaves | In salads or for flavouring soups, omelettes and entrées |
| Coriander | Seeds | In pickles or for flavouring cakes, sauces and drinks |
| Dill | Leaves | Flavouring soups and sauces |
| | Seeds | In preserves or pickles |
| Fennel | Leaves | As a garnish or for flavouring sauces |
| Garlic | "Clove" (bulb) | In salads or for flavouring soups and stews |
| Horseradish | Root | Flavouring sauces |
| Hyssop | Leaves | Flavouring soups |
| Marjoram | Leaves | In stuffings or for flavouring soups, stews or sauces |
| Mint | Leaves | As a garnish or for flavouring sauces, soups or vegetables |
| Parsley | Leaves | As a garnish, in salads or for flavouring soups and sauces |
| Purslane | Leaves | In salads or for flavouring soups and sauces |
| Rosemary | Leaves and shoots | In salads or for flavouring stews, sauces and fruit cups |
| Rue | Leaves | Flavouring fruit cups—use sparingly |
| Sage | Leaves | In stuffings or for flavouring soups, sauces and stews |
| Savory | Leaves | As a garnish, in stuffings or for flavouring stews, sauces and vegetables |
| Sorrel | Leaves | In salads, as a vegetable or for flavouring soups |
| Southernwood | Leaves | Flavouring cakes |
| Tansy | Leaves | As a garnish, in salads or for flavouring cakes, puddings and stews |
| Tarragon | Leaves | In salads, for making Tarragon vinegar or flavouring omelettes, sauces and stews |
| Thyme | Leaves | In stuffings or for flavouring soups and stews |

# SUGGESTIONS FOR MENUS AND DIETS

Meal patterns vary widely, from community to community, and even from family to family. In most cases, the type of meal and the hour at which it is eaten depend for the most part on the occupations of the individual members of the family. In general, most families are accustomed each day to taking the three set meals—breakfast, lunch and dinner or supper, with one or more subsidiary snacks.

**Breakfast:** The breakfast of porridge, other cereal dish, or fruit with cereal, followed by tomato, egg, bacon or fish, or a combination of any two of these and toast, butter and marmalade with tea or coffee, is an adequately balanced meal with which to start the day. A hasty bite of toast and black coffee taken on the run is not at all a good nutritional beginning as numerous advertisements remind us.

**Main meal:** The main meal of the day, whether midday or evening, should contain meat or fish or an equivalent source of protein served with potatoes and a second or even a third vegetable. This is usually followed by a second course planned to give extra energy with a light first course or to avoid heaviness after, for example, a meal of roast meat and Yorkshire pudding.

**Third meal:** The third meal should again, if possible, contain either meat, fish, cheese or egg. It is at most times of a simpler form than the main meal and it usually has a less defined pattern. This meal is often the opportunity for introducing fresh fruit or salad into the menu and for putting in a junket or similar dish which increases the milk consumption without offering too much liquid milk.

**Snacks:** The content of these snacks can make very important contributions when it is necessary to raise the nutritional value of the diet. Conversely it is often from these snacks that redundant food is obtained by those who find themselves more than adequately nourished. The snack meals should therefore be watched as carefully as the main meals by those who guard the family health.

**Season:** Although the general principles of menu planning always remain the same, it is known that a menu made out for summer differs in composition of actual foods from that made out for winter. This is because:

(*a*) foods which are in season are used, in order to reduce costs,

(*b*) in the cold weather the requirement for heat and energy is increased, with the result that heavier meals containing more carbohydrate and fat are needed.

Table III gives suggestions for a weekly menu in the winter. In the summer when it is hot, more salads and cold desserts replace some of the savoury dishes and the heavier baked desserts, see Table IV.

## TABLE I

### Table of Food Values for a Balanced Diet

| BODY BUILDING FOODS | ENERGY FOODS | |
|---|---|---|
| Meat | Butter | Dried peas |
| Offal | Margarine | Haricot beans |
| Poultry | Lard | Rice |
| Game | Cooking fats | Sago |
| Fish | Bread | Macaroni |
| Eggs | Potatoes | Spaghetti |
| Cheese | Oatmeal | |
| Milk | Biscuits | |
| Beans | Cakes | |
| Peas | Honey | |
| Nuts | Jam | |
| Wholemeal bread | Sugar | |

| FOODS THAT GIVE CALCIUM | FOODS THAT GIVE IRON | |
|---|---|---|
| Cheese | Lean meat | Wholemeal bread |
| Milk | Liver | Black treacle |
| Sardines | Kidney | Raisins |
| Herrings | Eggs | Currants |
| Eggs | Watercress | Dried Apricots |
| Green vegetables | Spinach | |
| Bread—white | Oatmeal | |
| Black treacle | Bread—white | |

| FOODS THAT CONTAIN VITAMIN A | FOODS THAT CONTAIN VITAMIN D |
|---|---|
| Butter | Butter |
| Margarine | Margarine |
| Eggs | Eggs |
| Milk | Milk |
| Liver | Halibut liver oil |
| Green vegetables | Cod-liver oil |
| Carrots | |
| Halibut liver oil | |
| Cod-liver oil | |

| FOODS THAT CONTAIN THE VITAMIN B GROUP | FOODS THAT CONTAIN VITAMIN C | |
|---|---|---|
| Liver | Blackcurrants | Parsnips |
| Meat | Rosehip syrup | Swedes |
| Yeast | Oranges | Tomatoes |
| Yeast extracts | Lemons | Potatoes |
| Eggs | Grapefruit | Lettuce |
| Milk | Green vegetables | |
| Cheese | Watercress | |
| Oatmeal | Parsley | |
| Wholemeal bread | Cauliflower | |

The vitamin containing foods are arranged roughly in order of their contribution to the diet.

## TABLE II

### Recommended Daily Calorie Allowances

| AGE AND SEX | | CALORIES | AGE AND SEX | | CALORIES |
|---|---|---|---|---|---|
| Children under 1 yr. | | 100 per kg. (2.205 lb.) | Women | light activity | 2000 |
| | 1–6 | 1000 to 1500 | | moderate activity | 2500 |
| | 7–10 | 2000 | | pregnant | 2500 |
| Boys | 11–14 | 2750 | | nursing | 3000 |
| | 15–19 | 3500 | Men | light activity | 2250 |
| Girls | 11–14 | 2750 | | moderate activity | 3000 |
| | 15–19 | 2500 | | heavy work | 3500 |

From Report of the Committee on Nutrition, British Medical Association.

### Portions of Common Foods which Yield 100 Calories

| FOOD | WT. | MEASURE | FOOD | WT. | MEASURE |
|---|---|---|---|---|---|
| Bread | 1½ oz. | 1 slice | Banana | 5 oz. | 1 large |
| Rice | 1 „ | 4 tablesp. | Orange | 10½ „ | 2 large |
| Sweet biscuits | ¾ „ | 2 small | Cabbage | 13½ „ | ½ |
| Bacon | ¾ „ | 1 rasher | Carrots | 16 „ | 5–6 medium |
| Cheese (Cheddar) | ¾ „ | 1 in. cube | Onion | 16 „ | 4 medium |
| Egg | 2¼ „ | 1 extra large | Potato | 4¾ „ | 1 medium |
| Steak | 1 „ | ¼ helping | Potato chips | 1½ „ | 1 packet |
| Butter | ½ „ | 1 tablesp. | Tomato | 25 „ | 10 medium |
| Cream, thick | 1 „ | 1¾ tablesp. | Marmalade | 1½ „ | 3 tablesp. |
| Margarine | ½ „ | 1 tablesp. | Toffee | ¾ „ | 3 |
| Milk | 6 „ | 1 teacup | Sherry | 2½ „ | 1 medium glass |
| Apples, cooking | 10 „ | 2 | Sugar | 1 „ | 2 tablesp. |

Note: Weights given are edible portion. Spoon measures are level measuring spoons.

## TABLE III

### Suggested Weekly Menu for the Main Meals of a Balanced Winter Diet

| | Breakfast | Lunch | Dinner |
|---|---|---|---|
| Sunday | Boiled egg<br>Toast<br>Butter and marmalade<br>Tea or coffee | Roast beef<br>Yorkshire pudding<br>Roast potatoes<br>Gravy<br>Brussels sprouts<br>Egg jelly | Cream of mushroom soup<br>Rolls<br>Cheese and bacon savouries<br>Raw fruit |
| Monday | Porridge<br>Mince meat on toast<br>Toast<br>Butter and marmalade<br>Tea or coffee | Savoury omelet<br>Watercress and chicory<br>Banana<br>Brown bread and butter | Cold beef<br>Mashed potatoes<br>Carrots and parsnips<br>Apple shortcake and custard |
| Tuesday | Porridge<br>Bacon and egg<br>Toast<br>Butter and marmalade<br>Tea or coffee | Sausage toad<br>Junket and stewed prunes<br>Cheese and biscuits | Steak pie<br>Boiled potatoes<br>Cabbage<br>Turnips—white<br>Steamed chocolate pudding and chocolate sauce |
| Wednesday | Porridge<br>Bacon and tomato<br>Toast<br>Butter and marmalade<br>Tea or coffee | Macaroni cheese<br>Fruit salad<br>Cheese and biscuits | Liver and bacon<br>Brussels sprouts<br>Mashed potatoes<br>Gooseberry sponge |
| Thursday | Grapefruit<br>Sausage and fried potatoes<br>Toast<br>Butter and marmalade<br>Tea or coffee | Barley broth<br>Fish soufflé<br>Grilled tomatoes<br>Apple, raw<br>Cheese and biscuits | Grilled lamb chops<br>Chipped potatoes<br>Spinach<br>Carrots<br>Lemon meringue pie |
| Friday | Porridge<br>Scrambled egg on toast<br>Toast<br>Butter and marmalade<br>Tea or coffee | Cream of celery soup<br>Curried vegetables<br>Chutney, rice<br>Rolls and butter | Fried fillet of cod<br>Green peas<br>Mashed potatoes<br>Apple crumble |
| Saturday | Stewed apples and cornflakes<br>Poached egg on toast<br>Toast<br>Butter and marmalade<br>Tea or coffee | Meat rissoles<br>Tomato sauce<br>Mashed potato<br>Raw fruit cheese and biscuits | Fricassée of rabbit<br>Jacket potatoes<br>Swedes<br>Pear upside-down |

## TABLE IV

### Suggested Weekly Menu for the Main Meals of a Balanced Summer Diet

| | Breakfast | Lunch | Dinner |
|---|---|---|---|
| Sunday | Boiled egg<br>Toast<br>Butter and marmalade<br>Tea or coffee | Roast beef<br>Roast potatoes<br>Gravy<br>Green Peas<br>Egg jelly | Clear vegetable soup<br>Rolls and butter<br>Cheese and bacon savouries<br>Raw fruit |
| Monday | Flaked cereal and milk<br>Mince meat on toast<br>Toast<br>Butter and marmalade<br>Tea or coffee | Savoury omelet<br>Watercress and tomato<br>Banana<br>Brown bread and butter | Cold beef<br>Mashed potatoes<br>Carrots<br>Apple shortcake and custard |
| Tuesday | Grapefruit<br>Bacon and egg<br>Toast<br>Butter and marmalade<br>Tea or coffee | Sausage toad<br>Lettuce<br>Junket and stewed plums | Salad: Lettuce, cress, tomato, cheese and sardines<br>Potato<br>Lemon meringue pie |
| Wednesday | Flaked cereal and milk<br>Bacon and tomato<br>Toast<br>Butter and marmalade<br>Tea or coffee | Creamed vegetables<br>Cheese and biscuits<br>Raw fruit | Liver—braised<br>Boiled potatoes<br>Green salad<br>Peach sponge |
| Thursday | Stewed fruit<br>Sausage and fried potatoes<br>Toast<br>Butter and marmalade<br>Tea or coffee | Clear soup<br>Rolls and butter<br>Cheese soufflé<br>Grilled tomatoes<br>Raw fruit | Grilled lamb chops<br>Mashed potatoes<br>Green beans<br>Moulded fruit salad |
| Friday | Grapefruit<br>Scrambled egg on toast<br>Toast<br>Butter and marmalade<br>Tea or coffee | Salad: Lettuce, cress, cheese, nuts, and tomato<br>Rolls and butter<br>Vanilla ice cream | Steamed fillet of sole and Hollandaise sauce<br>Potato chips<br>Green peas<br>Fruit trifle |
| Saturday | Flaked cereal and milk<br>Poached egg on toast<br>Toast<br>Butter and marmalade<br>Tea or coffee | Veal rissolettes<br>Tomato sauce<br>Watercress<br>Cheese and biscuits<br>Raw fruit | Braised steak<br>Mashed potatoes<br>Green salad<br>Fruit jelly whip |

The above menu shows how the "heavier" dishes, satisfactory for cold winter days may be replaced by "lighter" ones which are well suited to warmer summertime conditions.

# DIETS FOR VARIOUS CONDITIONS

Having considered diets which will keep the family in a state of good nutrition during normal and healthy activity, it is now time to discuss diets for people who are not in a state of good health. The person concerned may be either seriously ill and needing continual care, still carrying on with normal work but paying careful attention to the food which is eaten, or in a condition which is between these two extremes. Where special diets are required for special conditions, it is the doctor and the dietician who advise on the food to include or exclude, and the amounts of these which should be taken in. It must be understood that the following diets are simply *to act as a guide to the home nurse and should in no way replace the advice of a doctor.*

The diets to be considered are:

1. High calorie diet.
2. Low calorie diet.
3. Fluid diet.
4. Semi-solid diet.
5. Light diet.
6. Low residue diet.
7. High protein diet.
8. Low protein diet.
9. Low salt diet.

## 1. HIGH CALORIE DIET

This is suitable for:

(*a*) convalescence after fever or a severe and prolonged illness,
(*b*) underweight caused by certain nervous disorders,
(*c*) undernutrition due to the restriction of food taken, e.g. in unwise dieting.

It is easy to suggest a diet high in fat and rich in milk but this is very frequently unacceptable. The best way to increase food intake is by making up small attractive meals of the highest possible food value and giving them at frequent intervals. Glucose or ordinary sugar should be added to beverages, fruits, puddings, porridge, etc., whenever possible. Fresh fruit drinks with added sugar is a pleasant way of increasing calories, and sweetened coffee, cocoa, tea or other milky drinks may be taken between meals.

### DISHES SUGGESTED FOR A HIGH CALORIE DIET

**Soups:** Thick soups which include meat, vegetables and barley or other cereal. Cream soups, such as tomato or chicken, made with margarine or butter. Rolls and butter or fried croûtons to be used as an accompaniment to soups.

**Main Course**

Eggs: Eggs cooked by any method on buttered toast with or without bacon.
Fish: Any fried fish or fish baked in fat.
Fish in white sauce or as a soufflé.
Hollandaise sauce and chips as accompaniments where suitable.
Meat: All roasted or grilled meats, with gravy.
Pork, ham, and other fat meat.
Pies, puddings and stews with dumplings.
Vegetables: Green or root vegetables with potatoes.

**Desserts**

Suet and steamed puddings.
Pastry and cake puddings.
Stewed fruit with added glucose.
Ice cream, egg jelly and mousses.
Sweet sauces made from fruit juices or syrup, and sweet custards to be used liberally.

## 2. LOW CALORIE DIET

This is suitable for:

(*a*) enforced lack of exercise owing to heart disease, old age, rheumatism or fractures (after the first week),
(*b*) overweight.

Fundamentally, it is important to decrease the energy value of the food by eating as little as possible of sweet and starchy foods. A good mixed diet can be built up of lean meat and fish, eggs, milk, butter, margarine, green vegetables and fruit which can be satisfying. In between meals snacks should be avoided altogether.

### SUITABLE DISHES FOR A LOW CALORIE DIET

**Soups:** Clear soups made from vegetables, e.g. spinach, consommé, meat extract, chicken broth carefully freed from fat. Mixed vegetable soup.

**Main Course**

Eggs: Boiled or poached.
Fish: Steamed or poached white fish.
Meat: Lean meat, rabbit or chicken.

Vegetables: Green-leaf vegetables, marrow, cauliflower, celery, French and runner beans.
Tomatoes.
Small amounts of root vegetables and potatoes.

**Dessert**

Stewed fruit with no sugar.
Raw fruit except bananas.
Fruit salad with no sugar.
Fruit whip.
Fruit jellies, e.g. orange or lemon (made with pure fruit juice and gelatine).
Skimmed milk junket.

There should be no "in-between" meals or snacks, but tea with skimmed milk from the day's allowance, fruit drinks without sugar or a meat extract drink is permitted.

## FOODS FORBIDDEN ON A LOW CALORIE DIET

*Starchy foods:* Pastry, cakes, puddings of all types, suet crust, dumplings.
Barley, rice, tapioca, macaroni, spaghetti and similar cereals.
Bread, except for that allowed in the diet.

*Dairy products:* Cream, sweetened condensed milk.
Milk, butter, ice cream and margarine, except for that allowed in the diet.

*Meat and fish:* Fat meats such as ham, bacon, pork and the drippings from such meat.
All fried meat and fish.

*Fruit and nuts:* Dried fruits, stewed or preserved fruits which have sugar added.
All nuts.

*Vegetables:* Dried peas, beans and lentils.
All fried vegetables.
Potatoes, except for those allowed in the diet.

*Soups:* Thick soups, gravies and stews.

*Beverages:* Alcoholic beverages, e.g. beer, cocktails and wine.
Mineral waters, e.g. ginger ale.
Ginger beer, bottled fruit juices. (Soda water is excepted.)

*Condiments and flavourings:* Oil and salad dressings made with oil, salad cream.
Sugar and sweets, jams and marmalade.

## 3. FLUID DIET

This is suitable for a person who has:

(*a*) acute diarrhœa in the intermediate stages,

(*b*) fevers.

A person on such a diet should be given small feeds at frequent intervals, usually every two hours, as the amount of food which is tolerated, especially in the initial stages, is very little. With an increased tolerance to food, the patient should be fed increasing amounts to make sure that there is a sufficient intake of calories and other nutrients.

### SUGGESTIONS FOR A FLUID DIET

1. Milk mixture and glucose.
   The milk mixture is made by adding 2 oz. dried full-cream milk powder to each pint of fresh milk.
2. Yeast extract and milk mixture.
3. Junket or milk jelly made with fresh milk and with cream and glucose added.
4. Cream, glucose and milk mixture.
5. Boiled custard or ice cream, made with egg, milk mixture, cream and glucose.
6. Cocoa, or malt drink made with milk mixture and glucose.
7. Fruit juices such as lemon or orange with added glucose. Such juices should be strained through a double thickness of butter muslin, and should not be given if the patient's throat is sore.
8. Beef tea.

Some salt should be included in the foods, especially where there is a high fever.

## 4. SEMI-SOLID DIET

This is suitable for a person who has:

(*a*) had tonsils removed,

(*b*) tonsillitis,

(*c*) fever.

As soon as it is possible, a patient who has been on a fluid diet is put on to a diet which contains soft foods.

### SUITABLE DISHES FOR A SEMI-SOLID DIET

**Soups:** Clear soups and cream soups, both of which have been strained.

**Main Course**

Eggs: Soft cooked, poached, or scrambled.

Meat: Chicken or rabbit minced and mixed with a white sauce.

Fish: Minced and mixed with a white sauce or as a custard or soufflé.

Cheese: Cream cheese.

Vegetables: White potato mashed. Sieved vegetables.

**Dessert**

Cornstarch, bread, rice or tapioca pudding.

Custard, junket, jelly.

Plain ice cream, stewed and puréed apple or other fruit. Ripe banana.

Fresh tomato juice and fruit juice with sugar to taste should be given daily except in cases where the throat is sore, e.g. after the removal of tonsils.

### FOODS FORBIDDEN ON A SEMI-SOLID DIET

*Bread and cereals:* Whole-grain bread, fresh bread and biscuits, bran and any cereal unless well strained.

*Cheese:* Any hard or highly flavoured cheese.

*Dessert:* Any containing fruit, nuts or spices.
Pastries, pies, puddings.

*Eggs:* Fried.

*Fried foods:* All fried foods.

*Fruits:* All except strained juices, and stewed fruit.

*Meats:* All red meats.

*Seasonings:* All spices, vinegar and condiments.

*Nuts:* All nuts.

## 5. LIGHT DIET

This is suitable for:

(*a*) convalescence from fever, operations, or from any disease not requiring a special diet,

(*b*) dyspepsia,

(*c*) old age,

(*d*) pregnancy, where there is indigestion or vomiting.

A person who is on a light diet may have similar food, but with certain modifications, to that eaten by the healthy members of a family.

## SUITABLE DISHES FOR A LIGHT DIET

**Soups:** Cream soups and clear soups.

Broths made with chicken, rabbit, or beef stock with added rice, tapioca or macaroni.

(Onion should be avoided.)

### Main Course

Eggs: Eggs boiled, poached or scrambled.
Creamed eggs.

Cheese: Cream cheese.

Fish: Steamed, poached, grilled or baked fish.
Plain or tomato sauce may be served.
Fish soufflé.
Creamed fish.

Meat: Beef, chicken, lamb and rabbit, roasted, grilled, boiled, or steamed with a plain gravy or sauce.
Chicken or rabbit, creamed, in a custard or in a jelly.
Sweetbreads, brains or tripe stewed in milk, and served with a white sauce made from the milk.

Vegetables: Potatoes (boiled or steamed), mashed or sieved vegetables which do not contain much fibre.

### Dessert

Milk puddings or custards made with rice, tapioca, semolina, macaroni or sago.

Moulds (blancmange), junket or jellies made with milk or fruit juice.

Soufflés, meringues or egg custards.

Gelatine desserts e.g. Egg jelly, Bavarian cream, strained fruit whips or mousses.

Ice cream, trifle or Queen of puddings.

Stewed fruits, with the skins and tough fibres removed.

### Cakes and sweets

Sponge cake, butter cake, angel cake.

(No dried fruit or nuts should be eaten).

Small amounts of barley sugar, or plain or milk chocolate—after meals.

FOODS FORBIDDEN ON A LIGHT DIET

*Beverages:* Strong tea and coffee. Aerated mineral waters.

*Breads, cereals, etc.:* Wholemeal bread, new bread, rolls or biscuits, hot buttered toast.

Any whole-grain cereals or coarse porridge unless well strained.

Digestive, coconut, whole wheat and rye biscuits.

Pastry, suet puddings and crusts.

*Cheese:* Cheddar and all hard cheeses.

*Eggs:* Fried.

*Fish:* Herrings, bloaters, kippers, salmon, sardines, eels.

Shellfish, lobster, crab, etc.

Any fried fish.

*Meat:* Tough or fat meat, e.g. pork.

Fried meat or twice cooked meat.

Heart.

*Fruit:* Raw fruit which contains pips or coarse fibres, e.g. apples, gooseberries, pineapple, currants, strawberries.

Cooked fruits which contain pips, e.g. gooseberries.

*Nuts:* All nuts.

*Vegetables:* Roasted or fried potatoes.

Cabbage, turnips, swedes, dried or broad beans, dried peas or lentils.

Onions and leeks.

Celery and rhubarb.

All raw vegetables e.g. lettuce, cress and other vegetables which are used in salads.

*Condiments:* Pepper, mustard and ginger.

Vinegar, pickles, chutney and horseradish.

*Jams:* Those containing pips or peel, e.g. some marmalades.

## 6. LOW RESIDUE DIET

This is suitable for cases of:

(*a*) acute diarrhœa in its later stages,

(*b*) amœbic or bacillary dysentery.

The foods allowed and forbidden, and the suitable dishes, have already been outlined under a light diet. The patient may be given this diet provided that he does not take any fruit except well-strained orange, tomato or other fruit juice, or any vegetables except small amounts of mashed potato. Any foods which contain fibre or leave any residue on digestion must be avoided. Fruits, vegetables and whole grain cereals are the chief foods which come into this category.

For convalescence or mild forms of diarrhœa or dysentery, fruit and vegetable may be introduced gradually, provided that they are well-sieved and are free from stalks, skins and pips.

It is important that abundant fluid is given in order to compensate for the loss which occurs in the watery stools.

## 7. HIGH PROTEIN DIET

This is suitable for a person suffering from:

(*a*) severe burns,

(*b*) certain diseases of the kidney.

Any foods which have a high protein content may be included in the diet. To avoid spoiling the appetite for these foods, any which contain large amounts of fat or sugar and little protein, should be eaten in small amounts.

The protein intake may be increased by adding, where appropriate, skimmed milk powder to baked foods or made up dishes.

### SUITABLE DISHES FOR A HIGH PROTEIN DIET

Any dishes which have in them large amounts of any of the body building foods as listed in Table I will have a high protein content. Meat, fish, milk, eggs and cheese dishes are the important ones to be considered.

### FOODS FORBIDDEN ON A HIGH PROTEIN DIET

*Fried foods:* All fried foods.

*Sweets or dessert:* Any which provide no protein and large amounts of sugar and starches.

## 8. LOW PROTEIN DIET

This is suitable for:

(*a*) gradual heart failure,

(*b*) certain diseases of the kidney.

Any foods which have a low protein content may be included in a low protein diet. The foods which must be restricted and taken in small amounts only, are those given in Table I under the heading of body building foods.

### SUITABLE DISHES FOR A LOW PROTEIN DIET

Any dishes which have in them large amounts of sugar, starches and fat with little or no protein.

**Soups:** Clear soups made with vegetables or yeast extract. Cereals such as barley, macaroni, etc., may be added.

**Main course**

Meat and fish: Small amounts of chicken, rabbit, red meat or fish, roasted, grilled, braised, boiled or steamed.

Vegetables: All vegetables and salads, except dried peas, beans and lentils.

**Dessert**

Fruit—stewed or baked or raw.

Any dessert made with arrowroot, cornflour, rice, tapioca or sago.

Milk or eggs must not be used unless the protein which they contain is calculated in the diet.

Cream may be used.

**Beverages**

Lemonade and other fruit juices generously sweetened with glucose. Tea, coffee and cocoa with small amounts of milk.

**Bread, biscuits, etc.**

These may be taken in very restricted quantities if made from wheat flour.

**Condiments**

All condiments are allowed, but an excess of salt should be avoided.

### FOODS FORBIDDEN ON A LOW PROTEIN DIET

*Beverages:* Any made with large amounts of milk.

*Bread and cereals:* Pastry and puddings containing wheat flour, or puddings containing breadcrumbs unless these have been especially allowed for in the diet.

*Dairy products:* All cheese, milk or foods containing dried milk and eggs, unless these have been calculated for as part of the diet.

*Desserts:* Any desserts made with gelatine, eggs or milk unless the protein has been allowed in the diet.

*Nuts:* All nuts.

*Soups:* Meat soups and meat extracts.

*Vegetables:* Dried peas, beans and lentils.

## 9. LOW SALT DIET

This is suitable for:

(*a*) certain diseases of the kidney,

(*b*) certain conditions of the heart.

When a low salt diet is indicated, it means that not only must salt be eliminated from the diet, but also that any food which contains sodium must be taken in very restricted amounts. Hence, instead of naming the diet a low salt diet, it is really more correct to call it a low sodium diet.

### SUITABLE DISHES FOR A LOW SALT DIET

**Soups:** Cream soups and clear soups unsalted.

**Main Course**

Meat: Fresh or frozen beef, lamb, pork, veal; rabbit, chicken, duck or turkey, either grilled, roasted, stewed or boiled without salt.

Liver may be taken once every 10 days.

Fish: Fresh fish only, fried, steamed or poached without salt.

Eggs: One a day permitted.

Vegetables: All fresh vegetables (except celery) raw, boiled or steamed.

**Dessert**

Any desserts made with tapioca, rice, macaroni, sago or semolina which do not have salt added.

If an egg or milk is used, it must come from the day's allowance.

Fruits stewed or canned.

Custard and home-made ice cream, made from the milk and egg allowance.

Gelatine desserts with fruit juices and pulp.

Fruit pies with unsalted pie crust.

**Beverages**

Cocoa, coffee or tea made with small amounts of milk.

Carbonated beverages.

**Bread, cereals, etc.**

Unsalted or low salt bread should be used.

Cornflour, oatmeal, rice, spaghetti, etc.

Any baked products, such as buns, cakes or biscuits which have yeast or sodium-free baking-powder as a raising agent and no added salt.

**Fats**

Butter or margarine must be unsalted. Oil or lard may also be used.

**Condiments**

All spices, herbs and extracts of almond, lemon, orange, peppermint and vanilla.

FOODS FORBIDDEN ON A LOW SALT DIET

*Beverages:* Dutch process cocoa.

*Bread, cereals, etc.:* Salted bread and biscuits. All baked products which have baking soda or sodium baking-powder as the raising agent.
Proprietary breakfast cereals.
Self-raising flours.

*Cheese:* All types, except washed cottage cheese.

*Eggs:* All, except one per day.

*Desserts:* All cake desserts which contain baking-powder.
Desserts which contain milk or eggs not included in the allowance.

*Fats:* Salted butter and margarine.
Bacon fat.

*Fruit:* Those containing salt or sodium benzoate as a preservative.

*Meat:* Bacon, corned beef, ham, salt pork, meat extracts, sausages, canned meats, fresh brains or kidney.

*Fish:* Bloaters, kippers, smoked haddock, canned fish, sardines, shellfish, any frozen fish, fresh or canned lobster, shrimp or crab.

*Nuts:* Salted, peanut butter.

*Soups:* All canned soups, salted broths and soups

*Vegetables:* All canned vegetables, celery, baked beans.

*Condiments:* Celery salt, onion salt, meat flavourings, prepared mustard, bouillon cubes, catsup, olives, pickles, sauces, relishes, horseradish, soy sauce.